ASSYRIAN-ENGLISH-ASSYRIAN DICTIONARY

CUNEIFORM EDITION

PUBLICATIONS OF THE

FOUNDATION FOR FINNISH ASSYRIOLOGICAL RESEARCH

NO. 27

Assyrian-English-Assyrian Dictionary

Cuneiform Edition

THE NEO-ASSYRIAN TEXT CORPUS PROJECT
2023

This dictionary project was sponsored in part by Dr. Norman Sohlkhah,
Director of the Mesopotamian Museum (Chicago)

Published with the support of the
Foundation for Finnish Assyriological Research

Set in Times
The Assyrian Royal Seal emblem drawn by Dominique Collon from original
Seventh Century B.C. impressions (BM 84672 and 84677) in the British Museum
Copy editing and English language revision by Robert M. Whiting
Typesetting and Layout by Robert M. Whiting and Simo Parpola
Custom fonts by Robert M. Whiting
Cover design and typography by Mikko Heikkinen

Printed in the USA
Distributed by Eisenbrauns,
an imprint of Penn State University Press

ISBN 978-951-51-8580-8

Assyrian-English-Assyrian Dictionary

Cuneiform Edition

Editor-in-chief

Simo Parpola

Managing Editor and English Editor

Robert Whiting

Associate Editors

Zack Cherry

Mikko Luukko

Greta Van Buylaere

Editorial Assistants

Paolo Gentili

Stephen Donovan

Saana Svärd

FOREWORD

In March 2000, when the *Assyrian-English-Assyrian Dictionary* of the NATC Project was at its initial stages, Dr. Norman Solhkhah, founder of the Mesopotamian Museum of Chicago, turned to me asking whether it would be possible to publish a cuneiform edition as well, with the Assyrian headwords spelled and printed out in cuneiform. I welcomed the idea, because the sponsorship provided by Solhkhah offered the possibility of speeding up the completion of the dictionary, although in the end this took much longer than initially expected. Nevertheless, by 17 January 2003 the project had produced preliminary proofs of the cuneiform edition, which were sent to Solhkhah along with a detailed report on the progress of the work. Unfortunately, final proofs of the cuneiform edition could not be produced until 5 October 2005, when work on the dictionary proper was finally approaching completion.

Meanwhile Solhkhah, frustrated with the slow progress of the work, decided to use the proofs sent to him to produce a cuneiform edition on his own. On his web page, this book is titled *English-Assyrian / Assyrian-English Dictionary: The Dawn of Civilization* [...] Printed Exclusively for Mesopotamia Museum of Chicago", but it was also referred to as *The Helsinki Neo-Assyrian Dictionary* and credited to the NATC Project, although the project was not involved in its production. The book is advertised to be available at Assyrian Universal Alliance Foundation AUAF and Al-Itekal Bookstore, Chicago, but many potential clients, myself included, have failed to acquire a copy.

For these reasons, the NATC project has decided to reissue the cuneiform edition in a format similar to the *Assyrian-English-Assyrian Dictionary* published in 2007. The Assyrian and English sides are based on computer runs executed on 5 October 2005, and the Introduction is virtually identical with that of 2007, so the dictionary can be used without the necessity of purchasing or consulting AEAD.

Helsinki, 25 March 2023 Simo Parpola

CONTENTS

THE ASSYRIAN LANGUAGE

Assyrian is an extinct Semitic language spoken in ancient Mesopotamia from about 2300 until about 500 BC, after which it gradually merged with Aramaic.

Together with Babylonian, Assyrian forms the Akkadian branch of East Semitic. Throughout its history, Assyrian and Babylonian were in intensive contact with each other and in many ways developed parallelly. From the earliest times, however, Assyrian displays a number of differences from Babylonian that kept increasing with time, until by the end of the second millennium BC, the two languages were certainly no longer mutually intelligible. Many of the distinctive features of Assyrian are also found in the pre-Akkadian languages spoken at Ebla and Mari, which were cognate to Akkadian but distinct from it. Unfortunately, we know very little about the early phases of Assyrian.

The earliest known texts in Assyrian were written by Assyrian traders from the city of Assur doing business in Anatolia in the Old Assyrian period (c. 2000-1700 BC). It is possible that the city of Assur played a central role in long-distance overland trade already before the Akkadian Empire in the third millennium BC. Under the Akkadian Empire (c. 2340-2160 BC), Assur developed into a city-state, and afterwards became a province of the Sumerian Ur III Empire (c. 2100-2000 BC). The later kings of Assur observed the traditions of their Akkadian predecessors and fostered Standard Akkadian as a cultural language in which royal inscriptions, epical poetry, and other genres of literature were composed under strict observance of ancient stylistic conventions.

Other kinds of texts were, however, routinely written in Assyrian. The corpus of Old Assyrian currently consists of more than 23,000 texts, mainly letters and various legal, economic and administrative documents, but also treaties, eponym lists, incantations etc., and later corpora feature many other types of text, for example laws and edicts; cultic rituals; horse-training instructions; perfume, glass-making and medical recipes; astrological reports, and oracle queries and reports; prophecies; and even literary and scientific texts, epics, hymns, and prayers. Many of the latter are written in a mixture of Assyrian and Standard Akkadian.

From the beginning, Assyrian kings pursued a policy of territorial expansion designed to ensure the control of important trade routes, vital to the economy of their land. This policy gradually led to the creation of a large multi-national state, the Assyrian Empire, which dominated the Middle East for almost seven centuries. In the so-called Middle Assyrian period (c. 1350-1050 BC), vast areas previously controlled by Hurrian-speaking peoples were annexed and assimilated to the Assyrian heartland. In the Neo-Assyrian period (c. 930-600 BC), when Assyria controlled practically the entire Middle East, vast numbers of conquered, mainly Aramaic-speaking peoples were deported into central Assyria in an effort to create a linguistically uniform Assyrian nation. As a result, Aramaic was established as the lingua franca of the Empire, while Assyrian itself, heavily influenced by Aramaic, retained its status as the high language of the political elite.

The Assyrian language of the Neo-Assyrian period differs from its Middle and Old Assyrian predecessors in many details of grammar and lexicon. On the other hand, many central features of Assyrian grammar and vocabulary remained unchanged through the ages, and while new forms, words and phrases were constantly created, old forms, words and phrases were sometimes astonishingly long retained as variants alongside newer ones. Grammatical features characteristic of Neo-Assyrian may be sporadically attested already in Old or Middle Assyrian, and conversely words normally encountered only in Old or Middle Assyrian may occasionally turn up in Neo-Assyrian texts. This makes it legitimate to turn to Middle or Old Assyrian vocabulary whenever a particular word or concept known from these earlier varieties of Assyrian does not happen to be attested in Neo-Assyrian.

After the collapse of the Assyrian Empire, Neo-Assyrian continued to be spoken and written at least until the middle of the sixth century BC, but thereafter it gradually assimilated to Aramaic and became extinct as a spoken language by the end of the millennium at the latest. However, it did not disappear without a trace. Many Assyrian features still survive in the phonology, morphology, syntax and lexicon of the Neo-Aramaic dialects spoken in the ancient Assyrian heartland by the descendants of ancient Assyrians, the modern Assyrians. Probably one of the best indicators of the depth of this linguistic integration, the symbiosis and eventual merger of Assyrian and Aramaic, is that in later Greek usage, Aramaic language and script were commonly referred to as "Assyrian language and script."

THE AIM AND SCOPE OF THE DICTIONARY

The present dictionary does not cover the entire lexicon of Assyrian from the Old Assyrian through the Middle and Neo-Assyrian periods. Instead, it focuses on the vocabulary of the Neo-Assyrian period, which it seeks to present as completely and accurately as possible. In this, it follows the model of contemporary-language dictionaries, which likewise basically focus on just one language period (the contemporary one) instead of many. The aim has been to create a tool that can be profitably used not only for studying texts from the Neo-Assyrian period but also for composing new texts in the relevant languages, be it for purposes of experimental research and teaching, or simply for fun.

The dictionary contains all the words and phrases attested in Assyrian texts composed in the Neo-Assyrian period, including royal inscriptions and other texts written in Standard Akkadian. As already mentioned, Standard Akkadian had from earliest times been the literary language of Assyria, and it would be impossible to compose Assyrian text dealing with religious, scientific or other technical matters without recourse to its vocabulary. Words attested in Neo-Assyrian personal names only have also been taken into consideration, but with the exception of month names, only a few proper nouns (mainly names of stars, gods, places, and mythological figures) have been included. In all, Neo-Assyrian words and phrases constitute approximately 50% of the lexical material included in the dictionary, Standard Akkadian ones about 25%.

The remaining 25% are mainly words and phrases that are not attested in Neo-Assyrian sources but have been included in order to increase the usefulness of the English side (1373 additional Standard Akkadian words, 228 Middle- and Old Assyrian words, 303 Neo-Babylonian words attested in the Sargonid royal corresponce, and 401 Aramaic words). Many more words could of course have been added from these sources. However, the focus of the dictionary being on the Neo-Assyrian period, the number of words from other periods has been kept as low as possible consistent with a reasonably complete English vocabulary. Furthermore, since the primary purpose of this dictionary is to document the Neo-Assyrian lexicon, forms from other idioms that are identical to Neo-Assyrian are not noted unless there is a difference in meaning, and then only the different meanings are noted. Words from other idioms that have a different spelling from Neo-Assyrian without different meanings are usually noted as variants. Words from other idioms that are cited as headwords are given in their native form except for Aramaic.

In addition, the dictionary contains a number of asterisked words and meanings that can be assumed to have existed in Neo-Assyrian but are not actually attested in our sources. Including such items in the present dictionary is justified by the fact that many of the relevant words and meanings can be derived with certainty from the basic vocabulary of Assyrian.

In all, the dictionary contains about 13,000 Assyrian entries and about 23,000 English entries.

THE DESIGN OF THE DICTIONARY

The Assyrian and English sides of the dictionary have been electronically generated from the same set of basic data, so that there is an almost 100% agreement between the information contained in them. The English side is in effect an index to the translations of the Assyrian words, so that an English headword basically corresponds to an English meaning on the Assyrian-English side.

Note, however, that Assyrian compound words ending in the genitive (ab ababi, bēt ili, ša-rēši, etc.), cited in their full form on the English-Assyrian side, are not to be found in the expected alphabetic order on the Assyrian-English side but have to sought under their last element (abu, ilu, rēši, etc.). Some very common compounding elements (bēl, bēt, mār, rab, ša-) are also collected in alphabetical order under the first element; see in more detail below.

Structure of Entries

The entries in the dictionary consist of the following information:

- Assyrian or English headword
- Cuneiform spelling of the head-word (found in cuneiform edition of the dictionary only)
- English or Assyrian equivalents of the headword
- Idiom source symbol
- Grammatical information.

Order of Entries

Entries are arranged in alphabetic order by the head-words, except for Assyrian compound words, adverbial, nominal, prepositional and verbal phrases and idiomatic expressions, which are arranged under their most important elements according to rules defined below (p. xv).

The alphabetic order in Assyrian entries is:

a b d e g ḫ i j k l m n p q r s ṣ š t ṭ u w z

Aleph (') is ignored in sorting. Long vowels with macron and circumflex follow the respective short vowels (a ā â e ē ê i ī î u ū û).

English entries are arranged in the order of the English alphabet.

Spelling

Assyrian words are transcribed according to the conventions familiar from the glossaries of the State Archives of Assyria series (thus pirsu not persu, etc.), although there are a few differences (e.g., ammīu, annīu, egertu, ēkallu, ēkurru, kēttu, ṣāssu). The spelling of English words follows the American standard, although it should be noted that many of the meanings and senses of the English words correspond to the British usage as defined in the Oxford English Dictionary, and do not necessarily apply to American English.

Assyrian Entries

Headwords

The headwords (in bold type) are given in normalized form. Nouns are cited in the nominative singular, adjectives in their masculine form, verbs in the infinitive of the G stem (if attested). A few nouns (e.g., tabrâti) are cited in the nominative plural if a singular is not attested; a few verbs with no attested G stem (e.g., kallumu, šaklulu) are listed under the D or Š stem form. Quadriliteral verbs are listed under their N stem.

All Assyrian words are presented in Neo-Assyrian form (with vowel harmony), all Babylonian ones in Neo-Babylonian form. Standard Akkadian words follow the norm of Neo-Assyrian literary texts and royal inscriptions. Aramaic loanwords appear in Neo-Assyrianized form. In words subject to vowel harmony, the vowel affected is **not bolded**.

Most important ***variants*** are listed after the head-words (within parentheses) and cross-referenced in appropriate places in the alphabetic order.

Homonyms are differentiated with capital letters (A, B, C ...) following the head-word. The order of the homonyms reflects their frequency and/or the origin: more common homonyms are listed before less common; Neo-Assyrian ones come before > Standard Akkadian > Neo-Babylonian > Middle/Old Assyrian > Aramaic ones.

Compounds and Phrases

Compounds, phrases and idiomatic expressions are arranged under the head-words central to them according to the following rules:

- Compound words ending in the **genitive** (e.g., ab-abi, ab ab-abi, apāl bēt ili, mār šarri, ša-muhhi-āli) are listed under the last element (i.e., under abu, ilu, šarru, ālu, in the above examples). However, as a convenience, some of the extremely common initial elements (mār, bēl, bēt, rab, ša-) have been collected together in normal alphabetic sequence. Thus it is possible to look up mār šarri under both mār and šarru. The reason for this is that in many instances words of this type were treated as genuine compounds (e.g., mār šarri 'crown prince' → mār šarrūtu 'crown-princehood', ša-pētḫalli 'horseman' → ša-pētḫallūtu 'horsemanship').

- Compounds involving two words in the nominative (e.g., abu ummu, abnu aqartu) are listed under the first element (abu, abnu).

- Adverbial and prepositional phrases (im-magāni, ina mati, issu pān) are listed under the last element (magānu, mati, pān) even when the words have merged. However, some compound prepositions and subjunctions (e.g., ina libbi, ina maḫar, adi bēt), where the nominal element frequently no longer has its literal meaning, are listed both under the initial preposition/subjunction (ina, adi) and under the final element (libbu, maḫru, bēt). This treatment is not consistent throughout.

- Phrasal verbs (qarābu + ina muhhi), hendiadys constructions (našû rammû) and idiomatic verb phrases are listed under the verb (qarābu, ramû, etc.).

Idiom Source Symbols

The language of the Assyrian Empire was a blend of idioms, consisting principally of the current Assyrian vernacular (Neo-Assyrian), the current Babylonian vernacular (Neo-Babylonian), the Assyro-Babylonian literary language (Standard Akkadian), and Aramaic.

The symbols following the head-word indicate the source of the word. Neo-Assyrian words, which form the bulk of the vocabulary, are not marked. Standard Akkadian words are marked with ★. Neo-Babylonian words (culled from the Babylonian correspondence of Assyrian kings) are marked with ◊. Obsolete words (from Middle and Old Assyrian texts) are marked with †. Aramaic words (including Akkadian loanwords in Aramaic) are marked with +. Reconstructed or hypothetical words (whose existence has been posited not is not attested in our sources) are marked with an asterisk *.

Even though educated Assyrians could routinely switch from Neo-Assyrian to Standard Akkadian in writing, and to Aramaic or Neo-Babylonian in speech, and thereby would occasionally mix the relevant vocabularies and grammars, they on the whole carefully observed the grammatical and lexical distinctions between these idioms. *It is imperative therefore that these distinctions be carefully observed and taken into consideration by the users of the present dictionary as well*, especially in composing Neo-Assyrian or Standard Akkadian text. It is legitimate to resort to the vocabulary of other idioms if no suitable word or phrase is attested in a given idiom, but mixing idioms indiscriminately (when appropriate words exist in the idiom itself) is not acceptable and should be strictly avoided.

Cuneiform Spelling

The headword is in some editions of this dictionary followed by its standard cuneiform spelling in Neo-Assyrian sources. For words that could be written logographically, the most common logographic spelling is given. Otherwise the word is spelled syllabically, using the most typical Neo-Assyrian orthographic conventions and sign values. No consistency has been striven for in the rendering of those geminated consonants and long vowels which could be left unmarked in Neo-Assyrian orthography.

Words not attested in Neo-Assyrian sources are not given in cuneiform spelling.

Grammatical Information

The abbreviations following the headword indicate its part(s) of speech (n., adj., etc.), gender (f., for feminine nouns), inflectional class(es) (n. [1], etc., for masculine nouns), plurality (pl., for nouns cited in the plural form), and vowel class (a/u, a/i, etc., for verbs). The vowel class of middle-weak Assyrian verbs is generally not indicated since it can always be easily inferred from the form of the infinite (diānu = a/i, duālu = a/u, etc.).

The abbreviations used are listed on p. xx. Paradigms illustrating the declination of nouns and the conjugation of verbs belonging to different vowel classes are found on pp. xix-xx.

Meanings

The meaning of a word is defined by means of one or more English translations arranged in semantic groups. Distinct meanings are separated by semicolons, different senses by commas. In verbs with multiple meanings and senses, "to" only appears at the beginning of a list of different senses and is not repeated until the meaning changes. Clarifying or supplementary information is enclosed within parentheses, e.g., pistachio-like (garden herb), pistachio (nut). Meanings restricted to specific verbal stems are preceded by (D), (Š), etc.

Generic definitions or unclear meanings are enclosed within parentheses (e.g., 'a plant', 'a gold ornament', 'mng. unclear'). Uncertain meanings are indicated with a question mark (used perhaps too sparingly; our policy has been to omit the question mark, if no other Akkadian candidate has been found or suggested for the English word in question and there is no cogent reason to doubt the identification). Conjectural or tentative meanings are qualified with the word "perhaps."

English Entries

The Akkadian vocabulary is much more limited than in modern languages, and accordingly the semantic fields of Akkadian words often are much broader than in English. The reader should therefore not be surprised to find that the number of English entries in the present dictionary considerably exceeds that of Assyrian ones, and that the number of Assyrian equivalents of an English head-word usually is also much lower than the number of English equivalents of a given Assyrian headword on the Assyrian-English side.

Headwords

The English headwords include basically the same categories as the Assyrian ones (e.g., basic and derived words, compounds, proper nouns). Compound nouns, noun phrases, adverbial phrases, phrasal verbs, and verbal phrases are likewise basically listed under the relevant nouns and verbs with the listing being under the most "important" word in the phrase, a judgment that is often subjective. To conserve space, all words in which the headword appears in initial position have been grouped together under the headword. This includes not only compounds and phrases, but also words formed by the addition of suffixes, as long as the headword occurs in full in the word and the word is actually derived from the headword. Homographic homonyms are generally listed as separate headwords unless a context clue is included in the entry.

Meanings

The English headwords are followed by a list of all the Assyrian words they are associated with on the Assyrian-English side. Although listed in alphabetic order and separated by commas, these Assyrian words must not be understood as simple synonyms of the English word. Usually, they represent different meanings or senses of the latter and may even correspond to entirely different English words (homonyms), although some of them belong to different idioms and language periods and thus may indeed be truly synonymous. In some cases, context has been added to the English meanings, for example, to distinguish the 'bark' of a tree from the 'bark' of a dog, but in most cases it is necessary to back-check the English meaning by looking up the Assyrian word on the Assyrian side in order to determine the semantic domain of the Assyrian word and ensure that this word actually corresponds to the English meaning sought. The sources of the Assyrian words are indicated by the symbols already explained under the Assyrian entries (see p. xv). Naturally, to get a better grasp of the fine points in the semantics and usages of a word, one would have to consult more compresensive dictionaries (CAD or AHw).

[NB: The months of the old Assyrian calendar, glossed on the Assyrian side as 'first month' through 'twelfth month', are lemmatized on the English side in parentheses under the ordinal numbers.]

PARADIGMS

Nouns

n.[1]			*(with vowel harmony)*
Singular	ṣupru	didabû	akb**u**ru
Plural	**ṣuprē**	**didabê**	**akberē**
n.[2]			
Singular	šarru		nēr**u**bu
Plural	**šarrāni**		**nērabāni**
n.[3]			
Singular	ḫazannu		saps**u**pu
Plural	**ḫazannāti**		**sapsapāti**
n.[4]			
Singular	ēpišānu		
Plural	**ēpišānūti**		
n.[1,2]			
Singular	ilu		
Plural	**ilē, ilāni**		
n.[1,3]			
Singular	qātu		šem**u**ru
Plural	**qātē, qātāti**		**šemerē, šemerāti**
n.[2,3]			
Singular	dullu		
Plural	**dullāni, dullāti**		
f.			
Singular	egertu	dann**u**tu	
Plural	**egerāti**	**dannāti**	

Adjectives

m.				
Singular	damqu	dannu	šaniu	kēnu
Plural	damqūti	dannūti	šaniūti	kēnūti
f.				
Singular	de'iqtu	dattu	šanītu	kēttu
Plural	damqāti	dannāti	šaniāti	kēnāti

Verbs

	a/u	i/i	u/u	a/a	a/i	
Infinitive	šakānu	paqādu	maqātu	ṣabātu	alāku	tadānu
Present	išakkan	ipaqqid	imaqqut	iṣabbat	illak	iddan
Preterite	iškun	ipqid	inqut	iṣbat	illik	iddin
Perfect	issakan	iptiqid	ittuqut	iṣṣabat	ittalak	ittidin
Imperative	šukun	piqid	muqut	ṣabat	alik	dīni
Precative	liškun	lipqid	linqut	liṣbat	lillik	liddin
Stative	šakin	paqid	maqit	ṣabit	alik	tadin

ABBREVIATIONS

acc.	accusative
AEAD	Assyrian-English-Assyrian Dictionary (Helsinki, 2007)
AHw	Wolfram von Soden, Akkadisches Handwörterbuch (Wiesbaden, 1958-1981)
Aram.	Aramaic
adj.	adjective
adj. cp.	adjectival compound
adj. phr.	adjectival phrase
adv.	adverb
CAD	The Assyrian Dictionary of the Oriental Institute of the University of Chicago
CDA	A Concise Dictionary of Akkadian (Wiesbaden, 1999; 2nd, corrected printing, 2000)
conj.	conjunction
cp.	compound
dat	dative
D	D-stem
DAW	T. R. Kämmerer & D. Schwiderski, Deutsch-akkadisches Wörterbuch (Münster, 1998)
DN	divine nam
Dt(t)	reflexive/intransitive D-stem
Dtn	iterative D-stem
du.	dual
f.	feminine
gen.	genitive
G	G-stem
GN	geographical name
Gt(t)	reflexive/reciprocal G-stem
Gtn	iterative G-stem
hend.	hendiadys
imp.	imperative

int., interj.	interjection
interr.	interrogative word
iter.	iterative
leg.	legal
lit., liter.	literally
m.	masculine
MA	Middle-Assyrian
mng.	meaning
N	passive/reflexive N-stem
n. [1]	masculine noun of class 1 (pl. -ē, -ê)
n. [1, 2]	masculine noun of classes 1 and 2
n. [2]	masculine noun of class 2 (pl. -āni)
n. [2, 3]	masculine noun of classes 2 and 3
n. [3]	masculine noun of class 3 (pl. -āti)
n. [4]	masculine noun of class 4 (pl. -ūti)
n. cp.	composite noun
n. pl.	plural noun
NA	Neo-Assyrian
NATC	The Neo-Assyrian Text Corpus
NB	Neo-Babylonian
nf.	feminine noun
nom.	nominative
np.	noun phrase
Ntn	iterative N-stem
num.	numeral, number
OA	Old Assyrian
OB	Old Babylonian
obj.	object
obl.	oblique
o.s.	oneself
p.	person
part.	particle
pass.	passive
pf.	perfect
phr.	phrase
pl.	plural
PN	personal name
poss.	possessive
prec.	precative
pref.	prefix
pron.	pronoun, pronominal
prp.	preposition
prs.	present
prt.	preterite
q.	interrogative word

rdg.	reading
refl.	reflexive
RIM	The Royal Inscriptions of Mesopotamia (Toronto)
SAA	State Archives of Assyria (Helsinki)
sg.	singular
s.o.	someone
s.th.	something
stat.	stative
st. cstr.	status constructus
subj.	subjunction, subjunctive
suff.	suffix(es)
Š	causative stem
Št(t)	reflexive/reciprocal Š-stem
Štn	iterative Š-stem
trans.	transitive
uncert.	uncertain
uncl.	unclear
unkn.	unknown
v.	verb
v. a/a	verb of a class
v. a/i	verb of a/i class, like alāku, tadānu
v. a/u	ablaut class verb
v. i/i	verb of i class
v. u/u	verb of u class
vent.	ventive
vp.	verbal phrase

SYMBOLS

*	unattested form, or reconstructed word or meaning
+	word or meaning added from Aramaic
★	Standard Akkadian word or meaning
†	obsolete (MA/OA) word or meaning
◊	Neo-Babylonian word or meaning
~	repeated headword
→	main entry continues with associated word or expression
(D ≈ G)	D stem is similar in meaning to the G stem

[Hyphens suffixed to head-words indicate an obligatory possessive suffix (e.g., udē-) or a morpheme boundary (e.g., ša-).]

ENGLISH — ASSYRIAN

Ab *n.* Ābu (month)
aback *adv.* ana qinniš
abacus *n.* ša-manê; → **~(?)** *n.* māḫiṣāti☆
abaft *adv.* ina kutalli
abandon *v.* ezābu [o.], nadû☆, našû rammû, rammû (D), uššuru (D); → **~ed** *adj.* ezbu☆; → **be(come) ~ed** *v.* namû B☆
abase *v.* šapālu+ (D), šapālu☆ (Š); → **~d** *adj.* šappulu; → **~ment** *n.* tašpiltu☆
abash *v.* bâšu (D); → **be(come) ~ed** *v.* bâšu; → **~ment** *n.* būštu☆
abate *v.* naḫāsu◊, paḫāḫu, pašāḫu, šuḫarruru☆; → **~ment** *n.* baṭālu+
abbreviate *v.* karû (D); → **~d** *adj.* kapṣu+
abbreviation *n.* takrītu*
abdomen *n.* emšu☆, imšu☆, karšu+
abdominal *adj.* karšāiu+
abduct *v.* mašā'u, pa'āṣu (D), puāgu, zuāru (D) [o.]; → **~ion** *n.* ḫubtu
aberration *n.* sagûtu+
abet *v.* dabābu (Š); → **~ment** *n.* mušadbibūtu
abhor *v.* ziāru; → **~rence** *n.* zīru; → **~rent** *adj.* zēru☆
abide *v.* katāru+
ability *n.* lē'ûtu☆
abject *adj.* dallu☆, šappulu; → **~ion** *n.* tašpiltu☆
ablaze *adj.* napḫu☆; → **~** *adv.* išātiš☆
able *adj.* lē'û☆; → **be ~** *v.* maṣû (Š); → **be(come) ~** *v.* la'û; → **~-bodied** *adj.* damqu
abloom *adj.* unnubu☆
ablution *n.* rinku; → **~ ritual** *n.* bēt rinki
ably *adv.* lē'îš☆
abnegate *v.* rammû (D)
abnormal *adj.* aḫīu; → **~ly** *adv.* eli minâtīšu☆
abode *n.* šubtu
abolish *v.* nasāku☆ (Š)
abominable *adj.* gaṣṣu B☆, saliu+
abomination *n.* anzillu☆, ikkibu
abort *v.* nadû☆, ṣalā'u [o.]; → **make ~** *v.* ṣalā'u (Š) [o.]; → **~ion** *n.* nīd libbi☆
abound *v.* dešû☆ (Dt); → **make ~** *v.* utāru+ (D)
about *adv.* ammār, battibatti; → **~** *prep.* ina muḫḫi; → **get ~** *v.* namāšu (D)
above *adv.* elān☆, elāniš☆, elānu◊, eliš, ṣēriš☆; → **~** *prep.* ṣēr☆
abrade *v.* garādu+, marāṭu, pašāṭu
abrasion *n.* mirṭu
abreast *adv.* aḫia aḫia◊
abridge *v.* karû (D); → **~ment** *n.* takrītu*
abroad *adj./adv.* ina ḫūli [i.], ina māt nakiri [i.], ina nakiri [i.]

abscess *n.* sikru
abscond *v.* ḫalāqu
absence *n.* lā qurbūtu*, makûtu B; → **in the ~ of** *prep.* ela☆
absent *adj.* lā qurbu; → **~-minded** *adj.* sagû+; → **~ee** *adj.* lā qurbu
absolutely *adv.* ibašši; → **~ not** *adv.* laššu lā
absolve *v.* padû, pašāru; → **~r** *n.* pāširu
absorb *v.* alāṭu☆, ekēmu☆, la'āṭu☆
abstain *v.* šurrû B☆ (Dt)
abundance *n.* ḫiṣbu☆, lulû☆, malûtu+, nuḫšu, šumḫu☆, ṭuḫdu; → **~(?)** *n.* mēšertu☆
abundant *adj.* duššû☆, ḫabṣu☆, napšu, šundulu☆; → **be(come) ~** *v.* ṭaḫādu; → **make ~** *v.* šuparzuḫu☆; → **~ly** *adv.* rabîš☆
abuse *n.* bīštu☆, magrītu☆, pištu☆; → **~** *v.* parrû [o.], sanāqu+ (D)
abusive *adj.* ḫabbālu+
abut *v.* nakāpu☆ (Gtn)
abyss *n.* anzanunzû☆, apsû, lalgar☆
acacia *n.* ašāgu
accede *v.* erābu, kapātu+
accelerate *v.* arāḫu☆ (D)
accent *n.* dikšu☆
accentuate *v.* dakāšu☆; → **~d** *adj.* dakšu☆
accept *v.* magāru, maḫāru; → **~able** *adj.* maḫru; → **make ~able** *v.* ṭiābu☆ (Š); → **~ance** *n.* maḫāru, migru☆, mitgurtu
access *n.* alaktu☆; → **~ion year** *n.* rēš šarrūti☆
accident *n.* miḫru, miqtu; → **~ally** *adv.* ilāni ētapšū [i.]
acclaim *v.* na'ādu (D)
accommodate *v.* biādu (D), kannû (D) [o.]
accommodation *n.* mūšubu
accompaniment *n.* libītu+
accompany *v.* ina idi alāku [i.], labû+, radû
accomplice *n.* ša-issi
accomplish *v.* epāšu, kašāru, malû+ (Š); → **~ed** *adj.* gammuru, palkû☆, šallumu+; → **~ment** *n.* epšetu
accordant *adj.* mitguru☆
according → **~ to** *prep.* ina pitti, ina pūt, libbû◊, pitti; → **~ly** *adv.* iddāti, ina pitti, ina pūti; → **~ly** *subj.* pitti
accost *v.* ṭeḫû☆
account *n.* nikkassu; → **take ~ of** *v.* manû B [o.]; → **~ant** *n.* ša-pān-manê; → **chief ~ant** *n.* šandabakku☆; → **~ing** *n.* munūtu☆, nikkassu; → **chief of ~s** *n.* rab nikkassi
accrue *v.* rabû; → **~(?)** *v.* kapātu☆
accumulate *v.* kamāru; → **be ~d** *v.* kamāru☆ (Gt); → **~d property** *n.* sikiltu☆

accumulation *n.* kiriktu☆, nikimtu [o.], taqrintu☆

accuracy *n.* ḫarṣūtu*

accurate *adj.* ḫarṣu; → **~ly** *adv.* ina ṭūbi [i.]; → **do ~ly** *v.* ḫarāṣu

accurse *v.* nazāru; → **~d** *adj.* nazru

accusation *n.* bitqu; → **make ~s** *v.* bitqē batāqu [i.]

accuse *v.* batāqu, ubburu☆; → **~r (female)** *n.* mubbirtu◊

accustom *v.* sadāru (Š)

ache *n.* murṣu

achieve *v.* ammār X maṣû [i.], kašādu, kašāru; → **~d** *adj.* kašdu; → **~ment** *n.* epšetu; → **great ~ments** *n.* narbû☆; → **~r** *n.* ēpišu

Achilles tendon *n.* šašallu

acid *adj.* enṣu+, marru B+; → **be(come) ~** *v.* marāru+; → **~ity** *n.* emṣānūtu+

acknowledge *v.* idû☆ (Š); → **~d** *adj.* edû

acknowledgment *n.* tūdītu+

acme *n.* appu

acorn *n.* allānu

acquaint with *v.* ša'ūdu (Š)

acquaintance *n.* napṭaru☆

acquainted with *adj.* mūdû

acquiescence *n.* migru☆

acquiescent *adj.* salmu

acquire *v.* laqû, qanû B, rašû☆, sakālu☆; → **let ~** *v.* rašû☆ (Š); → **~ lawfully** *v.* zarāpu laqû; → **~d** *adj.* uppu [o.]

acquisition *n.* kišdu, qinītu

acquisitive *adj.* sākilu*

acquit *v.* uššuru (D), zakû+ (D); → **~tal** *n.* tazkītu☆

acre *n.* ikû

acrid *adj.* marru B

acrimonious *adj.* marru B

across → **get ~** *v.* ebāru; → **take ~** *v.* ebāru (Š), nabalkutu (Š)

Across-the-River *n.* Eber nāri

act *n.* epšetu; → **~** *v.* epāšu; → **~ amiss** *v.* ḫaṭû; → **~ing** *n.* epāšu; → **~ion** *n.* epšetu, ipšu☆, ṣibit ṭēmi☆; → **~ions** *n.* alkakāti☆; → **~ive** *adj.* ēpišu, tēbû☆; → **~ivity** *n.* epšetu, kušīru+, šipir qāti; → **~or** *n.* ēpišu, mēlulû☆, mummillu☆; → **~ress** *n.* mummiltu☆; → **she who ~s** *n.* ēpissu

actual *adj.* kēnu; → **~ly** *adv.* ibašši, kēttu

acute *adj.* ḫarīpu+, qatnu+

ad-lib *adv.* kî libbī-

adamant *adj.* ašṭu☆

adapt o.s. *v.* magāru☆ (Gt)

adaptable *adj.* mitguru☆

Adar *n.* Addāru (month)

add *v.* aṣābu◊, ṭapû, uṣābu; → **~ to** *v.* aṣābu (D), radû (D); → **~ up** *v.* kamāru☆; → **~ up to** *v.* kamāru☆ (Gt); → **~endum** *n.* ša raddê, tardītu; → **~er** *n.* bašmu

addition *n.* tardītu, ṭīpu☆; → **in ~** *adv.* issēniš, ittimma◊, kīma atartimma☆; → **in ~ to** *prep.* elat☆, ṣēr☆; → **~al** *adj.* utru; → **be(come) ~al** *v.* utāru; → **~al amount** *n.* tiṣābu; → **~ally** *adv.* elat☆

address *v.* ragāmu (vent.); → **~ee** *n.* māḫirānu [o.]

adduce *v.* ḫasāsu (Š)

adept *adj.* bēru B+

adequacy *n.* malûtu+, sapqūtu+

adequate *adj.* naṭû☆, sapīqu+

adhere *v.* dabāqu+; → **~ to** *v.* dabāqu+; → **~nce** *n.* ra'āmu; → **~nce (to)** *n.* dubqu+; → **~nt** *n.* rā'imānu

adhesion (to) *n.* dubāqu+

adjacent to *prep.* itê☆, ṭēḫi

adjoining *adj.* ṭāḫi, ṭēḫi; → **~ to** *prep.* gabdi

adjourn *v.* uḫḫuru+

adjunct *n.* šaniu, tardītu

adjuration *n.* māmītu+

adjure *v.* tamû (D), zakāru☆ (Š)

adjust *v.* tarāṣu B (D); → **~ o.s.** *v.* magāru☆ (Gt); → **~able** *adj.* mitguru☆; → **~ment** *n.* šunquttu☆

adjutant *n.* mār qāti, rādi qāti

administer *v.* apālu B, arû C☆ (Gtn), radû, šapāru☆

administration *n.* rēdûtu☆; → **public ~** *n.* rēdût māti☆

administrator *n.* šaknu (acting), šāpiru, šatammu☆; → **female ~** *n.* šakintu; → **~ of towns** *n.* ša-ālāni

admirable *adj.* ša tabrâti*

admiration *n.* tabrâti☆ (pl.)

admire *v.* barû B☆ (Gtn)

admission *n.* erābu

admittance *n.* erābu

admixture *n.* billutu☆

admonish *v.* qalālu (D)

ado *n.* ḫubūru☆

adolescence *n.* ṣuḫurtu

adolescent *adj.* muštēnû☆; → **~** *n.* batūlu, ṣaḫurtu, tariu [o.]

adopt *v.* ana mar'ūti laqû [i.], ṣabātu; → **~ (child)** *v.* laqû; → **~ion** *n.* mar'ūtu

adoration *n.* labān appi☆, palāḫu

adore *v.* appu labānu☆, karābu

adorn *v.* asāmu☆ (D), elāḫu (D) [o.], tullû☆, za'ānu☆ (D); → **~ with garlands** *v.* kallulu+ (D); → **~ed** *adj.* za''unu☆; → **~ment** *n.*

simtu, šumḫu*
adroit *adj.* lā'iu
adult *adj.* rabiu, šaklulu+; → **~erate** *v.* zuppu+ (D); → **~erer** *n.* naiāku*; → **~eress** *n.* naiāktu*; → **~ery** *n.* nīku; → **~hood** *n.* rūbu
advance *n.* alāku, ana pāni alāku [i.], tallu-ku*; → **~** *v.* etāqu, radû* (Š)
advantage *n.* kušīru+, tūmulu; → **take ~** *v.* ḫabālu B; → **~ous** *adj.* kāširu+, ṭābu
advent *n.* erābu
adventurous *adj.* nā'imu*
adversary *n.* bēl abiti, bēl amati◊, bēl da-bābi, gārû*, māḫiru B*, qardammu*; → **~ in court** *n.* bēl dēni
adverse *adj.* maḫḫuru; → **be(come) ~** *v.* maḫāru (D)
adversity *n.* miḫru
advice *n.* milku, mitluktu*
advise *v.* malāku; → **~dly** *adv.* ḫadīš*; → **~r** *n.* māliku, muštālu*
advocate *n.* rābiṣu [o.]
adze *n.* akkullu, pāšu*
aegis *n.* ṣillu; → **under the ~ of** *adv.* ina ṣilli
afar *adv.* rūqiš*
affair *n.* abutu
affect *v.* lapātu; → **~ation** *n.* nikiltu; → **~ed** *adj.* laptu B; → **be(come) ~ed by** *v.* rašû*; → **~ing** *n.* lāpitu*; → **~ion** *n.* rā'imū-tu*, ru'āmu*; → **~ionate** *adj.* rā'imānû◊
affiliated *adj.* ṣamdu+
affinity *n.* qurbūtu
affirm *v.* buāru (D) [o.], kuānu (D), šiāmu+
affirmative *n./adj.* annu kēnu
affix *v.* ṣabātu (D)
afflict *v.* lapātu, ṣarāpu+ (D); → **~ion** *n.* liptu
affluence *n.* nuḫšu, ṭuḫdu
affluent *adj.* šarû, ṭaḫdu
affront *v.* qulālē šakānu [i.]
afoot *adv.* ina šēpi
aforementioned → **(the) ~** *pron./adj.* šin-āti*, šuātu*; → **~ person** *n.* bēl zakār šumi*
afraid *adj.* ādiru*, palḫu, pardu*; → **be(come) ~** *v.* adāru, galādu, palāḫu, parā-du*, šaḫātu B*
afresh *adv.* eššiš*
after *prep./subj.* arki*, dāt, iddāt, ina dāt, ištu*, urkat, urki; → **~** *subj.* kīma; → **~birth** *n.* ipu*, silītu*
aftermath *n.* ṣītu*
afternoon *n.* muṣlālu, qiddat ūmi* (late); → **late ~** *n.* saḫār ūme
afterwards *adv.* arkāniš*, arkānu*, arkiš*, iddāti, urkēte
again *adv.* tūra; → **do ~** *v.* saḫāru, saḫāru (D), šanû (D), šanû* (Št), šanû*, tuāru (D) [o.], tuāru [o.]
against *prep.* ina irti, ina muḫḫi, innirti, kî lā, ṣēr*, ṣēriš*; → **~ the will** *adv.* kî lā libbi, ša lā
agate *n.* šubû+; → **~ with one white band** *n.* pappardaliu; → **~ with two white bands** *n.* papparmīnu
age *n.* dāru+; → **~** *v.* paršumu (D); → **~d** *adj.* paršumu; → **~d (x) years** *n.* mār [x] šanāti
agency *n.* ēpišānūtu◊
agent *n.* allāku [o.], muppišu
aggrandize *v.* rabû* (Š); → **~ment** *n.* tar-bītu
aggravate *v.* pašāqu B* (Š)
aggravating *adj.* mušapšiqu*
aggregate *v.* kannušu+
aggression *n.* tību; → **act of ~** *n.* nukurtu
aggressive *adj.* dapnu*, erḫu*, kadru*, nadru*, tēbû*; → **~ly** *adv.* dapniš*; → **act ~ly** *v.* erēḫu*; → **~ness** *n.* erḫūtu*
aggressor *n.* tēbû*
agile *adj.* ḫarīpu+, nammušīšu*, pazīzu+; → **be(come) ~** *v.* namāšu [o.]
agitate *v.* dabābu (Š), dalāḫu, tarāku (Š); → **~d** *adj.* dalḫu
agitation *n.* mušadbibūtu
agitator (of conspiracy) *n.* mušadbibu
aglow → **set ~** *v.* ḫamāṭu* (Š)
agonizing *adj.* marṣu
agony *n.* sinqu
agree *v.* magāru (N); → **~able** *adj.* magru; → **~ment** *n.* mitgurtu, rikistu*, riksu; → **be(come) in ~ment** *v.* magāru; → **in ~ment** *adj.* magru
agriculture *n.* ikkārūtu+
ague *n.* ḫurbāšu* (cold), kuṣṣu; → **~(?)** *n.* qūbāti
ahead → **be(come) ~** *v.* panû; → **~ (of)** *adv.* ina rēši
aid *n.* aiālu, ḫamāti*, kitru, nārārūtu*, nēr-āru*, nērārūtu*, rēṣūtu*, usutu; → **~** *v.* katā-ru, sêdu*, tappûti alāku [i.]
ail *v.* ḫâšu B*; → **~ing** *adj.* marṣu+; → **~ment** *n.* murṣānu+, murṣu
aim *n.* ṣammuru*, ṣumrāt libbi*; → **~ (for)** *v.* dagālu, ṣamāru*, ṣamāru*; → **~ at** *v.* pānē ana X šakānu [i.]
ain't *v.* laššu
air *n.* šāru; → **~** *v.* napāšu (D); → **~ vent** *n.* bāb zīqi*, nappāšu*; → **~ing** *n.* nupūšu [o.]

ajar *adj./adv.* ṣallupu*
akin *adj.* mušlu, qurbu ana
Akkadian *n./adj.* akkadāiu; → ~ **(language)** *n.* akkadītu; → **in ~ (writing)** *adv.* akkadatti◊
alabaster *n.* gišnugallu
alarm *n.* tukku B☆; → ~ *v.* etāku (D)
alas → ~ *interj.* aḫūla, aḫūlamma
alcoholic *n.* šakrānu; → ~ **drink** *n.* šikru☆
alcoholism *n.* šakrānūtu*
ale *n.* šikāru (strong); → **(diluted)** ~ *n.* billu (blended), billutu (blended); → **~-monger** *n.* ša-billēšu
Aleppo *n.* Hallaba
alert *adj.* etku; → ~ *n.* lē'i īni☆; → ~ *v.* etāku (D), ḫarādu (D); → **be(come)** ~ *v.* etāku
algae *n.* elapûa
alien *adj.* nakru; → **resident** ~ *n.* ubāru; → **~ate** *v.* nakāru (Š); → **~ate from** *v.* parāsu
alight *adj.* napḫu☆; → ~ *v.* urādu
alike *adj.* mušlu; → ~ *adv.* mitḫāriš☆; → **be(come)** ~ *v.* mašālu
alimentation *n.* akullû
alimony *n.* ma''uttu
alive *adj.* balṭu, balṭūssu☆; → **keep** ~ *v.* balāṭu (D); → **being** ~ *n.* balṭūtu
alkali *n.* lardu; → **~ne plant** *n.* uḫūlu+
all *n.* gimirtu, gimru, kalu☆, kullatu☆, nagbu B☆, napḫaru☆, puḫru☆; → ~ *n./adj.* gabbu; → ~ *pron.* kalāma☆; → **~-around** *adj.* ēpiš gabbu; → **~-powerful** *adj.* dandannu☆; → **~-powerfulness** *n.* dandannūtu☆; → ~ **... who/that** *subj.* ammār ...ni; → ~ **around** *adv.* nalbân☆, nalbâna [o.]; → ~ **but** *adv.* ubān☆; → ~ **kinds of** *pron.* kalāma☆; → ~ **kinds of X** *n.* siḫirti X [i.]; → **be(come)** ~ **right** *v.* tarāṣu B; → ~ **that** *subj.* mār; → ~ **together** *adv.* ina muḫḫi aḫāiš
allay *v.* nuāḫu (D), pašāḫu (Š)
allegation *n.* bitqu
allege *v.* baqāru
allegiance → **pledge of** ~ *n.* adê
alleviate *v.* pašāḫu (Š)
alleviation *n.* tapšīḫu☆
alley *n.* birītu B☆, dalbānu☆, suqāqu
alliaceous plant (kind of) *n.* kuniphu
alliance *n.* ebrūtu☆, ṭābūtu☆; → **conclude an** ~ *v.* ana aḫāmiš qerēbu [i.]; → **~(?)** *n.* kitrānūtu◊
allied *adj.* salmu
allocate *v.* paqādu
allocation *n.* esiḫtu, isḫu◊, išḫu [o.], piqittu, šikintu
allot *v.* zuāzu; → **~ment** *n.* iškāru
allow *v.* tadānu
alloy *n.* billu; → ~ *v.* balālu; → ~ **(kind of)** *n.* sādu
allure *n.* kazbatu☆, kuzbu; → ~ *v.* kazābu☆ (D)
alluring *adj.* kazbu☆, kuzbānu☆
ally *n.* bēl salāmi◊, kitru, nērāru☆, rēṣu☆
almighty *adj.* kaškaššu☆
almond *n.* šuqdu; → ~ **(tree)** *n.* duqdu; → ~ **tree** *n.* lammu
almug *n.* elammakku☆
aloe *n.* ṣiburu
aloft → **keep** ~ *v.* ṣapāpu☆ (D)
alone *adj.* ēdānu-☆, ēdiššī-☆, udē-; → ~ *adv.* ēdiš☆
along *prep.* šiddi; → **get** ~ *v.* dabāqu+; → ~ **with** *prep.* adi, adu; → **~side** *prep.* itê☆, šiddi
aloud *adv.* šaqīš☆
already *adv.* maṣi
also *adv.* issēniš, ū
altar *n.* parakku; → **reed** ~ *n.* paṭīru; → **room for portable ~s** *n.* bēt paṭīrāti
alter *v.* enû☆, šanû (Š), šanû (Š); → **~ation** *n.* ḫūlāpu+, šinītu☆, šunnūtu☆; → **be ~ed** *v.* enû☆ (N); → **~nate** *v.* enû☆ (Št), šanû☆ (Gtn); → **~natively** *adv.* šanīš, ulâ
although *gram.part.* lū; → ~ *subj.* ša
altitude *n.* mēliu
altogether *adv.* ana gammurti, ana māla; → ~ *n.* gimru
alum *n.* aban gabê☆, gabû, šikkatu C☆; → ~ **maker** *n.* ša-gabêšu; → **~nus** *n.* tarbiu
always *adv.* ina matēma, kaiamānu
Amanus *n.* Hamānu
amass *v.* kamāru (D), nakāmu☆; → **~ed** *adj.* karku, nakmu☆
amateur *n.* šarrāiu+
amaze *v.* šuqammumu☆; → **~d** *adj.* šuqammumu☆; → **be(come) ~d** *v.* tamû B☆; → **~ment** *n.* tabrâti☆ (pl.)
amazing *adj.* ša tabrâti*
ambassador *n.* ṣīru
amber *n.* elmēšu
ambiguity *n.* pitruštu☆
ambiguous *adj.* pitrusu☆; → ~ **omen** *n.* pitruštu☆
ambit *n.* pittu
ambition *n.* ṣumrāt libbi☆
ambulatory *adj.* muttalliku
ambush *n.* šubtu, taḫsītu☆
ameliorate *v.* ṭiābu (D)
amelioration *n.* tadmiqtu [o.]
amend *v.* taqānu+ (D), tarāṣu B+ (D); →

~ment *n.* tūrāṣu+
amenities *n.* ḫašaḫtu+ (pl.)
amid(st) *prep.* biri-☆, ina qereb☆
amiss *adj.* ḫaṭû☆
amity *n.* salīmu☆, ṭābūtu☆
ammi *n.* niniu
ammonia *n.* ṭābat Amāni
amnesia *n.* lā ḫasās amāti☆
amnesty *n.* durāru, šubarrû☆
amniotic fluid *n.* edamukku☆
amniotic sac *n.* edamukku☆
among *prep.* biri-☆, birti, ina libbi, ina puḫur☆, ina qereb☆
amorous *adj.* rā'imānû◊, rā'imu; → ~ **dalliance** *n.* ṣīḫtu
amortize *v.* karû (D) [o.]
amount *n.* manītu, mīnu B☆, minūtu, nību☆, nīpu
amphora *n.* agannu
ample *adj.* napšu, rapšu
amplify *v.* rapāšu (D)
amputate *v.* batāqu
amulet *n.* kišādu; → ~ **(kind of)** *adj.* ṣallumu; → ~ **for childbirth** *n.* aban ḫālti; → ~ **stone** *n.* aban lamassi; → **stone ~s** *n.* šūtabnī☆
amuse *v.* ṣiāḫu☆ (D); → **~d** *adj.* ṣuḫḫu☆, šuḫdû◊; → **~ment** *n.* mussa''ītu, ṣūḫu☆
amusing *adj.* muṣiḫḫu☆
analogy *n.* ittu☆
analysis *n.* bīru
analyze *v.* barû B☆, ḫiāṭu☆
anarchy *n.* saḫmaštu☆, tēšû☆
ancestor *n.* abu (pl.)
ancestry *n.* kisittu☆
anchorage *n.* makallû☆, maklūtu☆
ancient *adj.* labīru
and *conj.* u
anecdote *n.* tašnītu☆
anew *adv.* ana eššūti☆, eššiš☆
angel *n.* lamassu
anger *n.* libbāti, nuggatu☆, ru'ubtu◊, rūbu B☆, šibistu☆, šuḫuṭ libbi☆, tēgimtu☆, uzzatu☆, uzzu☆, zinūtu☆; → ~ *v.* agāgu☆ (D), zanû (Š)
angle *n.* zamītu+, zamû☆
angrily *adv.* aggiš☆, ezziš☆
angry *adj.* aggu☆, daḫru☆, ezzu☆, ra'bu, šabbāsu☆, šabsu◊, zenû☆; → **be(come) ~** *v.* agāgu☆, ezēzu☆, ra'ābu, ṣarāḫu (N), šabāsu☆, šaḫāṭu C☆, zenû☆; → **cause to be ~** *v.* zanû (Š); → **make ~** *v.* zenû☆ (D); → **be(come) ~(?)** *v.* sanû; → **very ~** *adj.* ugguguu☆; → **get ~ with s.o.** *v.* libbāt X malû [i.]
anguish *n.* sinqu; → **~ed** *adj.* nassu☆; → **be(come) ~ed** *v.* gaṣāṣu

angular *adj.* zamītāiu+
animal *n.* umāmu; → **bald ~** *n.* qarūḫu; → **old ~** *n.* qarūḫu; → **sea ~** *n.* binût tānti☆, umām tānti☆; → **select young ~** *n.* mūrnisqu☆; → **wild ~** *n.* nammaštu☆; → **~ (kind of)** *n.* ḫarušḫu; → **wild ~s** *n.* nammaššû☆
animate being *n.* šikin napišti☆
ankle *n.* kursinnu; → **~-chain** *n.* šemuru; → **~ bone** *n.* kiṣallu; → **~t** *n.* sabirru, šemuru
annals *n.* narû
annex *n.* bētu šaniu; → ~ *v.* sakālu☆
annihilate *v.* gamāru, pasāsu, šagāšu
annihilating *adj.* gāmiru☆
annihilation *n.* abtūtu☆, karašû☆, šaḫluqtu☆
announce *v.* barû B (D), idû☆ (D), idû☆ (Š), passuru; → **~ment** *n.* šisīt nāgiri☆, šūdûtu☆; → **~r** *n.* mubarriu*
annoy *v.* dalāḫu+, nazāqu☆ (Š), šīru saḫālu [i.]; → **~ance** *n.* lumun libbi, saḫāl šīri☆; → **~ed** *adj.* dalḫu+; → **~ing** *adj.* dāliḫu+
annul *v.* pasāsu; → **~ment** *n.* baṭālu+
anoint *v.* eqû, pašāšu, šammunu; → **~ o.s.** *v.* pašāšu (N); → **be ~ed** *v.* šammunu (Dtt); → **~ing** *n.* pašāšu, tēqītu
anomalous *adj.* uzzubu☆
anomaly *n.* izbu
another thing *n.* šanītu
answer *n.* gabrû, nāpaltu [o.], nāpassu, tūrti amati◊; → ~ *v.* apālu, apālu (Š); → ~ **(by)** *v.* šapēlu
ant *n.* kulbābu; → **~'s nest** *n.* qinnu+; → **~bear** *n.* dabbu ša namli+; → **~hill** *n.* qinnu+; → **like ~s** *adv.* kulbābiš☆
antagonist *n.* māḫiru B☆
antecedent *n.* abu (pl.), ālik pāni
antediluvian *adj.* ša pān abūbi☆
antelope *n.* sūsu B☆ (bubalis)
anterior *adj.* pānīu
anticipate *v.* ḫarāpu, panû
antimony *n.* ṣadīdu; → ~ **(paste)** *n.* guḫlu
antipathy *n.* zērūtu☆
antiphon *n.* miḫru
antique *adj.* labīru
antiquities *n.* ṣâti
antiquity *n.* ulla◊
antler *n.* qaran aiāli*
anus *n.* qinnutu, šaburru☆, šuburru
anvil *n.* šapiltu☆; → **~-stone** *n.* šapiltu☆
anxiety *n.* ḫīp libbi, nikittu
anxious → **be(come) ~** *v.* ḫâšu B☆, ikku karû [i.]
any *pron.* aiumma☆; → **~ kind of** *pron.* memmēni; → **~ time** *adv.* immatēma, imma-

timēni
anybody *pron.* mamman★, memmēni
anyhow *adv.* ū
anyone *pron.* aiumma★, mamma★, mammāna★, memmēni; → ~ **who** *pron.* mannu ša
anything *pron.* memmēni, mimma★, mimmû; → ~ **which** *pron.* mīnu ša
anytime *adv.* ina matēma
anyway *adv.* tūra, ū
anywhere *adv.* aiākamēni
apart *adv.* aḫamma; → **keep** ~ *v.* ḫarāmu★; → ~ **from** *prep.* alla◊, balāt, ela★, elat★, ullânu★; → **~ment** *n.* mūšubu
apathetic *adj.* lā ṣāḫitu*
apathy *n.* lā ṣaḫātu*
ape *n.* pagû★, uqūpu; → ~ *v.* paggû* (D); → **female** ~ *n.* uqūputu
aperture *n.* ḫurru+, pētu, pû
apex *n.* appu
aphasia *n.* kadibbidû★
apiece *adv.* iāmuttu
apologize *v.* tēgirtu šakānu [i.]
apology *n.* tēgirtu
apoplexy *n.* mišittu★ (apoplectic)
appall *v.* parādu★ (D)
apparel *n.* tēdīqu★
apparent *adj.* apû★, āṣiu, ṣillānīu+, šāpû; → **make** ~ *v.* kallumu (D)
apparition *n.* tabrītu★, tāmartu
appeal *v.* sullû★; → (**sex**) ~ *n.* kuzbu; → ~ **to** *v.* maḫāru, šasû★
appear *v.* amāru (N), apû★, naṭālu★ (N); → ~ **in court** *v.* zaqāpu; → **~ance** *n.* būnu, pānu (pl.), šikittu★, šiknu, tabrītu★, tāmartu, zīmu (pl.); → **outer ~ance** *n.* bunnannê★ (facial); → **terrifying ~ance** *n.* rašubbatu★
appease *v.* nuāḫu (D), pašāru, salāmu (D); → **~d** *adj.* pašru★
append *v.* radû (D); → **~age** *n.* tillē; → **~ix** *n.* tiṣābu
applaud *v.* na'ādu (D)
apple → **marsh** ~ *n.* ḫašḫūr api; → **mountain** ~ *n.* armannu; → ~ (**tree**) *n.* šaḫšūru
applicable *adj.* asmu★, qurbu ina muḫḫi
application *n.* ṭīpu★
apply *v.* qarābu+ (D), šamādu, ṭapû; → ~ **to** *v.* maḫāru, qarābu ina muḫḫi
appoint *v.* paqādu; → **~ed** *adj.* paqdu; → **~ee** *n.* šikin qāti★; → **~ment** *n.* piqittu
apposite *adj.* asmu★
appraisal *n.* kiṣiptu
appraise *v.* uqāru+ (Š)
appreciable *adj.* ša amāri*
appreciate *v.* ḫašāḫu★
appreciation *n.* ṭēmtu+

apprehend *v.* aḫāzu, lamādu, ṣabātu
apprentice *n.* ṣeḫru, šamallû, talmīdu, tarbiu; → **female** ~ *n.* talmittu [o.]; → **~ship** *n.* šamallûtu
apprise *v.* barû B (D)
approach *v.* maḫāru, qarābu, sanāqu★, ṭaḫû, ṭeḫû★; → ~ (**to city**) *n.* sippu+; → ~ **sexually** *v.* ṭeḫû★
appropriate *adj.* naṭû★, simtu (person or thing), šūsumu★; → ~ *v.* sakālu★; → **~ness** *n.* usmu★
approval *n.* annu, migru★, šalmūtu+
approve *v.* damāqu (D)
approximate *v.* qarābu+; → **~ly** *adv.* ammār
apricot *n.* šallūru
April *n.* Nisannu (month)
apron *n.* sasuppu
apropos (**of**) *prep.* ina muḫḫi, šuḫ
aquarium *n.* bēt nūni+
Aquarius *n.* Gula★
Arab *n./adj.* Arbāiu; → **~(s)** *n.* Arubu; → **~ia** *n.* Arubu; → **~ian** *n./adj.* Arbāiu; → **~ian Desert** *n.* Bāzu; → **~ian woman** *n.* Arbītu; → **~ic** *n.* Arbītu
Aram *n.* Arumu; → **~aic** *adj.* Armītu; → **write in ~aic script** *v.* sepēru◊; → **~ean** *n./adj.* Armāiu; → **~ean(s)** *n.* Arumu; → **~ean woman** *n.* Armītu
Arbela *n.* Arbail
arbiter *n.* pāris birti*
arbitrarily *adv.* kî libbī-, kî raminī-
arbitrary *adj.* šuḫdû◊
arbitrate between *v.* birti X parāsu [i.]
arbor *n.* qirsu B
arboretum *n.* kirimāḫu★
arc *n.* uskāru
arch *n.* qassu+, qumbutu+
arch-traitor *n.* sarsarru
archaic *adj.* ullû★
archaisms *n.* ṣâti
archenemy *n.* bēl dāmē
archer *n.* māḫiṣu, nāš qašti★; → **~(s)** *n.* ṣāb qassi; → (**light**) ~ *n.* Itu'āiu , Itu'u ; → **auxiliary** ~ *n.* Itu'āiu , Itu'u ; → **~y** *n.* ṣāb qassi; → **~y unit** *n.* ṣāb qassi
archetype *n.* gišḫurru★
archipelago *n.* nagû B+ (pl.)
architect → **~(?)** *n.* šelappāiu; → **chief** ~ *n.* rab šelappāie; → **~ural feature** (**kind of**) *n.* ṣimmittu
architrave *n.* ḫittu★
archive *n.* bēt ṭuppāti; → **~s** *n.* maštāru+
archivist *n.* ša-pān-bēt-ṭuppāti*
ardently *adv.* ṣarḫiš*

ardor *n.* ḫimiṭ libbi☆ (excessive)

arduous *adj.* marṣu, pašqu☆; → **be(come) ~** *v.* marāṣu

area *n.* eqlu, kaqquru, pāṭu☆; → **~ measure (kind of)** *n.* pānu B☆

aren't *v.* laššu; → **(they) ~ ...** *cop.* lā ... šina, lā ... šunu

argue *v.* dabābu, ṣâlu [o.], ṣāssu garû, šutābulu☆

argument *n.* dabābu, dibbē, ṣâlūtu [o.], ṣāssu; → **~ation** *n.* dabābu

arid *adj.* ablu; → **~ity** *n.* ablūtu

Aries *n.* agru, Agru☆

arise *v.* tabû

aristocracy *n.* mār damqūtu

aristocrat *n.* mār damqi; → **~ic** *adj.* damqu

ark *n.* ēkallu☆, eleppu

arm *n.* aḫu B, durā'u, idu☆, isḫu C☆, izirû, kappu B☆; → **upper ~** *n.* izirû; → **~-piece(?)** *n.* bēt aḫi; → **~ful** *n.* ammār durā'i+; → **~hole** *n.* šaḫātu+; → **~hole flap** *n.* aḫu B; → **~let** *n.* kirku+

armament *n.* anūt tāḫāzi☆, tillē

armannu-pomegranate → **like an ~** *adv.* armanniš☆

armature *n.* siriam+

armchair *n.* nēmattu

armed *adj.* labšu+, nāš kakki☆; → **~ forces** *n.* emūqu (pl.)

Armenia *n.* Urarṭu

armistice *n.* baṭāl kakkē*

armor *n.* ḫalluptu, qurpissu, sariānu, siriam☆; → **(felt) ~** *n.* naḫlaptu; → **~-maker** *n.* ša-ḫalluptēšu; → **~ plate** *n.* siriam+; → **~clad** *adj.* ḫallupu; → **~ed chariot** *n.* taḫlīpu (defensive); → **~er** *n.* ša-ḫalluptēšu; → **~ing** *n.* taḫlīpu (defensive); → **~y** *n.* bēt māšarti, ḫalluptu

armpit *n.* aruppu☆, suḫātu, šaḫātu+, uppi aḫi☆

arms *n.* tillē

army *n.* aḫu B (pl.), ellatu☆, emūqu (pl.), ḫi'ālu◊, ummānu☆; → **standing ~** *n.* kiṣir šarri; → **~ commander** *n.* rab ḫi'āli◊, rab ummāni; → **~ corps** *n.* kiṣru

aroma *n.* napīšu☆; → **~tic** *adj.* ṭābu; → **~tic** *n.* riqiu

around *adv.* battibatti; → **~** *prep.* itāt☆; → **get ~** *v.* labû

arousal *n.* tību

arouse *v.* dakû

arousing *n.* dīku

arrange *v.* sadāru, šakānu; → **~ment** *n.* riksu, šiknu

array *n.* sidru+; → **~** *v.* sadāru

arrears *n.* ḫibiltu (pl.)

arrest *v.* ṣabātu; → **~ed** *adj.* ṣabbutu; → **~ing** *adj.* ṣābitu

arrival *n.* erābu

arrive *v.* alāku (vent.), qarābu, ukkubu☆ (D); → **~ at** *v.* darāku+, kašādu

arrogance *n.* multarḫūtu☆

arrogant *adj.* multarḫu☆, muštarriḫu☆, šurruḫu☆; → **be(come) ~** *v.* kadāru C☆; → **act ~ly** *v.* šarāḫu☆ (Dt)

arrogate *v.* paqāru

arrow *n.* lištāḫu [o.], mulmullu, šiltāḫu, šukuddu☆, uṣṣu; → **like an ~** *adv.* šiltāḫiš☆; → **~-maker** *n.* sasin šiltāḫi, sasin uṣṣi, sasinnu; → **~-shaft** *n.* šurdu; → **~head** *n.* kaqqad šiltāḫi [o.], lūlītu◊, uṣṣu

arsenal *n.* bēt māšarti, bēt tilli, ēkal māšarti

arsenic(?) *n.* aškiqû

art *n.* nikiltu, šipru, ummânūtu+; → **work of ~** *n.* šipir nikilti☆; → **~efact** *n.* šipir nikilti☆, šipru; → **~ful** *adj.* naklu, nukkulu☆; → **be(come) ~ful** *v.* nakālu; → **~ifice** *n.* šipir nikilti☆; → **~ificer** *n.* ummânu; → **~ificial** *adj.* naklu; → **make ~ificially** *v.* nakālu☆ (D); → **~isan** *n.* ummânu; → **~ist** *n.* ummânu; → **~istic** *adj.* naklu, nukkulu☆; → **~istically** *adv.* nakliš☆; → **execute ~istically** *v.* nakālu☆ (D); → **make ~istically** *v.* niklāti nukkulu [i.]; → **~istry** *n.* ummânūtu, ummânūtu+; → **~s** *n.* nikiltu (pl.)

artery *n.* šer'ānu

arthritis *n.* maškadu☆

as *prep./subj.* akī, kî, kīma; → **(just) ~** *prep./subj.* akī ša, kî ša; → **~ far as** *prep./subj.* adi, adu, adu muḫḫi; → **~ follows** *gram.part.* mā; → **~ if** *subj.* akī, issu maṣin, kī maṣīma, kī maṣin; → **~ much/many as** *subj.* ammār, ammār ...ni, mala☆, mār; → **~ nought** *adv.* zaqīqiš☆; → **~ of now** *adj.* ša ūmi ana ūmi; → **~ soon as** *subj.* aššа◊, ištu☆, qanni; → **~ though** *subj.* issu maṣin, kī maṣin; → **~ to** *prep./subj.* aššu☆, ina muḫḫi, šuḫ; → **~ usual** *adv.* kī ša kāiamānu [i.]; → **~ well** *adv.* issēniš

asafoetida *n.* nuḫurtu, tiātu

ascend *v.* elû; → **~ancy** *n.* bēlūtu; → **~er** *n.* ēliu

ascension *n.* šūqu☆

ascent *n.* elû, mēliu, mūlû

ascetic *n./adj.* maḫḫû, nazīru+

ascribe *v.* šaṭāru+ (Š), ussuku (D)

ash *n.* tumru☆; → **~es** *n.* tumru☆, ṭikmēnu☆

ash (tree) *n.* murrānu
ashamed *adj.* baiāšu☆, buššu*; → **be(come) ~** *v.* bâšu
ashore *adv.* ina kibri
aside *adv.* aḫīta [o.]
ask *v.* ša'ālu; → **~ about** *v.* ša'ālu; → **~ for** *v.* erāšu, ša'ālu
askance *adv.* ṣalpiš☆
askew *adv.* ṣalpiš☆; → **~(?)** *adj.* ḫakê☆
asleep *adj.* ṣallu☆
asp *n.* bašmu+
aspect *n.* būnu, pānu+, pānu (pl.)
asphalt *n.* kupru
aspiration *n.* ṣumrāt libbi☆
aspire *v.* ṣamāru☆
ass → **she- ~** *n.* atānu; → **wild ~** *n.* sirrimu; → **~ (buttocks)** *n.* qinnutu
assail *v.* maqātu ina muḫḫi [i.], sabāku, šaḫāṭu C☆; → **~ant** *n.* tēbû☆
assassin *n.* dā'ikānu◊, dā'iku☆; → **~ate** *v.* duāku; → **~ation** *n.* nērtu☆
assault *n.* šiḫṭu, taḫsītu☆, tību; → **~** *v.* ḫasā'u, tabû
assay *n.* pidānu☆
assemblage *n.* paḫḫurtu
assemble *v.* kamāsu, kannušu+, paḫāru, paḫāru (D), rakāsu; → **be ~d** *v.* karāku (N)
assembly *n.* puḫru, šipāru☆; → **head of ~** *n.* rab puḫri☆; → **public ~** *n.* puḫru ša nišē; → **~ hall** *n.* bēt puḫri☆
assent *n.* annu; → **~** *v.* salāmu+
assert *v.* idû☆ (Š); → **~ion** *n.* zuqāru
assess *v.* ḫiāṭu☆; → **~ment** *n.* kiṣiptu
assets *n.* bišītu☆, nikkassu
asshole *n.* qinnutu
assiduity *n.* kušīru+
assiduous *adj.* kāširu+; → **be(come) ~ toward(s)** *v.* ašrāti še'û☆
assign *v.* kallumu (D), paqādu, ussuku (D); → **~ to** *v.* manû B, manû ana [i.]; → **~ work** *v.* epāšu☆ (Š); → **~ment** *n.* esiḫtu, ussuktu; → **military ~ment** *n.* ḫurādu
assist *v.* ina idi uzuzzu [i.], issi X uzuzzu [i.]; → **~ance** *n.* ḫamāti☆, rīṣu☆, šaḫātu [o.], tappûtu☆, usutu; → **come to ~ance** *v.* tappûti alāku [i.]; → **~ant** *n.* šaniu
assizes *n.* puḫru
associate *n.* aḫu+, šutāpu☆
assorted *adj.* sammuḫu, sanḫu
assortment *n.* liqtu
assuage *v.* nuāḫu+ (D); → **be(come) ~d** *v.* nuāḫu+
assume *v.* kaṣāpu
assuming that *conj.* issurri
assumption *n.* kiṣiptu

Assur *n.* Libbi-āli
assurance *n.* šūdûtu+
assure *v.* kuānu (D), pû tadānu [i.], takālu (D); → **~d** *adj.* kunnu
Assyria *n.* māt Aššūr; → **~n** *n./adj.* Aššūrāiu; → **~n(s)** *n.* Aššūru☆; → **~n (language)** *n.* Aššūrītu; → **~n (woman)** *n.* Aššūrītu
asterisk *n.* kakkabtu
astonish *v.* ta'ādu+ (Š); → **be(come) ~ed** *v.* ta'ādu+; → **~ed gaze** *n.* tabrâti☆ (pl.); → **~ing** *adj.* ša tabrâti*; → **~ment** *n.* tabrâti☆ (pl.)
astound *v.* ta'ādu+ (Š)
astragal *n.* kiṣallu
astride *adv.* ina pētḫalli
astringent *adj.* šēlu☆
astrologer *n.* ṭupšarru Enūma Anu Illil
astrological *adj.* [ša] Enūma Ānu Illil; → **~ omen series (name of an)** *n.* Enūma Anu Illil☆; → **~ work (name of an)** *n.* ṣarrat šamê
astrology *n.* ṭupšarrūt Enūma Anu Illil*
astronomer *n.* ṭupšarru Enūma Anu Illil
astute *adj.* naklu
asunder *adj.* ḫapiu
asylum *n.* marqītu☆
at *prep.* qanni
athlete *n.* bēl emūqi☆, bēl umāši, ša-umāši
athwart *adv.* parkiš☆
atone for *v.* šalāmu (D)
atrocious *adj.* gaṣṣu B☆
atrocity *n.* gaṣṣūtu*
atrophied part *n.* nēkemtu☆
attach *v.* aḫāzu (Š), radû (D), rakāsu, ṣamādu; → **~ed** *adj.* raksu; → **~ment** *n.* mandītu B◊, raksūtu*, tardītu, tillē
attack *n.* šiḫṭu, tīb tāḫazi☆, tību, tibûtu☆; → **~** *v.* erēḫu☆, maqātu, maqātu ina muḫḫi [i.], sabāku+, šaḫāṭu C☆, tabû, zaqāpu
attain *v.* ammār X maṣû [i.], kašādu; → **~ goal** *v.* ṣaḫittu kašādu [i.]; → **~ment** *n.* kišdu
attempt *v.* ba''û, kapādu
attend *v.* etāku (D), ḫarādu; → **~ to** *v.* apālu B; → **~ance** *n.* duālu+, libītu+; → **~ant** *n.* lamutānu◊, ša-bēt-kiṣri (linen); → **~ant of teams(?)** *n.* ša-urâni; → **~ant of the treasurer** *n.* rādi masenni
attention *n.* ḫarduttu, nasḫuru, tašmû☆, uznu; → *interj.*~ addānika
attentive *adj.* ḫardu, na'du☆, qaiālu☆; → **be ~** *v.* ḫarādu (N); → **be(come) ~** *v.* uznu bašû [i.]; → **~ly** *adv.* na'diš☆
attenuate *v.* qatānu☆ (D), raqāqu+ (Š)
attest *v.* kuānu (D)
attic *n.* elītu+

attire *n.* labussu, lubussu, lubūšu, nalbašu*; → **~ o.s.** *v.* šitpuru*
attitude *n.* kilītu+, miqit pāni◊
attorney *n.* rābişu [o.]
attract *v.* kazābu* (D); → **~ion** *n.* kazbatu*, kuzbu; → **~ive** *adj.* kazbu*, kuzbānû*, kuzzubu* (highly); → **be(come) ~ive** *v.* kazābu*; → **~iveness** *n.* kuzbu
attribute *v.* ussuku (D)
auburn *n./adj.* ruššû*
audacious *adj.* qardu
audacity *n.* qardūtu*
audience gift *n.* nāmurtu, tāmartu
auditor → **government ~** *n.* šatammu*
auditory meatus *n.* ruqqi uzni*
augment *n.* tardītu; → **~** *v.* uşābu, utāru (D)
augur *n.* dāgil işşūri; → **~y** *n.* ittu
august *adj.* şīru*
August *n.* Ābu (month)
aunt *n.* aḫāt abi, aḫāt ummi
aurochs *n.* rīmu
aurora *n.* šēru*; → **~ borealis** *n.* akukūtu
auspices *n.* şillu
auspicious *adj.* ṭābu
austere *adj.* dannu
authentic *adj.* kēnu; → **~ity** *n.* kēnūtu
author *n.* ēpišu, šāṭiru
authoritative *adj.* šalṭu B
authority → **claim ~** *v.* šalāṭu; → **having ~** *adj.* šalṭu B; → **position of ~** *n.* piqittūtu; → **give ~ over** *v.* šalāṭu (Š); → **have ~ over** *v.* šalāṭu
authorize *v.* šalāṭu (Š); → **~d** *adj.* šašluṭu
autobiography *n.* narû
autochthonous *adj.* unzarḫu
autocrat → **~(?)** *n.* parriku*; → **~ic** *adj.* šitluṭu*
autograph *n.* šumu šaṭru*
autopsy *n.* bīru
autumn(?) *n.* takrimāti
auxiliaries *n.* kitru
avail o.s. of *v.* utāru+
availability *n.* rāqūtu
available *adj.* bašiu, qurbu, rāqu; → **be(come) ~** *v.* rēšu kullu [i.], riāqu; → **make ~** *v.* rēšu kullu [i.], riāqu (Š)
avaricious *adj.* nāš ēni*
avenge *v.* gimillu turru*; → **~r** *n.* bēl dāmē, mutīr gimilli*
avenue *n.* muttalliktu*
average *adj.* maššuḫu+, sadru
averse *adj.* maḫḫuru
aversion *n.* zērūtu*
avert *v.* etāqu (Š); → **(act of) ~ing** *n.* šūtuqtu*
avid *adj.* nāš ēni*
avoid *v.* ruāqu, ziāru
await *v.* aqû* (D), ina pāni dagālu [i.], katāru+, qa''û
awake *adj.* ēru*; → **~** *v.* êru, ḫarādu, nagaltû*; → **keep ~** *v.* dalāpu (D); → **stay ~** *v.* dalāpu; → **~n** *v.* dakû; → **~ning** *n.* dīku
award *n.* tarīntu*
aware → **be(come) ~** *v.* ragāšu+, udû; → **~ of** *adj.* mūdû; → **~ness** *n.* mūdânūtu
away *adv.* pati
awe *n.* ḫurbāšu* (cold); → **~(?)** *n.* šuribtu*; → **~-inspiring** *adj.* rašubbu*, šugludu*; → **~some** *adj.* rašbu*, rašubbu*; → **~struck** *adj.* šuḫarruru*
awful *adj.* galtu*; → **~ly** *adv.* galtiš*
awkward *adj.* kēšu*, parku
awl *n.* marşā'u*
awning *n.* zārutu
awry *adj.* nabalkutu
axe *n.* ḫaşşinnu, kalappu, nargu+, pāšu*, qulmû*, ulmu; → **~ (kind of)** *n.* agasalakku*; → **~ maker** *n.* naggār pāši
axis *n.* sarnu+, šernu
axle *n.* bubūtu B*, šernu
ay(e) *n.* anni*, annu+
azure *n./adj.* iqnû, saggilmut
azurite *n.* saggilmut
baa *v.* pa'û+
babble *v.* ḫabāru, şabāru+; → **~r** *n.* ḫabbiru
baby *n.* lakû, šerru*
Babylon *n.* Bābili; → **citizen of ~** *n.* Bābilāiu; → **~ia** *n.* māt Akkadî; → **~ian** *n./adj.* Bābilāiu; → **~ian minister (kind of)** *n.* simmagir*
bachelor *adj.* sagdilû*
back *n.* kutallu, şēru*; → **get ~** *v.* saḫāru (D); → **give ~** *v.* saḫḫuru tadānu [i.]; → **keep ~** *v.* kalû; → **~(rest)** *n.* nēmattu; → **in the ~** *adv.* ina kutalli; → **on(to) the ~** *adv.* purqidam*; → **~ache** *n.* muruş kutalli*
backbite *v.* karşē akālu [i.]
backbiting *n.* akāl karşē, akāl karşē+
backbone *n.* eşenşēru
background *n.* arkatu*
backing *n.* tukultu; → **~ out** *n.* tūrtu
backside *n.* urkutu
backward *adj.* kutallānu [o.]; → **~(s)** *adv.* ana qinniš, arkiš*, qinniš
bad *adj.* bīšu+, bīšu◊, lā damqu, lamnu, masku [o.], massuḫu [o.], samku; → **be(come) ~** *v.* ba'āšu◊, be'āšu, be'ēšu◊, lamānu, masāku [o.], ragāgu*, samāku; → **consider as ~** *v.*

masāku⋆ (Š); → **make** ~ *v*. ba'āšu◊ (D), lamānu (D), masāku⋆ (D), samāku (D); → **very** ~ *adj*. lammunu; → **give a ~ name** *v*. masāku⋆ (Š)
badge *n*. simtu
badger *n*. kalab urṣi⋆, sapūnu+; → ~ *v*. bazāḫu [o.]; → **rock** ~ *n*. sapūnu+
badly *adv*. lamniš [o.], lemniš⋆
baffle *v*. dalāḫu; → **~d** *adj*. dalḫu
bag *n*. saqqu+, takāltu⋆; → **(leather)** ~ *n*. luppu, naštuq⋆; → **leather** ~ *n*. ḫintu, kunzu⋆, naruqqu, tukkannu; → **money** ~ *n*. kīsu; → **leather ~ (kind of)** *n*. maššiu
Bahrain *n*. Tilmun
bail *v*. pūtuḫu našû [i.]; → **~er** *n*. naḫbû
bailiff *n*. rābiṣu
bait *n*. laqtu+
bake *v*. epû◊, ṣarāpu; → **~d** *adj*. ṣarpu; → **~r** *n*. āpiu, nuḫatimmu+; → **chief ~r** *n*. rab āpie; → **female ~r** *n*. āpītu; → **~r of seven-tiered cakes** *n*. ša-siqqurrātēšu; → **~ry** *n*. bāb bēt tinūri, bāb tinūri, bēt āpie
baking pit *n*. tinūru+
balance *v*. šaqālu⋆; → **be in** ~ *v*. šaqālu⋆ (Gt); → **~d** *adj*. šitqulu⋆
balcony *n*. aptu, zamītānu+
bald *adj*. gubbuḫu⋆, gurrudu⋆, ḫamṣu⋆, qarīḫu+; → **be(come)** ~ *v*. garādu⋆; → **~ing** *adj*. gurrudu⋆; → **~ish** *adj*. gurrudu⋆
baldachin *n*. ermu⋆
bale *n*. makṣaru⋆, maqarrutu
balk *v*. sakālu B⋆
ball *n*. pukku⋆; → **roll/form/make into a** ~ *v*. kapātu⋆ (D); → **~ (of wool)** *n*. kunšu⋆; → **~ (up)** *v*. kapātu+
ballot *n*. passu+
baloney *n*. siliāti
ban *v*. ḫarāmu+ (Š), kalû
band *n*. ellatu⋆, meserru⋆, miṣru B (decorative), nēbuḫu, riksu, ṭurru; → **~(?)** *n*. sakannu; → **~ (for head or feet)** *n*. i'lu; → **~ together** *v*. paḫāru (Dtt)
bandage *n*. ṣindu, širṭu; → ~ *v*. rakāsu, ṣamādu; → **~/loincloth (kind of)** *n*. sunābu
bandit *n*. ḫabbātu, mār ḫabbāti⋆, parriṣu
bandy-legged *adj*. passulu⋆
bang *v*. maḫāṣu, napāṣu, tarāku
bangle *n*. šemuru
banish *v*. nasāḫu, uṣû (Š); → **~ment** *n*. ṭarīdūtu+
bank *n*. aḫātu B⋆, aḫu B, kibru, kišādu; → **~(ing house)** *n*. bēt tankāri; → **river** ~ *n*. kibir nāri; → **the other** ~ *n*. ebertu C⋆; → **~er** *n*. tankāru; → **~ruptcy** *n*. rāqānūtu+
banned *adj*. ḫarmu+; → **be(come)** ~ *v*. ḫarāmu+
banner *n*. šurinnu, urigallu
banquet *n*. qarētu; → **wedding** ~ *n*. quršu
banter *v*. lazānu
bar *n*. aškuttu⋆, mēdelu⋆, sukru+, ṣiṣṣu⋆; → ~ *v*. edālu, parāku, peḫû⋆; → **(cross)~** *n*. napraku⋆
barb *n*. paruššu+
barbarian *n./adj*. ḫalgatû⋆, nuā'u [o.], Qutû⋆; → **~(s)** *n*. zēr ḫalgatî◊; → **~ horde(s)** *n*. ummān-manda⋆
barbarous *adj*. nakru, saklu
barber *n*. gallābu; → **female** ~ *n*. gallābtu; → **~shop** *n*. bēt gallābi
bare *adj*. pattû, šamṭu+; → ~ *v*. patû; → **~faced** *adj*. lā kallulu*; → **~foot** *adj*. šamṭu+; → **~headed** *adj*. lā apru*; → **~ly** *adv*. pašqiš⋆
bargain *v*. tēgirtu šakānu [i.]; → **~(?)** *n*. tēgirtu
barge *n*. magillu⋆, makkūtu+
bark *n*. qulāptu [o.], qulpu, siḫpu; → **~ (of a dog)** *n*. rigmu; → **~ (of a dog)** *v*. nabāḫu◊
barley *n*. uṭṭutu; → **name of a dish made from fermented** ~ *n*. zannu; → **late** ~ *n*. šigūšu; → **roasted** ~ *n*. gubību, qalâti; → **~ groats** *n*. arsānu, arsu; → **~ ration** *n*. kurummutu
barmaid *n*. sābītu⋆
barman *n*. sābiu
barn(?) *n*. bēt talpitti
barracks *n*. bēt napṭarti
barrage *n*. erretu B⋆, errutu [o.], miḫru, sikru⋆
barrel *n*. dannu B
barren *adj*. lā ālidu⋆; → **~ness** *n*. lā ālidūtu⋆
barricade *v*. sakāru B+
barrier *n*. napraku⋆, sikru⋆
barter *v*. puḫḫu, šapēlu
basalt *n*. atbāru; → **~(?)** *n*. ṣallamtu⋆; → **~ (from Gasur)** *n*. kašurrû⋆
base *adj*. šaplu+; → ~ *n*. āl tukulti⋆ (military), duruššu⋆, išdu, kannu+, šaplu, šupku⋆, šuršu⋆; → **military** ~ *n*. bīrtu; → **~board (of a chariot)** *adj*. sassu
basement *n*. kalakku C◊
bashful *adj*. baiāšu⋆; → **be(come)** ~ *v*. bâšu
basics *n*. rēšēti*
basin *n*. ḫariu, kiūru⋆, saplu
basis *n*. išdu
bask *v*. šammušu+ (D)
basket *n*. kuruppu, masappu, quppu, sallu, sallu+, tuḫallu [o.]; → **~(?) master** *n*. rab

kaqqulti; → **reed ~** *n.* nakmuru; → **~-bodied** *n.* kakkullānu; → **~-like** *n.* kakkullānu; → **~-seller** *n.* ša-ḫuppānēšu; → **~ (kind of)** *n.* takpu; → **~ carrier** *n.* zābil kudurri☆; → **~ry** *n.* atkuppūtu☆

bast *n.* siḫpu

bastion *n.* bīrtu

bat *n.* suttinnu☆

batch *n.* šazbussu

bate *v.* baṣāru+

bath *n.* rinku; → **~ (kind of)** *n.* tuānu B

bathe *v.* ramāku (D); → **~ o.s.** *v.* ramāku; → **~d** *adj.* ramku☆

bathroom *n.* bēt ramāki

bathtub *n.* narmuku [o.]

baton(?) *n.* urāku◊

battalion *n.* sadirtu, sidirtu☆

battering ram *n.* nāpilu☆, šubû B☆

battle *n.* anuntu☆, ašgugu☆, qablu C☆, qarābu, ṣūlāti☆, tāḫāzu☆, tamḫāru☆, taqrubtu☆, tašnintu☆, tuquntu☆; → **fight a ~** *v.* ṣāltu epēšu☆; → **~ array** *n.* sadirtu, sidirtu☆; → **~ line** *n.* sadirtu, sidirtu☆, sidru☆; → **~field** *n.* ṣēru☆, tušāru☆; → **~ground** *n.* naqrabu☆; → **~ment** *n.* kulūlu, naburru☆, sa'ītu; → **~mented parapet** *n.* samītu☆; → **like ~ments** *adv.* naburriš☆

baulk *n.* bīru B☆

bawl *v.* nagāgu☆, nazāqu☆

bay *n.* ibratu☆, nērab tānti*; → **~(?) (horse)** *n.* ḫarbakannu; → **~ window** *n.* zamītānu+

bayou *n.* raṣīnu+

bazaar *n.* sūqu+

bdellium *n.* bidurḫu◊, budurḫu

be it *gram. part.* lū

beach *n.* kibru

bead *n.* erimmatu☆ (egg-shaped), ḫiddu; → **~(?)** *n.* šanduppu

beak *n.* appu, pû, ṣipru☆

beaker *n.* kāsu+

beam *n.* gišmaḫḫu☆; → **~** *v.* barāḫu☆, namāru; → **~ing** *adj.* namru

bean *n.* pūlu B☆; → **~(?) (kind of)** *n.* mangu B☆

bear *n.* asu B

bear *v.* našû, šadādu☆, ubālu, zabālu; → **~ (young)** *v.* alādu☆, ulādu; → **~ down** *v.* kanāšu☆ (Š); → **~ fruit** *v.* enēbu☆ (Dt); → **~ interest** *v.* rabû; → **~ the responsibility** *v.* pūtuḫu našû [i.]

beard *n.* ṭarru☆, ziqnu; → **~ed** *adj.* zaqnu☆; → **be(come) ~ed** *v.* zaqānu; → **~ed courtier** *n.* ša-ziqni; → **~ed man** *n.* darru☆, ziqnānu; → **~less** *adj.* lā ziqnānu*

beast *n.* umāmu

beat *v.* daqāqu+, maḫāṣu, nakādu, naṭû, rabāsu, rapāsu, tarāku; → **~ off** *v.* sakāpu☆; → **~ the ground** *v.* rapāsu+; → **~ thin** *v.* raqāqu+ (Š); → **~ together** *v.* rapāsu; → **~ up** *v.* napāṣu; → **~er** *n.* māḫiṣu; → **~ing** *n.* niṭūtu☆, tirku

beautiful *adj.* babbanû◊, banû☆, damqu; → **be(come) ~** *v.* banû B☆, damāqu

beautify *v.* damāqu (D)

beauty *n.* babbanītu◊, banītu☆, banūtu☆, dunqu

beaver *n.* garīdu☆

because *subj.* aššu☆, nēmel, nirit; → **~ of** *prep.* aššu☆, issu pān, šūt B☆

beckon *v.* ittu tadānu

become *v.* bašû (N), emû☆, tuāru

bed *n.* eršu, maiāltu☆, maiālu, namullu (plank); → **~ (part of)** *n.* sāḫiru; → **~ down** *v.* kanānu (Štn) [o.]; → **~clothes** *n.* dappastu (pl.); → **~cover** *n.* dappastu, qarrāru; → **~ding** *n.* dappastu (pl.), rubṣu☆; → **~ridden** *adj.* naiulu*; → **~rock** *n.* dunni qaqqari☆, kiṣir šaddê, šipik šaddê☆; → **~room** *n.* bēt erši, bēt maiāli, uršu B☆; → **~spread** *n.* qarrāru; → **~time** *n.* simin ṣalāli

bedeck *v.* labāšu☆ (Š), tullû☆

bee *n.* ḫabūbītu☆; → **~hive** *n.* bēt ḫabūbāti*, qinnu+; → **~line** *n.* ḫarrānu išartu*; → **~swax** *n.* pār nūbti☆

beech *n.* murrānu+

beef *n.* šīr alpi

beer *n.* billu (blended), billutu (blended), sirīšu☆, šikāru (strong); → **(strong) ~** *n.* šikru☆; → **bittersweet ~** *n.* alappānu; → **first class ~** *n.* kašmaḫḫu☆; → **~ (kind of)** *n.* amūmu, ḫammurtu, miḫḫu, ṣimtu; → **thin ~ (kind of)** *n.* našpu; → **~ jug** *n.* piḫiu; → **~ mash** *n.* agarinnu B☆, titābē; → **~ wort** *n.* narṭubu

beet *n.* silqu B+, šamuttu [o.], šumuttu☆; → **~root** *n.* silqu B+, šumuttu☆

befall *v.* maqātu ina muḫḫi [i.]

befit *v.* asāmu☆; → **~ting** *adj.* simtu (person or thing)

before *adv.* ina pānīti; → **~** *prep.* ellāmū-☆, ina maḫar☆, ina pān, ina pānāt, pān, pāna☆, pānāt, ullânu☆; → **~** *subj.* lām☆; → **~hand** *adv.* ina pānīti

befoul *v.* šaḫātu C+ (Š), ṭanāpu◊ (D)

befriend *v.* aḫû☆ (Gt)

beg *v.* ṣallû, ša'ālu+; → **~ humbly** *v.* appu labānu☆

beget *v.* reḫû☆; → **~ter** *n.* ālidu, bānû☆, zārû☆

beggar *n.* muškēnu; → **~y** *n.* muškēnūtu
begin *v.* šarrû; → **~ with** *v.* rēšu našû [i.]; → **~ner** *n.* šarrāiu+; → **~ning** *n.* kaqqudu, rēšu, šarrû, šurrâti*, tašrītu B*; → **at the ~ning** *adv.* ina rēši
beguile *v.* nakālu+
behavior *n.* alaktu*, riddu; → **proper ~** *n.* riddu kēnu*
behead *v.* kaqqudu nakāsu
behind *adv.* arkiš*, ina kutalli; → **~** *prep.* arki*, urkat, urki
behold *v.* dagālu
being *n.* bišītu*; → **come into ~** *v.* bašû (N)
Beirut *n.* Bērû
belch *n.* gišūtu*; → **~** *v.* gašû*; → **~ forth** *v.* nasāku
belief *n.* qēptu, qīptu*
believable *adj.* qēpu
believe *v.* qiāpu
belittle *v.* qalālu (D); → **~ment** *n.* qulālu
belittling *n.* qulālu+
bell *n.* tigû*
belle *n.* babbanītu◊, banītu*
belligerent *adj.* dāpinu*; → **~** *n.* qarābtānu+
bellow *v.* lebû*, nagāgu*, ramāmu*; → **~s** *n.* napūḫu
belly *n.* bandillu, karšu+; → **~ button** *n.* abunnutu*
belong to *v.* dagālu (N)
belonging to *adj.* attû*
belongings *n.* bīšu B*, bušû*
beloved *adj.* ra'mu, uqru+; → **~** *n.* narāmtu*, narāmu*, ra'īmu, ra'intu; → **~(?)** *n.* rēntu; → **~ one** *n.* namaddu B*
below *adv.* šapla, šaplāniš*, šaplānu-, šapliš; → **~** *prep.* šapal, šupāl*
belt *n.* ebḫu, ebīḫu*, ḫuṣannu*, meserru*, musāru, nēbuḫu, šibbu*; → **~ (for climbing palm trees)** *n.* tubalû*; → **~ up** *v.* ebēḫu*
bemoan *v.* damāmu*
bench *n.* gišḫummu*, kitturru
bend *v.* atāku* (D), kanāšu*, kapāṣu* (D), šarāru*; → **~ (back)** *v.* kepû*; → **~ back** *v.* kapāṣu*; → **~ down** *v.* kanāšu*, luādu, qadādu B*, šapālu (D); → **~ forwards** *v.* šurru*; → **~ one's mind toward(s)** *v.* pānē ana X šakānu [i.]
beneath *adv.* taḫtānu; → **~** *prep.* šupāl*
benediction *n.* karābu; → **recite ~s** *v.* dalālu
benefactor *n.* ṭābtānu
beneficence *n.* ṭēbūtu+
beneficial *adj.* ṭābu
benefit *n.* kušīru, nēmulu
benevolence *n.* nasḫuru
benevolent *adj.* damqu, ṭābu; → **~ly** *adv.* damqiš [o.]
benign *adj.* damqu; → **~ancy** *n.* sapqūtu+; → **~ant** *adj.* rēmānu; → **~ity** *n.* mitgurtu
bent *adj.* kappupu, kapṣu*, kuppupu* (very); → **be(come) ~** *v.* kapāṣu*; → **~ up** *adj.* kapṣu*
benumbed *adj.* kēru*; → **be(come) ~** *v.* kâru*
bequeath *v.* šiāmu
bequest *n.* qēssu
bereave *v.* ḫabālu B, puāgu; → **~d** *adj.* ekû*; → **~ment** *n.* ḫibiltu*
berry *n.* tūtu+
berth *n.* makallû*, maklūtu*
beryl *n.* burallu
beseech *v.* bâlu*
beside *prep.* gabdi, innidi, itu◊; → **~s** *adv.* kīma atartimma*; → **~s** *prep.* ela*
besiege *v.* esāru, labû; → **~d** *adj.* labû
besmirch *v.* ṭanāpu◊ (D)
best *adj.* utturu+; → **~** *n./adj.* ašarēdu; → **~ man** *n.* sūsabinnu*; → **role of ~ man** *n.* sūsabinnūtu*
bestir *v.* dalāḫu+; → **~ o.s.** *v.* ramanšu dakû*
bestow *v.* qiāšu, riāmu, šutlumu*
betoken *v.* kallumu (D)
betray *v.* nakālu+, nakālu+; → **~al** *n.* zabiltu*
betrothal *n.* ḫašaddu
better → **make ~** *v.* ṭiābu (D)
between *prep.* biri-*, birīt*, birti
beverage *n.* massītu
bevy *n.* rāpu+
bewail *v.* bakû
beware of *v.* naṣāru
bewilder *v.* dalāḫu, dalāḫu
bewitch *v.* kašāpu*; → **~ed** *adj.* kašpu*; → **~er** *n.* muštēpišu*
beyond *adv.* aḫūla, aḫullâ, aḫullû◊; → **~** *prep.* alla◊, elat*
bib *n.* sasuppu
biceps *n.* šer'ān izirê*
bicker *v.* ṣâlu [o.]
bid *v.* qabû
bide *v.* katāru+
bier *n.* eršu
big *adj.* da'nu, dannu, rabiu; → **~-bellied** *n.* karšānu; → **~-eared** *n.* uznānu; → **~ shot** *n.* dannatānu; → **~headed** *n.* kaqqadānu
bight *n.* gidiltu+

bile *n*. martu
bilge *n*. išid eleppi☆
bilious *adj*. marru B
billet *v*. biādu (D)
billow *n*. gillu+; → ~ *v*. sabā'u; → **~s** *n*. rubbu☆
bin → **grain ~** *n*. tuānu B+
bind *v*. kamû☆, kasû, rakāsu, ṣamādu+; → **~ (on)** *v*. ḫarāšu☆; → **~ legally** *v*. rakāsu; → **~ together** *v*. ṣamādu+; → **~ up** *v*. rakāsu, ṣamādu+; → **~ing** *n*. riksu
biography *n*. narû
bird *n*. iṣṣūru; → **crested (kind of) ~** *n*. kubšānu☆; → **female ~** *n*. iṣṣūrtu; → **like a ~** *adv*. iṣṣūriš☆; → **small ~** *n*. ṣepru+; → **young ~** *n*. nibṣu☆; → **~-cage** *n*. quppu; → **like a ~-catcher** *adv*. sandāniš☆; → **~-lime** *n*. dubāqu, tūbāqu; → **~-snare** *n*. ḫuḫāru; → **as with a ~-snare** *adv*. ḫuḫāriš☆; → **~ (kind of)** *n*. allallu B☆, anpatu☆, kupītu, šilû; → **mountain ~ (kind of)** *n*. udīnu☆; → **wild ~ (kind of)** *n*. marrutu; → **~ fodder** *n*. kupātu; → **~ of prey** *n*. zību
birth *n*. ilittu, talittu; → **give ~** *v*. alādu☆, bašû (Š), ḫarāšu B☆ (D), ulādu; → **~mark** *n*. šimit uzni☆, umṣatu☆
'bishop' *n*. šatammu☆
bison *n*. didānu☆
bit *n*. kirṣu; → **(bridle) ~(?)** *n*. mune''û◊; → **a ~** *adv*. ēṣe
bitch *n*. kalbatu☆; → **~y** *n*. kalbatānu*
bite *n*. nišku☆; → ~ *v*. našāku; → **~ up** *v*. našāku (D)
bitter *adj*. marru B, marṣu; → **be(come) ~** *v*. marāru; → **make ~** *v*. marāru◊ (D), marāru☆ (Š); → **~-tempered** *adj*. marru B; → **~ vetch** *n*. kišinnu; → **~ly** *adv*. marṣiš; → **~ness** *n*. martu+, murru; → **~sweet** *adj*. karān šēlibi+
bitumen *n*. kupīru, kupru; → **crude ~** *n*. iṭṭû
blab *v*. ḫabāru; → **~ber** *v*. dabābu (Gtn)
black *adj*. ṣalmu B; → **be(come) ~** *v*. ṣalāmu, ša'āru+; → **~ cumin** *n*. sabubānu, sibibiānu [o.], zibû☆; → **~ kohl** *n*. asḫar☆; → **~ spot** *n*. ṣulmu☆, tirik ṣulmi☆; → **~ star (Saturn)** *n*. kakkubu ṣalmu☆; → **~ stone** *n*. ṣallamtu☆; → **~ woman** *n*. ṣalintu; → **~ wood** *n*. ṣulmu☆; → **~bird** *n*. aškikītu ṣalintu☆; → **~en** *v*. ṣalāmu (D), ša'āru+ (D); → **~head** *n*. ṣulmu☆, umṣatu☆; → **~head Persian** *adj*. parsuāiu; → **~ness** *n*. ṣulmu☆, šu'ru+; → **~smith** *n*. nappāḫ parzilli
bladder *n*. libbuḫu; → **~ stone** *n*. aban muštinni☆
blade *n*. lišānu, šēssu, ziqpu
blame *n*. ḫiṭṭu; → ~ *v*. kasāsu+, ra'ābu; → **~less** *adj*. paṣiu+, zakû+
bland *adj*. lā parsu*
blank space *n*. puṣû
blanket *n*. dappastu
blare *v*. raṣānu☆
blaspheme *v*. karṣē akālu [i.], parrû [o.]
blasphemously *adv*. ana masikti [o.]
blasphemy *n*. miqit pê☆, šillatu☆, šukunnû◊
blast *n*. šāru; → ~ *v*. šabāṭu B☆
blaze *n*. akukūtu, nipḫu
blazing *adj*. āriru B☆; → ~ *n*. muštaḫmiṭu☆, nipḫu
blazon *v*. barû B (D)
bleach *v*. paṣû (D); → **~ed** *adj*. paṣiu; → **~er** *n*. pūṣāiu; → **~er (of garments)** *n*. ašlāku
bleak *adj*. adru B
bleary-eyed *adj*. dalpu
bleat *v*. lebû☆, pa'û+
bleed *v*. alāku [ša dāmi] [i.]; → **~ing heart** *n*. kusup libbi
blemish *n*. pindû☆, uršu☆
blend *v*. balālu, ḫiāqu
bless *v*. karābu; → **~ed** *adj*. rāš ili☆; → **~edness** *n*. rāšilūtu☆; → **~er** *adj*. kāribu; → **~ing** *n*. ikribu, karābu, kiribtu
blight *n*. kamūšu☆
blind *adj*. gallulu; → ~ *n*. upputu☆; → ~ *n./adj*. lā dāgilu, lā nāṭilu☆; → ~ *v*. gallulu, ḫuppudu☆, napālu☆ (D); → **~er(?)** *n*. ṣubāt ēni☆; → **~fold** *v*. arāmu; → **~ness** *n*. lā dāgilūtu*; → **night/day ~ness** *n*. sillurmû☆
blink *n*. ṣadāru☆; → ~ *v*. ṣabāru; → **~ers** *n*. ipu☆
bliss *n*. ulṣu☆; → **~ful** *adj*. elṣu☆
blister *n*. ebiānu+, ḫibṣu, nūpāḫu+
blithe *adj*. namru
blizzard *n*. riḫṣu
bloated → **be(come) ~** *v*. ṣemēru☆; → **~ness** *n*. ṣimirtu☆
block *n*. kubtu, šibirtu; → ~ *v*. ḫaṭāmu, kasāru, paḫû, parāku, peḫû☆, sakāku, sakāru B, šanā'u☆; → **~ade** *v*. esāru; → **~age** *n*. sikru☆; → **be(come) ~ed** *v*. napāqu☆, sakāku; → **~headed** *adj*. paḫiu, peḫû☆
blond *n./adj*. sāmu
blood *n*. dāmu; → **let ~** *v*. maḫāṣu; → **~-thirster** *n*. āmir dāmi☆; → **~ vessel** *n*. šer'ānu ša dāmi+; → **~curdling** *adj*. pardu☆; → **~letter** *n*. ummânu B+; → **~stained weapon** *n*. kak dāmi; → **~y** *adj*. dāmānāiu+
bloom *v*. enēbu☆

blossom *v.* enēbu*; → **~ of the vine** *n.* samādiru+
blot *n.* uršu*; → **~ out** *v.* pasāsu
blotch *n.* pi'āru
blow *n.* miḫṣu; → **~** *v.* napāḫu, šabāṭu B*, ziāqu; → **~ away** *v.* edēpu*, našābu*; → **~ down** *v.* edēpu*; → **~ out** *v.* balû (D), napāḫu+; → **~ over** *v.* nuāḫu; → **~n-up** *adj.* napḫu; → **~n on** *adj.* napḫu*
blubber *v.* bakû (Gtn); → **~ing** *n.* bikītu
blue → **dark ~** *n./adj.* takiltu+; → **light ~** *n./adj.* ḫašmānu; → **~-green** *n./adj.* ḫinziribu
bluff *n.* niklu; → **~** *v.* niklu nakālu
bluish green *n./adj.* ḫinziribu
blunder *v.* ḫaṭû
blunt *adj.* ḫasru*, kepû*; → **~** *v.* ḫasāru*, kepû*
blur *v.* dalāḫu; → **~red** *adj.* dalḫu+; → **~ry** *n.* barru*
bluster *n.* nullāti*; → **~** *v.* šarāḫu* (Dt), ziāqu
boar *n.* ḫuzīru+, šaḫû; → **marsh ~** *n.* šaḫāpu; → **wild ~** *n.* šaḫāpu
board *n.* adappu*, dappu*
board *v.* rakābu
boast *v.* paḫāzu, šarāḫu* (Dt); → **~er** *n.* paḫḫizu; → **~ful** *adj.* paḫḫuzû◊, paḫzu, utturu*
boat *n.* eleppu, rukūbu*, šapīnutu; → **propel a ~** *v.* maḫāru ša eleppi*; → **~-owner** *n.* bēl eleppi; → **~ of inflated skins(?)** *n.* kibarru*; → **~man** *n.* mallāḫu, parrisu*; → **chief ~man** *n.* rab mallāḫi; → **~swain** *n.* rab mallāḫē+, rab mallāḫi; → **~wright** *n.* mallāḫu
bob *v.* gazāzu, kamāmu*
bode *v.* qabû ana
bodily *adj.* pagrānu+; → **~ fluids** *n.* mê; → **~ nature** *n.* pagrānūtu+
bodkin *n.* pulukku+
body *n.* lānu, pagru, šalamtu*, zumru; → **lower ~** *n.* emšu*; → **main ~** *n.* ummatu*; → **~ part (kind of)** *n.* zirūtu; → **~guard** *n.* ša-qurbūti, ša-šēpi (personal); → **~guard (kind of)** *n.* ša-pānīti
boil *n.* bubu'tu*, sikru
boil *v.* baḫāru* (D), bašālu, salāqu; → **~ away** *v.* rabāku [o.]; → **~ up** *v.* zaqāru (D); → **~ed** *adj.* bašlu; → **~ed (meat)** *adj.* salqu; → **~ed meat** *n.* silqu; → **keep ~ing** *v.* baḫāru* (D); → **~ing hot** *adj.* baḫru*; → **~ing point** *n.* baḫrūtu*; → **~ing state** *n.* baḫrūtu*
boisterous *adj.* paḫḫuzû◊, paḫzu; → **be(come) ~** *v.* šagāšu+

bold *adj.* nā'imu*, qardu; → **~-faced** *adj.* erḫu*
bollard *n.* ṭarkullu*
bollocks *n.* ḫarbūtu+
bolster *n.* še'ītu [o.]
bolt *n.* mēdelu*, napraku*, sikkūru, sukru+, šigāru*; → **~** *v.* šaḫāṭu C*, zabābu*
bond *n.* e'iltu*, markāsu, riksu; → **~age** *n.* kabsūtu+, kamûtu*, nīru+
bone *n.* eṣentu
bonfire *n.* išātu
bonk *v.* niāku
bonny *adj.* damqu
boo *v.* muāqu+
boob *n.* lillu*; → **~y** *n.* lillu*
book of life *n.* lē'u ša balāṭi
bookkeeper *n.* šassukku*, ṭupšarru
bookworm *n.* ākilu B+
boost *v.* elû (Š)
boot *n.* šuḫupputu [o.]
booth *n.* raqpu+
bootleg *v.* pazzuru
bootlegger *n.* mupazziru*
booty *n.* ḫubtu, kišittu*, šallutu
border *n.* itû*, kisurru*, miṣru*, pattu, pāṭu*, pulukku*, qannu, taḫūmu; → **~-line** *n.* pattu; → **~ area** *n.* pattu; → **~ post** *n.* madgulu*
bore *n.* lazzuzu+; → **~** *v.* palāšu; → **~ through** *v.* patāḫu; → **~hole** *n.* pilšu
boring *adj.* lazzu+; → **be(come) ~** *v.* lazāzu+; → **~-worm** *n.* balṭītu+
born *adj.* uldu; → **be ~** *v.* alādu* (N); → **~ (in)** *n.* ilittu
borrow *v.* ana/ina pūḫi našû [i.], ḫabālu, ša'ālu+
bosom *n.* ḫabūnu, kirimmu*
boss-eyed *adj.* gallulu
boss (raised projection) *n.* nipḫu
both *pron./adj.* kilallān*, kilallē, kilattān*; → **~ ... and** *conj.* lū ... lū
bother *v.* narāṭu (D)
bottle *n.* laḫannu, ziqqu+ (leathern)
bottom *adj.* šaplu; → **~** *n.* išdu, šaburru*, šaplu; → **rock ~** *n.* šipik šaddê*; → **~ line** *n.* libbi abiti; → **~ part** *n.* šaplītu*
bough *n.* larû
bouillon *n.* mê šīri
bounce *v.* šaḫāṭu C* (Gtn)
bound *adj.* ḫarrušu*, raksu, ṣamdu+; → **~ up** *adj.* ṣandu*; → **~ary** *n.* itû*, miṣru*, puluggu*, taḫūmu; → **~ary (stake)** *n.* pulukku*; → **~ary mark(er)** *n.* kudāru, kudurru; → **~ary stone** *n.* kudurru; → **~er** *n.* kudurrānu

bounteous *adj.* ḫabṣu*, napšu, ṭābtānu
bountiful *adj.* ṭaḫdu
bounty *n.* tidintu
bout (of illness) *n.* šaggaštu*
bow *n.* qassu, tilpānu*; → **~-and-arrow case** *n.* salṭu; → **~-case** *n.* bēt qassi, šalṭu; → **~-maker** *n.* sasin qašāti, sasinnu; → **chief ~-maker** *n.* rab sasinni; → **~legged** *adj.* passulu*; → **~man** *n.* ša-qassi, ša-qašti*; → **~string** *n.* matnu
Bow-star *n.* qassu
bow *v.* kapādu, qadādu B*; → **make ~** *v.* kanāšu* (D); → **~ down** *v.* kanānu (Štn) [o.], kanāšu*; → **~ down to** *v.* appu labānu*; → **~ed** *adj.* kuppupu* (very); → **~el** *n.* tīru; → **~els** *n.* errē
bowl *n.* itqūru, kallu, mallatu*, pursītu (offering), qulliu, saplu, šappu; → **shallow ~** *n.* siḫḫāru; → **stone ~** *n.* pūru B; → **~/goblet (kind of)** *n.* dāpi'u; → **~/jug (kind of)** *n.* māsunu; → **~ (kind of)** *n.* burzigallu*, parsutu; → **~ for washing hands** *n.* ša-qāti
box *n.* pišannu◊, quppu, sussullu; → **~-tree** *n.* šimšālu; → **~/case (kind of)** *n.* ḫabaraḫḫu; → **~ (kind of)** *n.* ašḫulu; → **~thorn** *n.* eddettu
boxwood *n.* taskarinnu
boy *n.* mar'u, qallu; → **~hood** *n.* mar'ūtu, ṣeḫēru*; → **~ish** *adj.* ṣaḫūrānīu*
brace *v.* ṭiābu+ (D); → **~ o.s. (up)** *v.* qablē rakāsu [i.]
bracelet *n.* sa'uru, sabirru, samāru*, šemuru
brackish *adj.* marru B
brag *v.* paḫāzu, šarāḫu* (Dt); → **~gart** *n.* paḫḫizu
braid *n.* gidlu, kiplu, kunšu*
brain *n.* muḫḫu; → **~ matter** *n.* mūqaru+
bramble *n.* amurdinnu
bran *n.* kuspē
branch *n.* āru, ḫuṣābu, larû; → **~** *v.* bêšu*; → **~ (out)** *v.* larû, ṣurrušu*
brand *n.* gizilû; → **~** *v.* šamātu◊; → **~ mark** *n.* sinnutu, šindu◊; → **~ing** *n.* nakmû*; → **~ing-iron** *n.* nakmû*; → **~marked(?)** *adj.* simmatānu
brat *n.* ilittu
brave *adj.* ālilu*, allallu*, qardu; → **~ry** *n.* qardūtu*, qurdu
brawl *n.* puḫpuḫḫu*; → **~** *v.* ṣabāru+
bray *v.* daqāqu+; → **~ (of a donkey)** *v.* na'āru+, nagāgu*, naḫāru+
brazen *adj.* akṣu*
brazier *n.* kanūnu; → **~ (kind of)** *n.* ḫuluppāqu
breach *adj.* batqu; → **~** *n.* niksu, pilšu; → **~** *v.* parāṣu*; → **make ~** *v.* palāšu; → **~ed** *adj.* palšu
bread *n.* aklu, kusāpu; → **beer ~** *n.* pappīru*; → **flat/thin ~** *n.* kusīpu*; → **leavened ~** *n.* enṣu+; → **sour ~** *n.* enṣu; → **sweet ~** *n.* mutqû*; → **wheat ~** *n.* qadūtu; → **yeast ~** *n.* ḫumbiṣutu; → **~ (kind of)** *n.* diru'u, ḫuḫḫuru, midru, pasru, ripītu
break *n.* ḫipītu*, ḫippu, ḫīpu, kīlu*; → **~** *v.* ḫabāšu, ḫapû, ḫaṣāṣu, parāṣu, šabāru; → **~ down** *v.* ḫapû (N), naḫarmumu*; → **~ in** *v.* kabāsu+; → **~ inmake to** *v.* palāšu; → **~ into** *v.* parāṣu; → **~ loose** *v.* parāqu+; → **~ off** *v.* ḫaṣābu◊, karāṣu, karātu, kasāpu, parāqu+; → **~ open** *v.* šarāmu [o.]; → **~ out** *v.* šabābu+; → **~ the law** *v.* parāṣu*; → **~ through** *v.* palāšu, parāṣu; → **~ to pieces** *v.* napāṣu+ (D); → **~ up** *v.* ezābu (Gt) [o.], ḫesû*, parāru (D), paṣṣû, šabāru; → **~ up with** *v.* šalāmu+ (D); → **~able** *adj.* ša ḫapê; → **~age** *n.* šimṭu+; → **~down** *n.* ḫīpu; → **~er** *n.* agû B*; → **~ing** *n.* ḫipītu*; → **~through** *n.* pilšu
breakfast *n.* naptan šēri*
breast *n.* irtu, ṣerretu B*, tulû; → **~bone** *n.* kaskāsu; → **~feed** *v.* enāqu (Š); → **~feeding** *n.* tēnīqu*; → **~plate** *n.* siriam+, ša-irti B
breath *n.* napīšu*, šāru
breathe *v.* napāšu; → **~ into** *v.* napāḫu+
breathing *n.* napīšu*, nipšu B
breccia *n.* turminû; → **volcanic ~** *n.* turminabandû
breed *v.* rakābu (Š), ulādu, ulādu* (Š); → **~er** *n.* ālidu; → **~ing** *n.* tarkibtu*
breeze *n.* mānitu*, napīšu*, šarbillu*, zīqu
brevity *n.* kurûtu*
brew *v.* rasānu; → **~er** *n.* sirāšû; → **chief ~er** *n.* rab sirāšê, rab širāšê; → **~ing vat** *n.* nazzītu
bribe *n.* katrû*, šulmānu, ṭa'tu, ṭātu*; → **~** *v.* šulmānāti tadānu [i.]; → **~ry** *n.* ṭa'tūtu*
brick *n.* libittu; → **blue-glazed ~** *n.* agur uqnî*; → **burnt ~** *n.* agurru*; → **fired ~** *n.* ebertu; → **yellow-glazed ~** *n.* agur ešmarê*; → **~ course** *n.* nadbāku, tikpu; → **~ maker** *n.* lābinu; → **~ mason** *n.* urāsu; → **~ masonry** *n.* urāsūtu; → **~ mold** *n.* nalbantu*, nalbanu*; → **~ up** *v.* raṣāpu; → **~layer** *n.* urāsu; → **mold ~s** *v.* labānu; → **pile of ~s** *n.* amāru C*; → **~work** *n.* libittu
bridal → **~ chamber** *n.* bēt qurši; → **~ gift** *n.* terḫatu*; → **~ veil** *n.* raddīdu+
bride *n.* kallutu; → **~groom** *n.* ērišu*, ḫa-

daššû☆, ḫatannu
bridge *n.* gišru, titurru; → **~head** *n.* rēš gišri+
bridle *n.* malūṭu☆, rappu☆; → **~-bit** *n.* makṣaru☆
brief *adj.* kapṣu+, kuriu, qallīlu+; → **~** *v.* ḫakāmu (Š), lamādu (Š); → **~ly** *adv.* kaṣriš*; → **put ~ly** *v.* kapāṣu+
brier *n.* puqdutu
brigade *n.* mūgu
brigadier *n.* rab mūgi
bright *adj.* namru, napḫu☆, nebû☆; → **~** *n.* muttanbiṭu☆; → **be(come) ~** *v.* ba'ālu, ḫalû☆, namāru, napardû☆; → **make ~** *v.* ḫalû☆ (Š); → **~en** *v.* ḫalû☆ (Š), namāru (Š), namāru☆ (D), napardû☆ (Š); → **~ener** *adj.* munammiru☆; → **~ly** *adv.* namriš☆; → **~ness** *n.* namirtu☆, numru☆
brilliance *n.* namrirru☆ (pl.), namurratu☆, šarūru
brilliant *adj.* namru, namurru☆, šūpû☆; → **be(come) ~** *v.* namāru; → **make ~** *v.* namāru (Š); → **~ly** *adv.* namriš☆
brim *n.* ṣirû◊, šaptu; → **~** *v.* ana ṣirê malû [i.]; → **~ over** *v.* ana ṣirê malû [i.]
brimstone *n.* kibrītu+
brine → **fish ~** *n.* mê nūni☆
bring *v.* abālu B☆, našû (vent.), qarābu (D), ubālu; → **~ across** *v.* ebāru (Š); → **~ back** *v.* saḫāru (D); → **~ close** *v.* ṭaḫû (D); → **~ down** *v.* urādu (Š); → **~ forth** *v.* nabā'u+ (Š); → **~ in** *v.* erābu (Š); → **~ low** *v.* šapālu+ (D), šapālu+ (Š); → **~ out** *v.* uṣû (Š vent.); → **~ over** *v.* etāqu (Š), nabalkutu (Š); → **~ to** *v.* arû C☆; → **~ together** *v.* ḫarāšu☆ (D), kannušu+, paḫāru (D); → **~ up** *v.* elû (Š), rabû (D); → **~ing in** *n.* tērubtu [o.]
brink *n.* šaptu+
brisk *adj.* napšu
bristle *n.* zappu; → **~** *v.* zaqāpu+
brittle *adj.* paḫḫu+
broach *v.* patāḫu
broad *adj.* palkû☆, rapšu, šadlu☆; → **be(come) ~** *v.* rapāšu, šadālu☆; → **~ bean** *n.* pūlu B☆; → **~en** *v.* šadālu☆ (D), šuparruru☆; → **~minded** *adj.* libbu rapšu [i.], palka uzni☆
broil *v.* gabābu (D), gabbubu; → **~ed** *adj.* gabbubu
broken *adj.* ḫapiu, šabru; → **be ~** *v.* ḫapû (N); → **~ heart** *n.* kusup libbi; → **~ in** *adj.* kabsu+, lammudu; → **~ into** *adj.* palšu+; → **~ piece** *n.* šibru☆; → **~ up** *adj.* kabsu
bronchitis *n.* suālu
bronze *n.* siparru; → **~-colored** *adj.* siparrānu; → **~ object (kind of)** *n.* tabbilu☆, taturrû☆; → **~n** *adj.* siparrānu; → **~s** *n.* anūt erê; → **~smith** *n.* nappāḫ siparri
bronzy *adj.* siparrānu
brooch *n.* tudittu
brood *n.* ilittu, qinnu+; → **~** *v.* qapāpu+
brook *n.* naḫlu; → **~let** *n.* raṣīnu+
broom *n.* sāru B; → **~stick** *n.* qātu+
broth *n.* akussu; → **~el** *n.* aštammu☆; → **~er** *n.* aḫu, talīmu; → **~er's sister** *n.* aḫāt aḫi; → **~er's son** *n.* mār aḫi; → **equal ~er** *n.* talīmu; → **twin ~er** *n.* talīmu; → **younger ~er** *n.* duppussû☆; → **~er-in-law** *n.* ḫatannu, ikīsu, mār emi☆; → **~erhood** *n.* aḫḫūtu, atḫê☆; → **~erliness** *n.* aḫḫūtu; → **~erly relations or relationship** *n.* aḫḫūtu; → **become ~ers** *v.* aḫû☆ (Gt)
brought-up → **badly ~** *adj.* lā radiu+
brow *n.* pūtu
browbeat *v.* ḫanû☆
brown *n./adj.* sāmu
browse *v.* amāru; → **~ on(?)** *v.* nâku☆
bruise *n.* miḫṣu; → **~** *v.* ḫašālu, maḫāṣu, marāsu+, napāṣu, ṣalāpu+
brunt *n.* dannat miḫṣi
brush *n.* mušṭu☆; → **~** *v.* mašādu B☆; → **~ off** *v.* šamāṭu
brush pile *n.* abru
brushwood pile → **like a ~** *adv.* abriš☆
brutal *adj.* gaṣṣu B☆
brute *n.* nuā'u [o.]
brutish *adj.* lillu+, nuā'u [o.]
bryony *n.* gupnu+
bubble *n.* burbu'tu☆
buccaneer *n.* ḫabbāt tānti*
buck *n.* armu, kizzu , urīṣu; → **~ up** *v.* libbu rašû [i.]
bucket *n.* dālu, išpikku, madlû, naḫbû; → **leather ~** *n.* mašlû☆; → **~ irrigation** *n.* dilūtu☆
buckle *n.* qullu; → **~ (on/up)** *v.* ṣamādu+
buckle (collapse) *v.* qâpu☆, → **~d** *adj.* quppu B☆
bud *n.* pir'u; → **~** *v.* parā'u
buddy *n.* ša-qurubti
budge *v.* nadādu B☆, nâšu☆
buffoon *n.* aluzinnu☆, pāḫizu
bug *n.* kalmutu, pispisu
build *v.* banû, epāšu, raṣāpu; → **~ completely** *v.* raṣāpu gamāru, raṣāpu šaklulu☆; → **~ firmly** *v.* šaršudu☆; → **~ high** *v.* zaqāru (D); → **~ up** *v.* rabû; → **~er** *n.* bānû☆; → **~er's hod** *n.* kudurru B☆; → **chief ~er** *n.* šitimgallu☆; → **master ~er** *n.* etinnu, rab bānî, šitimgallu☆; → **head of master ~ers** *n.* rab etinnāti; → **~ing** *n.* bētu, rišpu☆; → **main**

~ing *n.* bētu dannu; → **~ing (kind of)** *n.* bēt ekiri, qumbutu

built *adj.* epšu, raṣpu; → **have ~** *v.* epāšu☆ (Š)

bulge *n.* dikšu☆, nupḫu+

bulging *n.* ebû+

bulk *n.* gipšūtu☆, kabittu☆, šipku, šuqlu [o.]; → **~y** *adj.* ḫabburu

bull *n.* lû, šūru B☆; → **(breeding) ~** *n.* puḫālu; → **choice ~** *n.* gummāḫu☆; → **like a wild ~** *adv.* rīmāniš☆; → **ungelded ~** *n.* šaklulu; → **wild ~** *n.* rīmu; → **young ~** *n.* mīru◊; → **~-man** *n.* kusarikku☆; → **~ calf** *n.* bīru C☆; → **~ colossus** *n.* aladlammû; → **~ of heaven** *n.* alû; → **~headed** *adj.* aštu☆; → **~ock** *n.* bīru C☆; → **~shit** *n.* dibbē lā šalmūti, zê alpi*

bully *v.* gašāru☆ (Dt)

bulrush *n.* urbatu☆

bulwark *n.* dūru

bumblebee *n.* zamīmtu+

bump *n.* ḫibṣu, maštu☆; → **~ into** *v.* emādu, ina irti X maqātu [i.]

bun *n.* gubāru◊

bunch *n.* sagullu+, sanbuku, tuganû; → **~(?)** *n.* rigāmu

bundle *n.* ebissu, ibissu, makṣaru☆, riksu, šutukku; → **~ carrier(?)** *n.* ša-ebissēšu

bung *n.* purussu☆

bungle *v.* dalāḫu epāšu

bunion *n.* ebiānu+

bunk(um) *n.* ḫarbūtu+

buoy *v.* šuā'u

burden *n.* biltu

bureau *n.* bētu

burglar *n.* nittamēlu, palliššu, sāru; → **~y** *n.* nabalkattu☆

burial → **~ ground** *n.* bēt qabūri+; → **~ place** *n.* naqburu

burly *adj.* kabra irti☆

burn *v.* dalāqu◊, ḫamāṭu☆, kabābu B◊, qâdu☆, qalû, qamû, ṣarāpu, šabābu☆, šarāpu; → **let ~** *v.* qamû☆ (Š); → **~-mark** *n.* qīlu; → **~ brightly** *v.* namāru; → **~ down** *v.* šarāpu; → **~ up** *v.* ḫamāṭu☆ (D), šabābu+; → **~ with zeal** *v.* qenû☆; → **~ing** *n.* maqlû, naqmūtu☆, qīlu, šuruptu; → **~ing fever** *n.* li'bu☆; → **give ~ing pain** *v.* ṣarāpu (D)

burnish *v.* kapāru

burnt-offering *n.* maqalūtu, šuruptu

burp *v.* gašû☆

burrow *n.* ḫurru; → **~(?)** *n.* ḫalīdu

bursary *n.* bēt quppi

burst *v.* balû☆; → **~ forth** *v.* nabā'u+; → **~ out** *v.* parā'u

bury *v.* qabāru, tamāru

bush *n.* gapnu, ziqpu; → **~y** *adj.* šamḫu☆; → **~el** *n.* pānu B☆

business *n.* alaktu, maḫīru, tankāruttu [o.]; → **do ~** *v.* makāru B [o.]; → **~ associate** *n.* tappû [o.]; → **~ partnership** *n.* itbārūtu [o.]; → **~ venture** *n.* ḫarrānu; → **~like** *n.* tankārānu☆; → **~man** *n.* tankāru

bustle *n.* ḫubūru☆, nugušsû☆

busy *adj.* ḫabru☆

but *conj.* ū, u

butcher *n.* nākisu, ṭābiḫu; → **~** *v.* ṭabāḫu; → **chief ~** *n.* rab ṭābiḫi

butler *n.* šāqiu

butt *v.* dapānu☆, nakāpu☆; → **~ each other** *v.* nakāpu☆ (Gt)

butter *n.* ḫimātu; → **~ trader** *n.* ša-ḫimāti [o.]; → **~cup** *n.* tiātu+; → **~fly** *n.* gurṣiptu

buttock *n.* šuḫḫu [o.]; → **~s** *n.* qinnutu

button/knob (kind of) → **ornamental ~** *n.* pīnu

buy *v.* laqû, mâru◊, miāru, qanû B, šâmu☆, šiāmu B; → **~er** *n.* māḫirānu [o.], musaḫḫiru◊, šā'imānu☆; → **~ing agent** *n.* musaḫḫiru◊

buzz *n.* ḫubbu☆; → **~** *v.* azāzu☆, ḫabābu☆, šagāmu, zamāmu+; → **~er** *n.* ḫabūbītu☆; → **~ing** *n.* šugummû

by *adv.* adi lā, adu lā; → **~** *prep.* qanni; → **~-street** *n.* suqāqu; → **~ (oath: in the name of)** *prep.* nīš☆

Byblos *n.* Gubla

bye (bye) *n.* ina šulmi alik*

bygone *adj.* gamru

bypass *v.* etāqu (Š)

byssus *n.* būṣu

bystander *n.* dāgilu

cabin *n.* kurḫu+, tū'u+; → **ship's ~** *n.* bēt eleppi☆, ḫinnu☆

cabinet *n.* kummu☆; → **kitchen ~** *n.* bēt ḫuruppi

cad *adj.* paḫḫuzû◊; → **~dish** *adj.* paḫḫuzû◊

cadaver *n.* pagru

cadence *n.* kīlu☆

cage *n.* bēt esēri☆, nābartu☆, quppu

cajole *v.* kazābu☆ (D)

cake *n.* garīṣtu+; → **(tiered) ~** *n.* siqqurrutu B; → **sweet ~** *n.* mutqītu; → **wedding ~** *n.* siqqurrutu B; → **chief ~-baker** *n.* rab ša-muttāqi; → **~ (kind of)** *n.* kukku; → **sweetened ~ (kind of)** *n.* kamānu; → **~ man** *n.* ša-muttāqi

Calah *n.* Kalḫu

calamity *n.* dibiru☆, karašû☆

calamus → **sweet ~** *n.* qanû ṭābu+

calcareous *adj.* gaṣṣānu
calcite *n.* elallu
calculate *v.* kaṣāpu, manû B
calculation *n.* igiarû☆, kiṣiptu
caldron *n.* ruqqu
calendar → **(royal)** ~ *n.* inbu bēl arḫi ; → ~ **month** *n.* urḫu ūmāti
calf *n.* mūru; → **young** ~ *n.* būru B; → ~ **of the leg** *n.* kinṣu
call *n.* nibītu☆, rigmu, šisītu☆; → ~ *v.* nabû☆, qarû, ragāmu, šasû☆, zakāru☆; → ~**-up age** *n.* eṭlūtu☆; → ~ **(out)** *v.* sasû; → ~ **by name** *v.* šumu nabû [i.]; → ~ **for** *v.* erāšu, ragāmu (vent.); → ~ **of herald** *n.* šisīt nāgiri☆; → ~ **out** *v.* ragāmu; → ~ **to account** *v.* ba''û, ina qāti ba''û [i.]; → ~ **up** *v.* dakû; → ~**ed (one)** *n.* nibītu☆; → ~**ing up** *n.* dakûtu, dikûtu
callus *n.* ebiānu+
calm *adj.* nēḫu; → ~ *n.* nūḫtu☆; → ~ *v.* nuāḫu (D), pašāḫu (Š); → **be(come)** ~ *v.* nuāḫu; → **keep** ~ *v.* libbu ṣabātu [i.]; → ~ **down** *v.* pašāḫu; → ~**ly** *adv.* nēḫiš☆
calumniate *v.* karṣē akālu [i.]
calumny *n.* karṣu (pl.), pištu☆
camel *n.* gammalu, udru (Bactrian); → ~**'s hump** *n.* gungulīpu☆; → **she-** ~ *n.* anāqutu, gammaltu; → ~ **driver** *n.* rādi gammali; → ~ **herder** *n.* rā'i gammali; → ~ **thorn** *n.* ašāgu
camelopard *n.* gamalnemru+
camp *n.* karāšu B☆; → **military** ~ *n.* madāktu, ušmannu☆; → ~**ing ground** *n.* bēt maškenē+
campaign *n.* gerru☆, ḫarrānu
can *n.* šāḫu
can → ~**'t** *gram. part.* lā mūqā-; → ~**not** *gram. part.* lā mūqā-
canal *n.* ḫarru, ḫirītu, nārtu, nēburu+, pattu, pātu; → **(small)** ~ *n.* atappu ; → **irrigation** ~ *n.* miṭirtu☆; → **like a** ~ *adv.* atappiš☆, pattiš☆; → **irrigation** ~**/ditch** *n.* miṭru☆; → ~**/ditch (kind of)** *n.* ḫālilu☆; → ~ **(part of)** *n.* šiliḫtu◊; → ~ **inspector** *n.* gugallu
cancel *v.* pasāsu; → ~**lation** *n.* pissatu☆, piššatu B☆
Cancer *n.* alluttu
candelabrum *n.* mušanmirtu
candid *adj.* zakû
candidate *n.* ša-paqādi*
candied *adj.* mattuqu
candle *n.* iškūrtu☆; → ~**light** *n.* nūr iškūrti*; → ~**stick** *n.* kannu+, nabraštu+; → ~**wick** *n.* būṣinnu
candor *adj.* kēttu; → ~ *n.* zakûtu
candy *n.* mutqītu; → ~ **peddler** *n.* ša-mutqītēšu
cane *n.* qanû; → **aromatic** ~ *n.* qanû ṭābu+; → ~**brake** *n.* apu B☆
canine *adj.* kalbānu B☆; → ~ **tooth** *n.* šinnu rabītu☆
Canis major *n.* qassu
canker-worm *n.* ṣarṣūru+
cannabis *n.* qunnubu
cannibal *n.* ākil amēli
canny *n.* ḫākimu+
canopy *n.* ermiānu☆ (Anu's), ermu☆, zārutu
canteen *n.* bēt ḫurši
canvas *n.* šaḫḫû☆, šaḫḫu◊
cap *n.* kubšu, mandītu B◊, pingu; → ~ *v.* panāgu; → ~**-maker** *n.* ša-kubšēšu
capability *n.* lē'ûtu☆
capable *adj.* lē'û☆; → **be(come)** ~ **of** *v.* ammār X maṣû (stat.) [i.]
capacity *n.* ṣibtu
cape (of land) *n.* rēš tānti☆
caper *v.* šaḫāṭu C☆ (Gtn)
capillary *n.* qû B☆
capital *n.* kaqqudu, namkūru☆; → **investment** ~ *n.* naruqqu; → **liquid** ~ *n.* rēš namkūri☆; → ~ **(of a column)** *n.* qumāšu☆
capitulate *v.* salāmu
caprice *n.* bibil libbi☆
capricious *adj.* mušpēlu☆
Capricorn *n.* suḫurmāšu, Suḫurmāšu☆
capricous → **be(come)** ~ *v.* nabalkutu☆
capsize *v.* nabalkutu (Š)
captain *n.* rab kiṣri
captivate *v.* esāru+, sarāḫu+ (Š)
captive *n.* šallutu; → **like a** ~ *adv.* kamīš☆; → **take** ~**/prisoner** *v.* pâdu☆, šalālu☆; → ~**s** *n.* ḫubtu
captivity *n.* galûtu+, ṣibittu☆, šallūtu☆
capture *v.* ṣabātu; → ~**d** *adj.* ṣabbutu, ṣabtu
car *n.* saparru
caracal *n.* zirqu☆
caravan *n.* alaktu, ḫarrānu; → ~ **entrepreneur** *n.* bēl ḫarrāni
caraway *n.* ḫaš[i]mur☆
carbon *n.* pe'mu+
carbuncle *n.* gumāru+, simmu, sūmu
carcass *n.* pagru, šalamtu☆
Carchemish *adj.* Gargamis
card *n.* pitqu B+, qulāpu+
card *v.* mašādu B☆, napāšu B; → ~**(ing device)** *n.* mušṭu☆
cardamom *n.* kudimmu, qāqullu☆
cardinal point *n.* šāru

care *n.* kunnūtu◊; → **~ for** *v.* kunnû* (D), rēšu kullu [i.]; → **~ of** *prep.* ina qāt; → **take ~ of** *v.* ašāru, ḫaṣānu, rēšu kullu [i.]; → **~d for** *adj.* kannû; → **~free** *adj.* ḫadiu; → **make ~free** *v.* libbu nammuru [i.]; → **~ful** *adj.* ḫardu; → **~less** *adj.* šēṭu; → **be(come) ~less** *v.* lētu nadû [i.], šelû◊; → **~lessly** *adv.* ina šēṭūti*; → **~lessness** *n.* egītu; → **~taker** *n.* uklu B+

caries *n.* balṭītu+

carnage *n.* šaggaštu*

carnal *adj.* pagrānu+

carnelian *n.* kasânītu (beet-like), sāntu

carnivorous *adj.* ākil šīri

carob (tree) *n.* ḫarūbu

carol *v.* nagû*

carp *n.* arsuppu*

carpenter *n.* naggāru; → **chief ~** *n.* rab naggāri

carpet *n.* nakbusu; → **~-knitter** *n.* kāmidu; → **~ weaver(?)** *adj.* ḫundurāiu

carriage *n.* rukūbu*, šazbussu, tallaktu, utnannu [o.]; → **~ shed** *n.* bēt utnannāti [o.]

carrier *n.* nāšiu

carrion *n.* pagru

carry *v.* abālu B*, našû, ubālu, zabālu; → **~ around** *v.* labû (Š); → **~ away** *v.* bašāmu C*, galû (Š), tabālu; → **~ near** *v.* qarābu+ (D); → **~ off** *v.* gazālu; → **~ on** *v.* lazāzu; → **~ out** *v.* epāšu, etāqu (Š), gamāru+ (D); → **~ to term** *v.* šaklulu*; → **~ing basket** *n.* kudurru B*; → **~ing stick** *n.* atḫusu

cart *n.* ereqqu*, qirsu, saparru, tallaktu; → **~ shed** *n.* bēt utnannāti [o.]; → **~wright** *n.* naggār magarri, naggār mugirri

cartilage *n.* naḫnāḫutu, naiabtu*

carve *v.* esēqu*, garāšu, naqāru, qarāšu; → **(stone) ~r** *n.* ēṣiru*

carving *n.* kapšarrūtu*; → **~ knife** *n.* karrāṭu+

cascade *n.* tibku*; → **~** *v.* gašāru* (Dt)

case *n.* kiṣirtu, takāltu*, unīnu; → **~ at law** *n.* dēnu

cash *n.* kaspu; → **~-box** *adj.* quppu+

cashier *n.* ša-muḫḫi-quppi

casing *n.* kabnu*, taḫbātu*

cask *n.* nazzītu+

casket *n.* pitnu*

cassia *n.* qulkullānu

Cassiopeia *n.* Sīsû*

cast *adj.* šapku*; → **~** *v.* karāru, nadû*, patāqu*, ṣalā'u [o.], šapāku*; → **~(?)** *v.* nabā'u* (Š); → **~ (metal)** *v.* riāqu (Š); → **~ away** *v.* selû+; → **~ down** *v.* daḫû+, saḫāpu+, šapālu+ (D); → **~ off** *v.* rammû (D), ṣalā'u [o.], šaḫāṭu; → **~ out** *v.* daḫû+

castaway *adj.* saliu+

castigate *v.* ana ḫiṭṭi šakānu [i.], qalālu (D)

casting *n.* pitqu*, šipku

castle *n.* bīrtu

castrate *n.* ša-rēši; → **~** *v.* ana ša-rēši turru [i.]

castration *n.* ša-rēšūtu, tapṭīru*

cat *n.* šūrānu, šurānu*

cataleptic → **be(come) ~** *v.* amāšu*

catapult *n.* uṣpu

cataract *n.* nadbāk mê*, tibku*, zīqu+ (violent)

catastrophe *n.* dibiru*, karašû*

catch *v.* ba'āru, kašādu; → **~ in** *v.* sabāku (D); → **~ up** *v.* kašādu; → **~ up with** *v.* kašādu; → **~y** *adj.* ṣābitu

cater *v.* apālu B; → **~er** *n.* laḫḫennu (temple); → **female ~er** *n.* laḫḫennutu

caterpillar *n.* burdišaḫḫi, mūnu, nappilu

cattle *n.* būlu

cauldron *n.* kiūru*, ruqqu; → **~ (kind of)** *n.* tapḫu

caulk *v.* peḫû*

cause to *v.* ša-

causeway *n.* arammu* (siege)

cauterize *v.* qamû

caution *v.* ḫarādu (D)

cautious *adj.* etku, muntalku*, pitqudu*

cavalry *n.* pētḫallu; → **~(man) of the royal guard** *n.* ša-pētḫal qurubte; → **~ commander** *n.* rab pētḫalli; → **~ unit** *n.* pirru; → **commander of ~ units** *n.* rab pirrāni; → **~man** *n.* ša-pētḫalli

cave *n.* ḫurru; → **~ in** *v.* qâpu*; → **~rn** *n.* gubbutu+, ḫurru

cavil *v.* karṣē akālu [i.]

cavity *n.* ḫalīdu, ḫurru, karšu+, ruqqu B*; → **~ of the ear** *n.* ruqqi uzni*

caw *v.* naqāḫu+, šasû*; → **~-caw** *n.* quaqua

cease *v.* baṭālu, kalû (N), naparkû*, nuāḫu+; → **~ doing** *v.* našû rammû; → **~d** *adj.* baṭlu; → **~less** *adj.* lā naparkû*

ceasing *adj.* mupparkû*

cedar *n.* erēnu; → **prickly ~** *n.* burāšu; → **~ balsam** *n.* dām erēni; → **~ mountain** *n.* šad erēni*; → **~ resin** *n.* qatrānu*, supuḫru

cede *v.* nadādu B*, naḫāsu◊, tadānu

ceil *v.* ṣallulu+; → **~ing** *n.* ūru

celebrated *adj.* edû

celebration *n.* rīštu◊, tašīltu*; → **house of ~s** *n.* bēt ḫidāti*

celebrity *n.* edûtu*

celerity *n.* ḫamuttu*

celestial → **~ body** *n.* kakkubu; → **~ firmament** *n.* burummu*

celibacy *n.* batūlūtu+

celibate *n.* nazīru+

cell *n.* kummu*, maštaku*, tū'u+

cella *n.* atmunu, kiṣṣu*, kummu*, papāḫu; → **~r** *n.* kalakku C◊

cement *n.* šelluru

cemetery *n.* qabūru

censer *n.* muqattirtu, nidnakku [o.], šēḫtu

censure *v.* dakû

census *n.* aširtu

centary(?) *n.* daddaru*

Centaurus *n.* Habaṣīrānu*

centaury(?) *n.* daddaru*

center *n.* abunnutu*, qabassu, qabsu, qerbītu*; → **city ~** *n.* qabsi āli

centipede *n.* ḫallulâ; → **like a ~** *adv.* ḫallālatti

central *adj.* qabassīu, qablīu*, qabsīu; → **~ part** *n.* durgu*

century *n.* dāru+

ceramics *n.* paḫḫārūtu+

cereal → **~(s)** *n.* ašnan B*; → **~ (kind of)** *n.* abuḫšinnu, gulbūtu, inninnu, kātu, sēpu B

ceremony *n.* kidudê*, parṣu; → **wedding ~** *n.* ḫatnūtu+; → **~ (kind of)** *n.* pandugānu; → **~ (kind of; lit. 'opening of the gate')** *n.* pīt bābi◊

certain *adj.* kunnu; → **~ly** *adv.* issurri, uddi [o.]; → **~ly not** *adv.* laššu lā; → **~ty** *n.* abutu kunnutu, kunnūtu*

certified *adj.* ḫarmu [o.], kunnu

certify *v.* kuānu (D)

certitude *n.* kunnūtu*

cervical vertebra *n.* kunuk kišādi*

cessation *n.* baṭlu

chafe *v.* kabādu+ (D)

chaff *n.* ḫāmu, iltu B, pu'ē, zê nissaba

chain *n.* ḫarḫarru, šeršerrutu

chair *n.* kussiu; → **sedan ~** *n.* kussiu; → **~man** *n.* rab puḫri*; → **~person** *n.* rab puḫri*

chaise *n.* utnannu [o.]

chalcedony *n.* ḫulālu; → **pale-blue ~** *n.* ašpû

chalice *n.* kāsu+

challenge *n.* migirtu*; → **~** *v.* garû*, paqāru

chamber *n.* massuku, maštaku*, tū'u*, tuānu B+

chamberlain *n.* ša-muḫḫi-bētāni

chameleon *n.* aiar ili, ḫulamēšu

chamois *n.* turāḫu+

champignon *n.* puṭuru

champion *n.* ašarēdu, etellu*, qarrādu

chance *n.* miqtu; → **by ~** *adv.* ilāni ētapšū [i.]

chandelier *n.* mušanmirtu, nabraštu+

change *n.* kasap kīsi*, šinītu*, šunnūtu*; → **~** *v.* enû*, nakāru (D), puḫḫu, šanû, šanû (Š), šupēlu*; → **~ (of clothes)** *n.* tēnû; → **~ into** *v.* emû* (Š); → **~able** *adj.* mušpēlu*; → **be ~able** *v.* šanû* (Gt); → **~d** *adj.* nakkuru; → **~d order** *n.* enītu*; → **~over** *n.* tēnītu*

changing *adj.* muštēnû*; → **keep ~** *v.* šanû* (Gtn)

channel *n.* bitqu B◊, ḫirīṣu, rāṭu; → **~** *v.* etāqu (Š)

chant *v.* la'āzu+, zamāru; → **~er** *n.* kalû B; → **chief ~er** *n.* kalamāḫu, rab kalê

chaos *n.* tēšû*

chap *n.* tappû; → **~el** *n.* kiṣṣu*, sukku; → **~el (kind of)** *n.* bēt natḫi*; → **~let** *n.* kilīlu+

chapter *n.* pirsu

char *v.* ša'āru+ (D)

character *n.* šiknu; → **~istic** *n.* ittu*, simtu; → **~ize** *v.* eṣāru+

charcoal *n.* pe'ettu, pēntu

chard *n.* silqu B+

charge *n.* bitqu, piqittu, qātu; → **be in ~** *v.* šalāṭu+; → **~ (an account)** *v.* manû B [o.]; → **~ against** *v.* manû ina muḫḫi [i.]

chariot *n.* magarru, mugirru, narkabtu; → **~(?) (part of)** *n.* aštillu*; → **large-wheeled ~** *n.* uttartu; → **~-drivership** *n.* mukīl appātūtu; → **~-knight** *n.* mār damqi; → **~-knighthood** *n.* mār damqūtu; → **~-man** *n.* sūsānu; → **~ (kind of)** *n.* dunānu, mašīru*; → **~ (part of)** *n.* ḫutnû*; → **~ (specification of a)** *n.* nagalmušu; → **~ driver** *n.* mukīl appāti, mukīl ašāti*; → **~ fighter** *n.* mār damqi; → **~ owner** *n.* bēl mugirri; → **~ supervisor** *n.* ša-pān-mugirri; → **~eer** *n.* assāru*, ša-narkabti

charisma *n.* kuzbu, lalû

charitable *adj.* rēmānu, ṭābtānu

charity *n.* ṭābtu

charm *n.* kuzbu, lulû*; → **~** *v.* kazābu* (D); → **love ~** *n.* aban rāmi; → **provide with ~** *v.* lullû*; → **~ed** *adj.* kašpu*; → **~ing** *adj.* kāšipu*, kazbu*, lullû*; → **be(come) ~ing** *v.* kazābu*

chart *n.* liṭṭu

chase *n.* ridpu; → **~** *v.* kašādu (D), radādu; → **~ around** *v.* našarbuṭu*; → **~ away** *v.* kašādu (D); → **~d away** *adj.* ṭardu*

chasm *n.* šitqu+

chaste *adj.* zakû; → **~ tree** *n.* šunû*

chastise *v.* ṣarāpu+ (D)

chastity *n.* zakûtu

chatter *n.* dabābtu; → ~ *v.* dabābu (Gtn), ṣabāru; → **~box** *n.* ṣābiru*

cheap *adj.* batqu [o.]; → **~en** *v.* batāqu [o.]; → **~ly** *adv.* maḫīriš☆

cheat *v.* dâṣu☆, salû, sarāru [o.], ṭalāmu+; → **~ing** *n.* sarrūtu☆

check *n.* maltaktu☆; → ~ *v.* ašāru, balāmu+, biāru, latāku, murruru◊, paqādu, rēšu našû [i.], sanāqu☆, tuāku+ (D); → **)keep in ~** *v.* lâṭu☆; → **~-list** *n.* amirtu☆; → **~-up** *n.* piqittu; → **~ on** *v.* rēšu našû [i.]; → **~ through** *v.* barû B☆; → **~ed** *adj.* ašru, latku; → **~ing** *n.* masnaqtu☆

cheek *n.* lētu; → **~bone** *n.* isu☆; → **~y** *adj.* erḫu☆

cheer → **~ up** *v.* libbu balluṭu [i.], namāru (Š), napardû☆ (Š); → **~ful** *adj.* namru; → **be(come) ~ful** *v.* napardû☆; → **make ~ful** *v.* libbu nammuru [i.]; → **~ful mood** *n.* nummur libbi☆; → **~ful song** *n.* elēlu☆; → **~less** *adj.* adru B

cheese *n.* eqīdu; → **~-mite** *n.* ākilu B+

cheetah *n.* mindīnu☆, senkurru

cherish *v.* ḫaṣānu, kunnû☆ (D), naṣāru; → **~ed** *adj.* kannû; → **~ing** *n.* kunnûtu◊

cherry(?) *n.* girīṣu☆

cherry plum *n.* šallūru

cherub *n.* kurību

chest *n.* bāntu B☆, irtu, pišannu◊, sussullu, šaddu◊, tupninnu, unīnu; → **~-plate** *n.* ša-irti B

chew *v.* kasāsu, lamāmu☆

chic *adj.* damqu

chick-pea *n.* ḫallūru☆, šu'u

chicken *n.* raṣṣīṣu☆; → **~ pox** *n.* samānu B☆, šagbānu☆

chickling vetch *n.* elmessu [o.], laṭiru☆

chicory *adj.* murāru☆; → ~ *n.* marurtu+

chide *v.* kasāsu+

chief *n.* rabiu; → **~ly** *adv.* parīsatti+; → **~tain** *n.* ra'su; → **(foreign) ~tain** *n.* ṣīru

child *n.* līdu, ṣeḫru, ṣīt libbi☆; → **(young) ~** *n.* šerru☆; → **~birth** *n.* talittu; → **~hood** *n.* lakûtu; → **~ish** *adj.* ṣeḫrānu*, [ša] šerri*

chiliarch *n.* rab līmi

chill *n.* kuṣṣu; → ~ *v.* kaṣû☆ (D); → **~y** *adj.* kaṣû☆; → **be(come) ~y** *v.* kaṣû☆

chime *n.* šugummû; → ~ *v.* ḫalālu B, šagāmu

chin *n.* zuqtu

chine *n.* rapassu

chink *n.* bitqu+, rigmu, ṣelpu+

chip *n.* ḫiṣibtu☆, ḫuṣābu; → ~ *v.* kasāmu [o.], kasāpu; → **~ off** *v.* ḫasāru☆

chirp *v.* ṣabāru

chirrup *v.* ṣabāru

chisel *v.* esēqu☆; → **~(?)** *n.* urāku◊

choice *adj.* libbu, nasqu; → ~ *n.* nisiqtu☆, nisqu☆, nišīt ēni☆; → **~st** *n.* nisqu☆; → **~st things** *n.* rēšāti

choir *n.* kalû B (pl.), kināltu+, šitru☆; → **~ boy** *n.* kulu'u

choke *v.* ḫanāqu

choking *adj.* ḫāniqu

choleric *adj.* ezzu☆, uggugu☆

choose *v.* amāru, atû B☆ (D), biāru, ḫiāru, nasāqu

choosy *adj.* nassiqu☆

chop *v.* ḫabāšu, nakāsu (D); → **~ down** *v.* kašāṭu☆; → **~ off** *v.* kasāpu; → **~ up** *v.* kasāmu [o.]; → **~ped** *adj.* kassupu

chord *n.* pirku☆, pitnu B☆

chores *n.* tupšikku

chorus *n.* zumāru

chosen *adj.* amru, bēru B, ummuru; → **~ (one)** *n.* nibītu☆; → **~ one** *n.* nīš ēni☆, nišītu☆

chronic *adj.* lazzu

chronicle *n.* narû

chronological order → **in ~** *adv.* ana sadīr aḫāiš

chubby *adj.* kabru, ṭapšu [o.]; → **be(come) ~** *v.* ṭapāšu☆

chuckle *v.* qarāqu+

chum *n.* ra'mu+, šutāpu+; → ~ *v.* aḫû☆ (Gt)

church *n.* ēkallu+

churn *n.* namāṣu☆; → ~ *v.* muāṣu☆

chute *n.* rāṭu

cider *n.* mēzu

Cilicia *n.* Hilakku

cinder *n.* tumru☆

cinnabar *n.* makru+

circle *n.* kilīlu+, kipputu; → ~ *v.* labû, maṣāru◊, sâru☆; → **set up in a ~** *v.* sâru☆ (D); → **~ in the air** *v.* gadālu+

circuit *n.* daiāltu (synodic), labītu

circular *n.* lābiu

circulate *v.* labû (Š)

circulation *n.* labītu

circumambulate *v.* labû; → **make ~** *v.* labītu labû

circumambulation *n.* labītu

circumcise *v.* gazāru+

circumference *n.* kipputu, nakuppu, siḫirtu☆, talbītu☆

circumspect *adj.* muntalku☆, muštālu☆, pitqudu☆

circumstances *n.* arkatu☆
circumvent *v.* labû
cistern *n.* būrtu, būru, gubbu, kuppu☆
citadel *n.* qabsi āli; → **~ wall(?) (part of)** *n.* šeḫenītu☆
citation *n.* nisḫu
cite *v.* nasāḫu
citizen *n.* mār āli, mār māti; → **senior ~** *n.* paršumu; → **~ry** *n.* nišē māti; → **~ship** *n.* mār ālānūtu*, mār mātūtu*
city *n.* ālu, māḫāzu; → **capital ~** *n.* āl bēlūti☆; → **dynastic ~** *n.* āl palê◊; → **entrance into ~** *n.* erāb āli; → **inner ~** *n.* libbi āli; → **privileged ~** *n.* āl kidinni☆; → **royal ~** *n.* āl bēlūti☆; → **supply ~** *n.* āl tuklāti☆; → **~-lordship** *n.* bēl ālūtu
civil → **~ servant** *n.* urdu ēkalli; → **~ity** *n.* rā'imūtu+; → **~ized** *adj.* radiu+
clack *v.* qarāqu+
clad *adj.* labšu☆, nanduqu☆
claim *n.* rugummû☆; → **~** *v.* ba''û, baqāru, paqāru; → **raise/lodge/make a ~** *v.* ragāmu, tuāru, zaqāpu; → **~ant** *n.* pāqirānu◊
clairvoyant *n.* šabrû☆
clam *n.* biṣṣūr atāni
clammy *adj.* salḫu [o.]
clamor *n.* ḫubūru☆, killu, rigmu, šisītu☆; → **~ous** *adj.* ḫabru☆
clamp *n.* rappu☆, umāšu☆; → **~(?)** *n.* gišginû☆; → **~s and chains (of a battering ram)** *n.* umāšu☆
clan *n.* ellatu☆, salātu B☆
clandestine *adj.* pesnu◊; → **~ly** *adj.* šapal qāti
clang *v.* ranānu+; → **~or** *n.* rigmu
clap *v.* maḫāṣu, rapāsu; → **~per** *n.* kanzabu☆; → **~pers** *n.* kiskilāti
clarification *n.* tazkītu☆
clarify *v.* ḫakāmu (Š), lamādu (D), ṣarāpu+ (D)
clarity *n.* zūku B☆
clash *n.* mitḫuṣu☆; → **~** *v.* maḫāṣu
clasp *n.* kirissu☆, malūṭu☆, qullu; → **~** *v.* šapāṣu☆
class *n.* dargu+
clatter *v.* ḫabāru
clause → **conditional ~** *n.* šummu☆; → **relative ~** *n.* šummu☆
clavicle *n.* kirru B☆
claw *n.* ṣupru; → **~ onto** *v.* šarāṣu
clay *n.* isikku☆ (potter's), ṭiṭṭu; → **potter's ~** *n.* kirinnu☆
clean *adj.* ebbu, zakû, zakû+; → **~** *v.* ebābu (D), ḫapāpu◊, zakû (D); → **be(come) ~** *v.* ebābu, zakû; → **keep ~** *v.* ebābu (D); → **~ed** *n.* masiu; → **~ed (barley)** *n.* zakûtu; → **~er** *n.* muzakkû☆; → **~liness** *n.* zakûtu; → **~ly** *adv.* zakîš*; → **~se** *v.* ḫâpu☆, kapāru, marāqu+; → **~sing** *n.* tazkītu+, tēlissu
clear *adj.* ḫakmu, murruqu◊, namru; → **~** *v.* ṣarāpu+, zakû+ (D); → **be ~** *v.* ḫakāmu (N); → **be(come) ~** *v.* zakû+; → **make ~** *v.* birti ēnē maddudu [i.], ḫakāmu (Š), lamādu (D); → **~-cut** *adj.* šarmu; → **~ away** *v.* pasāku (D), paṭāru, paṭāru (D); → **~ from the way** *v.* issu pī ḫūli paṭṭuru [o.]; → **~ o.s.** *v.* zakû+; → **~ off** *v.* našābu☆; → **~ out** *v.* pasāku (D); → **~ up** *v.* ḫarāṣu, namāru; → **~ance** *n.* pitru☆, tazkītu; → **~ed (plot of land)** *n.* paṣiu [o.]; → **~ing** *n.* pitru☆; → **~ing)** *n.* taptiu; → **~ly** *adv.* elliš☆
cleave *v.* dabāqu+, nakāsu, naqāpu+, natāru☆ (Š)
cleft *n.* šitqu☆
clemency *n.* ennānāti (pl.) [o.], rēmu
clement *adj.* rēmānu
clepsydra *n.* didibbu
clergy *n.* ērib bēti; → **~man** *n.* ērib bēt ili, ērib bēti, ša-ēkurri
cleric *n.* ērib bēti; → **~al** *adj.* [ša] ṭupšarrūti
clerk *n.* ṭupšarru
clever *adj.* ḫāsisu, ḫassu, naklu; → **act ~ly** *v.* nakālu; → **~ness** *n.* nikiltu
click *v.* naqāšu+
client *n.* aštapīru☆, ubru; → **~age** *n.* ubrūtu; → **~elage** *n.* ubrūtu; → **~ele** *n.* ubrūtu; → **~ess** *n.* uburtu
cliff *n.* kāpu, uḫummu☆; → **like a ~** *adv.* uḫummiš☆
climax *n.* ṭuḫdu
climb *n.* elû, mūlû; → **~** *v.* elû, šaqû B; → **~er** *n.* ēliu; → **~ing plant (kind of)** *n.* anḫurašru; → **~ing plant (kind of; lit. 'long plant')** *n.* šammu arku
cling *v.* dabāqu+; → **~ (to)** *v.* sabāku+, sabāku+ (D)
clinic *n.* bēt asê+
clink *n.* rigmu; → **~** *v.* ḫalālu B; → **~er** *n.* ḫaḫû B☆
clip *v.* gallubu, kaṣāṣu☆, naḫātu (D), nakāsu; → **~pers** *n.* magazzutu; → **~ping** *n.* gulībtu☆; → **~ping(?)** *n.* supīrtu; → **~pings** *n.* gizzutu
clitoris *n.* ḫanduttu☆
cloak *n.* ḫullānu, nalbašu☆; → **container for ~s** *n.* bēt kuzippi
clod *n.* kurbānu
clog *v.* kasāru, sakāru B; → **~ up** *v.* napāqu☆

clogged → **be(come) ~** *v*. sakāku
cloister *n*. gagû◊; → **~ing** *n*. sikru☆
close *adj*. qurbu; → **~** *n*. qerbu☆; → **~** *v*. edālu, ḫaṭāmu, paḫû, peḫû☆, sakāru B+, sakāru B; → **be(come) ~** *v*. qarābu; → **~ to** *adj*. qurbu; → **~ to** *prep*. innidi; → **keep ~ to** *v*. dabāqu+; → **~ together** *adv*. qanni aḫāiš; → **~d off** *adj*. kanku, peḫû☆; → **~ly joined** *adj*. ṣamdu+; → **~ness** *n*. qurbūtu
closet *n*. bēt kuzippi, bēt qāti
closure *n*. markāsu, sukurtu [o.]
clot *n*. kirṣu
cloth *n*. kuzippu, ṣubātu, šaḫḫu◊, šuḫattu; → **dirty ~** *n*. urāšu☆; → **~/leather item (kind of)** *n*. išḫu; → **~ (kind of)** *n*. gammīdutu
clothe *v*. edēqu☆, ḫalāpu☆; → **~ o.s.** *v*. labāšu (N), labāšu☆ (Gt); → **~ with** *v*. ḫalāpu☆; → **~d** *adj*. labšu☆, nanduqu☆; → **~s mender** *n*. mukabbû
clothing *n*. labussu, lubāru☆, lubšu☆, lubussu, lubūšu, talbuštu☆; → **~ (piece of)** *n*. ḫuzūnu
cloud *n*. erpetu☆, upû☆, urpatu☆, urpu; → **(cumulus) ~(?)** *n*. nīdu☆; → **like a ~** *adv*. urpāniš☆; → **~ formation (kind of)** *n*. ḫupû☆; → **~burst** *n*. rādu☆; → **~ed** *adj*. erpu; → **~less** *adj*. lā erpu☆, petû☆; → **~s** *n*. nalbaš šamê☆; → **~y** *adj*. erpu; → **be(come) ~y** *v*. arāpu
clove pink *n./adj*. illūru☆
clover *n*. neplu+
clown *n*. aluzinnu☆, muṣiḫḫu☆; → **~ish** *adj*. ṭapšu [o.]
cloy *v*. ziāru (N)
club *n*. itbārtu☆, nar'antu
clue *n*. naptāḫu+
clump *n*. kurbānu; → **~** *v*. kamāru (D)
clumsy *adj*. kēšu*
cluster *n*. sagullu+, sanbuku; → **~ed** *adj*. kaṣru
clutch *v*. karāmu, šarāṣu
co-owner *n*. bēl zitti
coach house *n*. bēt utnannāti [o.]
coal *n*. pe'ettu, pe'mu+; → **~(s)** *n*. pēntu; → **(live) ~** *n*. gumāru
coalition *n*. aḫḫūtu
coast *n*. aḫu B, kibru; → **~al** *adj*. ša šiddi tānti☆; → **~al plain** *n*. sapan tānti☆
coat *n*. naḫlaptu; → **~** *v*. šiālu; → **~ of mail** *n*. sariānu, siriam☆; → **~ with** *v*. aḫāzu (D), kapāru; → **~ing** *n*. iḫzu☆
cobbler *n*. aškāpu+
cobblestone *n*. paršu+
cobweb *n*. qê ettūti☆
cock *n*. akkadīja☆, tarnugallu
cockle *n*. lišān kalbati+
cockroach *n*. ṣeṣru+
cocoon *n*. biškānu
coerce *v*. tuāku+ (D)
coercion *n*. kaṣāru+
coexistence *n*. aḫḫūtu
coffer *n*. tupninnu; → **~-dam** *n*. mušašnītu (temporary); → **~ master** *n*. rab šaddāni
coffin *n*. arānu☆
cog *n*. šinnānu+
cogent *adj*. mušadbibu*
cogitate *v*. abālu B☆ (Št)
cognate *adj*. qurbu ana
cognizance of → **take ~** *v*. lamādu (Gtn) [o.]
cognizant *adj*. ḫāsisu, ḫassu+
cohere *v*. dabāqu+, maḫāru☆ (Gt), samāḫu; → **~nt** *adj*. mitḫuru*
cohort *n*. kiṣru; → **~ commander** *n*. rab kiṣri; → **rank of ~ commander** *n*. rab kiṣrūti
coiffure *n*. kizirtu; → **~** *v*. kazāru; → **~d man** *n*. kazru; → **~d woman** *n*. kazrutu
coil *n*. tīru; → **~** *v*. kanānu☆
coin *n*. zūzu+; → **cast ~** *n*. zi'pu☆
coincidence *n*. miqtu, mitḫurtu☆
coition *n*. nīku
coitus *n*. nīku, rikibtu☆
cold *adj*. kaṣû☆; → **~** *n*. kuṣṣu, šarbu; → **be(come) ~** *v*. karāsu, kaṣû☆; → **~-blooded** *adj*. lā pādû☆; → **~ cuts** *n*. nisḫāni; → **~ness** *n*. kuṣṣu
colic *n*. kīs libbi
collaborate *v*. dullu issāḫāiš epāšu; → **~ with** *v*. samāḫu (Dtt)
collaboration *n*. šutāpūtu+
collaborator *n*. ša-issi
collapse *n*. miqittu; → **~** *v*. abātu☆ (N), maqātu, naḫarmumu☆, qâpu☆; → **liable to ~** *adj*. qaiāpu☆; → **~d** *adj*. quppu B☆; → **~d part** *n*. miqittu
collar *n*. qullu; → **~bone** *n*. kirru B☆
collate *v*. barû B☆
colleague *n*. aḫu, itbāru [o.], kinattu
collect *v*. ḫamāmu☆, ḫarāšu☆ (D), kannušu, kapātu☆ (D), kaṣāru, laqātu, paḫāru (D), šabāšu, tadānu (Š); → **~ up** *v*. esāpu; → **~ion** *adj*. ḫimmatu☆; → **~ion** *n*. kiriktu☆, liqtu, paḫḫurtu, tapḫīru [o.], taqrintu☆; → **~ive mass** *n*. ummatu☆; → **~ively** *adv*. mitḫāriš☆; → **~or** *n*. laqqātu☆
collide *v*. emādu, maḫāṣu (N)
collision *n*. lipittu
colloquial *adj*. ša pî nišē
collyrium *n*. itqurtu ša abāri☆
colocynth *n*. peqqû☆, tigilû, zūmu

colonial *adj.* [ša] kāri
colonize *v.* ušābu (Š)
colony *n.* kāru
color *n.* šimtu*; → ~ *v.* barāmu B* (D), ṣapû; → **~(ed part)** *n.* burmu*; → **~ful** *adj.* barrumu; → **~ing** *n.* tiriptu [o.]
column *n.* gišmaḫḫu*, timmu; → **~-base** *n.* gišgallu*, gullutu; → **~ (of a book)** *n.* eqlu+
coma(?) *n.* kīrtu*
coma (of a comet) *n.* ṣipru*
comb *n.* muštu*; → ~ *v.* mašādu B*, nadādu (D) [o.], napāšu B; → **cock's ~** *n.* karballutu+; → **~ out** *v.* ḫalāṣu, mašādu B*; → **~ed** *adj.* ḫalṣu; → **~ings** *n.* mušādu*
combat *n.* mitḫuṣ kakkē*, mitḫuṣu*, tāḫāzu*, taqrubtu*, tašnintu*, tidūku*; → **~ant** *n.* muntaḫṣu*, ša-umāši; → **~ive** *adj.* šitnunu*
combine *v.* emādu (N), ṣamādu
combustible *n.* širpu
combustion *n.* maqalūtu, maqlû, šuruptu
come *v.* alāku (vent.); → **~ about** *v.* bašû (N); → **~ back** *v.* saḫāru alāku; → **~ back again** *v.* saḫāru erābu; → **~ by** *v.* kašādu, qarābu; → **~ close** *v.* sanāqu*, ṭeḫû*; → **~ down** *v.* urādu; → **~ forth** *v.* uṣû (vent.); → **~ forth (from an egg)** *v.* qalāpu*; → **~ in** *v.* erābu (vent.); → **~ near** *v.* qarābu+, ṭeḫû*; → **~ off** *v.* maqātu, paṭāru (N); → *interj.~ on* gana*; → **~ out** *v.* uṣû (vent.); → **~ suddenly upon** *v.* šaḫāṭu C*; → **~ to** *v.* ḫasāsu; → **~ up to** *v.* maṣû; → **~ upon** *v.* ina irti X alāku [i.]
comedian *n.* aluzinnu*, pāḫizu
comedienne *n.* aluzinnutu
comely *adj.* damqu
comet *n.* ṣallummû*
comfort *n.* nēḫtu*, taknû*, ṭūbu; → ~ *v.* libbu nuḫḫu [i.]; → **~able** *adj.* ṭābu
comfortably *adv.* ṭubbātiš*
comic → **~ actor** *n.* pāḫizu; → **~al** *adj.* muṣiḫḫu*
coming *n.* erābu
command *n.* pû, qibītu*, qību, siqru, ṣīt pî*, šikin ṭēmi, ūrtu*, zikru; → ~ *v.* mu''uru*, qabû; → **at the ~ of** *n.* ina muḫḫi pê [i.]; → **under the ~ of** *adj.* ša qāt; → **~ant** *n.* šikin ṭēmi; → **~er** *n.* mu'irru*, muma''iru*; → **fort ~er** *n.* rab bīrti, rab ḫalzi; → **supreme ~er** *n.* rab ummānāti rapšāti; → **~er-in-chief** *n.* turtānu; → **~er-of-fifty** *n.* rab ḫanšê; → **~er-of-ten** *n.* rab ešerti; → **~er-of-thousand** *n.* rab līmi; → **~ership** *n.* šikin ṭēmūtu; → **~ing** *n.* qābiu*; → **~ment** *n.* qību, tērtu*
commemorate *v.* ḫasāsu (Š)
commence *v.* aḫu ummudu [i.], šarrû; → **~ment** *n.* tašrītu B*
commend *v.* na'ādu (D)
comment *n.* qību; → ~ *v.* qabû; → **~ary** *n.* mukallimtu
commerce *n.* maḫīru, tankāruttu [o.]
commercial *adj.* [ša] kāri
commission *n.* tērtu*, ussuktu
commit *v.* epāšu; → **~ o.s.** *v.* pû tadānu [i.], rakāsu (N); → **~ perjury** *v.* tamīt šapti tamû [i.]; → **~ thefts** *v.* tablu tabbulu; → **~ment** *n.* raksūtu*, šūdûtu+; → **~ted** *adj.* raksu; → **~tee** *n.* kināltu
commodity (kind of) *n.* šunāgu
common *adj.* sadru; → **~ beet** *n.* kasiu; → **~ factor** *n.* makṣaru*; → **~ man** *n.* saklu, ṣāb ḫupši*; → **~ people** *n.* ḫupšu*, ṣāb ḫupši*, ṣindu u birtu*; → **~ soldiers** *n.* ṣāb ḫupši*; → **~er** *n.* ṣāb ḫupši*; → **~place** *n.* sadirtu
commotion *n.* ḫubūru*; → **be(come) in ~** *v.* ragāšu+
communicate *v.* qabû, ša'ūdu (Š)
communication *n.* ṭēmu
communicative *adj.* muštaddinu*
community *n.* kalzu
compact *adj.* kaṣru; → ~ *n.* adê
companion *n.* aḫu+, tappû; → **travel ~** *n.* bēl ḫarrāni; → **~ship** *n.* libītu+, tappûtu*
company *n.* kiṣru, libītu+, puḫru+
comparative *adj.* muštamḫiru*; → **~ly** *adv.* ana minâtīšu*
compare *v.* maḫāru (Š), mašālu+ (D)
compartment *n.* kummu*, tū'u+
compassion *n.* gimillu*, gimlu, rēmu, taiārtu*; → **have ~ on** *v.* rēmu ina muḫḫi/ana X šakānu [i.]; → **~ate** *adj.* rēmānu, rēmēnānû*
compatible *adj.* mitguru*; → **be ~** *v.* magāru* (Gt)
compatriot *n.* mār māti
compeer *n.* miḫru
compel *v.* dâṣu*, ša-
compensate *v.* kašāru B*, riābu
compensation *n.* rību C*, šalluntu, tašlimtu
compete *v.* šanānu* (Gt)
competence *n.* lē'ûtu*
competent *adj.* itpēšu*, lā'iu, lē'û*, sapīqu+; → **very ~** *n.* telītu*; → **~ly** *adv.* lē'îš*
competition *n.* šitnuntu*
competitor *n.* šāninu
compilation *adj.* ḫimmatu*

compile *v.* esāpu, ḫamāmu★, kannušu+, lapāpu+ (D)
complain *v.* bakû, nazāmu (Dtt); → **~ in tears** *v.* bakû (Gtn); → **~t** *n.* rigmu; → **~t against** *n.* miḫirtu★
complement *n.* šallāmu, šullāmu
complete *adj.* gamru, šaklulu+, šalmu; → **~** *v.* gamāru, gamāru (D), šaklulu★, šalāmu (D); → **be(come) ~** *v.* šalāmu+; → **~(?)** *v.* panāgu (D); → **~d** *adj.* qatû★; → **~ly** *adv.* ana gammurti, kališ★, nalbân★; → **do ~ly** *v.* gamāru (D), šalāmu (D); → **~ness** *n.* šuklultu★
completion *n.* šalluntu, šuklultu★, šullāmu+, tagmirtu★
complex *n.* itguru★
complexion *n.* būnu, simat pāni★
complexity *n.* billu★
compliance *n.* salmūtu+
compliant *adj.* māgiru, mundagru★, salmu+; → **make ~** *v.* dabābu (Š)
complicate *v.* kaṣāru+, pašāqu B★ (Š); → **~d** *n.* itguru★
complication *n.* itgurūtu★
compliment *n.* tanattu★
comply *v.* magāru (N)
compose *v.* kaṣāru, rakābu+ (D); → **~ o.s.** *v.* qablē rakāsu [i.]; → **~d** *adj.* nēḫu; → **~r** *n.* murakkibānu+
composite *adj.* rakkubu+
composition *adj.* kammu★ (esoteric)
composure *n.* nēḫtu★
compound *adj.* rakkubu+; → **~** *v.* rakābu+ (D), ṣamādu
comprehend *v.* ḫakāmu; → **~ing** *n.* ḫākimu
comprehensible *adj.* ša iḫakkimūni*
comprehension *n.* ḫasīsu
comprehensive *adj.* palkû★
compress *n.* markastu★; → **~** *v.* mazā'u
compromise *n.* mitgurtu; → **~** *v.* magāru★ (N)
compulsion *n.* da'ānu, tēkītu
compulsive *adj.* dannu
compunction *n.* muruṣ libbi
computation *n.* kiṣiptu, minītu
compute *v.* mašāḫu
comrade *n.* ebru★, illu★, ru'u★, tappû; → **~ship** *n.* tappūtu★
con man *n.* sarru★
conceal *v.* katāmu, pazzuru, pesēnu◊; → **~ed** *adj.* katmu★, pazru★, pesnu◊; → **~ment** *n.* tapzirtu★
conceit *n.* multarḫūtu★; → **~ed** *adj.* multarḫu★, muštarriḫu★
conceivable *adj.* ša iḫakkimūni*
conceive *v.* arû B, ḫasāsu, ṣabātu
concentrate *v.* ḫamāmu★, kaṣāru; → **~d** *adj.* kaṣru
concentration *n.* kiṣru; → **~ camp** *n.* karašû★
conception *n.* arûtu
concern *n.* duluḫtu◊, muruṣ libbi; → **~** *v.* qarābu ina muḫḫi; → **cause ~** *v.* naqādu★; → **~ o.s.** *v.* marāṣu★ (Št); → **be(come) ~ed** *v.* libbu marāṣu [i.]; → **be(come) ~ed about** *v.* issi libbi dabābu [i.]; → **~ing** *prep.* aššu★, aššut◊, ina muḫḫi, issu muḫḫi, šuḫ, šūt B★
concession *n.* mitgurtu
concierge *n.* ša-pān-nērebi
conciliable *adj.* musallimu★
conciliate *v.* magāru★ (D), salāmu (D)
conciliatory *adj.* musallimu★
concise *adj.* kapṣu+, kaṣru, pašqu+
conclude *v.* šakānu, šalāmu+ (D); → **be(come) ~d** *v.* šalāmu+
conclusive *adj.* parsu
concoct *v.* balālu; → **~ion** *n.* ribku★
concord *n.* mitgurtu, tašmû★; → **~ant** *adj.* mitguru★
concrete *adj.* šapû★; → **~** *n.* šelluru
concubinage *n.* abrakkūtu★
concubine *n.* esirtu, sekrutu
concur *v.* magāru (N)
concussion *n.* miḫṣu
condemn *v.* ḫiṭṭu emādu, nazāru; → **~ation** *n.* ḫalpūtu [o.]
condense *v.* šapû★ (D)
condiment *n.* šaḫītu B+; → **~ (kind of)** *n.* karkartu
condole *v.* libbu nuḫḫu [i.]; → **~nce** *n.* nēḫtu★
conduct *n.* riddu
cone *n.* sikkutu, terinnu★; → **~(?)** *n.* bunbullu
confection → **~ (kind of)** *n.* mirsu; → **~er** *n.* karkadinnu; → **chief ~er** *n.* rab karkadinni; → **female ~er** *n.* karkadinnutu; → **~ery** *n.* muttāqu
confederate *n.* bēl adê
confederation *n.* a'lu★, ebrūtu★
confer *v.* malāku (N), malāku★ (Gt), nadānu★ (Št); → **~ence** *n.* muštālūtu★; → **~ence room** *n.* bēt milki★
confess *v.* dabābu, idû★ (Š); → **~ion** *n.* šūdûtu★; → **~or** *n.* mušēdû★
confidant(e) *n.* qēpu
confide *v.* paqādu, qiāpu; → **~nce** *n.* tiklu+, tukultu+; → **give ~nce** *v.* takālu (D); → **place ~nce in** *v.* takālu+; → **be(come) ~nt** *v.* raḫāṣu; → **make ~nt** *v.* raḫāṣu (Š); →

~ntial *adj.* qēpu; → **~ntially** *adv.* ana lā amāri [i.]
confine *v.* esāru, lâṭu☆, pâdu☆, paḫû, peḫû☆, sakāru B+; → **~d** *n.* līṭu☆; → **~ment** *n.* mēsēru☆; → **woman in ~ment** *n.* ḫarištu☆; → **be in ~ment (of women in labor)** *v.* ḫarāšu B☆; → **~s** *n.* taḫūmu
confirm *v.* kuānu (D); → **~ation** *n.* piqittu, takittu☆; → **~ed** *adj.* kunnu
confiscate *v.* qātu šakānu [i.], ṣabātu
conflagration *n.* maqalūtu, naqmūtu☆
conflict *n.* ṣāssu, ṣēlūtu☆; → **~ing** *adj.* maḫḫuru; → **~ing** *n.* šitnû☆; → **be ~ing** *v.* šanû☆ (Gt)
confluence *n.* piāti
conform *v.* maḫāru☆ (Gt)
confound *v.* dalāḫu
confront *v.* maḫāru; → **~ation** *n.* ṣāssu
confuse *v.* ašû (Š), balālu, dalāḫu, ešû☆; → **~d** *adj.* ballu, dalḫu, ešû☆; → **be ~d** *v.* ešû☆ (N), parādu☆ (Dt); → **be(come) ~d** *v.* ešû☆
confusion *n.* daliḫtu☆, dilḫu☆, duluḫḫû☆, ešītu☆, ippiru☆, tēšû☆; → **throw into ~** *v.* ašû (Š); → **in ~** *adv.* dulluḫiš☆
confute *v.* saḫāpu+
congenial *adj.* mitguru☆
congenital *adj.* naṣību+
congestion *n.* gipšu☆
conglomerated *adj.* kupputu☆
congratulate *v.* karābu
congregate *v.* paḫāru, paḫāru (D)
congregation *n.* kinältu, puḫru
congress *n.* kinältu+, puḫru
congruent *adj.* mitguru☆
congruous *adj.* mitguru☆
conic(al) *adj.* sikkatānu*
conifer (kind of) *n.* argannu
conjecture *n.* sebru+
conjoined → **be ~** *v.* ṣamādu☆ (N)
conjunction *n.* šitqultu☆
conjurer *n.* āšipu
connect *v.* ṣamādu; → **~ed** *adj.* ṣabbutu; → **be ~ed with** *v.* aḫāzu☆ (Gt); → **~ion** *n.* qurbūtu; → **~ions** *n.* ṣindāti*
connive → **~at** *v.* katāmu (D); → **~with** *v.* dabābu issi [i.], laḫāšu+
connoisseur *n.* mūdānû◊
connotation *n.* ḫakimtu*
connote *v.* qabû ana
conquer *v.* kašādu, nêru☆; → **~ed** *adj.* kašdu; → **~ing** *adj.* kāšidu; → **~or** *n.* kāšidu☆
conquest *n.* kišittu☆
conscientious *adj.* ḫardu
conscious *adj.* ḫāsisu; → **be(come) ~** *v.* êru, ḫasāsu; → **~ of** *adj.* ḫassu+; → **~ly** *adv.* ina mūdānūti [i.]; → **~ness** *n.* ērūtu☆, ḫasīsu, mūdânūtu
conscript *n.* ālik ilki; → **~ion** *n.* ṣāb šarrūtu
consecrated *adj.* quddušu☆
consecration *n.* taqdīšu [o.]
consecutive *adj.* ṣabbutu☆, šutēmudu☆
consent *n.* annu, migru☆; → **~** *v.* magāru (N)
consequence *n.* ṣītu☆
consequent *adj.* āṣiu; → **~ly** *adv.* iddāti
conservation *n.* naṣāru+
conserve *v.* naṣāru+
consider *v.* abālu B☆ (Št), ana X kullu [i.], dagālu, manû issi [i.]; → **~ thoroughly** *v.* amatu šutābulu [i.]; → **~able** *adj.* kabbīru+, šūpû☆; → **~ate** *adj.* mitluku☆, na'du☆; → **~ation** *n.* muštālūtu☆; → **in ~ation of** *prep.* pitti; → **~ing that** *subj.* pitti
consign *v.* paqādu; → **~ee** *n.* māḫirānu [o.]; → **~ment** *n.* šazbussu, šēbultu☆
consistent *adj.* mitḫuru*; → **be ~** *v.* maḫāru☆ (Gt); → **~ with** *prep.* ša pitti
consolation *n.* nēḫtu☆
console *v.* libbu nuḫḫu [i.]
consolidate *v.* kuānu (D)
consort *n.* ḫarmu☆
consortium *n.* itbārtu☆
conspicuous *adj.* šūpû☆
conspiracy *n.* sīḫu B☆
conspirator *n.* mušadbibu
conspire *v.* dabābu issi [i.]; → **~ with** *v.* issi X udû [i.], pâ itti X šakānu [i.]
constable *n.* bēl birki☆, daiālu
constant *adj.* kaiamānīu, kaiānu☆; → **~ly** *adv.* ginâ☆, kaiamānu, kaiāna☆, santak☆
constellation *n.* kakkubu, lumāšu; → **~ (name of a)** *n.* angubbû☆
consternation(?) *n.* sipiḫ libbi◊
constipated → **be(come) ~** *v.* napāqu☆
constipation *n.* isiltu☆, kipṣu+
constituent *n.* ḫišiḫtu☆; → **~s** *n.* udê
constitute *v.* paqādu+, šiāmu
constraint *n.* kasītu☆ (magical), šapšāqu☆
constrict *v.* kabālu☆ (D), kapāṣu+, siāqu (D); → **~ion** *n.* ḫiniqtu☆, isiltu☆, kipṣu☆
construct *v.* kaṣāru, raṣāpu; → **have ~ed** *v.* rakāsu (Š); → **~ion** *n.* epšetu, nēpešu☆, riṣiptu☆, šikittu☆; → **~ive** *adj.* bāniu, bannāiu+; → **~or(?)** *n.* šelappāiu
consult *v.* ša'ālu; → **~ation** *n.* šitūltu☆; → **~ing** *n.* šittālu☆
consume *v.* akālu, rabāku [o.]; → **~d** *adj.* aklu

consuming *adj.* ākilu
consummation *n.* šullāmu+
consumption *n.* akiltu
contact *n.* siḫru
contagious *adj.* muštaḫḫizu⋆
contain *v.* tuāku+ (D); → **~er(?) (kind of)** *n.* lignu, mišlūtu; → **~er/measure (kind of; for fish and dates)** *n.* qapīru; → **~er (kind of)** *n.* adakurru, burzibandû⋆, darīku, ḫabnutu, ḫiburnu, išpu, kukkupu, lukannu, pāširtu, qabḫu, qablītu B, tanūku, tuppisannu⋆
contaminate *v.* parrû [o.]
contemplate *v.* abālu B⋆ (Št)
contemplative *adj.* muštābilu*
contemporary *n.* mār simini+
contempt *n.* qulālu+, šēṭūtu, šēṭūtu+; → **treat with ~** *v.* massuḫu [o.], mêšu⋆ (D), šiāṭu+
contemptibility *n.* šēṭūtu+
contemptible *adj.* šēṭu+
contemptuous *adj.* šaiāṭu+
contend *v.* gapāru⋆ (Dt), naṣû+, ṣâlu [o.], šanānu⋆ (Gt); → **~er** *n.* šāninu
content *adj.* libbu, ṭābu; → **~** *v.* libbu ṭubbu [i.], ṭiābu (D); → **~ed** *adj.* nēḫu, šabbu; → **~ment** *n.* ḫūd libbi, sapqūtu+
contention *n.* šitnuntu⋆
contest *n.* ṣēlūtu⋆; → **~** *v.* baqāru, dabābu, paqāru, ṣâlu [o.], šanānu⋆ (Gt); → **~ant** *n.* sēḫû◊
contiguous *adj.* ṭaḫiu*
continent *n.* nābalu⋆
contingency *n.* malʾētu [o.]
contingent *n.* kalzu; → **~(?)** *n.* mūgu
continual *adj.* lazzu, sadru
continue *v.* barû C⋆ (Št), lazāzu, radû+; → **~ doing** *v.* arāku (D)
continuity *n.* dūru B
continuous *adj.* sadru
contort *v.* ḫanāṣu⋆ (D)
contra *prep.* ina muḫḫi, ša lā
contraband *n.* pazzurtu
contract *n.* rikistu⋆; → **~ed** *adj.* raksu
contract *v.* kapāṣu+; → **~ o.s.** *v.* kalāṣu⋆; → **~ion** *n.* kilṣu⋆, kipṣu⋆; → **~ion (of eye)** *n.* gabāṣu⋆
contradict *v.* ṣâlu [o.]; → **~ion** *n.* ṣāssu; → **~ory** *adj.* pitrusu⋆; → **be ~ory** *v.* šanû⋆ (Gt)
contrary *adj.* maḫḫuru; → **be ~** *v.* lā magāru (N); → **be(come) ~** *v.* ṣâlu [o.]; → **~ to** *prep.* ina pūt, kî lā
contrast *n.* mitḫurtu⋆
contravene *v.* parāku
contribute *v.* zabālu+
contribution *adj.* ginû; → **~** *n.* igisû; → **~s (of food)** *n.* ilkakāti
contrivance *n.* šipir nikilti⋆
contrive *v.* nakālu
control *n.* bēlūtu, masnaqtu⋆, piqittu; → **~** *v.* âru⋆ (D), biālu, ḫiāṭu⋆, lâṭu⋆, šalāṭu; → **~ o.s.** *v.* libbu ṣabātu [i.]; → **assume ~ of** *v.* kašāšu⋆; → **~led** *adj.* ašru; → **~ler (of grain deliveries)** *n.* rab sūti
controversial subject *n.* abat ṣāssi
controversy *n.* ṣāssu
contusion *n.* miḫṣu, simmu
convalescent *n.* bāliṭu*
convenience *n.* bēt musâti⋆, ṭūbu
convenient *adj.* tarṣu
convention *n.* puḫru, tallaktu
converge *v.* emādu (N); → **~nce** *n.* mitḫurtu⋆
conversant *adj.* lamdu⋆; → **~ with** *adj.* mūdû
conversation *n.* dabūbu⋆
converse *v.* lišānu šakānu⋆, nadānu⋆ (Št); → **~ly** *adv.* enīta⋆
convert *v.* pašāru
convex *adj.* kappu C*
convey *v.* etāqu (Š), radû, zabālu (Š); → **~ance** *n.* šazbussu
convict *n.* ṣabtu; → **~** *v.* ḫiṭṭu emādu, kuānu (D); → **~ion (in law)** *n.* dēnu
convince *v.* dabābu (Š)
convincing *adj.* mušadbibu*
convoke *v.* kannušu+
convoy *v.* labû+
convulse *v.* arāru B⋆, damû◊
convulsion *n.* muggu
coo *v.* damāmu⋆
cook *n.* nuḫatimmu; → **~** *v.* bašālu, bašālu (Š); → **~'s prebend** *n.* nuḫatimmūtu⋆; → **chief ~** *n.* rab nuḫatimmi; → **temple ~** *n.* nuḫatim bēt ili, nuḫatim bēti; → **~ed** *adj.* bašlu, buḫra⋆; → **~ery** *n.* ḫuršu [o.]; → **~ing pot** *n.* diqāru; → **~ing pot (kind of)** *n.* dūdu; → **~ing vessel (kind of)** *n.* asallu; → **supervisor of ~s** *n.* ša-pān-nuḫatimmi
cool *adj.* karsu, kaṣû⋆; → **~** *v.* kaṣû⋆ (D); → **be(come) ~** *v.* karāsu, kaṣû⋆; → **~ down** *v.* pašāḫu; → **~er** *n.* mukaṣṣītu, ṣarṣāru; → **~ing** *n.* maqartu
coop *adj.* quppu+
cooper *n.* ša-dannēšu
cooperate *v.* dullu issāḫāiš epāšu
cooperation *n.* kitru
cooperative *adj.* kātiru*
cope with *v.* maṣû
copious *adj.* duššû⋆

copper *n.* erû, urudû*; → ~ **object (kind of)** *n.* inianu◊; → ~ **peddler** *n.* ša-erêšu; → **~plate** *n.* lē'u siparri; → **~smith** *n.* nappāḫ erê, qurqurru*
coppice *n.* qablu B
copse *n.* qablu B
copulate *v.* niāku, qarāšu B*, rakābu* (Gt)
copulating *n.* ritkubu*
copulation *n.* niāku, rikibtu*
copy *n.* gabrû, miḫirtu, miḫru, šaṭṭāru; → ~ *v.* mašālu* (D), nasāḫu
coquetry *n.* ṣīḫtu
coquette *n.* ṣaiāḫû*
coquettish *adj.* ṣaiāḫû*; → **behave ~ly** *v.* ṣiāḫu* (Gtn)
cor *n.* kurru B*
coral *n.* kasītu B+; → **~(?)** *n.* baḫrû
cord *n.* matnu, pitiltu
cordial *adj.* gāmilu*, libbānāiu+
core *n.* durgu*
coriander *n.* kisibarru
corn *n.* nissābu*, še'u; → **~-bin** *n.* padakku
corner *n.* tubqu*, zamītu+; → **~(?)** *n.* zamītu*; → **(outer) ~** *n.* zamû*; → **inside ~** *n.* šaḫātu*; → **~ pillar** *n.* zamû*; → **~stone** *n.* pūlu
cornice *n.* kulūlu, pasqu*
cornucopia *n.* per'ūtu+
coronary *n.* mišittu* (apoplectic)
coronation *n.* kullultu*
corporal *n.* rab ešerti
corps *n.* kiṣru; → **royal ~** *n.* kiṣir šarri
corpse *n.* pagru, šalamtu*
corpulence *n.* milītu*
corpulent *adj.* ḫabburu, kabru
corral *n.* ma'assu
correct *adj.* išaru*, tarṣu; → ~ *v.* tarāṣu B+ (D); → **be(come) ~** *v.* tarāṣu B (stat.); → **~ion** *n.* tūrāṣu+; → **~ly** *adv.* išariš*
correspond *v.* aḫāiš apālu; → **~ence** *n.* mitḫartu*; → **~ing** *adj.* māḫiru; → **~ing to** *prep.* tamšīl*
corridor *n.* barakku*, dalbānu*, dulbānu
corroborate *v.* kuānu (D)
corrode *v.* akālu+, šaḫāḫu (D) [o.]
corrosive *adj.* ākilu
corrupt *adj.* ṭappīlu+; → **~ible** *adj.* māḫir šulmānāti*; → **~ion** *n.* ṭappīlūtu+
corselet *n.* siriam+
cortex *n.* qulāptu [o.]
coruscate *v.* ṣarāḫu C+
corvée → ~ **(basket)** *n.* tupšikku; → ~ **worker** *n.* zābil kudurri*
corybant *n.* kurgarrû; → **female ~** *n.* kurgarrutu
cosmetics *n.* mēqû*
cost *n.* gimru [o.], šīmu; → **~ly** *adj.* uqru+; → **be(come) ~ly** *v.* uqāru+
coster(monger) *n.* bāqilu*
costume *n.* kuzippu, nalbašu*, talbuštu*, tēdīqu*
cottage *n.* kurḫu+
cotton(?) *n.* karpassu*
couch *n.* nēmattu, nēmudu
cough *n.* guḫḫu*; → ~ *v.* ganāḫu*; → ~ **with phlegm** *n.* suālu
council *n.* muštālūtu*, puḫru; → **city ~** *n.* puḫru ša āli*; → **~lor** *n.* māliku, muštālu*
counsel *n.* milku; → ~ *v.* malāku; → **take ~** *v.* malāku (N); → **~lor** *n.* māliku, muntalku*
count *v.* manû B; → **~among** *v.* manû issi [i.]; → ~ **as** *v.* manû ana [i.], manû issi [i.]; → ~ **on** *v.* takālu+; → **~ed** *adj.* manû; → **~enance** *n.* bunnu, būnu, zīmu (pl.); → **~er** *n.* abnu; → **~er** *v.* šapêlu; → **~erbalance** *v.* maḫāru; → **~erfeit** *v.* zuppu+ (D); → **~erpane** *n.* qarrāru; → **~erpart** *n.* maṭṭaltu*, miḫirtu, miḫru; → **~ing** *n.* munūtu*; → **~less** *adj.* ana lā māni*, lā manê*, lā mīnu*, lā nībi, ša lā nībi*, šār*; → **~less (times)** *n.* ana lā mīni*; → **all ~ries** *n.* mātitān*; → **~ry** *n.* mātu; → **enemy ~ry** *n.* māt nukurti; → **in every ~ry** *adv.* mātitān*; → **inhabitants of the ~ry** *n.* nišē māti; → **low-lying ~ry** *n.* unqu B+; → **open ~ry** *n.* bamāti*, ṣēru*; → **~ryman** *n.* mār māti; → **~ryside** *n.* kīdu*; → **~y** *n.* ḫalzu
coup *n.* nabalkattu*
couple *n.* ṣimittu*; → ~ *v.* ṣamādu; → **~d** *adj.* ṣandu
coupling *n.* ṣindu
courage *adj.* libbu; → **~ous** *adj.* qardu, rāš libbi*; → **be(come) ~ous** *v.* qarādu
courier *n.* daiālu, kalliu
course *n.* alaktu*, ḫarrānu, māluku, mētequ*, mētuqu, talluku*; → **change ~** *v.* ḫūlu nakkuru (D) [i.], šanītu alāku*; → **follow a ~** *v.* garāmu*
court *n.* bīrtu+; → ~ *v.* ḫašādu; → **president of the ~** *n.* ša-pān-dēnāni; → **president of the ~ of justice** *n.* rab dēnāni; → **~official (kind of)** *n.* ša-dabābi; → ~ **position** *n.* mazzāz pānūtu
courteous *n./adj.* amēlānu
courtesan *n.* abrakkatu*; → **~ship** *n.* abrakkūtu*
courtesy *n.* de'iqtu
courtier *n.* ērib ēkalli, gerseqû*, mār ēkal-

li, mazzāz ēkalli, mazzāz pāni, tīru B☆ (eunuch), urdu ēkalli; → ~ **status** *n.* mazzāz pānūtu; → ~ **training** *n.* mazzāz pānūtu; → **~s** *n.* libīt ēkalli, nišē ēkalli
courtyard *n.* kisallu, tarbāṣu; → **main ~** *n.* kisalmāḫu; → ~ **sweeper** *n.* kisalluḫḫu☆; → **female ~ sweeper** *n.* kisalluḫḫatu☆
cousin *n.* mār aḫ-abi
covenant *n.* adê
cover *n.* erintu, ḫillu, kutmu☆, kutummu☆, naktumu, siḫpu, ṣipputu, taktīmu, tapšû; → ~ *v.* apāru☆, arāmu, ḫalāpu☆, katāmu, katāmu (D), katāmu☆ (Š), labāšu☆ (Š), qarāmu, saḫāpu, ṣallulu, šiālu; → **stone ~** *n.* makkūtu B+; → **~-plate** *n.* taḫlīpu (defensive); → **~-up** *n.* tapzirtu☆; → ~ **each other** *v.* ḫalāpu☆ (Gt); → ~ **o.s.** *v.* ḫalāpu (N); → ~ **up** *v.* katāmu, katāmu (D), pesēnu◊; → ~ **with** *v.* malû☆ (Št); → ~ **with rust** *v.* šaḫātu C+ (Š); → ~ **with skin** *v.* qarāmu+; → **~age** *n.* ṣulūlu; → **~ed** *adj.* ḫallupu, ḫarmu [o.], kuttumu☆, ṣallulu; → **~ed up** *adj.* katmu☆, pussunu◊; → **be(come) ~ed with color** *v.* tarāpu☆; → **be(come) ~ed with patches** *v.* edēḫu☆; → **~ing** *n.* erintu, kutmu☆, qarūmu+, sasuppu+, siḫpu, ṣulultu☆, taḫlīpu (defensive), taḫluptu☆, taktīmu, tapšû; → **head ~ing** *n.* šakaqqidi; → **~ing-board** *n.* taḫlīpu (defensive); → **~t** *adj.* pazru☆
covet *v.* bibil libbi rašû☆, ēnu našû☆; → **be(come) ~** *v.* ṣaḫātu; → **~ous** *n.* ṣāḫitu
covey *n.* kināltu+
cow *n.* arḫu☆, littu; → **free-roaming ~** *n.* sāḫirtu☆; → **wild ~** *n.* rīmtu☆; → **~-dung** *n.* kabūt alpi; → **~-house** *n.* tarbāṣu; → **~-shed** *n.* tarbāṣu; → ~ **driver** *n.* rādi litti☆
coward *n.* pallāḫu☆; → **~ice** *n.* pallāḫūtu*; → **~ly** *adj.* šaplu+
cower *v.* kamāṣu
cowrie *n.* biṣṣūr atāni
coy *adj.* baiāšu☆
crab *n.* alluttu
crabby *adj.* adru B
crack *n.* bitqu+, nigiṣṣu☆, šitqu☆; → ~ *v.* ḫapû, naqāḫu+, paṣādu (Dtt)
crackle *v.* ṣarāḫu C+
cradle *n.* eršu
craft *n.* īnu☆, lipittu, šipru, ummânūtu+
craftiness deceit *n.* šipir nikilti☆
craftsman *n.* kiškattû☆, ummânu; → **military ~** *n.* kitkittû; → **~ship** *n.* ummânūtu
crafty *adj.* enqu☆, muštēpišu☆, nakkulu+, naklu
crag *n.* kāpu☆
cramp *n.* muggu; → ~ *v.* magāgu; → **have ~s** *v.* magāgu☆ (Gtn)
crane *n.* kurkû; → **~(?)** *n.* kāliu☆
cranial *adj.* gulgullāiu+
cranium *n.* kalli kaqqidi☆, muḫḫu
crank *n.* gamlu; → **~y** *adj.* parku
cranny *n.* bitqu+, ṣelpu+
crash *n.* miqittu; → ~ *v.* ḫapû (N), ṣarāḫu C+
crate *n.* ḫuppu; → **~r** *n.* pī mappūḫīti+
crave (for) *v.* puqqu
craven *n.* pallāḫu☆
craving *n.* puqqu*
crawl *v.* ḫalālu, pašālu☆, šapāpu+; → **~ing** *adj.* pašālatti☆
craze *n.* maḫḫûtu☆; → ~ *v.* maḫû* (D); → **become ~d** *v.* maḫḫûtiš alāku☆
craziness *n.* maḫḫûtu☆
crazy *adj.* maḫḫû☆
creak *v.* damāmu☆, na'āru+, naḫāru+, nazāmu
cream *n.* lišdu☆, muššu'tu☆, šamnu
create *v.* banû, bašāmu☆, bašû (Š), patāqu☆
creation *n.* binūtu, nabnītu☆, tabnītu☆, tabšūtu☆
creative *adj.* bāniu+
creator *n.* bānû☆, mummu☆
creature *n.* binūtu; → **~(s)** *n.* nabnītu☆
credence *n.* qēptu, qīptu☆; → **give ~** *v.* qiāpu
credibility *n.* qēpūtu
credible *adj.* qēpu
credit *n.* qēptu, rašûtu◊; → **~or** *n.* bēl ḫabulli, qā'ipānu [o.], rāšû◊, rašûtānu◊
credulous *adj.* saklu
creek *n.* atappu+
creel (for fish) *n.* lattu
creep *v.* ḫalālu, pašālu☆, šalālu B☆; → ~ **in** *v.* ḫalālu; → **~ing** *n.* ḫillutu
cremation *n.* šuruptu
crenellation *n.* kulūlu; → **~(?)** *n.* kullultu☆
crescent *n.* uskāru
cress *n.* kudimmu, saḫlû
crest *n.* karballutu, ṣipru☆; → **bird's ~** *n.* karballutu+; → **helmet ~** *n.* karballutu
Crete *n.* Kaptara☆
crevasse *n.* šitqu☆
crevice *n.* nigiṣṣu☆, šitqu☆
crew *n.* rakkābu☆, rikbu☆; → **ship's ~** *n.* ṣāb eleppi☆; → **~s** *n.* ba'ulāti☆
crib *n.* eršu
cricket *n.* ṣarṣāru B☆; → **~ (kind of)** *n.* upput eqli
crime *n.* annu B☆, arnu☆, gillatu☆, gullul-

tu*, ḫibiltu*, ḫiṭītu*, ḫiṭṭu, sartu, šērtu B*; → **commit a ~** *v.* ḫiṭṭu ḫaṭû
criminal *n.* bēl ḫiṭṭi, parriṣu, zēr nērti*; → **be(come) a ~** *v.* sarāru [o.]
crimson *n./adj.* argamannu
cringe *v.* napalsuḫu*, pašālu*
crinkle *v.* gamāzu+
crinkly *adj.* gammīzu+
cripple *n.* ḫummuru◊; → **~(d)** *adj.* kabbulu, pessû*; → **~d** *n.* ḫummuru◊; → **be(come) ~d** *v.* kabālu*
crisis *n.* naquttu◊, sinqu
crisp *adj.* paḫḫu+
criss-cross *n.* šuteṣlup*; → **~ed** *adj.* šuteṣlupu*
crisscross *n.* issu māka issu māka [i.]
criterion *n.* mašqālu+
critical *adj.* nakdu*; → **be(come) ~** *v.* naqādu*; → **~(ly ill)** *adj.* naqdu*; → **~ situation** *n.* naquttu◊
criticism *n.* muparrisūtu+
croak *v.* naqāḫu+, naqāqu+
crock *n.* ḫaṣbu; → **~ery** *n.* ḫaṣbu
crocodile(?) *n.* kušû*
crocus(?) *n.* andaḫšu
crony *n.* ra'mu+
crook *n.* gamlu, isḫappu*, parriṣu, šibirru*; → **~ed** *adj.* egru, ḫakê*, naklu+, paslu*, patlu+, ṣalpu*; → **~ed** *n.* itguru*
croon *v.* ḫabābu*
crop *n.* ebūru; → **~** *v.* qatāpu; → **grain ~** *n.* šegunû*; → **~ (of a bird)** *n.* pisurru+, quqqubānu+; → **~ year** *n.* mērēšu
cross *adj.* parku; → **~** *n.* ispillurtu; → **~** *v.* ebāru; → **be ~** *v.* egēru* (Gt); → **~-examination** *n.* tasniqtu*; → **~-examine** *v.* sanāqu (D); → **~-eyed** *n.* ṣudduru*; → **~ over** *v.* ebāru, nabalkutu
crossbar *n.* ḫūqu, pariktu, tallu
crossbeam *n.* adappu*, dappu*
crossed *adj.* egru
crossing *n.* nēburu; → **~ (place)** *n.* nēbartu*
crossroads *n.* ispillurtu
crosswise *adj.* parku; → **~** *adv.* parkiš*
crotch *n.* ḫallu
crouch *v.* kamāṣu
crow *n.* āribu*, qāribu; → **~d** *n.* ummānu*; → **~ded** *adj.* ḫabṣu+; → **~n** *n.* agû, kilīlu, kulūlu, qimmatu*, qimmu; → **~n** *v.* kallulu (D); → **like a mural ~n** *adv.* kilīliš*; → **mural ~n** *n.* kilīlu, kulūlu; → **~n as bride** *v.* kallulu+ (D); → **~n of the head** *n.* muḫḫu; → **~n prince** *n.* mār šarri; → **be ~ned** *v.* apāru* (N)
crucial *adj.* pārisu
crucible *n.* kūru, naṣraptu
crucified *adj.* zaqpu+
crucify *v.* zaqāpu+
crude *adj.* lā bašlu
cruel *adj.* gaṣṣu B*, marru B+; → **be(come) ~** *v.* gaṣāṣu B*; → **~ty** *n.* gaṣṣūtu*
cruise *v.* neqelpû*
crumb *n.* kirṣu
crumble *v.* naḫarmuṭu*
crummy *adj.* lammunu
crumple *v.* kapāṣu*; → **~d** *adj.* kapṣu*
crunch *v.* našāku (D)
crush *v.* ḫapû, ḫašālu, letû* (D), marāqu, marāsu+, mêsu*, napāṣu (D), paṣṣû, suāku; → **make ~** *v.* ḫašālu (Š); → **~ minutely** *v.* daqāqu◊ (D); → **be ~ed** *v.* parāru (N)
crust layer *n.* qarūmu+
crutch *n.* nēmattu
cry *n.* killu, šisītu*; → **~** *v.* bakû, nuāqu*, ṣiāḫu*; → **utter a ~** *v.* ṣarāḫu B*; → **~ aloud** *v.* ṣarāḫu B+; → **~ for help** *n.* killu; → **~ of distress** *n.* killu; → **~ out** *v.* lebû*, ragāmu, ṣarāḫu B*
crybaby *n.* bakkânu*
crying *n.* bikītu, rigmu
crystal *n.* gamēsu
cub *n.* mūrānu
cube *n.* pūru; → **~ root** *n.* basû*
cubit *n.* ammutu; → **(great) ~** *n.* aslu B*; → **big ~** *n.* ammutu rabītu; → **one third ~** *n.* šizû*
cuckoo *n.* rāqu+
cucumber *n.* qiššû
cucurbitaceous plant (kind of) *n.* naṣṣubu
cuddle up *v.* kanānu*
cuddly *adj.* rabbu B
cudgel *n.* nar'antu
cuff *v.* siparrē šakānu [i.]
cuirass *n.* siriam+
cuisine *n.* nabšaltu+
cul-de-sac *n.* ḫūlu karmu*
culinary *adj.* ṭabbāḫāiu+; → **~ art** *n.* nuḫatimmūtu*; → **~ dish (kind of)** *n.* ḫaršu, sapulḫu
cull *v.* biāru
culminate → **be(come) ~** *v.* zaqāru
culminating constellation *n.* ziqpu
culmination *n.* ziqpu
culprit *n.* bēl arni*
cult *n.* parṣu; → **~(ic rites)** *n.* pelludû*; → **~ center** *n.* māḫāzu; → **~ object (kind of)** *n.* ēqu, nasramû, ša-zuqiti, tallakku; → **~ ob-**

ject (kind of; lit. 'tree of absolution') *n.* gišburru; → **~ic act/ritual (kind of)** *n.* tamriqāti; → **~ic ceremony (kind of)** *n.* mudarriktu; → **~ivate** *v.* arāšu; → **~ivated** *adj.* radiu+; → **~ivation** *n.* ārišūtu, ikkārūtu⋆, mazrūtu, mērеštu B⋆, mērēšu; → **put under ~ivation** *v.* arāšu (Š); → **~ivation (contract)** *n.* errēšūtu⋆
culture *n.* mardûtu+
culvert *n.* asurrakku⋆
cumbersome *adj.* pašqu⋆
cumin *n.* kamūnu
cummerbund *n.* ṣipirtu (woven)
cuneiform sign *n.* miḫiṣtu
cuneiform wedge *n.* santakku⋆
cunning *adj.* naklu; → **~** *n.* nikiltu, niklu
cunt *n.* biṣṣūru⋆, ḫurdatu⋆
cup *n.* kāsu, qabūtu; → **~** *v.* takāpu; → **~ master** *n.* rab kāsāti; → **~bearer** *n.* šāqiu; → **chief ~bearer** *n.* rab šāqê; → **female ~bearer** *n.* šāqītu
cupboard *n.* bēt kāsāti
cups → **container for ~** *n.* bēt kāsāti
curb *v.* kabāsu, lâṭu⋆, sakāru B+
cure *n.* bulṭu, nablāṭu⋆
curio *n.* nukru⋆; → **~sity** *n.* nukru⋆
curious *adj.* aḫīu
curl *n.* kizirtu; → **~** *v.* kazāru; → **~ up** *v.* kanānu⋆; → **be(come) ~ed** *v.* kapāṣu⋆; → **~y** *adj.* qannunu⋆
current *n.* nāru
curriculum *n.* iškāru
curry *v.* nadādu (D) [o.]; → **~ favor with** *v.* ēnē X dagālu [i.]
curse *n.* arratu⋆, erretu⋆, izru⋆, izzirtu, māmītu⋆, nizirtu; → **~** *v.* arāru⋆, nazāru
cursory *adj.* lasmu
curt *adj.* kapṣu+, kuriu
curtail *v.* maṭû (D)
curtain *n.* pariktu; → **~(?)** *n.* maldudu
curve *n.* kinšu⋆; → **~** *v.* kapādu; → **~d** *adj.* kappu C*
cuscuta *n.* kasû B⋆
cushion *n.* ḫa'ūtu; → **~(?)** *n.* ḫabû B
Cushite *n./adj.* Kūsāiu
cushy *adj.* pašīqu+
cuss *v.* nazāru
custodian *n.* nāqidu+
custody *n.* qātu
custom *n.* parṣu, ussu⋆; → **~-house** *n.* bēt kāri; → **~ary** *adj.* kaiamānīu; → **~er** *n.* zabbānu+; → **~s** *n.* bēt kāri, miksu; → **~s duty** *n.* miksu
cut *adj.* batqu; → **~** *n.* ḫirṣu, niksu, nisḫu; → **~** *v.* baṣāru, batāqu, gazāru, ḫaṣābu◊, ḫaṣāṣu, nakāsu, ṣalāpu+, šalāqu, šarāmu, šatāqu⋆; → **~ (at an angle)** *v.* ṣalāpu⋆; → **~ (off)** *adj.* naksu; → **~ (stone)** *v.* naqāru; → **~ (up)** *v.* ṭabāḫu; → **~ away** *v.* qadādu+; → **~ down** *v.* gadāmu+, ḫaṣāṣu, kašāṭu⋆, maṭû (D), nakāsu, rasābu⋆; → **~ in pieces** *adj.* nukkusu⋆; → **~ into** *v.* ḫarāṣu, paṣādu; → **~ of meat (kind of)** *n.* bugurru; → **~ off** *v.* batāqu, gadāmu [o.], karātu, kašāṭu⋆, nakāsu, parā'u B⋆, parāsu, qadādu; → **~ off (tip of nose)** *v.* šarāmu+; → **~ out** *v.* batāqu; → **~ short** *v.* kaṣāṣu⋆; → **~ through** *v.* natāru⋆ (Š), salātu⋆ (D); → **~ to size** *v.* šarāmu; → **~ up** *v.* batāqu, salātu
cute *adj.* damqu
Cutha *n.* Kutê
cutler *n.* ša-patrēšu*; → **~y** *n.* anūt akāli
cutting *n.* bitqu B◊, kismu⋆, niksu; → **~ edge** *n.* šēssu⋆; → **~ tool** *n.* makkāsu⋆; → **~s** *n.* ḫibištu⋆
cycle *n.* adannu
cyclone *adj.* imsuḫḫu⋆
cyder *n.* mēzu
cylinder seal *n.* kišādu
cymbal *n.* tigû⋆
cynoglossum *n.* lišān kalbi⋆
cyperus *n.* suādu
cypress *n.* supālu⋆ (a kind of), šurmēnu; → **~ (kind of)** *n.* ḫašurru⋆
Cyprus *n.* Iadnāna
cyst *n.* diḫḫu; → **~ic duct** *n.* maṣraḫu⋆
daft *adj.* iaḫudû⋆
dagger *n.* ḫangaru, uṣultu; → **~-like** *n.* ḫangarānu
daily *adj.* [ša] ūmi; → **~** *adv.* ūmišam⋆, ūmišamma⋆, ūmussu◊
dainty *adj.* ṣaiāḫu⋆
dais *n.* parakku
dale *n.* unqu B+; → **~** *n./adj.* mušpalu⋆
dally *v.* namūtu epāšu [o.]
dam *n.* sikru⋆; → **~** *v.* sakāru B; → **~ for diverting watercourse** *n.* mušašnītu (temporary); → **~ of reeds** *n.* errutu [o.]; → **~age** *n.* batqu, ḫibiltu⋆; → **~age** *v.* ḫabālu B⋆ (D), ḫaṭû◊ (D), samāku (D); → **suffer ~age** *v.* marādu (N), marāṭu (N); → **be ~aged** *v.* marāṭu (N); → **~ages** *n.* ḫibiltu (pl.)
Damascus *n.* Dimašqa
dame *n.* bēltu
damn *n.* izzirtu; → **~** *v.* nazāru; → **~ed** *adj.* nazru
damp *adj.* raṭbu, salḫu [o.]; → **be(come) ~** *v.* raṭābu, salāḫu⋆ (stat.); → **~ course of a wall** *n.* asurrû⋆; → **~ness** *n.* ruṭbu⋆, ruṭibtu⋆
dance *n.* riqdu; → **~** *v.* rapāsu+, raqādu,

sâru☆; → ~ **(in a circle)** *v.* sâru☆; → **~r** *n.* raqqidu☆

dancing *n.* riqdu; → **~-girl** *n.* mummiltu☆

dandruff *n.* epqēnu☆, kibšu☆

danger *n.* puluḫtu; → **be in ~(ous condition)** *v.* naqādu☆; → **~ous** *adj.* akṣu☆, da'nu, [ša] puluḫti*, šaggīšu+

dangle *v.* šuqallulu☆

dapper *adj.* dammuqu, kannû

dappled *adj.* kakkullānu+

dare → **be(come) ~** *v.* ṣarāmu+

daring *adj.* qardu, ṣarmu+

dark *adj.* adru B, da'mu☆, eklu☆, eṭû☆, ṣalmu B, ṣullulu☆; → **be|)keep in the ~** *v.* adāru (Dtt); → **be(come) ~** *v.* adāru, da'āmu☆, ekēlu☆, eṭû☆, tarāku B☆; → **pitch ~** *adj.* ukkulu☆; → **~en** *v.* adāru (D), adāru☆ (Š), da'āmu☆ (D), ekēlu☆ (D); → **~ened** *adj.* udduru; → **~ly** *adv.* adriš☆; → **~ness** *n.* da'ummatu☆, ekeltu☆, ekletu☆, eṭūtu☆, igiltu, uklu C☆

darling *n.* namaddu B☆, narāmtu☆, narāmu☆, ru'ūmtu☆, tarāmu B [o.]

darnel *n.* lišān kalbati+; → **~(?)** *n.* elmessu

dart *v.* šaḫāṭu C☆

dash *v.* napāṣu; → **~ to pieces** *v.* napāṣu+ (D); → **~ing** *adj.* šurruḫu☆

date *n.* adannu, saluppu; → **dried ~** *n.* uḫinnu; → **set a ~** *n.* adannu šakānu; → **~ beer or wine** *n.* kurunnu☆; → **~ cultivation** *n.* nukaribbūtu☆; → **~ palm** *n.* gišimmaru; → **~ palm (wild species of)** *n.* alamittu☆; → **~ palm branch** *n.* libbi gišimmari☆; → **~d** *adj.* labīru; → **basket for ~s** *n.* šugurrû☆; → **rotten ~s** *n.* ṭanīpu◊; → **spoiled ~s** *n.* ṭanīpu◊

daub *v.* eqû; → **~ing** *n.* tēqītu

daughter *n.* bintu, bukurtu☆, mar'utu; → **king's ~** *n.* mar'at šarri; → **~-in-law** *n.* kallutu; → **status of a ~-in-law/bride** *n.* kallūtu; → **~ship** *n.* mar'atūtu

daunting *adj.* sāḫipu☆

dauntless *adj.* qardu

dawdle → **be(come) ~** *v.* kuāšu

dawn *n.* kallamāri, sāntu B, ṣiprāti+, šēru☆

day *n.* immu B☆, ūmu, urru☆; → **~'s work** *n.* addû☆; → **auspicious ~** *n.* ūmu šemû☆; → **by ~** *adv.* ša ūmi; → **every ~** *adj.* ša ūmi ša ūmi; → **evil ~** *n.* uḫulgalê☆; → **fair ~** *n.* ūmu lā erpu [i.]; → **fifteenth ~** *n.* šapattu☆; → **new moon ~** *n.* ūm bubbuli; → **turn of the ~** *n.* saḫār ūme; → **~ after day** *n.* ūmu ana ūmi; → **~ after tomorrow** *adv.* illīdiš, līdiš; → **~ before yesterday** *adv.* ina šalši ūmi, iššaššūmi; → **~ before yesterday** *n.* šalši ūmi, šaššūmi; → **~ to day** *n.* ūmu ana ūmi; → **~ without rain** *n.* ūmu lā erpu [i.]; → **~break** *n.* namārītu, ṣiprāti+; → **at ~break** *adv.* innamāri; → **like ~light** *adv.* ūmiš☆; → **in ~s to come** *n.* labāriš ūmē [i.]; → **~time** *n.* immu B☆, kal ūmi; → **at ~time** *adv.* ša ūmi

daze *n.* kīrtu☆, kūru B☆; → **~d** *adj.* kēru*, šuḫarruru☆; → **be(come) ~d** *v.* kâru☆, šuḫarruru☆

dazzle *v.* ḫuppudu☆

dead *adj.* mētu; → **spirit of the ~** *n.* eṭemmu; → **~ end** *n.* ḫūlu karmu*; → **~ of night** *n.* qūltu☆; → **~en** *v.* anāšu (D), kâru☆ (D); → **~line** *n.* adannu, edānu; → **~ly** *adj.* [ša] muāti; → **~ly crime** *n.* ḫiṭṭu ša muāti; → **~ly poison** *n.* imat mūti☆; → **~ness** *n.* mētūtu+

deaf *adj.* lā šāmiu*, lā šēmû☆, sakkuku, sukkuku◊; → **~** *n.* ḫaršu B+; → **~-mute** *adj.* peḫû☆; → **~-mute** *n.* ḫaršu B+, ḫašikku☆; → **~ness** *n.* ḫaršūtu+, sakkukūtu

deal in *v.* miāru

deal with *v.* kullu, pû ṣabātu [i.]

dealer *n.* muppišu; → **incense ~** *n.* ša-endēšu; → **~ in leather hides** *n.* ša-ṣallēšu

dear *adj.* uqru, uqru+

death *n.* mētūtu, mūtu; → **put to|cause the ~** *v.* muātu (Š); → **cause the ~ of s.o.** *v.* muātu (Š); → **~ rattle** *n.* ḫūqu B☆; → **~ sentence** *n.* dēnu ša muāti; → **~ly silence** *n.* šaḫrartu☆

debar *v.* parāku (D)

debase *v.* baṣāru+

debate *adj.* tēṣītu B☆; → **~** *n.* ṣâlūtu [o.]; → **~** *v.* darāsu

debauchery *n.* paḫzūtu+

debility *n.* lu'tu☆

debit *v.* manû B [o.]

debris *n.* nappaltu☆, sirḫu☆

debt *n.* e'iltu☆, ḫabullu, ḫibiltu; → **be in ~** *v.* ḫabālu (D stat.); → **~ remission** *n.* andurāru☆, durāru; → **~or** *n.* ḫabbulu

decad *n.* ešertu; → **~ent** *adj.* maqtu

decanted → **be ~** *v.* esāpu (N)

decapitate *v.* kaqqudu nakāsu

decare *n.* sūtu

decay *n.* sāsu+, šiḫḫutu, šīpu☆, zupru☆; → **~** *v.* zapāru☆; → **~ed** *adj.* abtu☆; → **~ed matter** *n.* sumkinnu☆

deceit *n.* niklu+, piriṣtu☆, pirṣāti☆; → **~ful** *adj.* naklu+, ṭullumâ; → **~ful omen** *n.* tasrirru☆; → **~fully** *adv.* ina pirṣāti [i.]; → **act ~fully** *v.* nakālu+

deceive *v.* lā kettu dabābu, niklu nakālu,

parāṣu☆ (Š), salû, ṭalāmu+

December *n.* Kanūnu (month), Kislīmu (month)

decency *n.* būštu☆

decent *adj.* baiāšu☆

deception *n.* nikiltu, sullû B☆, tašqirtu☆; → **~(?)** *n.* pīgu☆

deceptive *adj.* sarru☆; → **~ly** *adv.* sartatti◊

decide *v.* parāsu; → **~d** *adj.* parsu; → **~r** *n.* pārisu

deciduous tooth *n.* šinnu ša ḫilbi+

decision *n.* purussû, ṣibit ṭēmi☆; → **~-maker** *n.* pārisu

decisive *adj.* pārisu; → **~ action** *n.* ṣibit ṭēmi☆

deck *n.* šaburru☆; → **~** *v.* elāḫu (D) [o.]; → **furnish with a ~** *v.* ruggubu☆

declaim *v.* ragāmu

declaration *n.* nību☆, pû, šūdûtu+

declare *v.* kallumu (D), qabû, šiāmu+; → **~ allegience** *v.* qannu ṣabātu [i.]

decline → **be(come) ~** *v.* šiāṣu

decoct *v.* rabāku [o.]; → **~ion** *n.* ribku☆

decompose *v.* maḫāḫu

decorate *v.* za'ānu☆ (D); → **~d** *adj.* za''unu☆

decoration *n.* simtu, šakuttu, šumḫu☆

decorative inlay *n.* iḫzēti☆

decorative motif (kind of) *n.* usḫu

decrease *n.* miṭītu◊, nušurrû☆; → **~** *v.* maṭû, maṭû (D)

decree *n.* rikistu☆, ṭēmu; → **~** *v.* qabû, šiāmu; → **~ fate** *v.* šīmtu šiāmu

decurion *n.* rab ešerti

dedicate *v.* elû (Š); → **~ o.s. to** *v.* elû☆ (Št)

dedication *n.* ikribu, šēlûtu

deduce *v.* abāku, ḫarāṣu (Št) [o.]

deduct *v.* elû (D), ḫarāṣu (Št) [o.], našāru, ṣaḫāru (D); → **~ion** *n.* maššartu☆, niširtu☆, nišru, šunquttu☆, tušaḫruṣu [o.]

deed *n.* epšetu, ipšu☆; → **great ~(s)** *n.* qurdu; → **great ~s** *n.* narbû☆; → **heroic ~s** *n.* alkakāt qurdi☆

deep *adj.* ḫuddudu☆, rūqu☆; → **very ~** *n.* šuppulu☆; → **~-rooted** *adj.* šarrušu+; → **~ly cut** *adj.* ḫuddudu☆

deer → **red ~** *n.* lulīmu

deface *v.* sapānu

defamation *n.* tašqirtu☆

defamatory *adj.* muqallilu*

defame *v.* karṣē akālu [i.]

defeat *n.* abiktu, dabdû☆, dēktu, kamāru B☆, sikiptu☆, taḫtû☆; → **~** *v.* duāku, kamāru šakānu [i.], kašādu, lapātu☆ (Š), maḫāṣu, maqātu (Š), saḫāpu; → **~ completely** *v.* ana māla duāku [i.]; → **~ed** *adj.* šulputu☆

defecate *v.* teṣû☆

defect *n.* ḫiṭṭu; → **~** *v.* nabalkutu; → **~ive** *adj.* maṭiu; → **be(come) ~ive** *v.* maṭû; → **~or** *n.* maqtu

defend *v.* ḫaṣānu, naṣāru

defense *n.* ḫiṣnu☆, ṣulūlu+

deferment *n.* šiddu

defiance *n.* šipṣu☆

defiant *adj.* šapṣu☆

deficiency *n.* muṭê

deficient *adj.* maṭiu

deficit *n.* batqu, bitiqtu, imbû☆, miṭītu◊, muṭê

defile *n.* nērubu, pušqu☆; → **~** *v.* la'āšu☆, lapātu☆ (Š), lu''û☆, ṭanāpu+ (D); → **~d** *adj.* lu''û☆, ṭanpu+, ṭappīlu+

define *v.* parāsu, šiāmu

definite *adj.* parsu; → **~ly** *adv.* ra'i☆

definition *n.* šiknu

definitive *adj.* parsu

deflect *v.* nê'u☆

deflower *v.* ṭanāpu+ (D)

deform *v.* ḫabālu B+ (D); → **~ed** *adj.* pessû☆, uzzubu☆; → **~ity** *n.* ḫiṭṭu

defraud *v.* ḫabālu B, nakālu+

defray *v.* šalāmu (D)

defy *v.* maḫāru

degenerate *adj.* uzzubu☆; → **~** *v.* šaḫāḫu

degeneration *n.* šiḫḫutu

degradation *n.* būštu+, tašpiltu☆

degrade *v.* šapālu (D); → **~d** *adj.* šappulu

degrading *adj.* muqallilu*, mušappilu*

degree *n.* dargu+

deign *v.* magāru☆

dejection *n.* ašuštu☆, šuplu libbi

delay *n.* tazbiltu☆; → **~** *v.* kalû (Gtn), karāmu, katāru+, muqqu☆, namarkû (Š), saḫāru [o.], uḫḫuru; → **be(come) ~ed** *v.* kuāšu (D), namarkû

delegate *n.* qēpu, ṣīru+; → **~** *v.* paqādu

delegation *n.* šaprūtu

delete *v.* pasāsu, pašāṭu

deliberate *adj.* muštālu☆; → **~** *v.* abālu B☆ (Št), amatu šutābulu [i.], malāku (N), malāku☆ (Gt), šutaddunu☆; → **~ly** *adv.* ina ḫūd libbi [i.], ina mērešti [i.]

deliberation *n.* milku, mitluktu☆, muštālūtu☆, šitūltu☆

delicacy *n.* mutqītu

delicate *adj.* naḫsu☆ (very), qatnu

delicious *adj.* ṣaiāḫu☆

delight *n.* bulṭu libbi, lalû; → **~** *v.* libbu

balluṭu [i.]; → **be(come) ~ed** *v.* libbu balāṭu [i.]; → **~ful** *adj.* ṣaiāḫu☆, ta'īdu+

delimit *v.* kadāru; → **~ing** *adj.* māṣiru

delineate *v.* eṣāru+, ḫaṭāṭu+, palāku☆

delinquent *n.* ḫaṭṭā'u☆

delirious *adj.* maḫḫû☆, sarḫu

deliver *v.* ezābu+ (Š), ḫarāšu B☆ (D), tadānu, ubālu, ubālu (Š); → **~ to** *v.* ina qāti manû [i.], manû B; → **~ up** *v.* šalāmu+ (D); → **~y** *n.* šazbussu

dell *n.* unqu B+

delta *n.* pī nāri

delude *v.* sagû+ (Š)

deluge *n.* abūbu

delve *v.* tarāḫu [o.]; → **~ into** *v.* ḫarāṣu

demagogue *n.* mušadbibu

demand *n.* erištu☆; → **~** *v.* ba''û, erāšu; → **~ing** *n.* mūterrišu☆

demarcate *v.* maṣāru◊ (D), palāku☆

demeanor *n.* riddu

demerit *n.* miṭītu

demi- *adj.* mišil

demobilize *v.* paṭāru

demolish *v.* napālu☆, naqāru, natāru☆ (Š), paṭāru (D), saḫāpu+

demon *n.* gallû, šēdu+; → **~ (kind of)** *n.* alû, ḫultuppu☆, lilû☆; → **~strate** *v.* kallumu (D); → **~stration** *n.* taklīmu☆

demote *v.* šapālu (D)

demotion *n.* tašpiltu☆

den *n.* gubbutu+; → **~ial** *n.* nukurrû [o.], ullu☆

denigrate *v.* karṣē akālu [i.], ṭapiltu dabābu [i.]

denigration *n.* ṭapiltu☆

denounce *v.* karṣē akālu [i.], ubburu☆; → **~r** *n.* bātiqu

dense *adj.* ebṭu+, ebû+, ḫabburu, šapku☆, šapû☆; → **be(come) ~** *v.* šapû☆

dental infection *n.* muruṣ šinni☆

denude *v.* erû B (D) [o.], lubūšē šaḫāṭu [i.]

denunciation *n.* akāl karṣē, batiqtu

deny *v.* kalû, šarābu+

depart *v.* namāšu (D); → **~ing** *adj.* āṣiu

departure *n.* mūṣû

depend *v.* takālu+; → **~ on** *v.* takālu (D stat.); → **~ence** *n.* ḫanšūtu*; → **~ent** *adj.* ḫanšu B; → **~ent** *n.* aštapīru☆, ṣēnu B+

depict *v.* esēqu☆, eṣāru

deplete *v.* ḫabû

deplorable *adj.* bīšu+

deplore *v.* karrû+ (D)

depopulate *v.* nadû☆ (Š)

depopulation *n.* ḫarbūtu

deport *v.* galû (Š), nesû☆ (D); → **~ation** *n.* galītu, šaglūtu; → **~ed** *adj.* šallu☆; → **~ee** *n.* nasīḫu☆, šaglû; → **~ees** *n.* galītu; → **master of ~ees** *n.* rab šaglūti

depose *v.* nakāru (D); → **~d** *adj.* darsu

deposit *n.* maškānu, šibḫu☆; → **~ary** *n.* ṣābitu

depot *n.* maškattu◊

depraved *adj.* ṭappīlu+

depravity *n.* ṭappīlūtu+

depress *v.* libbu šappulu [i.]; → **be(come) ~ed** *v.* libbu šapālu [i.], šapālu; → **~ion** *n.* ašuštu☆, kūru B☆, mušpalu☆, sapannu☆, šīlu☆, šupālu☆, šuplu, šuplu libbi

deprive *v.* ekēmu☆, ḫabālu B, puāgu; → **~ of** *v.* zammû

depth *n.* mušpalu☆, šuplu

deputy *n.* šaniu; → **female ~** *n.* šanētu

derelict *adj.* ezbu☆

deride *v.* lazānu

derision *n.* liznu*

derive *v.* radû+

derogatory *adj.* muqallilu*

descend *v.* šutaktutu☆, urādu; → **~ant** *n.* lēpu, līp līpi

descent *n.* ilittu, kisittu☆, mūraddu☆

describe *v.* eṣāru+

description *n.* šiknu

desecrate *v.* lapātu☆ (Š)

desecration *n.* li'šu, šēṭūtu+

desert *adj.* madburu; → **~** *n.* ḫuribtu☆, mudāburu, namû☆; → **~** *v.* maqātu; → **~(ed place)** *n.* ḫurbu; → **sand ~** *n.* kaqqar bāṣi☆; → **~ someone** *v.* idu naparkû [i.]; → **be(come) ~ed** *v.* ḫarābu☆; → **~er** *n.* maqtu, muštaḫalqu◊; → **~ion** *n.* nabalkattu☆

deserve *v.* utāru (D)

design *n.* eṣurtu☆, gišḫurru☆, uṣurtu; → **~** *v.* eṣāru; → **long ~** *n.* ariktu☆; → **~ate** *v.* qabû; → **~er** *n.* ēṣiru☆; → **~er(?)** *n.* rab šiknāni

desirable *adj.* ṣaiāḫu☆

desire *n.* ba''ītu☆, bibil libbi☆, ḫišiḫtu☆, izimtu☆, nazmatu☆, nīš libbi☆, nizmatu☆, ṣaḫittu, ṣibūtu☆, ṣiḫittu, ṣummuru☆, ṣumru☆; → **~** *v.* erāšu, ḫašāḫu☆, ṣabû◊; → **be(come) ~** *v.* ṣaḫātu; → **sexual ~** *n.* nīš libbi☆; → **~d** *adj.* eršu, ṣaḫtu

desirous *n.* ṣāḫitu

desk *n.* paššūru

desolate *n.* šuḫrubu☆; → **~** *v.* saḫāpu+; → **make ~** *v.* šaḫruru; → **very ~** *n.* ḫitrubu☆

desolation *n.* namûtu☆

despair *n.* miqit ṭēmi☆; → **~** *v.* nazāqu☆

desperate *adj.* dalḫu; → **be(come) ~** *v.* ašāšu☆

desperation *n.* miqit ṭēmi☆
despicable *adj.* masku [o.], qallulu, šēṭu⁺
despise *v.* bašā'u, mêšu☆, selû◊, šâṭu B☆; → **~d** *adj.* šēṭu⁺; → **~r** *adj.* šaiāṭu⁺
despoil *v.* ḫamāṣu◊ (Š), ḫubtu ḫabātu
destination *n.* qītu
destine *v.* šiāmu
destiny *n.* šīmtu
destitute *adj.* katû☆, makiu, muškēnu
destitution *n.* makûtu
destroy *v.* abātu☆, diāšu☆, gamāru, ḫalāqu (D), ḫapû, ḫaṭû◊ (D), lapātu☆ (Š), magguru⁺, mêsu☆, qatû☆ (D); → **~ by burning** *v.* qamû; → **~ by fire** *v.* ina išāti šarāpu [i.]; → **~ed(?)** *adj.* šuḫḫû☆
destructible *adj.* ša ḫapê
destruction *n.* ḫapûtu, riḫiṣtu☆, šaḫluqtu☆
destructive *adj.* rāḫiṣu☆
desultory *adj.* lā kapdu*
detach *v.* šaḫāṭu; → **~ment** *n.* pursānu⁺
detail *n.* batiqtu; → **in ~** *adv.* šiddi arki [i.]; → **in ~** *n.* issu šiddi arki [i.]; → **~ed report** *n.* ḫariṣtu; → **send a ~ed report** *v.* ḫarāṣu šapāru
detain *v.* kalû; → **~ment** *n.* mēsēru☆
detect *v.* patû
detention *n.* maškānūtu; → **~ room** *n.* bīt siggi◊
deter *v.* galādu (D), palāḫu (D)
deteriorate *v.* lamānu (D)
determinate *adj.* parsu
determination *n.* ṣarmūtu⁺, ṣūrāmu⁺
determinative *adj.* pārisu
determine *v.* parāsu, šiāmu; → **~d** *adj.* ṣarmu⁺; → **be(come) ~d** *v.* ṣarāmu⁺
detest *v.* selû⁺, ziāru; → **~able** *adj.* nazru; → **be ~able** *v.* ziāru (N); → **make ~ed** *v.* nazāru (Š)
dethrone *v.* saḫāpu⁺, tabû (Š)
detract from *v.* baṣāru⁺
detriment *n.* bitiqtu
devalue *v.* baṣāru⁺
devastate *v.* abātu☆ (D), raḫāṣu B, šaḫruru
devastating *adj.* rāḫiṣu☆, šēru B☆
devastation *n.* naspantu☆, našpantu, riḫiṣtu☆, riḫṣu, saḫaptu☆
develop *v.* arû C☆ (Gtn), rabû (D); → **~ment** *n.* rūbu
deviate *v.* ḫūlu nakkuru (D) [i.], samû (Gtn)
deviation *n.* sagûtu⁺
devil *n.* gallû, šēdu⁺; → **little ~** *n.* šēdānu⁺; → **~ itself** *n.* ḫiriṣ gallê lemni☆
devise *v.* patāqu☆
devolve *v.* qiāpu
devote *v.* elû (Š); → **~ o.s.** *v.* tâpu☆; → **~ o.s. to** *v.* naqû⁺ (D); → **~d to** *adj.* šarbubu
devotee *n.* šēlūtu; → **~ of I&tar** *n.* ḫarmāku, kazru, kazrutu
devotion *n.* labān appi☆, šēlûtu
devour *v.* akālu; → **~ing** *n.* ukultu☆
devout *adj.* muštēmiqu☆
dew *n.* nalšu; → **~y** *adj.* raṭbu
dexterity *n.* nikiltu
dexterous *adj.* kāširu⁺, naklu; → **be(come) ~** *v.* nakālu
diadem *n.* aguḫḫu☆, pitūtu
diagnosis *n.* qību
diagnostics *n.* sakikkû
diagonal *n.* ṣiliptu☆ (diagonal)
diagram *n.* asarru
dialect *n.* lišānu
dialog(ue) *n.* dabūbu☆
dialogue *adv.* pī aḫāmiš☆
diameter *n.* kubru
diamond *n.* elmēšu⁺
diaphragm *n.* dikšu☆, ṣulultu☆
diarrh(o)ea *n.* nišḫu☆
diarrhoea → have ~ *v.* ṣanāḫu☆
dice *n.* pūru
dicker *v.* tēgirtu šakānu [i.]
dictate *v.* qabû
diction *n.* naqbītu
diddle *v.* niāku
die *v.* muātu, nammušīšu alāku [i.]; → **~ down** *v.* šuḫarruru☆; → **~ out** *v.* baṭālu⁺
differ → be ~ *v.* lā magāru (N); → **~ence** *n.* nappaltu B☆, sangilû☆, tašpiltu☆; → **~ent** *adj.* nakkuru, nakru, šaniu; → **~ent** *n.* šitnû☆; → **be(come) ~ent** *v.* nakāru, šanû; → **~entiate** *v.* parāsu; → **~entiate between** *v.* birti X birti Y ḫakāmu [i.]; → **~entiated** *adj.* parsu⁺; → **~entiation** *n.* pursānu⁺; → **~ently** *adv.* šanîš
difficult *adj.* da'nu, marṣu, pašqu☆, šupšuqu☆; → **be(come) ~** *v.* da'ānu, danānu☆, pašāqu B☆; → **~y** *n.* dannutu, namrāṣu☆; → **with ~y** *adv.* namrāṣiš☆, pašqiš☆, šupšuqiš☆
diffident → be ~ *v.* parādu☆ (Gtn)
diffuse *v.* tarāṣu
dig *v.* ḫarāru☆, ḫarāṣu, ḫarû, ḫaṭāṭu⁺; → **~ (up)** *v.* ḫapāru☆; → **~ out** *v.* ḫaṭāṭu; → **~ through** *v.* palāšu⁺; → **~ up** *v.* tarāḫu [o.]; → **~est** *v.* pašāru, pašāru⁺; → **~estible** *adj.* ša pašāri*; → **~estion** *n.* pušurtu⁺
digging work *n.* ḫirūtu☆
dignified *adj.* kabtu☆; → **~ conduct** *n.* uqrūtu⁺
dignitary *n.* kabtu☆
dignity *n.* būltu◊, būštu☆, uqrūtu⁺

dilapidated → **be(come)** ~ *v.* anāḫu, anāšu, labāriš alāku [i.], miqittu rašû [i.]; → **become** ~ *v.* labīrūtu alāku [i.]
dilapidation *n.* anḫūtu, enšūtu*, maqittu*
dilate *v.* rapāšu (D)
diligence *n.* ḫarduttu, kušīru+
diligent *adj.* ḫardu, kāširu+
dill *n.* šibittu*
dilute *v.* ḫiāqu, ramāku; → **~d** *adj.* ḫīqu
dim *n.* barru*; → ~ *v.* barāru (D); → **be(come)** ~ *v.* barāru, unnutu (D); → **~ension** *n.* middutu, mināti* (pl.), mišiḫtu*, namaddu
diminish *v.* maṭû, ṣaḫāru (D); → **be(come)** ~ *v.* šiāṣu; → **be(come) ~ed** *v.* naḫātu
diminution *n.* tamṭītu*
diminutive *adj.* ṣeḫḫeru
dimly *adv.* adriš*
dimness *n.* barāru
din *n.* ḫubūru*
dine *v.* akālu šatû
dingy *adj.* gammīzu+
dining room *n.* bēt naptini
dinner *n.* naptan līlāti*, naptunu; → **~-attendant** *n.* ša-naptini
diorite *n.* ušû
dip *v.* ṭabû
diphtheria *n.* bu'šānu*
diplomat *n.* ṣīru
dipper *n.* itqūru
direct *adj.* išaru*, tarṣu; → ~ *v.* abālu B* (Gtn), šapāru, tarāṣu B+ (D), tarāṣu B (D); → **~ion** *n.* šāru, tarṣu B, tirṣu; → **~ive** *n.* tērtu*; → **~ly** *adv.* ina muḫḫi ašli; → **~ory** *n.* rikis gerri*; → **~ress** *n.* šakintu
dirge *n.* taqribtu*
dirtiness *n.* aruštu*
dirty *adj.* lu''û*, ša''uru; → ~ *v.* la'āšu*; → **be(come)** ~ *v.* ša'āru, ṭanāpu◊; → **make** ~ *v.* ša'āru (D), ša'āru* (Š), urruzu
disability *n.* kabbulūtu*
disable *v.* kabālu* (D); → **~d** *adj.* kabbulu, ṣabbutānu
disadvantageous *adj.* lā kušīri*
disagree → **be** ~ *v.* lā magāru (N); → **~able** *adj.* zēru; → **~ment** *n.* lā magāru
disappear *v.* ḫalāqu, paṭāru (N), tabālu; → **make** ~ *v.* ḫalāqu (Š), pa'āšu (D)
disappoint *v.* bâšu+ (D); → **~ment** *n.* būštu+
disapproval *n.* sūlû+
disapprove *v.* selû+
disarrange *v.* seḫû* (D)
disaster *n.* karašû*, šaḫluqtu*
disband *v.* rammû (D)
disbelief *n.* lā qīptu*
disbelieve *v.* lā qiāpu
discard *v.* karāru, rammû (D)
discern *v.* ḫakāmu+; → **~ing** *adj.* rāš tašīmti*; → **~ment** *n.* tašīmtu*
discharge *v.* patû (D), radû+ (Š); → ~ **pus** *v.* šarāku B*
disciple *n.* talmīdu, talmīdu+; → **~ship** *n.* talmīdūtu+
discipline *n.* mardûtu+, sanqūtu*; → **~d** *adj.* radiu+, sanqu*
disclaim *v.* nakāru+
disclose *v.* kallumu* (Š), patû
disclosure *n.* taklimtu
discolor *v.* qašāpu+; → **~ation** *n.* ṣiriptu*, tiriptu [o.]
discomfit *v.* ana māla duāku [i.], dalāḫu+
disconcert *v.* ḫabālu B+ (D)
disconsolate *adj.* udduru
discontinue *v.* baṭālu* (Š)
discord *n.* lā mitgurtu*; → **~ant** *adj.* lā māgiru*
discourage *v.* libbu nasāḫu [i.], libbu šappulu [i.]; → **be(come) ~d** *v.* libbu šapālu [i.]
discourse *n.* dabābu
discover *v.* atû B*; → **~y** *n.* itūtu*
discredit *n.* qulālu; → ~ *v.* qalālu (D), qulālē šakānu [i.]; → **~able** *adj.* mušappilu*
discreet *adj.* pitqudu*; → **~ly** *adj.* šapal qāti; → **~ly** *adv.* ana lā amāri [i.], šapla qāti [i.]
discrepancy *n.* sangilû*
discrete *adj.* parsu
discriminate *v.* mussû*, parāsu
discrimination *n.* parsūtu+
discuss *v.* abālu B* (Št), amatu šutābulu [i.], amû* (Gt), dabābu, malāku (N); → **~ion** *n.* dabābu, šitūltu*
disdain *n.* bašā'u+, šēṭūtu; → ~ *v.* šêṭu*; → **~ful** *adj.* šaiāṭu+
disease *n.* masla'tu*, murṣu, sili'tu*; → **anal** ~ *n.* muruṣ šuburri*; → **head** ~ *n.* muruṣ qaqqadi*; → **heart** ~ *n.* muruṣ libbi; → **joint** ~ *n.* maškadu*; → **venereal** ~ *n.* muruṣ niāki*, rimṭu; → **~-causing demon (kind of)** *n.* asakku; → **~d** *adj.* marṣu
disembark *v.* ana kibri emādu [i.]
disembowel *v.* ṣarāku*
disengagement *n.* pitrustu*
disfavor *n.* lā ṭābtu
disfigure *v.* akālu
disgrace *n.* masiktu [o.]; → ~ *v.* bâšu (D), masāku* (D); → **~ful** *adj.* bīšu◊, masku [o.]; → **~fully** *adv.* ana masikti [o.]
disguise *n.* puṣūnu [o.]; → ~ *v.* paṣānu

(D) [o.]; → ~ **o.s.** *v.* ramanšu šannû
disgust *n.* zērûtu⋆, zīru; → **~ing** *adj.* zēru⋆; → **be ~ing** *v.* ziāru (N)
dish *n.* kallu, mākālu, mallatu⋆, saplu; → **(metal) ~** *n.* ḫuruppu⋆; → **wooden ~** *n.* mākassu; → **~ (kind of)** *n.* lummu, maziu; → **copper ~ (kind of)** *n.* mukarrisu; → **~earten** *v.* libbu nasāḫu [i.]
dishevelled *adj.* apparrû⋆
dishonest *adj.* sarru⋆; → **~y** *n.* sarrûtu⋆, sartu, ṣaliptu⋆
dishonor *v.* bâšu (D); → **bring ~ on** *v.* qulālē šakānu [i.]; → **~able** *adj.* bīšu◊
dishwasher(?) *n.* kāpir diqāri
disinfect *v.* marāqu+
disinherit *n.* ina mar'ūti nasāḫu [i.]
disintegrate *v.* naḫarmuṭu⋆ (Š), šaḫāḫu
disintegration *n.* naspuḫtu⋆, šiḫḫutu
disk *n.* kipputu, nipḫu
dislike *v.* ziāru
dislocate *v.* galû (Š), parāqu+
dislodge *v.* nâšu⋆, ruābu (D)
disloyal *adj.* lā kēnu; → **~ speech** *n.* sullû B⋆
dismantle *v.* naqāru, paṭāru
dismay *n.* idirtu; → **~** *v.* parādu⋆ (D); → **~ed** *adj.* pardu⋆
dismember *v.* batāqu
dismiss *v.* patû (D), paṭāru
dismount *v.* urādu
disobedience *n.* lā mitgurtu⋆
disobedient *adj.* lā māgiru⋆; → **be(come) ~** *v.* lā magāru; → **~ (person)** *adj.* lā šāmiu*
disobey *v.* lā šamû
disobliging *adj.* lā magru
disorder *n.* duluḫḫû⋆; → **~ly** *adj.* dalḫu, šaggīšu+; → **political ~s** *n.* ešītu⋆
disorganize *v.* dalāḫu
disown *v.* zakû+
disparage *v.* qulālē šakānu [i.]; → **~ment** *n.* qulālu
disparaging *adj.* muqallilu*
disparity *n.* parsûtu+
dispassionate *adj.* nēḫu
dispatch *n.* šēbultu⋆, šipirtu; → **~** *v.* abālu B⋆ (Š), šakātu (Š), šalāḫu B [o.], ubālu (Š); → **~ rider** *n.* kallāp šipirti
dispel *v.* kašādu (D)
dispensation *n.* ennānāti (pl.) [o.]
dispersal *n.* naparrurtu⋆
disperse *v.* parāru (D), sapāḫu; → **~(?)** *v.* šabāḫu◊ (D)
displace *v.* abāku (D), galû (Š), nabalkutu (Š), nasāḫu; → **~d person** *n.* nasīḫu⋆
display *v.* kallumu (D); → **~(?)** *n.* kullumūtu⋆; → **(funerary) ~** *n.* taklimtu
displease *v.* be'āšu+, libbu lummunu [i.]
displeasing *adj.* lā ṭābu; → **be(come) ~** *v.* marāṣu
displeasure *n.* lumun libbi
disposal of → **at the ~** *prep.* ina qāt
dispose *v.* karāru; → **~ of** *v.* ḫalāqu (D), nasāḫu, rammû (D); → **~ of (property)** *v.* šalāṭu
disposition *n.* miqit pāni◊, šīmtu, ṭēmu
disproportion *n.* lā mitḫārūtu*; → **~ate** *adj.* lā mitḫāru⋆
dispute *adj.* tēṣītu B⋆; → **~** *n.* ṣâlūtu [o.], ṣāssu, ṣēlūtu⋆, tapqirtu⋆; → **~** *v.* baqāru, dabābu, paqāru; → **have a ~** *v.* ṣāssu garû
disqualify *v.* lā damāqu*
disquiet *v.* dalāḫu+; → **~ed** *adj.* dalḫu
disregard *v.* egû, ezābu [o.], mêšu⋆, rammû (D), šêṭu⋆
disrepair *n.* maqittu⋆
disrespect → **treat with ~** *v.* dâṣu⋆; → **~ful** *adj.* lā ādiru⋆, lā pāliḫu
disruption *n.* dilḫu⋆
dissatisfaction *n.* lā ṭūb libbi*
dissect *v.* ṣalāpu⋆; → **~ion** *n.* ṣiliptu⋆ (diagonal)
disseminate *v.* zarû; → **~ slanders** *v.* ṭapālu⋆ (Š)
dissemination *n.* zarû
dissension *n.* lā mitgurtu⋆
dissent → **be ~** *v.* lā magāru (N)
dissentient *n.* ṣalīpu+
disservice *n.* lumnu
dissident *adj.* lā māgiru⋆
dissimulation *n.* niklu+
dissipate *v.* baddudu, parāḫu+ (D)
dissipation *n.* naspuḫtu⋆
dissociate *v.* parāqu+
dissolute *adj.* parruḫu+
dissolution *n.* naḫarmuṭu*, napšurtu⋆
dissolve *v.* maḫāḫu, naḫarmuṭu⋆, pašāru, zuābu [o.]
distaff *n.* pilaqqu
distance *n.* birītu B⋆, mardītu; → **long ~** *n.* rūqu⋆; → **~ o.s.** *v.* patû, ruāqu
distant *adj.* nesû⋆, patiu, rēqu⋆, rūqu⋆, ullû⋆; → **be(come) ~** *v.* nesû⋆, ruāqu
distaste *n.* zērûtu⋆
distemper *n.* muruṣ kalbi*
distend *v.* napāšu
distension *n.* ṣimirtu⋆
distill *v.* ḫalāṣu, šaḫālu+; → **~ation** *n.* šiḫiltu+
distinct *adj.* ḫakmu, parsu; → **be ~** *v.* ḫakāmu (N); → **~ion** *n.* pursānu+; → **~ive** *adj.*

parsu+; → **~ly** *adv*. pašīqatti+
distinguish *v*. birti X birti Y ḫakāmu [i.], ḫakāmu birti [i.], mussû◊, mussû⋆, parāsu; → **~ (between)** *v*. ḫakāmu; → **~ed** *adj*. ašû⋆, edû
distort *v*. kapāṣu⋆ (D), pasālu [o.], ṣalāpu⋆; → **~ed** *adj*. kapṣu⋆, patlu+
distract → **cause to ~** *v*. samû (D); → **~ed** *adj*. dalḫu; → **~ion** *n*. diliḫtu⋆
distress *n*. ašuštu⋆, daliḫtu⋆, nakuttu, pušqu⋆, sinqu; → **~** *v*. ašāšu⋆ (D); → **~ed** *adj*. uššušu⋆
distribute *v*. zarû, zuāzu (D); → **~ gifts** *v*. qiāšu (D)
distributing *n*. zarû
distribution *n*. za'uzzu, zarû
district *n*. bābtu, ḫalzu, nagītu⋆, nagiu
distrust *v*. lā takālu*; → **~ful** *adj*. lā taklu*
disturb *v*. ašāšu⋆ (D), dalāḫu, dalāpu (D), seḫû⋆ (D); → **~ance** *n*. daliḫtu⋆, diliḫtu⋆; → **~ed** *adj*. dalḫu, pardu⋆; → **be(come) ~ed** *v*. parādu⋆; → **~ed state** *n*. dilḫu⋆; → **~ing** *adj*. dāliḫu⋆
ditch *n*. atappu , īku, palgu; → **like a ~** *adv*. ikiš⋆, palgiš⋆
ditto *adv*. šanīš
diurnal *adj*. [ša] ūmi, [ša] ūmi
dive *v*. šalû⋆; → **be ~rge from** *v*. šanû⋆ (Gt); → **~rgence** *n*. naparrurtu⋆; → **~rse** *adj*. lā mitḫāru⋆; → **~rsion (canal)** *n*. takkīru⋆; → **~rt** *v*. batāqu, parāsu
divide *v*. ḫapû, parāsu, šatāqu+, zuāzu; → **~ inheritance** *v*. zittu batāqu [i.]; → **~ off** *v*. palāku⋆, parāqu⋆; → **~d** *adj*. parsu, zēzu; → **~d** *n*. ṣalīpu+; → **~nd** *n*. munūtu⋆
dividing baulk *n*. birītu B⋆
divination *n*. bārûtu, bīru
divine abodes *n*. ašrāti⋆ (pl.)
divine assembly hall *n*. ubšukkinakku⋆
divine garment (kind of) *n*. šer'ītu
divine protection *n*. kidinnu
divine supremacy *n*. illilūtu
diviner *n*. bāriu
divinity *n*. ilūtu
division *n*. pirsu, zittu
divorce *n*. uzubbû⋆; → **~** *v*. ezābu [o.], rammû (D); → **~d** *adj*. ezbu⋆; → **get ~d** *v*. ezābu (Gt) [o.]
divulge *v*. barû B (D), kallumu (D)
dizziness *n*. ṣidru+, ṣūd pāni⋆
dizzy *v*. neqelpû⋆; → **be(come) ~** *v*. šakāru+; → **become ~** *v*. ṣâdu (Gtn); → **make ~** *v*. ṣâdu⋆ (D)
do *v*. epāšu, epāšu (D); → **~-nothing** *adj*. lā ēpišu; → **~-nothing** *n./adj*. šēṭu; → **~ (something) well** *v*. damāqu (D); → **~ away with** *v*. duāku, gamāru; → **~ first** *v*. ḫarāpu; → **~ for** *v*. apālu B, gamāru; → **~ good deeds** *v*. damqāti saḫāru⋆; → **make ~ hastily** *v*. dalāḫu epāšu; → **~ in** *v*. duāku; → **~ in addition** *v*. radû (D); → **~ in an orderly manner** *v*. sadāru (D); → **~ more** *v*. radû (D); → **~ obedience** *v*. urdānūtu epāšu [i.]; → **be(come) ~ slowly** *v*. marû⋆; → **~ somersaults** *v*. nabalkutu⋆ (Gtn); → **~ up** *v*. epāšu (D); → **~ well** *v*. dammuqu epāšu; → **~ with success** *v*. kašāru+; → **~ without** *v*. šurrû B⋆ (Dt)
docile *adj*. kanšu⋆
dock *v*. emādu
doctor *n*. asû; → **chief ~** *n*. rab asê
document *n*. egertu, giṭṭu◊, giṭṭu+ (parchment), nibzu , sipru◊, šaṭṭāru, ṭuppu; → **~ary** *adj*. šaṭru
dodder *n*. kasūtu
dodge *v*. ḫalāqu (Gtn)
doe *n*. ṣabītu+; → **~r** *n*. ēpišu
dog *n*. kalbu; → **female ~** *n*. kalbatu⋆; → **like a ~** *adv*. kalbāniš⋆; → **mythical wild ~** *n*. urdimmu⋆; → **wild ~** *n*. uridimmu⋆; → **young ~** *n*. mūrānu; → **~ days** *n*. ūmē ša nanmurti Qašti⋆
doggedly *adv*. kalbāniš⋆
doghouse *n*. bēt kalbi+
dogs → **keeper of (hunting) ~** *n*. ša-kalbāni
doing *n*. epāšu
doll *n*. passu⋆
dolomite *n*. elallu
dolphin *n*. nāḫiru⋆
domain *n*. bētu, taḫūmu
dome *n*. qumbutu+; → **~stic** *adj*. bētānīu, unzarḫu; → **~stic** *n*. muttabbilu⋆; → **~stic (kind of)** *n*. ša-bēt-qiqî; → **~stic accoutrements** *n*. anūt bēti; → **~stic fittings** *n*. anūt bēti; → **~stic quarters** *n./adj*. bētānu; → **~stic servants** *n*. nišē bēti; → **~sticate** *v*. kabāsu; → **~sticated** *adj*. kabsu
domicile *n*. mūšubu
dominant *adj*. šitluṭu⋆; → **be(come) ~** *v*. ba'ālu
dominate *v*. biālu, šalāṭu
domination *n*. bēlūtu, etallūtu⋆
dominion *n*. bēlūtu, etallūtu⋆; → **complete ~** *n*. gamīrūtu⋆
don *v*. edēqu⋆; → **~ate** *v*. elû (Š), riāmu; → **~ation** *n*. rēmuttu
done with *adj*. gamru
donkey *n*. imāru; → **~'s cunt** *n*. biṣṣūr

atāni; → **riding** ~ *n.* agālu☆; → **wild** ~ *n.* akkannu; → **~-mare** *n.* atānu; → **~driver** *n.* rādi imāri; → **~foal** *n.* mār atāni☆
donor *n.* nādinu☆, šāriku☆; → **~(?)** *n.* šarrāku◊
doomed *adj.* dēnu+
Doomsday *n.* ūm epēš nikkassi
door *n.* dassu, ēdissu; → **double ~** *n.* mutīrtu☆, tu'intu; → **front ~** *n.* abullu+, bāb pūti; → **part or decoration of a ~** *n.* saramê; → **~-beam** *n.* šibšutu; → **~-leaf** *n.* ēdissu; → **~-pivot** *n.* ṣirru☆, šagammu☆; → **~ hasp** *n.* mukīl dassi☆; → **~ holder** *n.* mukīl dassi☆; → **~ pole** *n.* šukû☆; → **~ socket** *n.* ṣirru+ (upper or lower); → **~ with two leaves** *n.* ēdissu+ (pl.)
doorframe *n.* sippu
doorjamb *n.* sippu
doorkeeper → **chief ~** *n.* atūgallu
doorman *n.* atû
doorpost *n.* sippu; → **~(?)** *n.* šupšutu; → **socket for ~** *n.* ṣirru☆
doors → **double ~** *n.* ēdissu+ (pl.), ta''umāti+ (pl.)
doorsill *n.* askupputu
doorstop *n.* mukīl dassi☆
doorway *n.* bābu, dakkannu☆
dope *v.* kâru☆ (D)
dorbeetle *n.* muqappil zê☆
dormouse *n.* arrābû; → **female ~** *n.* arrābātu; → **(bag made of) ~ skin** *n.* mašak arabê
doss *v.* nuāmu+
dot *n.* tikpu B
double *adj.* eṣpu☆, ta''umu; → **~** *v.* eṣāpu, šanû☆ (Št), ta''umu (D); → **~(d)** *adj.* šannu'u, šunnû☆; → **~-pipe** *n.* ṣinnutu
doubt *n.* lā qīptu*, nirriṭu; → **~** *v.* lā qiāpu, pašāku+; → **make ~** *v.* pašāku+ (D); → **~ful** *adj.* lā qā'ipu*, lā qēpu; → **~less** *adv.* issurri
dough *n.* aṣūdu+, lēšu; → **lump of ~** *n.* aṣūdu+
dove *n.* su''u, summatu☆
down *adv.* šapliš; → **be(come)lbe(come) ~** *v.* libbu šapālu [i.]; → **get ~ to** *v.* aḫu ummudu [i.]
downcast *adj.* šappulu; → **be(come) ~** *v.* pānē guddudu [i.]
downfall *n.* miqittu
downheartedness *n.* šuplu libbi
downhill *adj.* āridu☆; → **~** *adv.* šapliš; → **~** *n.* kinšu☆
downpour *n.* riḫṣu
downright *adv.* ana gammurti
downstairs *adv.* ina šapliš
downstream *adv.* šapliš
downtown *n.* libbi āli
downtrodden *adj.* kabsu+
downward(s) *adv.* šapliš
downwards *adv.* ana šapliš, ana šupāl☆
dowry *n.* nadunnû
doxology *n.* dalīlu
doze *n.* munattu☆; → **~** *v.* nuāmu+; → **~ off** *v.* nuāmu+; → **~n** *n.* šinešertu+
drab *adj.* abārāiu+, lazzu
draft *n.* liṭṭu; → **~ee** *n.* ṣāb šarri; → **~sman** *n.* ēṣiru☆
drag *v.* mašāru, šadādu; → **~ around** *v.* mašāru (Gtn)
dragoman *n.* targumānu
dragon *n.* bašmu, mušḫuššu☆, šungallu; → **~fly** *n.* kallat Šama&☆, kulīlītu☆, kulīltu, kulīlu☆
dragoon *v.* radāpu+
drain *n.* rāṭu; → **~** *v.* nazālu◊; → **~age channel** *n.* mušēṣītu☆
drainpipe *n.* naṣṣubu, pisannu, rāṭu
drainpipe,waste pipe *n.* bību
drake *n.* puḫālu
drama → **(cultic) ~** *n.* taklimtu
drape *v.* eṣāpu; → **~s** *n.* mardutu (pl.), pariktu
draught *n.* zīqu; → **~(-animal)** *n.* šaddidu☆; → **~sman** *n.* ēṣiru☆
draw *v.* eṣāru, šalāpu, šamāṭu+, šâṭu☆; → **~ across** *v.* parāku; → **~ back** *v.* qapālu+; → **~ breath** *v.* napāšu; → **~ close** *v.* ukkubu☆ (D); → **make ~ fine** *v.* raqāqu+ (D); → **~ in** *v.* karû; → **~ lots for** *v.* pūru karāru [i.]; → **~ nigh** *v.* qarābu+; → **~ out** *v.* arāku+ (Š), šamāṭu+; → **~ up** *v.* epāšu, sadāru
drawback *n.* sikru+
drawer *n.* ēṣiru☆
drawing *n.* eṣurtu☆, mēṣēru, uṣurtu; → **~ of water** *n.* dilūtu☆
drawn *adj.* eṣru
dread *n.* ḫurbāšu☆ (cold); → **~** *v.* palāḫu
dream *n.* šittu☆, šuttu; → **~** *v.* šuttu amāru; → **~ interpreter** *n.* ḫarṭibu (Egyptian), šā'ilu; → **female ~ interpreter** *n.* šā'iltu☆; → **~ ritual** *n.* mušuttu; → **~er** *n.* šabrû☆
dreary *adj.* adru B, lazzu
dregs *n.* qadūtu☆, šuršummu☆
drench *v.* ṣapû, taḫāḫu☆ (D); → **~ing** *n.* šīpu
dress *n.* labussu, lubussu, ṣubātu, tēdīqu☆; → **~** *v.* edēqu☆, labāšu; → **~ (hair)** *v.* kazāru, ṣapāru☆; → **~ ornament (kind of)** *n.*

tenšû◊; → ~ **pin** *n.* tudittu; → **make ~ up** *v.* kannû (D); → **get ~ed** *v.* edēqu☆ (N), labāšu (N); → **~ing** *n.* tal'ītu (absorptive)

dressmaker *n.* mukabbû, ša-kuzippēšu*

dribble *v.* šurruḫu B☆

dried up → **be(come) ~** *v.* paḫāḫu+

drift *v.* neqelpû☆, šapāpu☆, ziāqu; → **be(come) ~** *v.* samû; → **~ about** *v.* alāku (Gtn); → **~ing** *adj.* muqqelpû☆

drill *v.* palāšu, sadāru; → **~ through** *v.* palāšu; → **~er** *n.* pallišu

drink *n.* massītu, mašqītu, maštītu☆; → **~** *v.* šatû; → **give ~** *v.* šaqû; → **~er** *n.* šātiu; → **heavy ~er** *n.* šātiu; → **~ing-pot** *n.* massītu; → **~ing bowl** *n.* kappu; → **~ing place** *n.* mašqû; → **~ing tube** *n.* šulpu; → **~ing utensil** *n.* mašqû; → **~ing vessel** *n.* kāsu+; → **~ing vessel of ten seahs** *n.* massītu; → **serve ~s** *v.* šaqû; → **~s vendor** *n.* ša-naḫbêšu◊

drip *v.* natāku, ṣarāru, šaḫālu+; → **(let) ~** *v.* natāku (D); → **~ping** *n.* tattiktu☆; → **~ping(s)** *n.* nitku

drive *adj.* rīdu☆; → **~** *v.* radû; → **sexual ~** *n.* nīš libbi☆; → **~ around** *v.* mašāru☆; → **~ at** *v.* ṣamāru☆; → **~ away** *v.* abāku, daḫû+, parādu+ (D), radādu, ṭarādu☆; → **~ back** *v.* sakāpu☆; → **~ in** *v.* retû☆; → **~ off** *v.* ṭarādu☆; → **~ on** *v.* radāpu; → **~ out** *v.* ṭarādu+

drivel *n.* dibbē ša šāri, šārāti (pl.)

driven off *adj.* ṭardu☆

driver *n.* rādiu

driving *adj.* rīdu☆; → **~-platform** *adj.* sassu; → **~ stick** *n.* mekkû☆, nanḫuṣu

droll *adj.* muṣiḫḫu☆

dromedary *n.* gammalu+

drool *v.* šurruḫu B☆

droop *v.* urādu

drop *n.* nitku; → **~** *v.* nadû☆, natāku, rammû (D); → **let ~** *v.* ṣarāru (D); → **~ dead** *v.* našû rammû; → **~ off** *v.* parāṭu+; → **~ one's cheek** *v.* lētu nadû [i.]; → **~pings** *n.* pudru (animal); → **~sy** *n.* aganutillû☆

dross *n.* ziblu

drought *n.* ablūtu, sarābu, ṣētu

drove *n.* sagullu; → **~r** *n.* rā'i sagulli

droving *adj.* rīdu☆

drown *v.* ṭabû

drowse *v.* nuāmu+

drowsiness *n.* ṣūdāru+

drowsy *adj.* naiumu+

drudgery *n.* mānaḫtu

drug *n.* šammi pašāri, šammu; → **fatal ~** *n.* šammu ša muāti

druggist *n.* ša-gabêšu

drugstore *n.* bēt šammāni+

drum *n.* timbuttu☆, uppu B☆; → **copper ~** *n.* manzû; → **~skin** *n.* uppu B☆; → **~stick** *n.* sikkutu☆

drunk *adj.* šakru; → **be(come) ~** *v.* šakāru; → **make ~** *v.* šakāru (D)

drunkard *n.* šakkiru, šakrānu

drunkenness *n.* šakartu, šakrānūtu*

dry *v.* mazāqu (Dtt); → **be(come) ~** *v.* abālu, erēru☆, na'āpu☆; → **~ bed of torrent** *n.* naḫlu+; → **~ up** *v.* abālu (D); → **~ wood** *n.* bulê; → **~ing place** *n.* mašṭû☆

dual *adj.* ta''umu

dub *v.* nabû☆

dubious *adj.* lā qēpu

duck *n.* iṣṣūru rabiu, paspasu☆; → **she- ~** *n.* ālittu☆; → **~ling** *n.* lidānu; → **she- ~ling** *n.* parratu☆

duckweed *n.* elapûa

duct *n.* bību, nēburu+

due *n.* ilku; → **in ~ course** *adv.* bāsi; → **~s** *n.* ilkakāti

dug up *adj.* ḫarru

duke *n.* bukāšu☆

dull *adj.* lillu+; → **~** *v.* kepû☆; → **be(come) ~** *v.* šakāru+; → **grow ~** *v.* šaḫātu C+

duly *adv.* bāsi, išariš☆, kēniš

dumb *adj.* ḫarrušu☆, peḫû☆, sakkuku, šuḫarruru☆, uqququ☆; → **~** *n.* ḫaršu B+; → **be(come) ~** *v.* ḫarāšu C+, šuḫarruru☆; → **make ~** *v.* ḫarāšu C+ (D)

dumbbell *n.* lillu☆

dumbness *n.* ḫaršūtu+, paḫûtu*, sakkukūtu

dummy *n.* lillu☆

dump *v.* rammû (D); → **~ling(?)** *n.* ḫulūṭu; → **~y** *n.* kiqillānu

dunce *n.* lillu☆

dune *n.* šipik bāṣi☆

dung *n.* kabû◊, kabūtu, pudru (animal), rubṣu☆, ziblu+; → **~ beetle** *n.* muqappil zê☆; → **~ cake** *n.* pudru (animal); → **~ heap** *n.* kiqillutu, tubkinnu☆; → **~ house** *n.* bēt zibli

dungeon *n.* bēt kīli☆

dunghill *n.* kiqillutu

dupe *v.* dâṣu☆, sarāru [o.]

duplicate *n.* miḫru; → **~** *v.* šanû☆ (Št)

durable → **be(come) ~** *v.* bâru B☆

duration *n.* dūru B, tirṣu; → **long ~** *n.* labār ūmē

during *adv.* ina tarṣi; → **~** *n.* ana tarṣi◊; → **~** *prep.* adi, adu, ina; → **~ the night** *adv.* ša mūši

dusk *n.* barārītu; → **at ~** *n.* ina barāri [o.],

irti barāri; → **~y** *adj.* barārīu, ṣillānīu⋆; → **be(come) ~y** *v.* barāru

dust *n.* epru, tarbu'tu⋆ (cloud of); → **~-cloud** *n.* akāmu⋆; → **~-guard** *n.* saḫargû; → **~-heap** *n.* kiqillutu+; → **~ storm** *n.* ašamšūtu, turbu'u⋆; → **like a ~ storm** *adv.* ašamšāniš⋆

dustbin *n.* kakkul zibli*

duty *n.* esiḫtu, ilku, miksu; → **guard ~** *n.* maṣṣarūtu◊

dwarf *n.* kurû⋆, zizru

dwell *v.* ramû B⋆, ušābu; → **~ upon** *v.* arāku+ (D); → **city ~er** *n.* mār āli; → **~ing** *n.* mūšubu, rimītu⋆, šubtu; → **~ing house** *n.* mūšubu

dwindle *v.* ṣaḫāru+

dye (kind of) *n.* ḫuḫḫurāti

dye (kind of)+greenish-blue *n.* urṭû

dye (red) *v.* ṣarāpu

dyeing *n.* ṣīpu; → **~ vat** *n.* naṣraptu

dyer *n.* muṣappiu, ṣāpiu; → **female ~** *n.* muṣappītu; → **polychrome ~** *n.* mubarrimu

dyke *n.* īku

dynamic *adj.* gāmiru⋆

dynamism *n.* gāmirūtu⋆

dynasty *n.* bēt abi, palû

each *pron.* iāmuttu

eager *adj.* ḫarīpu+, ṣarramu⋆; → **be(come) ~** *v.* ḫarāpu; → **~ to write** *n.* šaṭṭiru⋆

eagle *n.* arû D⋆, nā'iru⋆; → **like an ~** *adv.* arāniš⋆; → **~-bearer** *n.* nuballu⋆

ear *n.* ḫasīsu, uznu; → **give ~** *v.* uznu ana X šakānu [i.]; → **~-man** *n.* ša-uzni; → **~-mark** *n.* šimit uzni⋆; → **~ (of barley)** *n.* šubiltu; → **~ blockage** *n.* sakāk uzni⋆; → **~ infection** *n.* ḫunṭu ša uzni*; → **~ache** *n.* muruṣ uzni*; → **~ed** *n.* uznānu

earlier *adj.* maḫrû, pānīu, rēssu◊

earlobe *n.* uzuntu⋆

early *adj.* ḫarpu; → **~** *adv.* ḫarpiš⋆; → **be(come) ~** *v.* ḫarāpu; → **do ~** *v.* ḫarāpu; → **~ bird** *n.* ḫāripānu; → **~ evening** *n.* saḫār ūme; → **~ moment** *n.* ḫarpūtu; → **~ riser** *n.* ḫāripānu

earn *v.* aḫāzu, qanû B+, utāru (D); → **~est** *adj.* nakdu⋆; → **~est talk(?)** *n.* šiāḫu; → **~ings** *n.* mānaḫtu (pl.)

earring *n.* anṣabtu, qudāsu

earth *n.* epru, erṣutu⋆, kaqquru; → **with ~** *adv.* epriš⋆; → **~en wall(?)** *n.* sirḫu⋆; → **~enware** *n.* karputu ; → **~ly** *adj.* [ša] kaqqiri

earthquake *n.* rību

earthworm *n.* maṣṣar ṭiṭṭi

earwax *n.* zê uzni

eary *n.* uznānu

ease *n.* pašīqūtu+; → **~** *v.* pašāḫu (Š); → **set at ~** *v.* napāšu (D); → **~ off/up** *v.* napāšu, napāšu, pašāḫu, pašāqu+, pašāqu+, ramû

easily *adj.* ša lā dulli; → **~** *adv.* išariš⋆, pašīqatti+, qalliš⋆

easiness *n.* pašīqūtu+

east *n.* napāḫ šamši, nipiḫ šamši⋆, ṣīt šamši⋆, šaddû; → **in the ~** *adv.* ṣītān⋆; → **to the ~** *n.* ana ṣīt šamši; → **~erly** *adj.* [ša] ṣīt šamši⋆; → **~ern** *adj.* [ša] ṣīt šamši⋆

eastward(s) *n.* ana ṣīt šamši

easy *adj.* pašīqu+, ṭābu; → **make ~** *v.* pašāqu+

eat *v.* akālu, leḫēmu◊; → **~ clean** *v.* malālu⋆; → **~ one's fill** *v.* malālu⋆; → **~able** *adj.* ša akāli; → **~en** *adj.* aklu; → **~ing** *adj.* ākilu; → **stop ~ing** *v.* šurrû B⋆ (Dt)

eaves *n.* gisallāti⋆ (pl.); → **~(?)** *n.* gišallû⋆

ebb *n.* esīgu⋆; → **~-tide** *n.* esīgu⋆

ebony *n.* ṣulmu⋆, ušû

echo *v.* apālu, apālu (Gtn)

eclipse *n.* attalû, tādirtu; → **~** *v.* katāmu; → **be ~d** *v.* adāru⋆ (N)

economy *n.* bētūtu, maššuḫūtu+

ecstatic *adj.* sarḫu, zabbu⋆; → **~** *n.* maḫḫû, ša-šēḫi, šēḫānu; → **be(come) ~** *v.* maḫḫûtiš alāku [i.]

ecstaticism *n.* zabbūtu⋆

eczema *n.* šīqu B⋆

edge *n.* pattu, šaptu; → **~(?)** *n.* maldu⋆

edgeways *adv.* battu ana batti

edgewise *adv.* battu ana batti

edible *adj.* ša akāli; → **~ bird (kind of)** *n.* tarmazillu, ušāmutu; → **~ plant (kind of)** *n.* murrutu◊

edict *n.* ṣindatu⋆, šūdûtu⋆

edifice *n.* bētu, riṣpu⋆

edifying *adj.* kāṣiru

edit *v.* tarāṣu B (D)

Edom *n.* Udūmu

educate *v.* arû C⋆ (Gtn), riddu šakānu [i.]; → **~d** *adj.* radiu+

education *n.* iḫzu⋆, mardûtu+, riddu, talmīdūtu+, tarbītu+, tarbûtu

eel *n.* kuppû B⋆

eerie *adj.* aḫīu

efface *v.* pašāṭu

effect *n.* ṣītu⋆; → **~** *v.* epāšu; → **~ive** *adj.* gamīru◊, gāmiru⋆

effectual *adj.* ēpišu

effeminate *adj.* sinnišānu⋆; → **~ man** *n.* assinnu

efficacy *n.* gāmirūtu★
efficiency *n.* ēpišūtu
efficient *adj.* ēpišu
effigy *n.* ṣalmu
effluent *n.* mê bībi*
effort *n.* dilpu; → **make an ~** *v.* maṣû★ (Št), ṣarāmu; → **~lessly** *adj.* ša lā dulli
effrontery *n.* miqit pê★
eft *n.* ṣurārītu+
egg *n.* pelû◊; → **insect ~** *n.* nābu★; → **fish ~s** *n.* binût nūni★
ego *pron.* anāku
egret *n.* anpatu+
Egypt *n.* Muṣur; → **~ian** *n./adj.* Muṣrāiu
eight *n./adj.* samāne★, šamāni; → **~een** *n./adj.* samānšer[et]★; → **~eenth** *adj.* samānšerīu★
eighth *n.* samnu★; → **one ~** *n.* samuntu; → **~ month)** *n.* uraḫ qarrāte [o.]
eightieth *adj.* šamānāiu
eighty *n./adj.* samānâ★
either *adv.* ḫadi; → **~ ... or** *conj.* ḫadi ... ḫadi, lū ... lū, šumma ... šumma
ejaculate *v.* reḫû★
ejaculation *n.* riḫūtu
eject *v.* nabā'u+ (Š), nasāku
elaborate *adj.* nukkulu★
Elam *n.* Elamtu
Elamite class of persons receiving rations *n.* šarnuppu◊
Elamite class of priests *n.* buḫlalû★
Elamite official *n.* zilliru◊
elapse *v.* alāku; → **~d** *adj.* gamru
elated *adj.* napḫu+
elbow *n.* kiṣir ammiti; → **~ grease** *n.* mānaḫtu
elder *n.* paršumu, šību; → **city ~** *n.* paršum āli; → **the ~ly** *n.* šībūtu
eldest *adj.* rēštû★
elecampane *n.* sapalgīnu★
elect *adj.* nasqu; → **~** *v.* biāru, nasāqu; → **~rum** *n.* elmēšu
elegant *adj.* damqu, ṣaiāḫu★
elementary *adj.* šarrāiu+
elephant *n.* pīru; → **~'s tusk** *n.* šinni pīri; → **~ skin** *n.* mašak pēri
elevate *v.* šaqû B★ (Š); → **~d** *adj.* ṣīru★, šaqiu, zuqquru★; → **be ~d** *v.* matāḫu (N); → **be(come) ~d** *v.* šaqû B, zaqāru
elevation *n.* nišītu★, zuqqurtu★
eleven *n./adj.* issēnšer[et]*; → **~th** *adj.* issēnšerīu*, issēššerīu; → **~th month)** *n.* kuzallu [o.]
elicit → **make ~** *v.* apû★ (Š)
eligible *adj.* sapīqu+
eliminate *v.* nasāku★ (Š)
elite *adj.* bēru B; → **~** *n.* gunnu★
ell *n.* ammutu; → **~-long** *adj.* ammār ammiti; → **~-wide** *adj.* ammār ammiti
elongated → **be(come) ~** *v.* šatāḫu◊
else *adv.* ulâ
elsewhere *adv.* aḫīta [o.]
elude *v.* ruāqu
Elul *n.* Elūlu (month)
elusive *adj.* ḫāliqu*
emaciated *adj.* aklu, nuḫḫuru★
emanate *v.* radû+
emancipate *v.* durāru šakānu [i.]
emasculated devotee (kind of) *n.* kulu'u
emasculation *n.* ša-rēšūtu
embalm *v.* ḫanāṭu+
embankment *n.* kāpu
embargo *n.* sukurtu [o.]
embark *v.* rakābu (Š), rakābu+
embarrass *v.* bâšu (D), dalāḫu; → **~ment** *n.* būltu◊, būštu+, būštu★
embassy *n.* bēt ṣīri*, šaprūtu
embed *v.* zaqāpu
embellish *v.* damāqu (D), za'ānu★ (D)
ember *n.* gumāru
embezzle *v.* akālu+, ḫabālu B
embitter *v.* marāru◊ (D); → **~ed** *adj.* marru B+, marru B
emblem *n.* itḫuru, kizirtu; → **~ (kind of)** *n.* ašannu◊
embodied *adj.* pagguru+
embrace *n.* ipqu★; → **~** *v.* aḫāzu, edēru★; → **~ one another (in affection)** *v.* edēru★ (N)
embrage *v.* ḫaṣānu
embroider *v.* laqātu+; → **~er** *n.* laqqātu+
embryo *n.* inbu, ša-libbi
emend *v.* tarāṣu B+ (D); → **~ation** *n.* tūrāṣu+
emerald *n.* barraqtu+, barraqtu★
emerge *v.* uṣû (vent.); → **~ncy** *n.* abūbu
emery *n.* šammu B★
emigrant *n.* galīu+
emigrate *v.* galû, galû+
emigration *n.* galûtu+
eminence *n.* ṣīrūtu★
eminent *adj.* ṣīru★, šēḫu B★; → **~** *n.* tizqāru★
emissary *n.* ṣīru+; → **city ~** *n.* ṣīr āli★
emit *v.* uṣû (Š)
emmer *n.* kunāšu, zīzu
emotion *n.* bibil libbi★, tirik libbi
emperor *n.* šarru rabiu
emphasis *n.* dikšu★
emphasize *v.* dakāšu★, šapû★ (D); → **~d**

adj. dakšu☆
empire *n*. bēlūtu
employ *v*. epāšu☆ (Š), rēšu našû [i.]; → **~ee** *n*. kinattu, ṣuḫāru☆; → **~er** *n*. bēlu; → **~ment** *n*. ummânūtu+
empress *n*. rubātu☆
emptiness *n*. rāqūtu, rīqūtu☆
empty *adj*. rāqu, rīqu☆, sarrīqu; → **~** *v*. erû B (D) [o.], riāqu (Š); → **be(come) ~** *v*. riāqu; → **~-handed** *adj*. rāqūtē-, rīqūtu☆; → **be(come) ~-handed** *v*. erû B [o.]; → **~out** *v*. pasāku (D), riāqu (Š), šapāku+
emulate *v*. mašālu (Š)
enable *v*. maṣû+ (D)
enact *v*. epāšu (D), šiāmu
enamel *v*. marāqu+, šaḫāṭu B
enamoured *adj*. rā'imu
enceinte *n*. amuḫḫu☆, limītu☆
enchant *v*. kašāpu☆; → **~ing** *adj*. kāšipu*; → **~ment** *n*. kišpu*
encircle *v*. epāqu [o.], labû, lâṭu☆, saḫāru☆ (Št); → **~ment** *n*. nītu☆
encircling *n*. labītu, lābiu
enclose *v*. esāru, lâṭu☆, maṣāru◊, peḫû☆
enclosing *adj*. māṣiru
enclosure *n*. limītu☆
encompass *v*. epāqu [o.]
encourage *v*. libbu šakānu [i.], qarādu (D), raḫāṣu (Š); → **~ment** *n*. tukkultu☆
encroach *v*. aḫu ubālu [i.]; → **~ on** *v*. kasāsu
encrust *v*. qarāmu+
end *n*. qītu☆, šullāmu+; → **~** *v*. balû☆, gamāru (Dtt), gamāru☆ (N), naparkû☆, qatû☆; → **bring to an ~** *v*. qatû☆ (D); → **come to an ~** *v*. šalāmu+; → **at the ~** *adv*. ina qīti☆; → **lower ~** *n*. šēpītu; → **be(come)+at the ~ of the tether** *v*. ana ṣirê malû [i.]; → **~ up** *v*. šalāmu+
endanger *v*. palāḫu☆ (Š)
endear *v*. ra'āmu+ (D)
endeavor *n*. ṣummurtu☆ (pl.); → **~** *v*. ṣarāmu
endive *adj*. murāru☆
endorse *v*. magāru☆; → **~ment** *n*. migru☆
endow *v*. šarāku
endued *adj*. labšu+
endurance *n*. zābilānūtu+
endure *v*. anāḫu☆ (Št), darû, lazāzu, šadādu (Gtn), šadādu☆
enduring *adj*. lazzu
enemy *n*. aiābu☆, bēl dabābi, bēl lemutti☆, bēl nakāri, nakīru, nakru, qardammu☆, zā'irānu☆, zā'iru☆, zāmānû☆, zāmānu☆; → **like an ~** *adv*. nakriš☆; → **mortal ~** *n*. bēl dāmē, bēl mūtāti
energetic *adj*. kāširu+
energy *n*. abāru B☆, aḫu B
enfeeble *v*. anāšu+ (D), kadāru B+ (D)
enfold *v*. duāru [o.], kasû+, šapāṣu☆; → **keep ~ed** *v*. šapāṣu☆ (D)
enforce *v*. da'ānu (D), gabāru+
enfranchise *v*. durāru šakānu [i.]
engage in *v*. aḫu ummudu [i.]; → **~ a fight** *v*. ṣāltu epēšu☆
engender *v*. ulādu
engine → **(siege) ~** *n*. nēpešu☆; → **~er(?)** *n*. šelappāiu
engrave *v*. esēqu☆, naqāru; → **~r** *n*. kapšarru
enigma *n*. ḫittu B☆
enjoin *v*. qabû, šapāru
enjoy *v*. akālu, šabû; → **~able** *adj*. ṣiāḫu☆; → **~ment** *n*. tarṣiātu☆
enkindled *adj*. napḫu
enlarge *v*. gapāšu (D), rabû☆ (Š), rapāšu (D), šadālu☆ (D), utāru (Š); → **~ment** *n*. tarbītu
enlighten *v*. uznē pattû [i.]; → **~ed** *adj*. nammuru+, palka uzni☆, palkû☆
Enlil *n*. Illil; → **~ship** *n*. illilūtu
enlist *v*. rakāsu (Š)
enliven *v*. balāṭu (D), napāšu+ (D)
enmesh *v*. šutēlupu☆
enmity *n*. nukurtu, ṣēlūtu☆; → **cause ~** *v*. nakāru (Š)
enormity *n*. samiktu
enormous *adj*. bitrû☆, šūturu☆
enough *adv*. ma'ad, maṣi; → *interj*.~ aḫulap☆; → **be(come) ~** *v*. maṣû, sapāqu
enquire *v*. ša'ālu; → **~ for** *v*. ba''û
enrage *v*. agāgu☆ (D); → **be(come) ~d** *v*. nadāru☆ (N), ṣarāḫu (N)
enrapture *v*. sarāḫu+ (Š); → **~d** *adj*. sarḫu+
ensign *n*. simtu
enslave *v*. ana rēšūti alāku (Š) [i.], ana urdānūti kabāsu [i.]
ensue *v*. šakānu (N)
ensure *v*. pūtuḫu našû [i.]
entail *v*. bazāḫu [o.]
entangle *v*. šatû B☆, šutēlupu☆; → **~d** *n*. itguru☆; → **~ment** *n*. itgurūtu☆
enter *v*. erābu; → **~er** *n*. ēribtu, ēribu
enteritis *n*. ḫunṭu ša errē*
enterprise *n*. epšetu, ṣibūtu☆
entertain *v*. kazābu☆; → **~er** *n*. aluzinnu☆, mupaggiānu+; → **~ing** *adj*. kazbu☆; → **~ment** *n*. kazbūtu☆
enthrone *v*. ušābu (Š)

entice *v.* kazābu* (D)
entire *n./adj.* gabbu; → ~ *pron.* kalāma*; → **~ly** *adv.* ištēniš*; → **~ty** *n.* gamirtu, gimirtu, nagbu B*, napḫaru*, pāṭ gimri*, siḫirtu*, siḫru
entitle to do s.th. *v.* šalāṭu (Š)
entitled *adj.* šašluṭu
entourage *n.* libītu, mazzāz pāni; → **royal** ~ *n.* libīt ēkalli, libīt šarri
entrails *n.* errē; → ~ **(part of)** *n.* uzuntu nītu
entrance *n.* erābu, nērubu, tērubtu [o.]; → ~ **(to a city)** *n.* sippu
entreat *v.* ṣallû, ša'ālu+, šutēmuqu*
entrust *v.* paqādu, qiāpu; → ~ **to** *v.* pān X šudgulu [i.]; → **~ed** *adj.* paqdu, qēpu
entry *n.* erābu, tarbāṣu+, tērubtu*, tērubtu [o.]
entwine *v.* šatû B*; → **~d** *adj.* patlu*
enumerate *v.* manû B
enunciation *n.* tēltu
envelop *v.* arāmu, ḫalāpu*, ḫarāmu (D) [o.]; → **put in** ~ *v.* ḫarāmu (D) [o.]
envelope *n.* erintu, kiṣirtu, maknaktu (sealed) [o.], urimtu◊; → **~d** *adj.* ḫarmu [o.]; → **be ~d** *v.* ḫalāpu* (Gt)
envious *adj.* qāni'u*; → ~ **person** *n.* ḫādiānu
environment *n.* aḫītu (pl.), limītu*, siḫirtu*
environs *n.* itāti*, kamītu* (pl.), qannu
envisage *v.* dagālu*, eṣāru+
envoy *n.* našpāru◊, ṣīru, šapru
envy *n.* qi''u; → ~ *v.* qenû*
ephemeris *n.* tērsītu*
epic *n.* zamāru
epidemic *n.* mūtānu, šibṭu; → **~s** *n.* asakku
epigastrium *n.* pī karši*
epilepsy *n.* bennu, miqtu, rihu:t Šulpaea*
epileptic *n.* rihu:t Šulpaea*
epilogue *n.* šullāmu+
epistle *n.* egertu+
epitaph *n.* šiṭir arāni*
epitomize *v.* kannušu+
epoch *n.* palû
eponymate *n.* limmu
equal *adj.* mitḫāru*, mušlu; → ~ *n.* miḫru, šinnatu*; → ~ *v.* šanānu; → **be(come)** ~ *v.* mašālu; → **make** ~ *v.* mašālu (Š), mašālu* (D); → **try to** ~ *v.* mašālu* (D); → **~ity** *n.* miḫrūtu*; → **~ity(?)** *n.* šinintu*; → **~ize** *v.* mašālu* (D); → **~ling** *prep.* tamšīl*; → **~ly** *adv.* ana mitḫār, mitḫāriš*
equanimity *n.* nēḫtu*
equate *v.* mašālu* (D)
equation *adj.* tamšiltu*
equestrian *n.* ša-pētḫalli
equilibrium → **be in** ~ *v.* šaqālu* (Gt)
equinox *n.* šitqultu*
equip *v.* rakāsu (Š), ṣabātu (Š); → **~ment** *n.* rikis qabli◊, simmānû*, tillē; → **chief of ~ment** *n.* rab tilli; → **house of ~ment** *n.* bēt tilli; → **~ped** *adj.* šaṣbutu, tallulu; → **~ping** *n.* rikis qabli◊
equity *n.* kēnūtu+
equivalent *n.* miḫru, tamšīlu B*
equivocal *adj.* mitḫāru*
era *n.* dāru; → **~dicate** *v.* nasāḫu; → **~se** *v.* garādu+, pašāṭu; → **~sure** *n.* pissatu*
Erbil *n.* Arbail
erect *adj.* zaqpu, zaqpu+; → ~ *v.* retû*, tabû (Š), uzuzzu (Š), zaqāpu; → **~ed** *adj.* zaqpu; → **~ion** *n.* tibûtu*; → **be(come)|get an ~ion** *v.* tabû; → **be(come)|have an ~ion** *v.* magāgu
erode *v.* akālu, šaḫāḫu
erosion *n.* šiḫḫutu
erotic *adj.* kuzbānu*
err *v.* ḫaṭû, ḫiṭṭu ḫaṭû, naḫalṣû, sagû+; → **liable to** ~ *adj.* ḫāṭiu*; → **~ance** *n.* ḫiṭītu*
errand boy *n.* šapru
erratum *n.* ḫiṭītu*
erring *adj.* ḫāṭiu*
erroneous *adj.* ḫaṭû*
error *n.* ḫiṭṭu; → **commit an** ~ *v.* ḫiṭṭu ḫaṭû; → **make an** ~ *v.* naḫalṣû
eructation *n.* gišūtu*
erudite *adj.* lamdu*, mūdû
erudition *n.* iḫzu*
erupt *v.* napāḫu+; → **~ion** *n.* nipḫu
escalate *v.* elû (Š), rapāšu (D)
escape *v.* ezābu (Š), ḫalāqu, naparšudu*, šētu*; → **help** ~ *v.* ḫalāqu (Š)
escapee *n.* multaḫṭu*
escort *n.* libītu+; → ~ *v.* radû
esoteric compendium (kind of) *n.* kakku sakku
especial *adj.* utru+; → **~ly** *adv.* issu pūte
espousals *n.* ḫatnūtu+
espouse *v.* aḫāzu
essay *n.* šiṭirtu*
essence *adj.* libbu; → ~ *n.* libbānu*
essentials *n.* rēšēti*
establish *v.* kuānu (D), šakānu, šaršudu*; → ~ **as** *v.* šiāmu; → ~ **communication** *v.* lišānu šakānu*; → ~ **o.s.** *v.* kuānu (Dtt); → ~ **victory** *v.* lītu šakānu [i.]; → **~ed** *adj.* kunnu, taqnu+; → **~er** *n.* mukinnu
estate *n.* eqlu, nikkassu, urkutu

esteem *v*. uqāru⋆ (Š); → **~ed** *adj*. uqru
estimate *v*. kaṣāpu
estimation *n*. kiṣiptu
estrange *v*. nakāru (Š)
estuary *n*. pī nāri
eternal *adj*. dārīu; → **be(come) ~** *v*. darû; → **~ life** *n*. dārūtu
eternity *n*. dāru
Ethiopia *n*. Meluḫḫa⋆; → **~n** *n./adj*. Kūsāiu, Meluḫḫāiu⋆
eulogy *n*. tanittu⋆
eunuch *n*. gerseqû⋆, ša-rēši, šūt-rēši⋆; → **chief ~** *n*. rab ša-rēši; → **office of chief ~** *n*. rab ša-rēšūtu; → **royal ~** *n*. ša-rēš šarri; → **~ship** *n*. ša-rēšūtu
Euphrates *n*. Purattu
evacuate *v*. pasāku (D)
evade *v*. ruāqu, uṣû
evaluate *v*. kaṣāpu
evaluation *n*. kiṣiptu
evaporate *v*. baḫāru⋆ (D), baḫāru⋆, sapāḫu⋆ (N)
evasive *adj*. ḫāliqu*
even *adj*. mitḫāru⋆, sapnu*; → **~** *conj*. u; → **be(come) ~** *v*. mašālu; → **make ~** *v*. sapānu+; → **~ before** *adv*. adi lā, adu lā; → **~ if** *gram. part*. lū; → **~ if** *n*. u kî◊, u lū; → **~ more** *adv*. eliš [o.]; → **~ though** *gram.part*. lū; → **~ though** *n*. u kî◊, u lū; → **~ing** *n*. bādu, līlāti⋆, nubattu, šimētān⋆; → **in the ~ing** *adv*. ana bādi, kî bādi, ša bādi; → **~ing watch** *n*. barārītu; → **~tually** *adv*. ina qīti⋆
ever *adv*. immatēma, immatimēni, ina matēma, ina matimēni; → **~-ignited** *n*. muštaḫmiṭu⋆; → **~ since** *subj*. issu bēt
everlasting *adj*. dārīu
every *n*. kalu⋆; → **~ kind of** *n*. mimmû; → **~ one (of)** *n*. gabbē-; → **~ one (of)** *pron*. gabbu, iāmuttu
everybody *n*. qallu dannu(lit. 'weak and strong') [i.], ṣeḫer u rabi(lit. 'small and great') [i.]; → **~** *pron*. iāmuttu
everyday *adj*. kaiamānīu
everyone *n*. qallu dannu(lit. 'weak and strong') [i.], ṣeḫer u rabi(lit. 'small and great') [i.]
everything *n*. kullutu; → **~** *pron*. kalāma⋆, mimmû; → **~ that** *subj*. mala⋆
everywhere *adv*. aiākamēni; → **~** *pron*. kalāma⋆
evidence *n*. mukinnūtu◊, mukīntu
evident *adj*. šāpû, šūpû⋆
evil *adj*. bīšu+, lamnu, raggu⋆, samku; → **~** *n*. lamuttu; → **be(come) ~** *v*. be'āšu+, lamānu; → **do ~** *v*. be'āšu+ (Š); → **~-smelling** *adj*. zapru+; → **~ demon (kind of)** *n*. mukīl rēš lemutti⋆; → **~ smell** *n*. zaprūtu+; → **~doer** *n*. bēl ḫiṭṭi, ḫabbilu⋆, targīgu⋆
evoke *v*. dakû
ewe *n*. agurrutu, immertu⋆, laḫru⋆; → **young ~** *adj*. kabsutu; → **~r** *n*. ša-mê-qāti
ex(-) *adj*. pānīu
exacerbate *v*. marāru+ (Š)
exact *adj*. ḫarṣu; → **~** *v*. nasāḫu; → **~ vengeance** *v*. tuktê turru [i.]; → **~ly** *adv*. ḫarṣiš*; → **~ly as** *subj*. libbû◊
exaggerate *v*. utāru (Š); → **~d** *adj*. utturu⋆
exalt *v*. rabû⋆ (Š), šaqû B⋆ (D); → **~ed** *adj*. elû⋆, mutlellû⋆, ṣīru⋆, šurbû⋆; → **~ed** *n*. tizqāru⋆; → **~edness** *n*. ṣīrūtu⋆
exam *n*. maš'altu⋆
examination *n*. bīru, maš'altu⋆
examine *v*. barû B⋆, biāru, ḫâṭu⋆, ḫiāṭu⋆, murruru◊, palāsu⋆ (Ntn), sanāqu⋆
example *n*. riddu⋆
exasperate *v*. nazāqu⋆ (Š)
excavate *v*. ḫarû, ḫaṭāṭu
excavation *n*. ḫirūtu⋆
exceed *v*. utāru; → **~ingly** *adv*. adanniš adanniš
excel o.s. *v*. utāru+
excellence *n*. mētellūtu⋆, meṭlūtu⋆
excellent *adj*. arattû⋆, babbanû◊, dammuqu, kāširu+, šūturu⋆; → **most ~** *adj*. utturu+
except *prep*. alla◊, ezib⋆; → **~ (for)** *prep*. ela⋆; → **~ for** *n*. allān [o.]; → **~ion** *n*. ezibtu*; → **~ional** *adj*. uqru; → **~ionally** *adv*. adanniš, adanniš adanniš, eli minâtīšu⋆; → **do ~ionally** *v*. nakāru (D); → **be(come) ~ionally big** *v*. ba'ālu
excess *n*. atartu⋆; → **~ive** *adj*. utru, uttāru; → **~ively** *adv*. utar*
exchange *n*. maḫīru, pūḫu, šapūssu; → **~** *v*. enû⋆ (Št), ḫalāpu D+, puḫḫu, šapêlu, šupêlu⋆; → **in ~** *adv*. ina pūḫi; → **item of ~** *n*. pūḫtu; → **~ advice** *v*. šutaddunu⋆; → **~ rate** *n*. maḫīru
excitable *adj*. ragšu*
excite *v*. dakû, tabû (Š); → **~ to rebellion** *v*. nabalkutu (Š); → **be ~d** *v*. ragāšu⋆ (N); → **be(come) ~d** *v*. nīš libbi rašû⋆, tabû; → **~ment** *n*. nīš libbi⋆, tibûtu⋆
exciting *adj*. mummilu⋆, mušatbiu*
exclaim *v*. ragāmu
exclamation *n*. rigmu
exclude *v*. daḫû, šēpu parāsu [i.]
exclusion *n*. parās šēpi
exclusive *adj*. ēdu
excommunicate *v*. ḫarāmu+ (Š), ṭarādu+

excrement *n*. kabû◊, zê, ziblu+; → **bloody ~** *n*. nīṭu⋆
excrescence *n*. ṣibāru⋆
excrete *v*. ṣanāḫu⋆, tabāku⋆ (D)
excretion *n*. ṣinḫu⋆
exculpate *v*. riāmu
excursion *n*. daiāltu⋆
excuse *n*. tēgirtu; → **~** *v*. riāmu
execute → **cause the ~** *v*. muātu (Š)
executioner *n*. ṭābiḫu
exemplar *n*. šaṭṭāru
exemplify *v*. mašālu+
exempt *adj*. zakkû, zakû; → **be(come) ~** *v*. zakû; → **~ from** *v*. zakû (D); → **~ed person** *n*. šubarrû⋆; → **~ion** *n*. zakûtu
exercise *v*. epāšu (D), sadāru; → **~ kingship** *v*. šarrūtu epāšu [i.]
exert *v*. anāḫu (Š); → **~ion** *n*. mānaḫtu
exhale *v*. napāḫu+, pašû⋆
exhaust *v*. anāḫu (Š); → **~ o.s.** *v*. ḫabû⋆ (Dt); → **~ed** *adj*. anḫu, šudlupu⋆; → **be(come) ~ed** *v*. anāḫu; → **~ing** *adj*. marṣu, mušāniḫu*; → **~ion** *n*. anḫūtu, tānīḫu⋆; → **~ive** *adj*. gamru
exhibit *n*. taklimtu; → **~** *v*. barû B⋆ (Š), kallumu (D); → **~ humility** *v*. appu labānu⋆, labānu B⋆; → **~ion** *n*. kullumūtu⋆, taklimtu
exhort *v*. dabābu (Š)
exile *n*. šaglūtu, ṭarīdūtu⋆; → **~** *v*. galû (Š); → **go into ~** *v*. galû
exist *v*. bašû; → **~ence** *n*. bišītu⋆; → **~ent** *adj*. bašiu; → **~ing** *adj*. bašiu
exit *n*. āṣītu, mūṣû, ṣītu⋆
exodus *n*. galûtu+
exonerate *v*. riāmu
exorbitant *adj*. utru+, uttāru
exorcism *n*. āšipūtu, kakugallūtu⋆
exorcist *n*. āšipu, išippu⋆, kakugallu⋆, muššipu⋆, ša-šipti, šagammāḫu⋆; → **chief ~** *n*. rab āšipi; → **~ic** *adj*. [ša] āšipūti
exotic *adj*. nesû⋆
expand *v*. kuššû⋆, napāšu, rapāšu (D), ṭapû; → **~able** *adj*. narbû⋆
expanse *n*. gipšu⋆, sapannu⋆; → **of great ~** *adj*. šundulu⋆
expansion *n*. ruppušu⋆
expansive *adj*. ritpāšu⋆; → **~ly** *adv*. rapšiš⋆
expect *v*. ēnē tarruṣu [i.], ina pāni dagālu [i.], pān X dagālu [i.]; → **~ation** *n*. puqqu*; → **~oration(?)** *n*. pašūtu
expedite *v*. šalāḫu B+ (D)
expedition *n*. ḫarrānu
expel *v*. daḫû+, nasāḫu, ṭarādu+
expend *v*. akālu
expenditure *n*. akiltu, nadbāku
expense *n*. gimru [o.]; → **~s** *n*. akiltu
expensive *adj*. batqu [o.], uqru, utturu [o.]; → **be(come) ~** *v*. uqāru
experience *v*. amāru, rašû⋆; → **~ hardship** *v*. dannutu amāru [i.]; → **~d** *adj*. amru, lamdu⋆; → **be ~d** *v*. aḫāzu⋆ (Gt)
experiment *n*. litku; → **~** *v*. latāku* (Gtn)
expert *adj*. itpēšu⋆; → **~** *n*. lē'i īni⋆, mūdānû◊, mūdû īni⋆, ummânu
expertise *n*. lē'ûtu⋆
expiation *n*. tazkītu+
expiration *n*. qītu⋆, šullāmu+
expire *v*. šalāmu+
explain *v*. ḫakāmu (Š), lamādu (D), pašāqu (D), pašāru
explanatory *n*. pāširu
explicable *adj*. ša pašāri*
explicit *adj*. mukallimu*
exploit *v*. ḫabālu B, šalālu+; → **~ation** *n*. ḫabālu⋆
explore *v*. ḫâṭu⋆, ḫiāṭu⋆
export *n*. āṣītu; → **~** *v*. uṣû (Š)
expose *v*. kallumu (D), patû
expositor *n*. pāširu
expound *v*. darāsu
express → **by ~** *adv*. ana kallie, ša kil; → **~ion** *n*. siqru; → **~ive** *adj*. mukallimu*; → **~ly** *adv*. issu pūte
expropriate *v*. kašāšu⋆
expropriation *n*. kiššāti⋆
expulsion *n*. ṭarīdūtu+
expunge *v*. pašāṭu
exstirpate *v*. pašāṭu
exta (part of) *n*. isru⋆
extend *v*. arāku (Š), kapātu◊, rapāšu (D), šadādu, šuparruru⋆, tarāṣu; → **~ed hand** *n*. tiriṣ qāti
extension (of time) *n*. tirṣu
extensive *adj*. palkû⋆, rapšu, ritpāšu⋆, šundulu⋆; → **be(come) ~** *v*. rapāšu; → **~ly** *adv*. rapšiš⋆, šiddi arki [i.]
extent *n*. māraku⋆, siḫpu B⋆, tarṣu B
extenuate *v*. labāku (D), rabābu (Š)
exterior *adj*. kīdû⋆; → **~** *n*. kīdītu⋆
exterminate *v*. gamāru
external *adj*. kīdānû◊, kīdû⋆
extinct *adj*. abtu+; → **~ion** *n*. abtūtu+
extinguish *v*. balû (D), kabāsu⋆ (D); → **be(come) ~ed** *v*. balû⋆
extispicy *n*. bārûtu, bīru
extol *v*. na'ādu⋆, rabû⋆ (Š), šamāru B⋆ (Gt)
extort *v*. bazāḫu [o.]
extra *adj*. utru, uttāru; → **~** *adv*. kīma

atartimma☆
extract *n*. mēzu, nisḫu; → ~ *v*. nasāḫu, šalāpu; → **~ion** *n*. milḫu
extraneous *adj*. aḫīu
extraordinary *n*. lā kaiamānīu*
extravagance *n*. pūrāḫu+
extravagant *adj*. uqru adanniš, uttāru
extreme *adj*. šūturu☆; → **~ly** *adv*. adanniš adanniš
exuberance *n*. lalû
exuberant → **be(come)** ~ *v*. ḫabāṣu☆
exudation *n*. ḫīltu [o.]
exude *v*. šaḫālu+
exult *v*. nagû☆, riāšu; → **~ation** *n*. rīštu◊, ulṣu☆
eye *n*. ēnu; → **rim of** ~ *n*. kibir ēni☆; → **~-ball** *n*. kakkultu; → **~-opener** *n*. pāti ēni; → **~-salve** *n*. šīpu B+; → **~-stone** *n*. ēnu; → ~ **disease** *n*. muruṣ ēni☆; → ~ **infection** *n*. ḫunṭu ša ēnāti; → **keep an** ~ **on** *v*. ana šiddi X naṭālu [o.]; → ~ **paint** *n*. mēqītu☆; → ~ **salve** *n*. itqurtu ša abāri☆; → ~ **shadow** *n*. ṣulūl ēni+; → **~brow** *n*. šuḫru☆, šūr īni☆
eyelash *n*. agap ēni☆, kappi ēni☆, sassaptu☆; → **~es** *n*. pappāt ēni☆
eyelid *n*. kappi ēni☆; → **upper** ~ *n*. quliptu☆
eyeliner *n*. kuḫlu+, makaḫalūtu
eyesight *n*. ēnu, niṭil ēnē
eyewitness *n*. āmirānu [o.], āmirānu [o.]
fable *adj*. tēṣītu B☆
fabric → **(fine)** ~ *n*. ṭuānu (fine); → **thin** ~ *n*. qatattu; → **~ate** *v*. epāšu, patāqu☆; → **~ation** *n*. epšetu
facade *n*. meḫretu☆
face *n*. bunnu, būnu, pānu+, pānu (pl.); → ~ *v*. maḫāru; → **make** ~ *v*. maḫāru (D); → **radiant** ~ *n*. nummur pāni☆; → ~ **down** *adv*. buppāniš☆; → ~ **one another** *v*. maḫāru☆ (Gt); → ~ **to face** *adv*. ina pūt aḫāiš*; → ~ **up** *adj*. naparqudu☆
facilities *n*. ḫašaḫtu+ (pl.)
facility *n*. pašīqūtu+
facing *adj*. māḫiru; → ~ *n*. kisirtu, meḫret☆, muḫḫurtu☆; → ~ **each other** *adj*. šutātû☆
fact *n*. abutu kunnutu, kēttu; → **in** ~ *adv*. ibašši, kēttu; → **~ion** *n*. pilku
factitious *adj*. naklu
factor *n*. arû E☆, makṣaru☆
factual *adj*. kēnu
fade *v*. kamādu+; → ~ **out** *v*. paṭāru (N)
fail *v*. ana qinniš alāku [i.], ḫaṭû☆, maṭû, mêšu☆, naparkû☆; → **~ing** *n*. ḫiṭṭu
failure → **heart** ~ *n*. mišitti libbi*, tirik libbi
faint *adj*. unnutu; → ~ *v*. ṣâdu (Gtn); → **be(come)** ~ *v*. unnutu (D)
fair *adj*. damqu; → **be(come)** ~ *v*. ešēru☆; → **~ly** *adv*. ibašši, išariš☆, kēniš+; → **~ness** *n*. kēnūtu+
faith → **give** ~ *v*. takālu (D); → **~ful** *adj*. kēnu, taklu+; → **~fulness** *n*. kēnūtu; → **~less** *adj*. naklu+, ṭalūmu+
fake *v*. zuppu+ (D)
falcon *n*. kasūsu, mesukku, surdû☆
fall *n*. miqittu; → ~ *v*. maqātu, qiālu [o.]; → **make** ~ *v*. maqātu (Š); → ~ **behind** *v*. namarkû; → ~ **down** *v*. abātu☆ (N), maqātu, qâpu☆; → ~ **for** *v*. maqātu ana [i.]; → **be(come)** ~ **in love with** *v*. ra'āmu; → ~ **in with** *v*. magāru (N); → **be(come)** ~ **into ruin** *v*. miqittu rašû [i.]; → ~ **off** *v*. maqātu, našāru (N); → ~ **out** *v*. maqātu, ṣâlu [o.], ṣâssu garû; → ~ **through** *v*. maqātu; → ~ **to** *v*. maqātu ana [i.], šarrû+; → ~ **upon** *v*. maqātu ina muḫḫi [i.]
fallacy *n*. surru*
fallen *adj*. maqtu
fallible *adj*. ḫāṭiu*
fallow *n*. karapḫu
false *adj*. lā kēnu, sarru☆; → ~ **accusation** *n*. šukunnû◊; → ~ **allegations** *n*. dibbē lā šalmūti; → **~hood** *n*. sartu; → **~ness** *n*. sarrāti☆
falsify *v*. dâṣu☆, zuppu+ (D)
falter *v*. egēru☆ (Ntn)
fame *n*. šumu; → **posthumous** ~ *n*. itḫurānūtu☆; → **~d** *adj*. edû
familiar *adj*. kaiamānīu; → **~ity** *n*. bētāiūtu+, šalmūtu+; → **~ize** *v*. idû◊ (Št); → **~ize o.s.** *v*. idû◊ (Št), lamādu (Gtn) [o.]
family *n*. bētu+, kimtu, qinnu, salātu B☆; → ~ **group** *n*. ellatu☆; → ~ **head** *n*. ḫammu◊
famine *adj*. ubbuṭu☆; → ~ *n*. aruštu B☆, bubūtu, ḫušaḫḫu, nebrītu☆, sunqu☆
famish *v*. barû; → **~ed** *adj*. bariu
famous *adj*. edû, šūpû☆
fan *n*. mudammiqtu (palm branch); → ~ *v*. napāḫu+
fanatic *adj*. zabbu☆; → **~al** *adj*. sarḫu+
fanaticism *n*. zabbūtu☆
fancy *adj*. ṣaiāḫu☆; → ~ *n*. bibil libbi☆; → ~ *v*. maqātu ana [i.]; → **be(come)** ~ *v*. ra'āmu; → **be(come)|take a** ~ **to** *v*. ra'āmu
fang *n*. šinnu
fantasize *v*. dagālu
fantastic *adj*. šarḫu☆
fantasy *n*. ḫissat libbi☆
far *adj*. patiu, rēqu☆; → ~ *adv*. rūqiš☆; →

~-off *adj.* patiu; → **~-off days** *n.* ṣâti
faraway *adj.* nesû☆, patiu, rūqu☆; → **~** *n.* rūqu+; → **~ place** *n.* rūqu☆
fare *v.* alāku
farewell *n.* ina šulmi alik*
farm *n.* iškāru+; → **~-hand** *n.* agru; → **~er** *n.* ikkāru; → **head ~er** *n.* rab ikkāri; → **tenant ~er** *n.* errēšu◊; → **~ing** *n.* ikkārūtu☆
Fars *adv.* Parsumaš
farsighted *n.* dāgil rūqi*
fart *v.* ṣarātu; → **~er** *n.* ṣarritu
farther *adv.* utar*
farthest *n.* rūqu+
fascinate *v.* kazābu☆ (D), sarāḫu+ (Š), ta'ādu+ (Š)
fascinating *adj.* kāšipu*
fashion *v.* bašāmu☆, patāqu☆
fast *adj.* kapdu◊, lasmu; → **~** *v.* šurrû B☆ (Dt); → **be(come) ~** *v.* ezû☆; → **~en** *v.* rapāqu (D), ṣabātu (D), ṣamādu+; → **~en on** *v.* sabāku+; → **~en together** *v.* ṣamādu+; → **~ened** *adj.* ṣabbutu; → **~ening** *n.* qullu, ṣindu
fastidious *adj.* nassiqu☆
fasting *n.* lā akālu, ṣūmu+
fat *adj.* kabburu, kabru, marû☆, ṭapšu [o.]; → **~** *n.* ḫinṣu, līpu, šamnu; → **be(come) ~** *v.* kabāru, marû☆, ṭapāšu☆; → **~al** *adj.* [ša] muāti
fate *n.* namtāru☆, šīmtu; → **ill ~** *n.* lumnu
father *n.* abu, zārû☆; → **~'s house** *n.* bēt abi; → **~-in-law** *n.* emu; → **~hood** *n.* abbūtu; → **~less** *adj.* sumaktar◊
fathom *v.* lamādu
fatigue *n.* anḫūtu, mānaḫtu; → **~d** *adj.* anḫu
fatness *n.* kabrūtu☆
fatten *v.* kabāru (D), marû☆ (Š); → **be(come) ~** *v.* marû☆; → **~ed** *adj.* kabburu, marû☆; → **~ing (technique)** *n.* mārûtu☆
fatty *adj.* kabburu; → **~ tissue** *n.* ḫinṣu
fatuous *adj.* lillu+
fault *n.* ḫiṭṭu; → **~-finding** *n.* qulālu; → **~less** *adj.* zakû; → **~y** *adj.* ḫāṭiu, ḫaṭû☆
favor *n.* ennānāti (pl.) [o.], ennu [o.], gimillu☆, ṭābtu; → **do a ~** *v.* gamālu, ṭābtu epāšu [i.]; → **return a ~** *v.* gimillu turru☆; → **in ~ of** *n.* rā'imānu; → **~able** *adj.* magru, mitgāru☆, ṭābu; → **~ed by god** *n.* ilānû☆
favorite *n.* bēl de'iqti, bibil libbi B☆, biblu C◊, kunnūtu◊, migru B☆, namaddu B☆, nīš ēni☆, nišīt ēni☆, nišītu☆
fawn *v.* ḫanāpu☆, kazābu☆ (D)
fear *n.* ḫūpu, nakuttu, nikittu, pulḫu, puluḫtu; → **~** *v.* adāru C☆, galādu, palāḫu, šaḫātu B☆; → **chilling ~** *n.* rašubbatu☆; → **in ~** *adv.* adīriš☆; → **~ed** *adj.* palḫu; → **~ful** *adj.* ādiru☆, galtu☆, palḫu, pardu☆; → **~fully** *adv.* galtiš☆, palḫiš☆; → **~less** *adj.* lā ādiru☆, lā pāliḫu, lādiru☆; → **~some** *adj.* galtu☆, nanduru☆, palḫu, rašbu☆; → **~somely** *adv.* pardiš☆; → **~someness** *n.* pulḫu
feasible *adj.* naṭû☆, tarṣu; → **be(come) ~** *v.* alāku, naṭû B☆, tarāṣu B
feast *n.* tašīltu☆
feat(s) *n.* qurdu
feather *n.* abru B+, kappu B☆; → **~s** *n.* nāṣu☆
feats *n.* narbû☆
feature *n.* ittu☆; → **~s** *n.* bunnannê☆ (facial), bunnu, būnu, zīmu (pl.)
February *n.* Šaba:#u (month)
fecund *adj.* unnubu☆
fed up *adj.* mal'u; → **be(come) ~** *v.* ana ṣirê malû [i.]
fee *n.* igrē+, miksu
feeble *adj.* enšu☆, muqqu☆, pisnuqu☆; → **~** *n.* anšu; → **be(come) ~** *v.* rabābu; → **~-minded** *n./adj.* ulālu; → **~-minded person** *n.* dunnamû☆; → **~-minded woman** *n.* ulāltu; → **~ness** *n.* lu'tu☆
feed *v.* akālu (Š); → **~ing** *n.* šākussu; → **~ing ritual** *n.* tākultu
feel *v.* muāšu+, ragāšu+; → **~ blue** *v.* libbu šapālu [i.]; → **~ down** *v.* libbu šapālu [i.]; → **~ gratitude** *v.* ṭābtu ḫasāsu [i.]; → **~ pity for** *v.* rēmu ina muḫḫi/ana X šakānu [i.]; → **~ing** *n.* rigšu+; → **bad ~ings** *n.* masiktu [o.]
feign *v.* nakālu; → **~ing** *n.* niklu+
felicity *n.* ulṣu☆
fell *v.* nakāsu, qiālu (D) [o.], rasābu☆; → **~ed** *adj.* naksu
fellow *n.* aḫu, tappû; → **~-craftsman** *n.* kinattu; → **~ merchant** *n.* ebru☆; → **~ traveller** *n.* tappû; → **~ treasurer** *n.* mār masenni; → **~ worker** *n.* kinattu; → **~ship** *n.* aḫḫūtu+, ebrūtu+
felony *n.* ḫiṭṭu dannu
felt *n.* taḫapšu (woven); → **(pressed) ~** *n.* biršu; → **~-worker** *n.* sēpiu; → **chief ~ worker** *n.* rab sēpî
female *adv.* sinniš☆
feminine *adv.* sinniš☆
fence *n.* dūru, kutlu [o.]; → **~** *v.* labû, tuāku+ (D); → **reed ~** *n.* kikkisu; → **~ in** *v.* labû
fencing *n.* limītu☆
fend for o.s. *n.* ramanšu naṣāru
fend off *v.* sakāpu☆
fender *n.* panantu

fennel *n.* simru, uriānu
fenugreek *n.* šabbaliltu⭑
ferment *v.* emēṣu+ (D), ḫaṭāṭu B⭑; → **~ation** *n.* emēṣu+
ferocious *adj.* ekdu⭑, nalbubu⭑
ferry *n.* mušēbirtu, nēburu+
ferryboat *n.* elep nēberi⭑, nēburu+
fertile *adj.* ālittu⭑, ḫabṣu⭑, unnubu⭑; → **be(come) ~** *v.* naḫāšu⭑
fertility *n.* nuḫšu
fertilization *n.* tarkibtu⭑
fertilize *v.* reḫû⭑; → **~r** *n.* ziblu+
fervent *adj.* ḫanṭu
fervor *n.* ḫimiṭ libbi⭑ (excessive), uzzu⭑
fester *v.* šarāku B⭑; → **~ing** *adj.* šarku*
festival *n.* isinnu; → **hold a ~** *v.* isinnu epāšu [i.]; → **hold a/make ~** *v.* nigūtu šakānu [i.]; → **victory ~** *n.* akītu; → **~ (kind of)** *n.* eššēšu, garmartu, pandugānu, qarrātu; → **~ house** *n.* akītu
festive garment *n.* ṣubāt balti⭑
festivity *n.* isinnu
fetch *v.* matāḫu, našû (vent.)
fetlock *n.* kursinnu
fetter *n.* birītu⭑; → **in ~s** *adv.* kamīš⭑, kamūssu⭑; → **put in ~s** *v.* pâdu⭑
feud *n.* nukurtu; → **~al tenure** *n.* zimbānu⭑
fever *n.* ḫimṭu⭑, ḫunṭu, ummu B⭑; → **be(come) ~ish** *v.* ṣarāḫu; → **~ish heat** *n.* anqullu⭑
few *adj.* ēṣu B; → **a ~** *adj.* qallīlu+; → **a ~** *adv.* šina šalāš
fez-maker *n.* ša-kubšēšu
fib *n.* tēgirtu
fickle *adj.* ḫalpu+, mušpēlu⭑
fiction *adj.* tēṣītu B⭑
fidelity *n.* kēnūtu
field *n.* eqlu, iškāru (institutional), qarbatu⭑, ugāru; → **manager of sustenance ~(s)** *n.* rab ma'utti; → **arable ~** *n.* zar'u; → **fallow ~** *n.* kišubbû⭑; → **irrigated ~** *n.* ruṭibtu; → **~ (kind of)** *n.* itḫiṣu, kuribtu; → **~ laborer** *n.* mār zēri⭑; → **~ mouse** *n.* akburu+; → **~ of labor** *n.* iškāru+; → **~ of sustenance** *n.* mu'untu◊; → **~ pest (kind of)** *n.* ākilu B
fierce *adj.* ekdu⭑, ezzu⭑, šamru, šēru B⭑; → **be(come) ~** *v.* šamāru⭑; → **make ~** *v.* kadāru C⭑ (Š); → **~ly** *adv.* šamriš⭑
fiery *adj.* rasmu; → **~ glow** *n.* anqullu⭑
fifteen *n./adj.* ḫamiššer[et]*; → **~th** *adj.* ḫamiššerīu*
fifth *adj.* ḫanšu; → **be(come) ~** *v.* ḫamāšu⭑; → **one ~** *n.* ḫamussu
fiftieth *adj.* ḫanšāiu*
fifty *n./adj.* ḫanšā
fig *n.* tittu; → **~(?)** *n.* ṭīṭu; → **~-pecker** *n.* kubšānu+
fight *n.* ašgugu⭑, mitḫuṣu⭑, qarābu, ṣāltu⭑, ṣāssu, tidūku⭑; → **~** *v.* duāku, maḫāṣu (N), maḫāṣu⭑ (Gt), ṣâlu [o.], ṣāssu garû, ṣelû◊; → **start a ~** *v.* garû⭑; → **~er** *n.* ēpiš tāḫāzi⭑, māḫiṣu, muntaḫṣu⭑, muqtablu⭑; → **~ing** *n.* dēktu, mitḫuṣūtu⭑, ṣūlāti⭑
figure *n.* bunnannê⭑ (facial), lānu, nabnītu⭑, ṣalmu; → **~** *v.* eṣāru+; → **~d** *adj.* eṣru
figurine → **(apotropaic) ~** *n.* timru
filament *n.* qû B⭑
filch *v.* kabāsu+
filigree *n.* murdû⭑
fill *v.* malû (D), malû⭑ (Š); → **~ out** *v.* malû (D); → **~ to the brim** *v.* ana ṣirê mallû [i.]; → **~ up** *v.* malû; → **~ with** *v.* šabû (D); → **~ed** *adj.* mal'u; → **~ing** *n.* tamlītu; → **~y** *n.* mūrtu [o.]
film *n.* šišītu⭑; → **~y** *n.* barru⭑
filter *n.* šāḫilu◊; → **~** *v.* ḫalāṣu, šaḫālu◊; → **~ed** *adj.* ḫalṣu
filth *n.* malû B⭑; → **~y** *adj.* ša''uru, ṭanpu+
fin *n.* abru B⭑, agappu+, isḫu C⭑; → **~al** *adj.* gamru, nagmuru; → **~al accounting** *n.* šalluntu (complete); → **~ale** *n.* kīlu⭑; → **~ally** *adv.* ina qīti⭑
financial *adj.* kaspānāiu+
finch *n.* ṣepru+
find *v.* amāru, atû B⭑; → **make ~ mercy** *v.* ana rēmi šakānu [i.]; → **~ out** *v.* amāru, ḫarāṣu, lamādu, mussû◊; → **~ing** *n.* itūtu⭑
fine *adj.* damqu, ḫiššamû⭑, naḫsu⭑ (very), qatnu, qattanu⭑, raqqu, raqqu⭑; → **~** *n.* sartu; → **be(come) ~** *v.* damāqu, qatānu⭑, raqāqu; → **~st wheaten flour** *n.* samīdu B+
finger *n.* ubān qāti⭑, ubānu; → **little ~** *n.* ubānu ṣeḫertu; → **middle ~** *n.* ubānu qablītu⭑; → **~breath** *n.* ammār ubāni; → **~nail** *n.* ṣupru, ṣupur ubāni⭑; → **~tip** *n.* kaqqad ubāni
finial *n.* pingu
finish *v.* gamāru, malû+ (Š), qatû⭑, šaklulu+; → **~ doing** *v.* šaklulu⭑, šalāmu (D); → **~ doing s.th.** *v.* gamāru (D); → **~ writing up** *v.* šaṭāru gammuru; → **~ed** *adj.* gamru, qatû⭑, šaklulu+, šallumu+; → **be ~ed** *v.* gamāru (Dtt); → **be(come) ~ed** *v.* šalāmu; → **~ing** *adj.* gāmiru⭑
fir *n.* meḫru
fire *n.* anqullu, girru⭑, išātu; → **~** *v.* bašālu (Š), patû (D); → **catch ~** *v.* ṣarāḫu C+; → **on ~** *adv.* išātiš⭑; → **~-brand** *n.* kibirru⭑; → **(bon)~ beacon** *n.* išātu; → **~ rake** *n.*

mutirru; → **set ~ to** *v.* išātu šāḫuzu [i.]; → **~d** *adj.* ṣarpu; → **~place** *n.* kanūnu
firewood *n.* bulê, gaṣṣutu; → **~ container** *n.* bēt giṣṣiti; → **~ peddler** *n.* ša-gaṣṣātēšu
firm *adj.* dunnunu*, kunnu; → **be(come) ~** *v.* bâru B*, kuānu
firmament *n.* šupku*
firmly *adv.* dunnuniš*; → **~ fixed** *adj.* šaršudu; → **~ founded** *adj.* rašdu*; → **~ joined** *adj.* kaṣru
firmness *n.* kūnu*
first *adj.* maḫrû, pānīu, rēštû*; → **~** *adv.* ittēltu◊; → **~** *n.* issēn; → **be(come) ~** *v.* ḫarāpu; → **~-class** *adj.* ašarēdu, rēštu*; → **~-in-esteem** *n.* ša-šumēli; → **~-ranking** *adj.* rēštû*; → **~-rate** *adj.* rēštû*; → **~ month)** *n.* uraḫ Bēlat ēkalli [o.]; → **~ly** *adv.* iltēnšu*
fish *n.* nūnu; → **big ~** *n.* maṣātānu; → **freshwater ~** *adj.* nūn apsê*; → **~-man** *n.* kulīlu; → **~-woman** *n.* kulīltu; → **~erman** *n.* bā'ir nūni, bā'iru; → **~ing** *n.* bā'irūtu; → **~y** *adj.* lā taklu*, [ša] nūni*
fissure *n.* piṭru B*; → **~** *v.* šatāqu* (D)
fist *n.* upnu
fit *adj.* sapīqu+, šūluku*; → **~** *n.* ṣibtu; → **~** *v.* asāmu* (D), asāmu*; → **~ for** *adj.* asmu*, simtu (person or thing); → **~ together** *v.* rakāsu; → **~ness** *n.* sapqūtu+, ṭūb šīri (physical); → **~ted out** *adj.* tallulu; → **~ted to each other** *adj.* ta''umu+; → **~ting** *adj.* asmu*, naṭû*, šūsumu*
five sixths *n.* parasrab
five times *adv.* ḫanšīšu; → **be(come) ~ as great** *v.* ḫamāšu*
fivefold *adj./adv.* ḫanšīšu
fix *v.* rapāqu, retû*, zaqāpu; → **~ eyes in a stare** *v.* balāṣu* (D); → **~ in place** *v.* ṣabātu (D); → **~ upright** *v.* zaqāpu; → **~ed** *adj.* kunnu, ṣabbutu
fizz *v.* ḫazû*
flabby *adj.* ramû
flaccid *adj.* ramû
flagon *n.* maštītu*
flagrant *adj.* šūpû*
flagstone *n.* paršu+
flake *n.* epqēnu*, ḫupû*; → **~ away** *v.* ḫasāru*; → **~ off** *v.* ḫasāru*, šaḫāḫu; → **~s** *n.* qulpu+
flaking off *n.* šiḫḫutu
flame *n.* nablu; → **~** *v.* ḫamāṭu*; → **tongue of ~** *n.* lišān girri*
flaming *adj.* ḫanṭu; → **~ red** *n./adj.* argamannu
flange (of folding-doors) *n.* naḫīru+
flank *n.* aḫītu, aḫu B, giššu
flap *n.* taṣpuptu*; → **~** *v.* ṣapāpu*
flare *n.* mišḫu*, ṣirḫu*; → **~-up** *n.* mišḫu*; → **~ up** *v.* ḫamāṭu*, mašāḫu B*, ṣarāḫu C*, ṣarāru B*
flaring-up *n.* munnaḫzu*
flash *n.* birbirru, mišḫu*, nablu, ṣirḫu*; → **~** *v.* barāqu*, ṣarāḫu C*, ṣarāru B*
flask (of perfume) *n.* šikkatu*
flat *adj.* sapnu*; → **~-nosed** *adj.* šarmu+
flatland *n.* sapannu*
flatten *v.* saḫāpu, sapānu; → **be(come) ~ed** *v.* šâbu* (stat.)
flatter *v.* ḫanāpu*, kazābu* (D); → **~ing** *n.* mukazzibu*; → **~y** *n.* kuzubtu [o.]
flatulent *adj.* šārānu
flatus *n.* šāru
flavor *n.* ṭēmtu+
flaw *n.* ḫiṭītu*
flax *n.* kitû
flay *v.* kuāṣu
flea *n.* paršu'u*
fled *adj.* ḫalqu
fledgling *n.* nibṣu*
flee *v.* abātu* (N), ḫalāqu, irtu nê'u [i.], parāḫu, parāšu* (N); → **be(come) ~ away** *v.* parādu+
fleece *n.* itqu, nalbaš ṣēni*
fleecy *adj.* itqānu*
fleet *adj.* lasmu; → **~ing** *adj.* ḫāliqu*, qallīlu+
flesh *n.* pagru, šīru; → **~ly** *adj.* pagrānu+; → **~y** *adj.* ebṭu+, ebû
flex *v.* eṣāpu
flexure of the groin *n.* kurru C*
flick *n.* miḫṣu; → **~** *v.* maḫāṣu; → **~er** *v.* parāṭu; → **~er(?)** *v.* malāḫu (D)
flight *n.* arbūtu*
flinch *v.* kapāṣu+, sagû
fling *v.* šalā'u, šalû B*
flint *n.* ṣurru; → **~ blade** *n.* ṣurtu*
flipper *n.* isḫu C*
flirt *adj.* ēpiš namūti [o.]; → **~** *n.* namūtu [o.]; → **~** *v.* namūtu epāšu [o.]; → **~ation** *n.* ṣīḫtu
flirtatious *adj.* ēpiš namūti [o.], ṣaiāḫû*
flit *v.* našarbuṭu*, ṣabāru
float *n.* makkūtu+; → **~** *v.* neqelpû*, parāḫu+, šuā'u
flock *n.* sagullu
flog *v.* rapāsu
flogging *n.* ḫisiāti
flood *n.* abūbu, biblu B*, bubbulu, edû B*, mīlu; → **~** *v.* raḫāṣu B; → **like a ~** *adv.* abūbāniš*; → **~-wave** *n.* agû B*
Flood monster *n.* abūbu

flooded *adj*. raḫṣu*
floodgate *n*. bāb sekri+
flooding *n*. riḫiṣtu*, riḫṣu
floor *n*. nakbāsu, riṣpu+; → ~ *v*. raqāpu+; → **lay a** ~ *v*. raqāpu+; → **bottom** ~ *n*. bētu šaplīu; → **first** ~ *n*. bētu šaplīu; → **ground** ~ *n*. bētu šaplīu; → **second** ~ *n*. bētu elīu; → **sweep the** ~ *v*. sārē šētuqu [i.]; → **threshing** ~ *n*. adru
florid *n*. lalânu*
flour *n*. qēmu; → **coarse** ~ *n*. tappinnu; → **fine** ~ *n*. samīdu B*; → ~ **(kind of)** *n*. ḫatamlu, ḫirgalû, išqūqu, kukkušu*, upuntu*; → ~ **offering** *n*. širqu; → **~ish** *v*. dešû* (Dt), enēbu*, ḫanābu, šamāḫu*, šiāḫu B+, šutēlupu*; → **make ~ish** *v*. šamāḫu* (D); → **~ishing** *n*. lalânu*
flout *v*. lazānu
flow *v*. ḫanānu*, nabā'u+, radû+, tabāku (N); → **let** ~ *v*. radû+ (Š); → **make** ~ *v*. radû* (Š); → ~ **down** *v*. urādu; → **be(come)** ~ **over** *v*. ṭaḫādu; → **~er** *n*. aiuru, inbu, samādiru; → **~er-bed** *n*. musarû B*; → **~ering rush** *n*. šīšnu+
flu *n*. murṣu šatti
fluctuate *v*. sabā'u, šanû* (Gtn)
fluff *n*. nipšu
fluid *n*. mê, nīlu
fluke *n*. miqtu
flurry *n*. duluḫtu◊, zīnu, zīqu
flute *n*. ebbūbu, malīlu; → **~-player** *n*. zammāru+
flutter *v*. ṣapāpu*; → **~ing** *n*. taṣpuptu*
flux *n*. nib'u*
fly *v*. parāḫu+, parāšu* (N), parāšu*; → **let** ~ *v*. parāšu* (Š); → ~ **(insect)** *n*. baqqu*, zumbu; → ~ **about** *v*. parāšu* (Ntn); → ~ **at** *v*. šaḫāṭu C*; → ~ **whisk** *n*. ša-zumbē; → **~ing** *n*. mupparšu*, muštaprišu*, muttaprišu*
foal *n*. bakru*, mūru, suḫīru*
foam *n*. ḫurḫummatu*, rupuštu*
focus *n*. adūgu+
fodder *n*. kissutu; → **provide with** ~ *v*. marû* (Š); → ~ **master** *n*. rab kissiti; → ~ **store** *n*. bēt šammi
foe *n*. gārû*, gaṣṣiṣu, zā'irānu*, zā'iru*; → **~tus** *n*. kūbu*, ša-libbi
fog *n*. imbāru, qutru; → **like a** ~ *adv*. imbāriš*
foggy *adj*. qatturu
fold *n*. pitqu, qiplu*; → ~ *v*. karāku; → ~ **(up)** *v*. karāku+; → ~ **of the groin** *n*. kurru C*
foliage *n*. ḫasḫaltu*, ḫašḫaltu
folks *n*. nišē+
follow *v*. radû; → ~ **after** *v*. radû+; → ~ **closely** *v*. nentû*; → ~ **in order** *v*. sadāru+; → **~er** *n*. qurbu, talmīdu+, urdu; → **~ing** *adj*. ēribu
folly *adv*. lillūtu+; → ~ *n*. saklūtu+
foment *v*. dabābu (Š)
fond *adj*. rā'imu; → **be(come)** ~ **of** *v*. ra'āmu
fondle *v*. lallû (D), ra'āmu (D)
fondness *n*. ra'āmu
food *n*. akālu, akullû, leḫmu, mākālu, pitennu, uklu, ukullu◊; → **supplier of** ~ *n*. mušākilu B*; → ~ **(kind of)** *n*. gabūdu, ḫabrû, kamēšu; → **official in charge of** ~ **(title of)** *n*. rab qaqqulāti; → ~ **allowance** *n*. akullû; → ~ **offering** *n*. kurummutu; → ~ **ration** *n*. simmānû*; → **~stuffs set aside** *n*. maššartu*
fool *adj*. lā ḫassu*, lillu+, saklu+; → ~ *n*. lillu*; → ~ *v*. sarāru [o.]; → **be a** ~ *v*. lallû B+ (Dt); → **make a** ~ *v*. lallû B+ (Dt); → **~ery** *n*. lillūtu*; → **~ish** *adj*. lillu+, saklu, saklu+; → **~ish talk** *n*. nullāti*; → **~ish woman** *n*. lillatu*; → **act ~ishly** *v*. lallû B+ (Dt); → **~ishness** *n*. lillūtu*, nullāti*; → **~proof** *adj*. taklu
foot *n*. eṣentu, šēpītu, šēpu; → **ball of the** ~ *n*. suḫār šēpi*; → **on** ~ *adv*. ina šēpi; → **~-board (of a chariot)** *n*. saḫargû; → ~ **end** *n*. šēpītu; → **~ing** *n*. kisû*; → **~print** *n*. eqbu+, kibsu+; → **~race** *n*. lisnu; → **~stool** *n*. kerṣappu*
for *prep*. ana; → **make** ~ *v*. pānē ana X šakānu [i.]; → **~age** *n*. kissutu+, tabriu; → **~age** *v*. ba''û
foray *n*. šiḫṭu
forbearance *n*. arāk ikki◊
forbearing *n*. lā kāṣir ikki*; → **be(come)** ~ *v*. ikku urruku [i.]
forbid *gram.part*. lā; → ~ *v*. kalû, tuāku+ (D); → **~den** *adj*. ḫarmu+; → **~den** *n*. ikkibu*; → **be(come) ~den** *v*. ḫarāmu+
force *n*. aḫu B, emūqu; → ~ *v*. da'ānu (D), dâṣu*; → **use** ~ *v*. gabāru+; → **auxiliary** ~ *n*. ḫamāti*; → **by** ~ *adv*. da'āni, danāniš*, dannatti, emūqatti [o.], ina danāni*, kî da'āni, ša da'āni; → **main** ~ *n*. gunnu*; → **take by** ~ *v*. puāgu; → ~ **into submission** *v*. kanāšu* (Š); → ~ **to** *v*. ša-; → **~d labor** *n*. kudurru B*; → **~s** *n*. aḫu B (pl.)
forcible *adj*. dannu
forcibly *adv*. da'āni, dannatti, ina danāni*, kî da'āni, ša da'āni
ford *n*. nēbartu*, nēburu

fore *n.* pānu
forearm *n.* ammutu
forecast *n.* qību; → ~ *v.* qību šakānu
forecourt *n.* tarbāṣu+
forefather *n.* abu (pl.)
forefinger *n.* ubānu šanītu☆
foreground *n.* pūtu
forehead *n.* pūtu
foreign *adj.* nakru; → ~ **guest** *n.* ubāru; → **~er** *n.* mār māt nakiri☆
foreleg *n.* durā'u
forelock *n.* abussāti
foremost *adj.* rēštû☆; → ~ *n./adj.* ašarēdu
forenoon *n.* pān muṣlāli
foreordain *v.* šiāmu
foresee *v.* dagālu
foresight *n.* kūn libbi☆
forest *n.* ḫalbu☆, qissu; → **~all** *v.* ḫarāpu; → **~er** *n.* maṣṣar qabli
forethought *n.* kūn libbi☆
forever *adv.* ana dāriš☆, ana dūr dāri☆, dāriš☆, dārišam☆, ṣātiš☆
foreword *n.* rēš dabābi*
forfeit *v.* ina X elû [i.]
forge *n.* kiškattû☆; → ~ *v.* patāqu☆, zuppu+ (D); → **~t** *v.* mašû; → **make ~t** *v.* mašû (D); → **~tful** *adj.* lā ḫāsisu☆; → **~tfulness** *n.* lā ḫasās amāti☆
forgive *v.* kabāsu, mêšu☆, padû, rēmu rašû [i.]; → **~ness** *n.* napšuru, taiārtu☆
forgiving *adj.* gammilu☆, pādû☆
forgotten *n.* mašiu; → **become ~** *v.* mašû (N)
fork *n.* mazluqu [o.]; → ~ *v.* bêšu☆; → **~ing off** *n.* silittu☆
form *n.* alandimmû☆, binītu☆, binūtu, gattu, nigdimdimmû☆, padattu☆, šikittu☆, uṣurtu+; → ~ *v.* eṣāru+, kaṣāru, patāqu☆; → ~ **into a knot** *v.* kapātu+ (D); → ~ **into a pod** *v.* kapātu+; → **~ation** *n.* šipku; → **~ed** *adj.* patqu☆; → **~er** *adj.* pānīu; → **~erly** *adv.* ina pānīti; → **~ing** *n.* šipku
formula *n.* gerrû
fornicate *v.* niāku
fornication *n.* niāku
fornicator *n.* naiāku☆
forsake *v.* rammû (D)
fort *n.* bīrtu, dunnu [o.], ḫalzu☆, kādu◊
forthcoming *adj.* qurbu+
fortieth *adj.* arbīu*
fortification *n.* bēt dūri, bīrtūtu☆, ḫalzu☆
fortified farm(stead) *n.* dunnu [o.]
fortified place *n.* bēt dūri
fortify *v.* buāru (D) [o.], danānu☆ (D)
fortitude *n.* qardūtu☆
fortnight *n.* šapattu☆
fortress *n.* bēt dūri, bīrtu, dunnu [o.]
fortunate *adj.* damqu, rāš ili☆; → **be(come) ~** *v.* damāqu, kašāru+; → **~ly** *adv.* damqiš [o.]
fortune *n.* dunqu, rāšilūtu☆
forty *n./adj.* arbâ
forum *n.* rebītu☆
forward *v.* etāqu (Š), qarābu (D); → **~s** *adv.* ana pāni
foster *v.* rabû (D), rabû+ (D); → **~ child** *n.* tarbītu; → ~ **son** *n.* tarbiu; → **~ling** *n.* kunnūtu◊, tarbītu
foul *adj.* šuḫtānu+, zapru+; → ~ *v.* ša'āru+ (D), ṭanāpu◊ (D); → **be(come) ~** *v.* zapāru+; → **~ed** *adj.* dalḫu+
found *v.* kuānu (D), rašādu☆ (Š); → **~ation** *n.* duruššu☆, išdu, šuršu☆, temennu☆, uššē; → **~ation deposit** *n.* timru; → **~ation document** *n.* temennu☆; → **~ation pit** *n.* bērūtu☆; → **~ation stone** *n.* pūlu; → **~ation structure** *n.* asurrû☆; → **~ation trench** *n.* tublu☆; → **~er** *n.* mukinnu, mušaršidu☆
fount *n.* namba'u+
fountain *n.* nagbu☆, namba'u+
four *n.* arbittu; → ~ *n./adj.* erbi; → **(group of) ~** *n.* erbettu☆; → **~ each** *adv.* rubāia, rubū'ā◊; → **the ~ quarters** *n.* kibrāt erbetti☆; → **~ quarters (of the earth)** *n.* kippat erbetti; → ~ **times** *adv.* arbīšu, erbīšu; → **~fold** *n.* rubbu'u☆; → **~teen** *n./adj.* arbēšer[et]; → **~teenth** *adj.* arbēšerīu*; → **~th** *adj.* rabbu; → **one ~th** *n.* rabuttu; → **~th month)** *n.* uraḫ muḫur ilāni [o.]
fowl fattener *n.* mušākil iṣṣūri
fowl herder *n.* rā'i iṣṣūri
fowler *n.* sandû, ušandû☆; → **like a ~** *adv.* sandāniš☆
fowlherdboy *n.* ṣeḫer iṣṣūrē
fox *n.* šēlubu; → **like a ~** *adv.* šēlabiš☆; → **~-wine** *n.* karān šēlibi☆; → **~y** *adj.* sarru☆
fraction *n.* igitennu☆, paras
fracture *n.* ḫīpu; → ~ *v.* ḫapû
fragile *adj.* qatnu; → ~ *n.* anšu
fragility *n.* anšūtu
fragment *n.* ḫiṣibtu☆, ḫupû☆, šibirtu; → **~ary** *adj.* ḫapiu; → **~ed** *adj.* ḫapiu; → **(metal) ~s** *n.* ḫušê
fragrance *n.* irīšu☆, sammūtu☆
fragrant *adj.* ṭābu
frail *adj.* qatnu
fram drum *n.* uppu B☆
frame *n.* nalbantu☆, padattu☆, šibšutu; → ~ *v.* esāru; → **~ of mind** *n.* ṭēmu; → **~work** *n.* nalbantu☆

franchise *n.* pursānu+
francolin *n.* tatidūtu
frankincense(?) *n.* kanaktu
frantic *adj.* šegû*, zabbu*
fraternal *adj.* aḫānāiu+
fraternity *n.* aḫḫūtu+
fraternize *v.* aḫû* (Gt)
fraud *n.* sarrāti*, sartu, tukku+
fraudulent *adj.* sarru*; → **be(come) ~** *v.* sarāru [o.]; → **~ly** *adv.* sartatti◊
fraught with *adj.* mal'u+
fray *n.* ašgugu*
freckle *n.* pi'āru
free *adj.* rāqu, zakû; → **~** *v.* paṭāru, zakû (D); → **be(come) ~** *v.* riāqu, zakû; → **set ~** *v.* durāru šakānu [i.], riāqu (Š), uṣû; → **~ from** *adj.* zakû+; → **~ of work** *v.* riāqu (Š); → **~ will** *n.* ḫūd libbi; → **~dom** *n.* durāru, šubarrû*; → **~ly** *adv.* im-magāni+
freeze *v.* qarāḫu, qarāḫu (D); → **~ up** *v.* qarāḫu
freight *n.* ṣēnu B+; → **~er** *n.* makkūtu*
frenzied *adj.* zabbu*; → **be ~** *v.* maḫû* (N); → **be(come) ~** *v.* maḫḫûtiš alāku [i.]
frenzy *n.* šēḫu, šinītu+; → **be in a ~** *v.* zabābu*
frequent *v.* dapāru*, še'û* (Gtn); → **~ly** *adv.* ma'ad
fresco *n.* birmu*
fresh *adj.* balṭu, raṭbu, ṭābu; → **~en** *v.* balāṭu; → **~en up** *v.* ḫapāpu+; → **~man** *n.* šarrāiu+
fret *v.* akālu+; → **~ful** *adj.* anšu+, nazziqu*
friction *n.* mirṭu
fried *adj.* gabbubu
friend *n.* aḫu+, bēl de'iqti, bēl ṭābti, ebru*, itbāru [o.], re'mu◊, ru'u*; → **~liness** *n.* ṭubbāti*; → **~ly** *adj.* gammilu*, salmu, ṭābu; → **make ~ly** *v.* ṭiābu* (Š); → **be(come) ~ly with** *v.* libbu pašāru [i.]; → **be/make ~s** *v.* aḫû* (Gt); → **~ship** *n.* bēl ṭābtūtu, ebrūtu*, rā'imūtu*, ru'ūtu*, ṭābūtu*
frieze *n.* nēbuḫu
fright *n.* gilittu*, perdu+, pirittu*; → **~en** *v.* galādu (D), galādu* (Š), garāru (Š), palāḫu (D), parādu* (D); → **~en off** *v.* palāḫu (D); → **~ened** *adj.* palḫu, pardu*; → **be(come) ~ened** *v.* gilittu rašû*, palāḫu; → **~ening** *adj.* pardu*, rašbu*; → **~ful** *adj.* pardu*
fringe *n.* qannu, qarnu, sapsupu [o.]
frisk *v.* pazāzu+, raqādu, šaḫāṭu C* (Gtn)
frit *n.* anzaḫḫu, ḫuluḫḫu (light-colored)
frivolity *n.* rāqānūtu+
frivolous *adj.* qallulu; → **~ly** *adv.* qalliš*
frizzle *v.* gabbubu
frock *n.* urnutu (dressing)
frog *n.* muṣa''irānu; → **large ~** *n.* kitturru B
frolic *n.* ṣūḫu*, tamgītu*
from *n.* la pān◊; → **~** *prep.* ina, issu, issu libbi, ištu*, la, ultu*, ultu qereb*; → **~ (the presence of)** *subj.* issu pān; → **~ afar** *adj.* nesû*; → **~ here** *adv.* sunnāka; → **~ the beginning** *adv.* issu rēši; → **~ under** *prep.* issu šapal; → **~ various directions** *n.* issu māka issu māka [i.]; → **~ where** *subj.* issu bēt; → **~ which there in no escape** *adj.* ša lā naparšudi*
frond *n.* āru, zinû
front *adj.* maḫru; → **~** *n.* meḫretu*, pānu, qudmu*; → **in ~** *adv.* pāniš*; → **~ (side)** *n.* pūtu; → **in ~ of** *n.* meḫret*; → **in ~ of** *prep.* ellāmū-*, pānāt, pūt
frontier *n.* miṣru*, taḫūmu
frost *n.* ḫurbāšu*, qarḫu, šurīpu*, šuruppû*
froth *n.* rupuštu*
frown *v.* nekelmû*
frozen *adj.* qarruḫu*; → **be(come) ~** *v.* qarāḫu
fructified *adj.* unnubu*
frugality *n.* maššuḫūtu+
fruit *n.* inbu, mutḫummu*, zamru; → **~** *v.* enēbu* (D), enēbu*; → **pick ~** *v.* enēbu* (Dt); → **~-basket** *n.* kakkullu; → **~-stone** *n.* abnu; → **~ bowl** *n.* aṣūdu; → **~ confection or sweet sauce (kind of)** *n.* budê; → **~ offering** *n.* aṣūdu; → **~ tree** *n.* mutḫummu*; → **~ tree/fruit (kind of)** *n.* titipu; → **~ tree (kind of)** *n.* ingirāšu*; → **~ful** *adj.* per'ānu+; → **very ~ful** *adj.* unnubu*; → **~less** *adj.* lā unnubu*; → **first ~s** *n.* rēšāti; → **room for first ~s** *n.* bēt rēšāti
frustrate *v.* anāḫu (Š); → **~d** *adj.* šūnuḫu*
fry *v.* gabābu (D), gabbubu, qalû+
fuck *v.* niāku; → **~ing** *n.* nīku
fuel *n.* širpu, šuruptu
fugitive *n.* munnabbitu◊, munnabtu*, munnarbu*; → **~** *n./adj.* ḫalqu, muttaprašši du*
fulfil *v.* malû (D), šalāmu+ (D); → **be(come) ~led** *v.* malû, šalāmu+; → **~ler** *n.* mumalliānu+; → **~ment** *n.* šumlû+
full *adj.* mal'u; → **~** *v.* kaṣāru+; → **be(come) ~** *v.* malû, šabû; → **~-grown** *adj.* šaklulu+, šīḫu*; → **~-scale** *adj.* šīḫu*; → **~ extent** *n.* pāṭ gimri*; → **~ flood** *n.* kiššatu*; → **~ month** *n.* urḫu ūmāti; → **~ to the**

brim *adj.* ana ṣirê◊; → ~ **well** *adv.* maṣi; →
~er's mallet *n.* mazūru⁺; → **~er's stick** *n.*
mazūru⋆; → **chief ~er** *n.* rab ašlāki; → **~ness**
n. malûtu⁺
    fume *n.* buḫru⋆; → ~ *v.* baḫāru⋆
    fumigant *n.* qutāru
    fumigate *v.* qatāru (D)
    fun *n.* ṣūḫu⋆; → **for ~** *n.* kî ṣūḫi⋆; →
make ~ of *v.* lazānu
    function *n.* parṣu
    fundamental *adj.* išdāiu⁺; → **~s** *n.* rēšēti⋆
    funds *n.* nikkassu; → **available ~** *n.* rēš
namkūri⋆
    funeral burning *n.* šuruptu
    funeral pile *n.* kurullu⋆
    funeral service *n.* dulli qabāri
    funerary inscription *n.* šiṭir arāni⋆
    funerary offering *n.* kispu
    fungous *adj.* puṭrānu
    fungus *n.* puṭuru
    fungy *adj.* puṭrānu
    funnel *n.* ittû B⋆
    funny *adj.* muṣiḫḫu⋆; → **~ stories** *n.* kaz-
būtu⋆
    fur *n.* gildu⁺
    furbish up *v.* utāru (Š)
    furious *adj.* aggu⋆, daḫru⋆, ezzu⋆, na-
dru⋆, nanduru⋆, šalbābu⋆, šamru, šegû⋆,
uggugu⋆; → **be ~** *v.* labābu⋆ (N), šegû⋆ (N);
→ **be(come) ~** *v.* agāgu⋆, ezēzu⋆, nadāru⋆;
→ **~ly** *adv.* ezziš⋆, šamriš⋆
    furlong *n.* šiddu
    furnace *n.* atūnu⁺, kūru, tinūru⁺
    furnish *v.* ṣabātu (Š); → **~ings** *n.* muttab-
biltu⋆
    furniture *n.* gašīrūtu⋆, muttabbiltu⋆
    furrier *n.* parrāiu⁺
    furrow *n.* apšinnu⋆, šir'u⋆
    further *adv.* û, utar⋆
    furthermore *adv.* û
    furtive *adj.* šarriqu⋆; → **~ly** *adv.* ḫallā-
lāniš⋆, šarrāqiš⋆
    fury *n.* uggatu⋆, uzzu⋆
    fuse *v.* peḫû⋆, ṣuādu
    fusion *n.* pašāru⁺, ṣūdu
    fuss *n.* nuguššû⋆; → ~ *v.* dalāḫu; → ~
over *v.* dalāpu ina muḫḫi
    futile *adj.* paḫḫu⁺, rāqu
    futility *n.* rāqūtu
    future *adj.* urkīu; → ~ *n.* aḫrāti⋆, arkītu◊,
urkītu; → **distant ~** *n.* labār ūmē; → **for the**
~ *adv.* ṣātiš⋆; → **in the ~** *adv.* urkiš
    fuzz *n.* itqu, šārtu⁺
    gab *v.* ḫabāru
    gad about *v.* saḫāru

    gadfly *n.* zumbi alpi⋆
    gadget *n.* nēpešu⋆
    gag *v.* balāmu⋆
    gage *n.* šapartu
    gaiety *n.* nummur libbi⋆, tamgītu⋆
    gaily *adv.* elṣiš⋆, ḫadīš⋆
    gain *n.* nēmulu; → ~ *v.* aḫāzu, qanû B,
utāru (D); → **be(come) ~say** *v.* lā magāru
    gait *n.* alaktu⋆, tallaktu B⋆, talluku⋆
    Galaxy *n.* ṣerret šamê
    gale *n.* ziqziqqu⋆
    gall (bladder) *n.* martu
    gallant *adj.* qardu; → **~ry** *n.* qardūtu⋆
    galley *n.* eleppu
    gallop *n.* lisnu; → ~ *v.* lasāmu
    gallstone *n.* ṣimirtu⁺
    gallus *n.* kurgarrû; → **chief ~** *n.* rab kur-
garrê
    galore *adj.* ana ṣirê◊
    gambol *v.* dakāku⋆, šaḫāṭu C⋆ (Gtn)
    game *n.* mēlultu⋆; → **~-piece** *n.* passu⋆;
→ ~ **preserve** *n.* ambassu
    gangster *n.* ḫabbilu⋆, sarsarru, šaršarrānu◊
    gaol *n.* bēt kīli⋆
    gap *n.* šitqu⋆
    gape *v.* puāqu⁺
    gaping *n.* pūqu⁺
    garbage *n.* tuḫḫu⋆; → ~ **collector** *n.* zab-
bālu⁺
    garden *n.* kirītu, kiriu; → ~ **bed** *n.* musa-
rû B⋆; → ~ **manager** *n.* rab kirie; → **~er** *n.*
nukaribbu; → **chief ~er** *n.* rab nukaribbi; →
~ing *n.* nukaribbūtu⋆
    garland *n.* kilīlu⁺; → **as with a ~** *adv.*
kilīliš⋆
    garlic *n.* šūmu
    garment *n.* kuzippu, labussu, lubāru⋆,
lubšu⋆, lubussu, ṣubātu; → **fine ~** *n.* qatattu;
→ **lower ~** *n.* šupālītu; → **outer ~** *adj.*
naḫtu⁺ (long); → **purple ~** *n.* argamannu⁺;
→ **upper ~** *n.* elītu; → **~/cloth (kind of)** *n.*
bēt rēši; → **~/item (kind of)** *n.* kandirši, kundirašši; → **~/textile (kind of)** *n.* ḫarīru, zazabtu; → ~ **(kind of)** *n.* gammīdu, guzguzu◊,
iaḫilu, iamnuqu, iarītu, kirbīnu, kirnāiu,
naḫtu, niksu, nimrā'u, paritītu, sibrītu, supāqu,
ša-pê, šaḫīlu; → ~ **(kind of; lit. 'moving like**
a snake') *n.* ša-tāluk-ṣirri; → ~ **with multi-**
colored trim *n.* ša-birme
    garner *n.* tuānu B⁺
    garnish *v.* za'ānu⋆ (D)
    garrison *n.* bēt maṣṣarti, šūlūtu⋆
    gas *n.* šāru
    gash *n.* ḫerṭu⁺; → ~ *v.* gêšu⋆
    gastric *adj.* [ša] karši⋆

gate *n.* bābu; → **city ~** *n.* abullu; → **~ (kind of)** *n.* mušlālu; → **~ (part of)** *n.* matgiqu*; → **~ guard** *n.* maṣṣar bābi; → **~ of the palace** *n.* bāb ēkalli; → **~ supervisor** *n.* ša-pān-bābi; → **~guard** *n.* atû
gatehouse *n.* bēt abulli; → **~ (kind of)** *n.* mušlālu
gates → **commander of city ~** *n.* rab abullāti
gateway *n.* abullu
gather *v.* ḫamāmu*, kamāsu, kannušu, karāku, laqātu, paḫāru, šabāšu; → **~ together** *v.* esāpu, šabāšu; → **~ up** *v.* laqātu; → **~ed** *adj.* karku; → **~ed together** *adj.* subbusu◊; → **~er** *n.* laqqātu*; → **~ing** *n.* puḫru, qitpu [o.]
gaudy *adj.* šamḫu*, šurruḫu*
gauze *n.* širṭu
gay *adj.* elṣu*
Gaza *n.* Hazzat
gaze *n.* imratu*, niṭlu*; → **~** *v.* dagālu, naṭālu*; → **~ at** *v.* palāsu* (N)
gazebo *n.* bēt ūri
gazelle *n.* ḫuzālu+, ṣabītu; → **young ~** *n.* ḫuzālu
gecko *n.* eṣṣu'u, ḫumbābītu, pizallūru
gem *n.* abnu, abnu aqartu*, digilu, kunukku; → **choice ~** *n.* aban nisiqti*; → **kidney-shaped ~** *n.* tukpītu
Gemini *n.* māšu*, tuāmē
gems → **choicest ~** *n.* nisiqti abnē*
general (of cavalry or chariotry) *n.* rab mūgi
generate *v.* banû
generation *n.* lēpu
generosity *n.* rabûtu
generous *adj.* qaiāšu*, ṭābtānu
genial *adj.* atra ḫasīsi*
genie *n.* šēdu
genitals *n.* qallû*; → **female ~** *n.* biṣṣūru*
genius *adj.* atra ḫasīsi*
genteel *adj.* damqu
gentle *adj.* pašru*, rabbu B, ṭābu; → **~** *n.* nēḫu+; → **~man** *n.* amēlu; → **~manlike** *n./adj.* amēlānu; → **~manly** *n./adj.* amēlānu
gentlewoman *n.* amēltu
gently *adv.* rabbiš*
gentry *n.* kināltu+
genuine *adj.* ḫīp šaddî
geometrician *n.* māšiḫu*
gepard *n.* mindīnu*
germ *n.* qarnu
gesture *n.* ittu
get *v.* aḫāzu, kašādu, našû, rašû*; → **~ as far as** *v.* maṣû* (Št); → **~ at** *v.* kašādu; → **~ away** *v.* ḫalāqu; → **~ mad at s.o.** *v.* libbāt X malû [i.]; → **be(come) ~ potency** *v.* nīš libbi rašû*; → **~ started with** *v.* aḫu ummudu [i.]
ghastly *adj.* pardu*
ghee *n.* ḫimātu; → **~ trader** *n.* ša-ḫimāti [o.]
ghost *n.* eṭemmu, utukku; → **like a ~** *adv.* zaqīqiš*
giant *adj.* šīḫu*, utturu*; → **~ reed** *n.* apu B*
gibberish *adj.* dibbē lā dibbē
gibbous *adj.* gabnu◊
gibe *n.* šinṣu*; → **~** *v.* lazānu
giddiness *n.* ṣūd pāni*
giddy *v.* neqelpû*; → **~ing** *adj.* mušaṣbiru*
gift *n.* katrû*, magānu, nidintu◊, nidnu*, nūptu◊, qēssu, šūbultu*, tarīntu*, tidintu, ṭa'tu, ṭātu*; → **wedding ~** *n.* zublānû
gigantic *adj.* šūturu*
giggle *v.* ṣiāḫu* (Gtn)
gild *v.* sakāru; → **~ed** *adj.* sakru
gilt *adj.* sakru
gimmick *n.* niklu
ginger(?) *n.* zinzaru'u
giraffe *n.* gamalnemru+
gird *v.* ebēḫu*, ezāḫu, rakāsu
girdle *n.* aguḫḫu*, ebīḫu*, meserru*, musāru, nēbettu, ṣipirtu (woven), šibbu*
girl *n.* batūssu, qallassu, qallutu (slave); → **beautiful ~** *n.* banītu*; → **young ~** *n.* qallassu, ṣeḫertu; → **~ friend** *n.* ra'imtu+, ruttu*; → **~ student** *n.* talmittu [o.]
girt → **be ~** *v.* alālu* (Gt)
gist *n.* riksu
give *v.* nadānu*, tadānu; → **~ away** *v.* riāmu, tadānu; → **~ credit** *v.* qiāpu; → **~ over** *v.* tadānu; → **~ up** *v.* rammû (D); → **~n** *adj.* qīšu*; → **~n up to** *adj.* na'du*; → **~r** *n.* nādinu*, tādinu
giving of name *n.* nibīt šumi*
gizzard *n.* pisurru*
glad *adj.* ḫadiu; → **be(come) ~** *v.* ḫadû; → **~ly** *adv.* ḫadīš*, ṭābiš*; → **~ness** *n.* ḫadûtu, ḫudû
glamor *n.* lulû*
glance *n.* imratu*, nīš ēni*, niṭlu*; → **~ (of favor)** *n.* nišīt ēni*; → **~ at** *v.* palāsu* (N)
glans *n.* appi ušāri*
glare *v.* barāṣu*, nekelmû*, zalāqu B+
glass *n.* mekku (raw), zakūkītu*, zukû*
glassblower *n.* zakūkīu+
glassy *adj.* zakūkāiu+
glaze *n.* zakūkītu*; → **~** *v.* šaḫāṭu B
glazier *n.* zakūkīu+

gleam *n.* nūru; → ~ *v.* nebû⋆
glean *v.* laqātu; → **~ing** *n.* liqtu
glee *n.* ḫaddânūtu*
glide *v.* neqelpû⋆, šapāpu⋆
gliding *adj.* muqqelpû⋆
glimmer *v.* barāru
glimpse *v.* palāsu⋆ (N)
glint *v.* zalāgu+
glisten *v.* nagālu⋆; → **~ing** *adj.* barḫu
glitter *n.* zīmu; → ~ *v.* zalāqu B+
gloat over *v.* ḫadû
gloater *n.* ḫādiānu
globule *n.* kupatinnu⋆
gloom *n.* šaqummatu⋆; → **~y** *adj.* adru B; → **be ~y** *v.* adāru (Dtt), adāru⋆ (Št); → **be(come) ~y** *v.* adāru
glorification *n.* tašrīḫu⋆
glorify *v.* šarāḫu⋆ (D)
glorious *adj.* šarḫu⋆; → **be(come)** ~ *v.* šarāḫu⋆
glory *n.* tašīltu⋆; → ~ **in** *v.* šarāḫu⋆ (Dt)
glossy *adj.* barḫu
glow *n.* anqullu, birṣu⋆; → ~ *v.* ḫamāṭu⋆, nagālu⋆, naqallulu, šabābu⋆; → **make** ~ *v.* ḫamāṭu⋆ (D); → **red** ~ *n.* akukūtu; → **~-worm** *n.* dallāqu+; → **~er** *v.* balāṣu⋆; → **~ing** *adj.* naggulu⋆; → **~ing** *n.* muštaḫmiṭu⋆
glue *n.* debqu+, dubāqu+, tūbāqu; → ~ *v.* dabāqu+ (D)
glum *adj.* adru B
glut *v.* la'ātu+; → **~ton** *n.* akkilu⋆; → **~tonize** *v.* malālu⋆; → **~tony** *n.* akkilūtu
gnarled *adj.* pessû⋆
gnarly *adj.* mašru
gnash (teeth) *v.* gaṣāṣu
gnat *n.* baqqu⋆, buqāqu⋆
gnaw *v.* kasāsu
gnome *n.* šēdānu+
gnosis *n.* mūdûtu⋆
go *v.* akāšu⋆, alāku, âru⋆, nagāšu⋆; → *interj.*~ likalka; → **~-between** *n.* pāris birti*; → ~ **about** *v.* segû◊; → **make ~ across** *v.* ebāru (Š); → ~ **again** *v.* saḫāru alāku; → ~ **ahead** *n.* ana pāni alāku [i.]; → ~ **ahead** *v.* etāqu, lazāzu, panû; → ~ **along** *v.* segû◊; → ~ **along with** *v.* magāru (N), radû; → ~ **around** *v.* labû; → ~ **around with** *v.* karāku+ (N); → ~ **astray** *v.* ḫaṭû; → ~ **away** *v.* alāku (Gtt), bêšu⋆, dapāru⋆ (D), naṣālu⋆; → ~ **back** *v.* saḫāru alāku; → ~ **by** *v.* alāku; → ~ **deep** *v.* šapālu; → ~ **directly** *v.* ašāru B, ešēru⋆; → ~ **down** *v.* šapālu, urādu; → ~ **earlier** *v.* ḫarāpu alāku; → ~ **far** *v.* nesû⋆; → ~ **first** *v.* ḫarāpu alāku; → ~ **forward** *v.* radû+; → ~ **in front** *v.* panû; → ~ **into** *v.* erābu; → ~ **mad** *v.* maḫḫûtiš alāku⋆; → ~ **off** *v.* alāku (Gtt); → ~ **on** *v.* barû C⋆ (Št), lazāzu; → ~ **out** *v.* balû⋆, uṣû; → ~ **past** *v.* etāqu; → ~ **round** *v.* labû, saḫāru; → ~ **round begging** *v.* saḫāru+; → ~ **shakily** *v.* ṭamû B⋆; → ~ **straight** *v.* ešēru⋆; → ~ **straightaway** *v.* etāqu alāku; → ~ **to fight against** *v.* sālti ana libbi X alāku [i.]; → ~ **up** *v.* elû; → ~ **with** *v.* labû+
goad *n.* karallu⋆, paruššu⋆; → ~ *v.* zaqātu⋆
goal *n.* qītu, ṣammuru⋆, ṣummurtu⋆ (pl.)
goat *n.* enzu; → **(male)** ~ *n.* kizzu ; → **male** ~ *n.* urīṣu; → **mountain** ~ *n.* turāḫu; → **young** ~ *n.* laliu; → **young she-** ~ *n.* unīqu; → **~-fish** *n.* suḫurmāšu
goatherd *n.* rā'i enzi
gobble *v.* la'ātu⋆
goblet *n.* kāsu
God *n.* ilāni
god *n.* ilā'u, ilu
God → **by** ~ *adv.* ilumma
god(s) → **house of** ~ *n.* bēt ilāni
god → **city** ~ *n.* il āli; → **great** ~ *n.* ilu rabiu; → **highest** ~ *n.* Illil; → **house of** ~ *n.* bēt ili; → **image of** ~ *n.* ṣalam ili
God → **serve** ~ *v.* palāḫu+; → **spirit of** ~ *n.* šār ilāni
god → **supreme** ~ *n.* Illil; → ~ **of gods** *n.* Illil; → **~dess** *n.* iltu, ištāru⋆; → **~head** *n.* ilūtu; → **~less(ly)** *adj.* ša lā ilāni⋆; → **~like** *adj.* [ša] kī ili*; → **~like** *n.* nūrtānu; → **~s** *n.* ilāni
goer *n.* āliku
going *adj.* āliku
gold *n.* ḫurāṣu, pašallu⋆ (a kind of); → **fine** ~ *n.* ṣāriru⋆; → **~-like** *n.* ḫurāṣānu [o.]; → ~ **object (kind of)** *n.* sabubu; → ~ **ornament (kind of)** *n.* gubāru B◊; → ~ **paste (kind of)** *n.* lēru; → ~ **plate** *n.* lē'u ḫurāṣi; → ~ **plated** *adj.* ḫurāṣu uḫḫuzu, sakru; → **~en** *adj.* [ša] ḫurāṣi
goldfinch(?) *n.* ḫurāṣānu⋆
goldsmith *n.* kuttimmu, ṣarrāpu; → **chief** ~ *n.* rab ṣarrāpi
goldy *n.* ḫurāṣānu [o.]
good *adj.* babbanû◊, banû⋆, damqu, ṭābu; → **be(come)** ~ *v.* banû B⋆, damāqu, ṭiābu; → **make** ~ *v.* ṭiābu (D), ṭiābu⋆ (Š); → **~-looking** *adj.* baltānû⋆; → **~-tasting** *adj.* ṭābu; → ~ **condition** *n.* šalmūtu⋆; → ~ **deed** *n.* de'iqtu; → ~ **fortune** *n.* kušīru; → **do a** ~ **job** *v.* dammuqu epāšu; → ~ **luck** *n.* dunqu; → ~ **name** *n.* šumu damqu; → ~ **order** *n.* tu-

qūnu; → **be in ~ order** *v.* taqānu+; → **~ reputation** *n.* šumu damqu; → **~ sense** *n.* tašīmtu★; → **~ word** *n.* de'iqtu
goodbye *n.* ina šulmi alik*
goodness *n.* būnu B◊, de'iqtu, ṭābtu, ṭēbūtu+, ṭūbu
goods *n.* anūtu, bušû★, būšu★
goodwill *n.* ṭābtu, ṭubbāti★
goose *n.* iṣṣūru rabiu, paspasu★
gore *v.* nakāpu★
gorge *n.* ḫurru, naḫlu, nērubu, pušqu★; → **~** *v.* akālu; → **~ous** *adj.* šurruḫu★
goring *adj.* kadru★
gossip *n.* dābibtu★, lišānu; → **~** *v.* ṣabāru+; → **~(?)** *v.* ša'ūdu (Štn); → **~y (woman)** *n.* dābibtu★
gouge out eyes *v.* napālu★ (D)
gourd *n.* qiššû
gout *n.* ṣennītu+
govern *v.* âru★ (D), radû, šapāru★; → **~ment** *n.* bēt bēli, rēdût māti★, rēdûtu; → **city of ~ment** *n.* āl bēlūti★; → **house of ~ment** *n.* bēt rēdûti; → **~or** *n.* bēl pīḫati◊, pāḫutu, šakin māti★, šakkanakku★, šaknu (acting); → **~or of Nippur** *n.* šandabakku★; → **~orship** *n.* pāḫatūtu, šaknūtu
gown *n.* maqāṭu, maqāṭutu, muqāṭutu, urnutu (dressing)
grab *v.* puāgu, ṣabātu
grace *n.* kuzbu, rēmu, ṭēbūtu; → **by ~ of** *n.* ina ṭēbūti ša; → **~ful** *adj.* kuzbānu★, lullû★
gracious *adj.* gāmilu★, pašru★, rēmānu, ṭābu; → **~ly** *adv.* ṭābiš★
grade *n.* dargu+
gradually *adv.* dargu ana dargi*
grain *n.* ašnan B★, nissābu★, še'u, uṭṭutu; → **roasted ~** *n.* qullītu; → **stored ~** *adj.* tabku; → **~-heap** *n.* karû B, tarāmu; → **~-store** *n.* bēt karmi, karû B; → **~ (kind of)** *n.* ṭuṭumēsu; → **~s of sesame** *n.* šawaššammē+
granaries → **chief of ~** *n.* rab karmāni
granary *n.* bēt ḫašīmi, bēt karmi, ḫašīmu, karmu; → **~ master** *n.* rab karmi
grandchild *n.* mār mar'i
granddaughter *n.* mar'at mar'iti
grandees *n.* rabrabāni
grandeur *n.* rabûtu
grandfather *n.* ab-abi; → **maternal ~** *n.* ab-ummi★
grandma *n.* umm-ummi★
grandmother *n.* umm-ummi★, ummu abi◊
grandparents *n.* ab-abi (pl.)
grandson *n.* mār mar'i
granny *n.* umm-ummi★
grant *n.* rēmuttu, širiktu; → **~** *v.* qiāšu, riāmu, šutlumu★; → **~ed** *adj.* qīšu★
grape-stone *n.* purṣīnu+
grapes *n.* karānu; → **bunch of ~** *n.* isḫunnu, isḫunnutu
grapevine *n.* tillutu
graphic *adj.* eṣru
grapple (with) *v.* šapāṣu★ (Gt)
grasp *v.* aḫāzu, karāmu, ṣabātu, tamāḫu★; → **~ the hem** *v.* qannu ṣabātu [i.]
grass *n.* dīšu★, sassutu; → **~ pea** *n.* laṭiru★
grasshopper *n.* erbiu, zirzirru★
grate *n.* kisukku; → **~** *v.* gaṣāṣu; → **~ful** *adj.* ḫāsis ṭābti★
gratification *n.* ṭūb libbi
gratify *v.* libbu ṭubbu [i.]
grating *n.* kisukku, murdû★
gratis *adv.* im-magāni
gratitude *n.* ḫasās ṭābti★; → **sign of ~** *n.* dumuqqû★
gratuitously *adv.* im-magāni, ina ḫadûti
gratuity *n.* tamgirtu [o.]
grave *adj.* kabtu★; → **~** *n.* naqburu, qabūru, qubūru; → **~digger** *n.* qabbiru★
gravel *n.* galālu B◊, ḫiṣṣu★
gravestone *n.* asumit qabūri
gravity *n.* kabdūtu*, kubtu
gray hair *n.* šīpu★; → **~s** *n.* paršumāti
grayness *n.* paršumāti
graze *v.* ra'û
grease *n.* līpu; → **~** *v.* pašāšu
greasy *n.* šaḫīmu+
great *adj.* rabbû★, rabiu; → **be(come) ~** *v.* rabû; → **~-grandfather** *n.* ab ab-abi★; → **reach a ~ age** *v.* paršumu (Dtt); → **~ly** *adv.* adanniš, ma'diš★, rabīš★; → **~ness** *n.* narbû★, narbûtu★, rabûtu
Greece *n.* Iauna
greed *v.* ēnu našû★; → **~y** *adj.* nāš ēni★; → **be(come) ~y for** *v.* ṣaḫātu
Greek *n./adj.* Iamnāiu★, Iaunāiu
green *n./adj.* erqu, urqu; → **be(come) ~** *v.* erāqu; → **~ery** *n.* urqītu
greengrocer *n.* bāqilu★, baqqālu+
greenish-blue *n./adj.* ḫašmānu
greeting *n.* šulmu
grid *n.* birru
grief *n.* ašuštu★, lumun libbi, niziqtu★
grieve *v.* ašāšu★ (D), nazāqu★ (D)
grievous *adj.* lazzu+, marṣu
grill *v.* gabābu (D), gabbubu; → **~ed** *adj.* gabbubu
grim *adj.* lā gāmilu★, lā pādû★, šamru
grimace *v.* ḫanāṣu★ (D), ḫanāṣu★
grimly *adv.* aggiš★

grimy *adj.* šuḫtānu+
grind *v.* gaṣāṣu, marāqu, ṭiānu; → **~stone** *n.* arû
grip *n.* naṣbutu, rappu☆, ṣibtu; → **~** *v.* ṣabātu, šapāṣu☆
grisly *adj.* pardu☆
gristle *n.* gīdu
grit *n.* ḫiṣṣu☆
groan *n.* ṣiriḫtu☆; → **~** *v.* lebû☆, nazāmu, nuāqu☆, ramāmu☆, ṣarāḫu B+; → **~ing** *adj.* nassu☆
groats *n.* dulīqāti, ḫašlāti, sindu; → **~ (kind of)** *n.* siltu
groceries *n.* urqu+ (pl.)
grocery *n.* baqqālūtu+
groin *n.* kappaltu☆, šapūlu
groom *n.* kartappu◊, kizû☆, sūsānu; → **~ of armored chariot** *n.* ša-taḫlīpi; → **~sman** *n.* sūsabinnu☆
groove *n.* ḫerṭu+, ḫirīṣu; → **~** *v.* ḫarāṣu
grope (about) *v.* muāšu+
gross *adj.* dannu, ebû+, ḫabburu, kabru
grotto *n.* ḫurru
grouch *v.* nazāmu; → **~y** *adj.* adru B
ground *n.* dunnu☆, erṣutu☆, kaqquru; → **~** *v.* šaršudu☆; → **high ~** *n.* mūlû; → **slippery ~** *n.* mušḫalṣītu☆; → **solid ~** *n.* danninu, dunni qaqqari☆; → **wet ~** *n.* reṭbu+, ruṭibtu☆
group *n.* ellatu☆, kiṣru; → **~ed** *adj.* kaṣru
grouse *v.* nazāmu
grove (of trees) *n.* qablu B
grovel *v.* nagarruru, napalsuḫu☆
grow *v.* rabû, šiāḫu B☆; → **~ abundantly** *v.* šamāḫu☆; → **~ densely** *v.* elēpu☆ (Št); → **~ dim** *v.* barāru; → **~ dimmer** *v.* barāru; → **be(come) ~ frail** *v.* qatānu+; → **~ in number** *v.* ma'ādu; → **~ round** *v.* epāqu [o.]; → **~ thick** *v.* ebēṭu+; → **be(come) ~ thickly** *v.* šamāḫu☆; → **be(come) ~ thin** *v.* qatānu+; → **~ together** *v.* elēpu☆ (Gt); → **~ up** *v.* rabû; → **~ing toward(s) maturity** *adj.* muštēnû☆
growl *v.* na'āru+, nadāru☆, naḫāru+, nazāmu (Dtt), ramāmu☆
grown-up *adj.* rabiu
growth *n.* rūbu, tarbītu+
grub *n.* ṣarṣūru+; → **~** *v.* tarāḫu [o.]; → **~ up** *v.* gêšu☆, ḫalāšu☆, tarāḫu [o.]
grubby *adj.* gammīzu+; → **~** *n.* aršu☆
grudge → **bear a ~** *v.* ikku kaṣāru [i.], ikku kullu [i.]
gruel *n.* pappāsu; → **~(l)ing** *adj.* marṣu, pašqu☆
gruesome *adj.* pardu☆
grumble *v.* nazāmu (Dtt)
grumpy *adj.* adru B, nazziqu☆
grunt *v.* nazāzu☆
guarantee *n.* maškānu, urkīu; → **~** *v.* pūtuḫu našû [i.]
guarantor *n.* bēl qātāti, ša-qātāti, urkīu
guard *n.* maṣṣartu, maṣṣuru, ša-maṣṣarti, ša-šēpi (personal); → **~** *v.* etāku (D), naṣāru; → **be(come) on ~** *v.* ḫarādu; → **hill ~** *n.* ša-mēlê; → **place on ~** *v.* ḫarādu (D); → **~ (over)** *v.* naṣāru☆ (Š); → **appoint a ~ (over)** *v.* naṣāru☆ (Š); → **~ian** *n.* nāṣiru; → **~ian angel** *n.* maṣṣar šulmi u balāṭi; → **~ian of a treaty** *n.* bēl adê; → **commander of ~s** *n.* rab maṣṣiri
guest *n.* bēl kusāpi, ubru; → **female ~** *n.* uburtu; → **~-friend** *n.* napṭaru☆
guesthouse *n.* bēt napṭiri☆
guffa *n.* quppu
guffaw *v.* nagāgu☆
guide *n.* rādiu; → **~** *v.* arû C☆ (Gtn), mu''uru☆, radû; → **~ to the right path** *v.* ešēru☆ (Št); → **~lines** *n.* tērtu☆ (pl.)
guile *n.* niklu+
guilt *n.* arnu, ḫiṭītu☆, šērtu B☆; → **~less** *adj.* zakû+
Gula → **temple of ~** *n.* bēt Gula
gulf *n.* nērab tānti*
gull *v.* nakālu+
gullet *n.* lu'u☆, mušēritti☆, quqqubānu+
gullible *adj.* saklu
gully *n.* nadbāktu, nadbāku
gulp *v.* la'ātu☆; → **~ down** *v.* šatû
gum *n.* dūru+; → **~(s)** *n.* laḫšu☆; → **~s** *n.* dūr šinni☆
gurgle *v.* ḫabābu☆
Gurrean *n./adj.* Qurrāiu; → **~(s)** *n.* Qurru
gush *v.* nabā'u☆; → **~ out** *v.* nabā'u☆
gust *n.* zīqu, ziqziqqu☆
gusto *n.* ikku+
gut *v.* ṣarāku☆
Gutian *n./adj.* Qutû☆
gutsy *adj.* rāš libbi☆
gutter *n.* bību, pisannu, rāṭu
gypsum *n.* gaṣṣu
gyrate *v.* gadālu+
haberdashery *n.* anūt kabbê*
habit *n.* kaiamānūtu*; → **~able** *adj.* ša ušābi*; → **~able world** *n.* dadmē☆; → **~ation** *n.* maškunu+; → **~ations** *n.* dadmī☆
habitual *adj.* kaiamānīu
habituate *v.* sadāru (Š)
hack *v.* ḫesû☆, parāmu; → **~ to pieces** *v.* nakāsu (D)
haematite *n.* šaddānu
haemorrhage *n.* naḫšāti☆

haft *n*. šikru B☆
hag *n*. kaššāptu
haggard *adj*. aklu, anḫu
haggle *v*. gamādu+
hail *n*. abnu, šulmu; → **~stones** *n*. aban šamê☆
hair *n*. pērtu, qimmatu☆, šārtu; → **lock of ~** *n*. itqu, kizirtu; → **strand of ~** *n*. apparrītu☆; → **tufted ~** *n*. apparrītu☆; → **~cloth** *n*. saqqu+
haircut *n*. gallābūtu
hairdo *n*. kizirtu
hairdresser *n*. gallābu; → **~'s (salon)** *n*. bēt gallābi
hairpin *n*. kirissu☆
hairslide *n*. kirissu☆
hairwash *n*. mīs pērti*
hairy *adj*. laḫīmu☆, laḫmu☆, šu''uru☆; → **be(come) ~** *v*. šu''uru☆
half *n*. mišlu, muttutu☆; → **in ~** *n*. ana šinīšu, issēn ana šinīšu; → **~-brother(?)** *n*. mār abi; → **~-circle** *n*. uskāru; → **~-cubit** *n*. rūṭu; → **~-grown** *n*. tariu [o.]; → **~-mina** *n*. paras+; → **~-rope (60 cubits = 30 metres)** *n*. ṣuppān☆; → **~-shekel** *n*. zūzu☆; → **~-wit** *n*. lā rāš tašīmti☆; → **~breed** *n*. ballulu
halfway *n*. ina mišil ḫūli [i.]
hall *n*. bētu dannu; → **city ~** *n*. bēt āli; → **~mark** *n*. ginnu☆
hallo *n*. allû☆
hallway *n*. ašlukkatu☆
halo *n*. supūru☆, tarbāṣu
halt *adj*. pessû☆; → **be(come) ~** *v*. uzuzzu; → **~er** *n*. erinnu☆, šummannu☆
halve *v*. ana mišlāni parāsu [i.], ḫapû
hamlet *n*. kapru
hammer *n*. maqqabu☆; → **~ thin** *v*. raqāqu (D)
hamper *n*. ḫuppu, kuruppu
hamster *n*. asqūdu
hand *n*. qātu, rittu; → **~'s breadth** *n*. pušku; → **at ~** *adj*. qurbu; → **back of the ~** *n*. irtu ša qāti☆; → **~ over** *v*. ana qāti mallû [i.], ina qāti manû [i.], manû B, manû ina qāti [i.], pān X šudgulu [i.], šalāmu+ (D), tadānu
handbag *n*. ḫintu
handcuffs *n*. eṣ qāti
handful *n*. upnu☆
handicap *n*. piriktu☆; → **be(come) ~ped** *v*. ina issēt šēpi uzuzzu [i.]
handicraft *n*. lipit qāti☆
handiwork *n*. epšetu, lipit qāti☆, šipir qāti
handkerchief *n*. sasuppu+
handle *n*. naṣbutu, qātu+, rittu; → **~** *v*. abālu B☆ (Gtn), kullu (D)
hands → **both ~** *n*. talīmāni☆, tulīmāni☆; → **lifting of the ~** *n*. nīš qāti☆
handsome *adj*. damqu; → **~ness** *n*. banūtu☆
handwriting *n*. qātu
handy *adj*. qurbu
hang *v*. ana zaqīpi šakānu, e'ālu, zaqāpu+; → **~ (down)** *v*. šuqallulu☆; → **~ on** *v*. kullu (D); → **~ up** *v*. alālu, e'ālu; → **~ing** *adj*. šuqallulu☆; → **~man** *n*. ṭābiḫu
hanker for → **be(come) ~** *v*. ṣaḫātu
happen *v*. bašû (N), epāšu (N), maqātu; → **make ~** *v*. bašû (Š); → **~ successively** *v*. sadāru+
happily *adv*. ḫadīš☆
happiness *n*. bu'āru☆, ḫadûtu, ḫudû, ṭubbāti☆, ṭūbu
happy *adj*. damqu, elṣu☆, ḫadiu, ṭābu; → **be(come) ~** *v*. ḫadû, libbu balāṭu [i.]; → **make ~** *v*. namāru☆ (D)
harass *v*. dalāpu (D), dalāpu (Š), ḫasā'u; → **~ed** *adj*. dalpu; → **~ment** *n*. ḫisiāti, taršītu☆
harbinger *n*. mupassiru
harbor *n*. kāru
hard *adj*. ašṭu☆, da'nu, dannu; → **be(come) ~** *v*. da'ānu, danānu☆; → **be(come) ~-pressed** *v*. siāqu; → **~ of hearing** *adj*. sakkuku; → **give a ~ time** *v*. marāṣu (Š), siāqu (D); → **have a ~ time** *v*. pašāqu B☆ (Št); → **~en** *v*. da'ānu (D), ebû+, šagāgu☆
hardihood *n*. ṣarmūtu+
hardly *adv*. pašqiš☆
hardness *n*. dunnu☆
hardship *n*. dannutu, maruštu☆, šapšāqu☆
hardwood *n*. ēṣu dariu☆
hardy *adj*. patnu☆
hare *n*. arnubu
harelip *n*. arnabānu*
harem *n*. bēt isāti; → **~ woman** *n*. sekrutu
hark *v*. šamû
harlot *adj*. šamḫatu☆
harm *n*. ḫiṭṭu, tukku+; → **~** *v*. be'āšu+ (Š), ḫaṭû, takāku+; → **~less** *adj*. qallīlu
harmonious *adj*. mitguru☆, mitḫāru☆; → **be ~** *v*. maḫāru☆ (Gt)
harmony *n*. mitḫartu☆, mitḫurtu☆
harness *n*. abšānu☆, ḫalluptu; → **~** *v*. rakāsu, ṣamādu; → **~-maker** *n*. ša-ḫalluptēšu; → **~-suit** *n*. ša-ḫallupti; → **~ed** *adj*. raksu, ṣandu☆; → **be ~ed** *v*. ṣamādu☆ (N)
harp *n*. pilaggu; → **small ~** *n*. šebītu
harpoon *n*. pariangu☆
harrow *v*. šakāku☆; → **~(s)** *n*. kibbāni, maškakāti☆; → **~ing** *adj*. kāsip libbi*
harry *v*. dalāḫu+

harsh *adj.* ašṭu☆, dannu, marru B+; → **~ly** *adv.* kî dannati☆; → **treat ~ly** *v.* samāku (D)
haruspex *n.* bāriu; → **chief ~** *n.* rab bārê; → **office of chief ~** *n.* rab bārūti
harvest *n.* ebūru, eṣādu; → **~** *v.* eṣādu; → **~ (grapes)** *v.* baṣāru; → **~ song)** *n.* alāla; → **~ time** *n.* ebūru; → **~er** *n.* ēṣidu
hashish *n.* qunnubu
hasp *n.* mēdelu☆, napraku☆
hassle *v.* ṣâlu [o.]
haste *n.* ḫamuttu☆; → **~n** *v.* arāḫu☆, dalāḫu (D), ḫamāṭu B☆, ḫiāšu☆, radāpu
hastily *adv.* ḫanṭūssu☆, urruḫiš☆; → **do ~** *v.* dalāḫu
hasty *adj.* ḫanṭu B☆; → **be(come) ~** *v.* ezû☆
hat *n.* kubšu
hatch *v.* qalāpu☆
hatchet *n.* akkullu; → **~-faced** *n.* akkullānu; → **~y** *n.* akkullānu
hate *n.* zērūtu☆, zīru; → **~** *v.* ziāru; → **~d** *adj.* zēru☆; → **~ful** *adj.* zēru; → **make ~ful** *v.* nazāru (Š); → **~r** *n.* gaṣṣiṣu, zā'irānu☆
hatred *n.* zērāti☆, zērūtu☆, zīru
hatter *n.* ša-kubšēšu
hauberk *n.* gurpissu, qurpissu
haughtily *adv.* šalṭāniš☆
haughty *adj.* multarḫu☆, šalṭānu☆, šurruḫu☆; → **be ~** *v.* šarāḫu☆ (Dt)
haul *v.* šadādu, zabālu; → **~er** *n.* šaddidu☆
haulm *n.* qanû+
haunch *n.* giššu, rapassu
haunt *v.* naqāpu+, še'û☆ (Gtn)
have *v.* išû☆, kullu (D); → **come to ~** *v.* rašû☆; → **~ difficulty breathing** *v.* na'āšu☆; → **~ enough and to spare** *v.* utāru+ (Š); → **~ hitched up** *v.* rakāsu (Š); → **~ illicit sex repeatedly** *v.* niāku (Gtn); → **~ mercy upon** *v.* rēmu ina muḫḫi/ana X šakānu [i.]; → **~ over and above** *v.* utāru+; → **~ patience** *v.* libbu urruku [i.]; → **~ served** *v.* rakābu (Š); → **~ sex with** *v.* ṭeḫû☆; → **~n** *n.* kāru
havoc *n.* ḫarbūtu+
hawk *n.* kasūsu, surdû☆; → **~er** *n.* saḫḫiru
hay *n.* kissutu+, pu'ē; → **~ field** *n.* tabriu; → **~rick** *n.* kurillu☆; → **~stack** *n.* kurillu☆
hazard *n.* puluḫtu; → **~** *v.* palāḫu☆ (Š); → **~ous** *adj.* [ša] puluḫti*
haze *n.* ḫillu, ripsu
he *pron.* šû, šūtu; → **~-man** *n.* zikāru☆
head *n.* kaqqudu, muḫḫu, rēšu; → **~-lift (part of the exta)** *n.* nīš rēši☆; → **~-scarf** *n.* ša-kaqqidi; → **~ first** *adv.* buppāniš☆; → **~ache** *n.* muruṣ qaqqadi☆, ṣidru+, ṣūdāru+
headband *n.* parsīgu☆, patinnu◊; → **(royal) ~** *n.* pitūtu
headdress *n.* upurtu☆; → **~ (kind of)** *n.* aparakku
headgear *n.* kubšu
heading *n.* elītu
headland *n.* rēš tānti☆
headlong *adv.* buppāniš☆; → **~** *n.* kaqqadānu
headscarf(?) *adj.* maklulu *n.* muklulu
headstrong *adj.* alṭu☆, ašṭu☆
headway *n.* alāk pāni
heal *v.* balāṭu (D); → **~er** *n.* asû+, muballiṭu, mušallimānu; → **~ing** *n.* nablāṭu☆; → **~ing art** *n.* asûtu+; → **~th** *n.* bu'āru☆, šalāmu, šalmūtu☆, šulmu; → **bad ~th** *n.* lā ṭūb šīri; → **ill ~th** *n.* murṣānu+; → **~thy** *adj.* naḫšu☆, šalmu
heap *n.* gurunnu☆, karmu, karmu☆ (ruin); → **~** *v.* kamāru, karāmu B, ṣiānu; → **into a ~** *adv.* gurunniš☆; → **~ of flour** *n.* zidubdubbû☆; → **~ up** *v.* garānu☆ (D), kamāru (D), nakāmu☆, šapāku☆; → **~ed (up)** *adj.* nakmu☆; → **~ed up** *adj.* kitmuru☆; → **be ~ed up** *v.* kamāru☆ (Gt); → **~ing up** *n.* nikimtu [o.]
hear *v.* šamû; → *interj.~ me* anīna; → **~er** *n.* šāmiu*; → **~ing** *n.* našmû☆; → **sense of ~ing** *n.* našmû☆; → **~say** *n.* lišānu; → **~say witness** *n.* šāmiānu☆; → **~t** *adj.* libbu; → **~t** *n.* nupāru☆, ṣurru B☆; → **~t-attack** *n.* tirik libbi; → **~t-beart** *n.* tirik libbi; → **~t-shaped cake** *n.* libbu B; → **~tache** *n.* muruṣ libbi; → **~tbreaking** *adj.* kāsip libbi*; → **~tburn** *n.* ḫimṭēti☆; → **~ten** *v.* libbu šakānu [i.]; → **~th** *n.* kanūnu; → **~tily** *adv.* ina gum libbi [i.]; → **~tless** *adj.* lā pādû☆; → **~ty** *adj.* gāmilu☆, libbānāiu+, rā'imu
heat *n.* ḫimṭu☆, ṣarḫūtu, ṣētu, ṣurḫu, ummu B☆, umšu☆; → **~** *v.* baḫāru☆ (D), ṣarāḫu (D); → **~ stroke** *n.* ḫimiṭ ṣēti☆; → **~ up** *v.* emāmu (D); → **~ing** *n.* taṣriḫtu*
heatwave *n.* umšu☆
heaven *n.* ermiānu☆ (Anu's), šamê; → **~(s)** *n.* šamāmī☆; → **like ~** *adv.* šamāmiš☆; → **~ly** *adj.* [ša] šamê
heaviness *n.* kabdūtu*, kubtu, ṣūdāru+
heavy *adj.* kabdu, kabtu☆; → **by the ~ (weight) standard** *n.* ina danniti [i.]
hectare *n.* imāru
heddle *n.* ṣiṣītu☆
hedge *n.* limītu☆; → **~** *v.* labû
hedgehog *n.* ḫurbabillu
heed *v.* aqû☆ (D), quālu, šamû; → **~ful** *adj.* na'du☆; → **~less** *adj.* lā ḫāsisu☆

heel *n.* asīdu★, eqbu
hegemony *n.* kiššūtu
heifer *n.* sāḫirtu★; → **~ calf** *n.* būrtu B
height *n.* lānu, mēliu, mūlû, šūqu★; → **~en** *v.* šaqû B★ (Š)
heir *n.* aplu, mār rēdûti★; → **~ess** *n.* apiltu★
heliacal rising *n.* nanmurtu★
hell *n.* rikalla; → **~ish** *adj.* adūgāiu+
hello *n.* allû★
helmet *n.* gurpissu, ḫuliam★
help *n.* aiālu, ḫamāti★, kitru, nārārūtu★, nērāru★, nērārūtu★, rēṣūtu★, usutu; → **~** *v.* issi X uzuzzu [i.], katāru, sêdu★, tappūti alāku [i.]; → **get as ~** *v.* katāru; → **~er** *n.* ālik tappūti★, nērāru★, rēṣu★; → **~ful** *adj.* kātiru*, ṭābu; → **~less** *adj.* makiu, pisnuqu★; → **~less** *n./adj.* ulālu; → **~lessness** *n.* ulālūtu★
helter-skelter *adj.* šabalkutu
hem *n.* sissiktu★; → **~erological omen series (name of a)** *adv.* iqqur īpuš; → **~erology** *n.* biblu, inbu bēl arḫi
hemi- *adj.* mišil
hemlock *n.* murdu+
hemming in *n.* mēsēru★
hemorrhage *n.* alāk dāmi
hemp *n.* qunnubu; → **~ flower** *n.* qunnabtu
hen *n.* akkadītu★, tarnugallutu+
henbane *n.* šakirūtu, šakrūnu+
heptad *n.* sebettu★
her *pron.* šāša, šāši, šiāti★; → **~ald** *n.* nāgiru
herb *n.* ḫaṭṭi balāṭi, šammu; → **~ (kind of)** *n.* ḫabbaqūku, ḫambaṣūṣu★; → **~ (kind of; lit. 'pistachio-like')** *n.* buṭnānu; → **~age** *n.* rītu★
Hercules *n.* Kalbu★ (constellation)
herd *n.* sagullu; → **~er** *n.* rā'i sagulli; → **~sman** *n.* nāqidu, rā'iu, utullu★ (chief)
here *adv.* akanna◊, annāka, ḫannāka
hereabouts *adv.* annāka
heritage *n.* zittu
hermit *n.* madbarāiu+, mudabbirānu+, nazīru+
hero *n.* mu'āru★, qarrādu, qurādu, uršānu★; → **~ic** *adj.* dāpinu★, mamlu★, qardu
heroine *n.* qarittu, uršānatu★
heroism *n.* qarrādūtu★, qurdu, uršānūtu★, zikrūtu★
heron *n.* anpatu+, igirû★
hesitant *adj.* nāriṭu
hesitate *v.* katāru B, narāṭu, samû
hesitation *n.* nirriṭu
hew *v.* batāqu, naqāru; → **~ down** *v.* gadāmu+; → **~ out** *v.* naqāru+; → **~ing off** *n.* ḫīpu
hiccup *v.* nuḫḫuṭu★ (D)
hidden *adj.* kanku, katmu★
hide *n.* gildu+, mašku, pāru★; → **~** *v.* katāmu, marqītu aḫāzu★, pazzuru, pesēnu◊, raqû; → **(ox) ~** *n.* gildu; → **tanned ~** *adj.* ṣallu; → **~ous** *adj.* gaṣṣu B★; → **~r** *n.* raqqiu
hiding → **go into ~** *v.* marqītu aḫāzu★, šaḫātu emādu [i.]; → **~ place** *n.* šaḫātu★
hierodule (kind of) *n.* kulmašītu
high *adj.* elû★, qatnu+, šaqiu, šēḫu B★, zaqru★; → **be(come) ~** *v.* šaqû B, zaqāru; → **make ~** *v.* šaqû B★ (D); → **~-handed** *adj.* šuḫdû◊; → **~-mettled** *adj.* šitmuru★; → **~ and low** *adv.* šībūti u ṣeḫrūti [i.]; → **~ up** *adv.* šaqīš★; → **make ~er** *v.* šaqû B★ (Š)
highland *n.* eliāti★ (pl.); → **~er** *n.* šaddāiu★
highlight *v.* šapû★ (D)
highly *adv.* šaqīš★
highness *n.* ṣīrūtu★
highway *n.* ḫūl šarri
hijack *v.* puāgu
hike *v.* alāku, rapādu
hilarious → **be(come) ~** *v.* nagû★
hilarity *n.* nummur libbi★
hill *n.* mēliu, mūlû, tillu; → **~ock** *n.* mēliu; → **~y** *adj.* tillāiu+
hilt *n.* šikru B★
him *pron.* šāšu, šuāšu★
hind part(?) *n.* aqqābu
hinder *v.* kalû, karāmu, parāku (D), sakāru B+
hindmost *adj.* urkīu
hindrance *n.* piriktu★
hinge *n.* mukīl dassi★, nukuššû; → **~ maker** *n.* ša-nukuššēšu
hip *n.* giššu; → **~bone** *n.* giššu; → **~s** *n.* ḫanṣāti★, qablu (pl.)
hire *v.* agāru; → **~(?)** *n.* nāgurtu; → **~d man** *n.* agru; → **~ling** *n.* agru, munnagru
his *pron.* iššû; → **~s** *v.* ḫazû★, lebû★, napāḫu; → **~tory** *n.* narû, ṭēmu
hit *v.* maḫāṣu, šabāṭu B★
hitch *v.* ṣamādu; → **~ up** *v.* rakāsu; → **~ed up** *adj.* ṣandu★
hither *adv.* an-akanna◊, ana annēša, ana nēša, annēša, ḫannēša
hoard *adj.* ḫimmatu★; → **~** *n.* sikiltu★; → **~** *v.* sakālu★; → **~ing** *n.* sikiltu★
hoarfrost *n.* ḫurbāšu★
hoarse *n.* ḫarrūšu+
hoax *n.* niklu; → **~** *v.* niklu nakālu

hobble *v.* egēru⋆ (N), ḫuzzû⋆, kabālu⋆
hoe *n.* allu
hog *n.* ḫuzīru+
hoist *v.* dalû
hold *n.* ṣibtu; → ~ *v.* kullu (D); → **~-up** *n.* uḫḫuru+; → **~ (out)** *v.* anāḫu⋆ (Št), lazāzu; → **~ back** *v.* kalû; → **~ fast** *v.* tamāḫu⋆; → **~ good** *v.* kullu (Dtt); → **~ in** *v.* sakāru B+; → **take ~ of** *v.* ṣabātu; → **take ~ of o.s.** *v.* libbu ṣabātu [i.]; → **~ on** *v.* kullu (D); → **~ out** *v.* qarābu (D); → **~ responsible for** *v.* ina qāti ba''û [i.]; → **~ rule** *v.* šalāṭu+; → **~ sway** *v.* šalāṭu+; → **~ sway over** *v.* biālu, piālu; → **~ to** *v.* kullu (D); → **~ up** *v.* kalû, kullu (Dtt); → **~er** *n.* mukillu
hole *n.* apu, gubbutu+, ḫarūru+, ḫuppu B, ḫuptu, ḫurru, ḫurru+, ḫurrutu, šīlu⋆, takkapu⋆; → **~ (in grindstone)** *n.* ḫarūru⋆; → **~y** *adj.* ḫarūrānu
holiday *n.* šēzubtu⋆, ūmu rāqu
holiness *n.* ellūtu⋆, zakûtu+
holler *v.* bakû (Gtn), ziāqu+
hollow *adj.* ḫarru, paḫḫu+; → ~ *n.* ḫuptu; → **~ out** *v.* ḫarāru⋆, naqāru+
holy *adj.* ellu, qašdu⋆, quddušu⋆; → **~ man** *n.* qašdu⋆, ramku⋆; → **~ of holies** *n.* papāḫu; → **~ person** *n.* qadīšu; → **~ places** *n.* ašrāti⋆ (pl.); → **~ room** *n.* sāgu B⋆
home *n.* bētu
homecoming *n.* erāb bēti*
homeless *n./adj.* muttaprašširu⋆, ša lā bēti
homely *adj.* kaiamānīu
homer *n.* imāru
homeward(s) *n.* ana bēti
homework *n.* liginnu
homicide *n.* nērtu⋆
homogeneous *adj.* mitḫāru⋆
honest *adj.* kēnu, šalmu, tarṣu; → **~ly** *adv.* ina kētti; → **~y** *n.* kēnūtu
honey *n.* dišpu, pār nūbti⋆; → **~-bee** *n.* nūbtu⋆; → **~ cake** *n.* pennigu
honk *n.* niḫru+; → ~ *v.* naḫāru+
honor *n.* nīš rēši⋆, takbittu⋆; → ~ *v.* kabādu (D), kabātu⋆ (D), rēšu našû [i.], uqāru⋆ (Š); → **give/make ~** *v.* uqāru+ (Š); → **~able** *adj.* kabtu⋆, uqru+; → **~ed** *adj.* kabbudu, kabdu, kabtu⋆, kannû, uqru+; → **~ific ceremony** *n.* takbittu⋆; → **~s** *n.* kubādu
hood *n.* ḫullānu
hoodlum *n.* ḫabbilu⋆
hoodwink *v.* sarāru [o.]
hoof *n.* ṣupru
hook *n.* nāqiru⋆ (wall), naṣru; → **~er** *n.* ḫarintu
hoop *n.* kipputu
hoopoe *n.* kubšānu⋆
hoot *v.* naḫāru⋆
hop *v.* raqādu; → **~(s)** *n.* kasūtu
hope *n.* tukultu; → **~ (for)** *v.* puqqu; → **~ in** *v.* takālu; → **~ that** *gram. part.* lū; → **~less** *adj.* lā lē'û⋆
hordes *n.* ummānāti⋆
horizon *n.* išid šamê⋆, nabṭû⋆, šupuk šamê⋆; → **~s** *n.* kibrāti⋆; → **~tal** *adj.* nasku
horn *n.* qarnu; → **~ed** *adj.* qarnānu⋆
hornet *n.* zabbūru+
hornless *adj.* qarūḫu+
horny *adj.* qarnīu
horrible *adj.* pardu⋆
horribly *adv.* pardiš⋆
horrid *adj.* gaṣṣu B⋆
horrify *v.* palāḫu (D)
horror *n.* ḫurbāšu⋆ (cold)
horse *n.* sissû; → **brown ~** *n.* sirpu⋆; → **riding ~** *n.* pētḫallu; → **~-doctor** *n.* muna''išu⋆; → **~-dung** *n.* kabūt sissê; → **~ (breed/color of)** *n./adj.* irginu; → **~ (breed of)** *n.* tuānu; → **~ collector** *n.* mušarkisu; → **office of ~ collector** *n.* mušarkisūtu; → **~ keeper** *n.* mukīl sissê; → **~ nettle** *adj.* karān šēlibi+; → **~ trader** *n.* tankār sissê; → **~ trainer** *n.* sūsānu; → **~ trainer of open chariot** *n.* sūsān ša-pattūti; → **~ trainer of the royal guard** *n.* sūsān ša-šēpi; → **~ trappings(?) (kind of)** *n.* asmāti⋆
horseback → **on ~** *adv.* ina pētḫalli; → **~ riding** *n.* rakāb sissê*
horsefly *n.* ḫanzizītu
horseman *n.* kallāpu (armored), ša-pētḫalli; → **~ship** *n.* ša-pētḫallūtu*
horseradish *n.* gargīru+
horses (kind of) *n.* miṣirānu
hose → **irrigation ~** *n.* zarūgu [o.]
hospitable *n.* māḫirānu+
hospital *n.* bēt Gula; → **~ity** *n.* taknû⋆
host *n.* bēl bēti, ellatu⋆; → **~age** *n.* līṭu⋆, maškānu; → **condition of a ~age** *n.* maškānūtu+; → **condition of being a ~age** *n.* līṭūtu⋆; → **~el** *n.* aštammu⋆, bēt ubri; → **~ess** *n.* bēlat bēti
hostile *adj.* muṣṣālu⋆, nakru, zāmānû⋆; → **be(come) ~** *v.* nakāru
hostilities *n.* zērāti⋆; → **begin ~** *v.* garû⋆
hostility *n.* girūtu, nakrūtu⋆, nukurtu, zērūtu⋆
hot *adj.* emmu [o.], ḫanṭu, ṣarḫu; → **be(come) ~** *v.* emāmu, ṣarāḫu, ṣarāḫu (N); → **very ~** *adj.* ḫummuṭu B⋆; → **~-tempered** *adj.* aggu⋆, ṣarḫu; → **be(come) ~ up** *v.* emāmu; → **~el** *n.* bēt ubri; → **~head** *adj.*

rasmu
hound *n.* kalbu, urgulû☆; → **~'s-tongue** *n.* lišān kalbi☆; → **~s-tongue** *n.* lišān kalbi⁺
hour *n.* bēru; → **double ~** *n.* bēru
house *n.* bētu; → **city ~** *n.* bēt āli; → **master of the ~** *n.* bēl bēti; → **road ~** *n.* bēt urḫi; → **supervisor of the ~** *n.* ša-pān-bēti; → **~-born (slave)** *adj.* unzarḫu; → **(employee) of the ~ of the prefects** *n.* ša-bēt-šaknūti; → **~breaker** *n.* pallišu, sāru
household *n.* bētu
househusband *n.* bēl bēti
housekeeper → **female ~** *n.* abrakkatu☆
housekeeping *n.* abrakkūtu☆
housewife *n.* bēlat bēti, šarrat bēti
housework *n.* dulli bēti
housing *n.* mūšubu
hovel *n.* kurḫu⁺
hover *v.* šuqallulu☆; → **~ about** *v.* parāšu☆ (Ntn)
how? *interr.* aiāka, akê, akkā'i◊, kīkî☆
how long still? *interr.* kī maṣi aḫḫūr
how many? *interr.* kī maṣi
how much? *interr.* kī maṣi, kīma'◊
however *adv.* ū; → **~** *conj.* u
howl *v.* lebû☆, nazāqu☆; → **~ing** *adj.* šegû☆
hub *n.* sarnu⁺
hubbub *n.* ḫubūru☆; → **happy ~** *n.* ḫabību☆
huckster *n.* sūqāiu⁺
hue *n.* ṣīpu
hug *n.* ipqu⁺; → **~** *v.* edēru☆ (N), ḫaṣānu
huge *adj.* gapšu, utru, uttāru; → **be(come) ~** *v.* gapāšu
hull *v.* qalāpu⁺; → **~ of a ship** *n.* išid eleppi☆
hullabaloo *n.* ḫubūru☆
hullo *n.* allû☆
hum *n.* ḫubbu☆; → **~** *v.* ḫabābu☆, lebû☆, zuāmu⁺
human *n./adj.* amēlānu; → **~ being** *n.* amēlu, ṣalmāt kaqqidi☆; → **the ~ species** *n.* amēlūtu
humane *adj.* ra'ūmtānu⁺
humanity *n.* amēlūtu
Humbaba-figurine(?) *n.* ḫumbābarītu
humble *adj.* ašru B☆, maṭiu [o.], šaḫtu☆; → **be(come) ~** *v.* ašāru C☆, šapālu; → **~ o.s.** *v.* qadādu B☆
humbly *adv.* ašriš☆, šukūniš☆
humdrum *adj.* lazzu
humid *adj.* raṭbu; → **~ity** *n.* raṭībūtu⁺
humiliate *v.* šapālu (D); → **~d** *adj.* šappulu
humiliation *n.* tamṭīt pî☆, tašpiltu☆
humility *n.* labān appi☆, makûtu⁺
humming *n.* rimmatu☆
hummus(?) *n.* ḫinḫinu
humor *n.* kabattu, ṣūḫu☆
hump *n.* guggalīpu
humpback *adj.* gabnu◊; → **~ed** *adj.* gabnu◊
hunch *n.* guggalīpu
hunchback *adj.* gabnu◊; → **~ed** *adj.* gabnu◊
hunched *adj.* kappupu, kuppupu☆ (very)
hundred *n./adj.* mēat; → **a ~ times** *adv.* mētāia*; → **~fold** *adj./adv.* mētāia*; → **~th** *adj.* mētāiu*
hundurean → **chief ~** *n.* rab ḫundurāie
hung *adj.* zaqpu⁺; → **~er** *n.* aruštu B☆, berūtu☆, bubūtu, nebrītu☆, unṣu☆; → **~ry** *adj.* bariu; → **be(come) ~ry** *v.* barû; → **make ~ry** *v.* barû (Š)
hunt *v.* ba'āru; → **~er** *n.* ṣaiādu☆; → **~er for blood** *n.* āmir dāmi☆; → **~ing expedition** *n.* daiāltu☆; → **~ing foray** *n.* daiāltu☆
hurdle *n.* sikru☆
hurl *v.* ṣê'u, šalā'u
hurrah → **~** *interj.* illūri
hurricane *n.* anḫullu☆, imḫullu☆
hurried *adj.* lasmu; → **~ly** *adv.* arḫiš, dulluḫiš☆
hurry *n.* duluḫtu◊; → **~** *v.* arāḫu☆, ezû☆, ḫamāṭu B☆, ḫiāšu☆, radāpu; → **~ up** *v.* ḫamāṭu B☆ (D)
hurt *v.* akālu, akālu⁺, be'āšu⁺ (Š), maḫāṣu☆ (D), marāṣu (Š), zaqātu☆; → **~ful** *adj.* marṣu
husband *n.* ḫā'iru☆, ḫābiru, ḫarmu☆, mutu; → **~ of wife's sister** *n.* ikīsu; → **~man** *n.* ikkāru⁺
hush(?) *v.* nazāzu☆ (D)
hush-hush → **~** *interj.* ši' ši'
hush-money *n.* tamgirtu [o.]
hush up *v.* katāmu (D), pesēnu◊
husk *n.* iltu B, pu'ē, qulāptu [o.], qulpu⁺; → **(carob) ~** *n.* ḫarūbu⁺; → **~s** *n.* kuspē; → **~y** *adj.* ḫazû☆; → **be(come) ~y** *v.* ḫazû☆
hussy *n.* ḫarintu
hustle *v.* zuāmu⁺; → **~r** *n.* naiāku☆
hut *n.* kurḫu⁺; → **reed ~** *n.* ḫuṣṣutu, kikkisu, šutukku
hyacinthine *n.* argamannu⁺
Hydra *n.* bašmu
hydrophobia *n.* kalbūtu⁺
hyena *n.* būṣu B☆
hymen *n.* šišītu☆
hymn *n.* pāru C [o.]; → **~ of blandishment** *n.* zamār taknê☆

hypotenuse *n.* ṣiliptu☆ (diagonal)
hyssop *n.* zūpu◊
I *pron.* anāku
ibex *n.* turāḫu
ice *n.* kupû, qarḫu, šurīpu☆; → ~ *v.* qarāḫu (D); → **like** ~ *adv.* šurīpiš☆; → **~-cold** *adj.* qarruḫu*; → **~up** *v.* qarāḫu; → **~box** *n.* bēt maqarti
icon *n.* ṣalmu
idea *n.* ḫissat libbi☆
ideal *adj.* gitmālu☆; → ~ *n.* riddu☆; → ~ **behavior** *n.* riddu
ideas → **ingenious** ~ *n.* nikiltu (pl.)
identical *adj.* mitḫāru☆, mušlu, šutāḫû☆; → **be(come)** ~ *v.* mašālu
identification *n.* messūtu☆
identify *v.* idû☆ (D), mussû◊, mussû☆
idiocy *n.* lillūtu☆, sakkukūtu
idiot *n.* lillu☆
idle *adj.* laššu, mušta''û☆, rāqu; → **be(come)** ~ *v.* riāqu; → **~ness** *n.* rāqūtu, šēṭūtu; → **~r** *n.* mākiu, šēṭu
idol *adj.* ṣalmu+
if *subj.* kî, kīma, šumma, šummu; → ~ **indeed** *subj.* issu maṣi, issu maṣin; → ~ **not** *subj.* ulâ
ignite *v.* napāḫu, napāḫu☆ (D), qâdu☆
ignominy *n.* qulālu+
ignoramus *n.* lā mūdû abiti, sakkuku
ignorance *n.* lā mūdânūtu
ignorant *n.* lā mūdû☆, lā mūdû abiti
ignore *v.* šâṭu B☆; → *interj.~! except for* uššer [o.]; → ~ **continually** *v.* etāqu (Štn)
ill *adj.* marṣu; → **be(come)** ~ *v.* marāṣu; → **fall** ~ *v.* marāṣu+; → **~-advised** *adj.* lā mitluku☆; → **~-fated** *adj.* lammunu, lumnānû☆; → **~-wisher** *n.* ḫādiānu
illegitimate *adj.* lā kēnu
illicit *adj.* ḫarmu+
illiterate *adj.* saklu
illness *n.* murṣu, sili'tu☆
illogical *adj.* lā mitḫuru
illuminate *v.* namāru (Š), namāru☆ (D), napardû☆ (Š)
illumination *n.* namirtu☆
illusion *n.* sebīrūtu+
illustrate *v.* namāru (Š)
illustrative *adj.* munammiru☆
illustrious *adj.* edû, šanu''udu☆, šāpû
image *n.* ṣalmu, uṣurtu+
imagination *n.* ḫissat libbi☆, sebīrūtu+
imagine *v.* dagālu*, eṣāru+
imbalanced *adj.* lā šitqulu☆
imbecile *n.* lā rāš tašīmti☆; → ~ *n./adj.* ulālu
imbibe *v.* šatû
imbue *v.* reḫû☆
imitate *v.* mašālu (Š), mašālu☆ (D), paggû* (D)
imitation *n.* muššultu☆
imitator *n.* mupaggiānu+, mupeggû☆
immaculate *adj.* šaklulu
immaterial *adj.* qallīlu
immature *adj.* lā bašlu
immediate *adj.* ḫanṭu B☆; → **~ly** *adv.* ina muḫḫi ašli, qerbiš☆
immerse o.s. *v.* šalû☆
immigrant *n.* ubāru; → ~ **(group)** *n.* ēribtu
immigration *n.* ubārūtu◊
imminence *n.* qurbūtu
imminent *adj.* qurbu; → **be(come)** ~ *v.* qarābu
immobile *adj.* lā āliku
immobilize *v.* ḫamû☆, kabālu☆ (D)
immoderate *adj.* paḫzu, sarḫu+
immolation *n.* zību B+
immortal *adj.* dārīu; → **~ity** *n.* dārūtu
immovable *n.* lā muttalliku*
immutable *adj.* ša lā šunnê
imp *n.* šēdānu+
impact *n.* miḫṣu
impair *v.* anāšu (D), lamānu (D); → **~ment** *n.* tānīštu [o.]
impale *v.* ana zaqīpē šēlû☆, ana zaqīpi šakānu, ana ziqīpi zaqqupu☆, zaqāpu☆ (D)
impart *v.* šamû (Š), zuāzu
impassable *adj.* lā etāqi☆
impatience *n.* karû ikki
impatient → **be(come)** ~ *v.* ikku karû [i.]
impeccable *adj.* zakû
impede *v.* parāku (D)
impediment *n.* piriktu☆
impel *v.* daḫû+
impending *adj.* qurbu
impenetrable *adj.* sakku☆; → **be(come)** ~ *v.* sakāku
imperative *adj.* dannu
imperceptibly *adv.* ana lā amāri [i.]
imperfect *adj.* lā gitmālu☆
imperial *adj.* [ša] šarrūti☆, šalṭānu☆, šitluṭu☆; → **~ly** *adv.* šalṭāniš☆, šalṭiš☆, šitluṭiš☆
imperil *v.* palāḫu☆ (Š)
imperious *adj.* šalṭānu☆; → **~ly** *adv.* šalṭāniš☆
impersonate *v.* epāšu (D)
impertinent *adj.* erḫu☆
imperturbable *adj.* nēḫu
impetuosity *n.* paḫzānūtu+

impetuous *adj*. rasmu, šamru, šitmāru*, šitmuru*; → **~ly** *adv*. šamriš*, šitmuriš*
impetus *n*. mudakkītu*
impish *adj*. lāzinu*
implacable *adj*. lā gāmilu*
implant *v*. zaqāpu; → **~ed** *adj*. naṣību+, zaqpu
implement *n*. nēpešu*; → **~ (kind of)** *n*. ḫutugu; → **iron ~ (kind of)** *n*. arsallu, qaspu; → **~s** *n*. anūtu, unūtu*
implicated *adj*. qurbu ina libbi; → **~** *v*. qarābu ina libbi
implication *n*. ḫakimtu*
implied *adj*. ḫakmu
implore *v*. sarruru
imply *v*. ḫakāmu, qabû
impolite *adj*. lā radiu+
imponderable *adj*. ḫasāsiš lā naṭû*
import *v*. miāru+; → **~ance** *n*. kubtu; → **~ant** *adj*. kabdu, kabtu*; → **be(come) ~ant** *v*. kabādu, kabātu*
importunate *adj*. lazzu+; → **~ person** *n*. lazzuzu+
importune → **be(come) ~** *v*. lazāzu+
impose *v*. emādu, emādu (D), nadû*
imposing *adj*. gapšu, rašbu*
imposition *n*. indu, šiknu
impossible *adj*. lā naṭû*
impost *n*. iškāru; → **~or** *n*. sarru*
impotence *n*. šarbābu*
impotent *adj*. šarbubu
impoverish *v*. lapānu* (D); → **~ed** *adj*. ekû*; → **~ment** *n*. ekūtu*
impracticable *adj*. ša ana epāši lā illakūni [i.]
impregnate *v*. reḫû*
impress *n*. ṭibḫu; → **~** *v*. takāpu; → **make ~ upon** *v*. birti ēnē maddudu [i.]; → **~ion** *n*. tikpu B, ṭibḫu; → **~ionable** *adj*. raggūštānu+
imprint *n*. tikpu B, unqu; → **~** *v*. takāpu
imprison *v*. kalû, pâdu*; → **~ment** *n*. mēsēru*, ṣibittu*
improbable *adj*. da'nu
improper conduct *n*. lā riddu*
improprieties *n*. nullāti*
improve *v*. damāqu (D), našāru (N), ṭiābu (D); → **~ment** *n*. tadmiqtu [o.]
imprudent *n*. lā muštālu*
impudence *n*. lā būštu*, miqit pê*, sullû B*, šillatu*
impudent *adj*. erḫu*, lā ādiru*; → **make ~** *v*. paḫāzu+ (Š)
impulse *n*. bibil libbi*
impurity *n*. aršūtu*, lu'āti*
in *prep*. ina, ina libbi, ina qereb*; → **give ~** *v*. kanāšu*, salāmu+; → **~-house** *adj*. [ša] bēti; → **~ every respect** *pron*. kalāma*; → **~ s.o.'s way** *n*. ina pī ḫūli (to be) [o.]; → **~ the way** *n*. ina pī ḫūli (to be) [o.]
inability *n*. lā lē'ûtu*
inaccessible *adj*. kuttumu*, lā a'āri*
inaccurate *adj*. lā ḫarṣu*
inactive → **be(come) ~** *v*. quālu
inadequate *adj*. lā naṭû*, lā sapqu*
inadvertently *adv*. ina lā mūdānūti [i.], ina šēṭūti*
inalterable *adj*. ša lā innennû*, ša lā šunnê
inamimate *adj*. lā balṭu*
inapt *adj*. lā simāti*
inarticulate *adj*. ḫazû*, lā ḫakmu, lā ḫarṣu*
inasmuch as *subj*. aššu*, issu maṣi
inattentive → **be(come) ~** *v*. šelû◊
inaugurate *v*. šarrû
inauguration *n*. šarrû; → **~ feast** *n*. tašrītu B*
inauspicious *adj*. lā ṭābu, lamnu
incalculably *adv*. ina lā minātīšu*
incantation *n*. šiptu; → **~ formula (kind of)** *n*. enūru*
incapacitated *adj*. ṣabbutānu
incarnate *adj*. pagguru+
incarnation *n*. pagrānūtu+
incendiary *n*. mušadbibu
incense *n*. suādu
incentive *n*. mudakkītu*
incessant *adj*. lā naparkû*; → **~** *n*. lā mupparkû*
inch *n*. ubānu
incidence *n*. miqtu
incident *n*. miqtu; → **~ally** *adv*. aḫīta [o.]
incipient *adj*. šarrāiu+
incise *v*. esēqu*, ḫarāṣu, naqāru+, uqqû*
incision *n*. niksu
incite *v*. aḫāzu* (Š), dabābu (Š), dakû, dakû◊ (D), kadāru C* (Š); → **~ment** *n*. dīku; → **~r** *n*. munappiḫu*
inclement *adj*. lā pādû*
inclination *n*. qūptu*
incline *n*. kinšu*; → **~** *v*. qâpu*, šapālu (D); → **~ towards** *v*. pānē ana X šakānu [i.]; → **~d** *adj*. quppu B*
inclining *adj*. qaiāpu*
include *v*. esāru, ṭaḫû (D)
including *prep*. adi, adu
incoherent *adj*. lā mitḫuru
income *n*. irbu, miḫirtu B*; → **~r** *n*. ēribtu, ēribu
incomparable *adj*. lā šanān*
incompatible *adj*. lā mitguru*

incompetence *n*. lā lē'ûtu☆
incompetent *adj*. lā lē'û☆, saklu
incomplete *adj*. lā gamru, maṭiu
incomprehensible *adj*. ša lā iḫakkimūni
inconceivable *adj*. ḫasāsiš lā naṭû☆
incongruous *adj*. lā mitguru*
inconsiderate *adj*. lā mitluku☆, rešû☆
inconsistent *adj*. lā mitḫuru, pitrusu☆
inconstant *n*. lā kaiamānīu*
incontestable *adj*. ša lā paqāri
inconvenience *n*. maruštu☆
inconvenient *adj*. lā tarṣu
incorrect *adj*. lā kēnu, lā tarṣu; → ~ **behavior** *n*. lā šalāmu☆
incorruptible *adj*. lā māḫir šulmāni*
increasable *adj*. narbû☆
increase *n*. rubê, šumūdu◊, tarbītu+; → ~ *v*. aṣābu◊, ma'ādu, rabû, šadālu☆ (D), uṣābu, utāru (D), utāru (Š); → **make** ~ *v*. ma'ādu (Š)
incredible *adj*. lā qēpu
incredulous *adj*. lā qēpu
incriminate *v*. ḫiṭṭu emādu
incubate *v*. qapāpu+
inculcate → **make** ~ *v*. birti ēnē maddudu [i.]
incur *v*. rašû☆; → **~able** *adj*. lā pašāḫi☆, lā paṭāri, ša lā balāṭi, ša lā paṭāri; → **~able** *n*. lā tēbû☆; → **~sion** *n*. šiḫṭu
indebted *adj*. ḫabbulu; → **be(come)** ~ *v*. ḫabālu
indecency *n*. lā būštu☆
indecision *n*. sūmu B☆
indeed *adv*. ibašši, kēttu
indefatigable *adj*. lā āniḫu☆
indefinite *adj*. lā parsu*
indemnify *v*. šalāmu (D)
independence *n*. lā ḫanšūtu*
independent *adj*. lā ḫanšu
index finger *n*. ubānu šanītu☆
India *n*. Sindu☆; → **~n** *n./adj*. Sindāiu☆
indicate *v*. kallumu (D), qabû, qabû ana, ša'ūdu (Š)
indictment *n*. ḫalpūtu [o.]
indifference *n*. šēṭūtu
indifferent *adj*. šēṭu
indigenous *adj*. unzarḫu
indignant *adj*. šabsu◊
indignation *n*. libbāti
indignity *n*. lā simtu☆
indigo-blue *n./adj*. ṣalittu
indiscreet *adj*. lā pitqudu*
indiscriminate *adj*. lā pārisu*
indisposed *adj*. marṣu
indisputable *adj*. ša lā paqāri
indissoluble *adj*. ša lā pašāri

individual *adj*. issēnīu; → ~ *n*. napšutu
indolence *n*. egûtu, makûtu B
indolent *adj*. makiu B, šēṭu
indoors *adv*. bētānu, ina bētāni
induce *v*. aḫāzu☆ (Š); → **~ment** *n*. šulmānu
indulge *v*. ramû; → **~nce** *n*. ennānāti (pl.) [o.], pīdu
industrious *adj*. ēpišu; → **~ness** *n*. ēpišūtu
industry *n*. ummânūtu+
inebriate → **make** ~ *v*. šakāru (D); → **be(come) ~d** *v*. šakāru
ineffectual *adj*. lā ēpišu, lā kušīri+
inefficiency *n*. lā ēpišūtu*
inefficient *adj*. lā ēpišu, lā lē'û☆
inept *adj*. lā lē'û☆, samû; → **be(come)** ~ *v*. samû
inequality *n*. lā mitḫārūtu*
inert *adj*. lā ēpišu; → **~ia** *n*. lu'tu☆
inescapable *adj*. lā šēzubi*
inessential *adj*. qallīlu
inevitably *adv*. ina šīmti*
inexact *adj*. lā ḫarṣu*
inexhaustible *adj*. ša lā iggammaru☆
inexorable *adj*. lā pādû☆
inexperienced *adj*. lā lamdu☆
inexpertly *adv*. ina lā mūdānūti [i.]
inexplicable *adj*. ša lā pašāri
infallible *adj*. lā māqitu*, ša lā paqāri, taklu
infamous *adj*. bīšu◊
infamy *n*. lā būštu☆, šumu lā damqu
infancy *n*. lakûtu, ṣeḫēru☆
infant *n*. lakû, šerru☆; → ~ **at the breast** *n*. ša-irti
infantile *adj*. [ša] šerri*
infantry *n*. kimarru☆, zūku; → **heavy** ~ *n*. zūk šēpi☆; → **~man** *n*. rādiu
infatuated → **be** ~ *v*. lallû B+ (Dt)
infect *v*. lapātu; → **~ion** *n*. masla'tu☆
infectious *adj*. muštaḫḫizu☆
infer *v*. ḫarāṣu (Št) [o.]; → **~ence** *n*. tušaḫruṣu [o.]
inferior (one) *n*. aḫurrû☆
infiltrate *v*. ḫalālu
infinity *n*. lā qītu*
infirmity *n*. lā ṭūb šīri
infixed *adj*. qablīu☆
inflamed *adj*. ḫanṭu; → ~ *n*. ḫitmuṭu☆; → **be(come)** ~ *v*. ḫamāṭu☆
inflamed,ardent *adj*. ṣarḫu
inflammable *n*. munnapḫu*
inflammation *n*. ḫunṭu, li'bu☆, ṣiriḫ libbi☆
inflammatory fever *n*. išāt ṣimirti+

inflated *adj.* napḫu; → **be** ~ *v.* napāḫu (N)
inflation *n.* isiltu★
inflexible *adj.* lā muktappu*
inflict *v.* nadû★
influence *v.* lapātu
influential person *n.* maṣātānu
influenza *n.* murṣu šatti
inform *v.* ḫakāmu (Š), idû★ (Š), lamādu (Š), qabû, ša'ūdu (Š), šamû (Š), udû (D) [o.], uznē pattû [i.]; → **~ant** *n.* lišānu; → **~ation** *n.* batiqtu, lišānu, mandītu◊, ša-pê; → **~er** *n.* bātiqu, lišānu, ša-lišāni
infrequent *adj.* uqru
infuriate *v.* agāgu★ (D); → **~d** *adj.* šegû★, uggugu★
infuse *v.* tabāku
infusion *n.* ribku★
ingenious *adj.* naklu
ingenuity *n.* nikil libbi★, nikiltu
ingenuous *adj.* atra ḫasīsi★
ingot *n.* lišānu
ingrafted *adj.* naṣību+, zaqpu
ingratitude *n.* lā ḫasās ṭābti★
ingredient *n.* ḫišiḫtu★; → **~s** *n.* maškattu◊
ingress *n.* nērubu
inhabit *v.* ušābu; → **~ant** *n.* āšibu; → **~ed** *adj.* ašbu★; → **~ed regions** *n.* dadmī★
inhale *v.* napāšu
inherit *v.* zittu batāqu [i.]; → **~ance** *n.* urkutu, zittu
inhibit *v.* parāku (D)
inhospitable *adj.* nanduru★
inhuman *n.* lā amēlu
inimical → **make** ~ *v.* nakāru (Š); → **~ly** *adv.* nakriš★
iniquity *n.* šillatu★
initial *adj.* šarrāiu+; → **~ly** *adv.* issu rēši
initiate *n.* mūdû; → ~ **proceedings** *v.* ṣāssu garû; → **~d** *adj.* lamdu★, lammudu; → **~d** *n.* mūdû pirišti★; → **be ~d** *v.* malû+ (Št)
injure *v.* maḫāṣu, takāku★; → **~d** *adj.* laptu B
injurious *adj.* lazzu+
injury *n.* miḫṣu, te'iqtu★, tukku+
injustice *n.* ḫabālu★, pariktu, pirku, riggatu
inland *n.* libbi māti
inlay *n.* niḫsu, tamlītu; → ~ *v.* aḫāzu (D), ra'āzu★, ṣapāru★
inlet *n.* pû
inmate *n.* āšibu, ṣabtu
inmost *adj.* bētānīu; → ~ **(part)** *n.* libbānu★
inn *n.* bēt ubri; → **~-keeper** *n.* sābiu
innards *n.* kabattu
innate *adj.* naṣību+, uldu
inner *adj.* bētānīu, ša bētāni; → ~ *n.* libbānu★
Inner City *n.* Libbi-āli
inner parts *n.* bētāniāti
innermost part *n.* durgu★
innocence *n.* zakûtu+
innocent *adj.* lā lamdu★, zakû+; → **hold** ~ *v.* zakû+ (D)
innocuous *adj.* šalmu
innovation *n.* tēdištu★
innovator *n.* muddišu★
innumerable *adj.* lā mīnu★, lā nībi
inordinate *adj.* paḫzu
inquest *n.* maš'altu★
inquire *v.* ša'ālu
inroad *n.* šiḫṭu
insane *adj.* maḫḫû★
insanity *n.* miqit ṭēmi★
insatiable *adj.* ša lā iššabbû★
inscribe *v.* šaṭāru, uqqû★; → **~d** *adj.* šaṭru; → **~d slab** *n.* asumittu
inscription *n.* malṭuru, musarû★, muššarû, šiṭir šumi★, šiṭru★, šumu šaṭru★
inscrutable *adj.* rūqu★
insect(s) *n.* kalmutu
insect (kind of) *n.* burbillutu, išdi bukāni, kuluppu, šubabītu
insecure *adj.* lā taqnu*
insert *v.* zaqāpu
inset *v.* ṣapāru★
inside *adj.* libbu; → ~ *n.* qerbēnu★, qerbu★; → ~ *n./adj.* bētānu, libbānu★; → ~ *prep.* ina qereb★, qabsi
insight *n.* ḫissat libbi★, pīt uzni★
insignia *n.* simtu; → **royal** ~ *n.* simāt šarrūti★
insignificant → **be(come)** ~ *v.* qalālu
insincere *adj.* lā kēnu, lā šalmu
insinuate *v.* laḫāšu+
insipid *adj.* lā ṭābu
insist *v.* radāpu; → **~ent** *n.* rādipu*
insolence *n.* mēreḫtu★, tuššu★
insolent *adj.* erḫu★, paḫḫuzû◊; → **be(come)** ~ *v.* erēḫu★, paḫāzu; → **~ly** *adv.* ekṣiš★
insoluble *adj.* ša lā pašāri
inspect *v.* amāru, ḫiāru, rēšu našû [i.], ṣubbû★; → **~ed** *adj.* amru; → **~ion** *n.* amirtu★, aširtu, masnaqtu★, māšartu; → **~or** *n.* ḫaiāṭu★, ḫazannu
inspiration *n.* nipḫu
inspire *v.* napāḫu+; → ~ **awe** *v.* palāḫu★

(Š); → **~d** *adj.* napḫu⁺, nappuḫu☆
install *v.* retû☆, ṣabātu (Š), šakānu, ušābu (Š); → **~ in a place of residence** *v.* ramû B☆ (Š), ušābu (Š); → **~ed** *adj.* ṣabbutu
instant *n.* riggu⁺, ṣibit appi☆
instantaneous *adj.* ḫanṭu B☆
instead *adv.* ina kūmi, ina kutalli, ina pūḫi, issi qanni, kīmu☆; → **~ (of)** *prep.* kūmu; → **~ of** *prep.* ina kūm, libbû◊
instep *n.* irat šēpi☆
instigate *v.* dabābu (Š), dakû◊ (D)
instigator *n.* ēpišānu, mušadbibu
institute *v.* kuānu (D), šakānu (Š)
instruct *v.* âru☆ (D), ḫakāmu (Š), lamādu (D); → **~ed** *adj.* lammudu; → **~ion** *n.* iḫzu☆, mardûtu⁺, tērtu☆; → **~ions** *n.* šipāru☆; → **~ive** *adj.* mušaḫkimu*; → **~or** *n.* mulammidu☆
instrument *n.* tiriṣ qāti
insubordinate *adj.* lā ḫanšu; → **be(come) ~** *v.* kadāru C☆
insubordination *n.* lā ḫanšūtu*
insubstantial *n.* daqqiqu☆
insufficient *adj.* ēṣu B, lā sapqu*, maṭiu; → **be(come) ~** *v.* mâṣu☆, šiāṣu
insular *adj.* nagiānu*, parsu⁺
insulate *v.* peḫû☆
insult *n.* magrītu☆, mēreḫtu☆, migirtu☆, pištu☆, qulālu, te'iqtu☆; → **~** *v.* massuḫu [o.], ṭapālu☆; → **~ing** *adj.* magrû☆
insuperable *adj.* lā šanān☆
insurgent *n.* bēl sīḫi, tēbû☆
insurmountable *adj.* lā elê☆
insurrection *n.* bārtu, nabalkattu☆
intact *adj.* balṭu, šalmu
integral *adj.* šallumu⁺
integrate → **make ~** *v.* pâ ištēn šuškunu [i.]; → **~ with** *v.* samāḫu (D)
integrity *n.* šalmūtu⁺
intellect *n.* murqu☆, ṭēmu
intelligence *n.* bišīt uzni☆, ḫasīsu, pīt ḫasīsi☆, pīt uzni☆, ṭēmu
intelligent *adj.* ḫāsisu, ḫassu, palka uzni☆, rāš uzni☆
intelligible *adj.* ḫakmu, murruqu◊
intemperance *n.* paḫzūtu⁺
intend *v.* ṣamāru☆
intense *adj.* dannu; → **be(come) ~** *v.* šapû☆; → **~ly** *adv.* adanniš
intensify *v.* da'ānu (D), danānu☆ (D), šapû☆ (D)
intensity *n.* dannutu
intent *adj.* ṣāmiru*; → **~** *n.* ṣumru☆; → **be ~ on** *v.* ṣamāru☆ (Gt); → **~ion** *n.* ṣammuru☆, ṣibūtu☆, ṣumrāt libbi☆; → **~ional** *adj.* ṣamru*; → **~ionally** *adv.* ina ḫūd libbi [i.]
interact *v.* aḫāiš uppušu
intercalary *adj.* diri; → **~ Adar** *n.* Addāru diri
intercalate *v.* darāru, darû B
intercede *v.* abbūtu ṣabātu [i.]
intercept *v.* kalû⁺
intercession *n.* abbūtu
intercessor *n.* ṣābit abbūti
interconnected *adj.* itḫuzu☆
interest *n.* rubê; → **~ (on money etc.)** *n.* ṣibtu B [o.]; → **be(come) ~ed in** *v.* uznu ana X šakānu [i.]
interfere *v.* aḫu tabālu [i.], aḫu ubālu [i.], qātu ubālu [i.]
interior *adj.* libbu; → **~** *n.* karšu, qerbītu☆; → **~** *n./adj.* bētānu
interlace *v.* šatû B☆
interlock *v.* elēpu☆ (Št); → **be ~ed** *v.* elēpu☆ (Gt)
intermeddle *v.* aḫu tabālu [i.]
intermediary *n./adj.* pāris birti*, ša birti
intermediate *adj.* qablīu☆, ša birti
intermingle *v.* balālu (N), issi aḫāiš sammuḫu, nadānu☆ (Št)
intermission *n.* baṭlu
intermittently *adv.* ina birīt
internal *adj.* bētānīu; → **~ disease (kind of)** *n.* tašnīqu☆; → **~ organ (kind of)** *n.* qarrurtu; → **~ organs** *n.* bētāniāti, unūt libbi
interpose *v.* birti X parāsu [i.], ina birti šakānu
interpret *v.* parāsu, pašāru, targumu⁺; → **~ation** *n.* pišru; → **~er** *n.* nāpalû☆, pāširu, targumānu
interrogate *v.* sanāqu (D), ša'ālu, ša'ālu⁺
interrogation *n.* maš'altu☆
interrogative *adj.* šā'ilu
interrupt *v.* baṭālu☆ (Š), murrû◊; → **~ed** *adj.* baṭlu; → **~ion** *n.* baṭiltu☆, baṭlu
intersection *n.* ispillurtu, sūq erbetti☆
interspace *n.* birītu B☆
interstice *n.* itannu☆
intertwine *v.* elēpu☆ (Št), kapālu☆ (Gt), qapālu☆ (Gt), šutēlupu☆; → **~d** *n.* itguru☆
interval *n.* baṭlu, birītu B☆, kīlu☆
intervene *v.* ebāru ina birti
interview *n.* šitūltu☆
interweave *v.* gadālu⁺, sabāku☆
intestine → **large ~** *n.* šammāḫu☆; → **~ (kind of)** *n.* naḫtu, umandu☆; → **~s** *n.* bētāniāti, errē; → **~s(?) (part of)** *n.* emātu
intimacy *n.* qurbūtu
intimate *adj.* qurbu; → **~** *v.* laḫāšu
intimidate *v.* galādu (D), šaḫātu B☆ (D)

intimidator *n.* mugallitu☆
into *prep.* ana, ina, ina; → **~lerant** *adj.* lā šādidu*; → **~nation** *n.* zimru☆; → **~ne** *v.* zamāru
intoxicate *v.* šakāru+ (D); → **~d** *adj.* šakru+
intrepid *adj.* lā ādiru☆, lā pāliḫu, ṣarmu+
intricate *adj.* naklu
intrigue *n.* niklu
introduce *v.* erābu (Š), qarābu (D)
introduction *n.* šērubtu*
intrude *v.* da'āni erābu [i.], erābu
intuition *n.* bišīt milki☆, ḫissat libbi☆
intuitive *adj.* rāš uzni☆
inundate *v.* bâ'u☆ (Š), raḫāṣu B
inundation *n.* šurdūtu◊
inure *v.* sadāru (Š)
invade *v.* maqātu
invalid *adj.* kabbulu, laššu, naḫru [o.]; → **~ate** *v.* naḫāru B☆ (D), pasāsu
invaluable *adj.* šūquru☆, uqru adanniš
invariable *n.* lā muštannû*
invasion *n.* tibûtu☆
invection *n.* ṭapiltu☆
invective *n.* pištu☆
inveigh against *v.* karṣē akālu [i.]
invent *v.* nakālu; → **~ory** *n.* amirtu☆
inverse *adj.* nabalkutu
inversion *n.* nabalkattu☆
invert *v.* nabalkutu (Š); → **~ed** *adj.* nabalkutu; → **be(come) ~ed** *v.* nabalkutu
invest *v.* šapāku☆, šapāku [o.]
investigate *v.* ḫâṭu☆, ḫiāṭu☆, uṣṣuṣu (D); → **~ thoroughly** *v.* ša'ālu uṣṣuṣu
investigation *n.* teb'ītu☆, ṭerdu☆
investiture *n.* piqittu
investment *n.* naruqqu
investor *n.* tankāru
inveterate *adj.* šarrušu+
invidious *adj.* mušanziru*
invigorate *v.* balāṭu (D)
invisibly *adv.* ana lā amāri [i.]
invitation *n.* qarētu+
invite *v.* qarû; → **~d (guest)** *n./adj.* sasiu
inviting *adj.* kazbu☆
invocation *n.* zakār šumi☆, zuqāru
invoke *v.* karābu, saqāru, šasû☆, zakāru☆
involuntary *n.* lā ḫādiu*
involved *adj.* qurbu ina libbi; → **be(come) ~ in s.th.** *v.* qarābu ina libbi
involvement *n.* qurbūtu
inwardly *adv.* ana bētāni, šaplānu-
inwards *adv.* ana bētāni
Ionia *n.* Iauna; → **~n** *n./adj.* Iamnāiu☆, Iaunāiu

irascible *adj.* aggu☆, šabbāsu☆
irate *adj.* zenû☆
iridescent *n.* šit'āru☆
iris *n.* burum ēni☆
irk *v.* nazāqu☆ (Š)
iron *n.* parzillu; → **scrap ~** *n.* ḫušê parzilli*; → **wrought ~** *n.* parzillu sakru; → **~-worker** *n.* tebīru; → **~ peddler** *n.* ša-parzilēšu; → **~y** *n.* šinṣu☆
irradiate *v.* barāḫu☆ (D)
irrational *n.* lā rāš ṭēmi u milki☆
irreal *adj.* lā kēnu
irreconcilable *adj.* lā māgiru☆, lā mitguru*
irregular *n.* lā kaiamānīu*; → **~ity** *n.* lā kaiamānūtu*
irrelevant *adj.* lā qurbu
irresistible *adj.* lā maḫār☆, ša lā immaḫḫaru☆
irresponsible *adj.* lā nāši pūtuḫi*
irreverent *adj.* lā pāliḫu
irreversible *adj.* lā mušpēlu
irrigate *v.* makāru☆, šaqû
irrigation *n.* mikru☆, šīqu; → **provide ~** *v.* makāru☆ (Š)
irritable *adj.* nazziqu☆; → **be(come) ~** *v.* ikku karû [i.]
irritate *v.* akālu, ikku karû* (D)
is not *gram. part.* ia'nu◊
ischias *n.* muruṣ qabli☆
island *n.* nagû B☆
isle *n.* nagû B☆
isn't *v.* laššu
isolate *v.* ḫarāmu☆, parāqu☆, parāsu, šēpu parāsu [i.]
isolation *n.* ašar šēpu parsat☆, mēsēru☆
Israel *n.* Bēt Humrî
issue *n.* ṣītu☆; → **~** *v.* radû+, uṣû
isthmus *n.* lišānu+, nēberānu+
it *pron.* šî, šīti; → **~ (is)** *pron.* šû
itch *n.* ḫarāsu☆, rišūtu☆; → **~** *v.* ekāku, ḫarāsu☆, rašû B☆; → **~ing** *n.* ekketu☆
item *n.* bābu☆
itinerary *n.* rikis gerri☆
itsy-bitsy *n.* daqqiqu+
itty-bitty *n.* daqqiqu+
Itu'ean *n./adj.* Itu'āiu; → **~(s)** *n.* Itu'u; → **commander of ~s** *n.* rab Itu'āiē
ivory *n.* šinni pīri
Iyyar *n.* Aiāru (month)
jab *v.* da'āpu
jackal *n.* zību
jackass *n.* imāru
jackdaw *n.* āribu☆, qāribu
jaded *adj.* anḫu

Jaffa *n.* Iappû
jagged *adj.* sikrānu+
jaggy *adj.* sikrānu+
jail *n.* bīt siggi◊; → **~er** *n.* ša-bēt-kīli☆
jam *v.* kasāru
jamb *n.* sippu
jangle *v.* ṣâlu [o.]
janitor *n.* maṣṣar bābi, ša-bābi
jar → **two-seah ~** *n.* kaptukku; → **~ (for ointment)** *n.* pūru B
jargon *n.* lišān ummâni*
jasper *n.* ašpû
jaundice *n.* aḫḫāzu☆, amurriqānu☆
javelin *n.* asmarû☆, ḫutennu☆; → **~ (kind of)** *n.* puašḫu☆
jaw *n.* isu☆; → **~s** *n.* pû
jay *n.* qīqu+
jealous *adj.* qāni'u*; → **be(come) ~** *v.* qenû☆; → **~ person** *n.* ḫādiānu; → **~y** *n.* ḫaddânūtu*
jeer (at) *v.* lazānu
jeering *n.* liznu*
jeopardize *v.* palāḫu☆ (Š)
jerboa *n.* akburu; → **female ~** *n.* akbartu
jerk *n.* giddagiddû☆, tību; → **~** *v.* damû◊, šalāḫu
Jerusalem *n.* Ursalimmu
jest *n.* namūtu [o.]; → **~** *v.* namūtu epāšu [o.]; → **~er** *adj.* ēpiš namūti [o.]; → **~er** *n.* aluzinnu☆, muṣiḫḫu☆
jet *v.* nabā'u☆ (Š), nabā'u☆; → **~ty** *n.* kāru
Jew *n.* Iaūdāiu
jewel *n.* aban balti, aban nisiqti☆, abnu aqartu☆, tiqnu☆; → **~er** *n.* zadimmu☆; → **~ry** *n.* dumāqu, šakuttu, šukānu☆; → **~ry(?) (piece of)** *n.* šikku; → **~ry (piece of)** *n.* algumiš☆, allu, gusīgu
Jewess *n.* Iaūdītu*
Jewish *adj.* Iaūdāiu
jingle *n.* ḫalālu B, tigû☆
job *n.* īnu☆
jocund *adj.* ḫadiu
join *v.* emādu, rakāsu, ṣamādu; → **~ in** *v.* samāḫu (Dtt); → **~ together** *v.* dabāqu+ (D); → **~ up** *v.* emādu (N); → **~ed** *adj.* ṣandu; → **~er** *n.* naggāru; → **~t** *n.* kiṣru, šer'ānu+; → **do ~tly** *v.* karāku
joker *adj.* ēpiš namūti [o.]; → **~** *n.* aluzinnu☆
jokester *adj.* ēpiš namūti [o.]; → **~** *n.* aluzinnu☆
jolly *adj.* elṣu☆
jolt *v.* narāṭu (D), nâšu☆ (D)
jostle *v.* zuāmu+
jot *n.* kirṣu; → **~ down** *v.* ana ḫissiti šaṭāru [i.], arḫiš šaṭāru
journey *n.* ḫarrānu, māluku, mardītu; → **~** *v.* alāku, radû+; → **~man** *n.* šamallû
jovial *adj.* elṣu☆
joy *n.* elēṣ libbi☆, ḫadûtu, ḫidâti, ḫidûtu, ḫidûtu☆, ḫudû, ḫūdu, ilṣu, mēleṣu☆, nummur pāni☆, rīšāti; → **~-maker** *n.* ḫidâtānu; → **~of heart** *n.* ḫūd libbi; → **~ful** *adj.* elṣu☆, ḫadiu; → **sing a ~ful song** *v.* alālu B☆ (Gt); → **~fully** *adv.* elṣiš☆, ḫadīš☆, ina ḫidâti [i.], ulṣāniš☆; → **~ous song** *n.* elēlu☆
jubilant → **make ~** *v.* šūlulu☆
jubilation *n.* elēlu☆, ḫidâti, rīštu◊
Judah *n.* Ia'ūdu☆
judge *n.* daiānu; → **~** *v.* diānu; → **chief ~** *n.* sartennu☆, šartennu; → **supreme ~** *n.* diqugallu☆; → **~-like** *n.* daiānānu; → **~ship** *n.* dā'inūtu☆, daiānūtu☆
judgment *n.* dēnu, šipṭu☆, tašīmtu☆; → **pass ~** *v.* diānu; → **~-like** *n.* dēnānu; → **~al** *n.* dēnānu
judicature *n.* daiānūtu☆
judicial *adj.* dēnāiu+
judiciary *n.* daiānūtu☆
judicious *adj.* muštālu☆
jug *n.* assammu☆
juice *n.* mê, mēzu
juicy *adj.* mēzīu*; → **~ part** *n.* nurbu☆
July *adv.* Ta'ūzu (month)
jump *v.* šaḫāṭu C☆
junction *n.* ispillurtu
June *n.* Simannu (month), Simānu☆ (month)
junior *adj.* arkû☆, qatnu, šūbulti inbi☆, urkīu; → **~** *n.* aḫurrû☆
juniper *n.* burāšu (prickly), daprānu (Syrian), duprānu☆, duprānu (Syrian), šimšālu+, tupru [o.]
Juniperus drupacea *n.* duprānu☆
Jupiter *n.* Bēl
just *adj.* išaru☆, kēnu; → **~** *adv.* annūrig; → **~ a little** *n.* ammār rūṭi; → **~ice** *n.* išartu◊, mēšāru, mīšartu◊; → **in ~ice** *adv.* mīšariš☆; → **~ification** *n.* tazkītu☆
justified, *adj.* kunnu
justify *v.* kuānu (D), zakû+ (D); → **~ o.s.** *v.* zakû+
justly *adv.* kēniš, mīšariš☆
jut (out) *v.* magāgu
juvenile *adj.* ṣaḫūrānīu*; → **~** *n.* ṣaḫurtu, ṣeḫru
Kanun *n.* Kanūnu (month)
kebab *n.* immeru gabbubu
keel *n.* eṣenṣēr eleppi☆; → **~ plank** *n.* eṣenṣēr eleppi☆

keen *adj.* ḫarīpu+, qatnu+; → **be(come) ~** *v.* šapû⋆; → **very ~** *adj.* ṣarramu⋆

keep *v.* kullu (D); → **~ from** *v.* sakāru B+, šēpu parāsu [i.]; → **~ on** *v.* kullu (D); → **~ to** *v.* kullu (D); → **~ up** *v.* kullu (D), zanānu B⋆; → **~er** *n.* mukillu, ṣābitu

kelek *n.* kalakku

ken *v.* udû+

kernel *n.* abnu, kullu B, še'u

kettle *n.* ruqqu, tapḫu; → **small ~** *n.* tamgussu; → **~-stand** *n.* kandalu⋆; → **~-stand-like** *n.* kandalānu; → **~ room** *n.* bēt asalli; → **~drum** *n.* lilissu; → **~r** *n.* ša-dūdēšu

key *n.* namzāqu⋆, naptû⋆, napṭartu⋆; → **~(?)** *n.* uppu

kick *v.* napāṣu, rapāsu+; → **~ up** *v.* šalû B⋆

kid *n.* laliu; → **(male) ~** *n.* gadiu; → **~ as expiatory sacrifice** *n.* mašḫultuppû⋆; → **~nap** *v.* bašāmu C⋆, mašā'u; → **~ney** *n.* kalītu; → **~ney stone** *n.* ṣimirtu+

kill *v.* duāku, nêru⋆, šagāšu; → **cause the ~** *v.* muātu (Š); → **~er** *n.* dā'ikānu◊, dā'iku⋆

kiln *n.* atūnu, kīru, kūru; → **~ (part of)** *n.* bubû

kilogram *n.* manû

kilt *n.* sāgu (short)

kin *n.* kimtu; → **~ by marriage** *n.* salātu B⋆; → **~d** *adj.* damqu, pašru⋆, ṭābu; → **~d** *n.* šiknu; → **~dle** *v.* aḫāzu (Š), namāru (Š), napāḫu, qâdu⋆, šarrû; → **~dle fire** *v.* išātu karāru [i.]; → **~dled** *adj.* napḫu⋆; → **~dling** *n.* qīttu⋆; → **chips for ~dling** *n.* gibillu??◊; → **~dly** *adv.* damqiš [o.], ṭābiš⋆; → **treat ~dly** *v.* kunnû⋆ (D); → **~dness** *n.* de'iqtu, gimillu⋆, ṭēbūtu, ṭūbtu◊; → **~dred** *adj.* qurbu

king *n.* etellu⋆, malku⋆, rubā'u [o.], šarru; → **~'s affair** *n.* abat šarri; → **would-be ~(?)** *n.* šaršarru; → **great ~** *n.* šarru rabiu; → **image of ~** *n.* ṣalam šarri; → **substitute ~** *n.* šar pūḫi; → **~dom** *n.* šarrūtu; → **~ship** *n.* malkūtu⋆, rubūtu B⋆, šarrūtu; → **would-be ~ship(?)** *n.* šaršarruttu

kink *n.* patlūtu+

kinsman *n.* aḫu+

kip (down) → **be(come) ~** *v.* ṣalālu⋆

Kislev *n.* Kislīmu (month)

kiss *v.* našāqu

kitchen *n.* bēt nuḫatimmi

kitten *n.* mūrānu

knack *n.* niklu

knead *v.* luāšu⋆; → **~ing-trough** *n.* aṣūdu+; → **~ing bowl** *n.* aṣūdu

knee *n.* birku⋆, burku

kneel *v.* kamāṣu; → **have ~ down** *v.* kamāsu B⋆ (Š)

knife *n.* patru; → **sharp ~** *n.* quppû⋆; → **small ~** *n.* uṣultu; → **~ (kind of)** *n.* pašultu⋆

knight *n.* kallāpu (armored)

knit *v.* kamādu◊; → **~ter** *n.* kāmidu

knitwear *n.* anūt kamādi*

knob *n.* karru⋆, pingu

knock *n.* miḫṣu; → **~** *v.* da'āpu, maḫāṣu; → **~ down** *v.* da'āpu, nakāpu⋆ (D); → **~ out** *v.* magguru+

knoll *n.* tillu, tilūlītu+

knot *n.* kiṣru; → **~** *v.* kaṣāru; → **~ together** *v.* šatû B⋆; → **~ted** *adj.* kaṣru; → **~ted(?)** *adj.* sāiu

know *v.* idû⋆, lamādu [o.], udû; → **let ~** *v.* ḫakāmu (Š); → **~-how** *n.* mūdût šipri; → **~ (sexually)** *v.* lamādu [o.]; → **~ing** *adj.* mūdû; → **~ledge** *n.* edûtu⋆, mūdânūtu, mūdûtu⋆, nindānu B⋆; → **possessor of secret ~ledge** *n.* mūdû pirišti⋆; → **~ledgeable** *adj.* mūdû; → **~n** *adj.* udû; → **~n** *n.* medû◊; → **make ~n** *v.* idû⋆ (Š), ša'ūdu (Š), udû (D) [o.]

knuckle *n.* kursinnu

kohl *n.* guḫlu; → **~ pen** *n.* makaḫalūtu

kor (c. 8 bushels) *n.* kurru B⋆

kowtow *v.* kanānu (Štn) [o.]

labdanum *n.* lādunu⋆

labia *n.* lipiššāti⋆

labor *n.* mānaḫu⋆; → **~** *v.* anāḫu, pašāqu B⋆ (Št); → **be in ~** *v.* ḫarāšu B⋆, ḫiālu, ḫiālu; → **woman in ~** *n.* ḫaiāltu, muštapšiqtu [o.]; → **~-duty superior** *n.* bēl ilki; → **~ pain** *n.* ḫilu B⋆; → **~er** *n.* ēpiš dulli, nasīḫu⋆

laborious *adj.* marṣu, šupšuqu⋆; → **~ly** *adv.* marṣiš, šūnuḫiš⋆; → **very ~ly** *adv.* šupšuqiš⋆

lace *n.* pitiltu; → **~** *v.* šapû B⋆; → **~rate** *v.* šalāqu, šatāqu+

lack *n.* mēkūtu◊, muṭê; → **~** *v.* maṭû, zammû; → **~ of strength** *n.* lu'tu⋆; → **~ of things** *n.* laššūtu; → **be(come) ~ work** *v.* riāqu

lackey *n.* ša-bēti-šanie

lacking *adj.* maṭiu; → **be(come) ~** *v.* maṭû

lactic *adj.* ḫilbānāiu+

lad *n.* qallu

ladanum *n.* lādunu⋆

ladder *n.* mašḫaṭu⋆, nabalkattu⋆, simmiltu; → **~s** *n.* mēliu (pl.)

laden (with) *n.* ṣēnu B⋆

laden with *n.* nāšiu

ladle *n.* gidimmu

lady *n.* bēltu, etellutu⋆, šarrutu; → **~ of the house** *n.* bēlat bēti, šarrat bēti; → **~like** *adv.*

bēltānu; → ~ly *adv*. bēltānu
lag (behind) → **be(come) ~** *v*. namarkû
lagoon *n*. agammu; → **~s** *n*. berāti☆
lair *n*. gab'u, narbāṣu☆
laity *n*. saklūtu*
lake *n*. tāntu; → **~-shore** *n*. kibri tānti☆; → **~side** *n*. aḫ tānti☆, kišād tānti☆
lamb *n*. kalūmu◊; → **(male) ~** *n*. puḫādu; → **female spring ~** *n*. ḫurāptu; → **spring ~** *n*. ḫurāpu; → **~ (female)** *n*. puḫattu; → **like ~s** *adv*. kalūmiš☆
lame *adj*. ḫunzû☆, kabbulu, pessû☆, ṣabbutānu, ṣabbutu☆; → **~** *n*. ḫummuru◊; → **~** *v*. šamāmu☆; → **~nt** *v*. nabû☆ (D), ṣarāḫu B☆; → **~ntation** *n*. arūrūtu, dimmatu☆, girrānu☆, killu, qubbû☆, sipittu☆, taqribtu☆, tazzimtu, tēnintu☆; → **perform a ~ntation** *v*. taqribtu epāšu [i.]; → **sing a ~ntation** *v*. ṣarāḫu B☆; → **~nt** *n*. rigmu
lamp *n*. bēt būṣinni, būṣinnu, mušanmirtu, nūru
lampblack *n*. šu'ru+
lamppost *n*. mukīl nūri*
lance *n*. asmarû☆, kutāḫu; → **~t** *n*. karzillu☆, uṣultu
land *n*. eqlu, erṣutu☆, kaqquru, mātu, unnātu☆; → **~** *v*. ana kibri emādu [i.], emādu; → **bare/undeveloped plot of ~** *n*. puṣû; → **bottom ~** *n*. ušallu; → **chief of untilled ~** *n*. rab ḫarbi; → **cultivated ~** *n*. mērēšu; → **dry ~** *n*. nābalu☆; → **enemy ~** *n*. māt nakiri; → **native ~** *n*. mātu; → **pasture ~** *n*. qarbatu☆; → **plot of ~** *n*. kaqquru, pūru; → **tilled ~** *n*. šabburtu☆; → **turn into dry ~** *v*. nābališ turru [i.]; → **uncultivated ~** *n*. kišubbû☆, nidūtu☆; → **uninhabited ~** *n*. nidūtu☆; → **untilled ~** *n*. ḫarbūtu, nidūtu☆; → **waterlogged ~** *n*. saḫḫu☆; → **~-surveyor** *n*. māšiḫ eqli☆; → **~ (kind of)** *n*. kabakku; → **~ newly brought into cultivation** *n*. taptiu; → **~ed (person)** *n*. bēl eqli; → **~ing** *n*. emādu; → **~ing-place** *n*. kāru; → **~ing stage(?)** *n*. ḫūqu
landlady *n*. šarrat bēti
landowner *n*. bēl eqli
lane *n*. sulû☆, suqāqu, sūqinnu [o.]
language *n*. lišānu; → **~d** *n*. bēl lišāni
languid *adj*. muqqu☆, šarbubu; → **be(come) ~** *v*. rabābu
lantern *n*. bēt nūri☆, dipāru, šāšītu☆
lap *n*. birku☆, burku, sīqu (pl.), sūnu
lapidary *n*. zadimmu☆
lapis lazuli *n./adj*. iqnû; → **greenish ~** *n*. zagindurû
lapse *n*. ḫiṭītu☆
larceny *n*. šarqūtu
lard *n*. nāḫu; → **~er** *n*. ḫuršu [o.]
large *adj*. rabbû☆, rabiu, rapšu; → **~-scale** *adj*. rapšu; → **by the ~ (measure)** *n*. ina danniti [i.]; → **~ly** *adv*. rapšiš☆
lark *n*. kubšānu+
larva *n*. mūnu
lascivious *adj*. paḫzu+; → **~** *n*. ṣāḫitu; → **~ness** *n*. paḫzūtu+
lash *n*. agap ēni☆, ṭīru; → **~** *v*. ṭerû; → **~ (of whip)** *n*. dirratu☆
lass *n*. qallassu
lassitude *n*. lu'tu☆
lasso(?) *n*. ašqulālu☆
last *adj*. urkīu; → **~** *v*. anāḫu☆ (Št); → **~ forever** *v*. darû; → **~ year** *adv*. šaddaqdiš; → **~ year** *n*. šaddaqad◊; → **~ly** *adv*. urkītu*
latch *n*. mēdelu☆, sukru+
late → **be(come) ~** *v*. kuāšu, namarkû, uḫḫuru; → **~ly** *adv*. issu ḫaramme; → **~r** *adj*. arkû☆, urkīu; → **~r** *adv*. ḫarammāma, ullīš☆, urkēte; → **do ~r** *v*. uḫḫuru; → **~r (on)** *adv*. arkiš☆; → **~r time** *n*. arkītu◊, urkītu; → **~ral** *adj*. [ša] batti*; → **~st** *adj*. urkīu
latrine *n*. asurrû☆
latter *adj*. urkīu
lattice *n*. birru
laud *v*. na'ādu (D)
laugh *n*. ṣūḫu☆; → **~** *v*. ṣiāḫu☆; → **make ~** *v*. ṣiāḫu☆ (D); → **~ a lot** *v*. ṣiāḫu☆ (Gtn); → **~able** *adj*. ṣuḫḫu☆; → **~ing** *adj*. ṣuḫḫu☆; → **~ingstock** *n*. ṣuḫītu◊; → **be(come)/made a ~ingstock** *v*. ana ṣuḫīti šakānu [i.]; → **~ter** *n*. ṣīḫtu☆, ṣūḫu☆
launch *v*. karāru; → **~ing roller** *n*. girmadû☆
launderer *n*. ašlāku, pūṣāiu
laundry *n*. bēt pūṣāie; → **~ work** *n*. pūṣammūtu☆
lavatory *n*. bēt musâti☆, musâti☆
lavish *adj*. šurruḫu☆
law *n*. dīnu☆
lawabiding *adj*. pāliḫ šarri
lawful *n*. šalṭu+; → **~ly acquired** *adj*. zarpu laqiu
lawman *n*. ša-dēnāni
lawn *n*. dīšu+
lawsuit *n*. dēnu; → **start a ~** *v*. ṣāssu garû
lax *adj*. ramû; → **~ity** *n*. nīd aḫi☆
lay *v*. karāru; → **~ (down)** *v*. šalā'u [o.]; → **~ across** *v*. parāku; → **~ aside** *v*. šalāḫu+; → **~ bare** *v*. garādu+; → **~ claim to** *v*. paqāru; → **~ down** *v*. nadû☆; → **~ down(?)** *v*. šerû☆; → **~ flat** *v*. niālu (D), saḫāpu, sapānu; → **~ foundations of** *v*. rašādu☆ (Š); → **~ hands on** *v*. qātu šakānu [i.], qātu ummudu

[i.]; → ~ **hold (of)** *v*. sabāku+ (D); → ~ **in order** *v*. sadāru+; → ~ **low** *v*. šapālu+ (D); → ~ **near** *v*. qarābu+ (D); → ~ **off** *v*. patû (D), rammû (D), riāqu (Š); → ~ **on** *v*. šaṭāru+ (Š); → ~ **out** *v*. bašāmu☆, šeṭû☆; → ~ **rafters or planks** *v*. ṣallulu+; → ~ **under spell** *v*. kašāpu☆; → ~**er** *n*. nadbāku, šibḫu☆, šišītu☆, tikpu; → ~**er of straw (under or over a stack of corn)** *n*. tarāmu+
layout *n*. šikittu☆, šiknu, uṣurtu
laziness *n*. egûtu, makûtu B
lazy *adj*. egû, makiu B; → **be(come)** ~ *v*. egû, makû B; → ~**bones** *n*. naiālu
lead *n*. abāru, annuku, ṣerretu☆; → ~ *v*. radû; → ~**-gray** *adj*. abārāiu+; → ~ **astray** *v*. sagû+ (Š); → ~ **away** *v*. abāku; → ~ **in** *v*. abāku; → ~ **into exile** *v*. galû (Š); → ~ **rope** *n*. ṣerretu☆; → ~**en** *adj*. abārāiu+; → ~**er** *n*. ālik pāni, massû◊, rādiu; → ~**er** *n./adj*. ašarēdu; → ~**ership** *n*. ālik pānûtu◊, ašarēdūtu, rā'iūtu
leaf *n*. dappu+, ḫasḫaltu☆
league *n*. bēr kaqqiri
leak *v*. natāku; → ~**age** *n*. tattiktu☆; → ~**ing** *adj*. šurdû☆
lean *adj*. qatnu+; → ~ **against** *v*. emādu; → ~ **on** *v*. emādu
leap *v*. pazāzu+, šaḫāṭu C☆; → ~ **up and down** *v*. šaḫāṭu C☆ (Gtn); → ~ **year** *n*. šattu diri [i.]
learn *v*. aḫāzu, lamādu; → ~**ed** *adj*. lamdu☆, litmudu☆; → ~**ed (man)** *adj*. mūdû; → ~**ing** *n*. iḫzu☆, ummânūtu
lease *n*. šūṣûtu☆, tēṣītu☆; → ~ *v*. uṣû (Š)
leaseholder *n*. bēl eqli*
leash *n*. ṣerretu☆
leather *n*. mašku; → **tanned** ~ *n*. duḫšiu, risittu◊; → ~**-worker** *n*. aškāpu; → ~ **(kind of)** *n*. tunimmu; → ~ **master** *n*. rab maški; → ~ **object (kind of)** *n*. ginisû, kāpilu; → **chief** ~**worker** *n*. rab aškāpi
leave *n*. rāqūtu; → ~ *v*. alāku (Gtt), ezābu [o.], rammû (D), uṣû; → ~**(?)** *v*. naṣālu☆; → ~ **behind** *v*. ezābu [o.], riāḫu (Š); → ~ **loose** *v*. paḫāzu (Š); → ~ **out** *v*. abāku; → ~ **overnight** *v*. biādu☆ (Š); → ~ **someone's side** *v*. idu naparkû [i.]; → ~**n** *n*. enṣu+, sikkatu; → ~**n** *v*. emēṣu+ (D); → **green** ~**s** *n*. ḫasḫaltu☆, ḫašḫaltu
Lebanon *n*. Labnāna
ledge *n*. pasqu☆; → ~**s** *n*. gisallāti☆ (pl.)
lee *n*. ṣulūlu
leech *n*. asû+
leek *n*. karšu B, kurissu; → ~ **(kind of)** *n*. bišru, giršānu, šušrāti
left *n*. šumēlu; → ~**-handed** *adj*. šumēlānu*; → ~**-sider (he who sits at the left side)** *n*. ša-šumēli
Left House → **(employee) of the** ~ *n*. ša-bēt-šumēli; → ~**/Palace** *n*. bēt šumēli
left over → **be** ~ *v*. ezābu (Š), riāḫu, šêtu☆; → **be(come)** ~ *v*. utāru+
leftover *n*. rēḫtu; → ~**s** *n*. rēḫāti (pl.)
leg *n*. purīdu, sisītu; → **lower** ~ *n*. kinṣu; → ~ **(of a piece of furniture)** *n*. kablu
legacy *n*. zittu
legal claim *n*. buqurrû◊
legal opponent *n*. bēl dabābi
legal provision *n*. dīnu☆
legally → **do** ~ *v*. zarāpu
legate *n*. qēpu; → ~**ship** *n*. qēpūtu
legation *n*. qēpūtu
legend *n*. narû
leggings *n*. šaḫarrāti (pl.)
legion(s) *n*. emūqu (pl.)
legitimacy *n*. kēnūtu
legitimate *adj*. kēnu
legs → **hind** ~ *n*. ḫallāni
leisure *n*. multa''ūtu☆, mussa''ītu; → **at** ~ *adj*. mušta''û☆, rāqu; → ~ **time** *n*. mussa''ītu; → ~**ly** *adv*. nēḫiš☆
lend *v*. ḫabālu (D), qiāpu; → ~**er** *n*. qā'ipānu [o.]
length *n*. māraku☆, mišiḫtu☆, mūruku☆; → ~**en** *v*. arāku (D), arāku (Š)
lengthwise *adj*. pūt šiddi*
lengthy *adj*. arku, urruku*
lenient *adj*. rabbu B
lens(?) *n*. ša-tāmarti
lentil *n*. abšu, kakkû☆
Leo *n*. urgulû☆
leopard *n*. nemru+; → **she-** ~ *n*. nemrutu+; → ~**ess** *n*. nemrutu+
leper *n*. garbānu
leprosy *n*. šaḫaršuppû
leprous → **be(come)** ~ *v*. garābu; → ~**(?)** *adj*. gurruṣu◊
lesion *n*. simmu, urāšu☆
less *prep*. maṭi; → ~**-** *adj*. ša lā; → ~**en** *v*. maṭû, maṭû (D), ṣaḫāru (D); → ~**er** *adj*. ṣeḫru
lesson *n*. liginnu
lest *subj*. kūm
let *gram.part*. lū; → ~ *v*. tadānu; → ~ **boil** *v*. bašālu (Š); → ~ **dwell in security** *v*. šubat nēḫti šūšubu [i.]; → ~ **go** *v*. segû◊ (Š), uššuru (D); → **be(come)** ~ **languish** *v*. rabābu; → ~ **languishing** *adj*. šarbubu; → ~ **let languish** *v*. rabābu (Š); → ~ **relax** *v*. rabābu (Š); → ~ **simmer** *v*. bašālu (Š)
lethal *adj*. [ša] muāti

letter *n.* egertu, našpartu; → **~-scroll** *n.* sipru◊
lettuce *n.* ḫāsu
level *adj.* nasku; → ~ *v.* sapānu; → **upper ~** *n.* rigbu⋆; → **~ with** *n.* sapnu issi [i.]
lever *n.* kalkaltu⋆
levy *n.* dakûtu, dikûtu, ullūtu; → ~ *v.* dakû; → **official in charge of ~** *n.* rab batqi
lewd *adj.* paḫzu+; → **act ~ly** *v.* paḫāzu+ (D)
lexicon/encyclopedia (name of a) *n.* urra ḫubullu⋆
liabilities *n.* u'iltu (pl.)
liability *n.* e'iltu⋆; → **guarantor's ~** *n.* tarkistu⋆
liable *adj.* nāši pūtuḫi*
liar *n.* parrāṣu⋆, sarru⋆
libate *v.* naqû, ṣarāru (D)
libation *n.* maqqītu, maqqû, ṣurāru; → **~ bowl** *n.* munaqqītu, pagulu; → **~ vessel** *n.* muṣarrirtu; → **~ vessel (kind of)** *n.* tirimtu
libel *v.* karṣē akālu [i.]
liberal *adj.* libbu rapšu [i.], qaiāšu⋆, ṭābtā-nu
liberate *v.* durāru šakānu [i.], paṭāru; → **~d** *adj.* paṭru
liberation *n.* piṭru C⋆
liberty *n.* zakûtu
libido *n.* nīš libbi⋆
Libra *n.* zibānītu
librarian *n.* ša-pān-girginakki*
library *n.* gerginakku⋆, girginakku⋆
licentious *adj.* paḫzu+; → **be ~** *v.* paḫāzu+ (Dt)
lichen *n.* katarru
lick *v.* lâšu B⋆, naṣābu⋆; → **~ (up)** *v.* liā-ku⋆
lid *n.* naktumu; → **stone ~** *n.* makkūtu B+
lie *v.* nadû⋆ (stat.), parāṣu⋆, salû, salû (Gtn), sarāru [o.]; → **~ down** *v.* niālu, sakāpu B⋆, utūlu⋆; → **be(come) ~ down** *v.* rabāṣu, ṣalālu⋆; → **~ flat** *v.* naparqudu⋆; → **~ in ruins** *v.* namû B⋆; → **~ in wait** *v.* rabāṣu; → **~ on back** *v.* naparqudu⋆; → **be(come) ~ round** *v.* saḫāru (stat.); → **be(come) ~ still** *v.* ṣalālu⋆; → **~ supine** *v.* naparqudu⋆; → **~ waste** *v.* ḫarābu⋆; → **~s** *n.* kazbūtu⋆, sar-rāti⋆, siliāti, surrāti⋆; → **tell ~s** *v.* parāṣu⋆
lieu of → **in ~** *prep.* ina kūm, kūmu
lieutenant *n.* laputtû◊, rab ḫanšê
life *n.* balāṭu, napšutu; → **prime of ~** *n.* lalû; → **~-giving** *adj.* [ša] balāṭi; → **~less** *adj.* lā balṭu*; → **~span** *n.* middat balāṭi*; → **~time** *n.* balāṭu, balṭūtu
lift *v.* elû (D), matāḫu, našû; → **~ (nose/lip)** *v.* ganāṣu⋆; → **~ up** *v.* zaqāpu+; → **be ~ed** *v.* matāḫu (N); → **~ing** *n.* nišītu⋆, nīšu
ligament *n.* šer'ānu
light *adj.* qallīlu+, qallu; → ~ *n.* būṣinnu+, namirtu⋆, nannaru⋆, numūru, nūru, ṣētu; → ~ *v.* napāḫu, napāḫu⋆ (D); → **be(come) ~** *v.* qalālu; → **red ~** *n.* sāntu B; → **~-minded** *adj.* qallulu; → **~ up** *v.* barāṣu⋆, namāru (Š), napāḫu; → **~en** *v.* namāru (Š), namāru⋆ (D), napardû⋆ (Š); → **~er** *n.* munappiḫu⋆; → **~ing** *n.* qīttu⋆; → **~ly** *adv.* qalliš⋆; → **~ning** *n.* birqu, išātu; → **strike by ~ning** *v.* ba-rāqu⋆ (Š); → **stroke of ~ning** *n.* miqitti išāti
like *adj.* mušlu; → ~ *prep.* libbû◊; → ~ *prep./subj.* akī, kî, kīma; → ~ *v.* ḫadû; → **make ~** *v.* maḫāru (Š); → **in ~ manner** *adv.* kî annimma; → **~able** *adj.* maḫru; → **~ness** *n.* bunnannê⋆ (facial), muššulu⋆, ṣalmu, tamšīlu B⋆; → **in the ~ness of** *n.* meḫret⋆
likewise *adv.* issēniš, kî annimma; → **make+do ~** *v.* maḫāru (Š); → **do ~** *v.* mašālu (Š)
Lilith *n.* lilītu⋆
lily *adv.* šūšanu+; → **~ of the valley** *n.* šūšan unqi+
limbs *n.* mešrēti⋆, mināti⋆ (pl.)
lime *n.* gaṣṣu, gaṣṣu+; → **~(?)** *n.* kiškanû; → **~-tree** *n.* kiškanû; → **~stone** *n.* pūlu; → **fossiliferous ~stone** *n.* ašnan A⋆; → **like ~stone** *adv.* pīlāniš⋆; → **~stone (kind of)** *n.* pindû; → **~stone peddler** *n.* ša-pūlēšu; → **~stone store** *n.* bēt pūli
limit *n.* pāṭu⋆, taḫūmu; → ~ *v.* maṣāru◊ (D); → **to the ~** *adj.* ana ṣirê◊; → **~ed** *adj.* sakkuku
limp *adj.* ḫunzû⋆, ramû; → ~ *v.* ḫuzzû⋆, kabālu⋆; → **be(come) ~** *v.* ramû
limpid *adj.* ḫalṣu
limping *adj.* kabbulu, pessû⋆
line *n.* kisittu⋆, qû B⋆ (measuring), sidru, šumu; → **front ~** *n.* taḫūmu; → **royal ~** *n.* zār šarri, zēr šarrūti⋆; → **~ up** *v.* sadāru; → **~age** *n.* kisittu⋆
lineaments *n.* zīmu (pl.)
linen *n.* kitû; → **fine ~** *n.* būṣu; → **~ gar-ment** *n.* kitû; → **~ master** *n.* rab kitê
linger *v.* kullu (D), saḫāru [o.]; → **~ on** *v.* dalāpu
lining *n.* tamlītu
link *n.* kiṣru, riksu, šeršerru⋆; → ~ *v.* rakāsu; → **~ together** *v.* ṣamādu
linseed *n.* zēr kitî⋆
lint *n.* širṭu; → **~el** *n.* ḫittu⋆
lion *adj.* lab'u [o.]; → ~ *n.* labbu⋆, nēšu,

ūmu B*, urmāḫu*; → **big ~** *n*. piriggallû*; → **like a ~** *adv*. labbiš*; → **~-eagle** *n*. anzû; → **~-headed demon (kind of)** *n*. ugallu*; → **~-like** *adv*. labbānu; → **~ess** *n*. labbatu*, nēštu*; → **~ly** *adv*. labbānu
lip *n*. šaptu; → **raise the ~** *v*. ḫanāṣu*; → **~ service** *n*. dabābti šapti
liquefaction *n*. šiḫiltu+
liquefy *v*. naḫarmuṭu* (Š), pašāru+
liquid *adj*. naḫarmuṭu*, pašru*; → **~ate** *v*. gamāru, naḫarmuṭu* (Š)
liquorice *n*. sūsu, šūšu*; → **~ tree** *n*. sūsu
lisp *v*. la'āzu+
list *n*. qātu; → **~en** *v*. šamû (Gtn); → **~en to** *v*. šamû; → **~ener** *n*. šāmiu*; → **~less** *adj*. lā ṣāḫitu*; → **~lessness** *n*. lā ṣaḫātu*
litany *n*. naqbītu
liter *n*. qû
literature *n*. ṭupšarrūtu
litigant *n*. bēl ṣāssi (legal)
litigate *v*. dabābu, dēnu garû, ṣāssu garû
litigation *n*. dabābu
litter *n*. eršu, ḫāmu, līdu, rubṣu*, ziblu
little *adj*. daqqu*, ēṣu B, qallīlu+, qallu; → **be(come)+too ~** *v*. mâṣu*; → **open a ~** *v*. ṣalāpu+ (D); → **a ~** *adj*. qallīlu+; → **a ~** *adv*. ēṣe; → **a ~** *n*. ammār rūṭi
live *v*. balāṭu, kamāsu (D), ušābu; → **~ in** *v*. kullu (D); → **make ~ in bondage** *v*. kamīš šūšubu [i.]; → **~ in peace** *v*. pargāniš rabāṣu [i.]; → **~ longer than** *v*. paršumu (D)
livelihood *n*. akullû
liveliness *n*. balṭūtu
lively *adj*. balṭu, tēbû*
liver *n*. amūtu*, kabattu, tērtu*; → **~ omen** *n*. tērtu*
livestock *n*. būlu, maršītu, umāmu
livid *adj*. abārāiu+
living *adj*. balṭu; → **~ being** *n*. šikin napišti*, šiknat napišti*; → **~ quarters** *n*. maštaku*; → **~ space** *n*. bēt ušābi*
lizard *n*. ṣurārītu*, ṣurīrītu, ṣurīrû; → **(yellow) ~** *n*. ṣurārītu+; → **~ (kind of)** *n*. anduḫallutu, ḫulmiṭṭu*
load *n*. biltu, ṣēnu B+, šuqlu [o.]; → **~** *v*. rakābu (Š), ṣiānu; → **~ (the bow)** *v*. malû (D)
loaf *n*. aklu, garīṣtu; → **be(come) ~** *v*. makû B; → **~er** *n*. baṭṭālu+, mākiu
loan *n*. pūḫu; → **~** *v*. ina pūḫi tadānu [i.]; → **on ~** *adv*. ina pūḫi
loath *adj*. lā māgiru*
loathe *v*. ziāru
loathful *adj*. zēru
loathing *n*. zīru
loathsome *adj*. zēru, zēru*
lobby *n*. ašlukkatu*
lobe *n*. uzuntu*
local (inhabitant) *n*. mār nagie
locality *n*. ašru*
locate *v*. atû B*, karāru, mussû*; → **be(come) ~d** *v*. karāru (stat.)
location *n*. ašru*, kaqquru, maškunu
lock *n*. ḫargullu*, sikkūru, šigāru*; → **~** *v*. edālu; → **put on a ~** *v*. ḫargullu nadû [i.]; → **~-box** *n*. pitnu*; → **~ master** *n*. rab sikkūri; → **~ up** *v*. paḫû; → **~ up horns** *v*. nakāpu* (Gt); → **~ed** *adj*. edlu; → **~ing ring** *n*. ḫargullu*
locust *n*. erbiu, ṣarṣūru+; → **leprosy(-covered) ~** *n*. erib garābi; → **migratory ~** *n*. kallabūnu, tibbuttu; → **~ (kind of)** *n*. ḫilimmu, irgilu, suḫsilu, zizānu, zizru; → **~ tree** *n*. ḫarūbu+; → **like ~s** *adv*. aribiš*, eribiš*
lodestone *n*. šaddānu ṣābitu
lodge *v*. biādu (D); → **~r** *n*. uššābu
lodging *n*. mūšubu; → **~ inn** *n*. bēt ubri; → **~s** *n*. bēt napṭiri*
loft *n*. rugubu
loftiness *n*. ṣīrūtu*
lofty *adj*. ṣīru*, šaqiu
log *n*. gašūru
logos *n*. zikru
loin *n*. birku*, burku; → **~-girding** *n*. rikis qabli◊; → **~cloth** *n*. sūnu B, ṣubāt qabli*; → **~cloth(?)** *n*. ša-qabli; → **~s** *n*. qablu (pl.)
loiter *v*. duālu, saḫāru [o.]
lolium *n*. lišān kalbati+
loll *v*. rabāṣu
lone (horse) *n*. ēdānīu
lonely *adj*. ēdumānu
long *adj*. arku; → **be(come) ~** *v*. arāku; → **make ~** *v*. arāku (D); → **make grow ~** *v*. šatāḫu◊ (D); → **very ~** *adj*. arraku*, šuḫḫu*; → **~-drawn-out** *adj*. urruku*; → **make ~-lasting** *v*. labāru* (D); → **~-standing** *adj*. labīru; → **~ (for)** *v*. puqqu; → **~ for** *v*. ēnē tarruṣu [i.], ḫasāsu (Gtn), pānē našû [i.]
longevity *n*. labār ūmē
longlegged *n*. ḫalli-arkāti
look *n*. imratu*, nīš ēni*, niṭlu*; → **~** *v*. dagālu, naṭālu*; → **make ~** *v*. dagālu (Š); → **~ after** *v*. rēšu kullu [i.], šalāmu (D); → **~ angrily** *v*. nekelmû*; → **~ at** *v*. dagālu, palāsu* (N), šubbû*; → **~ at repeatedly** *v*. barû B* (Gtn); → **~ at thoroughly** *v*. barû B* (Gt); → **~ for** *v*. ba''û, ina pāni dagālu [i.], pâru*; → **~ for s.o.'s favor** *v*. ēnē X dagālu [i.]; → **~ forward to** *v*. ina pāni dagālu [i.], pān X dagālu [i.], puqqu; → **~ into** *v*. uṣṣuṣu

(D); → **~ over** *v.* palāsu☆ (Ntn); → **~ up** *v.* amāru; → **be ~ed upon as** *v.* dagālu (N); → **~ing glass** *n.* ša-tāmarti

lookout *n.* nāmuru

looks *n.* būnu

loop *n.* kippu, kipputu; → **~hole** *n.* zamītānu+

loose *adj.* paḫzu+, tabiu; → **~** *v.* pašāru, uššuru (D); → **be(come) ~** *v.* paḫāzu, ramû, tabû (stat.); → **~d** *adj.* paṭru; → **~n** *v.* pašāru, paṭāru; → **be ~ned** *v.* paṭāru (N)

loot *n.* ḫubtu, šallutu; → **~** *v.* šalālu☆; → **~er** *n.* šālilu☆

lop *v.* arû F☆, batāqu; → **~-nose** *adj.* šarmu+; → **~-sided** *n.* lā šitqulu+

lord *n.* bēlu, etellu☆, šu'ītu☆; → **city ~** *n.* bēl āli; → **~like** *adv.* bēlānu; → **~ly** *adj.* [ša] bēlūti☆; → **~ly** *adv.* bēlānu; → **~ship** *n.* bēlūtu, ēnūtu☆

lore *adj.* ša pî; → **~** *n.* īnu☆

lose *v.* ḫalāqu (D); → **cause to ~ direction** *v.* samû (D); → **~ one's life** *v.* napšutu qatû [i.]

loss *n.* bitiqtu, bitqu [o.], ḫaliqtu, ḫibiltu☆, imbû☆, miṭītu◊, ṣītu☆, tukku+; → **inflict ~** *v.* maṭû (D)

lost *adj.* ḫalqu; → **be(come) ~** *v.* ḫalāqu

lot *n.* isqu, passu+, pūru; → **~ion** *n.* marḫuṣu; → **~tery** *n.* pūru

lotus *adv.* šūšanu+

loud *adj.* šapû☆; → **be(come) ~** *v.* šapû☆; → **~-voiced** *adj.* raṣmu☆, ruṣṣunu☆; → **~ and bitterly** *adv.* ṣarpiš☆; → **make a ~ noise** *v.* raṣānu☆; → **~ly** *adv.* šaqīš☆

louse *n.* kalmutu; → **~'s egg** *n.* nābu+

love *n.* dādu☆, ra'āmu, ru'āmu☆; → **be(come) ~** *v.* ra'āmu; → **make ~** *v.* ra'āmu (D); → **in ~** *adj.* rā'imu; → **~-bird** *n.* murtāmu☆; → **~ affair** *n.* ru'āmu☆; → **~ play** *n.* ṣīḫtu, ṣūḫu☆; → **~d** *adj.* ra'mu; → **~d** *n.* ra'īmu; → **~d one** *n.* ra'īmu, ra'intu; → **~liness** *n.* munammû☆; → **~ly** *adj.* ṣaiāḫu☆

lovemaking *n.* ru'āmu☆

lover *n.* ḫā'iru☆, ḫābiru, ḫarmu☆, murtāmu☆, rā'imānu, rā'imu

lovesickness *n.* muruṣ râmi☆

loving *adj.* rā'imu; → **~ care** *n.* taknītu☆, taknû☆

lovingkindness *n.* ṭēbūtu+

low *adj.* batqu [o.]; → **be(come) ~** *v.* šapālu; → **~-lying (place)** *n./adj.* mušpalu☆; → **~-value** *adj.* maṭiu [o.]; → **~ spirits** *n.* šuplu libbi; → **~ water** *n.* esīgu☆; → **~er** *adj.* šaplīu, šupālû◊; → **~er** *v.* šapālu (D); → **~er parts** *n.* šaplāti☆; → **~er stone (of door)** *n.* ṣirru+ (upper or lower)

Lower Zab *n.* Zāba šaplīu

lowering *n.* tašpiltu☆

lowland *n.* šupālu☆; → **~** *n./adj.* mušpalu☆

loyal *adj.* kēnu; → **be(come) ~** *v.* kuānu, libbu gammuru [i.]; → **~ly** *adv.* ina gammurti libbi; → **~ty** *n.* gammurti libbi, kēnāti, kēnūtu

lubricant *n.* lubku☆

lubricate *v.* labāku (D)

lucid *adj.* namru; → **make ~** *v.* barāṣu+ (D)

luck *n.* rāšilūtu☆; → **bad ~** *n.* lumnu

luckily *adv.* damqiš [o.]

lucky *adj.* damqu, rāš ili☆; → **~** *n.* ilānû☆

lucrative *adj.* [ša] nēmeli*

lucre *n.* išdiḫu

luggage *n.* anūt ḫūli

lukewarm *adj.* ṣarḫu lā ṣarḫu*

lumbago *n.* matnutu+

lumber *n.* ēṣu

lumberjack *n.* nākisu

luminary *n.* nannaru☆

luminosity *n.* namrirru☆ (pl.)

luminous *adj.* namru; → **make ~** *v.* barāṣu+ (D); → **~ phenomenon** *n.* birṣu☆; → **~ splendor** *n.* šalummatu☆

lump *n.* kirinnu☆, kubtu, kurbānu, šibirtu

lunacy *n.* šēḫu

lunar *adj.* [ša] sīn

lunatic *n./adj.* maḫḫû☆, šēḫānu

lunch *n.* naptan muṣulāli*

luncheon *n.* naptan muṣulāli*

lung (part of) (lit. 'finger of the lungs') *n* . ubān ḫašê☆

lungs *n.* ḫašû

lupin *n.* šammi nipši, tarmuš☆

Lupus *n.* uridimmu☆

lurch *v.* nâšu☆

lure *v.* kazābu☆ (D)

lurk *v.* rabāṣu; → **~er (demon)** *n.* rābiṣu

luscious *adj.* kuzzubu☆ (highly)

lush *adj.* šamḫu☆

lust *n.* dādu☆, nīš libbi☆; → **~ for** *v.* ēnu našû☆; → **be(come) ~ for** *v.* ṣaḫātu; → **~er** *n.* šarūru; → **~ful** *adj.* tēbû☆; → **~y** *adj.* naḫšu☆; → **~y** *n.* lalânu☆; → **be(come) ~y** *v.* naḫāšu☆

lute *v.* peḫû☆

luxuriance *n.* lalû, šumḫu☆

luxuriant *adj.* ḫabṣu☆, šamḫu☆, ṭaḫdu; → **~** *n.* lalânu☆; → **be(come) ~** *v.* ḫabāṣu☆, ḫanābu

luxury *n.* lalû, nam'udu; → **~ item** *n.*

ṣaḫittu
lye *n.* qīltu
lying *n.* pīgu*, ṣaliptu*
lynx *n.* azarru; → **(desert) ~** *n.* zirqu*; → **~ (female)** *n.* zirqutu
lyre *n.* sammû
mace *n.* miṭṭu, nar'antu
machination *n.* epšetu
machine *n.* nēpešu*
mad *adj.* lā ṭēmānu, maḫḫû*, šegû*
madam *n.* bēltu
madden *v.* agāgu* (D), maḫû* (D)
madder *n.* ḫūrutu
made *adj.* epšu; → **have ~** *v.* epāšu* (Š); → **~-up** *adj.* ebru*, epšu
madman *adj.* maḫḫû*; → **~** *n.* ša-šēḫi, šēḫānu
madness *n.* maḫḫûtu*, šēḫu
magazine *n.* bēt abūsāti, ursūtu, uṣṣāru◊
maggot *n.* ākilu B+, sāsu+, tu'issu
magic *n.* āšipūtu, kakugallūtu*; → **anti-witchcraft ~** *n.* ušburrudû*; → **~ circle** *n.* gišḫurru*; → **~ wand** *n.* e'ru; → **~al** *adj.* [ša] āšipūti; → **~al rite (kind of)** *n.* zikurudû; → **~al text (kind of)** *n.* maštilû*; → **~ian** *n.* āšipu, ḫarṭibu (Egyptian), kakugallu*
magistrate *n.* muparrisu+
magnanimity *n.* rabûtu, rapāš libbi*
magnanimous *adj.* libbu rapšu [i.]
magnate *n.* rabannu*, rabiu
magnetic *adj.* ṣābitu
magnetism *n.* ṣābitūtu*
magnetite *n.* šaddānu ṣābitu
magnificence *n.* rabûtu, šutarruḫūtu*, tašīltu*
magnificent *adj.* bitrû*, rabbû*, šarḫu*, šitrāḫu*; → **~ly** *adv.* rabīš*
magnify *v.* rabû* (Š)
magnitude *n.* rabûtu
maid *n.* amtu*, antu; → **~en** *n.* ardatu*; → **~enly** *adj.* batūlāiu+
mail *v.* ana kallie šēbulu; → **~-shirt** *n.* naḫlaptu; → **~ shirt** *n.* šupālītu ḫalluptu; → **~clad** *adj.* labšu+
maim *v.* nakāsu
mainland *n.* nābalu*
maintain *v.* ina qāti kullu [i.]; → **~er** *n.* muballiṭānu [o.]
maintenance *n.* zāninūtu*
majestic *adj.* šagapīru*
majesty *n.* rabûtu
major *adj.* rabiu; → **~-domo** *n.* rab bēti; → **office of ~-domo** *n.* rab bētūti; → **~ity** *n.* nam'udu, utrūtu+
make *v.* epāšu; → **~-up** *n.* taknītu*; → **~ an appointment** *n.* adannu šakānu; → **~ off** *v.* ḫalāqu, ruāqu; → **~ to** *v.* ša-; → **~ up** *v.* eqû (Gt), rakābu+ (D); → **~ up for** *v.* riābu, šalāmu (D); → **~ up with** *v.* magāru* (Gt); → **~r** *n.* ēpišu; → **~shift** *n.* pūḫu
makean effort *v.* anāḫu* (Št)
making *n.* epāšu
Makran *n.* Magan*
malaise *n.* lā ṭūb libbi
malaria *n.* dī'u
male *n.* zakkāru, zikāru*; → **~** *n./adj.* zikru*; → **~diction** *n.* arratu*, nizirtu; → **~factor** *n.* lā ṭābtānu
malformation *n.* izbu
malformed birth *n.* izbu
malice *n.* magrītu*, martu
malicious *adj.* bīšu◊, raggu*; → **~ness** *n.* nullāti*
malignant *adj.* bīšu+, lamnu; → **be(come) ~** *v.* lamānu
malingerer *n.* raqqiu
mallet *n.* mazūru+
malodorous *adj.* samku
malpractice *n.* ḫiṭṭu
malt *n.* buqlu; → **~** *v.* baqālu*; → **~reat** *v.* ašāšu* (D); → **~reatment** *n.* ḫisi'tu; → **~ster** *n.* bāqilu*; → **~ster(?)** *n.* barrāqu
man *n.* amēlu, mu'āru*, mutu, zikāru*; → **(able-bodied) ~** *n.* ṣābu; → **like ~** *adv.* amēliš*; → **old ~** *n.* paršumu; → **primal ~** *n.* lullû B*; → **primitive ~** *n.* lullû B*; → **sacred ~** *n.* qadīšu; → **she- ~** *n.* assinnu; → **young ~** *n.* batūlu, eṭlu; → **~-eating** *adj.* ākilu; → **~-woman** *n.* assinnu; → **~ of the king** *n.* ša-šarri
manacle *n.* illurtu*, semēru*; → **~s(?)** *n.* ṣiṣṣu*
manage *v.* abālu B* (Gtn), radû; → **~ to** *v.* šalāmu; → **city ~r** *n.* rab āli; → **~ress** *n.* šakintu
mandate *n.* piqittūtu
mandatory *adj.* eršu
mandrake *n.* pillû*
mane *n.* gubāru◊, qimmatu*
maneuver *n.* sadāru; → **~** *v.* sadāru
mange *n.* garābu*; → **~d** *adj.* gurrudu*
mangel-wurzel *n.* silqu B*
manger *n.* eršu
mangle *v.* gamādu+
mangy *adj.* gardu*, gurrudu*; → **be(come) ~** *v.* garādu*
manhood *n.* eṭlūtu*, meṭlūtu*, zikrūtu*
mania *n.* šidru+
maniac *n.* ša-šēḫi
manifest *adj.* apû*, šāpû, šūpû*; →

be(come) ~ *v.* apû☆; → **make ~** *v.* apû☆ (Š); → **~ation** *n.* ittu

mankind *n.* abrāti☆, amēlūtu, tenēšēti☆

manliness *n.* eṭlūtu☆, zikrūtu☆

manly *adj.* zikru☆; → **~ man** *n.* eṭlu

manna(?) *n.* ṣaṣumtu☆

manner *n.* alaktu☆, parṣu; → **~s** *n.* alkakāti☆

mannish *adj.* zikārānu*

manoeuvre *n.* sadāru, sadirtu

manpower *n.* aḫu B

manservant *n.* ṣeḫru

mansion *n.* bētu+

manslaughter *n.* nērtu☆

mantis *n.* šā'ilu B

manual *adj.* [ša] qāti*; → **~ly** *adv.* ina qāti

manufacture *n.* epāšu, epšetu, šipru; → **~** *v.* epāšu; → **~d** *adj.* epšu; → **~r** *n.* ēpišu

manumission *n.* tazkītu☆

manumit *v.* durāru šakānu [i.]

manure *n.* ziblu+

many *adj.* ma'du; → **be(come) ~** *v.* ma'ādu; → **~-sided** *adj.* ma'du

map *n.* liṭṭu

maraud *v.* ḫabātu

marble *n.* parūtu☆

march *n.* māluku, mardītu

March *n.* Addāru (month)

march *v.* alāku, âru☆, radû, šadāḫu☆; → **~-past** *n.* mēteqtu☆; → **~ about** *v.* alāku (Gtn)

Marchesvan *n.* araḫsamnu

mare *n.* atānu

margin *n.* aḫītu

marine *n.* ṣāb eleppi☆; → **~ creature** *n.* binût tānti☆; → **~r** *n.* mallāḫu+

marital status *n.* ḫā'irūtu☆, issūtu

maritime *adj.* [ša] tānti

marjoram *n.* zūpu◊; → **~(?)** *n.* qurnû☆

mark *n.* ittu, šimtu☆; → **~** *v.* idû☆ (D), šamātu◊; → **~ off** *v.* kadāru; → **~er** *n.* ittu☆; → **road ~er** *n.* ittu☆

market *n.* maḫīru, sūqu+; → **~ place** *n.* maḫīru

marking *n.* tirku B☆

marriage *n.* aššūtu◊; → **~ ceremony** *n.* ḫatnūtu+; → **~ festival** *n.* ḫašaddu; → **~ gift** *n.* nadunnû; → **~able** *n.* ḫašdānu

married *adj.* aḫzu◊

marrow *n.* līpu

marry *v.* aḫāzu; → **~(?)** *v.* šaḫāru

marsh *n.* agammu, appāru, nāriṭu☆, raqqatu☆, rušundu☆; → **like a ~** *adv.* apiš☆; → **reed ~** *n.* šūru; → **~all** *v.* sadāru+

marten *n.* šikkidirru☆

martial *adj.* dāpinu☆

marvel *n.* tabrâti☆ (pl.); → **~** *v.* barû B☆ (Gtn)

marvellous *adj.* ša tabrâti*

mascara *n.* amāmû☆

masculine *adj.* zikru☆

masculinity *n.* zikrūtu☆

mash *n.* sarbu, titābē; → **~** *v.* marāsu; → **~ tub** *n.* nazzītu

mask *n.* kutmu☆; → **~** *v.* katāmu (D); → **~ed** *adj.* katmu☆

mason *n.* urāsu; → **chief ~** *n.* rab urāsi; → **~ry** *n.* riṣiptu☆

mass *n.* gipšu☆, gupšu☆, šipku; → **~** *v.* kamāru (D); → **~ meeting** *n.* puḫru ša nišē

massacre *n.* dēktu, šaggaštu☆; → **~** *v.* šagāšu, ṭabāḫu

massage *v.* mašādu B☆ (D), maššu'u

massive *adj.* ešqu☆, kaššu☆, puggulu☆, pungulu☆, uppuqu☆, uttāru, zaqru☆

mast *n.* ṭarkullu☆; → **~(?)** *n.* karû C☆; → **~er** *n.* bēlu, ummânu; → **~erful** *adj.* šulluṭu☆; → **~erly** *adj.* ummânīu+; → **~erpiece** *n.* šipir nikilti☆; → **~ery** *n.* bēlūtu; → **have the ~ery** *v.* šalāṭu+; → **~icate** *v.* lamāmu☆ (D)

mat *n.* kutummu☆, nakbusu; → **reed ~(?) (kind of)** *n.* šugurru

match *n.* šitnuntu☆; → **~** *v.* maṣû, mašālu, mašālu☆ (D); → **~ed** *adj.* šutāḫû☆; → **~ing** *adj.* šutāḫû☆; → **~less** *adj.* lā šanān☆

matchmaker *n.* mummirtu [o.]

mate *n.* tappû; → **~** *v.* rakābu (Š); → **~rial** *adj.* šapû☆; → **~rial** *n.* ḫišiḫtu☆, simmānû☆; → **raw ~rial(s)** *n.* ḫišiḫtu☆; → **~rialize** *v.* bašû (N); → **~rials** *n.* maškattu◊; → **~rials needed** *n.* ḫišiḫtu☆; → **~rnity** *n.* ālidūtu

mathematical problem *n.* igiarû☆

mathematician *n.* ṭupšar arê

mathematics *n.* arû E☆

mating *n.* ritkubu☆

matrimony *n.* aššūtu◊

matrix *adj.* tamšiltu☆; → **~** *n.* nalbantu☆

matron *n.* šarrat bēti

matter *n.* abutu, amatu☆, qadūtu☆

mattress *n.* še'ītu [o.]

mature *adj.* bašlu; → **~** *v.* pašāru+

maturity *n.* rūbu

maul *v.* daqāqu+, napāṣu

mausoleum *n.* kimaḫḫu

mauve(?) *n./adj.* irginu

maximize *v.* rabû☆ (Š)

may *gram. part.* lū

May *n.* Aiāru (month)

may not *gram. part.* ai⋆, lū lā
maybe *adv.* mindēma⋆; → ~ **possibly** *adv.* issurri
mayfly *n.* kulīlu
mayor *n.* laputtû◊, ša-muḫḫi-āli; → **office of the** ~ *n.* ša-muḫḫi-ālūtu
me *pron.* aiāši, iāši, iāti⋆
meadow *n.* gipāru⋆, sa'du, sādu◊, saḫḫu⋆, tamirtu⋆, ušallu; → **marshy** ~ *n.* appāru; → ~ **plant (kind of)** *n.* sungirtu◊
meagre *adj.* diqqu⋆, ēṣu B, qatnu+; → ~ *n.* muškēnu+; → ~**ness** *n.* muškēnūtu+
meal *n.* mākālu, naptunu, pitennu, ṭa'ūmu+; → ~ **(kind of)** *n.* kirrutu; → ~**time** *n.* simin naptini
mean *adj.* raggu⋆, sadru; → ~ *v.* qabû, qabû ana; → ~**der** *v.* qarāru⋆ (D); → ~**ing** *gram. part.* mā; → ~**ing** *n.* pišru, ṭēmu; → ~**ingless** *adj.* rāqu; → **be(come)** ~**ingless** *v.* riāqu; → ~**s** *n.* makkūru, usutu; → **by** ~**s of** *prep.* ina
measurable *adj.* ša madādi*
measure *n.* middutu, mināti⋆ (pl.); → ~ *v.* madādu, mašāḫu; → **beyond** ~ *adv.* eli minâtišu⋆; → ~**d area** *n.* mišiḫtu⋆; → ~**ment** *n.* mišiḫtu⋆, namaddu; → ~**r** *n.* mādidu, māšiḫu⋆
measuring rod *n.* qanû; → ~**(?)** *n.* qanūnu; → ~ **(c. 6 m)** *n.* nindānu⋆
measuring rope (60 metres) *n.* ašlu
meat *n.* šīru; → **cooked** ~ *n.* šubê; → **roasted** ~ *n.* šīr šumê, šubê; → **salted** ~ *n.* midlu; → ~ **(kind of)** *n.* ḫallam, ianūqu; → **salt-** ~ **master** *n.* rab midli; → ~ **prepair (kind of)** *n.* saplišḫu; → ~ **stock** *n.* mê šīri; → **salt-** ~ **trader** *n.* ša-midlēšu; → ~**y(?)** *n.* širiat
medal *n.* simtu
meddle *v.* aḫu ubālu [i.]; → ~**some** *adj.* kaddāru+
Medes *n.* Mādāia
Media *n.* Mādāia
median *adj.* qablīu⋆
mediate *v.* birti X parāsu [i.]
mediation *n.* parās birti*
mediator *n.* pāris birti*, ṣābit abbūti
medical *adj.* [ša] asûti; → ~ **compendium (name of; lit. 'all diseases')** *n.* napḫar murṣi⋆; → ~ **literature** *n.* bulṭu; → ~ **recipe** *n.* bulṭu; → ~ **science** *n.* asûtu+; → ~ **skill** *n.* asûtu
medicinal plant (kind of) *n.* amīlānu⋆, anḫullīmu, atā'išu⋆, kurbān eqli, martakal
medicine *n.* asûtu, šammi pašāri, šammu+; → ~ **of life** *n.* šammu balāṭi
mediocre *adj.* sadru
meditate *v.* abālu B⋆ (Št)
meditative *adj.* muštābilu*
Mediterranean Sea *n.* tāntu elītu⋆, tāntu rabītu ša Amurri⋆, tāntu ša šalām šanši⋆
medley *n.* ballussu
meek *n.* makiu+, nēḫu+; → ~**ness** *n.* makûtu+
meet *v.* atû B⋆ (Št), edēru⋆, ina irti X alāku [i.]; → ~ **up** *v.* emādu (N); → ~ **with** *v.* amāru (N), emādu (N); → ~**ing** *n.* puḫru
melancholy *n.* šuplu libbi
mellow *adj.* bašlu+
melody *n.* zimru⋆
melon *n.* qiššû; → **green** ~ *n.* qiššāti marrāti; → **ripe** ~ *n.* qiššāti bašlāti; → ~**/cucumber (kind of)** *n.* šūḫu
melt *v.* bašālu (Š), naḫarmuṭu⋆ (Š), naḫarmuṭu⋆, ṣuādu (D); → ~ **(down)** *v.* ṣuādu; → ~ **away** *v.* naḫarmuṭu⋆; → ~**ed** *n.* ṣēdu; → ~**ing** *n.* bušlu⋆; → ~**ing pot** *n.* ša-ṣūdi
membership *n.* mar'ūtu
membrane *n.* ipu⋆, qarūmu+, šer'ānu+, šišītu⋆
memoirs *n.* narû
memorable *adj.* ša ḫasāsi*
memorandum *n.* ḫissutu
memorial *n.* asumittu, narû, taḫsistu⋆
memorize *v.* ḫasāsu* (Š)
memory *n.* ḫissutu
men *n.* ṣābu; → **king's** ~ *n.* ṣāb šarri
menace *n.* šipṭu
mend *v.* kabbû (D); → ~**icant** *n.* muškēnu
menstrual bandage *n.* sinbu⋆, ulāpu
menstrual period *n.* maruštu⋆
mentally handicapped *adj.* sakkuku
mention *v.* saqāru, zakāru⋆
mercantile *adj.* [ša] kāri, tankārānû⋆
mercenary(?) *adj.* raksu
mercer *n.* ša-ṣubātēšu*
merchandise *n.* qēptu, šīmu; → ~ **(kind of)** *n.* tūku
merchant *n.* tankāru; → **chief** ~ *n.* rab tankāri; → **like a** ~ *adj.* tankārānû⋆; → ~**hood** *n.* tankāruttu [o.]
merciful *adj.* gāmilu⋆, rēmānu, rēmānû◊, taiāru⋆
Mercury *n.* Ših#u
mercy *n.* ennu [o.], gimillu⋆, rēmu, rēmūtu⋆, taiāru⋆; → **have** ~ *v.* rēmu ina muḫḫi/ana X šakānu [i.], rēmu rašû [i.]
merely *adv.* udēšu
merge *v.* samāḫu
merit *v.* aḫāzu, utāru (D); → ~**orious** *adj.* lā'iu

mermaid *n.* kulīltu
merman *n.* kulīlu
merriment *n.* ḫidûtu☆
merry *adj.* elṣu☆, ḫadiu, namru; → **be(come) ~** *v.* ḫadû; → **make ~** *v.* libbu nammuru [i.], nigūtu šakānu [i.]
merrymaker *n.* ḫidâtānu
merrymaking *n.* nigūtu☆, rīštu◊
mesh *n.* birru, itannu☆
mess *n.* daliḫtu☆, paššūru, puḫru+; → **~ up** *v.* seḫû☆ (D); → **~age** *n.* našpartu, našpirtu [o.], šipirtu, šipru; → **~age master** *n.* rab šibirti; → **hateful ~ages** *n.* zērāti☆; → **~enger** *n.* allāku☆, mār šipri, našpāru◊, šapru; → **mounted ~enger** *n.* rakbû☆
metal → **molten ~** *n.* ṣūdu; → **~-worker** *n.* qurqurru☆, ṣarrāpu+; → **~/alloy (kind of)** *n.* ḫabalkinnu☆; → **~ container/weapon (kind of)** *n.* manziaše☆; → **~ container (kind of)** *n.* kurkurru; → **~ dish (kind of)** *n.* zūqutu; → **~ implement (kind of)** *n.* daššu; → **~ object (kind of)** *n.* ankūnu, pakku, purṭû, siddu
metamorphosis *n.* šinītu☆
meteor *n.* kakkubu rabiu; → **train of a ~** *n.* mišḫu☆; → **~ic iron** *n.* amūtu B [o.]
meteorite *n.* kakkubu rabiu
method *n.* tērsītu☆; → **do ~ically** *v.* sadāru (D)
meticulous *adj.* ḫardu
metoikos *n.* ubāru
mew *v.* niāwu+; → **~s** *n.* qabuttu
midday *n.* muṣlālu, ūmu mašil [o.]
middle *adj.* qabassīu, qabsīu; → **~** *n.* qabassu, qablu, qabsu; → **in the ~ of** *prep.* qabsi; → **~ parts** *n.* qablu (pl.)
midge *n.* dabbābītu+; → **~t** *n.* kurû☆
midnight *n.* mišil mūši☆, qereb mūšīti☆; → **at ~** *n.* ina mūši mašil☆
midrib *n.* zinû
midst of → **in the ~** *prep.* birīt☆, birti, ina qereb☆
midsummer *n.* mišlāti ša ebūri*
midway *n.* ina mišil ḫūli [i.]
midwife *n.* mušālittu☆, sabsūtu
miff *v.* zenû☆ (D); → **~ed** *adj.* ra'bu, zenû☆
might *n.* gipšu☆, kiššūtu, lē'ûtu☆; → **by ~** *adv.* danāniš☆, dannatti, ina danāni☆; → **massed ~** *n.* gipiš ummāni☆
mightily *adv.* lē'īš☆
mighty *adj.* gapšu, šagapīru☆; → **be(come) ~** *v.* gapāšu; → **~(?)** *adj.* dašnu☆
migrant labor *n.* munnagrūti*
migrant worker *n.* munnagru
migrate *v.* galû
migration *n.* galûtu+
milch camel *n.* mušēniqtu
mild *adj.* ḫīqu, rabbu B
mildew *n.* kammu B☆, kibšu☆
mildness *n.* qatnūtu+
milestone *n.* abullu+
militant *adj.* dāpinu☆
milk *n.* ḫilpu, zizibu; → **~** *v.* ḫalābu, ḫalāpu C; → **~-dealer** *n.* ša-zizibēšu; → **~-vendor** *n.* ša-zizibēšu; → **~ chicken(?)** *n.* ianūqu; → **~ product(?) (kind of)** *n.* marmēna; → **~ seller** *n.* ša-zizibēšu; → **~ trader** *n.* ša-zizibēšu; → **~er** *n.* ḫālipu*; → **~man** *n.* ša-zizibēšu; → **~y** *adj.* ḫilbānāiu+
Milky Way *n.* ṣerret šamê
mill *n.* arû (hand), bēt āriri☆, meṭēnu☆; → **~ennium** *n.* līm šanāti; → **~er** *n.* āriru, ṭē'inu [o.]; → **work of a ~er** *n.* ararrūtu☆
millet *n.* tuḫnu
milliner *n.* ša-kubšēšu; → **~y** *n.* bēt ša-kubšēšu, kubšu (pl.)
millstone *n.* arû; → **~ cutter** *n.* naqqār arê
mill *n.* bēt ararri☆
mime *n.* aluzinnu☆; → **~** *v.* mašālu (Š)
mimic *n.* mupaggiānu+, mupeggû☆; → **~** *v.* mašālu (Š), paggû* (D)
mina *n.* manû
mince *v.* ḫarāṭu, kasāmu [o.]
mind *adj.* libbu; → **~** *n.* kabattu, karšu, ṣurru B☆, ṭēmu; → **presence of ~** *n.* ṣibit libbi; → **~er** *n.* tāriu (child) [o.]; → **be(come) ~ful of** *v.* ḫasāsu, ḫissat X ḫasāsu [i.]
mine *n.* ḫurru; → **~** *pron.* ijû; → **~r** *n.* ḫarrā'u*; → **~ral** *n.* abnu
mingle *v.* balālu, ḫiāqu, samāḫu; → **~ with** *v.* samāḫu (Dtt)
mining *n.* ḫarû
minister → **chief ~** *n.* sukkalmaḫḫu☆; → **~ of defense** *n.* turtānu; → **~ of justice** *n.* šartennu; → **~ to** *v.* apālu B; → **~s** *n.* rabrabāni
minor *adj.* ṣeḫru, tardennu☆; → **be(come) ~** *v.* ṣaḫāru
minstrel *n.* zammāru
mint *n.* naniḫu; → **~(?)** *n.* urnû
minus *prep.* maṭi
minuscule *n.* zizru
minute *adj.* daqqu☆; → **be(come) ~** *v.* daqāqu◊
miracle *n.* tabrâti☆
miraculous *adj.* ta'īdu+
mire *n.* nāriṭu☆
mirror *n.* muššulu☆, nāmuru B; → **~ image** *n.* maṭṭaltu☆
mirth *n.* ḫidûtu☆, ḫūd pāni☆, ṣūḫu☆, ulṣu☆

misadventure *n.* maruštu☆
misanthrope *n.* zā'ir amēlūti*
misapprehend *v.* lā ḫakāmu*
miscalculate *v.* ḫaṭû
miscarry *v.* ṣalā'u [o.]; → **~ing woman** *n.* nādītu☆
miscellaneous *adj.* sammuḫu
mischance *n.* lumnu
mischief *n.* namūtu [o.]
mischievous *adj.* lāzinu*; → **be(come) ~** *v.* ragāgu☆
misconduct *n.* ḫiṭṭu
misdeed *n.* gillatu☆, gullultu☆, samiktu, šērtu B☆
misdemeanor *n.* gillatu☆, ḫiṭṭu, nerṭû☆
miser *n.* kāriṣu*; → **~able** *adj.* ašīšû☆, lammunu, muškēnu, šūnuḫu☆
miserably *adv.* pisnuqiš☆, šūnuḫiš☆
misery *n.* dullu☆, tukku+
misfit *adj.* parku
misfortune *n.* lamuttu, maruštu☆, miḫru
misgiving *n.* lā qīptu*
misguided *adj.* ḫaṭû☆, lā radiu+
mishap *n.* miḫru
misinform *v.* lā kettu dabābu
misinterpret *v.* lā ḫakāmu*
mislay *v.* ḫalāqu (D)
mislead *v.* sagû+ (Š); → **~ing** *adj.* sarru☆
miss *v.* ḫaṭû☆, mêšu☆, šêṭu☆, zammû; → **~(?)** *v.* muāqu; → **~ out** *v.* ḫaṭû☆
missile *n.* ḫutennu☆
missing *adj.* batqu; → **be(come) ~** *v.* maṭû; → **is ~** *v.* laššu; → **~ (sum)** *n.* muṭê
mission *n.* šipru
mist *n.* akāmu☆, imbāru, ripsu, tīku
mistake → **make a ~** *v.* ḫiṭṭu ḫaṭû
mistreat *v.* ašāšu☆ (D), ḫasā'u; → **~ment** *n.* ḫisi'tu
mistress *n.* bēltu, sekrutu
mistrust *v.* lā takālu*
misty *adj.* qatturu
misunderstand *v.* lā ḫakāmu*
misuse *v.* ḫasā'u
mite *n.* sāsu+; → **~r** *n.* kubšu
mitigate *v.* rabābu (Š)
mix *v.* balālu, ḫiāqu, samāḫu (D); → **~ up** *v.* balālu; → **~ed** *adj.* ballu, sammuḫu; → **be ~ed** *v.* samāḫu (Dtt); → **~ed (beer)** *adj.* ḫīqu; → **~ed up** *adj.* dalḫu; → **~ture** *n.* ballussu, billutu☆
mo(u)ld *n.* šuḫtu
mo(u)ld (fungus) *n.* kamunû
Moab *n.* Mūab
moan *n.* ṣiriḫtu☆; → **~** *v.* damāmu☆, nabû☆ (D), nasāsu☆, nazāmu, nazāzu☆; → **~ing** *n.* dimmatu☆, dimmu☆, tabbītu☆
moat *n.* ḫarru, ḫirīṣu
mob *n.* ḫupšu☆, ṣindu u birtu☆
mobile *adj.* muttalliku, nammušīšu☆
mobilization *n.* dīku
mobilize *v.* dakû; → **~r** *n.* dākiu
mock *adj.* sarru☆; → **~** *v.* lazānu; → **~ery** *n.* liznu*, ṣuḫītu◊; → **~ing** *n.* liznu*
mode *n.* pitnu B☆; → **~ of performance** *n.* nēpēšu
model *n.* gišḫurru☆, riddu☆
moderate *adj.* maššuḫu+; → **~** *v.* mašāḫu+ (D)
moderation *n.* maššuḫūtu+
modern *adj.* eššu
modest *adj.* baiāšu☆, maššuḫu+; → **~y** *n.* būltu◊, būštu☆
modify *v.* puḫḫu
moist *adj.* labku, raṭbu; → **be(come) ~** *v.* raṭābu; → **~ spot** *n.* nurbu☆; → **~en** *v.* labāku (D), na'ālu☆, raṭābu+ (D); → **~ness** *n.* ruṭibtu☆
moisture *n.* raṭībūtu+, reṭbu+, ruṭbu☆
mold *adj.* tamšiltu☆; → **~** *n.* kibšu☆, šīpu☆, zi'pu☆; → **(metal) ~** *n.* naptaqu☆; → **~er** *v.* balû+; → **~y** *adj.* erru☆
mole *n.* ḫarriru, kiplu, umṣatu☆; → **red ~** *n.* pindû☆; → **~st** *v.* ḫasā'u
mollification *n.* tanēḫtu [o.], tanīḫtu☆
mollify *v.* labāku (D), rabābu (Š)
molt *v.* napāru+; → **~en** *adj.* naḫarmuṭu☆; → **~en** *n.* ṣēdu; → **become ~en** *v.* ṣuādu
moment *n.* riggu+, simunu, ṣibit appi☆; → **at the ~** *adv.* annūrig; → **for a ~** *adv.* surriš☆; → **in a ~** *adv.* surriš☆; → **~ous** *adj.* kabtu☆
monarch *n.* etellu☆, šarru; → **~y** *n.* šarrūtu
monetary *adj.* [ša] kaspi
money *n.* kaspu; → **for ~** *adv.* ina kaspi; → **small ~** *n.* kasap kīsi*; → **~-box** *n.* quppu; → **~-box(?)** *n.* bēt kaqqidi; → **~-lender** *n.* tankāru
moneywise *adj.* ina kaspi
mongoose *n.* sikkû, šikkû☆; → **~(?)** *n.* puṣuddu☆
mongrel *n.* ballulu
monkey *n.* pagû☆; → **~ (female)** *n.* pagūtu☆
monotonous *adj.* lazzu
monster *n.* izbu, umāmu (mythological); → **sea ~** *n.* tabnīt tānti☆
monstrous *adj.* izbānu*
month *n.* urḫu; → **(name of the twelfth (OA)) ~** *n.* allānātu [o.]; → **coming ~** *n.*

ēribu; → **each ~** *adv.* arḫussu◊; → **next ~** *n.* ēribu; → **~ (name of a)** *n.* tamḫīru [o.]; → **~ after month** *n.* urḫu ana urḫi; → **~ly** *adj.* ša urḫi; → **~ly** *adv.* arḫišam*
monument *n.* asumittu
mood *adj.* libbu; → **~** *n.* gerrû, ikku, kabattu, nupāru*, ṭēmu; → **bad ~** *n.* karû ikki; → **happy ~** *n.* nummur kabatti*; → **~y** *adj.* adru B
moon *n.* sīnu; → **~light** *n.* nūr sīn, ṣēt sīn*; → **~stone** *n.* abašmu
moor *v.* rakāsu; → **~ing place** *n.* makallû*; → **~ings** *n.* markāsu
moorland *n.* kaqqar giṣṣi*
moot point *n.* abat ṣāssi
mop *v.* šakkulu
mope *v.* ikku kullu [i.]
moping *n.* karû ikki
morale *adj.* libbu
morbid *adj.* marṣu
more → **give ~** *v.* ma'ādu (Š); → **make ~** *v.* ma'ādu (Š); → **~ than** *prep.* aq-qāt [o.], eli*; → **~ than once** *n.* māla šinīšu; → **~over** *adv.* aḫamma; → **~s** *n.* riddu
morgue *n.* bēt pagri [o.]
moribund *n.* maitānu*
morning *n.* kaṣâtu*, ša-šērāti, šērtu, šēru*; → **early ~** *n.* kallamāri, ṣippirrāti; → **in the ~** *adv.* innamāri; → **tomorrow ~** *n.* kallamāri; → **~ and evening** *adv.* ša šiāri nubatti; → **~ and evening** *n.* šiāru nubattu
moron *n.* lillu*
morose *adj.* marru B+
morrow *n.* šiāru (the)
morsel *n.* karṣu, ukālu
mortal *adj.* [ša] muāti; → **~ity** *n.* mūtānu+; → **~ity (rate)** *n.* mētūtu+
mortar *n.* gaṣṣu+, kalakku B*, šallaru*, šelluru
mortgage *v.* ana šaparti šakānu
mortify *v.* šapālu (D)
mortuary *n.* bēt pagri [o.]
mosaic *n.* riṣiptu+ (tesselated)
mosquito *n.* baqqu*, buqāqu*, zaqqitu*
moss *n.* elapûa
mostly *adv.* kaiamānu
moth *n.* ākilu B+, sāsu; → **~er** *n.* agarinnu*, bāntu*, garinnu, ummu; → **bearing ~er** *n.* ālissu; → **like a ~er** *adv.* bāntiš*; → **natural ~er** *n.* ummu ālittu; → **queen ~er** *n.* ummi šarri; → **~er-in-law** *n.* emētu*; → **~er-of-pearl** *n.* namrūtu*; → **~erhood** *n.* ummūtu*
motif *n.* abutu
motion *n.* alāku; → **~** *v.* ittu tadānu; → **set in ~** *v.* namāšu (D); → **~less** *adj.* lā āliku
motive *n.* mudakkītu*
motley *adj.* barmu*
mottled *adj.* barmu*
mound *n.* bērūtu*, tillu
mount *n.* iḫzu*; → **~** *v.* aḫāzu (D), rakābu
mountain *n.* gennû*, ḫuršānu*, šaddû; → **like a ~** *adv.* ḫuršāniš*; → **~** *adj.* [ša] šaddê; → **~-dweller** *n.* šaddāiu*, šaddû'a*; → **~-quarried** *adj.* ḫīp šaddî; → **~ peak** *n.* zuqtu B*; → **like a ~ peak** *adv.* pulukkiš*; → **~ top** *n.* ubān šadê*; → **~eer** *n.* šaddāiu*; → **~ous** *adj.* [ša] šaddê
mounting *n.* mandītu B◊, rikibtu*; → **~s** *n.* iḫzēti*
mourn *v.* sapādu*; → **~er** *n.* bakkiu, bēl tādirti; → **~ful** *adj.* adru B, udduru; → **~ing** *n.* sipittu*, tādirtu; → **utter+cries of ~ing** *v.* ṣarāḫu B* (Š); → **~ing-place** *n.* kiḫullû*; → **~ing garment** *n.* karru B*
mouse *n.* akburu+, pērurūtu (house), piāzu*
moustache *n.* sapsupu
mouth *n.* pû; → **~-washing (ritual)** *n.* mīs pî*; → **~ cavity** *n.* ḫurri pê*; → **~ful** *n.* ammār pî
movable *adj.* muttalliku; → **~s** *n.* numāti*
move *v.* akāšu*, alāku, alāku (Š), nadādu B*, namāšu [o.], raḫāšu*; → **~ about** *v.* duālu, segû◊; → **~ ahead of** *v.* panû; → **~ along** *v.* radû+, šapāpu*; → **~ alongside** *v.* bâ'u (Š); → **~ back and forth** *v.* sabā'u; → **~ downstream** *v.* šapālu (Dtt); → **~ farther** *v.* patû; → **~ forward** *v.* šadāḫu*; → **~ in** *v.* erābu; → **~ off** *v.* šēpē pašāru [i.]; → **~ on** *v.* etāqu, etāqu alāku, namāšu [o.], ukkušu; → **~ out** *v.* uṣû; → **~ softly** *v.* šapāpu+; → **~ up** *v.* elû (Š); → **~ment** *n.* alaktu*
moving *adj.* āliku; → **~ upstream** *n.* māḫirtu (boat)
mow *v.* gadāmu+; → **~ down** *v.* eṣādu
much *adj.* ma'du; → **~** *adv.* ma'ad, ma'da, ma'diš*, magal*; → **be(come) ~** *v.* ma'ādu; → **too ~** *adv.* ma'ad; → **make ~ of** *v.* ma'ādu (Š); → **~ troubled** *adj.* šūnuḫu*
muck *n.* pudru (animal); → **~ up(?)** *v.* ururuzu
mucus *n.* ḫaḫḫu B*
mud *n.* qadūtu*, rušundu*, ṭēru*; → **~-guard** *n.* saḫargû; → **~ masonry** *n.* pitiqtu*; → **~ wall** *n.* pitiqtu*, pitqu*; → **~dle** *v.* dalāḫu
muffle *v.* ḫaṭāmu

mug *n.* luṭṭu⋆ (soup)
muggy *adj.* ṣarḫu
mulberry *n.* tūtu+; → **~ (tree)** *n.* tuttu◊
mule *n.* daddammu, kūdunu, parû; → **~-stable man** *n.* ša-bēt-kūdini; → **~ express** *n.* kalliu; → **~ express commander** *n.* rab kallî; → **~ man** *n.* ša-kūdini; → **~ stable** *n.* bēt kūdini
mullein *n.* būṣinnu
multi- *adj.* ma'du
multicolored *adj.* barmu⋆, barrumu, bitrumu⋆; → **~** *n.* tabrīmu; → **be(come) ~** *v.* barāmu B⋆
multiple *adj.* ma'du; → **~** *n.* uṣṣupu*
multiplication (table) *n.* arû E⋆
multiplier *n.* arû E⋆
multiply *v.* aṣābu (D), eṣāpu, ma'ādu, našû ana [i.]; → **~ by three** *v.* šalāšu B⋆ (D)
multitude *n.* gipšūtu⋆, mādû⋆, mu'dû
mumble *v.* ḫabābu⋆
mumps *n.* ḫuzīrtu+
munch *v.* kasāsu+, lamāmu⋆
mundane *adj.* [ša] kaqqiri
municipal *adj.* [ša] āli
munitions *n.* anūt tāḫāzi⋆
murder *n.* nērtu⋆, šaggaštu⋆; → **~** *v.* duāku, šagāšu; → **~er** *n.* dā'ikānu◊, dā'iku⋆, šaggāšu⋆, zēr nērti⋆; → **~ous** *adj.* dā'iku⋆, kāṣir nērti⋆, šaggāšû⋆
murmur *v.* ḫabābu⋆, laḫāšu, laḫāšu+, nazāmu (Dtt)
muscle *n.* šer'ānu
muscular *adj.* šer'ānīu*
muse upon *v.* abālu B⋆ (Št)
mush *n.* sarbu; → **~ed (together)** *adj.* ḫabṣu+; → **~room** *n.* puṭuru
music *n.* nârūtu⋆, zammārūtu+; → **make ~** *v.* nigūtu epēšu [i.]; → **(joyful) ~** *n.* nigūtu⋆; → **~ (vocal or stringed)** *n.* zamāru+; → **~al arts** *n.* nârūtu⋆; → **~al instrument (kind of)** *n.* dubdubbu; → **~ian** *n.* nargallu (senior), nuāru; → **female ~ian** *n.* nuārtu; → **~ianship** *n.* nârūtu⋆
musing *adj.* muštābilu*
mussel *n.* biṣṣūr atāni; → **~ silk** *n.* būṣu
must not *gram. part.* lū lā
muster *n.* dakûtu, dikûtu; → **~ courage** *v.* libbu rašû [i.]
musty *adj.* erru⋆
mute → **be(come) ~** *v.* ḫarāšu C+
mutilate *v.* nakāpu⋆, nakāsu
mutineer *n.* nabalkattānu⋆
mutiny *n.* nabalkattu⋆
mutter *v.* ḫabābu⋆, ṣabāru
mutton *n.* immeru
mutual(ly) *adv.* ša aḫāiš
mutually *adv.* aḫāiš; → **be ~ satisfactory** *v.* tarāṣu B⋆ (Gt)
muzzle *n.* ḫargullu⋆, ḫuṭṭimmu⋆; → **~** *v.* balāmu+, ḫaṭāmu
myriad *n./adj.* šār⋆
myrrh *n.* murru
myrtle *n.* asu
myself *pron.* raminī
mysterious *adj.* katmu⋆
mystery *n.* pirištu⋆
mystic *n.* mūdû pirišti⋆; → **~(al)** *adj.* ṣallulu
nag *v.* karṣē akālu [i.]; → **~ at** *v.* magādu
nail *n.* sikkutu, ṣupru; → **~** *v.* rapāqu; → **~-cutter** *n.* ša-ṣupri; → **~mark** *n.* ṣupru
naked *adj.* mērânû⋆, mērešīu, pattû; → **be(come) ~** *v.* erû B [o.]; → **~ness** *n.* mērânūtu⋆
name *n.* nibītu⋆, nību⋆, šumu, zikru; → **~** *v.* nabû⋆, zakāru⋆; → **give a ~** *v.* šumu nabû [i.]; → **bad ~** *n.* šumu lā damqu; → **proper ~** *n.* šumu; → **~-giving** *n.* nibīt šumi⋆; → **list of ~s** *n.* mudasû⋆; → **~sake** *n.* bēl šumi+
nanny *n.* tārītu
nap *n.* munattu⋆; → **~** *v.* nuāmu+
nape of the neck *n.* gubāru◊
naphtha *n.* napṭu
napkin *n.* sasuppu
napless *adj.* qalpu
nard *n.* lardu
narrate *v.* šanû (D)
narrative *n.* tašnītu⋆
narrator *n.* mušanniānu+, mušanniu*
narrow *adj.* naḫsu⋆ (very), pāqu, pašqu⋆, pīqu⋆, qatnu+, sāqu, sīqu◊, šupšuqu⋆; → **~** *v.* qatānu⋆ (D); → **be(come) ~** *v.* pašāqu B⋆, piāqu, qatānu⋆, siāqu; → **make ~** *v.* siāqu (D); → **be(come) ~ed** *v.* qatānu+; → **~s** *n.* ḫinqu⋆
nasal *adj.* [ša] appi
natality *n.* talittu
nation *n.* bētu+, lišānu+, mātu, ummatu⋆; → **~al assembly** *n.* puḫru ša māti; → **~ality** *n.* lišānu
native *n.* mār māti; → **~-born** *adj.* unzarḫu
nativity *n.* ilittu
natural *adj.* kaiamānīu; → **die a ~ death** *v.* ana šīmti alāku [i.]; → **~ize** *v.* issi nišē māti manû [i.]; → **~ly** *adv.* ina šīmti*
nature *n.* nabnītu⋆, šiknu; → **~ of things** *n.* šīmtu
naughty *adj.* raggu⋆
nausea *n.* erišti libbi⋆; → **~ting** *adj.*

zēru⋆
nave *n.* ēkallu+
navel *n.* abunnutu⋆
navigation *n.* mallāḫūtu⋆
nay *gram. part.* lā+
near *adj.* qurbu; → **~** *n.* qerbu⋆; → **~** *prep.* innidi, itu◊; → **~est** *adj.* qurbu; → **~ly** *adj.* qurbu+; → **~ly** *adv.* ubān lā⋆; → **~ness** *n.* qurbūtu
neat *adj.* kannû, sudduru
necessaries *n.* ḫašaḫtu+ (pl.), ḫišiḫtu⋆, mēreštu⋆
necessarily *adv.* ina šīmti*
necessary *adj.* eršu, ḫašḫu⋆
necessitate *v.* erāšu
necessities *n.* ḫišiḫtu⋆
necessity *n.* ḫašaḫtu+, ḫišaḫtu+, šīmtu, tēkītu
neck *n.* gubāru◊, kišādu, libānu, tikku⋆; → **~-stock** *n.* erinnu⋆, sigāru; → **~-stone** *n.* kišādu; → **~ muscles** *n.* dadāni⋆; → **~ ornament (kind of)** *n.* kurinnu
necklace *n.* erimmatu⋆ (egg-shaped), erintu, gāgu; → **~(?)** *n.* šeršerrutu; → **~ clasp** *n.* kuṣurtu⋆
nectar *n.* kurunnu⋆
need *adj.* ḫašḫu⋆; → **~** *n.* erištu⋆, ḫašaḫtu [o.], ḫišaḫtu+, ḫišiḫtu⋆, ḫušaḫḫu, mēreštu⋆, mērešu⋆, ṣibūtu⋆, ṣummû⋆; → **~** *v.* ḫašāḫu⋆, ṣabû◊; → **occasional ~** *n.* miqtu; → **~ed** *adj.* ḫašḫu⋆; → **~ful** *adj.* makiu
needle *n.* pulukku⋆; → **~ss** *adj.* lā eršu
needs *n.* ḫašaḫtu+ (pl.), mēreštu⋆
needy *adj.* ḫašḫu⋆, mērešīu, muškēnu
negate *v.* šarābu+
negation *n.* ullu⋆
negative answer *n.* ullu⋆
neglect *n.* šēṭūtu; → **~** *v.* egû, ḫaṭû⋆, mêšu⋆, šêṭu⋆, šiāṭu+; → **be(come) ~** *v.* makû B; → **~ed** *adj.* uzzubu⋆; → **~ful** *adj.* šēṭu; → **be(come) ~ful** *v.* šelû◊
negligence *n.* egītu, egûtu, makûtu B, nīd aḫi⋆, šēṭūtu
negligent *adj.* egû, makiu B, šēṭu; → **be(come) ~** *v.* makû B, šâṭu B⋆, šelû◊, šiāṭu; → **~ly** *adv.* ina šēṭūti⋆
negotiate *v.* dabābu, lišānu šakānu⋆
negotiations *n.* ṭubbāti⋆
negress *n.* Meluḫḫītu*
negro *n./adj.* Meluḫḫāiu⋆
neigh *v.* nagāgu⋆; → **~bor** *n.* bēl taḫūmi, itû B⋆, qurbu, šē'i bābi; → **~borhood** *n.* bābtu; → **~boring** *adj.* qurbu
neither ... nor *conj.* lā ... lā
nephew *n.* mār aḫāti, mār aḫi
nerve *n.* gīdu, šer'ānu
nervous → **be ~** *v.* parādu⋆ (Gtn)
nest *n.* qinnu; → **~** *v.* qanānu; → **make a ~** *v.* qanānu
nestle *v.* qanānu
net *n.* birru, pūgu⋆, salītu, saparru B⋆, šētu⋆, šuškallu⋆; → **like a ~** *adv.* šētiš⋆
nether *adj.* šaplīu
netherworld *n.* erṣutu⋆, rikalla, šaplāti⋆
nettle *n.* kurṣipti eqli⋆; → **~** *v.* nakātu+
never *adv.* immatimēni lā; → **~ ceasing** *n.* lā mupparkû⋆; → **~theless** *adv.* kēttu, tūra
new *adj.* eššu; → **be(come) ~** *v.* edēšu⋆, ešāšu; → **~ year** *n.* rēš šatti, šattu eššutu [i.]
New Year *n.* zammukku⋆; → **~'s Day** *n.* rēš šatti
newborn *n.* lakû, šerru⋆
newly *adv.* ana eššūti⋆
newness *n.* eššūtu⋆
news *n.* passurtu, ṭēmu; → **bring good ~** *v.* passuru; → **bringer of ~** *n.* mupassiru; → **good ~** *n.* bussurtu⋆, passurtu
newt *n.* ṣurārītu+
next *adj.* ēribu; → **~-door** *adj.* qurbu; → **~ to** *prep.* gabdi, itê⋆, qanni
nibble *v.* karṣē akālu [i.]
nice *adj.* damqu; → **~ness** *n.* dunqu; → **~ty** *n.* dunqu
niche *n.* aptu, ḫibšu, ibratu⋆
nicked *adj.* palšu+
nickname *n.* kinūtu⋆
niece *n.* mar'at aḫāti, mar'at aḫi
niggard *n.* kāriṣu*
nigh *adj.* qurbu+; → **~t** *n.* mūšītu⋆, mūšu; → **at ~t** *adv.* kî bādi, mūšiš⋆, mūšīta⋆, mūšītiš⋆, ša mūši; → **by ~t** *adv.* ša mūši; → **in the ~t** *adv.* ša mūši; → **remain all ~t** *v.* biādu; → **spend the ~t** *v.* biādu, šumšû⋆; → **wandering by ~t** *adj.* mušamšû⋆; → **wedding ~t** *n.* quršu; → **~t-watchman** *n.* ḫā'iṭu⋆; → **~tfall** *n.* pān mūši⋆; → **~tingale** *n.* zāmiru+; → **~tly** *adj.* [ša] mūši, [ša] mūšīti; → **~tmare** *n.* šuttu parittu⋆; → **~tshade** *adj.* karān šēlibi+; → **~ttime** *n./adj.* šāt mūši, šāt mūši⋆
nimble *adj.* lassumu, pazīzu+
nimbus *n.* melammu⋆
nineteen *n./adj.* tešēšer[et]⋆; → **~th** *adj.* tešēšerīu⋆
ninety *n./adj.* tiš'ā*
Nineveh *n.* Nīnuwa
ninny *n.* saklu
ninth *adj.* tešiu; → **one ~** *n.* tešiu; → **~ month)** *n.* uraḫ kalmarte [o.]
Ninurta-like *n.* nūrtānu

nip *v*. karāṣu⁺
nipple *n*. appi tulê☆, zīzu B
Nisan *n*. Nisannu (month)
Nisibis *n*. Naṣībina
nit *n*. nābu☆; → **~er** *n*. nitiru
no *gram. part.* lā; → **~ exaggeration!** *interj.* lā utar [o.]; → *interj.~ further* lā utar [o.]; → **~ gentleman** *n*. lā amēlu; → **~ one** *pron.* lā mammāna☆
nob *n*. rēšu⁺
nobility *n*. mār banî◊
noble *adj*. ašû☆, damqu, mamlu☆, muttallu☆, ṣīru☆; → **~** *n*. ṣīru; → **~man** *n*. mār banî◊, mār damqi, rubû☆; → **~man(?)** *n*. bir kabti◊
noblewoman *n*. mar'at damqi*
nobody *pron*. lā mamman☆, lā mammāna☆
nocturnal *adj*. [ša] mūši; → **~ ceremony** *n*. baiādu
nod off *v*. nuāmu⁺
nod the head *v*. itmû☆, kamāmu☆
node *n*. kiṣru
noise *n*. ḫubūru☆, killu, šisītu☆; → **~less** *adj*. qālu
noisy *adj*. ḫabru☆, ḫubburu; → **be(come) ~** *v*. ḫabāru
nomad(s) *n*. ṣāb ṣēri☆
nomenclature *n*. nibītu☆
nominate *v*. nabû☆, šumu nabû [i.]
nomination *n*. piqittu
non-payment *n*. lā tadānu*
nonaggression *n*. sulummû☆
noncompliance *n*. šipṣu☆
nonetheless *adv*. kēttu, ū
nonexistent *adj*. lā bašiu*
nonsense *adv*. lillūtu⁺
nook *n*. dūtu☆
noon *n*. muṣlālu; → **(at) ~(time)** *n*. ūmu mašil [o.]; → **~time** *n*. muṣlālu
noose *n*. kippu
nor *gram. part.* lā
normal *adj*. išaru☆, sadru; → **~ize** *v*. ešēru☆ (Št), kuānu (D), sadāru (D); → **~ly** *adv*. išariš☆
north *n*. iltānu☆, ṣapūnu◊, šumēlu; → **~east** *n*. šaddû; → **~ern** *adj*. [ša] imitti
northwest *n*. iltānu☆
nose *n*. appu, naḫīru⁺; → **aquiline ~** *n*. appi arê☆; → **~-ring** *n*. qudāsu; → **~ mucus** *n*. upāṭu
nostril *n*. naḫīru; → **~(s)** *n*. naḫīru⁺
not *gram. part.* lā, ul☆; → **~** *subj.* šumma (in oath); → **~ binding** *adj*. naḫru [o.]; → **~ seen** *adj*. lā amru; → **~ yet** *adv*. qudīni lā, udīna lā; → **~able** *adj*. edû; → **~ary** *n*. ṭupšarru
notch *n*. ḫirīṣu; → **~** *v*. ḫarāṣu
note *n*. ḫissutu; → **~** *v*. ḫasāsu, qabû; → **~ down** *v*. ana ḫissiti šaṭāru [i.]
noteworthy *adj*. edû
nothing at all *pron*. lā memmēni
nothing whatever *pron*. lā memmēni
notice *n*. ḫissutu, ṭēmu; → **~able** *adj*. apû☆
notification *n*. ḫissutu
notify *v*. šamû (Š); → **~(?)** *v*. muddû◊
notion *n*. ḫakimtu*; → **~s** *n*. anūt kabbê*
notoriety *n*. šumu lā damqu
notorious *adj*. bīšu◊
notwithstanding *gram. part.* lū
noun *n*. šumu
nourish *v*. akālu (Š), ma''unu; → **~ment** *n*. akālu, ma''uttu, tablittu☆, uklu
novelty *n*. eššūtu☆
November *n*. araḫsamnu
novice *n*. didabû, šarrāiu⁺
novitiate *n*. talmīdūtu⁺
now *adv*. adû◊, akanni, enna◊, inanna☆, ūmâ; → **(just) ~** *adv*. annūrig; → **~ ... now** *adv*. zamar ... zamar☆
nowadays *adv*. akanni
nowhere *adv*. aiākamēni lā
noxious *adj*. dāliḫu☆; → **~ insect (kind of)** *n*. samānu
nozzle *n*. naḫīru⁺
Nubia *n*. Meluḫḫa☆; → **~n** *n./adj.* Meluḫḫāiu☆
nucleus *n*. durgu☆
nude *adj*. mērânû☆
nuisance *n*. saḫāl šīri☆
null and void *adj*. laššu
nullify *v*. pasāsu
numb *adj*. kēru*; → **~** *v*. šamāmu☆; → **~ with fear** *adj*. šuḫarruru☆; → **~er** *n*. mīnu B☆, minūtu, nību☆, nīpu; → **~er** *v*. manû B; → **~ered** *adj*. manû; → **~erless** *adj*. lā manê☆, lā mīnu☆, lā nībi; → **~ness** *n*. rimûtu☆
numeral *n*. mīnānu⁺
numerous *adj*. gapšu, ma'du; → **make ~** *v*. ma'ādu (Š); → **~ness** *n*. gipšūtu☆, ma'dūtu☆
nun *n*. nadītu☆; → **~nery** *n*. gagû◊
nuptial chamber *n*. ḫammūtu
nuptials *n*. ḫatnūtu⁺
nurse *n*. tārītu; → **~** *v*. enāqu (Š), ḫaṣānu; → **wet ~** *n*. mušēniqtu; → **~ling** *n*. ša-irti
nursemaid *n*. tārītu
nursery *n*. bēt tārīti
nursing *n*. tēnīqu☆; → **~ home** *n*. bēt tārī-

ti
nurture *v.* arû C* (Gtn), rabû (D)
nut *n.* kullu B
nutmeat *n.* kullu B
nutriment *n.* akālu
nuts *adj.* maḫḫû*
oak *n.* allānu, ḫaluppu; → **Kani&** ~ *n.* allān kāniš; → **scarlet** ~ *n.* mēsu⁺
oar *n.* gišallu*, namḫaštu*; → ~**sman** *n.* ša-gišalli*
oasis *n.* qablu ša madbāri*
oath *n.* māmītu, māmītu*, nīšu B*, samnu*, tamītu
oats *n.* dišarru*
obduracy *n.* ašṭūtu*, šipṣu*
obdurate *adj.* alṭu*, ašṭu*; → **be(come)** ~ *v.* ašāṭu*
obedience *n.* našmû⁺, sanqūtu*, šamû
obedient *adj.* māgiru, magru, šarbubu; → ~ **(person)** *adj.* mundagru*, sanqu*; → ~ **(person)** *n.* dāgil pāni, šāmiu*, šuknušu*
obeisance *n.* kanāšu
obese *adj.* kabburu, marû*
obesity *n.* kabrūtu*
obey *v.* magāru, pān X dagālu [i.], šamû; → **make** ~ *v.* magāru* (D)
object *n.* izimtu*; → ~ *v.* parāku, ṣālu [o.], ṣelû◊; → ~ **(kind of)** *n.* diḫipu, ingu, ipinnutu, maṣarru, mašrutu, mutnāru, qanītu, qundu, sinpu, supuqtu, šakku; → **be(come)** ~ **of mockery** *v.* ana ṣuḫīti šakānu [i.]; → ~**ionable** *adj.* lā simāti*; → ~**ive** *n.* izimtu*, nizmatu*, ṣibūtu*, ṣummurtu* (pl.)
oblate *n.* širku
obligation *n.* eʾiltu*, riksu; → ~ **to work** *n.* indu
oblige *v.* magāru (N); → ~ **s.o.** *n.* etāqu ina muḫḫi [i.]
obliging *adj.* gammilu*, māgiru
oblique *adj.* ṣalpu*
obliterate *v.* pasāsu, pašāṭu
oblivion *n.* mišītu*; → **fall into** ~ *v.* mašû (N)
oblivious *adj.* lā ḫasisu*
obnoxious *adj.* sanku, zēru*
oboe *n.* ṣinnutu
obscene *adj.* paḫzu⁺
obscenity *n.* bīštu*
obscure *adj.* sakku*, ṣallulu, ṣullulu*; → ~ *n.* barru*; → ~ *v.* barāru (D); → **be(come)** ~ *v.* barāru
obscuring(?) *adj.* mummilu*
obscurity *n.* barāru
observance *n.* ṣullû*
observant *adj.* naʾdu*

observation *n.* amirtu*, madgulu*, qību, tāmartu, urutu*; → ~ **tower** *n.* madgulu*
observe *v.* amāru, naʾādu* (Gt), puqqu, qabû, ṣubbû*; → ~**d part** *n.* minītu; → ~**r** *n.* dāgilu, muppalsu*
obsessed *adj.* kaṣṣuru⁺
obsession *n.* kaṣṣurūtu⁺
obsidian *n.* ṣurru, ṣurtu*
obsolete *adj.* labīru
obstacle *n.* napraku*
obstinacy *n.* šipṣu*
obstinate *adj.* ašṭu*, šapṣu*
obstruct *v.* parāku, parāku (D), peḫû*; → ~**ion(?)** *n.* pirku
obtain *v.* kašādu, rašû*, utāru⁺; → ~ **legally** *v.* zarāpu laqû
obtrusive *adj.* kaddāru⁺
obtuse *adj.* sakku*, sakkuku
obvious *adj.* namru, šāpû
occasion *n.* simunu; → ~**ally** *adv.* ina birīt
occident *n.* rabā šamši; → ~**al** *adj.* [ša] erāb šamši*
occlude *v.* sakāru B⁺
occlusion *n.* sukurtu [o.]
occult *v.* katāmu
occupant *n.* āšibu
occupation *n.* ummânūtu⁺; → ~ **(kind of)** *n.* mār karšāni
occupied with → **be(come)** ~ *v.* issi X dalāpu [i.]
occupy *v.* kašādu, ušābu
occur *v.* amāru (N), maqātu; → ~ **regularly** *v.* sadāru (stat.); → ~**rence** *n.* miqtu
ocean *n.* marratu*, tântu, tântu rabītu*
ochre *n.* makru⁺
October *n.* Tašrītu (month)
oculist *n.* asû ša ēnāte⁺
odd *adj.* aḫīu, nakkuru, utru⁺; → ~**ity** *n.* aḫītu, izbu
ode *n.* zamāru
odious *adj.* zēru
odor *n.* irīšu*, nipšu B
oesophagus *n.* luʾu*, mušērittu*
of *prep.* ša; → ~ *pron.* šūt*; → ~ **course** *adv.* ina šīmti*; → ~ **late** *adv.* issu ḫaramme; → ~ **lower rank** *adj.* maṭiu; → ~ **no use** *adj.* lā kušīri⁺; → ~ **two kinds** *n.* ana šinīšu
off *adv.* pati; → **get** ~ *v.* ezābu (Š), urādu; → ~**ence** *n.* šērtu B*; → **commit an** ~**ence** *v.* ḫiṭṭu ḫaṭû; → ~**end** *v.* ḫaṭû, zenû* (D); → ~**ended** *adj.* zenû*; → **be(come)** ~**ended** *v.* zenû*; → ~**ensive** *adj.* tēbû*, zēru; → ~**ensive** *n.* tibûtu*; → ~**er** *v.* elû (Š), maḫāru

(D), naqû★ (D), qarābu (D); → **~ering** *n.* nidbû (food), nindabû★ (food), niqiu, surqinnu★, tamḫīru [o.], taqribtu★; → **strewn ~ering(?)** *n.* surqu★; → **as an ~ering** *adv.* maḫḫuriš★; → **free-will ~ering** *n.* šagigurû★; → **incense ~ering** *n.* qutrinnu; → **official in charge of the regular ~ering** *n.* šaginêšu; → **regular ~ering** *n.* ginû, sattukku★; → **regular sheep ~ering** *n.* dariu; → **~ering (kind of)** *n.* burgû★, bursaggû★, ēqūtu, qinnītu; → **monthly ~ering (kind of)** *n.* guqqanû★; → **~ering (of aromatics or flour)** *n.* sirqu; → **~ering table** *n.* maškittu, takmīsu; → **manager of the regular sheep ~erings** *n.* rab darî◊; → **room for regular ~erings** *n.* bēt ginê; → **~hand** *adj.* ḫanṭu B★; → **~hand** *adv.* ḫanṭiš★, ina muḫḫi ašli; → **~ice** *n.* bēl piqittūtu, bētu, parṣu, piqittu, piqittūtu, qīptu★; → **~ice (kind of)** *n.* bēl zarrūti◊; → **~ice holder** *n.* bēl maṣṣarti, rab piqitti; → **~icer** *n.* ša-ḫuṭāri; → **information ~icer** *n.* bēl ṭēmi, mutīr ṭēmi; → **high-ranking ~icers** *n.* rabrabāni; → **~icial** *n.* bēl piqitti; → **office of the+eponym ~icial** *n.* bēt limmi [o.]; → **~icial (kind of)** *n.* dišānu, guzalû★, ša-sikkāti, zazakku★; → **~iciant** *n.* bēl parṣi; → **~spring** *n.* ilittu, lillidu, papallu★, ṣīt libbi★

often *adv.* ma'ad; → **~** *n.* šinīšu šalāšīšu

oil *n.* šamnu; → **~** *v.* lu''û★, pašāšu; → **best ~** *n.* ūlu★; → **fine ~** *n.* rūštu★; → **first class ~** *n.* šaman rūšti★; → **mineral ~** *n.* napṭu; → **olive ~** *n.* šaman sirdi; → **perfumed ~** *n.* igulû★; → **rancid ~** *n.* ikūku★; → **sesame ~** *n.* ellu B★; → **sweet ~** *n.* šamnu ṭābu; → **virgin ~** *n.* rūštu★, ūlu★; → **~ container** *n.* bēt šamni; → **~ flask** *n.* naḫbuṣu; → **~ from bowl** *n.* šaman pūri★; → **~ master** *n.* rab šamni; → **~ of blossom** *n.* šaman samādiri; → **~ trader** *n.* ša-šamni [o.]; → **~presser** *n.* ṣāḫitu; → **chief ~presser** *n.* rab rāqūti, rab ṣāḫiti; → **~y** *adj.* [ša] šamni

ointment *n.* muššu'tu★, napšaltu, piššatu★, tēqītu; → **fine ~** *n.* igulû★; → **~ vase** *n.* naḫbuṣu

okay *adv.* tariṣ

old *adj.* labīru, rabiu; → **be(come) ~** *v.* labāriš alāku [i.], labāru★; → **grow ~** *v.* labīrūtu alāku [i.], paršumu (D); → **~ age** *n.* labīrūtu, paršamūtu, šībūtu; → **extreme ~ age** *n.* littūtu; → **to ~ age** *adv.* labāriš★; → **~en times** *n.* labīru

oleander(?) *n.* ballukku+

olive *n.* sirdu

Oman *n.* Magan★

omen *n.* giskimmu★, ittu; → **~-expert** *n.* ṭupšarru

ominous *adj.* laptu B

omission *n.* egītu

omit *v.* ḫaṭû★

omnipotent *adj.* lā'i gabbi*

omnipresent *adj.* āšib gimri*

omniscient *n.* mūdû kalāma★

on *prep.* ina muḫḫi; → **get ~** *v.* rakābu+; → **~ account of** *prep.* eli★; → **~ behalf of** *prep.* eli★; → **~ one's own** *adj.* udē-; → **~ the other shore or bank** *adv.* aḫullâ, aḫullû◊; → **~ the other side** *adv.* aḫūlamma; → **~ this side/bank** *adv.* aḫannâ★; → **~ top of** *prep.* ina muḫḫi, ṣēr★; → **~ager** *n.* parû, sirrimu; → **female ~ager** *n.* sirrimtu★

once *adv.* iltēnšu★, ištīššu★, ittēltu◊, māla, qanni; → **at ~** *adv.* ḫanṭūssu★, ina muḫḫi ašli, kapdu◊; → **~ again** *adv.* šanuttēšu; → **~ more** *adv.* šanuttēšu, tūra

one *adj.* ēdu; → **~** *n.* issēn; → **~** *n./adj.* iltēt★, issēt; → **give ~'s attention to** *v.* lētu nadû [i.]; → **give ~'s heart entirely** *v.* libbu gammuru [i.]; → **put on ~'s lips** *v.* ina šapti šakānu [i.]; → **at ~'s pleasure** *adv.* kî libbī-; → **~-tenth** *n.* ešrāti; → **~-to-one** *adv.* ana mitḫār; → **~-year-old** *n.* mār šatti (m.), mar'at šatti (f.); → **~ ... the other** *conj.* issēn ... issēn; → **with ~ accord** *adv.* mitḫāriš★; → **~ after another** *adv.* battatāia, iddāt aḫāiš; → **~ another** *adv.* aḫāiš; → **~ by one** *adv.* battatāia; → **~ time** *adv.* iltēnšu★

onion *n.* šamaškillu, šumku [o.]; → **red ~** *n.* zinzimmu; → **small ~** *n.* andaḫšu; → **~s** *n.* šunkē

onlooker *n.* dāgilu

only *adj.* ēdu; → **~** *adv.* udēšu

onset *n.* tību

onslaught *n.* tīb tāḫāzi★; → **sudden ~** *n.* šiḫṭu

onto *prep.* ina muḫḫi

onyx *n.* ḫulālu

ooze *v.* natāku, ṣarāru

opaque *adj.* kanku; → **~** *n.* barru★

open *adj.* patiu, pattû, petû★; → **~** *v.* patû; → **~-handed** *adj.* ṭābtānu; → **~ (space)** *n.* pitru★, sūqu+, tarpašû★; → **~ chariot** *n.* pattūtu, ša-pattūti; → **~ field** *n.* nabrarû★; → **~ sea** *n.* qabli tānti; → **~ thighs** *v.* ḫallu patû★; → **~ up** *v.* patû+; → **~ed** *adj.* pattû; → **~ed-up** *adj.* pattû; → **~er** *n.* naptû★; → **~ing** *n.* aptu, apu, bitqu B◊, pētu, pû; → **~ing device** *n.* naptû★; → **~ing of the mouth** *n.* pīt pî★; → **~ly** *adv.* šūpîš★

operate *v.* epāšu (D)
operation *n.* epšetu
opinion *n.* ṭēmu; → **public ~** *n.* pī māti*
opponent *n.* bēl ṣāssi (legal), gārû*, māḫiru B*
opportune *adj.* ṭābu
oppose *v.* parāku
opposing *adj.* māḫiru
opposite *adj.* ša pūti, šutātû*; → **~** *n.* meḫret*; → **~** *prep.* ina pūt, miḫret*, pūt; → **~ direction** *n.* muḫḫurtu*; → **~ side** *n.* meḫretu*
opposition *n.* miḫirtu*, mitḫurtu*, piriktu*, šitqultu*; → **be in ~** *v.* atû B* (Št)
oppress *v.* dalālu B* (D), ḫabālu B, se'û◊, takāku+; → **~ed** *adj.* dullulu.*; → **~ion** *n.* ḫabālu*, tukku; → **~ive** *adj.* ḫābilu*; → **~or** *n.* ḫabbilu*, ḫābilu*
opt (for) *v.* biāru
opulence *n.* mašrû
opulent *adj.* šarû, ṭaḫdu
or *conj.* ū lū, ulâ; → **~ else** *adv.* ulamâ
oracle *n.* tērtu*; → **~ query** *n.* tamītu
oral *adj.* ša pî; → **~ paralysis** *n.* kadibbidû*; → **~ tradition** *n.* pû
oration *n.* tanattu*
orator *n.* ša-lišāni
orb *n.* kakkubu
orchard *n.* kiriu, ṣippatu*; → **(watered) ~** *n.* miṭirtu*
orchestra *n.* šitru*
ordain *v.* qabû, šiāmu
ordeal *n.* ḫursān
order *n.* qibītu*, sadīru, sidru, ṭēmu, ūrtu*; → **~** *v.* qabû, šapāru; → **be(come) in ~** *v.* tarāṣu B; → **be in ~** *v.* taqānu; → **in ~** *adj.* taqnu; → **in ~** *adv.* tariṣ; → **put in ~** *v.* sadāru, taqānu (D); → **set in ~** *v.* ešēru* (Št), sadāru, taqānu (D); → **by ~ of** *prep.* issu pî; → **in ~ to** *prep./subj.* bāsi; → **~ly** *adj.* multēširu*, sadduru, sudduru, tarṣu; → **give ~s** *v.* ṭēmu šakānu [i.]; → **issue strict ~s** *v.* šapāṭu*
ordinance *n.* riksu, ṣindatu*, ūrtu*; → **~s** *n.* tērtu* (pl.)
ordinary *adj.* ginû, sadru
ore *n.* epru
organize *v.* kaṣāru; → **~d** *adj.* kaṣru; → **~r** *n.* mušēpišu*; → **~r of banquet** *n.* bēl qarīti
organs *n.* mešrēti*
oriental *adj.* [ša] ṣīt šamši*
orientate *v.* maḫāru (D); → **~ o.s.** *v.* pānē ana X šakānu [i.]
orientation *n.* šikin pāni*

orifice *n.* pû
origin *n.* kisittu*, ummu; → **~al** *adj.* labīru; → **~al amount** *n.* ummu; → **~ally** *adv.* issu rēši; → **~ate** *v.* bašû (N)
originator *n.* bānû*
ornament *n.* simtu, šakuttu, šukānu*, tiqnu*; → **~(?)** *n.* ḫiddu; → **~ (kind of)** *n.* gum'u, kakkussu, ṭūdu; → **~ (kind of; on doors/columns)** *n.* sakku B*; → **~ (part of)** *n.* mudakkiu
orphan *n.* ekû*; → **~ girl** *n.* ekūtu*; → **~ed** *adj.* ekû*
oscillate *v.* sabā'u
ostentation *n.* multarḫūtu*
ostler *n.* rammāku+, sūsānu+
ostrich *n.* lurmu
other *adj.* šaniu; → **each ~** *adv.* aḫāiš; → **~ side** *n.* nēbartu*
otherwise *adv.* ulâ, ulamâ
otter *n.* kalab mê*, tarpašu*
ought *gram. part.* lū
ours *pron.* innû; → **~elves** *pron.* ramnin-ni*
out *adv.* ana qanni; → **give ~** *v.* barû B (D), qiāšu (D), uṣû (Š), zuāzu; → **keep ~** *v.* šēpu parāsu [i.]; → **~ of** *prep.* qanni; → **~ of breath** *adj.* napḫu+
outbid *v.* utāru+ (D)
outbreak *n.* nipḫu
outbuilding *n.* barakku*
outcast *adj.* ṭardu*
outcome *n.* ṣītu*
outcoming *adj.* āṣiu
outdistance → **be(come) ~** *v.* panû
outdoors *adv.* ana qanni, ina qanni
outer *adj.* bābānû*, kamû B*, kīdānû◊; → **~ gate** *n.* bāb kamî*; → **~ part** *n.* kīdītu*; → **~ wall** *n.* šalḫiu
outfit *n.* labussu, lubussu, nalbašu*; → **~** *v.* šitpuru*
outgoing *adj.* āṣiu
outgrow *v.* rabû
outhouse *n.* bētu šaniu
outlast *v.* anāḫu* (Št)
outlaw *n.* parriṣu
outlay *n.* akiltu; → **~** *v.* akālu
outlet canal *n.* mušēṣiu
outlet of a canal *n.* arūru*
outlet pipe *n.* mušēṣiu
outline *n.* kabbusītu, mēṣēru
outlive *v.* paršumu (D)
outrage *n.* mēreḫtu*, ru'ubtu◊, ṭūnāpu+; → **~ous** *adj.* erḫu*
outrider *n.* kallāpu (armored); → **commander of ~s(?)** *n.* rab kallāpi

outright *adv.* ina muḫḫi ašli
outset *n.* šarrû
outside *adv.* ina qanni; → ~ *n.* gīdānu, kamītu*, kīdānu*, qannu; → ~ *prep.* qanni; → **to the** ~ *adv.* kamātiš*; → **~r** *n.* aḫīu
outsize *adj.* utru; → ~ *v.* utāru
outskirts *n.* qannu
outstanding *adj.* bitrû*, ṣīru*, šūtuqu*
outstay *v.* katāru+
outstrip *v.* kašādu
outward(s) *adv.* ana qanni
outward appearance *n.* bunnu
outward bound *adj.* āṣiu
outward form *n.* lānu
outweigh *v.* kabātu*
oven *n.* adūgu*, atūnu, kīru, tinūru; → ~ **door** *n.* bāb tinūri
over *adv.* elānu◊, eliš, ṣēriš*; → ~ *prep.* alla◊, aq-qāt [o.], eli*, ṣēr*; → **give** ~ *v.* rammû (D), utāru+ (Š); → ~ **against** *n.* ana tarṣi◊; → **~all** *adv.* ana gammurti, kalīš*; → **~bearing** *adj.* akṣu*
overcast *adj.* erpu*; → **be(come)** ~ *v.* arāpu
overcoat *n.* qirmu
overcome *v.* kašādu; → **make** ~ *v.* maṣû (Š)
overcrowded *adj.* ḫabṣu+
overdo *v.* utāru (Š)
overdue *adj.* namarkû
overestimate *v.* utāru (Š)
overflow *v.* ana ṣirê malû [i.], nabā'u+ (Š); → **be(come)** ~ *v.* ṭaḫādu; → **~ing** *adj.* šurdû*, ṭaḫdu
overlap *v.* aḫāiš katāmu
overlay *n.* nalbētu [o.], siḫpu, tamḫīṣu*; → ~ *v.* labāšu* (Š), qarāmu+; → ~ **with** *v.* qarāmu
overmuch *adj.* utru+
overnight → **stay** ~ *v.* biādu, šumšû*; → ~ **accommodation** *n.* išpattalu [o.]
overpower *v.* šapālu+ (Š); → **~ing** *adj.* dāpinu*, kaškaššu*; → **~ing (weapon)** *n.* kašūšu*
overriding *n.* baṭālu+
overrule *v.* nasāku
overseas *adj./adv.* aḫūla tānti, eberti tānti*, ina ebertān tānti*, ina nēbarti tānti*
overseer *n.* uklu B*; → **temple** ~ *n.* ša-muḫḫi-bēt-ili; → ~ **of (...)** *n.* ša-muḫḫi-x; → ~ **of reeds** *n.* ša-muḫḫi-qanāti; → ~ **of the šahūru building** *n.* ša-muḫḫi-šaḫūri; → ~ **of the city of Nineveh** *n.* ša-muḫḫi-Nīnua; → ~ **of the coiffured women** *n.* ša-muḫḫi-kezrēti; → ~ **of the gate** *n.* ša-muḫḫi-bābi; → ~ **of the herds** *n.* rab sagullāti; → ~ **of the household** *n.* ša-muḫḫi-bēti; → ~ **of the royal residence** *n.* ša-muḫḫi-bēt-šarri; → ~ **of the royal tombs** *n.* rab bēt šarrāni, ša-muḫḫi-bēt-šarrāni; → ~ **of the storehouse(?)** *n.* ša-muḫḫi-qāti; → ~ **of the Succession Palace** *n.* ša-muḫḫi-bēt-rēdûti; → ~ **of the temple** *n.* ša-muḫḫi-bēt-ilāni; → ~ **of the temple of A&&ur** *n.* ša-muḫḫi-bēt-Aššūr; → ~ **to the palace** *n.* ša-muḫḫi-ēkalli
overshadow *v.* ṣallulu+
oversight *n.* lā šaḫsasūtu
overspread *v.* qarāmu+
overstate *v.* utāru (Š)
overt *adj.* apû*
overthrow *n.* nabalkattu*, sikiptu*; → ~ *v.* maqātu (Š), nabalkutu (Š), saḫāpu, sakāpu*
overtly *adv.* šūpîš*
overturn *v.* abāku B*, nabalkutu (Š), saḫāpu+, sakāpu*
overvalue *v.* uqāru* (Š), utāru (Š)
overview *n.* rikis gerri*
overweening *adj.* muštarriḫu*
overwhelm *v.* katāmu, katāmu* (Š), magguru+, saḫāpu; → **~ing** *adj.* sāḫipu*; → **~ing attack** *n.* siḫpu
overwork *n.* dullu utru; → ~ *v.* anāḫu, anāḫu (Š)
owe *v.* ḫabālu; → **one who ~s somebody a favor** *n.* bēl gimilli*
owing to *prep.* ina muḫḫi, issu pān
owl *n.* eššebu, qadû; → ~ **(kind of)** *n.* akkû*, ḫusû
own *adj.* attû*, ša raminī-; → ~ **strength** *n.* emūq ramāni*; → **~er** *n.* bēlu; → **without an ~er** *adj.* ša lā bēli; → **~erless** *adj.* ša lā bēli; → **~ership** *n.* bēlūtu
ox *n.* alpu; → **draught** ~ *n.* alap epinni; → **water/river** ~ *n.* alap nāri*; → ~ **fattener** *n.* mušākil alpi; → ~ **herder** *n.* rā'i alpi
pace *n.* ebertu B
pacification *n.* tanēḫtu [o.], tanīḫtu*
pack *v.* darāku [o.], epāqu (D) [o.], sarādu [o.]; → **~-animal** *n.* aṣappu; → **commander of ~-animals** *n.* rab aṣappi; → ~ **in** *v.* baṭālu, rammû (D); → ~ **sack** *n.* zurzu; → ~ **up** *v.* baṭālu, rakāsu; → **~age** *n.* riksu; → **~aged** *adj.* raksu
packaging *n.* libītu [o.]
packer *n.* kaṣṣāru [o.]
packet *n.* šuqlu [o.]
packing *n.* kiṣirtu, sarādu [o.]; → **~-supervisor** *n.* kaṣṣāru [o.]
pact *n.* adê

pad *v.* šê'u [o.]; → **~ding** *n.* tamlītu; → **~dle** *n.* lēqu+, sikkannu☆; → **steering ~dle** *n.* lēqu◊, sikkannu☆; → **~dock(?)** *n.* gugamlu

page *n.* dappu+, dassu

paid off *adj.* uṭṭuru

pail *n.* bandudû, madlû; → **~ing** *n.* šupšutu

pain *n.* siḫiltu☆, siḫlu; → **be(come) in ~** *v.* ḫiālu; → **inflict severe ~** *v.* sanāqu+ (D); → **(continuous) ~** *n.* murṣu; → **be(come) ~ful** *v.* marāṣu; → **~fully** *adv.* marṣiš; → **~less** *adj.* lā marṣu*; → **~staking** *adj.* marṣu, mušāniḫu*; → **~t** *n.* šimtu☆; → **~t** *v.* eṣāru+, tarāpu☆ (D); → **~t (the face)** *v.* ebēru B☆; → **~t in several colors** *v.* barāmu B☆ (D); → **~t o.s.** *v.* eqû (Gt); → **~ted** *adj.* ebru☆; → **be(come) ~ted** *v.* tarāpu☆; → **~ting** *n.* birmu☆, tiriptu [o.]

pair *n.* ṣimittu☆; → **~ of** *n.* ana šinīšu; → **~ed** *adj.* ta''umu+

pal up → **be ~** *v.* aḫû☆ (Gt)

palace *n.* ēkallu; → **little ~** *n.* egalturrû☆

Palace → **Succession ~** *n.* bēt rēdûti

palace enterer *n.* ērib ēkalli

palace farmer *n.* ikkār ēkalli

palace herald *n.* nāgir ēkalli

palace maid *n.* amat ēkalli

palace manager *n.* rab ēkalli

palace official *n.* mār ēkalli

palace people *n.* nišē ēkalli

palace personnel *n.* mazzāz ēkalli, ṣāb ēkalli

palace scribe *n.* ṭupšar ēkalli

palace servant *n.* urdu ēkalli

palace supervisor *n.* ša-pān-ēkalli

palatable *adj.* ṭābu

palate *n.* ikku+, līq pî☆

palatial profession (kind of) *n.* ša-ēkallāt i

pale *adj.* erqu, paṣiu, unnutu; → **be(come) ~** *v.* erāqu; → **be(come)/be ~** *v.* unnutu (D); → **turn ~** *v.* erāqu (D), paṣû; → **~face** *n.* pūṣānu; → **~ness** *n.* murṣānūtu+, pūṣu

Palestine *n.* Pilistu

pall of death *n.* šibiḫ mūti☆

pallid *adj.* erqu

pallor *n.* murṣānu+, murṣānūtu+, pūṣu

palm *n.* pušku; → **trimmed ~-frond** *n.* našbaṭu◊; → **~-rib** *n.* zinû; → **~ frond** *n.* sāru B; → **~ tree** *n.* gišimmaru☆

palpable *adj.* apû☆

palpitate *v.* nakādu, tarāku

palpitation *n.* tirku

palsy *n.* mišittu☆ (apoplectic)

paltry *n.* makiu+

pan *n.* itqūru; → **~der** *n.* bēl ḫarimti; → **~der** *v.* zanānu B☆

panegyric *n.* tanittu☆

panel *n.* dappu☆

pang *n.* siḫlu

panic *n.* ḫaiattu☆, ḫattu☆, ḫīp libbi; → **~** *v.* arāru B☆

pannier *n.* nakmuru

pansy *n.* assinnu

pant *v.* laḫātu+, na'āšu☆

panther *n.* nemru

panting *n.* napīšu☆

pantomimic dancing *n.* reqdu+

pantry *n.* bēt ḫurši, ḫuršu [o.]

pap *n.* pappāsu; → **~er** *n.* niāru, urbānu; → **~yrus** *n.* niāru, urbānu

parable *adj.* tamšiltu☆; → **utter ~s** *v.* mašālu+ (Š)

parade *n.* mašdaḫu☆, mēteqtu☆; → **~** *v.* etāqu, šadāḫu☆

paragon *n.* riddu, riddu☆

paralyse *v.* kabālu☆ (D), šamāmu☆; → **be(come) ~d** *v.* kabālu☆

paralysis *n.* mangu, mišittu☆ (apoplectic), muggu, rimûtu☆, šimmatu

paramount *adj.* elīu

paranymph *n.* sūsabinnu☆

parapet *n.* gabadibbu☆, sa'ītu

paraphernalia *n.* udê

parasite *n.* kalmutu, naiālu

parasol *n.* ša-ṣilli

parcel out *v.* batāqu

parch *v.* erēru☆ (D), qalû+; → **~ed** *adj.* ḫamadīru☆; → **be(come) ~ed** *v.* erēru☆; → **~ing thirst** *n.* laplaptu; → **~ment** *n.* magallatu◊, mašku, qulāptu+; → **~ment scroll** *n.* magallatu☆

pardon *n.* pīdu, rēmūtu☆; → **~** *v.* kabāsu☆ (D), padû, rēmu rašû [i.], riāmu

pare *v.* qalāpu, qalāpu+; → **~ off(?)** *v.* kaṣābu☆; → **~nt** *n.* ālidu; → **~ntage** *n.* kisittu☆; → **~nthood** *n.* ālidūtu; → **~nts** *n.* abu ummu

parity *n.* miḫrūtu☆

park *n.* ambassu, kirimāḫu☆

part *n.* paras, pirsu, qātu, zittu; → **~** *v.* bêšu☆; → **front ~** *n.* pānāti; → **lower ~** *n.* šapiltu☆; → **main ~** *n.* kabittu☆; → **~ from** *v.* patû

partake *v.* zuāzu

participate in *v.* erābu ina muḫḫi [i.]

particular *adj.* parsu; → **~ly** *adv.* parīsatti+

partisan *n.* šaggāšu+

partition *n.* birītu B☆; → ~ *v.* batāqu
partner *n.* bēl zitti, ebru☆, illu☆, šutāpu☆, tappû; → **~ship** *n.* ebrūtu☆, itbārūtu [o.], šutāpūtu☆, tappūtu☆
partridge *n.* iṣṣūr ḫurri; → **(gray)** ~ *n.* kakkabānu
party *n.* battu, qarētu
pass *n.* nēbartu+, nērubu; → **narrow** ~ *n.* pušqu☆; → ~ **away** *v.* alāku nammušīšu [i.], nammušīšu alāku [i.]; → ~ **by** *v.* bâ'u☆, etāqu; → ~ **for** *v.* dagālu (N); → ~ **off** *v.* alāku; → ~ **on** *v.* etāqu (Š); → ~ **out** *v.* zuāzu; → ~ **over** *v.* bâ'u☆, etāqu; → ~ **the night** *v.* biādu; → **~age** *n.* alaktu☆, alāku, mētequ☆, mētuqu, nēburu+; → **narrow ~age** *n.* suqāqu+; → **~ageway** *n.* dalbānu☆, dulbānu; → **~enger** *n.* ālik ḫūli, āliku; → **~er(-)by** *adj.* ētiqu☆; → **~ing** *adj.* ētiqu; → **~ion** *n.* bibil libbi☆, nīš libbi☆; → **~ionate** *adj.* šamru; → **be(come) ~ive** *v.* quālu
password *n.* dibbē lammadūti, ittu☆
past *adj.* gamru; → ~ *n.* labīru, maḫirtu, pānītu; → ~ **time(s)** *n.* pānītu
paste *n.* muššu'tu☆
pastille *n.* kupatinnu☆
pastoral care *n.* rā'iūtu+
pastry *n.* pennigu
pasturage *n.* namû☆, rītu☆
pasture *n.* aburru☆, gipāru☆, mer'ītu☆, namû☆, sa'du; → ~ *v.* ra'û
pat *n.* tirku; → ~ *v.* tarāku
patch *v.* kabbû (D)
patent *adj.* patiu
paternal house *n.* bēt abi
paternity *n.* abbūtu+
path *n.* daraggu☆, gerru☆, ḫarrānu, kibsu, padānu, ṭūdu B☆, urḫu B☆; → **mountain ~(?)** *n.* sangu☆; → **narrow** ~ *n.* sūqinnu [o.]
pathetic *adj.* lammunu
patience *n.* arāk ikki◊, zābilānūtu+
patient *adj.* šādidu*; → ~ *n.* marṣu; → **be(come)** ~ *v.* ikku urruku [i.]
patina *n.* šuḫtu
patio *n.* kisallu
patrimony *n.* bēt abi
patrocinium *n.* abbūtu
patrol *n.* gudūdu◊; → ~ *v.* duālu
patron *n.* bēl ṭābti; → **~age** *n.* abbūtu, bēl ṭābtūtu, šumāku+; → **~ize** *v.* ḫaṣānu
patter *v.* nazāmu; → **~n** *n.* uṣurtu
patty *n.* libbu B+
paunch *n.* karšu+, šammāḫu☆; → **~y** *n.* karšānu
pauper *n.* muškēnu
pause *n.* kīlu☆

pave *v.* kasāru; → **make** ~ *v.* raṣāpu+; → **~d** *adj.* raṣpu+; → **~ment** *n.* muttalliktu☆, riṣiptu+ (tesselated), riṣpu+
pavilion *n.* bēt mussa''īti, qumbutu+
paving *n.* riṣpūtu+; → ~ **(block)** *n.* kisirtu
paw *n.* qātu, rittu; → ~ *v.* rapāsu+; → **~n** *n.* maškānu+, passu☆; → **~ning** *n.* maškānūtu+
pay *v.* apālu (D), eṭāru B, šaqālu☆; → **make** ~ *v.* tadānu (Š); → ~ **attention** *v.* lētu nadû [i.], na'ādu☆ (Gt); → ~ **attention to** *v.* ēnē šakānu [i.], puqqu, uznu ana X šakānu [i.]; → ~ **back** *v.* saḫḫuru tadānu [i.]; → ~ **compensation** *v.* rību riābu [i.]; → ~ **completely** *v.* gammuru tadānu, šallumu tadānu; → ~ **double** *v.* eṣāpu tadānu; → ~ **down** *v.* kaspu tadānu [i.]; → ~ **in full** *v.* eṭāru B (D), šallumu tadānu; → ~ **off (a debt)** *v.* eṭāru B (D); → **~able** *adj.* ša tadāni*; → **~ment** *n.* nidnu☆, nisḫu, nūptu◊; → **make a ~ment on** *v.* karû (D) [o.]; → **~ments** *n.* ilkakāti
payoff *n.* tašbītu [o.]
Pazuzu head (amulet) *n.* kaqqad Pazūzi
pea *n.* šu'u; → **Indian** ~ *n.* mangu B+
peace *n.* nēḫtu☆, nūḫtu☆, salīmu☆, sulummû☆, šalintu; → **make** ~ *v.* salāmu; → **universal** ~ *n.* salīm kiššati☆; → ~ **of mind** *n.* nēḫtu☆, ṭūb libbi; → **~able** *adj.* salmu; → **~ful** *adj.* nēḫu, salmu
peacemaker *adj.* musallimu☆
peach *n.* ḫaḫḫu
peacock(?) *n.* pa'û☆
peak *n.* appu, rēštu☆, ubān šadê☆, ubānu, ziqpu; → **(mountain)** ~ *n.* pulukku☆; → **~s** *n.* rēšāti
peal *n.* šugummû; → ~ *v.* ragāmu, šagāmu
pear *n.* angāšu+; → ~ **(tree)** *n.* kameššeru☆
pearl *n.* abnu, īn nūni◊
peas *n.* ḫallūru☆; → **~ant** *n.* ikkāru, qatinnu; → **~ant(?)** *n.* ša-eqli; → **~antry** *n.* qatinnūtu
pebble *n.* galālu B◊, išqillatu☆
peck *n.* sūtu; → ~ *v.* laqātu+, naqāḫu+
pectoral *n.* ša-irti B; → **~(?)** *n.* guggupinnu
peculiar *adj.* aḫīu; → **~ity** *n.* ittu☆
pecuniary *adj.* [ša] kaspi
peddle *v.* saḫāru; → **~r** *n.* saḫḫiru, sāḫiru B; → **~r (kind of)** *n.* ša-ḫusinnēšu
pedestal *n.* gišgallu☆, kerṣappu☆, kigallu
pedestrian *n.* āliku, allāku+
pedigree *n.* kisittu☆
pedlar *n.* saḫḫiru; → ~ **woman** *n.* saḫḫirtu

peek *v.* ḫiāru+
peel *n.* qulāptu [o.], qulpu+; → ~ *v.* qalāpu; → **~ off** *v.* qalāpu; → **~ed** *adj.* qallupu, qalpu; → **~ings** *n.* qalpē+
peep *v.* ḫiāru+, ṣabāru
peer *n.* miḫru, tamšīlu B☆; → **~ in at** *v.* šurru☆; → **~less** *adj.* lā šanān☆
peeve *v.* ikku karû* (D)
peevish *adj.* marru B+, nazziqu☆; → **~ness** *n.* martu
peg *n.* naṣru, sikkutu; → **~ master** *n.* rab sikkāti
Pegasus *n.* ikû
pelican *n.* kumû☆
pellet *n.* kupatinnu☆; → **form a ~** *v.* kapātu☆ (D)
pelt *n.* mašku, šārtu
pelvis *n.* rapassu
pen *n.* agappu+, pitqu, qarṭuppu, tarbāṣu; → **reed ~** *n.* qan ṭuppi☆, qanû+, qarṭuppu; → **~alize** *v.* šipṭu emādu; → **~alty** *n.* arnu☆, ḫiṭṭu, sartu, šipṭu; → **~dant** *n.* mašqaltu [o.], šuqullālu☆; → **~dant lamp** *n.* nabraštu+; → **~dent** *adj.* šuqallulu☆
penetrate *v.* erābu; → **make ~** *v.* palāšu; → **~ sexually** *v.* naqābu☆
penetration *n.* pilšu
peninsula *n.* rēš tānti☆
penis *n.* matnu, ušāru
penitence *n.* nasḫuru
penitent(?) *n.* bēl palluḫi
penitential psalm *n.* eršaḫungû
penitentiary *n.* bēt mēsiri☆
pennant *n.* urigallu
penny-pincher *n.* kāriṣu*
pensive *adj.* muštābilu*
pent-up *adj.* kabsu+
penury *n.* muškēnūtu
people *n.* ba'ulāti☆, lišānu+, nišē, ummatu☆, ūqu◊; → **lover of ~** *n.* rā'imu ša nišē
pep up *v.* balāṭu (D)
per *prep.* ša; → **~ cent** *n.* ana mēt
perambulation *n.* atalluku☆
perceive *v.* ḫakāmu, ragāšu+, ṭeāmu+
perceptible *adj.* ša iḫakkimūni*
perception *n.* ḫakimtu*, rigšu+, ṭēmtu+
perch *v.* sakātu+; → **~ance** *adv.* issurri
percussion *n.* miḫṣu
perdition *n.* šaḫluqtu☆
peremptory *adj.* ša lā paqāri
perfect *adj.* gamru, gitmālu☆, šaklulu; → ~ *v.* malû+ (Š), šaklulu☆; → **~ bull** *n.* šaklulu; → **~ likeness** *n.* kal muššuli☆; → **~ed** *adj.* šallumu+; → **be ~ed** *v.* malû+ (Št); → **~ion** *n.* gitmālūtu☆, šuklultu☆, šuklulūtu; → **~ly** *adv.* gitmāliš☆
perfidious *adj.* naklu+
perfidy *n.* niklu+
perforate *v.* naqābu+, palāšu
perforation *n.* ḫarūru+, pilšu
perform *v.* epāšu; → **~ completely** *v.* šallumu epāšu; → **~ s.th. jointly** *v.* karāku epāšu; → **grotesque ~er** *n.* paḫḫizu; → **~er of military or civil service** *n.* ālik ilki
perfume *n.* raqqūtu, riqiu, šamnu ṭābu; → **make ~** *v.* raqqû; → **~ maker** *n.* muraqqiu; → **female ~ maker** *n.* muraqqītu; → **~ peddler** *n.* ša-suādēšu; → **~d** *adj.* raqqû
perfunctory *adj.* šēṭu
pergola *n.* qirsu B
perhaps *adv.* issurri, piqtatti; → **~(?)** *adv.* pīqatti
peril *n.* puluḫtu; → **~ous** *adj.* [ša] puluḫti*
perimeter *n.* kipputu, limītu☆, siḫirtu☆
period *n.* adannu, palû; → **~ical** *adj.* ša adanni*; → **~icity** *n.* adannūtu
periphery *n.* siḫirtu☆
perish *v.* ḫalāqu, napšutu qatû [i.]; → **~able** *adj.* ša ḫalāqi*
perjure o.s. *v.* tamīt šapti tamû [i.]
perjury *n.* tamītu ša dabābti šapti
perk (up) *v.* qablē rakāsu [i.]
perk up *v.* balāṭu
permanence *n.* malduru
permanent *adj.* kaiamānīu
permeate *v.* ḫalālu
permission → **give ~** *v.* šalāṭu+ (Š)
permissive *adj.* naddinu*
permit *v.* tadānu; → **~ted** *n.* šalṭu+
pernicious *adj.* [ša] muāti
perpendicular *adj.* zaqpu; → ~ *n.* ziqpu; → **~ (line)** *n.* muttarrittu☆
perpetrate *v.* epāšu☆ (Gtn)
perpetrator *n.* ēpišānu
perpetual *adj.* lazzu
perpetuate *v.* lazāzu
perplex *v.* dalāḫu, ešû☆; → **~ed** *adj.* dalḫu; → **~ing** *adj.* dāliḫu☆; → **~ity** *n.* duluḫḫû☆, ešītu☆
persecute *v.* radādu, radāpu
persecution *adj.* rīdu☆; → ~ *n.* ridpu, tukku
persecutor *n.* raddādu☆
perseverance *n.* lazzūtu*
persevere *v.* barû C☆ (Št), lazāzu
Persia *adv.* Parsumaš; → **~n (sheep)** *adj.* parsuāiu; → **~n Gulf** *n.* Marratu☆, tāntu ša Kaldi☆, tāntu šaplītu☆; → **~n lilac** *n.* zanzaliqqu

Persis *adv*. Parsumaš
persist *v*. lazāzu; → **~ence** *n*. lazzūtu*; → **~ent** *adj*. lazzu; → **~ently** *adv*. lazziš☆
person *n*. amēlu, napšutu; → **in ~** *adv*. qātā-; → **~age** *n*. kaqqudu; → **~al attendant** *n*. kizû☆; → **~ally** *adv*. qātā-; → **~ally(?)** *n*. qarbāti-; → **~ate** *v*. epāšu (D); → **~nel** *n*. mazzāzu; → **temple ~nel** *n*. mazzāz ēkurri
perspective *n*. madgulu☆
perspicacity *n*. ḫassūtu☆
perspiration *n*. zūtu
perspire *v*. zūtu karāru
persuade *v*. dabābu (Š)
persuasive *adj*. mušadbibu*
pert *adj*. erḫu☆
pertain to *v*. qarābu ina muḫḫi
pertinacious *adj*. ašṭu☆
pertinent *adj*. qurbu ina muḫḫi
perturb *v*. dalāḫu, narāṭu (D)
peruse *v*. šasû☆ (Gtn)
pervade *v*. parāḫu+
perverse *adj*. egru, patlu+; → **be ~** *v*. egēru☆ (Gt)
pervert *adj*. patlu+; → **~** *v*. egēru☆ (D), patālu+; → **~ed** *adj*. egru
pester *v*. dalāḫu, marāṣu (Š)
pestilence *n*. dibiru☆, mūtānu
pestle *n*. bukānu☆, esittu☆
pet *n*. dādu☆; → **come to an ~er out** *v*. balû☆
petition *n*. ša'altu+, taslītu☆, taṣlītu☆, un-ninnu☆
petrified *adj*. šuḫarruru☆; → **be(come) ~** *v*. šuḫarruru☆
petticoat *n*. ša-ḫurdati
pettish *adj*. nazziqu☆
petty *adj*. baṣru+, qallulu
petulant *adj*. nazziqu☆
phalanx *n*. sadirtu, sidirtu☆
phantom *n*. zakīqu
pharaohh *n*. pir'û☆
pharmacist *n*. ša-gabêšu
pharmacy *n*. bēt gabê*
phase *n*. adannu
philanthropist *n*. rā'imu ša nišē
Philistea *n*. Pilistu
phlegm *n*. ḫaḫḫu B☆, suālu, uḫḫu☆
phlegmatic *adj*. marû☆
phosphorescent *adj*. naggulu☆
phrase *n*. siqru, tēltu
phrenitis *n*. ummu ša muḫḫi☆
phylactery *n*. mē'elu
physical *adj*. [ša] šīri; → **~ condition** *n*. šīru
physician *n*. asû; → **chief ~** *n*. rab asê; → **chief woman ~** *n*. azugallatu
physiognomy *n*. alandimmû☆
physique *n*. nabnītu☆
pick *v*. baṣāru, laqātu, laqātu+; → **~ clean** *v*. ḫarāṭu; → **~ fruit** *v*. magādu; → **~ off** *v*. qatāpu; → **~ on** *v*. magādu; → **~ out** *v*. biāru, ḫiāru, rēšu našû [i.]; → **~ quarrel** *v*. magādu; → **~ up** *v*. laqātu, matāḫu
pickaxe *n*. akkullu, kalappu
picked *adj*. madlu
picket *n*. zaqīpu
pickle *v*. madālu
picnic table *n*. paššūr gerri☆
picture *adj*. ṣalmu+; → **~** *n*. uṣurtu+
piebald *n*. paṣiu ṣalmu
piece *n*. ḫirṣu, ḫuṣābu, passu☆, šibirtu, tak-kassu; → **~ of cloth** *n*. lubāru☆, muṣiptu◊
pied *adj*. barmu☆; → **~** *n*. paṣiu ṣalmu
piedmont *n*. šēpītu
pier *n*. kāru
pierce *v*. dakāšu☆, naqābu+, palāšu, patā-ḫu, saḫālu, šaqāru☆; → **~ through** *v*. dakāšu+; → **~d** *adj*. dakšu☆, palšu
piercing pain *n*. dikšu☆, siḫlu
piety *n*. palāḫ ili
pig *n*. ḫuzīru, šaḫû; → **female ~** *n*. ḫuzīr-tu, šaḫītu☆; → **young ~** *n*. kurkizānu; → **~ fat** *n*. nāḫu
pigeon *n*. su''u, summatu☆; → **carrier ~** *n*. su''u; → **wild ~** *n*. amuršānu☆, tamšīlu; → **~-hole** *n*. aptu; → **~ (kind of)** *n*. pudri sūqi
piggishness *n*. ḫuzīrūtu+
piggy *n*. ḫuzīrānu☆
piglet *n*. kurkizānu
pigment *n*. da'mutu, šammu+; → **red ~** *n*. makru+
pigmy *n*. kurû☆
pigsty *n*. erretu B☆
pike *n*. ziqtu+
pile *n*. dintu B☆, gurunnu☆, isītu; → **~** *v*. ṣiānu, šapāku☆; → **~ o.s. up** *v*. tabāku (N); → **~ of barley** *n*. karû B; → **~ of grain** *n*. karmu; → **~ on** *v*. garānu☆ (D), qarānu☆; → **~ up** *v*. garānu☆, kamāru, kamāru (D), ka-rāmu B, nakāmu☆, tabāku; → **~d up** *adj*. kamru☆
pilfer *v*. kabāsu+
pilgrim *adj*. kāribu
pill *n*. kakkultu+, kupatinnu☆; → **form a ~** *v*. kapātu☆ (D); → **~age** *n*. miši'tu☆
pillar *n*. timmu
pillory *n*. malūṭu☆
pillow *n*. ḫa'ūtu
pilot *n*. mallāḫu+
pimp *n*. bēl ḫarimti

pimple *n.* ziqtu
pin *n.* kirissu☆, sikkutu+
pincers *n.* allunāti [o.]
pinch off *v.* karāṣu
pine *n.* ašūḫu
pinion *n.* abru B☆
pink (a flower) *n./adj.* illūru☆
pink (a flower)ily *adv.* illūriš☆
pink (a flower)ish *adj.* illūrānu
pink carnation *n./adj.* illūru☆
pinkly *adv.* illūriš☆
pinky *adj.* illūrānu
pinnacle *n.* pulukku☆
pious *adj.* ašru B☆, mutnennû☆, na'du☆, pāliḫ ili; → **be(come) ~** *v.* ašāru C☆; → **~ly** *adv.* na'diš☆
pip *n.* abnu
pipe *n.* bību, ebbūbu, qanû, rāṭu, takkussu; → **~** *v.* ḫalālu B, nabābu☆; → **~s** *n.* bībāni; → **~tte** *n.* takkussu, uppu
piping hot *adj.* baḫru☆
piquant *adj.* šēlu☆
pirate *n.* ḫabbāt tānti*, ḫabbātu; → **~** *v.* ḫabātu
Pisces *n.* Nūnē☆, Zibbāti (pl.)
piss *n.* šīnāti; → **~** *v.* šiānu
pistachio *n.* buṭuttu; → **~ (nut)** *n.* buṭnu; → **~ nut** *n.* buṭnu+
pit *n.* gab'u, gubbu, gubbutu+, šuttatu☆; → **clay ~** *n.* issû☆
pita *n.* kusīpu☆
pitch *n.* ittû☆, iṭṭû, qīru; → **~** *v.* nadû☆, retû☆; → **~er** *n.* assammu☆, kandu, qulliu
piteous *adj.* lammunu
pitfall *n.* šuttatu☆
pith *n.* līpu
pithos *n.* kirru
pitiful *adj.* lammunu, rēmānu
pitted *adj.* naqquru+
pity *n.* rēmu; → **~** *v.* rēmu ina muḫḫi/ana X šakānu [i.]; → **have ~** *v.* rēmu ina muḫḫi/ana X šakānu [i.], rēmu rašû [i.]
pivot *n.* nukuššû
placable *adj.* musallimu☆
placate *v.* nuāḫu (D)
place *n.* ašru☆, maškunu; → **~** *v.* karāru, šakānu, uzuzzu (Š); → **put in ~** *v.* ṣabātu (Š); → **~nta** *n.* ipu☆
placid *adj.* nēḫu, pašḫu
plague *n.* dibiru☆, lipit Erra☆, mūtānu, šibṭu
plain *adj.* apû☆; → **~** *n.* bamāti☆, nabrarû☆, ṣēru☆; → **make ~** *v.* pašāqu+; → **~ly** *adv.* pašīqatti+, šūpîš☆; → **~tive** *adj.* nazziqu☆
plait *n.* gidlu; → **~** *v.* eṣāpu, gadālu+, ṭamû☆; → **~ed** *adj.* raksu, ṭamû☆
plan *n.* eṣurtu☆, gišḫurru☆, kipdu☆, liṭṭu, ṣibūtu☆, šibqu☆, uṣurtu; → **~** *v.* kapādu, ṣubbû☆ (Š)
plane tree *n.* dulbu☆
planet *n.* bibbu
plank *n.* dappu+; → **~ (resting on pillars)** *n.* ḫittu+; → **~ bridge** *n.* ḫittu+; → **~ing** *n.* raqpu+
planned *adj.* kapdu*
planner *n.* kāpidu☆; → **chief ~** *n.* rab šiknāni
plans → **make ~** *v.* kaṣāpu (D)
plant *n.* šammu, ziqpu; → **~** *v.* satālu☆, zaqāpu; → **name of an ill-smelling and thorny ~** *n.* daddaru☆; → **~(?) (kind of)** *n.* šadê◊; → **~/stone (kind of)** *n.* arzallu; → **~ (kind of)** *n.* abiūru, alamû☆, billu B, ḫaltappānu, kamantu, kušru, qutratu, sagalmušu, suḫsi Issār; → **aromatic ~ (kind of)** *n.* ballukku, kurdinnu; → **~ (trees)** *v.* ḫarāšu☆ (D); → **~ation** *n.* mērēšu, qablu B; → **~ed** *adj.* zaqpu; → **~er** *n.* zāqipu*; → **~ing** *n.* mērēštu B☆
plaster *n.* gaṣṣu+, šallaru☆, šelluru; → **~** *v.* siāru; → **(wall-)~** *n.* sīru; → **~ed** *adj.* sēru
plate *n.* adappu☆, dappu☆, dassu, kussimtu, luṭṭu☆ (soup), siḫḫāru; → **~** *v.* aḫāzu (D), qarāmu+
plateau *adj.* madburu
plated with *adj.* uḫḫuzu
platform *n.* du'u☆; → **~(?)** *n.* ḫutû
platoon *n.* ešertu; → **~ commander** *n.* rab ešerti
platter *n.* siḫḫāru
plausible *adj.* qēpu
play *n.* mēlulu; → **~** *v.* namēlulu; → **~ (a stringed instrument)** *v.* lapātu☆ (D), zamāru+; → **~ the flute** *v.* nabābu☆; → **~er** *n.* mēlulû☆; → **~ful** *adj.* mēlulāiu☆
playmate *n.* illu☆
plaza *n.* rebītu☆
plea *n.* taṣlītu☆; → **~d** *v.* dabābu; → **~sant** *adj.* ṭābu; → **make ~sant** *v.* damāqu (D), ṭiābu☆ (Š); → **~se** *v.* libbu ṭubbu [i.]; → *interj.~se* addānika, apputtu [o.]; → **be(come) ~sed** *v.* napardû☆; → **~sing** *adj.* maḫru, ṭābu; → **~sure** *n.* lalû, multa''ūtu☆, mussa''ītu, tarṣiātu☆, ṭūb libbi, ulṣu☆; → **~sure** *v.* lullû☆; → **give ~sure** *v.* lallû (D); → **at ~sure** *adv.* ina ḫadûti; → **with ~sure** *adv.* ḫadīš☆; → **~sure-house** *n.* bēt mussa''īti
plebeian *n.* ṣāb ḫupši☆; → **like a ~** *adv.*

ḫupšiš*
pledge *n.* maškānu, maškānūtu, šapartu, šapru B; → ~ *v.* ana šaparti šakānu
plentiful *adj.* ḫabṣu*, napšu; → **very** ~ *adj.* ṭuḫḫudu*
plenty *n.* nam'udu, ṭuḫdu; → ~ **of** *adj.* ma'du
pleurisy *n.* ḫunṭu ša ḫašê*
pliable *adj.* kanšu*
pliers *n.* allunāti [o.]
plight *n.* sinqu
plinth *n.* kisû*
plot *n.* niklu+, šibqu*; → ~ *v.* dabābu; → **~ter** *n.* dābibānu
plough *n.* epinnu; → **subsoil-** ~ *n.* ḫarbu
Plough → **the** ~ *n.* ereqqu*
ploughman *n.* ikkāru+, ša-epinni
ploughshare *n.* sikkutu
pluck *v.* baqāmu, marāṭu+, qatāpu; → ~ **(wool)** *v.* napāšu B; → ~ **out** *v.* ḫasāpu, šamāṭu; → **~ing** *n.* qitpu [o.]; → **~y** *adj.* ṣarmu+
plug *n.* purussu*, sikkat mê*
plum *n.* angāšu, ḫaḫḫu; → **~age** *n.* kappu B*, nāṣu*, šārtu; → **~ber** *n.* pallišu
plumbing *n.* bībāni
plume *n.* abru B*, qimmatu*
plump *adj.* kabburu, ṭapšu [o.], ubbuṭu*; → **be(come)** ~ *v.* ṭapāšu*; → **~-bellied** *adj.* ṭappušu*; → **~-faced** *adj.* ṭappušu*; → ~ **down** *v.* maqātu; → **make** ~ **up** *v.* ebēṭu* (D)
plunder *n.* šallutu; → ~ *v.* gazālu+, ḫabātu, ḫubtu ḫabātu, mašā'u, šalālu*; → **~ed** *adj.* šallu*; → **~er** *n.* mār ḫabbāti*, nābi'u*, nāpi'u*, šālilu*; → **~ing** *n.* miši'tu*, nēkemtu*, šilpu*
plunge *v.* maqātu, šaḫāṭu C*; → ~ **under water** *v.* šalû*
plural *adj.* ma'du; → ~ *n.* ma'dūtu*; → **~ity** *n.* ma'dūtu*
plus *prep.* adi, adu
plush *adj.* šamḫu*
ply *n.* qiplu*; → ~ *v.* kanāšu*
pneumonia *n.* muruṣ ḫašê*
pocket *n.* takāltu*; → **~ful** *n.* ammār takālti
pockmark *n.* birdu*; → **~(?)** *n.* šullu* (big)
pod → **(carob)** ~ *n.* ḫarūbu+
podium *n.* du'u*, mazzassu
poem *n.* zamāru
poignant *adj.* sāḫilu*
point *n.* dikšu*, ṣipru*, ziqtu; → ~ **out** *v.* kallumu (D), ša'ūdu (Š); → **~ed** *adj.* eddu, zaqtu*; → **be(come)** **~ed** *v.* edādu
poised *adj.* zaqpu+
poison *n.* imtu, šammu+, šammu ša muāti; → ~ *v.* sammumu+ (D), šammu ša muāti šaqû [i.]; → **~ous** *adj.* [ša] imti*; → **~ous matter** *n.* sumāmītu
poke *v.* utāru (Š); → **~r** *n.* mutirru; → **~r face** *n.* pānē ḫardūti [i.]
pole *n.* makūtu (shaduf), mašaddu (yoke), ṭarkullu*, zaqīpu, ziqpu; → **mooring** ~ *n.* namḫaru*, ṭarkullu*; → **punting** ~ *n.* parīsu*
polecat *n.* kakkišu
polemic *n.* gārû*; → **~s** *n.* ṣāssu
polish *v.* kapāru, marāqu+; → **~ed** *adj.* ebbu, ṣuppu
pollen(?) *n.* sēpu
pollinate *v.* rakābu* (D)
pollination *n.* rikibtu*
pollute *v.* lu''û*, ṭanāpu+ (D); → **~d** *adj.* lu''û*, ṭanpu+
pollution *n.* aruštu*
pomegranate *n.* armannu, lurintu, nurmû; → ~ **pip** *n.* aban nurmî*; → ~ **seed** *n.* purṣīnu
pommel *n.* karru*
pomposity *n.* multarḫūtu*
pompous *adj.* multarḫu*
pond *n.* iarḫu; → **~er** *v.* abālu B* (Št), amatu šutābulu [i.], amû* (Št), ḫarāṣu (Št) [o.], nadānu* (Št); → **be(come)** **~er** *v.* issi libbi dabābu [i.]; → **~ering** *n.* tušaḫruṣu [o.]; → **~erous** *adj.* kabru, marû*
pontoon *n.* maškuru
pony *n.* kūdunu
pool *n.* agammu, iarḫu; → **deep** ~ *n.* nērubu+
poor *adj.* katû*, lapnu; → ~ *n.* makiu+, muškēnu+; → **be(come)** ~ *v.* lapānu*; → **the** ~ *n.* mār muškēnūtu; → **~man** *n.* muškēnu; → **~ly** *adv.* lamniš [o.], marṣiš; → **~ness** *n.* muškēnūtu, muškēnūtu+
poplar *n.* adāru B; → **Euphrates** ~ *n.* ṣarbutu; → **resin of** ~ *n.* ḫīli ṣarbiti; → ~ **wood** *n.* ṣarbutu
poppet *n.* dādu*
poppy *n.* rezpu+
populace *n.* ūqu◊
popular *adj.* ra'mu, ša pî nišē
populate *v.* ušābu (Š)
population *n.* ba'ulāti*, nišē
porch *n.* bēt mutirrēti*, sippu+
porcupine *n.* burmāmu*
pore *n.* ḫarūru+; → **~-skinned** *adj.* ḫarūrānu; → **~d** *adj.* ḫarūrānu

pork *n.* šīr šaḫî★
porous *adj.* ḫarūrānu, paḫḫu+; → **be(come) ~** *v.* paḫāḫu+; → **~(?)** *adj.* šaḫarru★
porpoise *n.* massāru+
porridge *n.* pappāsu
port *n.* kāru; → **~able** *adj.* muttalliku; → **~able stove** *n.* adūgu+; → **~ent** *n.* giskimmu★, ittu; → **~er** *n.* nāšiu; → **head ~er** *n.* rab atê; → **~ico** *n.* bēt appāti★, bēt ḫillāni, bēt mutirrēti★; → **~ion** *n.* ḫirṣu, nisḫu, zittu; → **~ion out** *v.* zuāzu; → **~ly** *adj.* ebû, kabburu; → **~ray** *v.* eṣāru
position *n.* gisgallu★, mazzassu, nanzāzu★, šiknu
positive answer *adj.* annu kēnu
positively *adv.* kēniš
possess *v.* išû★; → **~ed** *adj.* maḫḫû★, ṣabtu; → **~ion** *n.* qātu; → **~ion(s)** *n.* namkūru★; → **~ions** *n.* anūtu, maršītu, mimmû; → **~ive** *adj.* išānû★; → **~or** *n.* bēlu
possibility *n.* mal'ētu [o.]
possible *adj.* naṭû★; → **be(come) ~** *v.* alāku, naṭû B★
post *n.* mazzassu, mazzāzu; → **~** *v.* ana kallie šēbulu; → **by ~** *adv.* ana kallie; → **~-** *adj.* ša urki; → **~-horse** *n.* kūdunu ša kallie; → **~-rider** *n.* kalliu; → **~-stage** *n.* bēt mardēti, kalliu; → **~ (troops)** *v.* ḫarāku◊; → **~ service** *n.* kalliu; → **~erior** *adj.* urkīu; → **for ~erity** *adv.* aḫrātaš★
posthaste *adv.* ana kallie
postman *n.* kalliu
postmaster *n.* rab kallî
postpone *v.* uḫḫuru
postulant *n.* šarrāiu+
postulate *v.* šiāmu+
posture *n.* šiknu
pot *n.* ḫaṣbu, karputu ; → **clay ~** *n.* ḫaṣbu; → **like a ~** *adv.* ḫaṣbattiš★, karpāniš★, karpatiš★; → **small ~** *n.* qadurtu+; → **~ caulker** *n.* kāpir diqāri; → **~ stand** *n.* gangannu★, kankannu, kannu
potash *n.* idrānu★, uḫūlu★
potency *n.* nīš libbi★; → **sexual ~** *n.* kuzbu
potent *adj.* dannu; → **~ial** *adj.* naṭû★
potion *n.* mašqītu
potsherd *n.* ḫaṣbattu★
potter *n.* paḫḫāru; → **~ (about)** *v.* riāqu+; → **master of ~s** *n.* rab paḫḫāri; → **~y** *n.* ḫaṣbu
pouch *n.* takāltu★
poultice *n.* mē'elu, ṭīpu★; → **~ (kind of)** *n.* ṣilbānu
poultry *n.* iṣṣūru
pounce *v.* maḫāṣu; → **~ upon** *v.* maqātu
pound *v.* daqāqu+, suāku, tarāku
pour *v.* naqû, šapāku★, tabāku; → **~ (over)(?)** *v.* taḫāḫu★; → **~ forth** *v.* nabā'u+ (Š); → **~ in** *v.* reḫû★; → **~ off** *v.* šaḫālu+; → **~ out** *v.* nazālu◊, šapāku+, tabāku, zanānu★ (Š); → **make ~ out** *v.* tabāku★ (Š); → **~ed out** *adj.* tabku; → **~ing** *n.* šipku
poverty *n.* muškēnūtu; → **~-stricken** *n.* muškēnu+
powder *n.* qēmu, tābīlu [o.]
power *n.* danānu★, dannūtu★, dunnu★, emūqu, kubukku★, lē'ûtu★, lītu★; → **give ~** *v.* šalāṭu+ (Š); → **have ~** *v.* šalāṭu+; → **(world) ~** *n.* kiššūtu; → **~ base** *n.* dannūtu★; → **~ful** *adj.* allallu★, dannu, gašru, mitru★; → **(more) ~ful** *adj.* guššuru★; → **~ful (person)** *n.* dannatānu; → **~less** *adj.* lā lē'û★, makiu, pisnuqu★; → **be(come) ~less** *v.* parāru; → **~lessness** *n.* lu'tu★
practicable *adj.* naṭû★, ša ana epāši ṭābūni
practically *adv.* ibašši
practice *n.* parṣu, ussu★; → **~** *v.* epāšu (D)
practitioner *n.* muppišu
praise *n.* dalīlu, tanattu★, tanittu★; → **~** *v.* dalālu, na'ādu (D), na'ādu★, šamāru B★ (Gt); → **~d** *adj.* na'du B★, šanu''udu★
praiseworthy *adj.* na'du B★
prance *v.* rapāsu+
prank *n.* namūtu [o.]; → **~ster** *adj.* ēpiš namūti [o.]
prate *v.* ṣabāru+
prattle *v.* ṣabāru; → **~r** *n.* ḫabbiru
pray *v.* sarruru, suppû★, ṣallû; → **~ devoutly** *v.* šutēmuqu★; → **~ to** *v.* sullû★; → **~er** *n.* ikribu, nīš qāti★, pīt upnē★, sīpu★, suppû★, surāru, ṣullû★, taslītu★, taspītu★, taṣlītu★, tēmēqu★ (deep), tiriṣ qāti; → **hand-lifting ~er** *n.* šuillakku; → **humble ~er** *n.* labān appi★; → **intense ~er** *n.* šutēmuqu★; → **~er bowl** *n.* pūt upni; → **~ing mantis** *n.* ša'ilu B
pre- *adj.* ša pān
pre-eminence *n.* ašarēdūtu
pre-eminent *adj.* ašarēdu
preach *v.* ragāmu; → **~er** *n.* raggimu
prebend *n.* isqu
precarious *adj.* lā šalmu
precaution *n.* ḫirdu
precede → **be(come) ~** *v.* panû; → **~nce** *n.* ālik pānûtu◊
preceding *adj.* pānīu
precept(s) *n.* iḫzu★

precinct → **sacred** ~ *adj.* ḫamru
precious *adj.* nasqu, uqru; → **be(come)** ~ *v.* uqāru; → **most** ~ *adj.* šūquru*; → ~ **item (kind of)** *n.* irṣiṣu, nītu; → ~ **object (kind of)** *n.* būn abni; → ~ **stone (kind of)** *n.* ḫusāru [o.], išḫu B, sīlu; → ~ **stone inlay** *n.* digilu
precipice *n.* kāpu*, nērubu+
precipitate *v.* arāḫu* (D)
precipitious *adj.* pašqu*
precise *adj.* ḫarṣu; → ~**ly** *adv.* ḫarṣiš*
precision *n.* qatnūtu+
preclude *v.* parāku (D)
precociously *adv.* ina lā ūmi
precursor *n.* ālik pāni
predator *n.* zību; → ~**y** *adj.* maššiʾu*; → ~**y bird** *n.* nāʾiru*
predecessor *n.* ālik maḫri*, ālik pāni
predestined *adj.* šēmu*
predetermined *adj.* šēmu*
predicament *n.* dannutu
predict *v.* qību šakānu; → ~**ion** *n.* qību; → **make a** ~**ion** *v.* qību šakānu
predominance *n.* šalṭūtu+
predominate *v.* šalāṭu* (Gt)
prefect *n.* šaknu (acting); → ~**ship** *n.* šaknūtu
prefer → **be(come)** ~ *v.* ṣabû+; → ~**able** *adj.* maḫru
preferably *adv.* ibašši
preference *adj.* libbu
prefix *n.* elītu*
pregnancy *n.* mērû*, tašḫītu*
pregnant → **be(come)** ~ *v.* arû B; → **get** ~ *v.* reḫû* (Dt); → ~ **woman** *n.* arītu B, erītu*
prehistoric *adj.* ša pān abūbi*
prelacy *n.* šatammūtu*
prelate *n.* šatammu*
preliminary *adj.* pānīu
premature *adj.* ḫarpu; → ~ **baby** *n.* kūbu*; → ~ **birth** *n.* nīd libbi*; → ~**ly** *adv.* ina lā simānīšu*, ina lā simini
premeditated *adj.* ṣamru*
premises *n.* bētu
preoccupation *n.* muruṣ libbi, nikittu
prepair *n.* epāšu, tērsītu*; → ~**s** *adj.* šaṣbutu
prepare *v.* epāšu, kaṣāru, rēšu našû [i.], ṣabātu (Š), šutērsû*, ṭiābu+ (D); → **make** ~ **(for burial)** *v.* kannû (D); → ~ **for journey or career** *v.* ḫūlu ana šēpi šakānu [i.]; → ~ **o.s. (for war)** *v.* qablē rakāsu [i.]; → ~**d** *adj.* epšu, šaṣbutu; → ~**dness** *n.* rikis qabli◊
preponderate *v.* kabātu*
prerogative *n.* pursānu+
prescribe *v.* qabû, uqqû*
prescription *n.* malṭuru
presence *n.* pānāti, pānu, ušuzzu◊; → **in the** ~ **of** *prep.* ina pān, ina pānāt, pānāt
present *adj.* qurbu; → ~ *n.* igisû, katrû*, nidintu◊, qēssu, širiktu, šūbultu*, šulmānu; → ~ *v.* maḫāru (D), qarābu (D), qiāšu, šarāku, šutlumu*; → **be(come)** ~ *v.* qarābu, uzuzzu; → **at** ~ *adj.* ša ūmi ana ūmi; → **at** ~ *adv.* annūrig; → ~ **(tense)** *n.* marû*; → ~ **o.s.** *n.* ramanšu kallumu; → ~**ation** *n.* taklimtu, tamḫīru [o.]; → ~**er** *n.* muqarribu*; → ~**ly** *adv.* annūrig
preserve *v.* eṭāru, ezābu+ (Š), naṣāru; → ~ **in salt** *v.* madālu; → ~ **life** *v.* šaṭāpu*; → ~**r** *n.* nāṣiru
press *v.* daʾāpu (D), emādu (D), ḫanāqu, mazāʾu; → ~ **(out)** *v.* ṣaḫātu B*; → ~ **down** *v.* ṣapāru*; → ~ **hard(?)** *v.* gammuzu; → ~ **hard upon** *v.* kabāsu+; → ~ **heavily** *v.* gamādu+; → ~ **out** *v.* mazāʾu; → ~ **strongly** *v.* bazāḫu [o.]
pressgang *v.* bazāḫu [o.]
pressure *n.* tēkubtu* (time); → ~ *v.* bazāḫu [o.]; → ~**(?)** *n.* siʾūtu*
prestige *n.* kabdūtu*
prestigious *adj.* kabtu*
presumably *adv.* issurri
presume *v.* kaṣāpu, šiāmu+
presuming *adj.* multarḫu*
presumption *n.* mēreḫtu*
presumptuous *adj.* multarḫu*; → ~**ness** *n.* multarḫūtu*
pretence *n.* sebīrūtu+
pretend *v.* nakālu; → ~**er** *n.* ḫammāʾu*
pretentious *adj.* multarḫu*
preterite *n./adj.* gamartu*, ḫanṭu B*
pretext(?) *n.* tēgirtu
pretty *adj.* damqu
prevail *v.* biālu, šalāṭu* (Gt); → **be in** ~ *v.* šalāṭu+; → ~ **over** *v.* maṣû; → ~**ing** *adj.* bāʾilu*
prevalence *n.* bāʾilūtu*
prevalent *adj.* bāʾilu*
prevent *v.* kalû, parāku (D); → ~**ion** *n.* piriktu*; → ~**ive** *adj.* pāriku*
previous *adj.* maḫrû, pānīu; → ~ **to** *prep.* pānāt, ullânu*; → ~**ly(?)** *adv.* ina maḫirti
prey *n.* šallutu; → ~ *v.* ḫabātu, šalālu*
price *n.* šīmu; → **go beyond the** ~ *v.* batāqu [o.]; → **market** ~ *n.* maḫīru; → **reduce the** ~ *v.* batāqu [o.]; → ~**less** *adj.* uqru adanniš
prick *n.* miḫṣu; → ~ *v.* saḫālu, takāpu, zaqātu*; → ~**ly** *adj.* siḫlānu*
pride *n.* bāltu*, gipiš libbi*; → ~ **o.s.** *v.*

šarāḫu☆ (Dt)
priest *n*. sangû; → **chief lamentation ~** *n*. kalamāḫu; → **high ~** *n*. ēnu B☆; → **lamentation ~** *n*. kalû B; → **position of a purification ~** *n*. išippūtu☆; → **purification ~** *n*. išippu☆; → **~-confectioner** *n*. sangû karkadinnu; → **~ (kind of)** *n*. lagāru☆, lumaḫḫu☆, maqaltānu, nēšakku☆, pašīšu☆, zabardabbu☆; → **~ess** *n*. ēntu☆; → **~ess (kind of)** *n*. aššat ili☆; → **~hood** *n*. sangûtu; → **~s (kind of)** *n*. angubbû☆
primacy *n*. ālik pānûtu◊
primary *adj*. rēštû☆
prime *adj*. rēštû☆
primeval *adj*. rēštû☆
primitive *adj*. rēštû☆
prince *n*. mār šarri☆, rubû☆; → **~ly** *adj*. muttallu☆; → **~ship** *n*. mār šarrūtu; → **~ss** *n*. etellutu☆, mar'at šarri, rubūtu☆, šanukkatu☆
principal *n*. kaqqudu; → **~ity** *n*. šarrūtu
print *n*. ṭibḫu
prior to *prep*. pānāt, ullânu☆
priority *n*. ālik pānûtu◊
prison *n*. bēt kīli☆, bēt ṣabti, bēt ṣibitti; → **~ official** *n*. ša-bēt-kīli☆; → **~er** *n*. ṣabtu; → **~er of war** *n*. līṭu [o.], šallutu; → **~ers of war** *n*. ḫubtu
privacy *n*. ašar šēpu parsat☆
private *adj*. parsu; → **~ (soldier)** *n*. rādiu
privation *n*. tamṭītu☆
privilege *n*. ikkibu; → **~d status** *n*. kidinnūtu
privy to *adj*. ḫassu+
prize *v*. naṣāru
pro- *n*. rā'imānu
probably *adv*. issurri, uddi [o.]
probe *n*. litiktu☆; → **~** *v*. latāku
problem *n*. ḫittu B☆
problematic *adj*. ašṭu☆
procedure *n*. kūn qāti☆, nēpēšu; → **~s** *n*. tallaktu B (pl.) [o.]
proceed *n*. ana pāni alāku [i.]; → **~** *v*. etāqu, ḫarrānu šutēšuru [i.], parāṣu, radû, radû☆ (Š), šadāḫu☆; → **(legal) ~ings** *n*. dēnu; → **~s** *n*. mānaḫtu (pl.)
process *n*. dabābu; → **~** *v*. epāšu (D); → **start a ~** *v*. dēnu garû; → **~ion** *n*. māluku, tabūtu; → **~ion (street)** *n*. mašdaḫu☆; → **~ional way** *n*. muttalliktu☆
proclaim *v*. apû☆ (Š), idû☆ (Š); → **~er** *n*. mubarriu*
proclamation *n*. šisīt nāgiri☆
procuration *n*. taḫḫūtu☆
procure *v*. qarābu (D), zanānu B☆; → **~r** *n*. zāninu☆; → **~ss** *n*. mummirtu [o.]
prod *v*. zaqātu+, zaqātu☆
prodigal *adj*. mubaddidu*, sappiḫu☆
prodigy *n*. tabrâti☆
produce *n*. biblu B☆ (pl.), miḫirtu B☆, miširtu☆; → **~** *v*. bašû (Š), qarābu (D); → **~d** *adj*. epšu
product *n*. arû E☆, epšetu, pāru B☆, tarbītu; → **~ion** *n*. miḫirtu B☆
profane *v*. ṭanāpu+ (D)
profess *v*. idû☆ (Š); → **~ion** *n*. šūdûtu☆, ummânūtu+; → **~ion (kind of)** *n*. bādisu, gaddāiu, ḫataššu◊, nisiu, šālipu; → **~ional (soldier)** *adj*. zakkû
proficiency *n*. lē'ûtu☆
profile *n*. lānu
profit *n*. kušīru, nēmulu; → **~-making** *n*. tadmiqtu [o.]; → **~able** *adj*. mudammiqu, ša kušīri*; → **~less** *adj*. lā kušīri☆
profound *adj*. rūqu☆; → **~** *n*. šuppulu☆; → **be(come) ~** *v*. ruāqu
profuse *adj*. šamḫu☆; → **be(come) ~** *v*. šamāḫu☆
progenitor *n*. ālidu
progenitress *n*. ālissu, ālittu☆
progeny *n*. nannabu☆
prognosis *n*. qību; → **make a ~** *v*. qību šakānu
prognostic *n*. ittu; → **~ate** *v*. qību šakānu
progress *n*. alāku, ana pāni alāku [i.]; → **~** *v*. ukkušu; → **~ion** *n*. talluku☆
prohibit *v*. kalû, lâṭu☆, parāku (D); → **~ed** *adj*. ḫarmu+
project *v*. kapādu, magāgu (D); → **~ed** *adj*. kapdu*; → **~ion** *n*. āṣītu☆, ḫandūru☆
proletariat *n*. mār muškēnūtu, ṣindu u birtu☆
prolific *adj*. unnubu☆
prolong *v*. arāku (D), arāku (Š), labāru☆ (Š); → **~ed** *adj*. arku+, urruku*
promenade *n*. māluku
prominent *adj*. āṣiu, šaqiu; → **~** *n*. tizqāru☆
promiscuity *n*. naiākūtu*
promiscuous *adj*. ballu, nā'iku; → **be ~** *v*. niāku (Gtn)
promise *n*. nidin pê☆, qibīt pî☆; → **~** *v*. pû tadānu [i.], qabû; → **break a ~** *v*. pašāru [o.]
promissory note *n*. u'iltu
promontory *n*. nakkāpu☆
promote *v*. elû (Š), rabû (D)
promotion *n*. šēlûtu, tarbītu☆ (pl.)
prompt *v*. ḫarādu (D); → **~ly** *adv*. ana ūmi, qerbiš☆
promulgate *v*. barû B (D)
prone *adj*. qaiāpu☆

prong *n.* zāqiptu+
pronounce *v.* zakāru☆; → **~ment** *n.* qibītu☆, zikir šapti☆
pronunciation *n.* lišānu+, rigmu, tēltu
proof *n.* mukinnūtu◊, mukīntu
prop *n.* šumāku+; → **~ (up)** *v.* našû
propagate *v.* rapāšu (D)
propense *adj.* quppu B☆
propensity *n.* qūptu*
proper *adj.* asmu☆, kēnu, sadduru, tarṣu, ṭābu; → **be(come) ~** *v.* asāmu☆, naṭû B☆, tarāṣu B; → **~ly** *adv.* ṭābiš☆; → **~ty** *n.* anūtu, bišītu☆, bīšu B☆, bušû☆, būšu☆, makkūru, maršītu, namkūru☆, nikkassu, qinītu
prophecy *n.* amat qibīt ilūti☆
prophesy *v.* ragāmu
prophet *n.* raggimu; → **~** *n.* maḫḫû; → **~ess** *n.* maḫḫūtu, raggintu
propitious *adj.* mitgāru☆, šalmu
proportion *v.* mašāḫu+ (D); → **~al** *adj.* mitḫāru☆; → **be ~al** *v.* maḫāru☆ (Gt); → **~ally** *adv.* mitḫāriš☆; → **~ate** *adj.* mitḫāru☆; → **~s** *n.* minâti☆ (pl.)
proposal *n.* milku
propose *v.* malāku; → **~ (marriage)** *v.* ḫašādu
proposition *n.* milku
proprietor *n.* bēlu
propriety *n.* simtu
prosecute *v.* ragāmu
prosecution *n.* dēnūtu+
prosecutor *n.* bēl dēni
prospect *n.* diglu
prosper *v.* ašāru B, ešēru☆, kašāru+, naḫāšu☆; → **~ity** *n.* bu'āru☆, dunqu, ḫegallu☆, išdiḫu, kušīru+, nuḫšu, ṭūbu; → **grant ~ity** *v.* naḫāšu☆ (D); → **~ous** *adj.* naḫšu☆, šamḫu☆
prostitute *adj.* šamḫatu☆; → **~** *n.* ḫarintu; → **sacred ~** *n.* qadissu
prostitution(?) *n.* ḫarmūtu
prostrate *adj.* maqtu; → **~ o.s.** *v.* napalsuḫu☆, šukênu
prostration *n.* labān appi☆
protect *v.* ḫaṣānu, ḫatānu☆, ina idi alāku [i.], kunnupu☆ (D), naṣāru; → **~ed** *adj.* ḫallupu; → **~ion** *n.* ḫiṣnu☆, ṣalūlu, ṣillu, ṣulūlu; → **~ive** *adj.* nāṣiru; → **~or** *n.* nāṣiru; → **~or (on chariot)** *n.* tašlīšu
protege *n.* kidinnu, kidinnû◊
protest *v.* bakû, pû patû [i.]
protract *v.* arāku (D); → **~ed** *adj.* urruku*
protrude *v.* magāgu, uṣû (vent.)
protrusion *n.* āṣītu☆
protuberance *n.* dikšu☆, nakkāpu☆, nipḫu
proud *adj.* muštarriḫu☆, šarḫu☆, šitruḫu☆; → **be(come) ~** *v.* šarāḫu☆; → **make ~** *v.* šarāḫu☆ (D); → **~ly** *adv.* šamḫiš☆
prove *v.* buāru (D) [o.], kuānu (D); → **~d** *adj.* kunnu; → **~n** *adj.* latku; → **~nder** *n.* kissutu+; → **~rb** *n.* tēltu
provide *v.* mânu◊, rēšu kullu [i.], tadānu; → **~ (food)** *v.* apālu B; → **~ abundantly** *v.* ṭaḫādu (D); → **~ for** *v.* zanānu B☆; → **~ with** *v.* ašāru, ṣabātu (Š), šakānu (Š); → **~nce** *n.* āširtu; → **~r** *n.* zāninu☆
province *n.* pāḫutu, pīḫatu☆
provisional *adj.* simanīu*
provisioner *n.* zāninu☆
provisioning *n.* šaṣbutu, zinnāti☆
provisions *n.* eṣidītu◊ (travel), ṣuddê☆ (travel); → **travel ~** *n.* ṣidītu☆
provocation *n.* mēreḫtu☆
provocative *adj.* erḫu☆; → **be(come) ~** *v.* erēḫu☆
provoke *v.* dabābu (Š)
prow *n.* rēšu; → **~ess** *n.* meṭlūtu☆
prowl *v.* ṣâdu, ṣâdu◊
proximity *n.* qurbūtu, ṭēḫu
prudence *n.* kūn libbi☆, sanqūtu☆, tašīmtu☆
prudent *adj.* mitluku☆, muštālu☆, pitqudu☆, sanqu☆
prune *n.* šallūru; → **~** *v.* arû F☆, batāqu
pry *v.* eṣānu, ḫiāṭu☆
psalm *n.* eršemmû
psoriasis *n.* epqu☆
psyche *n.* napšutu
pub *n.* bēt sābê☆, bēt šikāri; → **~erty** *n.* ṣaḫūrānūtu
public works → **chief of ~** *n.* rab pilkāni, rab pilki
publicity *n.* edûtu☆
publicize *v.* idû☆ (Š), udû (D) [o.]; → **~d** *adj.* uppû
publicly *adv.* šūpîš☆
pucker (up) *v.* kalāṣu☆
pudding *n.* pappāsu
puddle *n.* iarḫu
pudgy *adj.* kabburu
puff *v.* napāḫu, napāšu; → **~ up** *v.* napāḫu+; → **~ed-up** *adj.* napḫu+; → **~er** *n.* nāḫirānu☆; → **~y** *adj.* napḫu+
pugnacious *adj.* muṣṣālu☆
pull *v.* šadādu, šaḫāṭu, šâṭu☆; → **~ down** *v.* napālu☆, naqāru, saḫāpu+; → **~ o.s. together** *v.* libbu ṣabātu [i.]; → **~ off** *v.* nasāḫu, qatāpu, šaḫāṭu, šamāṭu+; → **~ out** *v.* marāṭu+, nasāḫu, šalāḫu, šalāpu, šamāṭu+; → **~ taut** *v.* magāgu (D); → **~ violently** *v.* pašānu☆; →

~ed-out (part) *n.* našmaṭu☆
pulmonary *adj.* [ša] ḫašê*
pulsate *v.* sabā'u, tabû☆ (Gtn)
pulse *n.* sakikkû, šer'ānu+; → ~ *v.* tabû☆ (Gtn)
pulsing *adj.* tēbû☆
pulverize *v.* suāku, ṭiānu
pumice (stone) *n.* qasūru+
pump *v.* nasāku+
punch *n.* miḫṣu; → ~ *v.* maḫāṣu
punctilious *adj.* ḫardu
punctually *adv.* adi ṭuppišu, ṭuppišu
puncture *v.* naqābu+, palāšu, patāḫu, takāpu
pungent *n.* ṣāripu+
punish *v.* enēnu☆, ḫiṭṭu emādu, sanāqu+ (D), ṣarāpu+ (D), šipṭu emādu; → **~ment** *n.* annu B☆, arnu☆, ennettu☆ (divine), ḫiṭṭu, šērtu B☆, šipṭu; → **inflict ~ment** *v.* šipṭu emādu
puny *adj.* qātnu
pup *n.* mūrānu
pupil *n.* talmīdu, tarbiu
pupillage *n.* talmīdūtu+
puppet *n.* passu☆
puppy *n.* mūrānu
purchase *n.* qinītu, šīmu; → ~ *v.* laqû, šâmu☆; → **~r** *n.* māḫirānu [o.], šā'imānu☆
purchasing venture *n.* šīmūtu◊
pure *adj.* ebbu, ellu, zakû; → **be(come) ~** *v.* ebābu, elālu, qadāšu☆, zakû; → **~ly** *adv.* elliš☆, udēšu
purge *v.* ešēru☆ (Š), ṣarāpu+
purification *n.* kupartu◊, takpirtu, taqdīšu [o.], tazkītu, tēlissu; → **~ (ritual)** *n.* šuluḫḫu☆; → **~ device** *n.* ša-tēlissi; → **~ ritual (kind of)** *n.* bēt salā' mê☆
purifier *n.* mullilu
purify *v.* elālu (D), ḫâpu☆, kapāru, qadāšu☆ (D)
purity *n.* ellūtu☆, zakûtu; → **~(?)** *n.* ḫūptu◊
purl *v.* ḫabābu☆
purple *n./adj.* argamannu, takiltu+; → **(blue) ~ (wool)** *n.* takiltu☆
purpose *n.* ṣummuru☆, ṣumru☆; → **~ly** *adv.* ina ḫūd libbi [i.]
purr *v.* ḫabābu☆
purse *n.* ḫintu, kīsu; → **(leather) ~** *n.* naštuq☆
purslane *n.* parparḫû [o.], purpuḫinnu
pursue *v.* kašādu (D), radādu, radāpu, radû
pursuit *adj.* rīdu☆; → ~ *n.* ridpu
purulent *adj.* šarku*
purvey *v.* zanānu B+; → **~or** *n.* mušākilu B☆, rab šīmāni, zāninu☆
pus *n.* qadūtu☆, šarku
push *v.* da'āpu, daḫû, nakāpu☆; → **~ away** *v.* napāṣu; → **~ back** *v.* sakāpu☆; → **~ down** *v.* napāṣu; → **~ over** *v.* nabalkutu (Š); → **~er** *n.* sakkāpu☆
pussy *n.* ḫurdatu☆
pustule *n.* bubu'tu☆
put *v.* nadû☆, ṣalā'u [o.], šakānu; → **~ across** *v.* ḫakāmu (Š); → **~ around** *v.* labû (Š), saḫāru☆ (Š); → **~ aside** *v.* bêru☆; → **~ away** *v.* elû (D); → **~ down** *v.* ana ḫissiti šaṭāru [i.], kabāsu, karāru, ṣalā'u [o.]; → **~ hands on** *v.* aḫu ummudu [i.]; → **~ off** *v.* šalāḫu+, uḫḫuru; → **~ on** *v.* apāru☆ (D), emādu (D), labāšu (N); → **~ out** *v.* balû (D); → **~ s.o. up for night** *v.* biādu (D); → **~ together** *v.* esāpu, kaṣāru, rakābu+ (D); → **~ up** *v.* kannû (D) [o.]; → **~ up with** *v.* zabālu+; → **~refaction** *n.* zupru☆
puzzle *v.* pašāku+ (D)
puzzling *adj.* dāliḫu☆
pygmy *n.* kurû☆
pyramid *n.* dintu B☆, isītu, sikkutu
pyre *n.* išātu, kurullu☆, šuruptu
pythia *n.* šā'iltu☆
qabu^ to deny → **(...) ~** *gram.part.* lā
quadrangle *n.* mitḫartu☆
quadrilateral *n.* mitḫartu☆
quadruple *n.* rubbu'u☆
quail *n.* urballu☆
quake *n.* ratātu+; → ~ *v.* narāṭu, nâšu☆, râdu☆, ruābu
qualification *n.* sapqūtu+; → **~ (kind of)** *n.* sisalḫu
qualified *adj.* damqu; → **be(come) ~ for** *v.* damāqu ana
qualify *v.* damāqu (D)
quality *n.* ṭēmtu+; → **average ~** *adj.* gurnu☆; → **first ~** *adj.* rēštu☆; → **of bad ~** *adj.* massuḫu [o.]; → **of inferior ~** *adj.* maṭiu [o.]
qualms *n.* erišti libbi☆
quantity *n.* middutu; → **large ~** *n.* mādû☆
quarrel *n.* ṣāssu, ṣēlūtu☆; → ~ *v.* ṣâlu [o.], ṣāssu garû; → **have a ~** *v.* ṣāssu garû; → **~some** *adj.* muṣṣālu☆
quarter *n.* rabuttu; → **city ~** *n.* bābtu
quartermaster *n.* rab tilli
quartet *n.* arbittu
quartz *n.* duḫšiu
quasi *prep.* tamšīl☆
quaver *v.* narāṭu
quay *n.* kāru; → **~-bank** *n.* kāru; → **~ and ferry dues** *n.* miksi kāri nēberi
queasy *n.* qā'iu*

queen *n*. issi ēkalli, malkatu⋆, rubātu⋆, rubūtu⋆, sēgallu, šarrutu; → **~-consort** *n*. sēgallu
queer *adj*. aḫīu
quell *v*. balû (D), kabāsu
quench *v*. balû (D)
querulous *adj*. nazziqu⋆
query *n*. zakār šumi⋆
quest *n*. teb'ītu⋆; → **~ion** *n*. maš'altu⋆; → **~ion** *v*. lā qiāpu, sanāqu (D), ša'ālu, ša'ālu+; → **~ionable** *adj*. lā taqnu*; → **~ioning** *n*. maš'altu⋆
queue *n*. šidlu+
quibble *v*. dabābu (Gtn)
quick *adj*. ḫanṭu B⋆, ḫummuṭu◊; → **be(come) ~** *v*. ḫamāṭu B⋆; → **~-tempered** *adj*. aggu⋆, rasmu; → **~-witted** *adj*. ḫarīpu+, ḫassu; → **~en** *v*. arāḫu⋆ (D), balāṭu, ḫamāṭu B⋆ (D); → **~ening** *adj*. [ša] balāṭi; → **~ly** *adv*. arḫiš, ḫanṭiš⋆, radpi◊, surriš⋆, zamar⋆; → **do ~ly** *v*. ḫamāṭu B⋆ (Š); → **make+too ~ly** *v*. dalāḫu epāšu; → **very ~ly** *adv*. arḫiš arḫiš, ḫitmuṭiš⋆, urruḫiš⋆
quiescent *adj*. qālu
quiet *adj*. nēḫu, qālu; → **~** *n*. nēḫtu⋆; → **be(come) ~** *v*. nuāḫu; → **keep ~** *v*. qapāpu+; → **stay ~** *v*. quālu, sakātu+; → **~ly** *adv*. nēḫiš⋆; → **~ness** *n*. qūlu
quietude *n*. qūlu
quill *n*. kappu B⋆
quilt *n*. tapšû
quince *n*. supurgillu
quints *n*. ḫanšat tuāmē+
quintuple *v*. ḫamāšu⋆ (D); → **~ts** *n*. ḫanšat tuāmē+
quit *adj*. uṭṭuru; → **~** *v*. rammû (D)
quite *adv*. adanniš
quits *adv*. uṭṭuru issu pān aḫāiš [i.]
quiver *n*. azannu, išputu, salṭu; → **~** *v*. katātu⋆, narāṭu; → **~ing** *n*. nurruṭu⋆
quota *n*. iškāru, munūtu⋆; → **~tion** *n*. nisḫu
quote *gram.part*. mā; → **~** *v*. nasāḫu
quotient *n*. bandû⋆, igitennu⋆
rabbit *n*. arnubu
rabble *n*. ḫalgatû⋆
rabid *adj*. šegû⋆
rabies *n*. šegûtu*
race *n*. bētu+, būnu, lisnu; → **~** *v*. lasāmu; → **~r** *n*. munnarbu⋆
rack *n*. naṣru; → **~(?)** *n*. maḫruṣu
radiance *n*. birbirru, melammu⋆, šarūru; → **gain ~** *v*. nabāṭu⋆ (Ntn)
radiant *adj*. barḫu, namru; → **be(come) ~** *v*. napardû⋆; → **make ~** *v*. namāru⋆ (D); → **awe-inspiringly ~** *adj*. namurru⋆; → **~ly** *adv*. namriš⋆
radiate *v*. barāḫu⋆, namāru, zalāgu+ (D)
radically *adv*. šuršiš⋆
radish *n*. puglu
radius *n*. pirku⋆; → **~ and ulna** *n*. ibrēti⋆
raffle (off) *v*. pūru karāru [i.]
raft *n*. amu◊, ḫallimu◊, kalakku, makkūtu+; → **big ~ (kind of)** *n*. magulû⋆; → **~er** *n*. gašūru
rag *n*. lubāru⋆, ulāpu; → **~ (for wiping)** *n*. šuḫattu
rage *n*. ru'ubtu◊, tēgimtu⋆, uggatu⋆, uzzu⋆; → **~** *v*. agāgu⋆, labābu⋆, nadāru⋆, ra'ābu, šagāšu+, šegû⋆; → **~r** *n*. nā'iru⋆
ragged *adj*. šarṭu
raging *adj*. nadru⋆, nalbubu⋆, nanduru⋆, šalbābu⋆, šitmuru⋆
raid *n*. šiḫṭu
rail *n*. kutlu [o.]; → **~** *v*. tuāku+ (D); → **~ at** *v*. ṭapālu⋆; → **~ing** *n*. šupšutu
rain *n*. šamūtu⋆, zīnu, zīqu+ (violent), zunnu; → **~** *v*. zanānu; → **bring ~** *v*. zanānu⋆ (Š); → **violent ~** *n*. riḫṣu; → **~ down** *v*. salāḫu⋆
rainbow *n*. manzāt⋆
raindrop *n*. tīku
rainfall *n*. zunnu
raise *v*. dakû, elû (D), elû (Š), matāḫu, rabû (D), tabû (Š); → **~ up** *v*. šaqû B⋆ (D); → **be ~d high** *v*. elû⋆ (Št)
raisin *n*. muzzīqu⋆, purṣīnu+
raising *n*. nišītu⋆, nīšu
rally *v*. paḫāru
ram *n*. iābilu, puḫālu; → **mountain ~** *n*. sappāru; → **young ~** *adj*. kabsu; → **make ~ in** *v*. raṣāpu+
ramble *v*. nagāšu⋆ (Gtn), rapādu; → **~ about** *v*. alāku (Gtn)
ramify *v*. larû
ramp *n*. arammu⋆ (siege), nabalkattu⋆; → **go on a ~age** *v*. nadāru⋆ (N); → **~ant** *n*. tābiu
rampart *n*. dūru, šalḫiu
rancid → **be(come) ~** *v*. zapāru+
rancor *n*. martu; → **~ous** *adj*. marru B
random *adj*. muqqelpû⋆
range *n*. tarṣu B; → **~** *v*. sarāḫu+; → **~r** *n*. maṣṣar qabli
rank *n*. be'šu, dargu+, sidru+; → **first ~** *n*. ašarēdūtu; → **~ and file** *n*. ḫupšu⋆, ṣeḫru◊ (pl.); → **~ing** *adj*. ašarēdu
rankle → **make ~** *v*. marāru⋆ (Š)
ransack *v*. maša'u
ransom *v*. ezābu+ (Š), padû (D), paṭāru

rap *n.* miḫṣu; → ~ *v.* maḫāṣu
rapacious *adj.* ekkimu☆, maššiʾu☆
rape *n.* nīku; → ~ *v.* ḫamāṣu◊ (Š), mazāʾu (D), niāku; → **~d** *n.* nēku
rapid *adj.* lasmu, qallīlu+
rapist *n.* nāʾikānu [o.]
rapt *adj.* sarḫu
rapture *n.* surḫu*
rapturous *adj.* sarḫu
rare *adj.* uqru; → **be(come) ~** *v.* uqāru; → **make ~** *v.* uqāru☆ (D), uqāru☆ (Š)
rarefy *v.* raqāqu (D), uqāru☆ (D)
rarely *adv.* uqur*; → **do ~** *v.* uqāru
rarity *n.* uqurtu*
rascal *n.* ḫappu, ḫarḫaru☆
rash *adj.* lasmu, rasmu; → ~ *n.* undē; → **~ness** *n.* paḫzānūtu+
rasp *v.* garādu+
rat *n.* ḫabaṣīru☆; → **mole ~** *n.* ušummu
rate *n.* middutu
rather *adv.* ibašši
ratify *v.* kuānu (D)
rating *n.* dargu+
ratio *n.* apšitû☆; → **~n out** *v.* zuāzu; → **~nal** *adj.* rāš ṭēmi u milki☆, ṭēmānu
rattle *v.* ramāmu☆
ratty *adj.* akbarāiu+
ravage *v.* akālu, ḫalāqu (D), ḫarābu☆ (Š)
rave *v.* maḫû☆, šegû☆; → **~n** *n.* āribu☆, ḫaḫḫūru☆, qāribu; → **~nous** *adj.* gašru+
ravine *n.* ḫurru, nadbāktu, nadbāku
ravish *v.* niāku, sarāḫu+ (Š); → **~ed** *n.* nēku; → **~ing** *adj.* kuzzubu☆ (highly)
raw *adj.* balṭu
ray *n.* šarūru
raze *v.* napālu☆, naqāru
razor *n.* naglubu
razzia *n.* šiḫṭu
re-enter *v.* saḫāru erābu
re-establish *v.* ana ašrīšu turru [i.], edēšu☆ (D), kaṣāru
reach *n.* tarṣu B; → ~ *v.* ammār X maṣû [i.], kašādu; → **make ~** *v.* maṣû☆ (D); → **~ out** *v.* tarāṣu; → **~ the lowest point** *v.* šapālu
react *v.* apālu; → **~ion** *n.* nāpaltu [o.], nāpassu
read *v.* šasû☆ (Gtn); → **~ (out)** *v.* sasû, šasû☆; → **~er** *n.* sāsiu*
readily *adv.* pašīqatti+
readiness *n.* rikis qabli◊
reading *n.* sasûtu, šitassû☆
ready *adj.* gamru, tēbû☆; → ~ *v.* ṭiābu+ (D), zakû (D); → **be(come) ~** *v.* rēšu kullu [i.]; → **get ~** *v.* qablē rakāsu [i.]; → **make ~** *v.* rēšu kullu [i.], ṣabātu (Š), šutērsû☆; → **get ~ for battle** *v.* idē patû [i.]; → **get ~ with** *v.* rēšu našû [i.]
real *adj.* kēnu; → **~ estate (kind of)** *n.* šaprutu; → **~ity** *n.* kēttu
realization *n.* ḫakimtu*
really *adv.* issu maṣin, kēttu; → **~not** *adv.* laššu lā
realm *n.* namlaktu☆
reap *v.* eṣādu
reappear *v.* amāru (N)
rear *n.* kutallu, urkītu; → ~ *v.* rabû (D); → **in the ~** *adv.* ina kutalli
Rear Palace *n.* bēt kutalli
rear part *n.* arkatu☆
rearguard *n.* urkītu
rearing *n.* tarbûtu
rearmost *adj.* urkīu
reason *n.* murqu☆, pakku B☆, ṭēmu; → **loss of ~** *n.* miqit ṭēmi☆; → **~able** *adj.* ṭēmānu
reasonably *adv.* ibašši
rebel *adj.* bārānû☆; → ~ *n.* šaršarrānu◊, tēbû☆; → ~ *n./adj.* nabalkattānu☆; → ~ *v.* nabalkutu, nakāru, seḫû☆
rebellion *n.* bārtu, gabaraḫḫu☆, sīḫu B☆; → **instigation to ~** *n.* mušamḫiṣūtu; → **instigator of ~** *n.* mušamḫiṣu
rebellious *adj.* bārānû☆, multablakkitu◊, nabalkattānu☆, nabalkutu
rebuff *v.* daḫû
rebuild *v.* šaklulu+
rebuke *v.* kasāsu+, qalālu (D)
recalcitrant *adj.* šapṣu☆
recall (to mind) *v.* ḫasāsu
recapitulate *v.* kapāṣu+
recede *v.* naḫāsu◊
receding (water) *n.* qarūru☆
receipt *n.* maḫāru, namḫartu☆, nibzu+
receive *v.* laqû [o.], maḫāru, našû; → **~r** *n.* māḫirānu [o.]
recently *adv.* issu ḫaramme
receptacle *n.* namḫāru [o.]
reception *n.* maḫāru, pānāti
recess *n.* ḫibšu, ibratu☆
recipient *n.* bēl maḫāri, māḫirānu [o.]
reciprocal *n.* igû☆; → **~ of reciprocal** *n.* igibû☆
reciprocate *v.* aḫāiš apālu (Gtn)
recitation *n.* naqbītu
recite *v.* manû B
reckless *adj.* rešû☆; → **be(come) ~** *v.* paḫāzu
reckon *v.* kaṣāpu, manû B; → **~ among** *v.* manû issi [i.]; → **~ as,** *v.* manû issi [i.]; → **~ in** *v.* manû ina libbi [i.]; → **~ on** *v.* takālu+;

→ **~ing** *n.* minītu
recline *v.* emādu, rabāṣu
recognize *v.* idû⋆ (D)
recoil on *v.* ana ḫiṭṭi tuāru [i.]
recollect *v.* ḫasāsu; → **~ion** *n.* ḫissutu, šaḫsasūtu
recommendation *n.* taḫsistu⋆
recompense *n.* rību C⋆, tamgirtu [o.], tašlimtu; → ~ *v.* riābu, šalāmu+ (D)
reconcile *v.* magāru⋆ (D), salāmu (D)
reconciliation *n.* bibil pāni⋆, salīmu⋆, tašmû⋆; → **~ payment** *n.* tamgirtu [o.]
recondite *adj.* šapšuqu
reconstruct *v.* eššiš epēšu⋆
record *n.* immu◊; → **~ed** *adj.* šaṭru
recount *v.* manû B, saḫḫuru manû*, šanû (D)
recourse *n.* marqītu⋆
recover *v.* balāṭu, tuāru (D); → **~y** *n.* balāṭu
recreation *n.* tablittu⋆
recruit *n.* raksu; → ~ *v.* rakāsu (Š); → **~ as ally** *v.* katāru; → **~ment officer** *n.* mušarkisu; → **commander of ~s** *n.* rab raksi
rectify *v.* ešēru⋆ (Š)
rectitude *n.* taqnūtu+
rectum *n.* šuburru
recumbent → **be(come) ~** *v.* rabāṣu
recuperate *v.* balāṭu
recur *v.* tuāru; → **~rence** *n.* tuāru; → **~rent** *adj.* taiāru⋆
red *n./adj.* ḫuššû⋆, ruššû⋆, sāmu; → **be(come) ~** *v.* pelû B◊, siāmu; → **~-haired** *adj.* barruqu; → **~-handed** *adj.* qāt ṣibitti; → **~-hot** *adj.* baḫru⋆; → **~-hued** *adj.* pelû⋆; → **~den** *v.* siāmu (D); → **~dening** *n.* ṣiriptu⋆; → **~dish** *adj.* pelû⋆, ruššû⋆
redecorate *v.* za'ānu⋆ (D)
redeem *v.* ezābu+ (Š), padû (D), paṭāru, uṣû; → **~er** *n.* paddi'u⋆
redemption *n.* pīdu
redhead *adj.* barruqu
redness *n.* sāntu B, su'mu, sūmu
redo s.th. *v.* saḫāru
redouble *v.* eṣāpu
reduce *v.* kaṣābu⋆, maṭû (D), ṣaḫāru (D)
reduction *n.* miṭītu◊, nušurrû⋆
redundant *adj.* utru
reed *n.* apu B⋆, kuppû, qanû; → **sweet ~** *n.* qanû ṭābu; → **~-bed** *n.* kuppû; → **build a ~ hut** *v.* ḫaṣāṣu; → **~ stalk** *n.* adattu; → **~ thicket** *n.* apu B⋆, kuppû, ṣūṣû⋆; → **~ worker** *n.* atkuppu
reef *n.* kāp tānti*
reek *n.* bu'šu⋆; → ~ *v.* be'ēšu◊, qatāru
reel *v.* galālu+, ṭamû B⋆
reestablish *v.* eššiš šakānu⋆
refer to *v.* qabû ana
reference *n.* ḫissutu
refill *v.* malû (D), saḫḫuru mallû*
refine *v.* bašālu, damāqu (D), qalû, ṣarāpu, ṣarāpu+, ṣuādu (D); → **~ (metals)** *v.* sakāru; → **~d** *adj.* bašlu, dammuqu, sakru, ṣarpu; → **~ment** *n.* tadmiqtu [o.]
refining-pot *n.* kūru
reflect *v.* mašālu⋆ (D); → **~ing** *adj.* mumaššilu*; → **~ion** *n.* ḫissutu, maṭṭaltu⋆, muššultu⋆; → **~ive** *adj.* mumaššilu*
reflex *n.* nāpaltu [o.]
reflux *n.* esīgu⋆
reform *n.* tēdištu⋆; → ~ *v.* edēšu⋆ (D), tarāṣu B+ (D); → **~er** *n.* muddišu⋆
refract *v.* šabāru+; → **~ory** *adj.* aštu⋆
refrain *n.* zumāru
refresh *v.* balāṭu (D); → **~ment** *n.* tablittu⋆
refuge *n.* marqītu⋆, puzru; → **place of ~** *n.* narqītu⋆; → **give ~ to** *v.* raqû
refugee *adj.* ḫalqu; → ~ *n.* munnabtu⋆
refusal *n.* lā magāru, sūlû+, ullu⋆
refuse *adj.* ḫimmatu⋆; → ~ *n.* zê, ziblu; → ~ *v.* daḫû, kalû, lā magāru (N), nakāru; → **~ (ordeal)** *v.* tuāru; → **~ access** *v.* parāku; → **~ dump** *n.* kiqillutu; → **~ to obey** *v.* qātu napāṣu [i.]
refute *v.* nasāku
regain *v.* saḫāru (D)
regal *adj.* [ša] šarri, [ša] šarrūti⋆; → **~ia** *n.* simāt šarrūti⋆
regard *v.* dagālu; → **~ as** *v.* ana X kullu [i.]; → **with ~ to** *prep.* ina muḫḫi; → **~ing** *prep.* ina muḫḫi; → **~ing** *subj.* aššu⋆; → **~less of** *adj.* ša lā
regenerate *v.* balāṭu (D)
regeneration *n.* tablittu⋆
regent *n.* šar pūḫi
regime *n.* rēdûtu⋆; → **~n** *n.* rēdûtu
region *n.* kaqquru, nagiu, siḫru; → **~s** *n.* kibrāti⋆
register *n.* mudasû⋆, sidru; → ~ *v.* šaṭāru
registrar *n.* ṭupšarru
registry *n.* bēt ṭuppāti
regnal *adj.* [ša] šarrūti⋆
regress *v.* ana qinniš alāku [i.]
regret *v.* saḫāru (N)
regular *adj.* kaiamānīu, sadru; → **~ly** *adv.* kaiamānu, kaiāna⋆; → **do ~ly** *v.* sadāru; → **~ly occurring** *adj.* sadru
regulate *v.* rakāsu, sadāru (D)
regulation *n.* riksu, ṣindatu⋆; → **~s** *n.*

rikistu⭑ (pl.), šipāru⭑
rehabilitate *v.* kaṣāru
rehearse *v.* šanû (D)
reign *n.* palû, tarṣu B, tirṣu; → **in the ~ of** *adv.* ina tarṣi
reimbursement *n.* tašlimtu
reinforce *v.* da'ānu (D); → **~ the construction** *v.* riksu dannunu [i.]; → **~ment** *n.* tadnintu⭑
reins *n.* appāti, ašāti⭑
reiterate *v.* šanû (D)
reject *v.* dabû+, nasāku, rammû (D), sakāpu⭑ (D), selû◊; → **~ alliance** *v.* qātu napāṣu [i.]; → **~ion** *n.* sikiptu⭑, sūlû+
rejoice *v.* elēṣu⭑, ḫadû, ḫamû B◊, nagû⭑, riāšu, šūlulu⭑
rejoicing *n.* ḫadûtu, ḫidâti, ḫidûtu⭑, ḫudû, rīštu◊, tamgītu⭑, ulṣu⭑
rejuvenate *v.* ana ṣuḫri turru (D) [i.]
relate *v.* passuru, šanû (D); → **~d (to)** *adj.* qurbu ana; → **~d to** *adj.* qurbu ina muḫḫi
relationship *n.* qurbūtu
relative *adj.* mitḫāru⭑; → **~** *n.* kinattu, mammannu⭑; → **~ly** *adv.* ana minâtīšu⭑; → **~s** *n.* nišūtu⭑
relax *v.* libbu pašāru [i.], nuāḫu, pašāḫu, pašāru, rabābu; → **~ation** *n.* mussa''ītu, tarmītu⭑; → **~ed** *adj.* pašḫu
relay *n.* ḫilpu B+
release *n.* napšurtu⭑, piṭru C⭑, tapṭirtu⭑, tarmītu⭑; → **~** *v.* pašāru, paṭāru, rammû (D), riāqu (Š), uṣû, uššuru (D); → **~d** *adj.* paṭru; → **~d person** *n.* šubarrû⭑; → **~r** *n.* pāširu
relegate *v.* nasāḫu paqādu [i.]
relent *v.* nuāḫu, pašāru (N), saḫāru (N); → **~ing** *adj.* taiāru⭑; → **~lessly** *adv.* lā taiār⭑
relevant → **be(come) ~** *v.* qarābu ina muḫḫi; → **~ (to)** *adj.* qurbu ina muḫḫi
reliability *n.* kēnūtu, takiltu B⭑
reliable *adj.* kēnu, šalmu, taklu, ummuru
reliance *n.* tukultu
reliant *adj.* takkulu
relics *n.* rēḫāti (pl.)
relief *n.* šēzubtu⭑, tapšuḫtu⭑, tēnītu⭑; → **~(?)** *n.* kabbusītu
relieve *v.* nuāḫu+ (D), pašāḫu (Š)
religion *n.* palāḫ ili
religiosity *n.* palāḫ ili
religious *adj.* pāliḫ ili; → **~ness** *n.* palāḫ ili
reluctance *n.* zīru
reluctant *adj.* parku; → **~ly** *adv.* ina marušti⭑
rely on *v.* takālu, takālu ana [i.], takālu ina muḫḫi [i.]
remain *v.* kalû (N), riāḫu, šêtu⭑; → **~der** *n.* rēḫtu, sittu⭑, sittūtu⭑, šittu B◊; → **~s** *n.* rēḫāti (pl.)
remark *n.* qību; → **~** *v.* qabû; → **~able** *adj.* edû
remarkably *adv.* adanniš
remedy *n.* bulṭu, šammu+
remember *v.* ḫasāsu
remembrance *n.* ḫissutu
remind *v.* ḫasāsu (Š); → **~er** *n.* ḫissutu, šaḫsasūtu, taḫsistu⭑
reminiscence *n.* ḫissutu
reminiscent *adj.* mušaḫsisu*
remiss *adj.* šēṭu
remit *v.* kabāsu, riāmu; → **~tance** *n.* šēbulti kaspi*
remnant *n.* rēḫtu
remonstrate *v.* ragāmu
remorse *n.* muruṣ libbi; → **~less** *adj.* lā gāmilu⭑, lā pādû⭑
remote *adj.* nesû⭑, patiu, rēqu⭑, rūqu⭑, ullû⭑; → **~ness** *n.* narqītu⭑
removal *n.* nēkemtu⭑, niširtu⭑, nišru, passuku*
remove *v.* abāku, dakû, elû (D), ḫasāpu, nakāru (D), nasāḫu, nasāku⭑ (Š), našāru, našû, nesû⭑ (D), pa'āṣu (D), pasāku (D), tabû (Š); → **~ from office** *v.* patû (D)
remunerate *v.* riābu
remuneration *n.* tašlimtu
remunerative *adj.* mudammiqu
rend *v.* parāmu, parāṭu+, šatāqu+; → **~ off** *v.* qadādu+; → **~er culpable** *v.* ḫaṭû⭑ (D); → **~er desolate** *v.* ḫarābu⭑ (Š); → **~er firm** *v.* ṭiābu+ (D)
renew *v.* edēšu⭑ (D), ešāšu (D); → **~al** *n.* tēdištu⭑; → **~er** *n.* muddišu⭑
renounce *v.* nadû⭑, rammû (D)
renovate *v.* ana ašrīšu turru [i.], edēšu⭑ (D), ešāšu (D)
renovation *n.* tēdištu⭑
renovator *n.* muddišu⭑
renown *n.* šumu damqu; → **~ed** *adj.* edû
rent *adj.* šarṭu; → **~** *n.* biltu, tēṣītu⭑; → **~** *v.* agāru, uṣû (Š); → **~al** *n.* tēṣītu⭑
renunciation *n.* tarmītu⭑
reorganize *v.* ana eššūti ṣabātu⭑
repair *n.* takšīru⭑; → **~** *v.* badāqu, batqu kaṣāru, batqu ṣabātu, edēšu⭑ (D), kašāru B⭑; → **~ work** *adj.* badqu; → **~er** *n.* bēl batqi
repast *n.* naptunu
repay *v.* riābu; → **~ment** *n.* šalluntu (complete)
repeal *v.* nasāku⭑ (Š)
repeat *v.* saḫāru (D), šanû (D), tuāru (D)

[o.], tuāru [o.]; → **~edly** *adv*. šalāšīšu arbīšu
repectfully *adv*. palḫiš*
repel *v*. daḫû+, irtu nê'u (D) [i.], sakāpu*, ziāru (N)
repellent *adj*. zēru*; → **be ~** *v*. ziāru (N)
repent *v*. saḫāru (N); → **~ance** *n*. nasḫuru
repercussion *n*. ṣītu*
repetition *n*. taiārtu*, tašnītu*, tašnû*
replace *v*. riābu; → **~ment** *n*. rību C*, šiḫlu, tēnītu*, tēnû
replenish *v*. malû (D), malû+, šalāmu (D)
replica *n*. muššultu*, muššulu*, tamšīlu B*; → **~te** *v*. mašālu* (D)
reply *n*. gabrû, nāpassu, tūrti amati◊; → **~** *v*. apālu
report *n*. ṭēmu, u'iltu; → **~ back** *v*. ṭēmu turru [i.]; → **~er** *n*. bēl ṭēmi
repose → **be(come) ~** *v*. rabāṣu
represent *v*. eṣāru+, kūm X apālu [i.]
representative *adj*. iššakku*, ša-kīma [o.]; → **~** *n*. šakkanakku*, šaknu (acting)
repress *v*. kabāsu; → **~ion** *n*. kabsūtu*
reprieve *n*. uzubbatu*
reprimand *v*. qalālu (D), ra'ābu
reprisal *n*. tuktê*
reproach *n*. qulālu+; → **~** *v*. qalālu (D), ra'ābu
reproduce *v*. mašālu* (D)
reproduction *n*. tamšīlu B*
reptile *n*. mušlallilu*
repudiate *v*. rammû (D)
repudiation *n*. tarmītu*
repugnance *n*. zērūtu*
repugnant *adj*. zēru*
repulse *v*. sakāpu*; → **~(?)** *v*. ṣê'u
repulsive *adj*. zēru*; → **be ~** *v*. ziāru (N)
reputable *n*. bēl šumi damqi
reputation *n*. gerrû, šumu; → **bad ~** *n*. masiktu [o.], šumu lā damqu
repute *n*. šumu
request *n*. erištu*, mēreštu*, ša'altu+; → **~** *v*. erāšu; → **~ed** *adj*. eršu; → **~er** *n*. mūterrišu*
require *v*. erāšu, ḫašāḫu*; → **~d** *adj*. ḫašḫu*; → **~ment** *n*. ḫašaḫtu [o.], ḫišiḫtu*
requisite *adj*. eršu; → **~** *n*. ḫišiḫtu*, ša'altu+; → **~s** *n*. mēreštu*
requisition *n*. erištu*
requital *n*. gimlu, rību C*
requite *v*. gimillu turru*, riābu
rescue *n*. ḫamāti*; → **~** *v*. ezābu (Š); → **~r** *n*. mušēzibu, ša-šēzubi [o.]
research *v*. barû B*
resemblance *n*. mušlānūtu*
resemble *v*. mašālu
resent *v*. ikku kaṣāru [i.], ziāru; → **~ful** *adj*. kāṣir ikki*; → **~ment** *n*. zīru
reserve *v*. kalû (Š); → **~s** *n*. kutallu
reservoir *n*. bēt mê
resettle *v*. ušābu (Š)
reside (in) *v*. ušābu
residence *n*. rimītu*, šubtu; → **royal ~** *n*. bēt šarri; → **take up ~** *v*. ramû B*; → **~ (of high priestess)** *n*. gipāru B*
residency *n*. ubārūtu
resident *n*. āšibu; → **be ~** *v*. kamāsu (D)
residue *n*. tuḫḫu; → **~ (of sesame)** *n*. kuspē
resign *v*. ramanšu paṭāru*
resin *n*. ḫīlu, za'u* (aromatic)
resist *v*. maḫāru; → **~ance** *n*. miḫirtu*; → **~ant** *adj*. patnu*; → **~ant** *n*. māḫiru B*; → **~er** *n*. māḫiru B*
resolute *adj*. šēmu*
resolution *n*. pīt pāni*, ṣūrāmu+, šīmtu
resonant *adj*. ruṣṣunu*
resort *n*. manāḫtu
resound *v*. raṣānu*, šagāmu
resource *n*. tukultu; → **~s** *n*. emūq ramāni*, nakkamtu
respect *n*. pulḫu, puluḫtu; → **~** *v*. adāru C*, palāḫu, uqāru* (Š); → **~able** *adj*. baiāšu*, kabtu*; → **~ed** *adj*. palḫu; → **be(come) ~ed** *v*. kabādu, kabātu*; → **highly ~ed** *adj*. dunnunu*; → **~ful** *adj*. na'du*, pāliḫu; → **~ively** *adv*. mitḫāriš*
respiration *n*. napīšu*
respite *n*. šiddu
resplendent *adj*. namurru*, šarḫu*, šūpû*
respond *v*. apālu, apālu (Gtn)
response *n*. gabrû, miḫru, tūrti amati◊
responsibility *n*. pūtuḫu
responsible *adj*. nāši pūtuḫi*
responsive *adj*. itpālu*
rest *n*. rēḫtu, sittu*, sittūtu*, šittu B◊, tapšuḫtu*; → **~** *v*. nuāḫu, pašāḫu, rabāṣu, sakāpu B*, sakātu+; → **give ~** *v*. nuāḫu+ (D), sakātu+ (D); → **put to ~** *v*. ṣalālu* (Š); → **at ~** *n*. nēḫu+; → **at ~** *v*. nuāḫu+, ṣalālu*; → **~house** *n*. maṣallutu; → **~ room** *n*. bēt musâti*, maṣallutu; → **~ful** *adj*. pašḫu; → **~ing** *adj*. pašḫu; → **~ing** *n*. sākipu*; → **~ing place** *n*. maiālu, manāḫtu, maṣallu
restitution *n*. šalluntu (complete); → **make ~** *v*. šalāmu+ (D)
restive *adj*. muqqu*
restless *adj*. dalpu, lā ṣālilu*, muttaggišu*, ṣā'idu*; → **~ness** *n*. diliptu
restoration *n*. takšīru*

restore *v.* batqu ṣabātu, edēšu⋆ (D), kašāru B⋆, saḫāru (D), saḫḫuru tadānu [i.], šaklulu⋆, šalāmu (D), tuāru (D); → **~ to a previous position** *v.* ana ašrīšu turru [i.]; → **~r** *n.* bēl batqi, muddišu⋆
restrain *v.* kalû, kapāṣu+, karāmu, sakāru B+; → **~t** *n.* kilītu⋆
restrict *v.* siāqu (D)
result *n.* arû E⋆; → **~** *v.* šakānu (N); → **~ing** *adj.* āṣiu
resupply *n.* šallāmu
resurgence *n.* balāṭu
resuscitate *v.* balāṭu (D)
resuscitation *n.* tablittu⋆
retail *v.* makāru B [o.]; → **~ merchant** *n.* pāširu [o.]; → **~er** *n.* saḫḫiru
retain *v.* kalû, kullu (D); → **~er** *n.* urdu
retaliate *v.* tuktê turru [i.]
retard *v.* namarkû (Š); → **~ation** *n.* tazbiltu⋆; → **~ed** *adj.* namarkû
retch *v.* a'āšu⋆ (Gtn)
retention *n.* ḫiniqtu⋆ (urine)
reticent *adj.* qaiālu⋆
retire *v.* nuāḫu
retort *v.* apālu
retrace *v.* ḫiāṭu⋆
retreat *n.* nabalkattu⋆, tūru [o.]; → **~** *v.* ana kutalli neḫēsu◊, saḫāru; → **~ (of army)** *n.* suḫḫurtu⋆
retrench *v.* maṭû (D)
retribution *n.* tūr gimilli⋆, turru tuktê⋆
retrieve *v.* saḫāru (D), šalāḫu
retrograde *v.* ana qinniš saḫāru [i.], saḫāru; → **be(come) ~** *v.* ramanšu da'āpu [i.]
retrogress → **be in ~** *v.* ana qinniš alāku [i.]
return *n.* saḫāru, taiārtu⋆, taiāru, tuāru, tūrtu, tūru [o.]; → **~** *v.* naḫāsu◊, saḫāru, tuāru, tuāru (D); → **~ing** *adj.* taiāru⋆
reunion *n.* puḫru
reveal *v.* barû B (D), barû B⋆ (Š), kallumu (D), kallumu⋆ (Š), patû; → **~ o.s.** *n.* ramanšu kallumu
revelation *n.* taklimtu
revelling *n.* reqdu+
revenge *n.* gimillu⋆, gimlu, tuktê⋆, tūr gimilli⋆, turru tuktê⋆
revenue *n.* taiāru; → **~(s)** *n.* irbu
revere *v.* adāru C⋆, na'ādu⋆ (Gt), palāḫu; → **~nce** *n.* palāḫu; → **treat with ~nce** *v.* uqāru+ (D); → **~nt** *adj.* na'du⋆, palḫu, pāliḫu, šaḫtu⋆; → **make ~nt** *v.* palāḫu⋆ (Š); → **~ntly** *adv.* na'diš⋆, palḫiš⋆
reversal *n.* nabalkattu⋆, suḫurrû⋆, tūrtu
reverse *adj.* nabalkutu; → **~** *v.* ana qinniš saḫḫuru [i.], nabalkutu (Š)
reversion *n.* turrūtu, tūrtu
revetment *n.* riṣiptu⋆, sa'ītu, samītu⋆
review *n.* aširtu, māšartu; → **~** *v.* ašāru, paqādu; → **~ palace** *n.* bēt māšarti, ēkal māšarti
Review Palace → **manager of ~** *n.* rab ēkal māšarti
reviewed *adj.* ašru
revile *v.* masāku⋆ (D), ṭapālu⋆
revise *v.* barû B⋆, tarāṣu B (D)
revision *n.* tūrāṣu+
revival *n.* tablittu⋆
revive *v.* balāṭu (D); → **~d** *adj.* balluṭu
revocation *n.* tuāru
revoke *v.* tuāru; → **be ~d** *v.* enû⋆ (N)
revolt *n.* bārtu, nabalkattu⋆, sīḫu B⋆; → **~** *v.* bâru⋆, nabalkutu, nakāru, seḫû⋆; → **~ing** *adj.* zēru⋆
revolution *n.* daiāltu (synodic), nabalkattu⋆; → **~ary** *n./adj.* nabalkattānu⋆; → **~ize** *v.* nabalkutu (Š)
revolve *v.* saḫāru
revulsion *n.* zīru
reward *n.* nidnu⋆, rēmuttu; → **~** *v.* riābu; → **~ing** *adj.* mudammiqu
rheumatic fever *n.* ḫunṭu ša eṣmāti*
rheumatism *n.* ḫunṭu ša eṣmāti*, muruṣ eṣenti*
rhinoceros *n.* sadēia⋆
rhombus *n.* keppû⋆
rhubarb *n.* nappu+
rib *n.* sikkat ṣēli, ṣēlu; → **floating ~** *n.* naiabtu⋆
ribbon *n.* ṭurru
ribcage *n.* bāntu B⋆
rice *n.* kuraggu
rich *adj.* šarû; → **be(come) ~** *v.* šarû; → **~ man** *n.* šarû; → **~es** *n.* mašrû
rick *n.* kurillu⋆
rickety *adj.* pisnuqu⋆
rickshaw *n.* ša-šadādi; → **~ supervisor** *n.* ša-pān-ša-šadādi
rid *v.* pasāku (D); → **~dle** *n.* ḫittu B⋆
ride *v.* ḫallu patû⋆, rakābu; → **make ~** *v.* rakābu (Š); → **~r** *n.* rakbû⋆, rakbu⋆, ša-pēthalli
ridge *n.* bīru B⋆, zuqtu B⋆
ridicule *n.* liznu*; → **~** *v.* lazānu
ridiculous *adj.* ṣuḫḫu⋆
riding *n.* rakāb sissê*, tarkubtu⋆
rifraff *n.* ṣindu u birtu⋆
rift *n.* ṣelpu+, šitqu⋆
rig *n.* martû⋆; → **~** *v.* retû⋆; → **~ up** *v.* rakābu+ (D)

right *adj.* kēnu, tarṣu+; → **be(come) ~** *v.* ašāru B, ešēru*; → **~-hand** *adj.* [ša] imitti; → **~-handed** *adj.* imittānu*; → **~-sider (he who sits at the right side)** *n.* ša-imitti; → **~ hand** *n.* imittu; → **~ side** *n.* imittu, imnu

righteous *adj.* išaru*, kēnu; → **~ness** *n.* išarūtu*, kēnāti, kēnūtu, mēšāru

rightful *adj.* kēnu

rightly → **do ~** *v.* tarāṣu B+ (D)

rigid *adj.* maggu; → **be(come) ~** *v.* magāgu

rigor *n.* aštūtu*; → **~ous** *adj.* aštu*

rile *v.* agāgu* (D), zanû (Š)

rill *n.* raṣīnu+

rim *n.* ḫūpu B* (wheel), kilīlu+, sippu, šaptu, šuḫuppu*

rime *n.* ḫurbāšu*

rind *n.* qulāptu [o.], qulpu

ring *n.* ḫūpu B* (wheel), malūṭu*, sabirru; → **~** *v.* ḫalālu B, šagāmu; → **signet ~** *n.* unqu; → **~let** *n.* kizirtu

rinse *n.* marḫuṣu, šiḫṭu B; → **~** *v.* raḫāṣu B, šaḫāṭu B

rinsing *n.* šiḫṭu B

riot *n.* ḫubūru*

rip off *v.* šamāṭu

ripe *adj.* bašlu; → **~n** *v.* bašālu

ripper(?) *n.* parritu

ripple *v.* katātu*

rise *n.* elû; → **~** *v.* matāḫu (N), nabā'u*, tabû; → **~ (heliacally)** *v.* napāḫu; → **~ higher** *v.* matāḫu (N); → **~ up** *v.* gapāšu, seḫû*, zaqāpu

rising *adj.* tēbû*; → **~** *n.* elû, tibûtu*; → **(heliacal) ~** *n.* nipḫu

risk *n.* puluḫtu; → **~y** *adj.* [ša] puluḫti*

rite *n.* kidudê*, parṣu

ritual *n.* dullu, epištu*, nēpeštu*, nēpēšu, parṣu; → **apotropaic ~** *n.* namburbû; → **~ (name of a)** *n.* egalkura◊, nāṭu, šurpu*; → **~ hut** *n.* urigallu; → **~ procedure** *n.* kikiṭṭû*; → **~ regulation** *n.* sakkû*; → **~ly unclean/impure person** *n.* musukku*

rival *n.* šāninu, šinnatu*; → **~** *v.* šanānu; → **~ry** *n.* šitnuntu*, tašnuntu*

rive *v.* šatāqu+; → **~r** *n.* nāru; → **like a ~r** *adv.* nāriš*; → **mouth of the ~r** *n.* pī nāri; → **~r-bed** *n.* māluku; → **~r-flats** *n.* raqqatu*; → **~r-gravel** *n.* abattu; → **~rside** *n.* šiddi nāri; → **~t** *v.* rapāqu

rivulet *n.* naḫlu

road *n.* gerru*, ḫarrānu, ḫūlu, mētequ*, mētuqu, ṭūdu B*, urḫu B*; → **access ~** *n.* māluku; → **royal ~** *n.* ḫūl šarri; → **side ~** *n.* ummu; → **take the direct ~** *v.* ḫarrānu šutēšuru [i.]; → **~side inn** *n.* bēt mardēti

roam *v.* rapādu; → **~ about** *v.* alāku (Gtn), ṣâdu◊; → **~ing about** *adj.* ṣā'idu*

roan *n.* sirpu*

roar *n.* rigmu; → **~** *v.* na'āru*, nadāru*, naḫāru+, ragāmu, ramāmu*, raṣānu* (Dt), šagāmu; → **~er** *n.* nā'iru*; → **~ing** *n.* murtaṣnu*, šāgimu*

roast *v.* qalû

rob *v.* gazālu+, ḫabātu, ḫamāṣu◊, mašā'u; → **~ber** *n.* ekkēmu*, ḫabbātu, mār ḫabbāti*, maššī'u*, šaggāšu*; → **~bery** *n.* naḫbutu

robe *n.* kusītu; → **~ (kind of)** *n.* lamaḫuššû; → **purple ~s** *n.* takiltu+ (pl.)

robust *adj.* gašru, puggulu*, pungulu*

rock *n.* abnu, kāpu, kīpu; → **~** *v.* sabā'u; → **mountain ~** *n.* aban šadî*; → **steep ~** *n.* kāpu*; → **~-crystal** *n.* duḫšiu

rocket *n.* gargīru; → **~(?) (a plant)** *n.* šurdunû; → **~ salad** *n.* gingīru

rockrose *n.* lādunu*

rocky *adj.* [ša] abni; → **~** *n.* abnānu

rod *n.* ḫuṭārtu*, ḫuṭāru, nanḫuṣu, qanû; → **~ent (kind of)** *n.* kursissu*

roe *n.* binût nūni*; → **~ deer** *n.* nālu

rogue *n.* ḫappu, ḫarḫaru*, isḫappu*

roil *v.* dalāḫu, sabā'u

roll *n.* kirku; → **~** *v.* galālu, nagarruru, sabā'u, šugarruru [o.]; → **~ about** *v.* nagarruru; → **~ along** *v.* dapānu*; → **~ aside** *v.* qapālu+; → **~ away** *v.* qapālu+; → **~ out** *v.* nagarruru (Š); → **~ out thin** *v.* raqāqu (D); → **~ round** *v.* karāku+; → **~ together** *v.* karāku+; → **~ up** *v.* kanānu*, kapālu*, karāku, qapālu*; → **~ed up** *adj.* qannunu*; → **~er** *n.* agû B*; → **~ing** *n.* gallatu*

romp *v.* dakāku*

roof *n.* tarānu*, ūru; → **~** *v.* ruggubu*, ṣallulu; → **~-beam** *n.* gašūru; → **~ pavilion** *n.* bēt ūri; → **~ed** *adj.* ruggubu*; → **~ing** *n.* ṣulultu*, ṣulūlu

rook *n.* āribu*, qāribu; → **~ery** *n.* qinnu+

room *n.* bētu, kaqquru, tuānu B+; → **front ~** *n.* bēt pūti; → **inner ~** *n.* kummu*; → **supply ~** *n.* bēt tilli; → **upper ~** *n.* rugubu; → **~ on roof** *n.* rugubu; → **~y** *adj.* rapšu, šadlu*

roost *v.* kepû+; → **~er** *n.* akkadīja*

root *n.* išdu, šuršu*; → **~ about** *v.* ḫarāru*; → **~ out** *v.* nasāḫu; → **by the ~s** *adv.* šuršiš*

rope *n.* ašlu, eblu, pitiltu, šummannu*; → **mooring ~** *n.* ṭarkullu*; → **skipping ~** *n.* keppû*; → **tow ~** *n.* ašlu

roquette *n.* gingīru

rosaceous *adj.* amurdinnāiu+

rose *n.* amurdinnu+; → **~ water** *n.* lādunu☆; → **~tte** *n.* aiuru, kakkabtu

rosewood *n.* musukkannu (Indian)

rosy *adj.* amurdinnāiu+

rot *n.* sumkinnu☆, šiḫḫutu, zupru☆; → **~** *v.* zapāru☆; → **be(come) ~** *v.* masāku [o.]; → **~ate** *v.* sâru☆; → **~ation** *n.* daiāltu (synodic); → **~ten** *adj.* masku [o.]; → **be(come) ~ten** *v.* masāku [o.]; → **become ~ten** *v.* zapāru☆

rouge *n.* illūr pāni☆

rough *adj.* da'nu, dannu; → **~ it** *v.* dannutu amāru [i.]; → **be(come) ~ up** *v.* šagāšu+; → **~ened** *adj.* mašru; → **~ly** *adv.* ammār, kî dannati☆

round *adj.* saḫru; → **be(come) ~** *v.* saḫāru (stat.); → **~ up** *v.* paḫāru (D), šabāšu

roundabout *n.* lābiu

roundup *n.* tapḫīru [o.]

rouse *v.* dakû

rout *n.* arbūtu☆

route → **roundabout ~** *n.* ḫūlu lābiu*

routine *adj.* kaiamānīu; → **~** *n.* kaiamānūtu*

rove *v.* rapādu, sarāḫu+

row *n.* sidru; → **~** *v.* maḫāru ša eleppi☆; → **~(?)** *v.* qadāpu☆

royal *adj.* [ša] šarri; → **~ty** *n.* šarrūtu

rub *v.* marāṭu, mašādu B☆ (D), maššu'u; → **~ away** *v.* marāṭu; → **~ down** *v.* siāru, ṣuppu [o.]; → **~ out** *v.* pašāṭu

rubbed *adj.* marṭu

rubbish *adj.* ḫimmatu☆; → **~** *n.* ḫāmu, siliāti; → **~ bin** *n.* kakkul zibli*

rubble *n.* ḫiṣṣu☆, nappaltu☆

rudder *n.* sikkannu☆

ruddy *adj.* sāmu

rude *adj.* erḫu☆, nuā'u [o.]

rudiments *n.* šuršē+ (pl.)

ruffian *n.* guzallu☆, šaggāšu+

ruffle *v.* dalāḫu; → **be(come) ~** *v.* šagāšu+; → **~d** *adj.* dalḫu+

rug *n.* mardutu, taḫapšu (woven)

rugged *adj.* da'nu, dannu

ruin *n.* karmūtu☆, šalputtu; → **~** *v.* abātu☆, ḫapû, lapātu☆ (Š); → **~ mound** *n.* tillu; → **~ation** *n.* šalputtu; → **~ed** *adj.* abtu☆, maqtu; → **~ed(?)** *adj.* šuḫḫû☆; → **~ous** *adj.* mušaḫribu*, rāḫiṣu☆, uqru adanniš; → **~s** *n.* abtāti☆, ḫarbāti, ḫarbatu☆; → **into ~s** *adv.* ḫarbiš☆; → **to ~s** *adv.* karmiš☆; → **turn into ~s** *v.* namû B☆ (D)

rule *n.* riksu, rubūtu B☆, tērtu☆; → **~** *v.* bêlu☆, biālu, piālu, radû, šalāṭu, šapāru, šarrūtu epāšu [i.]; → **~ justly** *v.* ešēru☆ (Št); → **~r** *n.* muma''iru☆, rubû☆; → **~r's staff** *n.* ušpāru☆; → **~rship** *n.* mētellūtu☆, rubūtu B☆

rumble *n.* rimmatu☆; → **~** *v.* ramāmu☆, raṣānu☆ (Dt)

rumbling *n.* rigmu

ruminate *v.* pašāru+

rummage *n.* teb'ītu☆; → **~** *v.* ba''û

rumor *n.* dabābu, lišānu; → **spread a ~** *v.* ša'ūdu (Štn); → **~(?)** *n.* batiqtu; → **~-monger** *n.* munappiḫu☆

rump *n.* rapassu, talammu☆

rumpus *n.* ḫubūru☆

run *v.* lasāmu; → **~-down** *adj.* anḫu; → **~-in** *n.* ṣāssu; → **~ about** *v.* duālu; → **~ away** *v.* abātu☆ (N), ḫalāqu, rapādu; → **~ down** *v.* anāḫu, gamāru (Dtt); → **~ into** *v.* emādu, ina irti X alāku [i.], ina muḫḫi maqātu [i.]; → **~ off** *v.* rapādu; → **~ out** *v.* ina X elû [i.]; → **~ out (of s.th.)** *v.* ṣappuḫu☆; → **be(come) ~ over** *v.* ṭaḫādu; → **be(come) ~ wild** *v.* paḫāzu

runaway *n.* munnarbu☆; → **~** *n./adj.* ḫalqu

rung *n.* ḫūqu

runner *n.* bēl birki☆, lāsimu, munnarbu☆, šānû☆; → **swift ~** *n.* pētān birki☆; → **~-up** *n.* šiḫlu

running *n.* lisnu

runny *adj.* naḫarmuṭu☆, nātiku

rupture *n.* taḫṣību☆; → **~** *v.* parāru (D)

ruse *n.* šipru; → **invent a ~** *v.* niklu nakālu

rush *n.* urbatu☆; → **~** *v.* ḫiāšu☆; → **~ (kind of)** *n.* šīšnu☆; → **~ against** *v.* erēḫu☆; → **~ on** *v.* radāpu; → **~es** *n.* kuppû

rust *n.* šuḫtu; → **~** *v.* šaḫātu C+; → **rub off ~** *v.* marāqu+; → **~icity** *n.* ikkārūtu+

rustle *v.* damāmu☆, ḫadādu, nazāzu☆

rusty *adj.* šuḫtānu+

rut *n.* ḫirṣu

ruthless *adj.* lā gāmilu☆

s.o.'s own expense → **at ~** *n.* ina memmēnī- [i.]

s.th. hastily → **do ~** *v.* dalāḫu (D)

saber *n.* gamlu

sable *n.* sammūru+

sack *n.* aza'illu [o.], naruqqu, saqqu [o.]; → **~** *v.* ḫubtu ḫabātu, patû (D); → **grain ~(?)** *n.* ittussu; → **~cloth** *n.* bašāmu B☆, saqqu [o.]

sacred *adj.* qašdu☆, quddušu☆; → **be(come) ~** *v.* qadāšu☆

sacrifice *n.* niqiu, zību B☆; → **~** *v.* naqû, qarābu+ (D); → **~ (kind of)** *n.* ḫitpu; → **~r** *n.*

bēl niqê
sacrilege *n.* gillatu*, gullultu*, šillatu*
sad *adj.* adru B, marru B+; → ~ *n.* libbu marșu [i.]; → **be(come) ~** *v.* marāșu; → **~den** *v.* libbu šappulu [i.]; → **~dle** *n.* taḫapšu (woven); → **~dlebag** *n.* zurzu; → **~dlecloth** *n.* taḫapšu (woven); → **~ist** *n.* ḫādi-ūa*; → **~ly** *adv.* marșiš; → **~ness** *n.* šuplu libbi
safe *adj.* šalmu, taqnu; → **be(come) ~** *v.* šalāmu; → **~box** *n.* pitnu*; → **~guard** *v.* nașāru; → **~ly** *adv.* šalmiš; → **~ty** *n.* šalintu; → **in ~ty** *adv.* aburriš*
saffron *n.* azupirānu*
sag *v.* qâpu*
sagacious *adj.* enqu*
sagacity *n.* tašīmtu*
sagapenum *n.* barīlāti*, barīlu
sage *n.* apkallu, barīlāti*, barīlu
sagging *adj.* qaiāpu*, quppu B*
Sagittarius *n.* Pabilsag*
said *pron./adj.* šuāti*
sail *n.* šaḫḫû*; → ~ *v.* rakābu
sailboat *n.* šaḫḫītu*
sailing *n.* rakkābūtu*; → **~boat** *n.* šaḫḫītu*
sailor *n.* mallāḫu; → **~'s trade** *n.* mallāḫūtu*; → **chief of the ~s** *n.* rab mallāḫi
saint *n.* qadīšu+, qašdu*; → **~ly** *adj.* qašdu*
salad *n.* ḫassē*
salamander *n.* șurārītu+
salary *n.* igrē
sale *n.* pašurtu*; → **~able** *adj.* ša tadāni*; → **~sman** *n.* muttaddinu*, sāḫiru B
salicornia *n.* uḫūlu+
salient *adj.* āșiu, kabtu*
saline *adj.* [ša] ṭābti
saliva *n.* ru'tu*
sallow *adj.* erqu
sally *v.* ușû
salt *n.* idrānu*, ṭābtu; → **put in ~** *v.* madālu; → **red ~** *n.* amānu; → **sea ~** *adj.* baḫru; → **~ (kind of)** *n.* ummišallu; → **~ mine** *n.* bēt ṭābti; → **~ trader** *n.* ša-ṭābti [o.]; → **~ water** *n.* marratu*; → **~ed** *adj.* madlu
saltpeter *n.* idru*
salty *adj.* madlu
salutary *adj.* mušallimu
salutation *n.* šulmu
salute *v.* šulmu qabû
salvage *v.* ezābu+ (Š)
salvation *n.* šulmu
salve *n.* lubku*, napšaltu, šīpu B+
Samaria *n.* Sāmirīna; → **~n** *n./adj.* Sāmirīnāiu
Samaritan *n./adj.* Sāmirīnāiu
same *n.* annīumma; → **by the ~ amount** *adv.* ana mitḫār; → **at the ~ time** *adv.* issēniš; → **in the ~ way** *adv.* kî annimma
sample(?) *n.* litku
sanctified *adj.* quddušu*
sanctify *v.* qadāšu* (D)
sanctimonious *adj.* qašdu*
sanction *n.* annu, migru*; → ~ *v.* magāru*
sanctity *n.* qašdūtu*
sanctuary *n.* eširtu*; → **~ (kind of)** *n.* šaḫūru
sanctum *n.* atmunu
sand *n.* bāșu*; → **like ~** *adv.* bāșiš*; → **~-dune** *n.* šipik bāși*; → **~al** *n.* mašennu, šēnu; → **~s** *n.* kaqqar bāși*; → **~stone** *n.* immanakku; → **red ~stone** *n.* sû; → **~y** *adj.* [ša] bāși*
sane *adj.* šalmu, ṭēmānu
sanitary napkin *n.* ulāpu
sanitary towel *n.* ša-ḫurdati, ulāpu
sanity *n.* šulum ṭēmi*
sap *n.* mê, ru'tu*
sapient *adj.* ḫassu
sapling *n.* piri'tu, ziqpu
sarcasm *n.* liznu*, šinșu*
sarcastic *adj.* lāzinu*, šānișu*
sarcophagus *n.* arānu*
saros (3600) *adj.* šār*
sash *n.* nēbettu, nēbuḫu, patinnu◊, șipirtu (woven); → **~-weaver** *n.* ušpār șiprāti; → **~ holder** *n.* nașbutu
sate *v.* šabû (D); → **~d** *adj.* šabbu, šebû*; → **be(come) ~d** *v.* šabû
satin *n.* šaddīnu
satisfaction *n.* tašbītu [o.]; → **give ~** *v.* libbu patû [i.]
satisfactory *adj.* ṭābu; → ~ *n.* mušabbiu*
satisfied *adj.* šabbu, šebû*, ṭābu; → **be(come) ~** *v.* lalû šebû [i.], šabû
satisfy *v.* libbu ṭubbu [i.], šabû (D), ṭiābu (D)
satrap *n.* pāḫutu
saturate *v.* marāsu+
Saturn *n.* Kaiamānu
sauce *n.* šaḫītu B+; → **~r** *n.* mākassu
saucy *adj.* erḫu*
saunter *v.* alāku (Gtn)
savage *adj.* ekdu*, šamru
savant *n.* apkallu, mūdû, ummânu
save *v.* eṭāru, ezābu (Š), ezābu [o.], šaṭāpu*
saving *adj.* mušallimu; → **~s** *n.* eṭrāti*

savior *n.* ēṭiru, mušēzibu, ša-šēzubi [o.]
savor *n.* ṭēmu+
saw *n.* massāru☆; → ~ *v.* nasāru☆; → **~dust** *n.* eper šaššāri*; → **~yer** *n.* naggāru+
say *v.* qabû; → **~ing** *n.* tēltu
scab *n.* garābu☆, sikru, simmu
scabbard *n.* kutummu☆
scabies *n.* ekketu☆, garābu☆, ḫarāsu☆
scald *v.* bašālu
scale *n.* epqēnu☆, kussimtu, qulāptu [o.], quliptu☆; → **~ armor** *n.* sariānu; → **~ off** *v.* qalāpu; → **~d** *adj.* qalpu; → **~s** *n.* zibānītu; → **housing for ~s** *n.* bēt zibāni; → **~s (of fish)** *n.* qulpu+
scaling/climbing over *n.* nabalkattu☆
scalpel *n.* karzillu☆, quppû☆
scamp *n.* ḫappu; → **~er** *v.* šaḫāṭu C☆
scan *v.* dagālu, ḫiāṭu☆; → **~dal** *n.* pištu☆, ṭūnāpu+; → **~dalize** *adv.* pišāti uppušu [i.]; → **~dalmonger** *n.* šaḫšaḫḫu☆; → **~dalous** *adj.* bīšu◊; → **~t** *adj.* ēṣu B
scapegoat *n.* mašḫultuppû☆
scar *n.* ibāru☆
scarce *adj.* ēṣu B, uqru; → **make ~** *v.* uqāru☆ (D), uqāru☆ (Š)
scare *v.* galādu (D), garāru (Š), palāḫu (D), šaḫātu B☆ (D); → **~ away/off** *v.* galādu☆ (Š), parādu+ (D); → **~d** *adj.* pardu☆; → **be(come) ~d** *v.* garāru, parādu☆; → **be(come) ~d away** *v.* parādu+
scarf *n.* kindabassu
scaring *adj.* galtu☆
scarlet *n./adj.* inzurātu
scatter *v.* našābu☆, parāru (D), sapāḫu, sarāqu, ṣappuḫu☆, zarāqu, zarû; → **~ed** *adj.* saphu☆; → **~ing** *n.* zarû
scavenger *n.* kannāšu+
scene *n.* diglu
scent *n.* irīšu☆, napīšu☆, šīr šumê; → ~ *v.* eṣānu; → **~ed flour (kind of)** *n.* maṣḫutu
scepter *n.* ḫaṭṭu, ḫuṭārtu☆, ḫuṭāru, šabbiṭu☆, šibirru☆, ušpāru☆
sceptical *adj.* lā qā'ipu*
schedule *n.* riksu; → **on ~** *adv.* ana ūmi; → **~d** *adj.* raksu
scheme *n.* uṣurtu; → **~ ?kapa:pu to bend** *v.* kapādu
schism *n.* šitqu+; → **cause a ~** *v.* šatāqu+
schismatic *adj.* parsu
scholar *n.* ummânu; → **~ly** *adj.* [ša] ummânūti; → **~ship** *n.* ummânūtu
scholastic explanations *n.* ṣâti
scholia *n.* ṣâti
school *n.* bēt ṭuppi
schoolboy *n.* talmīdu
schoolchild *n.* talmīdu
schoolfellow *n.* tappû
schooling *n.* tarbûtu
schoolmate *n.* tappû
scimitar *n.* gamlu
scintillate *v.* ummulu☆
scintillatingly *adj.* ummulu☆
scintillation *n.* šibūbu☆
scion *n.* ḫabbūru, ilittu, pir'u
scoff *n.* šinṣu☆; → **~ at** *v.* šanāṣu☆
scold *v.* qalālu (D); → **~ing** *n.* qulālu
scoop *n.* mussipu☆; → **~ up** *v.* esāpu☆ (D), šabāšu
scope *n.* tarṣu B
scorch *v.* qamû; → **~ing** *adj.* ḫummuṭu B☆
scorn *n.* baša'u+, šēṭūtu, šēṭūtu+; → ~ *v.* mêšu☆, šanāṣu☆; → **~er** *n.* šaiāṭu+; → **~ful** *adj.* šaiāṭu+
Scorpio *n.* zukiqīpu
scorpion *n.* zukiqīpu; → **~-man** *n.* girtablilû☆
scoundrel *n.* guzallu☆, ḫappu, ḫarḫaru☆
scour *v.* kapāru, marāqu+
scourge *n.* qinnāzu+; → ~ *v.* naṭû
scout *n.* daiālu; → **chief ~** *n.* rab daiāli
scowl *v.* ḫanāṣu☆ (D); → **~ing(?)** *adj.* šakṣu☆
scrape *v.* garādu+; → **~ off** *v.* garādu+, ḫalāšu☆, marāṭu; → **~ out** *v.* naqāru; → **~ up** *v.* esāpu (Š), sakālu☆ (D)
scraps → **(metal) ~** *n.* ḫušê
scratch *n.* ḫerṭu+; → ~ *v.* ekāku (D), ḫarāsu☆, marāṭu, naqāru; → **~ together** *v.* sakālu☆ (D); → **~ up** *v.* sakālu☆ (D); → **~ing** *n.* mirṭu
scream *n.* killu; → ~ *v.* ṣarāḫu B+; → **~ing** *n.* rigmu
screech *v.* ṣarāḫu B+; → **~ like an owl** *v.* qadû B☆
screen *n.* taḫlīpu (defensive)
scribal *adj.* [ša] ṭupšarrūti; → **~ art** *n.* ṭupšarrūtu; → **~ corpus** *n.* ṭupšarrūtu; → **~ practice** *n.* ṭupšarrūtu
scribble *v.* šaṭāru
scribe *n.* ṭupšarru; → **chief ~** *n.* rab ṭupšarri; → **female ~** *n.* ṭupšarrutu; → **military ~** *n.* ṭupšar ummāni; → **temple ~** *n.* ṭupšar bēt ili, ṭupšar ēkurri; → **~ (of Aramaic)** *n.* sepīru☆; → **office of ~ of the house** *n.* ṭupšar bītūtu◊; → **~ writing on waxed boards** *n.* ṭupšar lē'i
scriptorium *n.* bēt ṭuppāti
scrofula *n.* ḫuzīrtu+ (pl.)
scroll *n.* kirku, miglu

scrotum(?) *n.* lipšutu
scrub *v.* marāṭu
scruple *n.* būštu☆
scrupulous *adj.* nāriṭu
scrupulous, *adj.* ḫardu
scrutinize *v.* barû B☆, ḫâṭu☆, ḫiāru, marāru (D)
scrutiny *n.* bīru
scud *v.* arāḫu☆, ṣarāḫu C☆, šaḫāṭu C☆
scuffle *v.* rapāsu
scull *n.* lēqu+
sculpting *n.* kapšarrūtu☆
sculptor *n.* parkullu
sculpture *n.* urrākūtu☆
scum *n.* ḫurḫummatu☆
scurf *n.* rišūtu☆; → ~ *v.* garāṣu☆; → **~y** *adj.* garruṣu
scurry *n.* šiḫṭu; → ~ *v.* šaḫāṭu C☆
scurvy *n.* garābu☆
scuttle *n.* kakkullu
sea *n.* tāntu; → **~-shore** *n.* kibri tānti☆; → **~-water** *n.* marratu☆
seabed *n.* išdi tānti*
seabird *n.* iṣṣūr tānti*
seafood *n.* binût tānti☆
seah *n.* sūtu; → **~ master** *n.* rab sūti
seal *n.* kunukku; → ~ *v.* barāmu, kanāku; → **~ (an opening)** *v.* peḫû☆; → **~ (with a cylinder seal)** *v.* šugarruru [o.]; → **~ impression** *n.* birimtu
Sealand *n.* māt tānti
sealed *adj.* kanku; → **~ container** *adj.* maknuku [o.]; → **~ document** *n.* kanīku; → **~ house** *n.* bēt kanīki; → **~ order** *n.* unqu; → **~ room** *adj.* maknuku [o.]; → **~ storeroom** *n.* bēt unqi; → **~ tablet(?)** *n.* kasilaqqu◊
sealing *n.* šapassu
seam *n.* šipītu☆
seaman *n.* mallāḫu, ṣāb eleppi☆; → **~ship** *n.* mallāḫūtu☆
seamless *adj.* ša lā ḫiṭṭi+
seamster *n.* mukabbû
seamstress *n.* mukabbītu*
sear *v.* qalû, qamû
search *n.* teb'ītu☆; → ~ *v.* ba''û, ḫâṭu☆, še'û☆; → **~ out** *v.* ḫiāṭu (D)
seashore *n.* kibru
seasick *n.* marṣu ša tānti*; → **~ness** *n.* muruṣ tānti*
seaside *adj.* ša šiddi tānti☆; → ~ *n.* aḫ tānti☆, kišād tānti☆
season *n.* simunu; → **~able** *adj.* asmu☆; → **~al** *adj.* [ša] šatti; → **~al disease** *n.* murṣu šatti; → **~ing** *n.* riqiu

seat *n.* gišgallu☆, kussiu, šubtu; → **be(come) ~ed** *v.* ramû B☆
seaweed *n.* elapûa
seaworthy *adj.* lā'i tānti*; → **~ ship** *n.* muštabrītu☆
seclude *v.* esāru, šēpu parāsu [i.]; → **~d** *adj.* parsu
seclusion *n.* ašar šēpu parsat☆, sikru☆, sukurtu [o.]
second *adj.* arkû☆, šaniu, tardennu☆; → **~-best** *adj.* šiḫlu; → **~-hand** *adj.* labīru; → **~-in-esteem** *n.* ša-imitti; → **~-rate** *adj.* šiḫlu; → **~ cousin** *n.* mār mār aḫ-abi*; → **~ month)** *n.* uraḫ ša-sarrāte [o.]; → **a ~ time** *adv.* tūra; → **do for a ~ time** *v.* šanû☆; → **for the ~ time** *adv.* šaniānu☆; → **~ary** *adj.* šaniu, tardennu☆; → **~ly** *adv.* šaniānu☆, šanītu
secrecy *n.* pašīru☆; → **in ~** *adv.* ina aḫītēšu
secret *adj.* pesnu◊; → ~ *n.* katimtu☆, niṣirtu☆; → **keep ~** *v.* pesēnu◊; → **in ~** *adj.* šapal qāti; → **in ~** *adv.* pazriš☆, šarrāqiš☆; → **~ (lore)** *n.* pirištu☆; → **~ mission** *n.* pazzurtu; → **~ place** *n.* dūtu☆; → **~ary** *n.* ṭupšarru; → **city ~ary** *n.* ṭupšar āli; → **royal ~ary** *n.* ṭupšar šarri; → **~ion** *n.* ḫīltu [o.]; → **~ly** *adj.* šapal qāti; → **~ly** *adv.* ina aḫītēšu, pašīratti◊, šapla qāti [i.], šarqiš☆
sect *n.* pilku; → **~ion** *n.* kiṣru, pilku, pirsu, sadīru☆; → **~or** *n.* pilku
secure *adj.* taqnu; → ~ *v.* kuānu (D), rapāqu; → **be(come) ~** *v.* taqānu; → **make ~** *v.* taqānu (D)
security *n.* nēḫtu☆, tuqūnu, urkīu
sedate *adj.* pašḫu; → ~ *v.* nuāḫu (D), pašāḫu (Š)
sedge *n.* urbānu+; → **~(-tuber)** *n.* suādu; → **~ tuber** *n.* saggilatu☆
sediment *n.* qadūtu☆, sakīku☆, šuršummu☆
sedition *n.* sīḫu B☆
seduce *v.* kazābu☆ (D), sagû+ (Š)
seduction *n.* kuzubtu [o.]
see *v.* amāru, dagālu, naṭālu☆; → **~ off** *v.* radû; → **~ to** *v.* uznu ana X šakānu [i.]; → **~d** *n.* zar'u; → **~d** *v.* zarû; → **~d-corn heap** *n.* parūgu; → **~d-funnel** *n.* ittû B☆; → **~dbed** *n.* musarû B☆; → **~ding** *n.* zarû; → **~ing** *n.* nāṭilu☆
seek *v.* ba''û, pâru☆, še'û☆; → **~ out** *v.* ba''û, ḫiāru, ḫiāṭu (D); → **~ refuge** *v.* šaḫātu emādu [i.]; → **be(come) ~ to** *v.* ṣabû+
seem evil *v.* be'āšu+; → **make ~** *v.* be'āšu+ (Š)
seeming *adj.* ṣillānīu+

seen *adj.* amru
seep *n.* namba'u☆
seer *n.* šabrû☆
seethe *v.* bašālu+
segregate *v.* parāqu☆
seize *v.* aḫāzu☆, karāmu, sabāku (D), ṣabātu; → **~r (a demon)** *n.* aḫḫāzu☆
seizure *n.* ṣibtu
seldom *adv.* uqur*
select *adj.* nussuqu☆; → **~** *v.* amāru, atû B☆ (D), biāru, ḫiāru, nasāqu; → **~ed** *adj.* nasqu; → **~ion** *n.* itūtu☆, nisiqtu☆, nisqu☆
self *n.* ramunu; → **~-contained** *adj.* kapṣu+; → **~-control** *n.* kabsūtu+, ṣibit libbi; → **~-important** *adj.* muštarriḫu☆; → **~-possessed** *adj.* nēḫu
sell *v.* šiāmu B, tadānu; → **~ lawfully** *v.* zarāpu tadānu; → **~er** *n.* muttaddinu☆, tādinu; → **~er of tanning fluid** *n.* ša-kurrēšu; → **~ing** *n.* pašurtu☆
semblance *n.* būnu
semen *n.* nīlu, zar'u; → **~ duct** *n.* maslaḫ ušāri☆
semicircle *n.* qassu+, uskāru
semolina *n.* sasqû☆; → **~ broth** *n.* mê sasqî☆
senate *n.* paršamūtu
send *v.* abālu B☆ (Š), mu''uru☆, šapāru, ubālu (Š); → **~ away** *v.* uṣû (Š); → **~ back** *v.* tuāru (D); → **~ down** *v.* urādu (Š); → **~ earlier** *v.* ḫarrupu šapāru; → **~ first** *v.* ḫarrupu šapāru; → **~ in** *v.* erābu (Š); → **~ off** *v.* šalāḫu B [o.]; → **~ out** *v.* uṣû (Š); → **~ posthaste** *v.* ana kallie šēbulu; → **~ up** *v.* ina bēt kīli šapāru [i.]; → **~ word** *v.* šapāru; → **~er** *n.* šāpiru
senile *adj.* paršumu
senility *n.* paršamūtu
senior *adj.* pānīu; → **~** *n.* paršumu
sense *n.* pakku B☆, pišru, rigšu+; → **~** *v.* ragāšu+; → **~less** *adj.* lā ṭēmānu, lillu+; → **~lessness** *n.* saklūtu+
sensible *adj.* raggūšu+
sensitive *adj.* raggūštānu+
sensual *adj.* kuzbānu☆
sentence *n.* qibītu☆, šumu; → **~** *v.* qabû; → **~ (in law)** *n.* dēnu
sentimental *adj.* raggūštānu+
sentinel *n.* ša-maṣṣarti
sentry *n.* maṣṣuru, ša-maṣṣarti
separate *adj.* parsu; → **~** *v.* parāqu☆, parāsu, šatāqu+; → **~ from** *v.* parāqu+, parāsu; → **~ly** *adv.* aḫamma, aḫê◊; → **each ~ly** *adv.* aḫennâ☆
separation *n.* pirsu, uzubbû☆

September *n.* Elūlu (month)
sepulchre *n.* kimaḫḫu, naqburu
sequence *n.* sidru; → **in ~** *adv.* ana sadīr aḫāiš
sequential *adj.* sadru
sequester *v.* sakāru B+; → **~ed** *adj.* parsu
serf *n.* qatinnu; → **~ master** *n.* rab qatinnē; → **~dom** *n.* qatinnūtu
series *n.* iškāru, sidru+
serious *adj.* dannu, kabtu☆, nakdu☆; → **~ness** *n.* uqrūtu+
serpent *n.* ṣerru
serpentine *n.* muššāru
servant *n.* ardu◊, muttabbilu☆, urdu, urdu bēti; → **female ~** *n.* amtu☆, antu, muttabbiltu☆; → **temple ~** *n.* lamutānu◊
serve *v.* apālu B, duālu, lasāmu, palāḫu; → **be(come) ~** *v.* rēšu kullu [i.]
service *n.* apāl bēt ili, duālu+, nīru+; → **military ~** *n.* ṣāb šarrūtu; → **~able** *adj.* ša kušīri*, ṭābu
servile *adj.* urdānīu*
servitude *n.* ardūtu◊, nīru+, rēšūtu☆, urdānūtu
sesame *n.* šamaššammē; → **~ seed(s)** *n.* šawaššammē+
session *n.* ušābu+
set *v.* karāru, rabû B, šakānu; → **~-up** *n.* riksu; → **~ (sun)** *v.* erābu; → **~ afire** *v.* išātu ummudu [i.]; → **~ ajar** *v.* ṣalāpu+ (D); → **~ apart from** *v.* parāsu; → **~ aright** *v.* ešēru☆ (Št); → **~ aside** *v.* elû (D); → **~ course** *v.* ḫarrānu šutēšuru [i.]; → **~ down** *v.* šakānu; → **~ forth** *v.* kallumu (D), namāšu (D), uṣû; → **~ in** *adj.* uḫḫuzu; → **~ in** *v.* aḫu ummudu [i.]; → **~ in array** *v.* sadāru+; → **~ in place** *v.* retû☆, uzuzzu (Š); → **~ off** *v.* namāšu (D); → **~ on** *v.* sabāku+; → **~ on fire** *v.* išātu šāḫuzu [i.]; → **~ out** *v.* namāšu (D); → **~ right** *v.* ešēru☆ (Š), taqānu+ (D), tarāṣu B+ (D); → **~ straight** *v.* ešēru☆ (Š), tarāṣu B (D); → **~ the table** *n.* paššūru karāru; → **~ the table** *v.* paššūru rakāsu [i.]; → **~ to** *v.* aḫu ummudu [i.]; → **~ up** *adj.* zaqpu; → **~ up** *v.* karāru, kuānu (D), ṣabātu (Š), ṣalā'u [o.], šakānu, uzuzzu (Š), zaqāpu+; → **~ up a lament** *v.* taqribtu šakānu [i.]; → **~ upright** *v.* tarāṣu B+ (D)
setback *n.* miḫru
setting *n.* iḫzu☆, siḫru, šiknu; → **~ (of planet)** *n.* rību B☆, rūbu B; → **~ (of sun)** *n.* erābu
settle *v.* ramû B☆ (Š), ṣabātu (Š), šakānu (Š), ušābu (Š); → **~ down** *v.* ramû B☆, sakātu+; → **~ for** *v.* magāru (N); → **~ in** *v.* ušābu;

→ ~ **up** *v.* eṭāru B (D); → **~d** *adj.* kunnu; → **~ment** *n.* maškunu, šubtu, tazkītu*; → **~r** *n.* uššābu; → **~rs** *n.* galītu

seven *n./adj.* sebe*, sebettu*; → ~ **times** *adv.* sebīšu*; → **~teen** *n./adj.* sebēšer[et]*; → **~teenth** *adj.* sebēšerīu*; → **~th** *adj.* sabiu; → **~th heaven** *n.* šamû ša Ani*; → **~th month)** *n.* ṣippu [o.]; → **~tieth** *adj.* sebāiu*; → **~ty** *n./adj.* sebâ*

sever *v.* arû F*, nakāsu, parā'u B*, parāsu; → **~al** *adv.* ḫamiš šeš; → **~al times** *adv.* šalāšīšu arbīšu; → **~al times** *n.* šinīšu šalāšīšu

severe *adj.* dannu; → **be(come)** ~ *v.* da'ānu

severity *n.* danānu*, dannutu

sew *v.* kabbû (D), takāpu; → **~age** *n.* mê bībi*; → **~er** *n.* bību; → **~ing materials** *n.* anūt kabbê*

sex *n.* kuzbu; → ~ **organ** *n.* ūru B*

sexual intercourse *n.* niāku, nīku, rikibtu*; → **have** ~ *v.* niāku, rakābu* (Gt)

sexual union *n.* quršu, rikibtu*

sexuality *n.* kuzbu

sexy *adj.* kuzbānu*

shabby *adj.* qalpu

shack *n.* asuppu◊

shackles *n.* siparru

shade *n.* ṣillu, ṣulūlu; → ~ *v.* ṣallulu+; → **~-loving** *adj.* ṣillānīu*; → **~d** *adj.* ṣallulu

shadow *n.* ṣillu, ṣulūlu; → **in** ~ *adv.* ina ṣilli; → **~y** *adj.* eṭû*, ṣillānīu*

shaduf *n.* dilūtu*, makūtu*

shady *adj.* lā taklu*, ṣillānīu*

shaft *n.* qanû, šurdu, ziqpu; → ~ **(of a sedan chair)** *n.* sirdû*

shaggy *adj.* apparrû*

shake *n.* ratātu+; → ~ *v.* arāru B*, narāṭu, narāṭu (D), nâšu*, nussusu*, râdu*, ruābu (D), tarāku (Š), tarāru*; → ~ **down** *v.* šâbu*; → ~ **off** *v.* napāṣu+, napāṣu+ (D)

shaky *adj.* nāriṭu; → **be(come)** ~ *v.* nâšu*

shall *gram. part.* lū

shallot *n.* šamaškillu, zinzimmu

shallow *adj.* ēṣu B, qatnu, raqqu+; → ~ *n.* raqrāqu+

shambles *n.* tēšû*

shame *n.* bāltu*, būltu◊, būštu*; → **come to** ~ *v.* bâšu, luādu; → **put to** ~ *v.* bâšu (D); → **sense of** ~ *n.* būštu*; → **~d** *adj.* buššu*; → **~lessness** *n.* šillatu*

shan't *gram. part.* lā

shank *n.* kinṣu, piṭru, sisītu; → **~-band** *n.* piṭru+

shanty *n.* kurḫu+

shape *n.* binūtu, nigdimdimmû*, šikittu*; → **change** ~ *v.* emû*; → **~ly** *adj.* damqu

share *n.* isqu, zittu; → ~ *v.* zuāzu

shareholder *n.* bēl zitti, itbāru [o.]

sharer *n.* bēl zitti

sharp *adj.* ḫarīpu+, qatnu+, šēlu*; → **~-sighted** *adj.* ša ēnšu namratūni [i.]; → **~en** *v.* šêlu*; → **~ly incised** *adj.* šarmu; → **~ness(?)** *n.* šilītu*

shatter *v.* ḫapû, ḫašālu, letû* (D), napāṣu (D), parāru (D); → **~ed** *adj.* ḫabšu; → **be(come) ~ed** *v.* paḫāḫu+; → **~ing** *n.* nipṣu*

shave *v.* gallubu

shaving *n.* gallābūtu; → ~ **blade** *n.* naglubu; → **~s** *n.* ḫibištu*

shawl *n.* kindabassu, kirimmu*; → **(fringed)** ~ *n.* elītu

she *pron.* šî, šīti

sheaf *n.* kurillu*, ṣarru

shear *v.* gallubu, gazāzu; → **~er** *n.* gazzizu; → **~ing** *n.* gizzu; → **~s** *n.* magazzutu

sheath *n.* kutummu*, takāltu*

Shebat *n.* Šaba:#u (month)

shed *n.* asuppu◊, kurḫu+; → ~ *v.* naqû, šalāḫu+, tabāku

sheen *n.* birbirru, birṣu*

sheep *n.* immertu*, immeru, šu'u B*; → **carrier of** ~ *n.* zābil immeri; → **fat** ~ *n.* aslu*; → **fat-tailed** ~ *n.* gukkallu; → **fattened** ~ *n.* takbāru; → **like fat** ~ *adv.* asliš*; → **live** ~ *n.* udutilû*; → **mountain** ~ *n.* immer šaddi; → **wild** ~ *n.* immer šaddi; → **young** ~ *adj.* kabsu; → ~ **(designation of)** *n.* ṣu'ubtu; → ~ **(kind of)** *n.* šūbu*; → ~ **and goatherd** *n.* rā'i ṣēni*; → **flock of** ~ **and goats** *n.* ṣēnu*; → ~ **offering (kind of)** *n.* kimru, takmīsu; → **~fold** *n.* pitqu, supūru*; → **~ish** *adj.* immerānu

sheepmaster *n.* nāqidu+

sheet *n.* sasuppu, šaddīnu+; → **~/plaque (of metal)** *n.* lē'u

sheikh *n.* nasīku

shekel *n.* šiqlu

shelf *n.* rāpu+

shell *n.* aiartu, išqillatu*, kallu, qulāptu [o.]; → ~ *v.* qalāpu; → **~ed** *adj.* qalpu; → **~s** *n.* qulpu+

shelter *n.* maṣallu, muṣallutu, puzru, ṣalūlu, ṣillu, ṣulūlu, tarānu*; → ~ *v.* ḫaṣānu, ḫatānu*

shepherd *n.* rā'i immeri, rā'iu, utullu* (chief); → ~ *v.* ra'û; → **~'s hut** *n.* bēt rē'ê, gubru*; → **~'s staff** *n.* šibirru*; → **chief** ~ *n.* rab rā'î; → ~ **boy** *n.* kaparru*; → **~ing** *n.*

rā'iūtu+; → ~ship *n.* rā'iūtu
sherd *n.* ḫaṣbu
shield *n.* arītu (round), kabābu⋆ (heavy); → **(leather) ~** *n.* tukšu⋆; → **protective ~** *n.* mušēzibtu; → **~-boss** *n.* kammutu; → **~-man** *n.* ša-arīti; → **~-owner** *n.* bēl arīti; → **protective ~ carrier** *n.* ša-mušēzibti
shift *v.* nâšu⋆; → **~ to** *v.* abāku (D); → **~y** *adj.* lā taklu*
shimmer *v.* zalāgu+
shin *n.* kinṣu, kurītu⋆; → **~(bone)** *n.* kurītu⋆
shine *n.* nūru; → **~** *v.* barāḫu⋆, barāqu⋆, barāṣu⋆, ḫalû⋆, nabāṭu⋆, namāru, napardû⋆, naqallulu, nebû⋆; → **let ~** *v.* namāru (Š); → **make ~** *v.* nabāṭu⋆ (Š); → **~ brightly** *v.* ḫalû⋆ (Gt), mašāḫu B⋆; → **~ forth** *v.* apû⋆
shining *adj.* barḫu, ebbu, namru, napḫu⋆, nebû⋆, šāpû; → **~** *n.* muttanbiṭu⋆; → **be(come) ~** *v.* ebābu
shiny *adj.* barḫu, ebbu, namru
ship *n.* eleppu, šapīnutu+; → **~** *v.* zabālu (Š); → **cargo ~** *n.* makkūtu⋆; → **~-owner** *n.* bēl eleppi; → **~ment** *n.* šazbussu, šēbultu⋆, šūbultu⋆; → **~shape** *adj.* tarṣu; → **~wright** *n.* mallāḫu
shirk *v.* issu pān X ḫalāqu [i.], ruāqu
shirt *n.* šupālītu
shit *n.* zê; → **~** *v.* teṣû⋆
shiver *v.* ḫapû, ratātu⋆, tarāru⋆; → **~ing** *n.* kuṣṣu, ratītu⋆; → **~y** *adj.* rattitu⋆
shoal *n.* raqrāqu+
shock *n.* kurillu⋆, miḫṣu, miḫṣu*, tarāmu; → **~** *v.* palāḫu (D), parādu⋆ (D); → **~ing** *adj.* pardu⋆
shoe *n.* mašennu, šēnu
shoemaker *n.* aškāpu, aškāpu+, ēpiš šēni⋆
shoes → **put on ~** *v.* šēnu⋆
shoot *n.* ḫabbūru, kannu B, papallu⋆, pir'u, piri'tu, ziqpu; → **~** *v.* nasāku, šalā'u; → **~ up** *v.* nabā'u+
shop *n.* kurḫu; → **~** *v.* laqû, makāru B [o.], miāru
shore *n.* aḫātu B⋆, kibru, kišādu
short *adj.* karrû⋆, kuriu; → **be(come) ~** *v.* karû; → **~-tempered** *adj.* aggu⋆; → **in ~ supply** *adj.* batqu [o.]; → **~age** *n.* batqu, muṭê, tēkītu
shortcoming *n.* ḫiṭītu⋆, ḫiṭṭu
shorten *v.* karû (D); → **~ing** *n.* takrītu*
shortfall *n.* miṭītu◊, muṭê
shortly *adv.* arḫiš, ēṣiš [o.], zamar⋆
shortness *n.* kurûtu*
shot *n.* nisku⋆, šilūtu [o.]
should *gram. part.* lū; → **~ not** *gram. part.* lū lā; → **~er** *n.* būdu◊, imittu, kumāru; → **~er-blade** *n.* rapšu B+; → **~er blade** *n.* naglubu
shout *n.* aiārurutu, rigmu, šisītu⋆; → **~** *v.* ragāmu, sasû, šasû⋆
shove *v.* da'āpu
shovel *n.* marru, nēsupu
show *v.* barû B⋆ (Š), kallumu (D); → **make ~** *v.* dagālu (Š); → **~ mercy** *v.* rēmu ina muḫḫi/ana X šakānu [i.]; → **~ off** *v.* šarāḫu⋆ (Dt); → **~ up** *v.* qarābu; → **~er** *n.* zīnu; → **~y** *adj.* šamḫu⋆, šurruḫu⋆
shred *n.* širṭu; → **~** *v.* parāmu, šarāṭu⋆ (D)
shrew *n.* ḫulû, pušḫu; → **female ~** *n.* ḫulūtu; → **~d** *adj.* naklu
shriek *n.* rigmu
shrill *adj.* qatnu+, zēqu+
shrine *n.* aiakku, kiṣṣu⋆, parakku, parakku+, sāgu B⋆
shrink *v.* kalāṣu⋆, ṣaḫāru, ṣaḫāru (N); → **~ from** *v.* naḫāsu◊; → **~age** *n.* kilṣu⋆
shrivel → **be(come) ~** *v.* abālu; → **~ing** *n.* kilṣu⋆; → **~led** *adj.* ḫamadīru⋆; → **~led** *n.* ḫummuru◊; → **be(come) ~led** *v.* naḫāru B⋆
shroud *v.* karāku+, katāmu (D)
shrub *n.* gapnu
shrug off *v.* nasāku⋆ (Š)
shrunken *n.* ḫummuru◊
shudder *n.* ratātu+
shun *v.* nesû⋆, ruāqu
shut *adj.* edlu; → **~** *v.* ḫaṭāmu, sakāru B+; → **~ down** *n.* sakāru+; → **~ down** *v.* baṭālu; → **~ in** *v.* esāru, pâdu⋆; → **be ~ in** *v.* esāru⋆ (Dt); → **~ o.s. in** *v.* esāru (N); → **~ o.s. up** *v.* edālu (N); → **~ off** *v.* edālu, esāru, parāsu; → **~ up** *v.* kalû, peḫû⋆, quālu; → **~tle** *n.* ukû⋆
shy *adj.* baiāšu⋆; → **be(come) ~** *v.* sakālu B⋆; → **~ at** *v.* nesû⋆, palāḫu; → **~ away (from)** *v.* nesû⋆; → **~ from** *v.* nesû⋆, ruāqu
sick *adj.* marṣu; → **be(come) ~** *v.* marāṣu; → **~ person** *n.* marṣu; → **be(come) ~en** *v.* marāṣu
sickle *n.* ingallu
sickly *adv.* marrāṣu⋆; → **be ~** *v.* marāṣu (Gtn); → **be(come) ~** *v.* kadāru B+
sickness *n.* murṣānu+, murṣu
side *n.* aḫītu, aḫu B, battu, idu⋆, lētu, šaḫātu⋆; → **~(?)** *n.* maldu⋆; → **long ~** *n.* šiddu; → **upper ~** *n.* ṣēru⋆; → **~ by side** *adv.* aḫia aḫia◊; → **~ with** *v.* issi X šakānu [i.]
sideboard *n.* bēt ḫuruppi
sidepiece *n.* amāru B
siderites *n.* aprušu
sideways *adv.* ṣēlāniš⋆

Sidon *n*. Ṣīdūnu
siege *n*. nītu☆, usurtu☆; → **~-instrument(?) (kind of)** *n*. lulīmītu; → **~-shield** *n*. mušēzibtu; → **~ engine (kind of)** *n*. kalbānu☆, nimgallu☆; → **~ wall** *n*. dā'iqu☆
siesta *n*. muṣlālu
sieve *n*. mašḫulu, nappītu, nappû??◊; → **~** *v*. naḫālu☆, napû◊, šaḫālu◊; → **~d** *adj*. naḫlu B [o.]
sift *v*. naḫālu☆, napû◊, šaḫālu◊
sigh *n*. inḫu; → **~** *v*. anāḫu; → **~ing** *n*. tānīḫu☆; → **~t** *n*. diglu, niṭlu☆
sign *n*. ittu, ṣaddu☆; → **~al** *n*. ittu, ṣaddu☆; → **~al** *v*. ittu tadānu
signature *n*. šumu šaṭru☆
significance *n*. pišru
significant *adj*. ma'du
signification *n*. pišru
signify *v*. qabû ana
signpost *n*. ittu☆
silence *n*. qūltu☆, qūlu, šaqummatu☆; → **~** *v*. ḫarāšu C+ (D), sakātu◊ (D), šuqammumu☆; → **awesome ~** *n*. šaḫurratu☆
silent *adj*. qālu, šuḫarruru☆, šuqammumu☆; → **be(come) ~** *v*. ḫarāšu C☆, quālu, sakātu◊, šuqammumu☆; → **~ly** *adv*. qāliš☆, šaqummiš☆
silhouette *n*. ṣūrat ṣilli+
silk *n*. šaddīnu; → **sea ~** *n*. būṣu
sill *n*. sippu+; → **~y** *adj*. saklu
silo *n*. išpikku, padakku, šutummu☆; → **grain ~** *n*. kalakku C◊
silt *n*. sakīku☆, ṭēru☆
silver *n*. ṣarpu; → **refiner of ~** *n*. ṣarrāp kaspi, ṣarrāpu+; → **~ (kind of)** *n*. ruqpu; → **~ alloy** *n*. zaḫalû☆; → **~ alloy (kind of)** *n*. ešmarû☆; → **~smith** *n*. ṣarrāp kaspi
silver *n*. kaspu☆
similar *adj*. mušlu; → **make ~** *v*. mašālu☆ (D); → **~ity** *n*. mušlānūtu*; → **~ly** *adv*. kî annimma, mitḫāriš☆; → **do ~ly** *v*. mašālu (Š)
simile *adj*. tamšiltu☆; → **use a ~** *v*. mašālu+ (Š)
simmer *v*. bašālu; → **~ overnight** *v*. biādu☆ (Š)
simple *adj*. iaḫudû☆, saklu; → **~-minded** *adj*. saklu; → **~ton** *n*. dunnamû☆, saklu
simplicity *n*. saklūtu*
simply *adv*. sakliš*
simulate *v*. mašālu (Š)
simultaneously *adv*. issēniš
sin *n*. arnu, gillatu☆, gullultu☆, ḫiṭītu☆, ḫiṭṭu, nerṭû☆, šērtu B☆; → **~** *v*. ḫaṭû; → **mortal ~** *n*. ḫiṭṭu ša muāti; → **~ against** *v*. ḫiṭṭu ḫaṭû
since *prep*. ištu☆, ultu☆; → **~** *subj*. issu bēt, issu mār, issu maṣi, kī maṣin; → **~re** *adj*. šalmu, zakû+; → **~rely** *adv*. ina kētti; → **~rity** *n*. kēnūtu, zakûtu+
sinew *n*. gīdu, šer'ānu
sinful *adj*. ḫāṭiu, ḫaṭû☆
sing *v*. zamāru, zamāru+; → **~ joyfully** *v*. nagû☆; → **~ softly** *v*. laḫāšu+
singe *v*. gabābu (D); → **~r** *n*. nargallu (senior), nuāru, zammāru; → **chief ~r** *n*. rab nuāri, rab zammāri; → **female ~r** *n*. nargallutu, nuārtu
single *adj*. ēdānīu, ēdu, ēdumānu, issēnīu, sagdilû☆; → **~ door** *n*. ēdānītu; → **~ out** *v*. nasāqu
singly *adv*. aḫennâ☆
singular *adj*. ēdānīu
sinister *adj*. bīšu+
sink *n*. narmaktu, narmuku [o.]; → **~** *v*. ṭabû, ṭabû (D)
sinless *adj*. zakû
sinner *adj*. ḫāṭiu; → **~** *n*. bēl arni☆, ḫaṭṭā'u☆
sinter *v*. paṣû (D)
sip *v*. sarāpu+
sir *n*. bēlu
sire *n*. abu, bēlu; → **~n** *n*. nāḫiru☆
Sirius *n*. šukuddu☆
sister *n*. aḫātu; → **~'s son** *n*. mār aḫāti; → **~-in-law** *n*. alti aḫi*, issi aḫi [i.], mar'at emi☆; → **~hood** *n*. aḫātūtu; → **~ly** *adv*. aḫātānu*
sit *v*. kamāsu (D), ušābu; → **~ (on eggs)** *v*. qapāpu+; → **~ astride** *v*. ḫallu patû☆; → **~ down** *v*. ušābu; → **~ up** *v*. dalāpu
site *n*. ašru☆, maškunu
situate *v*. karāru; → **be ~d** *v*. nadû☆ (stat.); → **be(come) ~d** *v*. karāru (stat.), ṣalā'u (stat.) [o.]
situation *n*. šiknu
Sivan *n*. Simannu (month), Simānu☆ (month)
six times *adv*. šeššīšu
sixfold *adj./adv*. šeššīšu
sixteen *n./adj*. šediššer[et]*; → **~th** *adj*. šediššerīu*
sixth *adj*. šeššu; → **one ~** *n*. šadussu, šeššu; → **~ month)** *n*. uraḫ Hibur [o.]
sixtieth *adj*. šūšīu☆
sixty *n./adj*. šeššā, šūši
size *n*. lānu, mišiḫtu☆, rabûtu; → **normal ~** *n*. mināti☆ (pl.)
sizzle *v*. gabbubu
skeleton *n*. eṣentu
sketch *n*. liṭṭu, uṣurtu

skew *adj.* ṣalpu★; → ~ *v.* zuppu+ (D)
skilful *adj.* naklu; → **be(come) ~** *v.* nakālu; → **~ technique** *n.* šipir nikilti★; → **~ly** *adv.* nakliš★; → **execute ~ly** *v.* nakālu★ (Š); → **make ~ly** *v.* nakālu★ (D)
skill *n.* le'ûtu★, nikiltu, šipru; → **~ed** *adj.* enqu★, lā'iu; → **be(come) ~ed** *v.* damāqu
skim *v.* qalāpu; → **~ (through)** *v.* amāru
skin *n.* mašku, pāru★, qarūmu+, šišītu★; → **~** *v.* qalāpu; → **(ox) ~** *n.* gildu; → **scaly ~** *n.* quliptu★; → **~ disease (kind of)** *n.* ṣennītu★; → **~ of scales** *n.* qulāptu [o.]
skinflint *n.* kāriṣu*
skinny *adj.* aklu; → **~(?)** *adj.* nuḫḫuru★
skip *v.* etāqu (Š), raqādu; → **~ (out)** *v.* rammû (D); → **~per** *n.* mallāḫu
skirmish *n.* tāḫāzu★
skittish *adj.* pazīzu+
skulk *v.* ḫalālu
skull *n.* gulgullu, muḫḫu
sky *n.* ermiānu★ (Anu's), šamê; → **~-blue** *n./adj.* iqnû; → **~-high** *adj.* zuqquru★
slab(?) *n.* nišru
slab → **stone ~** *n.* askuppu★
slack *adj.* ramû; → **be(come) ~ off** *v.* ramû; → **~en** *v.* ramû; → **~er** *adj.* ḫalqu
slag *n.* ḫaḫû B★, ḫuluḫḫu (light-colored); → **~(?)** *n.* luliu
slam *v.* maḫāṣu, napāṣu
slander *n.* akāl karṣē, bīštu★, karṣu (pl.), ṭapiltu★, ṭiplu★, ṭupullû★; → **~** *v.* karṣē akālu [i.], lazānu, ṭapālu★; → **~ed** *adj.* ṭaplu★; → **~er** *n.* ākil karṣē, šaḫšaḫḫu★; → **~ous** *adj.* ṭappilu★
slang *n.* lišān nišē*
slant *v.* qâpu★
slap *n.* miḫṣu; → **~** *v.* maḫāṣu
slash *v.* naṭû
slate *n.* paršu+
slaughter *n.* mūtānu+, šaggaštu★; → **~** *v.* ḫatāpu, palāqu★, šagāšu, ṭabāḫu; → **~-bench** *n.* makāṣu★; → **make a ~-offering** *v.* ḫatāpu (D); → **~er** *n.* ṭābiḫu
slaughterhouse *n.* bēt ṭābiḫi
slave *n.* ardu◊, qallu, urdu; → **be(come) a ~** *v.* ana rēšūti alāku [i.]; → **bought ~** *n.* mār šīmi, ša-šīmi; → **house ~** *n.* urdu bēti; → **~-girl** *n.* amtu★, antu; → **~ master** *n.* rab urdāni; → **~ry** *n.* rēšūtu★
slay *v.* maḫāṣu, napāṣu (D), nêru★, sâdu★, šagāšu; → **cause the ~** *v.* muātu (Š)
sled *n.* iannusu
sledge *n.* iannusu; → **threshing ~** *n.* daiaštu★
sledgehammer *n.* akkullu
sleep *n.* ṣallūtu★, šittu★; → **~** *v.* niālu, utūlu★; → **be(come) ~** *v.* ṣalālu★; → **let ~** *v.* ṣalālu★ (Š); → **make ~** *v.* niālu (Š); → **~ around** *v.* niāku (Gtn) [o.]; → **be(come) ~ in** *v.* ṣalālu★; → **~ing** *adj.* ṣallu★; → **~ing** *n.* ṣālilu★; → **~ing place** *n.* muṣallutu; → **~less** *adj.* dalpu, lā ṣālilu★, pardu+, šudlupu★; → **be(come) ~less** *v.* dalāpu; → **~lessness** *n.* diliptu, perdu+; → **~y** *adj.* ṣallu★; → **~y** *n.* ṣālilu★; → **~y-head** *n.* ṣālilu★
sleet *n.* šalgu★
sleeve *n.* aḫu B
sleigh *n.* iannusu
slender *adj.* qatnu
slice *n.* ḫirṣu; → **~** *v.* karātu, parā'u B★; → **~d** *adj.* ṣalpu★
slick *adj.* naklu
slide *v.* naḫalṣû
sliding *n.* muḫḫalṣû*
slight *adj.* qallīlu+, qallu; → **~** *v.* qalālu (D); → **be(come) ~** *v.* piāqu, qalālu; → **~ing** *n.* qulālu+; → **~ly** *adv.* qalliš★
slim *adj.* qatnu, raqqu, raqqu★
slime *n.* ḫaḫḫu B★
sling *n.* aspu★, uṣpu; → **~er** *n.* sādiu; → **~stone** *n.* abattu
slink *v.* ḫalālu; → **~ing** *n.* ḫillutu
slip *v.* naḫalṣû; → **~-up** *n.* ḫiṭītu★; → **~ away** *v.* ḫalāqu; → **~ in** *v.* ḫalāpu B★; → **~ out** *v.* ḫalāqu; → **~ through** *v.* ḫalāpu B★; → **~ped with clay** *adj.* sēru; → **~pery** *n.* muḫḫalṣû*, mušḫalṣû★; → **~shod** *adj.* šēṭu
slit *v.* parā'u B★; → **~ open** *v.* šalāqu
slither *v.* šalālu B★
sliver *n.* ḫirṣu
slop *v.* šapāku+, tabāku, tabāku+
slope *n.* kinšu★, taraḫḫu★
sloping *adj.* āridu★
sloppy *adj.* makiu B
slot *n.* ḫurru
sloth *n.* egûtu, makûtu B, šēṭūtu; → **~ful** *adj.* egû, makiu B, šēṭu
slouch *v.* pānē guddudu [i.]
slough (off) *v.* šalāḫu+
slow *adj.* arku+, marû★; → **be(come) ~** *v.* marû★, muqqu★
sludge *n.* rušundu★
slug *adj.* egû
sluggard *adj.* egû, šēṭu; → **~** *n.* mākiu
sluggish *adj.* muqqu★; → **be(come) ~** *v.* muqqu★
sluice *n.* bitqu B◊; → **~ gate** *n.* bāb bitqi◊
slum *n.* bābti muškēnūti*; → **~ber** *v.* nuāmu+; → **morning ~ber** *n.* munattu★
slur *v.* ḫabābu★

slush *n.* sarbu, šalgu☆
slut *n.* ḫarintu
sly *adj.* naklu
small *adj.* dallu☆, diqqu☆, qallīlu+, qallu, ṣeḫru; → ~ *v.* dalālu B☆, daqāqu◊, naḫātu, qalālu, ṣaḫāru; → **very** ~ *adj.* ṣeḫḫeru, ṣuḫḫuru☆
smallpox *n.* samānu B☆, šagbānu☆, šallāqītu+
smaragd *n.* barraqtu☆
smart *adj.* ḫassu, kannû; → **make ~en** *v.* kannû (D)
smash *v.* napāṣu (D), pasāsu; → **~ing** *n.* nipṣu☆
smear *v.* eqû, kapāru, pašāšu, siāru
smell *n.* irīšu☆, napīšu☆, nipšu B; → ~ *v.* eṣānu; → ~ **bad** *v.* be'āšu, be'ēšu◊; → ~ **evil** *v.* zapāru+; → ~ **rank** *v.* be'āšu
smelt *v.* ṣarāpu, ṣuādu, ṣuādu (D); → **~ed** *n.* ṣēdu; → **~ing** *n.* bušlu☆
smile *v.* ṣiāḫu☆
smiling *adj.* ṣuḫḫu☆
smite *v.* maḫāṣu, napāṣu (D), palāqu☆, rasābu☆
smith *n.* nappāḫu; → **female** ~ *n.* nappāḫtu; → **master of ~s** *n.* rab nappāḫi; → **~y** *n.* bēt nappāḫi☆
smitten *adj.* maḫṣu
smoke *n.* qutru; → ~ *v.* qatāru; → **~d** *adj.* qatturu, qutturu☆; → **~less** *adj.* lā qatru
smoky *adj.* qatru, qatturu, qutturu☆
smolder *v.* šabābu+
smooth *adj.* sapnu*; → **be(come)** ~ *v.* mašālu; → ~ **(away/out/down)** *v.* sapānu; → ~ **the path** *v.* ḫūlu ana šēpi šakānu [i.]; → **~ly** *adv.* ṭābiš☆
smudge *v.* ṭanāpu◊ (D); → **~d** *n.* aršu☆
smuggle *v.* pazzuru; → **~r** *n.* mupazziru☆
smuggling *n.* pazzurtu
smutty *adj.* ša''uru
snack *n.* ṭa'ūmu+
snaffle *n.* makṣaru☆
snake *n.* ṣerru; → **~-like** *adj.* ṣerrānu; → ~ **charmer** *n.* mušlaḫḫu☆
snakish *adj.* ṣerrānu
snaky *adj.* ṣerrānu
snappish *adj.* aggu☆, marru B
snare *n.* gišparru☆, kippu
snarl *v.* na'āru☆
snatch *v.* puāgu, šamāṭu; → **~ed away** *adj.* šallu☆
sneak *v.* ḫalālu, šapāpu+; → **~y** *n.* ḫālilānu*
sneer *n.* šinṣu☆; → ~ *v.* ganāṣu☆ (Dt), šanāṣu☆
sneeze *n.* ni'šu☆; → **~(?)** *v.* na'āšu☆
sniff *v.* našāšu B☆; → ~ **at** *v.* eṣānu
sniffle *v.* naḫāsu B☆
snigger *v.* ṣiāḫu☆ (Gtn)
snip *v.* kaṣāṣu☆
snivel *v.* naḫāsu B☆
snooze *v.* nuāmu+
snore *v.* naḫāru☆
snort *n.* nipšu B; → ~ *v.* naḫāru☆, napāšu, nazāzu☆; → **~er** *n.* nāḫirānu☆; → **~ing** *v.* naḫāru☆
snot *n.* ḫaḫḫu B☆
snout *n.* ḫuṭṭimmu☆
snow *n.* kupû, šalgu☆; → ~ *v.* šalāgu☆
snowfall *n.* kupû
snowstorm *n.* meḫû ša kuppi*
snub-nose *adj.* šarmu+
snuff *v.* eṣānu; → ~ **at** *v.* eṣānu
snuffle *v.* eṣānu
snug *n.* šaḫīnu+
snuggle *v.* kanānu☆
so *adv.* akē; → **~-called** *adj.* iqabbûniššu; → ~ **(that)** *subj.* bāsi; → ~ **far** *adv.* adakanni, adi akanni, adinakanni; → ~ **that** *subj.* aššu☆; → ~ **that(?)** *subj.* bis
soak *v.* labāku (D), ramāku, rasānu, raṭābu (D), ṣapû; → **~ed malt** *n.* risittu☆; → **~ing** *n.* risittu☆, ṣīpu; → **~ing (wet)** *adj.* raṭṭubu
soap *n.* lardu; → ~ *v.* ḫapāpu+
soapwort (kind of) *n.* tullal☆
soar *v.* gadālu+, parāšu☆ (Ntn); → **~(?)** *v.* šuā'u
sob *v.* naḫāsu B☆, nuḫḫuṭu☆ (D)
sobbing *n.* bikītu, itḫusu☆
sober *adj.* lā šakru*, nēḫu, šalmu
sobriety *n.* nēḫtu☆
socket *n.* ḫuppu, uppu
socle *n.* kerṣappu☆, kigallu
soda *n.* aḫussu☆; → **washing** ~ *n.* nitiru; → ~ **ash** *n.* nitiru
sofa *n.* nēmattu
soft *adj.* labku, rabbu B; → **be(come)** ~ *v.* labāku, rabābu; → **very** ~ *adj.* nurrubu☆; → ~ **mass** *n.* mūqaru☆; → ~ **place** *n.* nurbu☆; → **~en (up)** *v.* labāku (D), rabābu (Š)
softhearted *n.* libbu rabbu [i.]
softly *adv.* rabbiš☆
soil *n.* epru, erṣutu☆, kaqquru; → ~ *v.* ša'āru (D), ṭanāpu◊ (D); → **~ed** *adj.* lu''û☆, ša''uru; → **~ed** *n.* aršu☆
solace *n.* nēḫtu☆
solder *n.* debqu+; → ~ *v.* bašālu (Š)
soldier *n.* rādiu, ṣābu; → **~ing** *n.* muntaḫṣūtu☆; → **~s (kind of)** *n.* zunzuraḫḫu
sole *n.* mašennu; → ~ **of the foot** *n.* šaplān

šēpi☆; → **~ly** *adv.* udēšu
solemn *adj.* kabtu☆; → **~ity** *n.* kabdūtu*, uqrūtu+; → **~ly** *adv.* rabīš☆
solicit *v.* ba"û+; → **~or** *n.* rābiṣu [o.]; → **~ous** *adj.* ḫardu, na'du☆, naqdu☆
solid *adj.* dunnunu☆, ešqu☆, ḫabburu, kaṣru, kunnu, raṣpu+, uppuqu☆; → **be(come) ~** *v.* kuānu; → **make ~** *v.* ḫubburu☆ (D), raṣāpu+
solidarity *n.* gammurti libbi, tappūtu☆
solidity *n.* šipku
solidly *adv.* dunnuniš☆
solitary *adj.* ēdumānu, madbarāiu+
solitude *n.* ēdumānūtu
solo *adj.* ēdumānu
soluble *adj.* ša pašāri*
solution *n.* piširtu; → **clear ~** *n.* pīt pāni☆
solve *v.* pašāru; → **~nt** *adj.* šalmu; → **~nt** *n.* piširtu
somber *adj.* adru B, eklu☆, ṣillānīu☆
some ... others *conj.* annūti ... annūti, issēnūti ... issēnūti
some kind of *pron.* memmēni
some or other *pron.* memmēni
somebody *pron.* mamman☆, mammāna☆, manāma☆
somehow *adv.* akêmēni*
someone *pron.* memmēni
somersault *n.* nabalkutu☆; → **do a ~** *v.* nabalkutu☆
something *pron.* memmēni
sometimes *adv.* ina birīt
somewhat *adv.* ēṣe
son *n.* bukru☆ (first-born), mar'u; → **posthumous ~** *n.* ḫurdu; → **~-in-law** *n.* emu, ḫatannu
song *n.* zamāru, zimru☆; → **~ (kind of)** *n.* araḫḫu☆; → **~ of praise** *n.* zamār taknê☆
sonhood *n.* mar'ūtu
sonorous *adj.* raṣmu☆, šapû☆
sonship *n.* mar'ūtu
soon *adv.* bāsi, ēṣiš [o.], surriš☆, zamar☆; → **~(?)** *n.* bis; → **very ~** *adv.* arḫiš arḫiš, urruḫiš☆
soot *n.* šu'ru+
soothe *v.* nuāḫu (D), pašāḫu (Š)
sooty *adj.* ša"uru+; → **be(come) ~** *v.* ša'āru+; → **make ~** *v.* ša'āru+ (D)
sophisticated *adj.* naklu, nukkulu☆
soporific *n.* šakrūnu+
sorcerer *n.* kaššāpu, multēpišu☆, muštēpišu☆
sorceress *n.* kaššāptu
sorcery *n.* kišpē
sordid *n.* aršu☆
sore *n.* simmu; → **~ly** *adv.* marṣiš; → **~s** *n.* ḫuzīrtu+ (pl.)
sorrow *n.* idirtu, niziqtu☆
sorry *n.* libbu marṣu [i.]; → **be(come) ~** *v.* libbu marāṣu [i.]
sought one *n.* ba"ītu☆
soul *n.* napšutu
sound *adj.* šalmu; → **~** *n.* rigmu; → **~** *v.* ḫalālu B, maḫāṣu, ragāmu; → **be(come) ~** *v.* šalāmu; → **make ~** *v.* ḫalālu B (D)
soup *n.* akussu; → **~ vendor** *n.* ša-akussēšu
sour *adj.* enṣu, marru B+; → **~** *v.* marāru+ (Š); → **be(come) ~** *v.* emēṣu☆, marāru+
source *n.* nagbu☆, namba'u☆, ummu
south *n.* imittu, šūtu B; → **~east** *n.* šūtu B; → **~ern** *adj.* [ša] šūti
southwest *n.* amurru; → **~erly** *adj.* [ša] amurri
souvenir *n.* ḫissutu
sovereign *n.* etellu☆, malku☆; → **~ty** *n.* etallūtu☆, šāpirūtu☆
sow *n.* ḫuzīrtu, šaḫītu☆; → **~** *v.* zarû; → **~ing** *n.* zarû
space *n.* kaqquru, rāqtu*, tarpašû☆; → **~ between** *n.* birītu B☆
spacious *adj.* rapšu, šadlu☆
spade *n.* marru
spadix *n.* sissinnu☆
span *n.* rūṭu, ūṭu◊; → **about a ~** *n.* ammār rūṭi
spangle *v.* zalāqu B+
spank *v.* naṭû
spare *adj.* utru; → **~** *v.* eṭāru, ezābu [o.], gamālu, padû; → **be ~d** *v.* šêtu☆
spark *n.* šibūbu☆
sparkle *n.* birbirru; → **~** *v.* nebû☆
sparkling *adj.* ummulu☆; → **~ly** *adv.* ummuliš☆
sparrow *n.* ṣepru+, ṣibāru B☆
sparse *adj.* ēṣu B; → **be(come) ~** *v.* raqāqu
spasm *n.* giddagiddû☆
spasmatic *n.* gidgiddānu
spasmodic *n.* gidgiddānu
spasms → **have ~** *v.* magāgu☆ (Gtn)
spate *n.* bubbulu, edû B☆
spatter *v.* raḫāṣu B, salāḫu☆
spatula *n.* mulappitu
spawn *n.* riḫūtu
speak *v.* amû☆, dabābu, qabû; → **~ for** *v.* abbūtu ṣabātu [i.]; → **~ in parables** *v.* mašālu+; → **~ low** *v.* laḫāšu+; → **~ out** *v.* dabābu, pû patû [i.]; → **~ slander** *v.* ṭapiltu dabābu [i.]; → **~ up** *n.* elīta dabābu☆; → **~er**

n. dābibu☆, qābiānu; → **one who ~s the language** *n.* bēl lišāni
spear *n.* asmarû☆, šukurru☆; → **~man** *n.* na:& kaba:bi (u) asmare^☆ (armored); → **(light) ~man** *n.* Qurrāiu , Qurru ; → **(regular) ~man** *n.* ša-arīti; → **auxiliary ~man** *n.* Qurrāiu , Qurru
spearmint *n.* nanihu
special *adj.* parsu; → **~ist** *n.* lē'i īni☆, ummânu
specific *adj.* ḫarṣu
specify *v.* mussû◊, šiāmu, ussuku (D)
speck *n.* uršu☆; → **~led** *adj.* barmu☆, kakkullānu+; → **be(come) ~led** *v.* barāmu B☆; → **be(come) ~led(?)** *v.* matāru☆
spectacle *n.* taklimtu
spectator *n.* dāgilu
specter *n.* eṭemmu, utukku
speculate *v.* kaṣāpu (D)
speech *n.* atmû☆, dabābu, lišānu+, šikin pî☆; → **~less** *adj.* šuqammumu☆
speed *n.* ḫamuttu☆; → **~** *v.* arāḫu☆ (D); → **~ (up)** *v.* arāḫu☆ (D)
speedily *adv.* ana kallie, ḫitmuṭiš☆
speedy *adj.* lasmu, lassumu
spell *n.* šiptu; → **~** *v.* šaṭāru
spellbound *adj.* raksu, uššupu*
spend *v.* akālu; → **~rift** *n.* musappiḫu☆; → **~thrift** *adj.* parruḫu+, sappiḫu☆
sperm *n.* nīlu, riḫûtu
spew *v.* ḫaḫû☆
sphere *n.* kilīl lumāšē+; → **~ of responsibility** *n.* pittu
sphinx *n.* apsasītu☆
Spica *n.* Šubiltu+
spice *n.* raqqūtu, riqiu; → **~/vegetable (kind of)** *n.* saḫunu; → **~ (kind of)** *n.* samīdu, sibbirru; → **~ plant (kind of)** *n.* ṣumlaliu; → **~d** *adj.* raqqû
spicy *adj.* raqqû
spider *n.* ettūtu☆; → **~-web** *n.* qê ettūti☆
spike *n.* puqdutu, ṣipru☆
spill *n.* gišgirru; → **~** *v.* sapāḫu, ṣappuḫu☆, tabāku
spilt *adj.* tabku
spin *v.* ṣabāru B, ṣâdu, šatû B☆, ṭamû☆; → **make ~** *v.* ṣabāru B (Š); → **~ round and round** *v.* ṣâdu (Gtn); → **~al column** *n.* eṣenṣēru; → **~dle** *n.* pilaqqu
spine *n.* eṣenṣēru
spinster *n.* ṣābirtu*
spiral *n.* tīru
spire *n.* siqqurrutu
spirit *adj.* libbu; → **~** *n.* šāru, utukku, zakīqu; → **protective ~** *n.* lamassu; → **~ed** *adj.* rāš libbi☆, šamru; → **be(come) ~ed** *v.* šamāru☆; → **~s** *n.* kabattu
spit *v.* šalû B☆; → **~ (of land)** *n.* lišānu+; → **~ out** *v.* ḫaḫû☆
spite *n.* martu; → **~(ful act)** *n.* magrītu☆; → **~ful** *adj.* raggu☆
spitfire *adj.* uggugu☆
spittle *n.* ru'tu☆
splash *n.* riḫṣu; → **~** *v.* raḫāṣu B, sapāḫu (D); → **~ing** *n.* riḫṣu
splatter *v.* raḫāṣu B
spleen *n.* ṭulīmu
splendid *adj.* nussuqu☆, šāpû, šarḫu☆, šitrāḫu☆, šitruḫu☆, šūpû☆, šurruḫu☆; → **be(come) ~** *v.* šarāḫu☆; → **make ~** *v.* šarāḫu☆ (D); → **~ly** *adv.* namriš☆
splendor *n.* lulû☆, melammu☆, tašīltu☆, tašriḫtu☆, zīmu; → **terrifying ~** *n.* namurratu☆
splice *v.* dabāqu+ (D)
splinter *n.* ḫuṣābu, sikkutu+; → **~** *v.* parāmu
split *n.* piṭru B☆, šitqu☆; → **~** *v.* letû☆, natāru☆ (Š), salātu, salātu☆ (D), šatāqu☆; → **~ in many places** *v.* šatāqu☆ (D); → **~ up** *v.* ezābu (Gt) [o.], parāsu; → **~ting off** *n.* silittu☆
splutter *v.* nazāzu☆
spoil *n.* kišittu☆, šallutu; → **~** *v.* ḫaṭû◊ (D), masāku☆ (D); → **~ed** *adj.* massuḫu [o.]; → **~s** *n.* ḫinsāti
spongy *adj.* puṭrānu
spontaneity *n.* ḫūd libbi
spontenously *adv.* ina ḫūd libbi [i.]
spook *n.* eṭemmu, utukku
spoon *n.* itqūru; → **~ful** *n.* ammār itqūri
sporadically *adv.* ina birīt
spot *n.* kakkultu+, pi'āru, tirku B☆, uršu☆; → **dark ~** *n.* uršu☆; → **red ~** *n.* sūmu; → **~less** *adj.* zakû; → **~ted** *adj.* kakkullānu+
spouse *n.* ḫīrtu
spout *n.* eṣennû☆; → **~** *v.* nabā'u☆
spray *v.* qarruru, zarāqu; → **~ (of fruit)** *n.* tuganû
spread *v.* parāḫu+, šeṭû☆; → **~ abroad** *v.* udû (D) [o.]; → **~ out** *v.* šuparruru☆, tarāṣu
sprig *n.* kannu B
spring *n.* dīšu☆, ēnu, nagbu☆, namba'u☆, pān šatti; → **~** *v.* šaḫāṭu C☆; → **~ back** *v.* nabalkutu; → **~ from** *v.* šiāḫu B+; → **~ up** *v.* nabā'u+, parā'u, šiāḫu B☆; → **~time** *n.* pān šatti
sprinkle *v.* qarruru, salā'u, salāḫu☆, šabāḫu◊, zarāqu; → **~(?)** *v.* bakāru; → **~r** *n.* musalliḫtu, ša-salā'i, zarriqu
sprinkling can *n.* ša-salā'i

sprint *v*. šaḫāṭu C*; → **~er** *n*. lāsimu
sprout *n*. ḫabbūru, papallu*, qarnu; → ~ *v*. baqālu*, dešû*, parā'u, ṣurrušu*, šiāḫu B+; → **~ed** *adj*. pur'u, qarnānu*
spruce up → **make ~** *v*. kannû (D)
spry *adj*. napšu
spun *adj*. ṭamû*
spunk *n*. ṣūrāmu+
spur *v*. zaqātu*
spurge *n*. nikiptu
spurn *v*. mêšu*
spurt *v*. nabā'u*
sputum *n*. uḫḫu*
spy *n*. dāgilu, daiālu, ḫaiāṭu*; → ~ *v*. dagālu, ḫiāṭu*
squabble *n*. puḫpuḫḫu*
squad *n*. pirru; → **~ron(?)** *n*. mūgu
squalid *adj*. gammīzu+
squall *v*. ṣarāḫu B+
squalor *n*. šuḫtu+
squander *v*. akālu+, baddudu, parāḫu (D), sapāḫu (D), sapāḫu*
square *n*. mitḫartu*, rebītu*, sūqu+; → **~(-form)** *n*. nalbantu*; → ~ **root** *n*. basû*, ibsû*
squash *n*. sarbu; → ~ *v*. marāsu
squat *v*. kamāṣu, napalsuḫu*; → **make ~** *v*. napalsuḫu* (Š)
squeak *v*. nazāqu*; → **~ing** *adj*. nazziqu*
squeal *v*. lebû*, nazāqu*, ziāqu+
squeeze *v*. mazā'u, ṣaḫātu B*; → **~r** *n*. mazzā'u
squint *n*. ṣadāru*; → **~-eyed** *adj*. gallulu; → **~ing** *n*. ṣudduru*
squirm *v*. ḫiālu
squirt *v*. nabā'u*
stab *v*. dakāšu*, maḫāṣu* (D), patāḫu; → ~ **in the back** *v*. issu kutalli maḫāṣu [i.]
stability *n*. kūnu*, taqnūtu+
stabilize *v*. kuānu (D)
stable *adj*. kunnu, taqnu+; → ~ *n*. bēt umāmi; → **be(come) ~** *v*. kuānu, taqānu+; → **~man** *n*. rammāku+
stack *n*. kurillu*; → ~ **up** *v*. garānu* (D), qarānu*
stadium *n*. šiddu
staff *n*. ḫuṭāru, mazzāzu, šabbiṭu*, šibirru*; → **hooked/curved ~** *n*. gamlu; → **~-bearer** *n*. ša-ḫuṭāri; → ~ **(kind of)** *n*. ḫaṭṭi balāṭi; → ~ **maker** *n*. ša-ḫuṭārēšu
stag *n*. aiulu, lulīmu
stage *n*. du'u*, mardītu
stagger *v*. narāṭu, ṭamû B*
stagnate *v*. kapāṣu+ (Gt)
stain *n*. uršu*; → ~ *v*. katāmu, ṭanāpu◊ (D); → **~ed** *n*. aršu*; → **be(come) ~ed** *v*. ṭanāpu◊; → **~less** *adj*. zakû
stair *n*. dargu*, mēliu
staircase *n*. mēlītu*, mēliu, simmiltu; → ~ **owner** *n*. bēl simmilti
stairs *n*. mašḫaṭu*, mēlê
stairway *n*. mēlītu*, mēliu
stake *n*. gašīšu, pulukku*, sikkutu, zaqīpu, ziqīpu; → **on ~s** *adv*. gašīšiš*
stale *adj*. erru*; → ~ *n*. be'šu
stalk *n*. ḫabbūru, kannu B+, qanû+, šulpu
stall *n*. qabuttu, tarbāṣu; → **~ion** *n*. mūrnisqu*
stalwart *adj*. kabra irti*
stamen (of date palm) *n*. taltallu
stamina *n*. abāru B*
stammer *v*. egēru* (Ntn)
stamp *n*. unqu; → ~ **out** *v*. kabāsu; → ~ **seal** *n*. unqu; → **~ede** *v*. palāḫu (D), rapādu
stance *n*. išdu
stand *n*. mazzassu, mazzāzu; → ~ *v*. našû, ušuzzu◊, uzuzzu; → **incense ~** *n*. maksūtu; → **king's ~-by** *n*. qurubtu; → **~-by cavalryman** *n*. ša-qurubti; → **~-in** *n*. pūḫu; → **~/pedestal (kind of)** *n*. labbunu; → ~ **at someone's side** *v*. ina idi uzuzzu [i.]; → ~ **by** *v*. issi X uzuzzu [i.]; → ~ **out** *v*. apû*; → ~ **up** *v*. tabû; → ~ **up for** *v*. ḫaṣānu
standard *adj*. sadru; → ~ *n*. šurinnu, urigallu
standstill *n*. kīlu*; → **be(come) ~** *v*. uzuzzu
star *n*. kakkubu; → **big ~** *n*. kakkubu rabiu; → **falling ~** *n*. kakkubu rabiu; → **morning ~** *n*. šēru*; → **shooting ~** *n*. kakkubu rabiu, zīqtu+; → **~-shaped object** *n*. kakkabtu; → ~ **of Marduk (Mercury)** *n*. kakkab Marduk*
stare *v*. palāsu* (Ntn); → ~ **(with wide-open eyes)** *v*. balāṣu*; → **~y** *adj*. balṣu
staring *adj*. balṣu
starling *n*. zanzīru*
starry *n*. kakkabānu
start *v*. šarrû; → ~ **out** *v*. aḫu ummudu [i.], namāšu (D), šarrû; → ~ **up** *v*. aḫu ummudu [i.], šarrû; → **~ing point** *n*. tašrītu B*
startle *v*. parādu* (D)
starvation *n*. berūtu*, bubāti◊, bubūtu
starve *v*. barû
state *n*. mātu; → ~ *v*. idû* (Š), qabû; → **the ~** *n*. ēkallu; → ~ **of affairs** *n*. mīnu [ša] šīṭni; → ~ **of health** *n*. šulmu; → **holder of ~ property** *n*. bēl iškāri; → ~ **service** *n*. ilku; → **~ly** *adj*. šēḫu B*; → **~ment** *n*.

abutu, pû, qibītu*, qību; → **make a ~ment** *v*. qību šakānu
station *n*. gisgallu*, mazzassu+, mazzāzu, nanzāzu*; → **~** *v*. uzuzzu (Š); → **road ~** *n*. bēt mardēti; → **be(come) ~ary** *v*. uzuzzu
statue *n*. ṣalmu; → **royal ~** *n*. ṣalam šarri
stature *n*. gattu, lānu, nabnītu*, šikittu*
statute *n*. dīnu*
staunch *adj*. taklu, taqnu+; → **~** *v*. balû (D), kasāru, nê'u*
stave *n*. ḫuṭāru; → **~ off** *v*. nê'u* (D)
stay *v*. biādu, kalû (N), kamāsu (D), kullu (D); → **be(come) ~ awake with** *v*. issi X dalāpu [i.]; → **~ clear (of) (of)** *v*. dapāru* (D); → **~ on** *v*. katāru+; → **~ permanently** *v*. barû C* (Št); → **be(come) ~ quiet** *v*. nuāḫu+; → **be(come) ~ up** *v*. dalāpu
steadfast *adj*. kunnu
steady → **be(come) ~** *v*. kuānu
steak *n*. šubê
steal *v*. gazālu, šarāqu; → **~(?)** *v*. pa'āṣu (D); → **in ~th** *adv*. šarrāqiš*; → **~thily** *adv*. ḫallālāniš*, šarqiš*; → **~thy** *adj*. šarriqu*
steam *n*. buḫru*; → **~** *v*. baḫāru*; → **~ing hot** *adj*. baḫru*
steel *n*. parzillu sakru
steep *adj*. pašqu*, zaqru*; → **~** *v*. marāsu+, rasānu
steer *v*. abālu B* (Gtn), arû C* (Gtn), kullu (D)
stele *n*. asumittu, narû
stem *n*. kannu B+, kisittu*, šulpu; → **~(?)** *n*. tarbītu; → **~ from** *v*. nabā'u*
stench *n*. bu'šu*
step *n*. ebertu B; → **~** *v*. kabāsu; → **~ (of a staircase)** *n*. ebertu B, nakbāsu; → **~ (of a staircase) (of a staircase)** *n*. mēlītu*
steppe *adj*. madburu; → **~** *n*. mudāburu, namû*, ṣēru*
sterile *adj*. lā ālidu*
sterility *n*. lā ālidūtu*
sterilize *v*. ana lā ālidi/ālitti turru [i.]
stern *adj*. ašṭu*
stew *v*. bašālu, bašālu (Š), sakāru B
steward *n*. abarakku*, laḫḫennu (temple); → **~ess** *n*. laḫḫennutu
stick *n*. ḫuṣābu, sikkutu*; → **sharp ~** *n*. paruššu*; → **~ out** *v*. magāgu, talālu*; → **~ to** *v*. dabāqu+, naqāpu+; → **~y** *adj*. dābiqu+
stiff *adj*. ašṭu*, maggu; → **be(come) ~** *v*. ašāṭu*, magāgu; → **~en** *v*. magāgu (D), šagāgu*; → **~ening** *n*. muggu; → **~ness** *n*. ašṭūtu*
stifle *v*. ḫanāqu, šanā'u*
stifling *adj*. ḫāniqu
stigma *n*. uršu*
stiletto *n*. quppû*
still *adj*. šuḫarruru*, šuqammumu*; → **~** *adv*. aḫḫūr, ana ḫūru; → **~-born child** *n*. kūbu*; → **awesome ~ness** *n*. šaḫurratu*
stimulate *v*. dakû◊ (D)
stimulus *n*. dīku
sting *n*. miḫṣu, siḫiltu*, ziqtu; → **~** *v*. zaqātu*; → **~-mark** *n*. ziqtu
stink *n*. bu'šu*, zaprūtu+; → **~** *v*. be'āšu, be'ēšu◊, zapāru+; → **~ing** *adj*. zapru+; → **~ing** *n*. be'šu
stint *n*. addû*
stir *v*. dalāḫu; → **~ up** *v*. dakû, dalāḫu; → **~rer** *n*. munappiḫu*; → **~ring** *adj*. mummilu*
stitch *v*. kabbû (D), takāpu; → **~er** *n*. mukabbû
stoa *n*. bēt ḫillāni
stock *n*. ilittu, nakkamtu; → **~** *v*. nakāmu*; → **~-dove** *n*. amuršānu*; → **~ up** *v*. karāmu B; → **~ade** *n*. māḫiru, šupšutu; → **~breeder** *n*. nāqidu; → **~s** *n*. malūṭu*; → **~taking** *n*. piqittu; → **~y** *adj*. ebû, kabra irti*
stolen *adj*. ekmu*, šarqu*; → **~ property** *n*. qāt ṣibitti
stomach *n*. karšu, tākaltu*; → **~-ache** *n*. tākaltu*; → **~ (of a pig)** *n*. quqqubānu*; → **~ (of a ruminant)** *n*. pisurru+
stone *n*. abattu, abnu, kīpu; → **love ~** *n*. aban rāmi; → **mountain ~** *n*. aban šadî*; → **precious ~** *n*. aban nisiqti*, abnu aqartu*; → **red-hot ~** *n*. gumāru+; → **shiny ~** *n*. zalāqu; → **~-** *adj*. [ša] abni; → **~-deaf** *adj*. peḫû*; → **~-like** *n*. abnānu; → **~ (kind of)** *n*. engisû*, ḫaltappû*, kasītu B*, mēṣu, mūṣu, šinni ṣabīti*; → **multicolored ~ (kind of)** *n*. luludānītu; → **red ~ (kind of)** *n*. sābu*; → **red-black ~ (kind of)** *n*. turminabandû; → **semi-precious ~ (kind of)** *n*. girim-ḫilibê, igizaggû, šubû; → **~ implement (kind of)** *n*. mušākilu; → **~ of pride** *n*. aban balti; → **~borer** *n*. pallišu; → **female ~borer** *n*. pallissu
stonecutter *n*. parkullu
stonemason *n*. parkullu
stoneware *n*. abnu
stony *adj*. [ša] abni; → **~** *n*. abnānu
stook *n*. kurillu*
stool *n*. kitturru; → **three-legged ~** *n*. taškû; → **~-bearer** *n*. ša-kitturrēšu
stoop *v*. qadādu B*; → **~ed** *adj*. kappupu, kuppupu* (very)
stop *n*. kīlu*; → **~** *v*. baṭālu, kalû, kalû (N), naparkû* (Š), naparkû*, parāsu; → **come**

to ~ *v.* uzuzzu; → ~ **up** *v.* ḫaṭāmu
stoppage *n.* sukurtu [o.]
stopper *n.* purussu*
storage *n.* nakrumu [o.]; → ~ **bin** *n.* išpikku; → ~ **jar** *n.* kirru; → ~ **jar (kind of)** *n.* ḫābû*
store *n.* nakkamtu; → ~ *v.* garānu*, karāmu B, nakāmu*, tabāku; → **underground** ~ *n.* kalakku C◊; → ~ **away** *v.* paḫû; → ~**d** *adj.* tabku
storehouse *n.* abusāti, bēt ḫurši, bēt qāti, nakkamtu, šutummu*, ubsāti, ursūtu, uṣṣāru◊; → **supervisor of the** ~ *n.* ša-pān-bēt-qāti
storeroom *n.* ašlukkatu*, kadammu
storey *n.* rigbu*; → **upper** ~ *n.* bēt rugbi, bētu elīu, rigbu*
stork *n.* igirû*, laqlaqqu*
storm *n.* anḫullu*, imḫullu*, meḫû; → **like a** ~ *adv.* ūmiš*; → ~**y** *adj.* adadānu, meḫānu*
story *n.* ṭēmu
stout *adj.* kabru, qardu
stove *n.* mušaḫḫinu
stow *v.* ṣiānu
straggle *v.* nagāšu* (Gtn)
straight *adj.* išaru*, šūšuru*, tarṣu; → ~ *adv.* išariš*; → **be(come)** ~ *v.* ešēru*
straightaway *adv.* ina muḫḫi ašli
straighten *v.* ešēru* (Š)
straightforward *adj.* išaru*, tarṣu+
strain *v.* ḫalāṣu, šaḫālu+; → ~**ed** *adj.* ḫalṣu, naḫlu B [o.]
strait *adj.* qatnu+, šupšuqu*; → ~ *n.* nēburu+, pušqu*; → ~**en** *v.* pašāqu B* (Š), siāqu (D); → ~**ened** *adj.* sāqu
strand *n.* pitiltu+; → ~ *v.* ṣapāru*
strange *adj.* aḫīu, nakru; → **be(come)** ~ *v.* nakāru; → ~**ly** *adv.* nakriš*; → ~**r** *n.* aḫīu, ubāru
strangle *v.* ḫanāqu; → ~**r** *n.* ḫāniqu
stranguary *n.* ḫiniqtu*
strangulation *n.* ḫinqu*
strangury *n.* ṣimirtu+
strap *n.* kurussu, tamšāru; → ~**(?)** *v.* qamāru; → **leather** ~**(?)** *n.* kursiu; → **leather** ~ *n.* maršu
stratagem *n.* šibqu*
stratified *adj.* tabku
stratum *n.* nadbāku
straw *n.* qanû+, šulpu, tibnu; → **accountant of** ~ *n.* ṭupšar tibni; → **pile of** ~ *n.* kurdiššu; → ~**berry** *n.* gergiššu*; → ~**berry tree** *n.* girgiššu*
stray *v.* sagû+, samû (Gtn); → **cause to** ~ *v.* samû (D); → ~**ing** *n.* ripittu*
streak *n.* ussu B*
stream *n.* naḫlu, nāru; → **(small)** ~ *n.* atappu+ ; → ~**er** *n.* urigallu
street *n.* sulû*, suqāqu, sūqu; → **main** ~ *n.* rebītu*; → **narrow** ~ *n.* suqāqu; → **side** ~ *n.* suqāqu; → ~ **inspector** *n.* ša-pān-sūqi; → **supervisor of the** ~**s** *n.* ša-pān-sūqi
streetwalker *n.* ḫarintu
strength *n.* abāru B*, danānu*, dannūtu*, dunnu*, emūqu, idu*, kubukku*; → ~**en** *v.* da'ānu (D), danānu* (D), patānu◊ (D), qarādu (D); → ~**ening** *n.* tadnintu*
strenuous *adj.* lā āniḫu*
stress *n.* ašuštu*; → ~ *v.* ašāšu* (D); → ~**ed** *adj.* uššušu, uššušu*; → **be(come)** ~**ed** *v.* ašāšu*
stretch *n.* mardītu, siḫpu B*; → ~ *v.* šadādu; → ~ **out** *v.* makāku◊, talālu*, tarāṣu; → ~ **over** *v.* tarāṣu* (Š); → ~**er** *n.* maiālu
strew *v.* sarāqu, zarāqu
stricken → **be** ~ *v.* mašādu* (N)
strict *adj.* dannu; → ~ **orders** *n.* šipṭu*; → **give** ~ **orders** *v.* šipṭu šakānu [i.]
stricture *n.* ḫinqu*
stride *n.* pīt purīdi*; → ~ *v.* šadāḫu*
strife *n.* ṣāssu, tašnuntu*
strike *n.* baṭlu, miḫṣu; → ~ *v.* lapātu, maḫāṣu, maqātu (vent.), nêru*, ṭerû; → ~ **down** *v.* napāṣu, palāqu*, rasābu*, šagāšu; → ~ **out** *v.* pasāsu; → ~ **with great force** *v.* gašāru* (Dt); → ~ **with palsy** *v.* mašādu*; → ~**r** *n.* baṭṭilu*, māḫiṣu
string *n.* ašlu, eblu, isḫu B*, matnu, pitiltu, qû B*, ṭimītu, ṭurru; → ~ *v.* šakāku [o.]; → ~ **(of a musical instrument)** *n.* pitnu B*; → ~ **of beads** *n.* šeršerrutu; → ~ **together** *v.* šakāku [o.]; → ~**ed instrument (kind of)** *n.* inu*; → ~**ent** *adj.* dannu
strip *n.* širṭu; → ~ *v.* erû B (D) [o.], šaḫāṭu; → ~ **(of field)** *n.* qutānu; → ~ **bare** *v.* erû B (D) [o.]; → ~ **by force** *v.* ḫamāṣu◊; → ~ **off** *v.* ḫarāṭu, šalāḫu+, šamāṭu
stripe *n.* ussu B*; → ~**d** *n.* širṭānu+; → ~**d agate** *n.* ḫulālu
strive *v.* ṣarāmu; → ~**(?)** *v.* naṣû; → ~ **constantly for** *v.* ašrāti še'û*; → ~ **for** *v.* ṣamāru*, še'û*; → ~ **for doggedly** *v.* ṣamāru* (Gt)
stroke *n.* miḫṣu, mišittu* (apoplectic), ussu B*; → ~ **(nose)** *v.* labānu B*
stroll *v.* alāku (Gtn)
strong *adj.* da'nu, dannu, ešqu*, gamīru◊, gašru, kaššu*, mitru*, puggulu*, pungulu*; → **be(come)** ~ *v.* da'ānu, danānu*, patānu◊; → ~**(er)** *adj.* guššuru*; → ~**-box** *n.* pitnu*;

→ **~-willed** *adj.* šitmāru*; → **~ man** *n.* bēl emūqi*; → **~est** *adj.* dandannu*
stronghold *n.* dannutu, dannūtu*
structure *n.* binītu*, kiṣru, šikittu*
struggle *n.* ippiru*
strut *n.* pariktu
stub *v.* nakāpu*
stubble *n.* šulpu
stubborn *adj.* atmāṣu*
stuck *adj.* kal'u*, ṣabtu
stud *n.* ālidu, ma'assu, naiāku*, puḫālu; → **~ent** *n.* talmīdu; → **female ~ent** *n.* talmittu [o.]; → **~entess** *n.* talmittu [o.]
studious *adj.* ēpišu
study *n.* iḫzu*; → **~** *v.* barû B*, lamādu (Gtn) [o.]
stuff *v.* ḫanāṭu+, malû (D); → **~ed** *adj.* mal'u; → **be(come) ~ed with** *v.* šê'u (stat.) [o.]; → **~ing** *n.* še'ītu [o.], tamlītu; → **~y** *n.* emmu+
stumble *v.* egēru* (Ntn), naḫalṣû
stump *n.* išdu, kisittu*; → **~(?)** *n.* urmazillu*; → **~y** *n.* kurû*
stun *v.* ḫamû*; → **~t** *n.* niklu; → **~t** *v.* kalû; → **~ted** *adj.* dallu*; → **be(come) ~ted** *v.* dalālu B*
stupefied *adj.* šuḫarruru*; → **be(come) ~** *v.* ta'ādu+
stupid *adj.* ḫuzzumu◊, lillu+, paḫiu, peḫû*, saklu+; → **turn ~** *v.* lallû B+ (Dt); → **~ity** *n.* lillūtu*, paḫûtu*, sakkukūtu
stupor *n.* kūru B*; → **fall into ~** *v.* kâru*
sturdy *adj.* kabra irti*
stutter *v.* egēru* (Ntn)
sty *n.* merḫu*
stylus *n.* qan ṭuppi*, qanû+, qarṭuppu
suave *adj.* rabbu B
Subarean *n./adj.* Subarû◊
subdue *v.* ḫanāšu (D), kabāsu, kapādu, laqātu; → **~d** *adj.* kabsu+; → **~r** *n.* muniḫḫu*
subject *n.* abutu, urdu; → **~** *v.* ḫanāšu (D), kanāšu* (D); → **~ to** *prep.* ša pitti; → **~ to** *v.* pān X šudgulu [i.]; → **be ~ to** *v.* dagālu (N); → **~ion** *n.* kabsūtu+; → **~s** *n.* ba'ulāti*
subjugate *v.* ḫanāšu (D), kabāsu+, kabāsu* (Š), kanāšu* (D), kanāšu* (Š)
sublime *adj.* ṣīru*, šaqiu
submerge *v.* šalû*, ṭabû; → **~d** *adj.* raḫṣu*; → **be(come) ~d** *v.* ṭabû
submersion *n.* ṣīpu, ṭību B*
submissive *adj.* ḫanšu B, kanšu*, māgiru; → **~ly** *adv.* kanšiš*; → **~ness** *n.* ḫanšūtu*
submit *v.* qannu ṣabātu [i.]; → **make ~** *v.* kamāsu B* (Š), kanāšu* (Š); → **~ o.s.** *v.* ḫanāšu; → **~ to** *v.* kanāšu*
subordinate *adj.* ḫanšu B; → **~** *n.* urdu
subordination *n.* ḫanšūtu*, šupālu*
subsequently *adv.* ḫarammāma, iddāti
subservient *adj.* urdānīu*
subside *v.* naḫāsu◊, nuāḫu, pašāḫu, šuḫarruru*
subsidiary *adj.* tardennu*
subsist *v.* balāṭu; → **~ence** *n.* ma''uttu
substance *adj.* libbu; → **~** *n.* riksu
substantial *adj.* šapû*
substitute *n.* dinānu, pūḫtu, pūḫu; → **~** *v.* ḫalāpu D+, puḫḫu
subtle *adj.* qatnu+, raqqu+; → **~ty** *n.* nikiltu
subtract *v.* ḫarāṣu, nasāḫu; → **~ion** *n.* nisḫutu [o.]
suburb *n.* qanni āli
subversive *adj.* saḫḫāpu+
subvert *v.* saḫāpu+
succeed *v.* kašāru, šalāmu
success *n.* kišru, kušīru; → **~ful** *adj.* kašru, šalmu; → **be(come) ~ful** *v.* kašāru, šalāmu; → **~ion** *adj.* rīdu*; → **~ion** *n.* rēdûtu, sidru+; → **in ~ion** *adv.* dārat aḫāiš, iddāt aḫāiš; → **~ive** *adj.* ṣabbutu*; → **~ively** *adv.* dārat aḫāiš; → **~or** *n.* ḫalputu, mār rēdûti*, mardû, tēnû
succinct *adj.* pašqu+
succulent *adj.* mēzīu*
succumb *v.* maqātu
suck *v.* enāqu, mazāqu, naṣābu*; → **~ out** *v.* mazāqu (D); → **~er** *n.* ēniqu*, ša-zizibi
suckle *v.* enāqu (Š)
suckling *n.* ēniqu*, ianūqu+, ša-zizibi, tēnīqu*
suction *n.* enāqu
sud *n.* ḫurḫummatu*; → **~den** *adj.* ḫanṭu B*; → **~denly** *adv.* radpi◊, ullānumma◊, ultu ullānumma*, zamarānu*
sue *v.* ragāmu, ṣāssu garû
suffer *v.* zabālu; → **be(come) ~** *v.* gaṣāṣu; → **cause to ~** *v.* rašû* (Š); → **make ~** *v.* marāṣu (Š); → **~ paralysis** *v.* rimûtu rašû*
suffice *v.* sapāqu; → **be(come) ~** *v.* maṣû
sufficiency *n.* sapqūtu+
sufficient *adj.* sapīqu+; → **be(come) ~** *v.* maṣû, sapāqu
suffiently *adv.* maṣi
suffix *n.* šaplītu*
suffocate *v.* ḫanāqu
suffocating *adj.* ḫāniqu
suffocation *n.* ḫinqu*
suggest *v.* malāku; → **~ion** *n.* milku; → **~ive** *adj.* mušaḫkimu*

suit *v*. asāmu☆; → **spare ~** *n*. tēnû; → **~ (of clothes) (of clothes)** *n*. kuzippu; → **~able** *adj*. asmu☆, šūluku☆; → **be(come) ~able for** *v*. damāqu ana
suitably *adv*. asmiš☆
suited *adj*. asmu☆
suitor *n*. ḫā'iru☆
sulk *v*. ikku kullu [i.]; → **~ing** *n*. karû ikki; → **~y** *adj*. adru B
sullen *adj*. adru B
sullied *adj*. lu''û☆
sully *v*. šaḫātu C+ (Š), ṭanāpu◊ (D)
sulphur *n*. kibrītu☆, ru'tītu☆; → **~ic acid** *n*. mê kibrīti+
sultriness *n*. kūrūtu+
sultry *adj*. rasmu, ṣarḫu
sum *n*. napḫaru☆; → **~ total** *n*. siḫirtu☆; → **~ up** *v*. kamāru☆, rakāsu
Sumerian *n./adj*. Šume:ru
summarize *v*. rakāsu
summary *n*. riksu
summer *n*. ebūru; → **early ~** *n*. ḫarpē; → **~-time** *n*. ebūru
summit *n*. rēštu☆, ubān šadê☆; → **~s** *n*. rēšāti
summon *v*. dakû, rēšu našû [i.], šasû☆; → **~er** *n*. dākiu; → **~ing** *n*. dīku, našû rēši; → **~s** *n*. našû rēši, šisītu☆
sumptuous *adj*. šadlu☆
sun *n*. šamšu, šanšu; → **like the ~** *adv*. šamšiš☆; → **~ disk** *n*. nipḫu, šanšāntu
sunbeam *n*. šarūr šanši
sunburn *n*. ḫimiṭ ṣēti☆; → **~t** *n*. qummû☆
sunflower *n*. šammi Šamaš☆
sunken *adj*. ṭabiu*
sunlight *n*. nūr šamši, ṣēt šamši; → **like ~** *adv*. šarūriš☆
sunlike *n*. šanšānu
sunny *adj*. namru; → **~** *n*. šanšānu
sunrise *n*. napāḫ šamši, nipiḫ šamši☆, ṣīt šamši☆; → **at ~** *n*. im-matāḫi
sunset *n*. erēb šamši☆, rabā šamši, šalām šamši☆, šulum šamši☆
sunshade *n*. ša-ṣilli
sunshine *n*. šarūr šanši
sunstroke *n*. ḫimiṭ ṣēti☆
sup *v*. sarāpu☆; → **~erb** *adj*. bitrû☆, ḫiššamû☆, šarḫu☆, šitrāḫu☆; → **~erfluous** *adj*. utru+, uttāru; → **~erimposed** *adj*. šutēmudu☆; → **~erintend** *v*. ašāru; → **~erintendent** *n*. ḫazannu; → **office of ~erintendent** *n*. ḫazannūtu; → **~erior** *adj*. elīu, gapru☆, šūturu☆, utru; → **be(come) ~erior** *v*. gapāru☆; → **~erstructure** *n*. rigbu☆; → **~ervise** *v*. ḫâṭu☆

supine *adj*. naparqudu☆; → **~** *adv*. purqidam☆
supple *adj*. labku; → **be(come) ~** *v*. labāku; → **~ment** *n*. tardītu, ṭīpu☆
suppliant *adj*. muštēmiqu☆
supplicate *v*. ṣallû
supplicating *adj*. muštēmiqu☆
supplication *n*. unninnu☆, utninnu☆
supplier *n*. mumalliānu+
supplies *n*. šaṣbutu
supply *n*. bābu [o.]; → **~** *v*. apālu B, miāru+; → **~ abundantly** *v*. ṭaḫādu (D); → **~ the deficit** *v*. batqu tadānu; → **~ with** *v*. ṣabātu (Š)
support *n*. kannu+, mukillu, nēmattu, šaḫātu [o.], taḫḫūtu☆, tukultu; → **~** *v*. našû, sêdu☆; → **~ (with food)** *v*. ma''unu; → **~er** *n*. rā'imānu, rēṣu☆
suppose *v*. kaṣāpu
supposing *conj*. issurri
supposition *n*. sebru+
suppository *n*. allānu☆
suppress *v*. kabāsu
suppurate *v*. šarāku B☆
suppuration *n*. šarku
supremacy *n*. ṣīrūtu☆
supreme *adj*. šurbû☆, šūturu☆
sure *adj*. kunnu; → **~ thing** *n*. abutu kunnutu; → **~ly** *adv*. issurri, piqtatti; → **~ness** *n*. kunnūtu*; → **~ty** *n*. urkīu
surf *n*. agû B☆
surface *n*. kaqquru, muḫḫu, siḫpu
surge *n*. gupšu☆; → **~** *v*. šapû☆
surly *adj*. adru B
surmise *v*. kaṣāpu
surmount *v*. maṣû, nabalkutu, rakābu
surpass *v*. utāru; → **~ing** *adj*. šūtuqu☆, utru+
surplus *adj*. uttāru
surprise *v*. maqātu ina muḫḫi [i.], ta'ādu+ (Š); → **~ (attack)** *n*. mandītu B◊, šiḫṭu
surrender *v*. salāmu+
surreptitious *adj*. katmu☆, pazru☆, pesnu◊; → **~ly** *adv*. šalāliš☆
surround *v*. duāru [o.], kapādu, labû, labû (Š), saḫāru☆ (Š); → **~ing** *n*. lābiu; → **~ings** *n*. aḫītu (pl.), itāti☆, libītu, limītu☆, siḫirtu☆, siḫru
survey *v*. ḫiāṭu☆, madādu; → **~or** *n*. ḫaiāṭu☆, māšiḫu☆, šādid ašli; → **female ~or** *n*. šādidat ašli
survival *n*. šalāmu
survive *v*. balāṭu, ezābu (Š)
surviving *adj*. balṭu
survivor *n*. multaḫṭu☆

Susa *n.* Šūšan
susceptible *adj.* raggūšu+
suspect *adj.* lā taklu*; → ~ *v.* lā qiāpu, palāḫu, pašāku+
suspend *v.* alālu, šaqālu⋆
suspense *n.* mašqalālu⋆
suspension *n.* sukurtu [o.]
suspicion *n.* lā qīptu*, puluḫtu, ṭupullû⋆
suspicious *adj.* lā qēpu
sustain *v.* našû; → **~er** *n.* zāninu⋆
sustenance *n.* bubūtu, ma''uttu, zāninūtu⋆
suture *n.* šipītu⋆
swab *n.* mukappirānītu+
swagger *v.* paḫāzu
swallow *n.* sinūntu, šinūntu⋆; → **~ (up)** *v.* alātu⋆, la'ātu⋆
swamp *n.* appāru, nāriṭu⋆, raqqatu⋆, rušundu⋆; → **~(?)** *n.* abbu⋆
swan *n.* usu, uzzu B+
swanky *adj.* šitrāḫu⋆
swarm *v.* dapāru⋆; → **~(ing)** *n.* tibûtu⋆
swarthy *adj.* ṣallumu; → ~ *n.* šaḫīmu+
swathe *v.* karāku+
sway *n.* bēlūtu; → ~ *v.* šâbu⋆
swear *v.* tamû
swearword *n.* arratu⋆, izzirtu
sweat *n.* zūtu
sweep *n.* kalkaltu⋆; → ~ *v.* ešēru⋆ (Š), šabāṭu B⋆; → **~ across** *v.* bâ'u⋆; → **~ away** *v.* raḫāṣu B; → **~ up** *v.* sārē šētuqu [i.]; → **~er** *n.* mušētiq sāri*; → **~ing** *n.* mukannišu+; → **~ings** *adj.* ḫimmatu⋆
sweet *adj.* dašpu⋆, duššupu⋆, matqu, ṭābu; → **be(come) ~** *v.* dašāpu⋆, matāqu, ṭiābu; → **~en** *v.* dašāpu⋆ (D), matāqu (D); → **~ened** *adj.* mattuqu
sweetheart *adj.* duššupu⋆
swell *n.* gupšu⋆; → **~ (up)** *v.* ebēṭu⋆, ebû+, gapāšu, nabā'u⋆, napāḫu+, ṣemēru⋆; → **~ (up) und down** *v.* šapû⋆; → **~ing** *n.* dikšu⋆, ebû+, gipšu⋆, isiltu⋆, nib'u⋆, simmu; → **~ings** *n.* ḫuzīrtu+ (pl.)
sweltering *adj.* ṣarḫu
swerve *v.* sagû, sagû+
swift *adj.* ḫanṭu B⋆, lasmu, qallīlu+; → **~ly** *adv.* arḫiš, urruḫiš⋆; → **~ness** *n.* ḫamuttu⋆
swill *v.* raḫāṣu B, šaḫāṭu B
swim *v.* mê la'û [i.], šuā'u; → **able to ~** *adj.* lā'i mê*
swimming *n.* šiḫītu+
swindle *n.* sarrūtu⋆; → ~ *v.* sarāru [o.]; → **~r** *n.* sarru⋆
swine *n.* ḫuzīru
swing *v.* šâbu⋆, tuāru (D)
swinishness *n.* ḫuzīrūtu+
swirl *v.* ṣâdu; → **make ~** *v.* ṣabāru B (Š)
swish *v.* ḫadādu
switch *v.* šupêlu⋆
swollen *adj.* ebṭu⋆, ebû, ebû+, napḫu, ubbuṭu⋆, ulluṣu⋆; → **be ~** *v.* napāḫu (N); → **be(come) ~** *v.* ṣemēru⋆; → **make ~** *v.* ebēṭu⋆ (D)
swoop *v.* maqātu; → **~ing** *adj.* sāḫipu⋆
sword *n.* namṣāru⋆, patru; → **~man** *n.* ṭābiḫu
sworn name *n.* šumu zakru [i.]
sycamore *n.* tuttu◊, urzinnu
syllabus *n.* iškāru
symbol *n.* kizirtu, simtu, urigallu
symmetric(al) *adj.* mitḫāru⋆
sympathetic *adj.* gammilu⋆, ḫassu+
sympathize *v.* rēmu ina muḫḫi/ana X šakānu [i.]
sympathy *n.* gimlu
symptom *n.* sakikkû
synonym *n.* miḫir šumi*
synthesis *n.* riksu
syrup *n.* dišpu
systematically → **do ~** *v.* sadāru (D)
tabernacle *n.* maškunu+, qumbutu+
table *n.* paššūru; → **cutting(?) ~** *n.* maḫruṣu; → **~ top** *n.* qāru; → **~cloth** *n.* kindabassu
tableland *n.* eliāti⋆ (pl.)
tablet *n.* immu◊, ṭuppu; → **(clay) ~** *n.* nibzu ; → **(horizontal) ~** *n.* u'iltu; → **oblong ~** *n.* giṭṭu◊; → **one-column ~** *n.* liginnu; → **school exercise ~** *n.* liginnu; → **~ box** *n.* ṭupšinnu; → **~ cover** *n.* urimtu◊; → **~ of destinies** *n.* ṭup šīmāti⋆
tableware *n.* udê
taboo *n.* anzillu⋆, asakku, ikkibu; → **like ~** *adv.* asakkiš⋆
tacit *adj.* qālu
taciturn *adj.* qaiālu⋆
tackle *v.* aḫu ummudu [i.]
tail *n.* zibbutu; → **~-end** *n.* zibbutu; → **~or** *n.* kāṣiru; → **chief ~or** *n.* rab kāṣiri
taint *v.* ṭanāpu◊ (D)
take *v.* aḫāzu⋆, laqû, našû; → **~ (time)** *v.* anāḫu⋆ (Št); → **~ after** *v.* ana X mašālu [i.]; → **~ aim (for)** *v.* pānē ana X šakānu [i.]; → **~ as a loan** *v.* ana/ina pūḫi našû [i.]; → **~ as replacement** *v.* ana batqi ṣabātu [i.]; → **~ away** *v.* baṣāru+, ekēmu⋆, eṭāru, našāru, puāgu; → **~ care of o.s.** *n.* ramanšu naṣāru; → **~ fire** *v.* ṣarāḫu C+; → **~ fire slowly** *v.* šabābu+; → **~ for** *v.* kī X dagālu [i.], kullu (D); → **~ fright** *v.* gilittu rašû⋆; → **~ off** *v.* ḫamāṣu◊, šaḫāṭu, šalāḫu+; → **~ on** *v.* ṣabātu;

→ ~ **out** *v.* šalāḫu; → ~ **over** *v.* ṣabātu; → ~ **pains** *v.* anāḫu⋆ (Št); → ~ **place** *v.* bašû (N), šakānu (N); → ~ **possession of** *v.* kašādu; → ~ **refuge** *v.* marqītu aḫāzu⋆; → ~ **revenge** *v.* tuktê turru [i.]; → ~ **to** *v.* aḫu ummudu [i.], arû C⋆; → ~ **up** *v.* ṣabātu; → **~n** *adj.* ṣabtu; → **~n away** *adj.* ekmu⋆; → **~n away** *n.* pēgu; → **be ~n away** *v.* našāru (N); → **be ~n for** *v.* kullu (Dtt)

tale *n.* tašnītu⋆; → **~bearer** *n.* ṣābiru*; → **~nt** *n.* lē'ûtu⋆; → **assayed ~nt** *n.* bilat maltakti⋆; → **~nt (weight)** *n.* biltu; → **spread ~s** *v.* ša'ūdu (Štn)

talisman *n.* kišādu

talk *n.* dabābtu, dabābu; → ~ *v.* dabābu; → ~ **foolishly** *v.* ṣabāru+; → ~ **idly** *v.* dabābu (Gtn); → **empty ~er** *adj.* šārānu

tall *adj.* arku, arraku⋆, elû⋆, šēḫu B⋆; → **be(come) ~** *v.* šatāḫu◊, šiāḫu B⋆; → **grow ~** *v.* šiāḫu B⋆

tallow *n.* līpu

talon *n.* ṣupru

tamarisk *adj.* ṭarpu'u; → ~ *n.* bīnu

tamborine *n.* ḫalḫallatu⋆

tame *v.* kabāsu+; → **~d** *adj.* kabsu+

Tammuz *adv.* Ta'ūzu (month)

tamper *v.* aḫu ubālu [i.]

tampon *n.* lippu, maššītu⋆

tangible *adj.* šapû⋆

tangle *v.* elēpu⋆ (Št); → **be ~d** *v.* ḫalāpu⋆ (Gt)

tank → **washing ~** *n.* namsû⋆

tanner *n.* ṣāripu; → **~'s paste** *n.* kurru; → ~ **of colored leather** *n.* ṣārip duḫšî

tanning *n.* risittu◊

tantalizing *adj.* dāliḫu⋆

tantrum *n.* ru'ubtu◊

tap *v.* radû⋆ (Š), tarāku; → **~er** *n.* kibirru⋆; → **~estry** *n.* mardutu

tar *n.* ittû⋆, qatrānu⋆, qīru; → **~dy** *adj.* namarkû

target *n.* nanḫaṣtu

tariff *n.* miksu, nisḫu

tarnish *n.* šuḫtu; → ~ *v.* šaḫātu C+ (Š), ṭanāpu◊ (D)

tarragon *n.* nūbu+

tarry *v.* biādu, katāru+, kuāšu (D), namarkû, saḫāru [o.]; → **be(come) ~** *v.* kuāšu, uḫḫuru

Tarsus *n.* Tarzi

tartar (on the teeth) *n.* šuḫtu+

task *n.* dullu, esiḫtu, šipru

tassel *n.* šikkatu B⋆

taste *n.* ṭēmtu+, ṭēmu; → ~ *v.* leḫēmu◊, liāmu, ṭeāmu+; → **~less** *adj.* lā ṭābu

tasty *adj.* raqqû, ṭābu

tatter *n.* širṭu; → **~ed** *adj.* šarṭu

tattler *n.* ṣābiru*

tattletale *n.* ṣābiru*

taught *adj.* lammudu

taunt *n.* šinṣu⋆; → ~ *v.* šanāṣu⋆

Taurus *n.* alû, Lû⋆

taut *adj.* maggu

tavern *n.* bēt sābê⋆, bēt šikāri

tawdry *adj.* šamḫu⋆

tax *n.* biltu, maddattu, miksu; → **collector of straw ~** *n.* šābišu; → **grain ~** *n.* nusāḫu (pl.); → **import ~** *n.* nisḫutu [o.]; → **straw ~** *n.* šibšu; → ~ **(kind of)** *n.* bitqu, ḫamussu; → ~ **collection** *n.* pirru; → ~ **collector** *n.* mākisu; → **~ation** *n.* maddattu; → **collect ~es** *v.* makāsu

Tayma *n.* Tēmâ

teach *v.* kallumu (D), lamādu (D); → ~ **to fly** *v.* kappu ṣapāpu [i.], ṣapāpu⋆ (Š); → **~er** *n.* mulammidu⋆; → **~ing** *n.* iḫzu⋆, talmīdūtu+

teak *n.* ušû

team *n.* naṣmadu⋆, ṣindu; → **(yoked) ~** *n.* ṣimittu⋆; → ~ **(of horses)** *n.* urû; → ~ **commander** *n.* rab urāti; → **~ed** *adj.* šutāḫû⋆; → **~s** *n.* ṣamadāni⋆

tear *n.* dintu, šitqu⋆; → ~ *v.* parāṭu, šarāṭu⋆; → ~ **apart** *v.* baṣāru (D); → ~ **asunder** *v.* šatāqu+; → ~ **away** *v.* ḫasāpu, nasāḫu, parāṭu+, qadādu+; → ~ **down** *v.* magguru, naqāru; → ~ **into strips** *v.* šarāṭu⋆ (D); → ~ **off** *v.* marāṭu+, šaḫāṭu, šalāḫu, šamāṭu; → ~ **out** *v.* nasāḫu, šalāpu, šamāṭu+; → ~ **out(?)** *v.* malāḫu; → ~ **out eyes** *v.* ēnē nappulu⋆; → **~ing out** *n.* milḫu; → **~s** *n.* diāti⋆ (pl.); → **draw ~s** *v.* dammû

tease → **be(come) ~** *v.* lazāzu+

teat *n.* zīzu B; → **~(?)** *n.* sīsu

technique *n.* šipir nikilti⋆

tedious *adj.* lazzuzu*

teem *v.* dapāru⋆

teenage(d) *n.* tariu [o.]

teenager *n.* ṣaḫurtu

teens *n.* ṣaḫūrānūtu

teeth → **bare the ~** *v.* ḫanāṣu⋆

tell *n.* tillu; → ~ *v.* qabû; → ~ **apart** *v.* mussû◊; → ~ **stories** *v.* kazābu⋆; → **~er** *n.* dābibu⋆; → **~er of lies** *n.* dābib ṣalipti⋆; → **~tale** *n.* dābibtu⋆, ṣābiru*

temper *n.* ikku, kabattu; → ~ *v.* balālu, ḫiāqu; → **ill ~** *n.* martu

temperament *n.* būnu

temperate *adj.* ḫīqu, maššuḫu+

temperature *n.* ṣurḫu; → **cold ~** *n.* kuṣṣu

tempest *n.* meḫû; → **~-tossed** *adj.* dalḫu+
tempestuous *adj.* adadānu, meḫānu*
template *adj.* tamšiltu☆
temple *n.* aiakku, bēt ilāni, bēt ili, bētu, ēkallu+, ēkurru, nakkaptu☆; → **(small) ~** *n.* parakku+ ; → **high ~** *n.* paramāḫu; → **raised ~** *n.* gigunû☆; → **supervisor of the ~** *n.* ša-pān-ēkurri; → **chief ~ administrator** *n.* šatam ekurrāti☆; → **~ enterer** *n.* ērib bēt ili; → **~ furniture (piece of)** *n.* sibkarû; → **master of ~ oblates** *n.* rab širki◊; → **~ warden** *n.* ša-ēkurri; → **chief of the ~s** *n.* rab ēkurrāti
temporal *adj.* simanīu*
temporarily *adv.* ana simini
temporary *adj.* simanīu*, ša simini*
temptation *n.* kuzubtu [o.]
tempting *adj.* kazbu☆
ten *n./adj.* ešer, ešertu; → **~ (times) each** *adv.* ešrāia; → **~ times** *adv.* ešrīšu; → **~ times** *n.* adi ešrīšu; → **~able** *adj.* kunnu
tenacious *adj.* dābiqānu+
tenant *n.* āšibu, uššābu
tend *v.* ra'û; → **~er** *adj.* labku, rabbu B; → **~er part** *n.* nurbu☆; → **~erhearted** *adj.* rēmānu; → **~erhearted** *n.* libbu rabbu [i.]; → **~erly** *adv.* rabbiš☆; → **~erness** *n.* taknû☆; → **~ing** *n.* rā'iūtu+
tendon *n.* gīdu, matnu, šer'ānu; → **hoof ~** *n.* šašallu
tendril *n.* samādiru+
tenfold *adj./adv.* ana ešrāti, ešrāia
tense *adj.* maggu, šaddu◊
tent *n.* kultāru☆, maškunu, zārutu
tenth *adj.* ešrû☆, ešru [o.]; → **one ~** *n.* ešrû☆; → **~ month)** *n.* uraḫ Sîn [o.]; → **~ part** *n.* ešrūtu
tenuous *adj.* qatnu
tepid *adj.* ṣarḫu lā ṣarḫu*
terebinth *n.* buṭnu, buṭuttu; → **~-berries** *n.* buṭnu+ (pl.)
term *n.* adannu, edānu; → **~ of office** *n.* pūru
terminate *v.* balû (D)
termination *n.* gamartu☆, qītu☆, taqtītu☆
termite *n.* balṭītu
terms *n.* šummu☆ (pl.); → **come to ~** *v.* magāru☆ (Gt)
terra firma *n.* nābalu☆
terrace *n.* tamlīu, temennu☆
terracotta *n.* ḫaṣbu
terrain *n.* kaqquru
terrestrial *adj.* [ša] kaqqiri
terrible *adj.* akṣu☆, galtu☆, šēru B☆
terribly *adv.* galtiš☆
terrific *adj.* rašubbu☆
terrified *adj.* pardu☆; → **be(come) ~** *v.* parādu☆
terrify *v.* galādu (D), galādu☆ (Š), palāḫu (D), parādu☆ (D); → **~ing** *adj.* galtu☆, pardu☆, pitluḫu☆, rašbu☆, rašubbu☆, šugludu☆; → **be(come) ~ing** *v.* rašābu☆
territory *n.* eqlu, kaqquru, kisurru☆, mātu, miṣru☆, puluggu☆, taḫūmu
terror *n.* ḫaiattu☆, ḫattu☆, ḫurbāšu☆ (cold), šuribtu☆; → **~ist** *n.* mugallitu☆; → **~ize** *v.* galādu (D)
terse *adj.* kapṣu+
test *n.* litiktu☆, litku, maltaktu☆, tasniqtu☆; → **~** *v.* biāru, latāku
testament *n.* šīmtu
tested *adj.* latku
testicle *n.* išku
testify *v.* kuānu (D)
testimony *n.* mukinnūtu◊
tether *n.* šummannu☆; → **~** *v.* ina ṣerreti kullu [i.], ṣerretu šakānu [i.]
tetrad *n.* arbittu, erbettu☆
text *adj.* kammu☆ (esoteric); → **~** *n.* dabābu, malṭuru, šaṭṭāru, šiṭirtu☆
textile *n.* ṣubātu; → **multicolored ~** *n.* birmu; → **~/garment (kind of)** *n.* ḫuzīqutu, raddīdu; → **~ (kind of)** *n.* massuku, šītu
texts → lamentation ~ *n.* kalûtu
thank *v.* karābu; → **~(s)** *n.* dalīlu; → **~ful** *adj.* kāribu; → **~less** *adj.* lā kāribu*; → **~sgiving** *n.* šūdûtu☆
that *pron.* ša; → **~** *pron./adj.* ammiu, šiāti☆, šû, šuāšu☆, šuāti☆, šuātu☆, ullû☆; → *interj.~'s enough* lā utar [o.]; → **~ which** *pron.* mīnu ša
thatch *n.* tarāmu+
thaw *v.* naḫarmuṭu☆
the passage of time → with ~ *n.* labāriš ūmē [i.]
the round → make ~ *v.* labītu labû
the sunset *v.* ana rabā šamši
the support of → with ~ *n.* ina tukulti [i.]
theft *n.* sartu, šarqūtu, tablu; → **commit a ~** *v.* tablu tabālu
their *pron./adj.* iššanû
them *pron.* šâšina☆, šâšunu, šâtina☆, šināšina, šunāšunu, šunūši◊, šunūti☆; → **~selves** *pron.* ramanšunu
then *adv.* iddāti, inūma☆, inūmīšu☆, inūšu☆; → **~** *n.* ina ūmīšu [i.]
thence *adv.* iddāti
therapy *n.* bulṭu
there *adv.* akannaka◊, ammāka; → **~ and then** *prep.* ullânu☆; → **~ is** *v.* ibašši; → **~ is not** *v.* laššu

thereabout(s) *adv.* ammāka

thereafter *adv.* iddāti, ullīš★

thereupon *adv.* ḫarammāma

they (f.) *pron.* šina

they (m.) *pron.* šunu

thick *adj.* ebû, ebû+, kabru, šapû★; → **~** *v.* ebû, kabāru; → **make ~** *v.* ḫubburu★ (D); → **~ (loaf)** *n.* ebbītu; → **~en** *v.* ebû+, kapātu+ (D); → **be(come) ~en (itr.)** *v.* kabāru; → **~en (tr.)** *v.* kabāru (D); → **~ly grown** *adj.* ebṭu+; → **~ness** *n.* ebû+, kabrūtu★, kubru, mūbû; → **~set** *adj.* ebṭu+, šamḫu★

thief *n.* ekkēmu★, sāru, šarrāqu★; → **like a ~** *adv.* šarrāqiš★

thieving *adj.* ekkimu★

thievish *adj.* šarriqu★

thigh *n.* pēmu (upper), sīqu, sūnu, šapru C★; → **inner ~** *n.* šapūlu; → **upper ~** *n.* ḫallu

thin *adj.* naḫsu★ (very), qatnu, qattanu★, raqqu, raqqu★; → **be(come) ~** *v.* daqāqu◊, qatānu★, raqāqu; → **make ~** *v.* raqāqu+ (D); → **~-drawn** *adj.* raqqu+; → **~ (out)** *v.* qatānu★ (D); → **~ part** *n.* qutnu

thine *pron./adj.* ikkû

think *v.* abālu B★ (Št), kaṣāpu (D), qabû ina libbi; → **be(come) ~ about** *v.* issi libbi dabābu [i.]; → **~ constantly** *v.* ḫasāsu (Gtn); → **~ of** *v.* ḫasāsu; → **be(come) ~ of** *v.* ḫissat X ḫasāsu [i.]

thinness *n.* qutnu

third *adj.* šalšu; → **one ~** *n.* šallussu, šulšu◊; → **~ (extispicy)** *n.* šalultu★; → **~ (in age)** *adj.* šalšāiu★; → **~ man** *n.* tašlīšu; → **office of ~ man (in a chariot team)** *n.* tašlīšūtu; → **~ month)** *n.* uraḫ ša-kēnāte [o.]; → **do for a ~ time** *v.* šalāšu B★ (D); → **for the ~ time** *adv.* šalšūtīšu; → **~ly** *adv.* šalšiš★

thirst *n.* ṣumāmītu, ṣummû★, ṣūmu; → **~** *v.* ṣamû◊, ṣamû◊; → **be(come) ~y** *v.* ṣamû◊; → **make ~y** *v.* ṣamû◊ (D)

thirteen *n./adj.* šalāššer[et]★; → **~th** *adj.* šalāššerīu★

thirtieth *adj.* šalāšāiu★

thirty *n./adj.* šalāšā★

this *pron.* annīu, ḫannīu; → **~** *pron./adj.* agâ◊, agannû◊, agātu◊, šû; → **~ instant** *adv.* annūrig; → **~tle** *n.* ašāgu, daddaru★

thither *adv.* ammēša

thong *n.* eblu

thorax *n.* bāntu B★, irtu

thorn *n.* giṣṣu, siḫlu; → **~ bush** *n.* ašāgu, baltu; → **~ plant** *n.* puqdutu

thoroughbred *adj.* ḫiššamû★

thoroughfare *n.* rebītu★

thoroughly → do ~ *v.* malû+ (Š)

those *pron./adj.* šātunu★, šināti★, šuātina★, šuātunu★, šunātunu★, šunūti★; → **in ~ days** *adv.* inūmīšu★

thou *pron.* atta (m.)

though *subj.* ša; → **~t** *n.* abat libbi, libbu [o.]; → **~tful** *adj.* ḫāsisu, muštālu★; → **~tless** *adj.* lā ḫāsisu★

thousand *n./adj.* līmu; → **~ years** *n.* līm šanāti; → **~th** *adj.* līmīu*

thrash *v.* darāku+ (D), rapāsu, rasābu★; → **~ing** *n.* niṭūtu★

thread *n.* qû B★, ṭību, ṭimītu, ṭuānu (fine); → **~** *v.* šakāku [o.]

threadbare *adj.* qalpu

threads → like ~ *adv.* qū'iš★

threat *n.* šipṭu; → **~en** *v.* šapāṭu★

three *n./adj.* šalāšu; → **~-year-old** *adj.* šulušīu; → **~ each** *adv.* šulšāia, šulūšâ◊; → **~ times** *n.* šalāšīšu; → **~ years ago** *adv.* rabušeni; → **~fold** *adj./adv.* šallušu

thresh *v.* darāku+ (D), darāsu (D), diāšu★, rapāsu

threshold *n.* askupputu, sippu+

thrice *n.* šalāšīšu

thrill *v.* tarāru★

thrive *v.* ešēru★, ḫanābu, naḫāšu★, šamāḫu★, šiāḫu B+; → **~(?)** *v.* šerû★

thriving *adj.* naḫšu★, unnubu★

throat *n.* ḫarurtu, lu'u★, napšutu

throb *v.* nakādu, tabû★ (Gtn), tarāku

throbbing *n.* tirku

throne *n.* kussiu; → **accede to the ~** *v.* ina kussê ušābu [i.]; → **base of the ~** *n.* nīd kussî★; → **~-base** *n.* gišgallu★; → **~-platform** *n.* di'u★, du'u★

throng *n.* ummānu★

throttle *v.* ḫanāqu

through *adj.* gamru; → **~** *prep.* birīt★, birti, ina qāt

throughout *adv.* ana gammurti, kalīš★

throw *v.* karāru, nadû★, ṣalā'u [o.], ṣê'u; → **~ away** *v.* rammû (D), selû+; → **~ down** *v.* napāṣu+, nasāku, saḫāpu+; → **~ o.s. down** *v.* napalsuḫu★; → **~ off** *v.* ṣalā'u [o.]; → **~ out** *v.* nasāku; → **~ up** *v.* ešēru★ (Š), karāru, qiā'u; → **~n down** *adj.* nasku

thrush *n.* ḫabbābītu+

thrust *n.* miḫṣu; → **~** *v.* daḫû+, dakāšu★, nakāpu★, saḫāpu+; → **~ away the hand** *v.* qātu napāṣu [i.]; → **~ out** *v.* daḫû+

thud *n.* tirku

thug *n.* šaggāšu★

thumb *n.* ubānu rabītu★

thump *n.* tirku; → ~ *v.* tarāku
thunder *n.* addu☆, rigim Adad; → ~ *v.* ramāmu☆, raṣānu☆ (Dt), šagāmu; → **~bird** *n.* anzû
thunderbolt *n.* birqu, miqitti išāti
thundering *n.* šāgimu☆
thunderous *adj.* adadānu
thunderstorm *n.* addu☆
thunderstruck *adj.* šuḫarruru☆
thundery *adj.* adadānu
thurible *n.* muqattirtu
thus *adv.* akî, kî annie, kīam☆, muk, umma◊; → ~ *gram. part.* mā; → ~ **(I/we)** *gram. part.* mūku, nuk, nūku
thwart *v.* parāku
thy *pron./adj.* ikkû
thyme *n.* ḫašānu, ḫašû B, zambūru☆; → ~ **or savory(?)** *n.* sataru☆
tiara *n.* agû
tibia *n.* kinṣu, kurītu☆
tickle(?) *v.* nadāqu☆
tidal wave *n.* edû B☆
tidbit *n.* mutqītu, ukālu
tide *n.* agû B☆, edû B☆
tidings *n.* passurtu; → **bring ~** *v.* passuru; → **(oral) ~** *n.* lišānu
tidy *adj.* zakû
tie *n.* riksu; → ~ *v.* kaṣāru, rakāsu, ṣamādu+; → **~ on** *v.* rakāsu; → **~ together** *v.* rakāsu; → **~ up** *v.* rakāsu, sarādu [o.]; → **~d** *adj.* kaṣru, raksu; → **be ~d** *v.* rakāsu (N)
tiger *n.* dumāmu☆
tight *adj.* maggu, pāqu, pīqu☆, sāqu, sīqu◊; → **be(come) ~** *v.* siāqu; → **~en** *v.* siāqu (D)
Tigris *n.* Diglat
tile *n.* agurru☆, ebertu; → **~(?)** *n.* makkūtu B◊; → **glazed ~** *n.* ebertu šaḫittu
till *adj.* quppu+; → ~ *prep.* adi, adu; → **~er** *n.* qatinnu
tilt *v.* kaṣṣû [o.]
timber *n.* gašūru
time *n.* adannu+, dāru+, simānu☆, simunu, tarṣu B, tirṣu; → **at that ~** *adv.* inūmīšu☆, inūšu☆; → **at that ~** *n.* ina ūmīšu [i.]; → **distant ~** *n.* ṣâti; → **free ~** *n.* rāqūtu; → **normal ~** *n.* minâti☆ (pl.); → **pass ~** *v.* ūmu šētuqu*; → **primeval ~** *n.* qudmu☆; → **spare ~** *n.* mussa''ītu; → **~-consuming** *adj.* ākil simini; → **long ~ ago** *n.* ultu ulla☆; → **~ for** *n.* simunu; → **~ frame** *n.* šikin adanni☆; → **at the ~ of** *adv.* ina tarṣi
timid *adj.* palḫu; → ~ **person** *n.* pallāḫu☆; → **~ly** *adv.* palḫiš☆
timorous *adj.* ādiru☆
tin *n.* annuku; → **~ ore** *n.* immanakku
tine *n.* šinnu
tinge *v.* ṣapû, tarāpu☆ (D)
tinkle *v.* zamāmu+
tiny *adj.* daqqu☆, qallu, ṣeḫḫeru; → **very ~** *n.* daqqiqu☆
tip *n.* appu; → **~ over** *v.* nabalkutu (Š); → **~s of the toes** *n.* appāt ubānāt šēpi☆; → **~sy** *adj.* šakru; → **~toe** *v.* ina appāt ubānāti alāku*; → **on ~toe** *n.* ina appāt ubānāti*; → **~toes** *n.* appāt ubānāt šēpi☆
tire *n.* ḫūpu B☆ (wheel), šuḫuppu☆; → ~ *v.* anāḫu; → **~(?)** *n.* kabnu☆; → **~ s.o.** *v.* anāḫu (Š); → **~d** *adj.* muqqu☆; → **be(come) ~d** *v.* anāḫu; → **~some** *adj.* lazzu+, mušāniḫu*
tiring *adj.* āniḫu☆, mušāniḫu*
Tishri *n.* Tašrītu (month)
tissue *n.* šuḫattu
tit *n.* ṣerretu B☆, zīzu B
tithe *n.* ešrūtu; → **~s** *n.* ešrâti
title deed *n.* dannutu
titled *adj.* iqabbûniššu
titter *v.* qatā'u*
to *prep.* ana, ina, ina muḫḫi; → ~ *v.* ezābu (Š); → **~-and-fro** *adv.* pāniš u arkiš☆
toad *n.* kitturru B
today *n.* ūmu annīu
toddle *v.* ṭamû B☆
toe *n.* ubān šēpi☆, ubānu; → **~nail** *n.* ṣupur ubān šēpi☆
toga *n.* kusītu
together *adv.* iltēniš☆, issi aḫāiš, ištēniš☆, kî aḫāiš; → **get ~** *v.* emādu (N), paḫāru; → **~ with** *prep.* adi, adu, qanni
toggle *n.* suppinnu☆
toil *n.* mānaḫtu; → ~ *v.* anāḫu, kadāru B, šâṭu☆
toilet *n.* asurrû☆, bēt musâti☆, musâti☆
toiling *n.* mānaḫtu
token *n.* itḫuru, ittu, šimtu☆
token, *n.* passu☆
tolerably *adv.* ibašši
tolerance *n.* zābilānūtu+
tolerant *adj.* šādidu*
tolerate *v.* našû, šadādu☆, zabālu
toll *n.* miksu; → **~ collector** *n.* mākisu
tomb *n.* kimaḫḫu, naqburu; → **royal ~** *n.* bēt šarri; → **~stone** *n.* asumit qabūri
tomorrow *adv.* ina šiāri, iššiāri; → ~ *n.* šērtu, šiāru (the)
tone *n.* ḫalīlu*; → **~ down** *v.* raqāqu (D)
tongs *n.* aruthē, maššânu
tongue *n.* lišānu; → **~-tied** *adj.* ḫarrušu☆, uqququ☆; → **be(come) ~-tied** *v.* ḫarāšu C+
tonight *n.* mūšu annīu
tonsil *n.* šuqdu+

tool *n*. mānaḫtu, nēpešu☆, tiriṣ qāti; → ~ **(kind of)** *n*. mušanniktu; → ~ **shed** *n*. bēt akkulli; → **~s** *n*. anūtu, unūtu☆
toot *v*. naḫāru☆
tooth *n*. šinnu; → **~ache** *n*. muruṣ šinni☆
top *n*. appu, muḫḫu, qimmatu☆, qimmu, rēšu; → ~ **level** *n*. rigbu☆; → ~ **part** *n*. rigbu☆; → **~ic** *n*. abutu
topknot *n*. qimmatu☆
topmost *adj*. elēnīu☆, elīu
topographical feature (kind of) *n*. kūsu
topographical term (kind of) *n*. ša-patri, tisarru
topple over *v*. nabalkutu
topsy-turvy *adj*. šabalkutu
torc *n*. sabirru
torch *n*. dipāru, numūru, zīqtu; → ~ **of reed** *n*. gizilû
torment *n*. šūnāqu+; → ~ *v*. ašāšu☆ (D)
torn *adj*. nukkusu☆; → **~-out (piece)** *n*. nusāḫu B
tornado *adj*. imsuḫḫu☆; → ~ *n*. anḫullu☆
torpid *adj*. kēru*
torpor *n*. kūru B☆
torrent *n*. naḫlu+
tortoise *n*. raqqu☆
tortuous *adj*. egru
torture *n*. šūnāqu+; → ~ *v*. sanāqu+ (D), ṣarāpu (D)
toss *v*. nadû☆, nasāku, raqādu (Š); → ~ **about** *v*. nabalkutu☆; → ~ **off** *v*. šatû
tot (up) *v*. kamāru☆
total *adj*. gamru; → ~ *n*. gimru; → ~ **(up)** *v*. kamāru☆; → **~ity** *n*. gamartu☆, gammurtu, gimirtu, gimru, gummurtu☆, kiššatu☆, kullatu☆, kullutu, nagbu B☆, napḫaru☆, puḫru☆, siḫirtu☆; → **~ly** *adv*. ana māla, kalīš☆
tote *v*. našû
totter *v*. narāṭu, nâšu☆, ṭamû B☆; → **~ing** *adj*. qaiāpu☆
touch *n*. liptu; → ~ *v*. lapātu; → ~ **(a woman)** *v*. qarābu+; → **~ed** *adj*. laptu B; → **~ing** *n*. lāpitu*; → **~y** *adj*. ragšu*
tough *adj*. da'nu, dannu, patnu☆; → **be(come)** ~ *v*. da'ānu
tour *n*. ḫūlu; → **~ist** *n*. āliku
tow *n*. ašlu; → ~ *v*. šadādu
toward(s) *adv*. ina tarṣi; → **toward(s)** *n*. ana tarṣi◊; → **toward(s)** *prep*. ana, ina irti, innirti, pūt, ṣēr☆, ṣēriš☆; → **toward(s)** *subj*. nirit
towel *n*. sasuppu; → **hand** ~ *n*. ša-qāti
tower *n*. asītu [o.], ašītu◊, dintu B☆, isītu, nāmuru, ṣāpītu☆, šaddidu☆; → **~(?)** *n*. saḫaru; → **temple** ~ *n*. siqqurrutu; → **~ing** *adj*. zuqquru☆
town *n*. ālu; → **~council** *n*. puḫru ša āli☆; → ~ **hall** *n*. bēt āli; → ~ **manager** *n*. rab āli
townie *n*. mār āli
township *n*. ālu
townsman *n*. ālāiu, mār āli
toxic *n*. sammānu+
toy *n*. passu☆
tochat *v*. ṣabāru
trace *v*. ḫiāṭu☆, kibsu radû [i.]
trachoma *n*. merḫu☆
track *n*. daraggu☆, ḫirṣu, kibsu, sulû☆; → ~ **down** *v*. kibsu radû [i.]; → ~ **master** *n*. rab kibsi; → **~er** *n*. rādi kibsi; → **chief ~er** *n*. rab rādi kibsi
tract *n*. adannu, kaqquru
trade *n*. maḫīru, tankāruttu [o.], ummânūtu+; → ~ *v*. šapêlu; → **chief of ~** *n*. rab kāri; → ~ **colony** *n*. kāru; → ~ **in** *v*. šapêlu; → ~ **route** *n*. ḫarrānu; → **~r** *n*. tankāru
trading partner *n*. tappû [o.]
trading post *n*. bēt kāri
trading station *n*. kāru
tradition *n*. ṭupšarrūtu; → **(oral)** ~ *adj*. ša pî; → **~al** *adj*. labīru
traffic, *n*. alaktu
trail *n*. kibsu; → ~ *v*. mašāru
train *v*. rabû (D); → **~ee** *n*. tarbiu; → **~er** *n*. murabbânu; → **~er of reserve horses** *n*. sūsān nakkanti; → **~ing** *n*. tarbûtu; → **~ing(?)** *n*. ṣibittu☆
trait *n*. ittu; → **~or** *n*. parriṣu
tramp *n*. saḫḫiru, zilullû☆
trample *v*. diāšu☆ (D), kabāsu; → ~ **down** *v*. darāsu; → ~ **upon** *v*. diāšu☆; → **have ~d** *v*. kabāsu☆ (Š)
trance *n*. šinītu+
tranquil *adj*. nēḫu; → ~ *n*. nēḫu+; → **be(come)** ~ *v*. pašāḫu; → **~ity** *n*. nēḫtu☆, nūḫtu☆
tranquillize *v*. sakātu+ (D)
transcend *v*. nabalkutu
transfer *v*. etāqu (Š), šapêlu
transfix *v*. dakāšu+
transform *v*. emû☆ (Š), tuāru (D); → **~ation** *n*. šinītu☆
transgress *v*. ḫaṭû, nabalkutu, parāṣu
transient *n./adj*. ētiqu
transit *n*. nēburu; → **~ion** *n*. nēbartu☆; → **~ory** *adj*. ētiqu
translate *v*. targumu+
translator *n*. nāpalû☆, targumānu
translucent *adj*. barḫu
transparent *adj*. barḫu
transpire *v*. zuātu+

transport *v.* miāru⁺, zabālu
Transpotamia *n.* Eber nāri
transverse *adj.* egru, parku, purruku*
transvestite *n.* assinnu
trap *n.* gišparru*, ḫuḫāru, kippu, nābartu*, nuballu*, šuttatu*
trapezoid *n.* apsammikku*, nalbantu*, pūt alpi*
trapper *n.* ḫābilu B*
trappings *n.* tallultu, tillē
trash *n.* ziblu; → ~ **can** *n.* kakkul zibli*
trauma *n.* simmu
travail *n.* pušqu*; → ~ *v.* pašāqu B* (Št); → ~**ing woman** *n.* muštapšiqtu [o.]
travel *n.* māluku; → ~ *v.* alāku, radû⁺; → ~ **about** *v.* nagāšu* (Gtn); → ~**ler** *n.* ālik ḫūli, ālik urḫi*, allāku*
traverse *v.* nabalkutu
tray *n.* eršu; → ~ **(kind of)** *n.* šunannu
treacherous *adj.* ṭullumâ; → ~**ly(?)** *adv.* napādiš*
treachery *n.* ṣaliptu*
tread *v.* darāku⁺, darāsu; → ~ **down** *v.* diāšu*, kabāsu; → ~ **harshly** *v.* darāsu; → ~ **upon** *v.* kabāsu
treason *n.* surrāti*
treasure *n.* išittu*, kasilaqqu◊, nakkamtu, niṣirtu*; → ~ *v.* naṣāru; → ~ **house** *n.* bēt niṣirti*; → ~**r** *n.* abarakku*, masennu; → **female** ~**r** *n.* masennutu
treasury *n.* ganūnu*, nakkamtu, šutummu*
treat *v.* abālu B* (Gtn), epāšu, epāšu (D); → ~ **abusively** *adv.* pišāti uppušu [i.]; → ~ **badly** *v.* massuḫu [o.]; → ~ **with care** *v.* kunnû* (D); → ~**ment** *n.* dullu; → ~**y** *n.* adê
treble *adj.* šallušu; → ~ *v.* šalāšu B* (D); → ~**d** *adj.* šallušu, šušlušu*
tree *n.* ēṣu, gapnu, gupnu; → **sacred** ~**(?)** *n.* ēqu; → **cosmic** ~ *n.* mēsu*; → **silk** ~ *n.* iṣṣu nāš šīpāti*; → ~**-trunk** *n.* gišmaḫḫu*, gupnu; → ~**/bush (kind of)** *n.* ṣadānu*; → ~**/wood (kind of)** *n.* elammakku*; → ~ **(kind of)** *n.* ellūtu B*, ḫammar ṭīṭi, musku, samullu◊, ṣippūtu, šaššūgu, šedû, šuratḫu*, tatīdu*; → ~ **of chastity** *n.* šunû⁺
trek *n.* ripittu*; → ~ *v.* rapādu
trellis *n.* birru
tremble *v.* arāru B*, narāṭu, râdu*, ratātu*, ruābu, tarāru*; → **make** ~ *v.* narāṭu (D); → ~ **all over** *v.* garāru (Ntn)
trembling *n.* nirriṭu, ratītu*
tremendous *adj.* šūturu*
tremor *n.* nirriṭu; → ~**s** *n.* ḫurbāšu* (cold)
tremulous *adj.* rattitu*
trench *n.* ḫirīṣu; → ~**ant** *adj.* šēlu*
trespass *v.* ḫaṭû
trespass: to deceive *v.* parāṣu*
tress *n.* kizirtu
trial *n.* dēnu, litku
triangle *n.* santakku*; → **right** ~ *n.* santakku*
tribunal *n.* bēt dēni; → **president of** ~ *n.* ša-pān-daiāni
tribute *n.* biltu, maddattu
trick *n.* nikiltu, niklu, šibqu*, tukku⁺; → ~ *v.* nakālu; → **play a** ~ *v.* niklu nakālu; → ~**ery** *n.* šipir nikilti*
trickle *v.* natāku, ṣarāru, šaḫālu⁺
tricky *n.* itguru*
trident *n.* mazluqu [o.]
tried → **be** ~ *v.* kuānu (Dtt)
trifle *n.* abutu qallissu; → ~ *v.* namūtu epāšu [o.]; → ~ **with** *v.* mēlulu issi [i.]; → ~**s** *n.* buṣaṣê*
trifling *adj.* qallīlu
trim *adj.* tarṣu; → ~ *v.* garāšu, ḫasāru*, kaṣāṣu*, qarāšu, šarāmu; → ~ **away** *v.* ṣapāru*
trimmings *n.* qiršu (pl.), šikkatu B*
trinket *n.* zalāqu
trip *n.* alaktu, ḫarrānu, ḫūlu; → ~ **up** *v.* naḫalṣû
tripe *n.* karaš alpi⁺
triple *adj.* šallušu, šušlušu*; → ~ *v.* šalāšu B* (D); → ~**t** *n.* taškû; → ~**ts** *n.* taškâti
tripod *n.* taškû
trite *adj.* darsu⁺
triumph *n.* erāb āli, irnittu*, lītu*; → ~**ant** *adj.* šitluṭu*, šulluṭu*; → ~**antly** *adv.* šitluṭiš*
trivial *adj.* darsu⁺, qallulu, ṣuḫḫu*
trodden *adj.* darsu⁺
troop *n.* kiṣru (military); → ~**(s)** *n.* ummānu*; → ~ **commander** *n.* rab ṣābi; → ~ **formation(?) (kind of)** *n.* kitullu*; → ~**s** *n.* baʾulāti*, emūqu (pl.), ṣāb kakki*, ṣābu, ummānāti*; → **(enemy)** ~**s** *n.* ellatu*; → **auxiliary** ~**s** *n.* kitru, nērāru*, tillāti*; → **combat** ~**s** *n.* ṣāb tāḫāzi*; → **commander of** ~**s** *n.* rab ummānāti; → **crack** ~**s** *n.* ašarissu*, šarissu; → **elite** ~**s** *n.* gunnu*; → **garrison** ~**s** *n.* ša-bīrti, šūlû*; → **massed body of** ~**s** *n.* gipiš ummāni*; → **paramilitary** ~**s** *n.* kitkittû; → **professional** ~**s** *n.* zukkû◊; → **released** ~**s** *n.* rammûti; → **shock** ~**s** *n.* ašarissu*
trophy *n.* zīm pāni*

trotter *n.* šānû☆
trouble *n.* dibiru☆, dilḫu☆, duluḫḫû☆, idirtu, maruštu☆; → ~ *v.* dalāḫu, marāṣu (Š); → **take ~** *v.* anāḫu, marāṣu☆ (Št); → **~d** *adj.* dalḫu
troublemaker *n.* mugallitu☆
troublesome *adj.* marṣu; → **be(come) ~** *v.* marāṣu
trough *n.* bukinnu, kuninnu, rāṭu
truce *n.* baṭāl kakkē*
truck *n.* ereqqu☆
true *adj.* kēnu; → **be(come) ~** *v.* kuānu
truffle *n.* puṭuru
truly *adv.* ina kētti, kēniš, kēttu
truncheon *n.* duqdu+, šabbiṭu+
trundle *v.* galālu+
trunk *n.* kisittu☆, pagru, šaddu◊, unīnu
trust *n.* qēptu, tukultu; → ~ *v.* qiāpu, raḫāṣu; → **position of ~** *n.* qīptu☆; → **~ in** *v.* takālu; → **put ~ in** *v.* takālu+; → **put one's ~ in** *v.* takālu (N); → **~ed** *adj.* qēpu; → **royal ~ee** *n.* qēpu; → **~ful** *adj.* takkulu, taklu+; → **~fulness** *n.* takiltu B☆; → **~ing** *adj.* takkulu
trustworthiness *n.* takiltu B☆
trustworthy *adj.* taklu, tuklātānu☆
trusty *adj.* taklu, taqnu+
truth *n.* kēttu; → **~ful** *adj.* kēnu; → **~fully** *adv.* ina kētti; → **~fulness** *n.* kēnāti, kēnūtu
try *v.* ba''û, ṭeāmu+; → **~ hard** *v.* maṣû☆ (Št); → **~ on** *v.* latāku; → **~ out** *v.* latāku; → **~ to** *v.* ṣarāmu; → **~ to kill** *v.* duāku
tube *n.* eṣennû☆, rāṭu, takkussu, uppu
tuck *n.* ḫabūnu; → **~ away** *v.* elû (D); → **~ in** *v.* akālu (Gtn); → **~ up** *v.* kanānu☆, katāmu
tuft *n.* karballutu+, qimmatu☆
tug *v.* šadādu, šalāḫu
tumble *n.* miqittu; → **~ (down)** *v.* maqātu; → **be(come) ~ down** *v.* ramanšu da'āpu [i.]
tumescent → **be(come) ~** *v.* ebû
tumid *adj.* ebû; → **be(come) ~** *v.* ebû
tummy *n.* bandillu
tumor *n.* ebiānu+
tumult *n.* ḫubūru☆, rigmu
tumultuous *adj.* ḫabru☆
tune *n.* zimru☆
tunic *n.* gulēnu, sāgu (short); → **~ peddler** *n.* ša-sāgātēšu
tuning *n.* pitnu B☆
tunnel *n.* pilšu; → ~ *v.* palāšu; → **~ler** *n.* pallišu
turbid *adj.* dalḫu, ebû; → **be(come) ~** *v.* ešû☆; → **~ity** *n.* duluḫḫû☆
turbulent *adj.* meḫānu*
turf *n.* nadbāk dīši*, sassutu
turgid *adj.* ebû
turmeric(?) *n.* kurkānû
turmoil *n.* rūbu B☆, tēšû☆
turn *n.* saḫāru, siḫru; → ~ *v.* saḫāru; → **~(ing)** *n.* turrūtu; → **ill ~** *n.* lumnu; → **~ (round)** *v.* zuāru [o.]; → **~ about** *v.* saḫāru, ṣâdu◊; → **~ acid** *v.* emēṣu+; → **~ against** *v.* ina muḫḫi X saḫāru [i.]; → **~ around** *v.* pasālu☆; → **~ aside from normal route** *v.* ḫūlu nakkuru (D) [i.]; → **~ away** *v.* nê'u☆, zuāru (D) [o.]; → **~ back** *v.* ana qinniš saḫāru [i.], nê'u☆, pasālu☆, saḫāru; → **~ down** *v.* selû+; → **~ hostile** *v.* garû☆; → **~ in** *v.* tuāru (D); → **~ into** *v.* emû☆, manû ana [i.], tuāru; → **to ~ into uncultivated land** *adv.* emû qišubbiš [i.]; → **~ off** *v.* balû (D); → **~ on** *v.* tabû (Š); → **~ out** *v.* ṭarādu☆, uṣû (Š); → **~ over** *v.* gêšu☆, nabalkutu, nabalkutu (Š); → **~ round** *v.* labû; → **~ sour** *v.* emēṣu+; → **~ the breast** *v.* irtu nê'u [i.]; → **~ to** *v.* maḫāru, saḫāru; → **~ towards** *v.* pānē ana X šakānu [i.]; → **~ up** *v.* amāru (N), apû☆; → **~ up (soil)** *v.* napālu☆ (D); → **~ upside down** *v.* nabalkutu (Š); → **~ing** *n.* siḫru, tūrtu; → **~ing point** *n.* bēt siḫri
turnip *n.* laptu; → **pomegranate-like ~** *n.* lapat armanni
turnover *n.* maḫīru
turret *n.* isītu
turtle *n.* raqqu☆, šelappû; → **~dove** *n.* sukanninu
tussle *v.* rapāsu
tutelary deity *n.* lamassu
tutelary god *n.* ilu mušallimu☆
tutor *n.* murabbânu
twaddle *n.* dibbē ša šāri, šārāti (pl.); → ~ *v.* ṣabāru+
twang *n.* rigmu
tweezers *n.* allunāti [o.], ša-ḫassupi
twelfth *adj.* šinšerû☆
twelve *n./adj.* šinšer[et]☆
twentieth *adj.* ešrīu*
twenty *n./adj.* ešrā
twice *adv.* šinīšu
twiddle *v.* ṣâdu
twig *n.* ḫuṣābu, larû
twilight *n.* barārītu, namārītu
twin *adj.* ta''umu; → ~ *n.* maššû☆, māšu☆, tu'āmu; → ~ *v.* ta''umu (D)
twine *n.* kiplu, ṭību, ṭimītu; → ~ *v.* gadālu+, karāku, patālu☆; → **~d** *adj.* eṣpu☆
twinge *v.* zaqātu+
twining *n.* gidlu

twinkingly *adv*. ummuliš*
twinkle *v*. ṣabāru, ṣarāru B*, ummulu*
twinkling *adj*. ummulu*
twirl *n*. sūrtu*; → ~ *v*. sâru*
twist *v*. atāku* (D), egēru* (D), gadālu+, kanānu*, pasālu*, patālu*, zuāru [o.]; → ~ awry *v*. patālu+; → ~ed *adj*. egru, paslu*, patlu*; → be ~ed *v*. egēru* (Gt)
twitch *n*. giddagiddû*, ṣadāru*, tību; → ~ *v*. šalāḫu; → ~ing *n*. giddagiddû*; → ~y *n*. gidgiddānu
twitter *v*. ṣabāru
two *n./adj*. šina B, šitta; → **in** ~ *n*. ana šinīšu, issēn ana šinīšu; → **~-humped** *adj*. ša šunāia guggalīpi-*, ša šunāia karrūni, ša šunāia ṣēri-*; → **~-valved** *n*. ta''umāti+ (pl.); → **~-year-old** *adj*. šunu'īu; → ~ **each** *adv*. šunāia; → ~ **thirds** *n*. šinip, šittān*; → ~ **years ago** *adv*. šaluššeni; → **~fold** *adj*. ta''umu+
tycoon *n*. šarû
type *n*. šiknu
Tyre *n*. **Ṣurru**
typify *v*. eṣāru+
tyro *n*. šarrāiu+
ubiquitous *adj*. āšib gimri*
udder *n*. ṣerretu B*
ugliness *n*. masiktu [o.]
ugly *adj*. lā damqu, masku [o.], mussuku*; → **be(come)** ~ *v*. masāku [o.]; → **~-looking** *adj*. mussuku*
ulcer *n*. šūḫānu+
ulterior *adj*. katmu*, pazru*
ultimate *adj*. nagmuru; → **~ly** *adv*. ina qīti*
umbilical cord *n*. abunnutu*
umbrella *n*. ša-ṣilli
un- *gram. part*. lā
unaccompanied *adj*. ēdumānu
unaccustomed *adj*. aḫīu
unalterable *adj*. ša lā šunnê
unanimity *n*. mitḫurtu*, pû ištēn [i.]
unanimous *adj*. mitḫāru*; → **make** ~ *v*. pâ ištēn šuškunu [i.]; → **~ly** *adv*. kī pî issēn [i.], mitḫāriš*, šēpu ana šēpi [i.]
unarmed *n*. lā nāš kakki*
unattached *adj*. lā raksu
unattended *adj*. lā naṣru*
unauthorized *adj*. ša lā pî; → ~ *n*. lā šalṭu*
unavailable *adj*. batqu, lā qurbu
unaware *n*. lā mūdû*; → **~s** *adv*. ina lā mūdānūti [i.]
unbalanced *adj*. lā šitqulu*
unbelievable *adj*. lā qēpu
unbend *v*. ešēru* (Š), nuāḫu; → **~ing** *adj*. lā ḫanšu
unbidden *adj*. lā qariu*
unblemished *adj*. šaklulu
unbroken *adj*. lā kabsu*
unbuckle *v*. paṭāru
unburden o.s. *v*. libbu patû [i.]
unbutton *v*. patû+
uncalled-for *adj*. lā eršu
uncanonical *adj*. aḫīu
uncastrated *adj*. šaklulu
unceasing *n*. lā mupparkû*
unchangeable *adj*. lā mušpēlu, ša lā šunnê
unchanged *adj*. lā nakkuru*
unchecked *adj*. paḫzu
uncle *n*. aḫ-abi; → **maternal** ~ *n*. aḫ-ummi
unclean *n*. aršu*; → **~liness** *n*. lu'āti*
unclear *adj*. lā ḫakmu
uncomfortable *adj*. lā ṭābu
uncommitted *adj*. lā raksu
uncommon *n*. lā kaiamānīu*
uncompromising → **be(come)** ~ *v*. lā magāru
unconcerned *adj*. lā qurbu
unconscious *adj*. lā ḫāsisu*; → **become** ~ *v*. kâru*
uncooked *adj*. balṭu
uncooperative *adj*. lā māgiru*
uncountable *adj*. lā mīnu*
uncover *v*. patû
unction *n*. pašāšu
uncultivated *n*. šuḫrubu*
undamaged *adj*. šalmu
undaunted *adj*. qardu
undeniable *adj*. ša lā paqāri
under *adv*. šapla, šaplānu-, taḫtānu; → ~ *prep*. šapal, šupāl*; → **keep** ~ *v*. kabāsu+; → **~age** *adj*. ṣeḫru; → **~brush** *n*. sassutu; → **~estimate** *v*. maṭû* (Š)
undergo *v*. zabālu+
underground *n*. kaqquru
undergrowth *n*. sassutu
underhand *adj*. šapal qāti
underling *n*. urdu
undermine *v*. palāšu+, saḫāpu+
underneath *adv*. šaplāniš*
underside *n*. šaplu, šupālu*
undersigned *n*. šāṭir šumi*
understand *v*. ḫakāmu, ḫasāsu*; → **~able** *adj*. ḫakmu; → **~ing** *n*. ḫākimu, ḫasīsu, ḫissat libbi*, uznu
understate *v*. maṭû* (Š)
undertake *v*. epāšu, ṣabātu; → **~r** *n*. qabbiru*

undervalue *v.* maṭû* (Š)
underwear *n.* dīdū [o.], šupālītu
underworld *n.* arallû★, ganṣir★, kigallu
undesirable *adj.* lā ṣaḫtu
undisciplined *adj.* lā radiu+
undisturbed *adv.* pargāniš★
undivided *adj.* lā zēzu
undo *v.* pašāru, paṭāru
undoubtedly *adv.* piqtatti
undress *v.* lubūšē šaḫāṭu [i.]
undue *adj.* lā simāti★
undulate *v.* qarāru★
unduly *adv.* lā simāti-★
unearthly *adj.* aḫīu
uneasy *adj.* lā ṣālilu★
uneducated *adj.* nuā'u [o.]
unemployed *adj.* rāqu, rīqu★; → **be(come) ~** *v.* riāqu
unemployment *n.* rāqūtu
unequal *adj.* lā mitḫāru★
unequipped *adj.* lā šaṣbutu*
unerring *adj.* lā ḫāṭiu*
unestablished *adj.* lā kunnu*
uneven *adj.* utru+
unexpectedly *adv.* ina lā mināti̇̄šu★
unfailing *n.* lā mupparkû★
unfamiliar *adj.* aḫīu
unfasten *v.* paṭāru
unfathomable *adj.* rūqu★
unfavorable → **be(come) ~** *v.* lamānu; → **make ~** *v.* lamānu (D)
unfinished *adj.* lā gamru
unfit *adj.* lā simāti★
unflagging *adj.* lā āniḫu★
unflinching *adj.* lā nāriṭu*
unfold *v.* patû
unforeseen *adj.* lā amru; → **~ly** *adv.* ina lā minātīšu★
unforgettable *adj.* ša lā mašê
unfortunate *adj.* bīšu+, lā damqu, lamnu, lumnānû★; → **~ly** *adv.* lamniš [o.]
unfounded *adj.* lā šalmu
unfriendly *adj.* lā magru, lā salmu
unfurl *v.* patû
ungirt → **be ~** *v.* paṭāru (N)
ungrateful *adj.* lā ḫāsis ṭābti★, ṭalūmu+
unguarded *adj.* lā naṣru*
unguent *n.* piššatu★
unhappily *adv.* adriš★, lamniš [o.]
unhappiness *n.* lā ṭūb libbi, lumun libbi
unhappy *adj.* adru B
unhealthiness *n.* lā ṭūb šīri
unhealthy *adj.* lā šalmu
unhitch *v.* paṭāru; → **~ed** *adj.* paṭru
unhurt *adj.* šalmu
unified → **be(come) ~** *v.* samāḫu
uniform *adj.* mitḫāru★; → **~ly** *adv.* mitḫāriš★
unify *v.* pâ ēda šuškunu [i.]; → **make ~** *v.* pâ ištēn šuškunu [i.]
unimportant *adj.* qallīlu
uninhibited *adj.* paḫzu
uninitiated *adj.* lā lammudu★
unintelligible *adj.* lā ḫakmu, nakru, ša lā iḫakkimūni
unique *adj.* ēdu; → **~** *n.* issēn
unison *n.* pû ēdu★
unit *n.* ištēnūtu★, kiṣru (military); → **~ commander** *n.* bēl pirri (cavalry)
unite *v.* pâ ēda šuškunu [i.], samāḫu (D); → **~ in marriage** *v.* kallulu+ (D); → **be ~d** *v.* samāḫu (Dtt)
unity *n.* pû ēdu★
universal *adj.* [ša] kiššati★
universe *n.* kiššatu★
unjust *adj.* ṭalūmu+
unjustified *adj.* lā kunnu*
unjustly → **treat ~** *v.* dâṣu★, ṭalāmu+
unkind *adj.* lā ṭābu
unknown *adj.* nakru; → **~** *n.* lā īdû★
unleash *v.* dakû
unless *subj.* ulâ
unlike *adj.* lā akī, lā mušlu; → **~** *n.* šitnû★; → **~ly** *adj.* da'nu
unload *v.* paṭāru, riāqu (Š)
unlock *v.* paṭāru; → **~ed** *n.* lā sakru*
unloving *adj.* lā rā'imu
unlucky *adj.* bīšu+, laptu B, lumnānû★
unmask *v.* patû
unmatched *adj.* lā šanān★
unmistakable *adj.* namru
unmoved *adj.* nēḫu
unnatural *n.* lā kaiamānīu*
unnecessary *adj.* lā eršu
unnerve *v.* dalāḫu+, garāru (Š)
unnoticed *adj.* lā amru
unobjectionable *adj.* ša lā paqāri
unobliging *adj.* lā māgiru★
unoccupied *adj.* rāqu, rīqu★; → **be(come) ~** *v.* riāqu
unopposable *adj.* lā maḫār★
unopposed *adv.* šitluṭiš★
unpack *v.* paṭāru
unpredictable *adj.* rasmu
unpredictably *adv.* ina lā minātīšu★
unprepared *adj.* lā šaṣbutu*
unprofitable *adj.* lā kušīri+
unpropitious *adj.* lā damqu
unqualified *adj.* lā damqu
unquestionable *adj.* ša lā paqāri

unravel *v.* patû
unreasonable *adj.* lā ṭēmānu; → ~ *n.* lā rāš ṭēmi*
unrefined *adj.* lā bašlu
unrelenting *adj.* lā pādû*
unreliable *adj.* lā taklu*
unrest *n.* diliptu; → **~rained** *adj.* paḫzu+, sarḫu+
unripe *adj.* lā bašlu
unrivalled *adj.* lā šanān*, ša lā iššannanu*
unruly *adj.* akṣu*
unsafe *adj.* lā šalmu
unsatisfactory → **be(come)** ~ *v.* lamānu
unseal *v.* patû
unseasonably *adv.* ina lā simānīšu*
unseemly *adj.* lā amru; → ~ **behavior** *n.* lā šalāmu*
unseen *adj.* lā amru
unsettled *adj.* dalḫu+, šaggīšu+
unshakable *adj.* lā nāriṭu*
unshaven *adj.* šu''uru*
unsheathe *v.* šalāpu, šamāṭu+
unshod *adj.* šamṭu+
unshorn *adj.* šu''uru*
unskilled *adj.* lā lē'û*
unsound *adj.* lā šalmu
unspecified *adj.* lā mīnānu
unsteadiness *n.* barāru
unsubmissive *adj.* lā ḫanšu
unsuccessful *adj.* lā kašru*
unsuitable *adj.* lā naṭû*
untamed *adj.* lā kabsu*
unthinkable *adj.* ḫasāsiš lā naṭû*
untidy *n.* aršu*
untie *v.* paṭāru
until *prep./subj.* adi bēt, adi, adu, adu bēt, adu muḫḫi; → ~ **dawn** *n.* adi namiranni; → ~ **non-existence** *n.* adi lā bašê*; → ~ **now** *adv.* adakanni, adi akanni, adinakanni
untimely *adv.* ina lā simānīšu*
unto *prep.* ana; → **~ld** *adj.* lā mīnu*, lā nībi
untouchable *adj.* ḫarmu+, qašdu*
untoward *adj.* lamnu
untrained *adj.* lā lammudu*
untried *adj.* lā lammudu*
untrustworthy *adj.* paḫḫu+
untruth *n.* lā kettu
ununderstandable *adj.* ša lā iḫakkimūni
unusual *adj.* aḫīu
unvaried *adj.* lā šāniu+
unveil *v.* patû; → **~ed** *adj.* lā kallulu*
unwanted *adj.* lā ṣaḫtu
unwarranted *adj.* lā šalmu
unweaned child *n.* ēniqu*
unwell *adj.* marṣu
unwilling *adj.* lā māgiru*
unwind *v.* patû
unwise *adj.* lā ḫassu*
unwittingly *adv.* ina lā mūdānūti [i.]
unwrap *v.* patû
unyielding *adj.* lā ḫanšu
up → **get** ~ *v.* tabû; → **make** ~ *v.* kannû (D); → ~ **to** *prep.* adi maḫar*; → **be(come)** ~ **to** *v.* maṣû; → **~braiding** *adj.* ra'bu; → **~bringing** *n.* tarbītu+, tarbûtu
upcoming *adj.* ēribu
upheaval *n.* šabalkutu
uphill *adv.* elānu◊, eliš
uphold *v.* našû
upholster *v.* šê'u [o.]
upkeep *n.* kullu ša rēši*
upland *n.* eliāti* (pl.)
uplift *n.* nīš rēši*; → ~ *v.* elû (Š), rēšu našû [i.]
upon *prep.* eli*, ina muḫḫi, ṣēr*
upper *adj.* elēnīu*, elīu, elû*; → ~ **lands** *n.* eliāti* (pl.); → ~ **part** *n.* elītu, muḫḫu; → ~ **world** *n.* eliāti* (pl.)
Upper Zab *n.* Zāba elīu
uppermost *adj.* elēnīu*, elīu
upright *adj.* išaru*, tarṣu+, zaqpu; → ~ *adv.* ziqpa*
uprising *n.* nabalkattu*
uproar *n.* ḫubūru*, killu, rigmu
uproot *v.* nasāḫu
upset *adj.* pardu*; → ~ *v.* abāku B*, dalāḫu, nabalkutu (Š), parādu* (D)
upshot *n.* ṣītu*
upside down *adj.* šabalkutu
upstairs *adv.* elānu◊
upstart *n.* saklu
upstream *adv.* ana maḫirti, elān*, elānu◊; → ~ **direction** *n.* maḫirtu
upwards *adv.* ana eliš, elān*, elāniš*, elānu◊, eliš
Ur *n.* Ūru
Urartu *n.* Urarṭu
urban *adj.* [ša] āli
urethra *n.* muštinnu*, pilšu ša ušāri*
urge *v.* dabābu (Š), qarādu (D); → ~ **on** *v.* radāpu; → **~nt** *adj.* murriḫu*; → **be(come)** **~nt** *v.* arāḫu*
urinate *v.* šatānu*, šiānu
urine *n.* šīnāti
Urmia → **Lake** ~ *n.* tāntu ša Nairi*
urn *n.* kallu
Ursa Major *n.* ereqqu*
us *pron.* niāši*; → **~age** *n.* parṣu, ussu*
use *n.* ḫašaḫtu+, ḫišaḫtu+; → ~ **up** *v.*

akālu, gamāru, uqāru☆ (D); → **be ~d up** *v.* gamāru☆ (N); → **~ful** *adj.* ša kušīri*, ṭābu; → **be(come) ~ful** *v.* ṭiābu; → **~less** *adj.* lā kušīri+, lā ṭābu; → **~r** *n.* mukillu
usual *adj.* kaiamānīu, sadru; → **~ly** *adv.* ginâ☆, kaiamānu; → **do ~ly** *v.* sadāru
usurp *v.* puāgu; → **~er** *n.* ḫammā'u☆
utensil *n.* udê; → **~s** *n.* anūtu, unūtu☆; → **household ~s** *n.* anūt bēti
uterus *n.* šassūru☆
utility *n.* ḫašaḫtu+, ḫišaḫtu+
utilize *v.* akālu
utmost *adj.* šūturu☆
utter *v.* ina šapti šakānu [i.], saqāru; → **~ance** *n.* atmû☆, gerrû, kataduqqû☆, nību☆, pû, siqru, ṣīt pî☆, zikru; → **~ly** *adv.* ana māla
uttermost *adj.* šūturu☆
uvula *n.* napšāru☆
vacancy *n.* rāqūtu
vacant *adj.* rāqu
vacate *v.* riāqu (Š)
vacation *n.* rāqūtu
vacillate *v.* narāṭu, samû
vacuum *n.* rāqtu*
vagabond *n.* saḫḫirtu, saḫḫiru
vagary *n.* bibil libbi☆
vagina *n.* biṣṣūru☆, ūru B☆
vagrant *n.* saḫḫiru, ṣaiādu☆, zilullû☆
vague *adj.* lā mīnānu, lā parsu*, unnutu
vain → **be(come) in ~** *v.* riāqu; → **be in ~** *v.* ana qinniš alāku [i.]; → **in ~** *adv.* im-magāni; → **~ (words)** *n.* šāru
vainglorious *adj.* multarḫu☆, sarrīqu
vainglory *n.* multarḫūtu☆
vale *n.* unqu B+; → **~t** *n.* ša-bēti-šanie
valiant *adj.* qardu; → **~ness** *n.* qardūtu☆
valid → **remain ~** *v.* kullu (Dtt); → **~ document** *n.* dannutu
valley *n.* naḫlu+, unqu B+; → **~** *n./adj.* mušpalu☆; → **~(?)** *n.* saḫimtu B☆; → **abrupt ~** *n.* nērubu+; → **deep ~** *n.* nērubu; → **flooded ~** *n.* na'īlu☆
valor *n.* qardūtu☆, qurdu
valuable *adj.* uqru; → **make ~** *v.* uqāru+ (Š); → **~s** *n.* uqurtu* (pl.)
value *n.* emūqu, šīmu; → **~** *v.* uqāru☆ (Š); → **make ~** *v.* uqāru+ (Š); → **article of ~** *n.* ṣaḫittu; → **current ~** *n.* pašāru; → **~less** *adj.* rāqu
vamp *v.* kazābu☆ (D)
vane *n.* iṣṣūr šāri☆
vanguard *n.* nuballu☆, pānāti, sagbû☆
vanish *v.* paṭāru (N)
vanity *n.* rāqūtu, šāru
vanquish *v.* kamû☆, kašādu; → **~er** *n.* muniḫḫu☆
vapid *adj.* rāqu
vapor *n.* buḫru☆; → **~ize** *v.* baḫāru☆ (D), baḫāru☆
variable *adj.* muštēnû☆
variance → **at ~** *n.* šitnû☆
variegated *adj.* barmu☆; → **be(come) ~** *v.* barāmu B☆
vary *v.* šanû☆ (Gtn)
vase *n.* qadurtu+
vassal *n.* dāgil pāni; → **~age** *n.* ardūtu◊
vast *adj.* palkû☆, rapšu, ritpāšu☆; → **~ly** *adv.* ma'diš☆; → **~ness** *n.* rapšūtu*
vat *n.* ḫariu, namḫāru [o.]
vault *n.* qumbutu+
vaunt *v.* šarāḫu☆ (Dt)
veal *n.* būru B
veer *v.* labû
vegetable(s) *n./adj.* urqu
vegetable-bed *n.* musarû B☆
vegetable (kind of) *n.* il'ūtu, šišanibu
vegetable gardener *n.* nukarib urqi
vegetation *n.* urqītu
vehemence *n.* ḫimiṭ libbi☆ (excessive)
vehement *adj.* dannu; → **~ly** *adv.* šitmuriš☆
vehicle *n.* rukūbu☆; → **small ~** *n.* marturrû☆; → **two-wheeled ~** *n.* mugirru
veil *n.* kutummu☆, paṣṣuntu, pusummu☆, puṣūnu [o.], sasuppu+; → **~** *v.* kallulu (D), katāmu (D), paṣānu (D) [o.], pesēnu◊; → **~ed** *adj.* paṣṣunu [o.], pussumu☆, pussunu◊
vein *n.* šer'ānu, umunnû☆, ušultu☆
velocity *n.* nisḫu☆
vendor *n.* bēl tadāni, sāḫiru B
veneer(?) *n.* tamḫīṣu☆
venerable *adj.* kabtu☆
venerate *v.* palāḫu
veneration *n.* kubādu, palāḫu
vengeance *n.* gimillu☆, gimlu, tuktê☆
venom *n.* imtu; → **~ous** *adj.* [ša] imti*
vent *n.* nappāšu☆
ventilate *v.* napāšu (D)
ventilation hole *n.* bāb zīqi☆
venture → **be(come) ~** *v.* ṣarāmu+; → **joint ~** *n.* šutāpūtu☆
venue *n.* bēt puḫri☆
veracity *n.* kēnūtu
verbascum *n.* būṣinnu
verbatim *adj./adv.* abutu ana abiti
verdict *n.* dēnu, šipṭu☆
verdigris *n.* šuḫtu
verdure *n.* reṭbu+
verge *n.* qannu
verification *n.* piqittu

verify *v*. kuānu (D)
verily *adv*. kēttumma
veritable *adj*. kaiamānīu
vermilionion *n*. makru+
vermin *n*. kalmutu, zērmandu*
vernacular *adj*. ša pî nišē
versatile *adj*. ma'du
versed in *adj*. mūdû
versus *prep*. ina muḫḫi
vertebra *n*. kunukku
vertebral column *n*. eṣenṣēru
vertical *adj*. zaqiptu*, zaqpu; → **~ly** *adv*. ziqipta*, ziqpa*
vertigo *n*. ṣādānu, ṣūd pāni*
very *adv*. adanniš; → **~ charming** *adj*. kuzzubu* (highly)
vessel → **(clay) ~** *n*. karputu ; → **glass ~** *n*. būzu; → **~/container (kind of)** *n*. alūtu; → **~ (kind of)** *n*. kūtu, masrāḫu; → **(clay) ~ (with two handles)** *n*. ḫaṣbu+
vest in *v*. paqādu, qiāpu, šalāṭu+ (Š)
vestibule *n*. nēburu+
vestige *n*. kibsu
vestry *n*. bēt qāti
vet *n*. ṣābu pānīu; → **~eran** *n*. ṣābu pānīu; → **~erinarian** *n*. muna''išu*; → **~erinary surgeon** *n*. muna''išu*
vex *v*. dalāḫu, dalāpu (D), nazāqu* (Š); → **~ation** *n*. dilḫu*; → **~ed** *adj*. dalpu
viable *adj*. ša ana epāši ṭābūni, [ša] balāṭi
viaduct *n*. titurru
viaticum *n*. ṣidītu*
vibrate *v*. katātu*, ratātu*
vibration *n*. ratītu*
vicar *adj*. iššakku*
vice *n*. ḫiṭītu*, šērtu B*; → **~-regency** *n*. iššakkūtu*; → **~-regent** *adj*. iššakku*; → **~ versa** *adv*. enīta*; → **~roy** *n*. šakkanakku*
vicinity *n*. limītu*; → **immediate ~** *n*. ṭēḫu
vicious *adj*. raggu*
vicissitude(s) *n*. pušqu*
victim *n*. iklu*, niqiu
victor *n*. kāšidu*
victorious *adj*. kāšidu; → **be(come) ~** *v*. bêlu*; → **~ly** *adv*. šalṭāniš*
victory *n*. irnittu*, lītu*
victual *n*. tablittu*; → **chief ~ler** *n*. rab danibāti; → **~s** *n*. eṣidītu◊ (travel), leḫmu, uklu
vie *v*. šanānu
view *n*. diglu, niṭlu*; → **~er** *n*. dāgilu; → **~ing** *n*. tāmartu
viewpoint *n*. madgulu*
vigil *n*. baiādu; → **~ance** *n*. ḫarduttu, maṣṣartu; → **~ant** *adj*. ḫardu; → **be ~ant** *v*. ḫarādu (N); → **~ante** *n*. ḫā'iṭu*
vigor *n*. balṭūtu, lalû; → **~ous** *adj*. balṭu
vile *adj*. qallulu
vilify *v*. qalālu (D)
village *n*. ālu, kapru; → **~ manager** *n*. rab ālāni; → **~r** *n*. ālāiu
villain *n*. ḫappu, ḫarḫaru*, isḫappu*; → **~y** *n*. ḫappūtu*, riggatu
vine *n*. gapnu+, tillutu; → **(wild) ~** *n*. gupnu+
vinegar *n*. ḫālu, karān ḫāli, ṭābāti, ṭābāti*
vineyard *n*. kiri tilliti
violate *v*. ḫaṭû; → **~d** *n*. nēku
violence *n*. dāṣtu*, ḫabālu*
violent *adj*. dannu, šamru; → **~ly** *adv*. emūqatti [o.], kî da'āni
violet *n./adj*. takiltu+
viper *n*. bašmu
virgin *n*. ardatu*, batūssu; → **~ goat** *n*. unīqu lā patītu; → **~al** *adj*. lā patītu; → **~ity** *n*. batūlūtu
Virgo *n*. Šer'u*, Šubiltu+
virility *n*. zikrūtu*
virtually *adv*. ibašši
virtues *n*. kēnāti
virtuous *adj*. kēnu, utturu+
viscous *adj*. dābiqu+
visibility *n*. tāmartu
visible *adj*. apû*; → **be ~** *v*. naṭālu* (N); → **be(come) ~** *v*. apû*; → **make ~** *v*. apû* (Š)
vision *n*. diglu, tabrītu*; → **~ary** *n*. šabrû*
visit *v*. erābu, pān X amāru [i.]; → **~or** *n*. ubāru
visualize → **make ~** *v*. apû* (Š), dagālu (Š)
vital *adj*. [ša] balāṭi; → **~ity** *n*. lalû
vitreous *adj*. zakūkāiu+
vivacity *n*. balṭūtu
vivid *adj*. balṭu; → **~ness** *n*. balṭūtu
vivifying *adj*. [ša] balāṭi
vixen *n*. šēlabtu
vizier *n*. šukkallu; → **chief ~** *n*. rab sukkalli; → **grand ~** *n*. šukkallu rabiu
vocation *n*. nibītu*, ummânūtu+
vociferous *adj*. ruṣṣunu*
voice *n*. rigmu; → **~ (from heaven)** *n*. tukku B*; → **~d** *adj*. zamru B*
void *adj*. rāqu; → **~** *n*. rāqtu*; → **~** *v*. nasāku, riāqu (Š); → **is ~** *v*. laššu
volatile *n*. muppaṛšu*
volcano *n*. mappūḫītu+
vole *n*. ḫarriru
volume *n*. epru*

voluntarily *adv.* ḫadīš★, ina ḫadûti
voluntariness *n.* ḫadûtu
voluntary *adj.* ḫadiu
voluptuous *adj.* paḫzu+; → **be ~** *v.* paḫāzu+ (Dt)
vomit *v.* ḫaḫû★, mâ'u★, qiā'u
voracious *adj.* karšānu+
votaress *n.* šēlūtu; → **~ (kind of)** *n.* mašītu; → **master of ~es** *n.* rab mašiāti
votary *n.* šēlūtu; → **~ (kind of)** *n.* mašû B
votive gift *n.* šēlūtu
votive offering *n.* ša-kāribi
vouch *v.* kuānu (D)
vow *v.* tamû
voyage *n.* ḫūlu
vulgar *adj.* paḫzu
vulnerable *adj.* ša maḫāṣi*
vulture *n.* zību
vulva *n.* biṣṣūru★, ḫurdatu★, qallû★, ūru B★
vying *adj.* šitnunu★
wad *n.* itqu, lippu; → **~dle** *v.* duālu+
wade *v.* šalû★; → **~ in(to)** *v.* aḫu ummudu [i.]
wadi *n.* naḫlu
wafer *n.* kamānu
waft *v.* ziāqu
wag one's tail *v.* sabā'u
wage(s) *n.* igrē
wage earner *n.* māḫir igrē*
wagon *n.* ereqqu★, ṣumbu★, tallaktu; → **~ master** *n.* rab tallakti
wail *n.* ṣiriḫtu★; → **~** *v.* bakû (Gtn), damāmu★, nabû★ (D), nasāsu★, nuāqu★, ziāqu; → **~(ing)** *n.* killu; → **~ing** *n.* arūrūtu, bikītu, dimmatu★, girrānu★; → **~ings** *n.* urubāti★
waist *n.* qablu (pl.); → **~-belt** *n.* ṣipirtu (woven)
wait *v.* aqû★, katāru B; → **~ for** *v.* katāru+, pān X dagālu [i.], qa''û, rēšu kullu [i.]; → **~ on** *v.* qa''û; → **~er** *n.* muttabbilu★, šanaptini
wake *v.* ḫarādu; → **~ up** *v.* dakû, nagaltû★; → **~ful** *adj.* ḫardu, mušamšû★; → **~fulness** *n.* ērūtu★, ḫarduttu; → **~n** *v.* êru (D), ḫarādu (D)
waking *adj.* ḫardu
walk *n.* māluku; → **~** *v.* akāšu★, šadāḫu★; → **~ about** *v.* alāku (Gtn); → **~ about about** *v.* alāku (Gtn); → **~ along** *v.* bâ'u★; → **~ away** *v.* alāku (Gtt); → **~ out** *v.* alāku ina qanni [i.]; → **~er** *n.* āliku; → **~ing distance** *n.* māluku
walkout *n.* baṭlu
walkover *n.* kišittu★
walkway *n.* māluku, tallaktu B★
wall *n.* igāru, kikkisu; → **city ~** *n.* amuḫḫu★, dūru; → **stone ~** *n.* dūr abni★; → **supporting ~** *n.* kisû★; → **~-plinth** *n.* samītu★; → **~ cone** *n.* sikkutu; → **~ up** *v.* raṣāpu
wallop *n.* miḫṣu
wallow *v.* nagarruru; → **allow to ~** *v.* nagarruru (Š)
walnut or mulberry(?) *n.* ṣūṣunu
wander *v.* rapādu, sagû+, segû◊; → **~ about** *v.* alāku (Gtn), nagāšu★ (Gtn)
wane → **be(come) ~** *v.* šiāṣu
want *n.* muškēnūtu, sunqu★, ṣummû★; → **~** *v.* ṣaḫātu; → **be(come) in ~** *v.* maṭû; → **~ed** *adj.* ṣaḫtu; → **~ing** *adj.* makiu; → **be(come) ~ing** *v.* maṭû
wanton *adj.* paḫzu+; → **cause to ~** *v.* paḫāzu+ (Š); → **~ness** *n.* paḫzūtu+
war *n.* qarābu+, tuquntu★; → **make ~** *v.* garû★; → **cease from ~** *v.* sakātu+
warble *v.* ṣabāru
ward *n.* piqittu; → **~ off** *v.* etāqu (Š); → **~en** *n.* rabiu; → **~er** *n.* maṣṣuru; → **~robe** *n.* bēt kuzippi
wares *n.* anūtu, udê, unūtu★
warfare *n.* kakku, qablu C★
warhorse *n.* ḫarbakannu, mūrnisqu★
warlike *adj.* dāpinu★, qardu; → **~** *n.* qarābtānu+; → **be(come) ~** *v.* qarādu
warm *adj.* ṣarḫu; → **~** *n.* šaḫīnu+; → **be(come) ~** *v.* ṣarāḫu, šaḫānu◊; → **keep ~** *v.* ṣarāḫu (D); → **~ up** *v.* ṣarāḫu (D)
warmhearted *n.* libbu pašru [i.]
warmly *adv.* ṣarḫiš*
warmonger *n.* kāṣir qarābi*
warmth *n.* ṣurḫu
warn *v.* ḫarādu (D); → **~ing** *n.* tukku B★
warp *n.* dēpu★, šutû [o.]
warrant *n.* šūdûtu+
warrior *n.* muntaḫṣu★, muqtablu★, qarrādu, qurādu, uršānu★; → **~(s)** *n.* ṣāb kakki★
warship *n.* elep qarābi
wart *n.* šullu★ (big)
wary *adj.* etku, pitqudu★; → **be(come) ~** *v.* etāku
wash *n.* mīsu★; → **~** *v.* ḫapāpu◊, masû; → **~ (away)** *v.* šaḫāṭu B; → **~ o.s.** *v.* ramāku; → **~ out** *v.* raḫāṣu B
washbasin *n.* namsētu★, narmaktu
washbowl *n.* namsû★, narmaktu, narmuku [o.]
washed *n.* masiu
washerman *n.* ašlāku
washing *n.* mīsu★; → **~-up** *n.* mīsu★; → **~ place** *n.* namsû★

washout *n.* abbu⋆

wasp *n.* adammumu, nambūbtu

waste *n.* šuḫrubu⋆, ziblu; → ~ *v.* baddudu, ḫarābu⋆ (Š), parāḫu+ (D), rabāku [o.], sapāḫu⋆, šaḫāḫu (D) [o.]; → **lay** ~ *v.* abātu⋆, ḫarābu⋆ (Š), namû B⋆ (D), šaḫruru, šuḫruru⋆; → **into a** ~ *adv.* kišubbāniš⋆, kišubbiš⋆; → **~-basket** *n.* kakkullu; → ~ **away** *v.* balû+, šaḫāḫu; → ~ **bin** *n.* kakkul zibli*; → ~ **matter** *n.* ziblu; → ~ **product** *n.* tuḫḫu; → **~ful** *adj.* mubaddidu*, sappiḫu⋆

wasteland *n.* ḫarbatu⋆, ḫurbu, namûtu⋆, nidūtu⋆; → **like a** ~ *adv.* ḫarbiš⋆

wastrel *n.* musappiḫu⋆

watch *n.* ḫarduttu, maṣṣartu; → ~ *v.* ḫarādu, naṣāru; → **middle** ~ *n.* qablītu; → **morning** ~ *n.* namārītu, šāt urri⋆; → ~- *adj.* nāṣiru; → ~ **out** *v.* ḫarādu (N); → ~ **over** *v.* ḫâṭu⋆; → ~ **over,supervise** *v.* ḫiāṭu⋆; → **~er** *n.* dāgilu; → **river ~er** *n.* dāgil nāri; → **~ful** *adj.* dalpu, ḫardu; → **be(come) ~ful** *v.* etāku; → **~man** *n.* ḫā'iṭu⋆, ḫaiāṭu⋆; → **~tower** *n.* madgaltu, nāmiru, nāmuru

watchword *n.* dibbē lammadūti

water *n.* māmū⋆, mê; → ~ *v.* makāru⋆, raṭābu+ (D), šaqû; → **draw** ~ *v.* dalû, ḫabû; → **cosmic subterranean** ~ *n.* lalgar⋆; → **high** ~ *n.* edû B⋆; → **sea** ~ *n.* mê tānti*; → **spring** ~ *n.* mê ēni; → **underground** ~ *n.* nagbu⋆; → **washing** ~ *n.* musâti⋆; → **~-channel** *n.* rāṭu; → **~-clock** *n.* didibbu; → **~-source** *n.* kuppu⋆; → **~-table** *n.* anzanunzû⋆; → ~ **administrator** *n.* ša-muḫḫi-mê; → ~ **buffalo(?)** *n.* alap kīši⋆; → ~ **channel** *n.* butuqtu⋆; → ~ **closet** *n.* bēt musâti⋆; → ~ **conduit(?)** *n.* butiqtu; → ~ **drawer** *n.* dāliu, ḫābiu; → **woman** ~ **drawer** *n.* ḫābītu; → ~ **drawing device** *n.* dilūtu⋆; → ~ **hole** *n.* namba'u⋆; → ~ **lily(?)** *n.* ašqulālu⋆; → ~ **of delivery** *n.* mê ḫâli; → ~ **scoop** *n.* gidimmu; → ~ **tank** *n.* bēt mê; → ~ **trough** *n.* pisannu; → ~ **vessel** *n.* bukinnu

waterfall *n.* nadbāk mê⋆, nadbāktu, nadbāku, tibku⋆

watering place *n.* mašqītu

waters → **subterranean** ~ *n.* anzanunzû⋆, apsû, asurrakku⋆; → **swamp** ~ *n.* berāti⋆

waterskin *n.* maškuru, mazzā'u, nādu

watertight *adj.* peḫû⋆

watery *adj.* raṭbu

wave *n.* gillu⋆; → ~ *v.* nussusu⋆; → **~r** *v.* narāṭu; → **~r to and fro** *v.* šâbu⋆; → **~s** *n.* rubbu⋆

wavy → **be(come)** ~ *v.* qarāru⋆

wax *n.* iškuru, kusup dišpi

way *n.* alaktu⋆, daraggu⋆, gerru⋆, ḫarrānu, ḫūlu, tallaktu B⋆; → **give** ~ *v.* nâšu⋆, ramû; → **give ~(?)** *v.* nadādu B⋆; → **roundabout** ~ *n.* ḫūlu lābiu*; → ~ **down** *n.* mūraddu⋆; → ~ **in** *n.* nērubu; → ~ **of life** *n.* alaktu⋆; → ~ **out** *n.* mūṣû

wayfarer *n.* ālik ḫūli

waylay *v.* ana šubti šēšubu [i.]

ways *n.* alkakāti⋆

wayward *adj.* šapṣu⋆

we *pron.* anēnu

weak *adj.* enšu⋆, makiu, qatnu; → ~ *n.* anšu; → ~ *n./adj.* ulālu; → **be(come)** ~ *v.* anāšu, kadāru B+, makû, rabābu; → **~en** *v.* anāšu (D), rabābu (Š); → **be(come) ~ened** *v.* nâšu⋆, paḫāḫu; → **~ly** *adv.* anšiš; → **~ness** *n.* anšūtu, enšūtu⋆, makûtu, tānīštu [o.]

wealth *n.* mašrû; → **~y** *adj.* šarû; → **be(come) ~y** *v.* šarû

wean *v.* parāsu; → **~ed** *adj.* parsu; → **~ed child** *n.* pirsu

weapon *n.* kakku; → **(divine)** ~ *n.* miṭṭu; → **clash of ~s** *n.* mitḫuṣ kakkē⋆

wear *v.* kullu (D); → ~ **down** *v.* anāḫu (Š); → ~ **off** *v.* gamāru⋆ (N); → ~ **out** *v.* balû+, marāṭu

wearied → **be(come)** ~ *v.* kadāru B+

wearily *adv.* šūnuḫiš⋆

weariness *n.* anḫūtu, mānaḫtu, mēnēšu, tānīḫu⋆

weary *adj.* anḫu, āniḫu⋆, muqqu⋆, šūnuḫu⋆; → ~ *v.* anāḫu; → **be(come)** ~ *v.* anāḫu, muqqu⋆; → **~-eyed** *adj.* dalpu

weasel *n.* kakkišu

weather *n.* ūmu (pl.); → **cold** ~ *n.* kuṣṣu, takṣiāti; → **rainy** ~ *n.* šarbu

weathercock *n.* iṣṣūr šāri⋆

weave *v.* maḫāṣu B, šatû B⋆; → ~ **colored cloth** *v.* barāmu B⋆ (D); → **~r** *n.* ušpāru; → **chief ~r** *n.* rab ušpāri; → **female ~r** *n.* ušpārtu; → **~r of multicolored trim** *n.* ušpār birmi

weaving *n.* šatūtu [o.]

web *n.* qû B⋆, šētu⋆

wed *v.* aḫāzu; → **~ding** *n.* emūtu⋆, quršu

wedge *n.* aškuttu⋆, santakku⋆, sikkutu+

wee *adj.* qallīlu; → **~d** *n.* uḫīru⋆; → **~d** *v.* nasāḫu; → **~ding** *n.* kismu⋆

week *n.* ḫamussu [o.]

weep *v.* bakû; → **make** ~ *v.* dammû; → **~er** *n.* bakkiu; → **~ing** *n.* bikītu, tēnintu⋆

weevil *n.* ākilu B+

weft *n.* nīru+

weigh *v.* ḫiāṭu, šaqālu⋆; → **~ed out** *adj.* šaqlu⋆; → **~er** *n.* ḫā'iṭānu⋆; → **name of a**

device for ~ing *n.* kaššadūtu; → ~t *n.* kubtu, mašqaltu [o.], šuqultu; → **loss of ~t** *n.* ḫaliqti šīri; → **~t-carrier** *n.* mubabbilu☆; → **~t-lifter** *n.* mubabbilu☆; → **~ty** *adj.* kabtu☆; → **be(come) ~ty** *v.* kabātu☆

weir *n.* erretu B☆, errutu [o.], miḫru; → **~d** *adj.* aḫīu, nakkuru

welcome *adj.* magru, maḫru; → ~ *v.* ḫaṣānu, maḫāru; → *interj.*~ lū maḫrāka*

welfare *n.* šalāmu, šulmu

well *adv.* damqiš [o.], ṭābiš☆; → ~ *n.* būrtu, būru, ēnu, gubbu, nagbu☆; → **keep ~** *v.* šalāmu (D); → **~-being** *n.* šalāmu, šalmūtu☆, šulmu; → **~-bred** *adj.* radiu+; → **~-chosen** *adj.* nussuqu☆; → **~-constructed** *adj.* epšu; → **~-founded** *adj.* rašdu☆; → **~-informed** *adj.* mūdê abiti; → **~-known** *adj.* edû; → **~-meaning** *adj.* ṭābu; → **~-off** *adj.* damqu, šarû; → **~-organized** *adj.* kaṣru; → **~-packed** *adj.* kaṣru, kaṣru [o.]; → **~-to-do** *adj.* damqu; → **~-versed** *adj.* itḫuzu☆, mūdû; → **be ~-versed in** *v.* aḫāzu☆ (Gt); → **~-wisher** *adj.* rā'imu; → **~-wisher** *n.* rā'imānu; → **~ administrator** *n.* ša-būri; → **~ enough** *adv.* maṣi; → **~ guard** *n.* maṣṣar ēni

wench *n.* antu

west *n.* amurru, erēb šamši☆, rabā šamši, šalām šamši☆, šulum šamši☆; → ~ *v.* ana rabā šamši; → **in the ~** *n.* šillān☆; → **~ern** *adj.* [ša] erāb šamši☆

westward(s) *v.* ana rabā šamši

wet *adj.* raṭbu; → ~ *v.* raṭābu+ (D); → **be(come) ~** *v.* raṭābu+; → **~-nurse** *v.* enāqu (Š)

wether *n.* immeru

wetness *n.* raṭībūtu+

wetted through *adj.* raṭṭubu

whack *n.* miḫṣu; → ~ *v.* maḫāṣu

whack, *v.* maḫāṣu

whale *n.* nāḫiru☆, sissû ša tānti☆

wham *n.* tirku

wharf *n.* kāru

what *pron./subj.* bēt, ša

what? *interr.* aiu, mīnu

what else? *interr.* mīnu aḫḫūr

what for? *interr.* mīnu

whatever *pron.* minimmēni, mīnu ša

wheat *n.* kibtu

wheedle *v.* kazābu☆ (D)

wheel *n.* magarru, mugirru; → **~-maker** *n.* naggār magarri

wheeze *v.* ḫalālu B, na'āšu☆

wheezing *n.* ni'šu☆; → ~ *v.* naḫāru☆

whelp *n.* mūrānu

when *adv.* enūma☆, inum☆, inūma☆; → ~ *subj.* akī, bēt, kīma

when? *interr.* immati

whenever *adv.* immatēma, ina matēma

where *subj.* ašar☆, bēt

where? *interr.* aiāka, alê, ali, ēkâ◊, ēkamma◊, ēkānu◊, ēkīam☆

where (from)? *interr.* ajinna☆

where to? *interr.* ajiš☆

whereabouts *n.* bēt ...ni

whereto *adv.* adi bēt; → ~ *subj.* bēt

wherever *adv.* ēma☆

whet *v.* šêlu☆

whether *subj.* kî, šumma, šummu; → **~ ... or** *conj.* šumma ... šumma

whetstone *n.* mušēltu

whey *n.* agakku☆

which? *interr.* aiu

whiff *n.* šīr šumê

while *n.* riggu+; → ~ *subj.* adi, adu; → **~ away** *v.* ūmu šētuqu*; → **~ hot** *adj.* baḫrūssu☆

whilst *prep.* adi, adu

whim *n.* bibil libbi☆; → **~per** *v.* nuāqu☆

whine *n.* inḫu; → ~ *v.* anāḫu, ḫalālu B, lebû☆, nazāqu☆

whinny *v.* nagāgu☆

whip *n.* ištuḫḫu☆, maḫītu, qinnāzu; → ~ *v.* naṭû; → **~-lash** *n.* tamšāru; → **~ container** *n.* bēt maḫītāti

whipcord *n.* tamšāru

whir *v.* zamāmu+

whirl *v.* sâru☆, sâru☆, ṣâdu, ṣâdu (Gtn), ṣâdu◊; → **~ing** *adj.* mummilu☆; → **~ing** *n.* ṣūdu B☆; → **~ing wind (kind of)** *n.* simurru☆

whirlwind *adj.* imsuḫḫu☆

whisker *n.* ziqnu; → **by a ~** *adv.* ubān☆; → **~s** *n.* šārat lēti☆

whisper *n.* liḫšu; → ~ *v.* laḫāšu, ratānu◊

whistle *v.* ḫalālu B

white *adj.* paṣiu; → **be(come) ~** *v.* paṣû; → **be(come) ~-hot** *v.* paṣû; → **~ cedar** *n.* liāru☆, tiālu; → **~ color** *n.* puṣû; → **~ cow** *n.* paṣītu; → **~ glow** *n.* pūṣu; → **~ honey** *n.* lallāru☆; → **~ of the eyes** *n.* pūṣ ēni☆; → **~ spot** *n.* pūṣu; → **~n** *v.* paṣû (D); → **be(come) ~n (itr.)** *v.* paṣû; → **~ness** *n.* puṣû

whitewash *v.* paṣû (D)

whither? *interr.* aiēša, ēkīam☆

whittle *v.* karātu

who *pron.* šūt☆ (he); → ~ *subj.* ša (he)

who? *interr.* mannu

who are you (pl.)? *interr.* ma''attunu

who are you (sg.)? *interr.* ma''atta

who else? *interr.* mannu aḫḫūr

whoever *pron.* mannu ša
whole *adj.* šallumu+, šalmu; → ~ *n.* gimirtu, kalu*, napḫaru*; → ~ *n./adj.* gabbu; → ~ *pron.* kalāma*; → **be(come)** ~ *v.* šalāmu
wholeheartedly *adv.* ina gammurti libbi, ina gum libbi [i.]
wholesome *adj.* mušallimu
wholly *adv.* kalīš*; → ~ *n.* gimirtu
whore *n.* ḫarintu
why? *interr.* atâ, mīnu
wick *n.* būṣinnu, pitiltu+; → **~ed** *adj.* raggu*, ṣalpu*, ṣennu*, šakṣu*; → **be(come) ~ed** *v.* ragāgu*; → **~edness** *n.* lamuttu; → **~erworker** *n.* ḫuppu C
wide *adj.* arku+, palkû*, rapšu, šundulu*; → **be(come)** ~ *v.* napalkû*, rapāšu; → **make** ~ *v.* rapāšu (Š); → **~ly** *adv.* rapšiš*; → **~n** *v.* rapāšu (D), šadālu* (D); → **~spread** *adj.* rapšu
widow *n.* almattu; → **~ed** *adj.* almattu+, almunu+; → **~er** *n.* almānu
width *n.* rupšu
wield *v.* kullu (D), tarāku (Š)
wife *n.* altu, aššatu*, aššutu [o.], ḫīrtu, issu B, marḫītu*; → ~ **of the king** *n.* sēgallu; → **~hood** *n.* issūtu
wig *n.* pursāsu*, upurtu*
wiggle *v.* narāṭu (D)
wild *adj.* ekdu*, kadru*, lā kabsu*, nadru*, nanduru*, šakṣu*, šamru; → **be** ~ *v.* šegû* (N); → **be(come)** ~ *v.* kadāru C*, nadāru*, šamāru*, šegû*
wildcat *n.* murasû
wilderness *n.* madburu+, ṣēru*
wildfire *n.* išāt api*
wildfowl *n.* iṣṣūr ṣēri*
wildlife *n.* nammaššû*, umām ṣēri*
will *n.* giṭṭu+ (parchment), šīmtu, ṭēmu; → ~ *v.* ḫadû; → **be(come)** ~ *v.* ṣabû+; → **make a** ~ *v.* šīmtu šiāmu; → **~ing** *adj.* ḫadiu; → **be(come) ~ing** *v.* ḫadû, ṣabû+; → **~ingly** *adv.* ḫadīš*, ina ḫadûti, ina mūdānūti [i.]
willow *n.* ḫilēpu*; → **~(?)** *n.* šakkullu
wilt → **be(come)** ~ *v.* abālu
wily *adj.* nakkulu+, naklu
win *v.* kašādu, utāru+
wince *v.* garāru, pazāzu+
winch *n.* makūtu
wind *n.* mānitu*, šāru; → ~ *v.* patālu*; → **boisterous** ~ *n.* ziqziqqu*; → **cold** ~ *n.* erijāti*; → **east** ~ *n.* šaddû; → **north** ~ *n.* iltānu*; → **south** ~ *n.* šūtu B; → **storm** ~ *n.* ziqziqqu*; → **west** ~ *n.* amurru; → ~ **(kind of)** *n.* šaparziqqu*; → ~ **up** *v.* kapālu*, qapālu*
windbag *n.* dābib šāri, šārānu
windlass *n.* makūtu
window *n.* aptu; → **through the** ~ *adv.* apāniš*
windpipe *n.* ebbūb ḫašî*, ur'udu*
windward *adj.* pān šāri*
wine *n.* karānu; → **choice** ~ *n.* mutinnu*; → **full-bodied** ~ *n.* karānu ḫabburu; → **~-bud** *n.* samādiru+; → **~-can master** *n.* rab kūtāti; → **(large) ~-jar** *n.* ḫaṣbu+; → ~ **(kind of)** *n.* karān lā'i, lā'u, mēzu, naḫanṣû, sarḫu B; → ~ **cellar** *n.* bēt karāni; → **keeper of the** ~ **cellar** *n.* ša-muḫḫi-kanni; → ~ **flask** *n.* šazamû; → ~ **jar/jug (kind of)** *n.* šapputu; → ~ **master** *n.* rab karāni; → **~skin** *n.* ziqqu; → **~skin raft** *n.* maškuru
wing *n.* abru B*, agappu, isḫu C*, kappu B*, nuballu*; → **take under one's** ~ *v.* kunnupu* (D); → **~ed** *n.* mupparšu*, muštaprišu*, muttaprišu*; → **spread ~s** *v.* ṣapāpu*
wink *v.* barāru, ṣabāru, ṣapāru*; → ~ **at** *v.* ezābu [o.]
winner *n.* kāšidu*
winning *adj.* kuzzubu* (highly)
winnow *v.* našābu*, zarû; → **~(?)** *v.* parāzu; → **shovel for ~ing** *n.* rapšu B*; → **~ing-fan** *n.* rapšu B+
winter *n.* kuṣṣu, takṣiāti
wintry *adj.* [ša] kuṣṣi
wipe *v.* kapāru, šakkulu; → ~ **away** *v.* šamāṭu; → ~ **clean** *v.* kapāru; → ~ **out** *v.* raḫāṣu B, sapānu
wire *n.* ṭurru; → ~ **cable** *n.* guḫaṣṣu
wiry *adj.* šer'ānīu*
wisdom *n.* bišīt uzni*, gigallūtu*, ḫasīsu, ḫassūtu*, mūdûtu*, nēmēqu
wise *adj.* enqu*, eršu B*, gigallu*, ḫāsisu, ḫassu, mūdû, palkû*, šalbābu*, ṭēmānu; → **exceedingly** ~ *adj.* atra ḫasīsi*
wish *adj.* libbu; → ~ *n.* bibil libbi*, izimtu*, mēreštu*, mērešu*, nazmatu*, ṣaḫittu, ṣammuru*, ṣibūtu*, ṣiḫittu, ṣummurtu* (pl.), ṣummuru*; → ~ *v.* ḫadû; → ~ **(for)** *v.* erāšu, ṣabû◊, ṣamāru*; → **be(come)** ~ **(for)** *v.* ṣabû+
wisp *n.* nipšu
wit *n.* pīt ḫasīsi*
witch *n.* kaššāptu, kaššāpu
witchcraft *n.* kišpē
with *prep.* gadu*, ina, ina libbi, issi, itti*; → **~draw** *v.* bêšu*, irtu nê'u [i.], naḫāsu◊, nasāḫu, našāru, nesû*, pa'āṣu, paṣāṣu, ruāqu; → **~drawal** *n.* maššartu*, niširtu*, suḫḫurtu*; → **~drawal(?)** *n.* sinnu*; → **~er** *v.*

abālu, na'āpu☆; → ~ered *adj.* ḫamadīru☆; → **be(come) ~ered** *v.* naḫāru B☆
withhold *v.* kalû
within *prep.* ina, ina libbi, ina qereb☆; → **~ agreed time** *adv.* ṭuppišu
without *prep.* balāt, balu☆, ša lā, šalānu◊, ullânu☆; → **~ any trouble** *adj.* ša lā memmēni; → **~ expense** *adv.* im-magāni+; → **~ permission** *adj.* ša lā, ša lā pî; → **~ question** *adv.* ra'i☆; → **~ respite** *adv.* lā taiār☆; → **~ work** *adj.* ša lā dulli
withstand *v.* maḫāru; → **~ing** *adj.* māḫiru
witless *adj.* lā ḫassu☆
witness *n.* mukinnu, paršumu, šību
wits *n.* pakku B☆
wizard *n.* multēpišu☆
wobble *v.* ṭamû B☆
woe → **~** *interj.* aḫūla, aḫūlamma, ūa
wolf *n.* barburu; → **she- ~** *n.* barbartu☆; → **~-like** *adj.* barbarānu; → **~ish** *adj.* barbarānu
woman *n.* amēltu, issu B; → **like a ~** *adv.* sinnišāniš☆; → **old ~** *n.* paršuntu; → **sacred ~** *n.* qadissu; → **unclean ~** *n.* musukkatu☆; → **wailing ~** *n.* bākītu, lallarītu☆; → **wise ~** *n.* apkallatu☆; → **young ~** *n.* ardatu☆; → **~hood** *n.* issūtu; → **~izer** *n.* naiāku☆
womankind *n.* isāti (pl.)
womanly *adv.* sinnišāniš☆
womb *n.* karšu+, rēmu B☆, šassūru☆, ūru B☆
women's area *n./adj.* bētānu
women's quarters *n.* bēt isāti
women → master of (harem) ~ *n.* rab isāti
won't *gram.part.* lā
wonder *n.* tabrâti☆ (pl.); → **~** *v.* barû B☆ (Gtn); → **~ful** *adj.* babbanû◊, ša tabrâti*; → **~ment** *n.* tabrâti☆ (pl.)
wondrous *adj.* ša tabrâti*
woo *v.* ḫašādu
wood *n.* ēṣu, qissu; → **Indian ~** *n.* sindû☆; → **~-pigeon** *n.* amuršānu☆, tamšīlu; → **~ fretter** *n.* balṭītu; → **~ store** *n.* bēt ēṣi; → **~ed** *n.* ḫalip qissi*; → **~en** *adj.* [ša] ēṣi; → **~pecker** *n.* nāqiru+; → **thick ~s(?)** *n.* armaḫḫu☆; → **~work** *n.* anūt ēṣi; → **~worm** *n.* balṭītu; → **~y** *adj.* [ša] ēṣi
wool *n.* šāptu; → **blue(-green) ~** *n.* uqniāti☆; → **blue-black ~** *n./adj.* ṣalittu; → **colored ~** *n.* barruntu; → **cotton ~** *n.* biršu; → **like red ~** *adv.* nabāsiš☆; → **multicolored ~** *n.* barmāti; → **plucked ~** *n.* gerdu; → **polychrome ~** *n.* tabrīmu; → **red ~** *n.* nabāsu☆, ṣirpu, tabarru☆, tabrību; → **speckled ~** *n.* barmāti; → **tuft of ~** *n.* itqu, nipšu, siggu; → **violet ~** *n.* sūntu; → **yield of ~** *n.* gizzutu; → **~ (color/quality of)** *n.* šeburtu; → **~ (kind of)** *n.* ḫuḫḫurāti, šur'ītu; → **light-blue ~ (kind of)** *n.* urṭû; → **~ felt** *n.* biršu; → **~ trader** *n.* ša-šāpti [o.]; → **~ly** *adj.* [ša] šāpti
word *n.* abutu, amatu☆, inimmû☆, siqru, zikru; → **king's ~** *n.* abat šarri; → **~ing** *n.* dabābu, naqbītu, pû; → **~s** *n.* dibbē
work *n.* dullu, epšetu, lipittu, šipru; → **~** *v.* dullu epāšu [i.]; → **~ assignment** *n.* addû☆, pilku; → **make ~ hard** *v.* anāḫu (Š); → **~ master** *n.* bēl dulli; → **~ out** *v.* epāšu; → **~ procedures** *n.* ṣibittu☆; → **~ song)** *n.* alāla; → **~ up** *v.* ḫamāṭu☆ (Š); → **~ed** *adj.* epšu; → **~er** *n.* ēpiš dulli, ša-šipri [o.]; → **~ing** *n.* epāšu; → **~man** *n.* ēpiš dulli; → **~manship** *n.* epšetu, nēpeštu☆, ummânūtu; → **~shop** *n.* kurḫu; → **temple ~shop** *n.* mummu
world *n.* adnāti☆, kiššatu☆; → **the ~** *n.* kibrāti☆; → **whole ~** *n.* kibrāt erbetti☆; → **~ly** *adj.* [ša] kaqqiri
worldwide *adj.* [ša] kibrāt erbetti☆
worm *n.* sāsu+, tu'issu; → **~ (kind of)** *n.* išqippu
wormwood *n.* sīḫu
worn *adj.* darsu+, labšu☆, qalpu; → **~-out** *adj.* marṭu, šūnuḫu☆
worried *adj.* uššušu☆; → **be(come) ~** *v.* ašāšu☆
worries *n.* niziqtu☆
worry *n.* ašuštu☆, muruṣ libbi, nikittu, nissatu☆, niziqtu☆; → **~** *v.* ašāšu☆ (D), ašāšu☆, ḫâšu B☆ (D), issi libbi dabābu [i.], nakādu, nazāqu☆; → **~ing** *adj.* dāliḫu☆
worse → **be(come) ~** *v.* ba'āšu◊; → **~n** *v.* ba'āšu◊ (D), lamānu (D), samāku (D)
worship *n.* labān appi☆, palāḫ ili; → **~** *v.* appu labānu☆, palāḫu, uqāru+ (D); → **~per** *adj.* pāliḫu; → **~per(?)** *n.* bēl palluḫi
worst *adj.* lamnu
worth *n.* simtu (person or thing); → **be(come) ~** *v.* ammār X maṣû (stat.) [i.]; → **~less** *adj.* rāqu, šēṭu+; → **~y of** *adj.* simtu (person or thing); → **~y ornament** *n.* usmu☆
would *gram.part.* lū
wound *n.* miḫṣu, pitḫu, simmu; → **~** *v.* maḫāṣu, ṣalāpu+; → **septic ~** *n.* urāšu☆; → **~ed** *adj.* maḫṣu; → **~ed** *n.* ṣalīpu+
woven material *n.* šutû [o.]
wow *n.* māmītu☆
wrangle *v.* ṣâlu [o.], ṣāssu garû
wrap *n.* ḫullānu, qirmu; → **~ (up)** *v.* ḫalāpu☆, kanānu☆, karāku, karāku+, labû, panāgu, šapû B☆; → **~per** *n.* mašlû☆, nalbētu [o.],

šaddīnu+; → ~ping *n.* ḫillu, libītu [o.], nalbētu [o.], ṭīpu*; → ~ping (kind of) *n.* taḫbātu*
wrath *n.* ibbû, libbāti, nuggatu*, šibistu*, uggatu*, uzzu*
wreath *n.* kilīlu+; → **like a ~** *adv.* kilīliš*
wreck *n.* niqru*; → ~ *v.* naqāru* (Š); → **~age** *n.* niqru*; → **~er** *n.* nāqiru*
wrench *v.* dapānu+ (D); → **~ out** *v.* ekēmu*
wrest *v.* puāgu
wrestle (with) *v.* ṣabātu* (Gt), šapāṣu* (Gt)
wrestler *n.* muštapṣu*, ša-abāri*, ša-umāši
wrestling *n.* šitpuṣu*
wretch *n.* muškēnu; → **~ed** *adj.* ašišû*, dallu*, nassu*, pisnuqu*, šaplu+; → **~ed** *n.* muškēnu+; → **be(come) ~ed** *v.* dalālu B*; → **~edly** *adv.* pisnuqiš*
wriggle *v.* ḫiālu
wring *v.* mazā'u; → **~er** *n.* mazūru*
wrinkle *v.* ganāṣu* (Dt); → **~d** *adj.* qaplu+
wrist *n.* rittu
writ *n.* šaṭṭāru
write *v.* šaṭāru; → **~ (songs)** *v.* rakābu+ (D); → **~ down** *v.* ana ḫissiti šaṭāru [i.], šaṭāru; → **~ to** *v.* šapāru; → **~r** *n.* šāṭiru
writhe *v.* ḫiālu
writing *n.* šaṭṭāru, šiṭirtu*, šiṭru*; → **~ board** *n.* gištû*, lē'u; → **~ reed** *n.* qarṭuppu
written *adj.* šaṭru; → **have ~** *v.* šaṭāru* (D), šaṭāru* (Š); → **~ down** *adj.* šaṭru; → **~ name** *n.* šumu šaṭru*
wrong *n.* ḫabālu*, ḫibiltu*; → ~ *v.* ḫabālu B; → **do ~** *v.* ḫaṭû; → **~ moment** *n.* lā simunu; → **~doer** *n.* bēl arni*, bēl lemutti*, ḫabbilu*; → **~doing** *n.* ḫabālu*, ḫibiltu*; → **~ed** *adj.* dullulu.*; → **~ful possessions** *n.* ḫinsāti
wrought up *adj.* dalḫu+
Yafo *n.* Iappû
yak *adv.* burṭiš
yank *v.* pašānu*, šalāḫu
yard *n.* tarbāṣu
yardarm *n.* karû C*
yarn *n.* ṭību, ṭimītu
yawn *v.* puāqu+; → **~ing** *n.* pūqu+
ye *pron.* atta (m.), attunu (pl.)
yea *n.* anni*
year *n.* šattu; → **eponym ~** *n.* limmu; → **every ~** *adj.* ša šatti ša šatti; → **~ after year** *n.* šattu ana šatti; → **the ~ before last** *adv.* šallašatti◊, šaluššeni; → **~ by year** *adv.* šattišam*; → **~ling** *n.* mār šatti (m.), mar'at šatti (f.); → **~ly** *adj.* ša šatti; → **~ly** *adv.* šattišam*
yearn → **~ (for)** *v.* puqqu; → **~ing** *n.* puqqu*
yeast *n.* saḫimtu*, sikkatu
yell *v.* ragāmu
yellow *n./adj.* erqu; → **be(come) ~** *v.* erāqu; → **~ paste** *n.* šīpu B*; → **~ish** *adj.* erqu
yelp *v.* nabāḫu◊
yes *n.* annu, kēn*
yesterday *adv.* ina timāli, ittimāli, timāli
yet *adv.* adīni◊
yield *n.* biltu, ḫiṣbu*, tēlītu; → ~ *v.* naḫāsu◊, salāmu+; → **~ing** *adj.* kanšu*, māgiru, nurrubu*
yoke *n.* abšānu*, apšānu*, nīru; → ~ *v.* ṣamādu; → **~ finial** *n.* ša-muḫḫi-nīri
yolk (of an egg) *n.* mūqaru+
yonder *adv.* aḫūla
you *pron.* atta (m.), kanāšunu, kāša; → **~ (f.)** *pron.* atti (f.), kāši; → **~ (pl.)** *pron.* attunu (pl.), kāšunu; → **~ng** *adj.* ṣeḫḫeru, šūbulti inbi*; → **be(come) ~ng** *v.* ṣaḫāru; → **~ng (of animals)** *n.* lidānu, suḫīru*; → **~nger** *adj.* tardennu*; → **~ngster** *n.* batūlu; → **~r** *pron./adj.* ikkanû, ikkû; → **~rs** *pron./adj.* ikkanû, ikkû; → **~rself** *pron.* ramanka; → **~rselves** *pron.* ramankunu; → **~th** *n.* batūlu, ṣaḫūrānūtu, ṣaḫurtu, ṣeḫēru*, ṣuḫrītu*, ṣuḫru*, ṣuḫurtu; → **~thful** *adj.* ṣaḫūrānīu*
yowl *v.* nazāqu*, ṣarāḫu B*
zeal *n.* uzzu*; → **~ous** *adj.* qāni'u*
zenith *n.* elât šamê*, ziqpu
ziggurat *n.* siqqurrutu; → **~-shaped cake** *n.* siqqurrutu B
zither *n.* kinnāru*
zodiac *n.* kilīl lumāšē+; → **sign of the ~** *n.* lumāšu; → **~al circle** *n.* kilīl lumāšē+; → **~al sign** *n.* lumāšu
zone *n.* pilku

ASSYRIAN – ENGLISH

a'āšu* *v.* $^{a/a}$ (Gtn) to retch
ab ab-abi* *n. cp.* great-grandfather
ab-abi *n. cp.* grandfather; (pl.) grandparents
ab-ummi* *n. cp.* maternal grandfather
abāku  *v.* $^{a/u}$ to lead away, leave out, drive away, remove; to lead in, to deduce*; (D) to shift to, to displace*
abāku B* *v.* $^{a/u}$ to overturn, upset
abālu  *v.* $^{a/a}$ to be dry, to shrivel*, wilt*, wither*; (D) to dry up
abālu B*  *v.* $^{a/i}$ to carry, bring; (Gtn) to handle, direct, treat, steer, manage; (Š) to send, dispatch; (Št) to discuss; to consider, deliberate, ponder, cogitate, contemplate, meditate, muse upon, think
aban balti  *n. cp.* stone of pride, jewel
aban gabê* *n. cp.* alum
aban ḫālti  *n. cp.* amulet for childbirth
aban lamassi  *n. cp.* amulet stone
aban muštinni* *n. cp.* bladder stone
aban nisiqti* *n. cp.* choice gem, jewel, precious stone
aban nurmî* *n. cp.* pomegranate pip
aban rāmi  *n. cp.* love charm, love stone
aban šadî* *n. cp.* mountain stone, rock
aban šamê* *n. cp.* hailstones
abārāiu+ *adj.* leaden, lead-gray, livid, drab
abarakku* 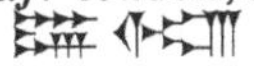 *n.* steward, treasurer
abāru  *n.* lead
abāru B* *n.* strength, energy, stamina
abašmu 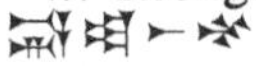 *n.* moonstone
abat libbi *n. cp.* thought*
abat ṣāssi *n. cp.* controversial subject*, moot point*
abat šarri *n. cp.* king's word, king's affair
abattu *nf.* river-gravel, slingstone, stone
abātu*  *v.* $^{a/u}$ to destroy, lay waste, ruin; (D) to devastate; (N) to collapse, fall down; to run away, flee
abbu* *n.* swamp(?), washout
abbūtu  *nf.* fatherhood, patronage, patrocinium; intercession
abbūtu+ *nf.* paternity
abbūtu ṣabātu‡ *vp.* to intercede, speak for
abiktu 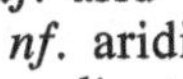 *nf.* defeat
abiūru 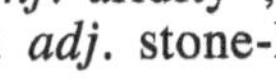 *n.* (a plant)
ablu *adj.* arid
ablūtu *nf.* aridity*, drought*
abnānu *adj.* stone-like, rocky, stony

abnu  *n.* ^{3}, *nf.* stone, rock, mineral; hail; gem, pearl; pip, kernel, fruit-stone; counter, stoneware
abnu aqartu* *np. f.* precious stone, gem, jewel
abrakkatu* *nf.* female housekeeper; courtesan
abrakkūtu* *nf.* concubinage, courtesanship; housekeeping
abrāti* *n. pl.* mankind
abriš* *adv.* like a brushwood pile
abru  *n.* brush pile
abru B* *n.* ^{1} wing, plume, pinion; fin
abru B+ *n.* ^{1} feather
abšānu* *n.* yoke, harness
abšu  *n.* ^{1} lentil
abtāti* *n. pl.* ruins
abtu* *adj.* decayed, ruined
abtu+ *adj.* extinct
abtūtu* *nf.* annihilation
abtūtu+ *nf.* extinction
abu  *n.* father; sire; (pl.) forefather, ancestor, antecedent
Ābu *n.* (month) Ab, August
abu ummu *np.* parents
abūbāniš* *adv.* like a flood
abūbu  *n.* $^{1/2}$ flood, deluge; Flood monster, emergency*
abuḫšinnu  *n.* (a cereal harvested when green)
abullu 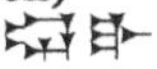 *nf.* city gate, gateway
abullu+ *nf.* front door, milestone
abunnutu* *nf.* umbilical cord, navel, belly button; center
aburriš*  *adv.* in safety
aburru* *n.* pasture
abusāti *n. pl.* storehouse
abussāti *n. pl.* forelock
abutu  *nf.* word, matter, affair; statement; motif, subject, topic
abutu ana abiti *adv.* verbatim*
abutu kunnutu *np. f.* sure thing, certainty, fact
abutu qallissu *np. f.* trifle
adadānu *adj.* stormy, tempestuous, thundery, thunderous
adakanni *adv.* until now, so far
adakurru  *n.* (a container used in cult)
adammumu  *n.* ^{3} wasp
adanniš  *adv.* very, quite; greatly, intensely, exceptionally*, remarkably*
adanniš adanniš *adv.* exceedingly, exceptionally, extremely
adannu  *n.* ^{3} term, deadline,

date; period, cycle, phase*, tract*
adannu+ *n.* ^{3} time
adannu šakānu *vp.* set a date, make an appointment
adannūtu *nf.* periodicity*
adappu* *n.* crossbeam; board, plate
adāru *v.* $^{a/u}$ to be dark, be gloomy, be afraid
adāru* *v.* $^{a/u}$ (Š) to darken; (Št) to become gloomy; (N) to be eclipsed
adāru *v.* $^{a/u}$ (D) to darken; (Dtt) to be gloomy, keep in the dark
adāru B *n.* poplar
adāru C* *v.* $^{a/u}$ to fear; to respect, revere
adattu *nf.* reed stalk
addānika *int.* attention, please
Addāru *n.* (month) Adar, March
Addāru diri *n.* intercalary Adar
addu* *n.* thunder, thunderstorm
addû* *n.* work assignment, day's work, stint
adê *n. pl.* treaty, covenant, pact, compact, pledge of allegiance
adi akanni *adv.* until now, so far
adi bēt *subj.* until; whereto
adi ešrīšu *adv.* ten times
adi lā *subj.* by, even before
adi lā bašê* *adv.* until non-existence
adi maḫar* *prp.* up to
adi namiranni *adv.* until dawn
adi ṭuppišu *adv.* punctually
adi, adu *prp.* until, till; during, while, whilst; as far as; plus, including, together with, along with
adinakanni *adv.* until now, so far
adīni◊ *adv.* yet
adīriš* *adv.* in fear
ādiru* *adj.* timorous, fearful, afraid
adnāti* *n. pl.* world
adriš* *adv.* darkly, unhappily; dimly
adru *adj.* threshing floor
adru B *nf.* dark, gloomy, sombre; sad, dreary, mournful, glum, sullen; cheerless, unhappy, bleak*, crabby*, grouchy*, grumpy*, moody*, sulky*, surly*
adû◊ *adv.* now
adu bēt *subj.* until
adu lā *subj.* by, even before
adu muḫḫi *prp.* as far as, until
adūgāiu+ *adj.* hellish
adūgu* *n.* oven
adūgu+ *n.* focus, portable stove
agâ◊ *pron.* this
agāgu* *v.* $^{a/u}$ to be angry, be furious, rage; (D) to anger, enrage, infuriate, madden, to rile*
agakku* *n.* whey
agālu* *n.* ^{1} riding donkey
agammu *n.* marsh, lagoon, pool
agannu *n.* ^{3} amphora
agannû◊ *pron.* this
aganutillû* *n.* dropsy
agap ēni* *n. cp.* eyelash, lash
agappu *n.* ^{2} wing
agappu+ *n.* ^{2} fin, pen
agarinnu* *nf.* mother
agarinnu B* *n.* beer mash
agāru *v.* $^{a/u}$ to hire, rent
agasalakku* *n.* (a kind of axe)
agâtu◊ *pron. f.* this
aggiš* *adv.* angrily, grimly
aggu* *adj.* angry, furious, hot-tempered, irascible, quick-tempered, short-tempered, snappish
Agru* *n.* Aries
agru *n.* ^{4} hired man, hireling, farm-hand; Aries
agû *n.* crown, tiara
aguḫḫu* *n.* girdle, diadem
agur ešmarê* *n. cp.* yellow-glazed brick
agur uqnî* *n. cp.* blue-glazed brick
agurru* *n.*, *nf.* burnt brick, tile
agurrutu *nf.* ewe
agû B* *n.* flood-wave, tide, roller, breaker, surf
aḫ tānti* *n. cp.* lakeside, seaside
aḫ-abi *n. cp.* uncle
aḫ-ummi *n. cp.* maternal uncle
aḫāiš *adv.* each other, one another; mutually
aḫāiš apālu *vp.* to correspond; (Gtn) to reciprocate
aḫāiš katāmu *vp.* overlap*
aḫāiš uppušu *vp.* to interact*
aḫamma *adv.* separately, apart, moreover
aḫānāiu+ *adj.* fraternal
aḫannâ* *adv.* on this side/bank
aḫāt abi *n. cp.* aunt
aḫāt aḫi *n. cp.* brother's sister
aḫāt ummi *n. cp.* aunt
aḫātānu* *adj.* sisterly
aḫātu *nf.* sister
aḫātūtu *nf.* sisterhood
aḫātu B* *nf.* bank, shore
aḫāzu *v.* $^{a/u}$ to grasp, embrace; to marry, espouse, wed; to learn, apprehend; to get, gain, earn, merit

aḫāzu*  *v.* $^{a/u}$ to take, seize; (Gt) to be connected with; to be experienced, well versed in; (Š) to incite, induce
aḫāzu  *v.* $^{a/u}$ (D) to mount, plate, coat with, inlay; (Š) to attach, kindle
aḫê◊  *adv.* separately
aḫennâ* *adv.* each separately, singly
aḫḫāzu* *n.* seizer (a demon); jaundice
aḫḫūr  *adv.* still
aḫḫūtu  *nf.* brotherhood, brotherliness, brotherly relations or relationship, coalition*, coexistence*
aḫḫūtu+ *nf.* fellowship, fraternity
aḫia aḫia◊ *adv.* side by side, abreast
aḫītа† *adv.* aside, elsewhere, incidentally*
aḫītu  *nf.* side, flank, margin*, oddity*; (pl.) surroundings, environment
aḫīu *adj.* strange, unaccustomed, unfamiliar, curious, odd, peculiar; abnormal, unusual, weird, queer, eerie; extraneous, uncanonical; stranger, outsider, unearthly*
aḫrātaš* 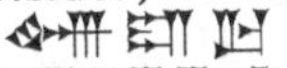 *adv.* for posterity
aḫrāti*  *n. pl.* future
aḫu  *n.* brother, colleague, fellow
aḫû*  *v.* (Gt) to become brothers, befriend, chum, fraternize, make friends, pal up
aḫu+ *n.* associate, companion, friend, kinsman
aḫu tabālu‡ *vp.* to interfere, intermeddle
aḫu ubālu‡ *vp.* to interfere, meddle, tamper, encroach
aḫu ummudu‡ *vp.* to put hands on, engage in, get down to, get started with, commence, set in, set to, start out, start up, tackle, take to, wade in[to]
aḫūla  *adv., int.* beyond, yonder; woe, alas
aḫūla tānti *adv.* overseas*
aḫūlamma *adv., int.* on the other side; woe, alas
aḫulap* *int.* enough!
aḫullâ  *adv.* beyond, on the other shore or bank
aḫullû◊ *adv.* beyond, on the other shore or bank
aḫurrû* *n.* junior, inferior (one)
aḫussu* *nf.* soda
aḫu B  *n.* ^{1} arm; side, flank; bank, coast; sleeve, armhole flap; energy, force, manpower; (pl.) forces, army
aḫzu◊ *adj.* married
ai*  *part.* may not
aiābu*  *n.* ^{1} enemy
aiāka  *q.* where?, how?
aiākamēni *adv.* anywhere, everywhere
aiākamēni lā *adv.* nowhere
aiakku  *n.* shrine, temple
aiālu  *n.* help, aid
aiar ili  *n. cp.* chameleon
aiartu 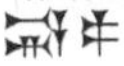 *nf.* shell
Aiāru *n.* (month) Iyyar, May
aiārurutu  *nf.* shout
aiāši  *obl. pron.* me
aiēša  *q.* whither?
aiu  *q.* what?, which?
aiulu  *n.* stag
aiumma*  *pron.* any, anyone
aiuru 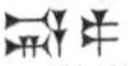 *n.* ^{1} rosette, flower
ajinna*  *q.* where (from)?
ajiš* *q.* where to?
akāl karṣē *n. cp.* slander, backbiting, denunciation
akāl karṣē+ *n. cp.* backbiting
akālu  *v.* $^{a/u}$ to eat, gorge, devour; to enjoy; to hurt, irritate; to ravage, disfigure; to erode; to consume, expend, outlay, spend, use up, utilize; (Gtn) to tuck in; (Š) to feed, nourish
akālu+ *v.* $^{a/u}$ to corrode, embezzle, fret, hurt, squander
akālu n. *n.* food, nourishment, nutriment
akālu šatû *vp.* to dine
akāmu* *n.* dust-cloud, mist
akanna◊  *adv.* here
akannaka◊ *adv.* there
akanni  *adv.* now, nowadays
akāšu* *v.* $^{u/u}$ to go, move, walk
akbarāiu+ *adj.* ratty
akbartu *nf.* female jerboa
akburu  *n.* ^{1} jerboa
akburu+ *n.* ^{1} mouse, field mouse
akē *adv.* so
akê  *int., q.* how?
akêmēni* *adv.* somehow
akī  *prp., subj.* when; as; as if; like
akî *adv.* thus
akī ša *subj.* (just) as
ākil amēli *n. cp.* cannibal*
ākil karṣē *n. cp.* slanderer
ākil simini *adj. cp.* time-consuming*
ākil šīri *adj. cp.* carnivorous*
akiltu  *nf.* consumption, expenditure, expenses, outlay
ākilu  *adj.* eating, man-eating; consuming, corrosive
ākilu B *n.* (a field pest)
ākilu B+ *n.* bookworm, cheese-mite, maggot, moth, weevil

akītu  *nf.* festival house; victory festival
akkadāiu *adj.* Akkadian
akkadatti◊ *adv.* in Akkadian (writing)
akkadīja* *n.* cock, rooster
akkadītu *nf.* Akkadian (language)
akkadītu* *nf.* hen
akkā'i◊  *q.* how?
akkannu 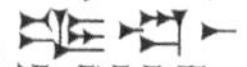 *n.* wild donkey
akkilu*  *n.* glutton
akkilūtu *nf.* gluttony*
akkû*  *n.* (a kind of owl)
akkullānu *adj.* hatchety, hatchet-faced
akkullu  *n.* $^{1/3}$ hatchet, pickaxe, adze, sledgehammer*
aklu  *n.* ^{1} bread, loaf
aklu a. *adj.* eaten, consumed; emaciated, skinny, haggard
akṣu* *adj.* dangerous, terrible, overbearing, brazen, unruly
akukūtu  *nf.* red glow, blaze, aurora borealis
akullû  *n.* food, food allowance, alimentation, livelihood
akussu  *nf.* soup, broth
āl bēlūti* *n. cp.* royal city, capital, city of government
āl kidinni* *n. cp.* privileged city
āl palê◊ *n. cp.* dynastic city
āl tuklāti* *n. cp.* supply city
āl tukulti* *n. cp.* (military) base
aladlammû  *n.* bull colossus
alādu*  *v.* $^{a/i}$ to give birth, bear (young); (N) to be born
ālāiu  *n.* townsman, villager
alāk dāmi *n. cp.* hemorrhage*
alāk pāni *n. cp.* headway*
alaktu  *nf.* caravan; business, trip; traffic;
alaktu*  *nf.* access, way, course; way of life, behavior, gait, manner; passage, movement
alāku  *v.* $^{a/i}$ to go, move, march, hike, fare, travel, journey; to go by, elapse, pass off; to be possible, be feasible; (Gtn) to roam, ramble, wander, walk, walk about, march about, drift about, saunter, stroll; (Gtt) to go away, leave, go off, walk away; (Š) to move; (vent.) to come
alāku ina qanni‡ *vp.* to walk out
alāku n. *n.* advance, progress, passage, motion
alāku nammušīšu‡ *vp.* to pass away
alāku (ša dāmi)‡ *v.* to bleed

alāla *n.* harvest song, work song
alālu  *v.* $^{a/u}$ to hang up, suspend
alālu*  *v.* $^{a/u}$ (Gt) to be girt
alālu B*  *v.* (Gt) to sing a joyful song
alamittu* *nf.* (a wild species of date palm)
alamû* 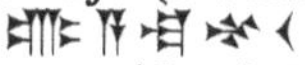 *n.* (a plant)
alandimmû*  *n.* form; physiognomy
alap epinni  *n. cp.* draught ox
alap kīši* *n. cp.* water buffalo(?)
alap nāri* *n. cp.* water, river ox
alappānu  *n.* bittersweet beer
alātu* *v.* $^{u/u}$ to absorb, swallow (up)
alê *q.* where?
algumiš* *n.* (a piece of jewellery)
ali  *q.* where?
ālidu  *n.* ^{4} begetter, progenitor, parent; breeder, stud
ālidūtu *nf.* maternity*, parenthood*
ālik ḫūli *n. cp.* traveller, wayfarer, passenger
ālik ilki  *n. cp.* conscript, performer of military or civil service
ālik maḫri* *n. cp.* predecessor
ālik pāni  *n. cp.* leader; antecedent, predecessor, precursor
ālik pānûtu◊ *nf. cp.* leadership, primacy, precedence, priority
ālik tappūti* *n. cp.* helper
ālik urḫi* *n. cp.* traveller
āliku *adj., n.* going, moving; goer, passenger, walker, pedestrian, tourist
ālilu* *n.* brave
ālissu  *nf.* bearing mother, progenitress
ālittu* *nf.* progenitress; she-duck
ālittu a.* *adj.f.* fertile
alkakāt qurdi* *n. cp. pl.* heroic deeds
alkakāti* *n. pl.* actions, manners, ways
alla◊  *prp.* except, beyond, apart from, over
allāku* *n.* traveller, messenger
allāku† *n.* agent
allāku+ *n.* pedestrian
allallu* *adj., n.* brave, powerful
allallu B* *n.* (a bird)
allān† *prp.* except for
allān kāniš *n. cp.* Kani& oak
allānātu† *nf.* (twelfth month)
allānu  *n.* oak, acorn
allānu* *n.* suppository
allu 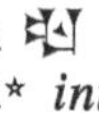 *n.* hoe; (a piece of jewellery)
allû* *int.* hallo, hello, hullo
allunāti† *nf. pl.* pincers, pliers*, twee-

zers*

alluttu *n.*^{3} crab; Cancer

almānu *n.* widower

almattu *nf.* widow

almattu+ *nf.* widowed

almunu+ *n.* widowed

alpu *n.*^{2} ox

alti aḫi* *nf. cp.* sister-in-law

altu *nf.* wife

alṭu* *adj.* obdurate, headstrong

a'lu* *n.* confederation

alû *n.* bull of heaven; Taurus; (a demon)

ālu *n.*^{2} city, town, township, village

alūtu *n.*^{1} (a kind of vessel or container)

aluzinnu* *n.* buffoon, clown, comedian, entertainer, jester, joker, jokester, mime

aluzinnutu *nf.* comedienne*

amāmû* *n.* mascara

amānu *n.* red salt

amāru *v.*$^{a/u}$ to see, inspect, observe; to experience; to look up, find, find out, choose, select, to browse*, skim [through]*; (N) to appear, reappear, turn up, occur; to meet with

amāru B *n.*^{1} sidepiece

amāru C* *n.* pile of bricks

amāšu* *v.* to be cataleptic

amat ēkalli *nf. cp.* palace maid

amat qibīt ilūti* *nf. cp.* prophecy

amatu* *nf.* word, matter

amatu šutābulu‡ *vp.* to consider thoroughly, to ponder, to deliberate, to discuss

ambassu *n.* game preserve, park

amēlānu *adj.* courteous, gentlemanlike, gentlemanly, human

amēliš* *adv.* like man

amēltu *nf.* woman, gentlewoman

amēlu *n.*^{1} man, person, human being, gentleman

amēlūtu *nf.* mankind, humanity, the human species

amīlānu* *n.* (a medicinal plant)

āmir dāmi* *n. cp.* blood-thirster, hunter for blood

āmirānu† *n.* eyewitness, eye-witness

amirtu* *nf.* inspection, observation; inventory, check-list

ammāka *adv.* there, thereabout[s]

ammār *pron., prp.* as much/many as; approximately, roughly, about

ammār ...ni *subj.* as much/many as, all ... who/that

ammār ammiti *np.* ell-wide, ell-long

ammār durā'i+ *np.* armful

ammār itqūri *np.* spoonful*

ammār pî *np.* mouthful*

ammār rūṭi *np.* about a span, a little, just a little

ammār takālti *np.* pocketful*

ammār ubāni *np.* fingerbreath

ammār X maṣû‡ *vp.* to achieve, attain, reach; (stat.) to be worth, be capable of

ammēša *adv.* thither

ammiu *pron.* that

ammutu *nf.* forearm, cubit, ell

ammutu rabītu *np.f.* big cubit

amru *adj.* seen, chosen, inspected; experienced

amtu* *nf.* maid, slave-girl, female servant

amu◊ *n.*^{3} raft

amû* *v.*$^{u/u}$ to speak; (Gt) to discuss; (Št) to ponder

amuḫḫu* *n.* city wall, enceinte

amūmu *n.* (a kind of beer)

amurdinnālu+ *adj.* rosy, rosaceous

amurdinnu *n.* bramble

amurdinnu+ *n.* rose

amurriqānu* *n.* jaundice

amurru *n.* west wind, west, southwest

amuršānu* *n.* wild pigeon, stock-dove, wood-pigeon

amūtu* *nf.* liver

amūtu B† *nf.* meteoric iron

an-akanna◊ *adv.* hither

ana *prp.* to, into, unto, towards, for

ana aḫāmiš qerēbu‡ *vp.* to conclude an alliance

ana annēša *adv.* hither

ana ašrīšu turru‡ *vp.* to restore to a previous position, re-establish, renovate

ana bādi *adv.* in the evening

ana batqi ṣabātu‡ *vp.* to take as replacement

ana bētāni *adv.* inwardly, inwards

ana bēti *adv.* homeward[s]*

ana dāriš* *adv.* forever

ana dūr dāri* *adv.* forever

ana eliš *adv.* upwards

ana ešrāti *adv.* tenfold

ana eššūti* *adv.* anew, newly

ana eššūti ṣabātu* *vp.* to reorganize

ana gammurti *adv.* altogether, completely, downright, overall, throughout

ana ḫissiti šaṭāru‡ *vp.* to jot down, note

down, put down, write down
ana ḫiṭṭi šakānu‡ *vp.* to castigate
ana ḫiṭṭi tuāru‡ *vp.* to recoil on
ana ḫūru *adv.* still
ana iānummeš *adv.* (an adverb, mng. unkn.)
ana kallie *adv.* posthaste, by express, by post, speedily
ana kallie šēbulu *vp.* to send post-haste, post, mail
ana kibri emādu‡ *vp.* to disembark, land
ana kutalli neḫēsu◊ *vp.* to retreat
ana lā ālidi/ālitti turru‡ *vp.* to sterilize
ana lā amāri‡ *adv.* confidentially, discreetly, invisibly, imperceptibly
ana lā māni* *adv.* countless
ana lā mīni* *adv.* countless (times)
ana maḫirti *adv.* upstream
ana māla *adv.* altogether, totally, utterly
ana māla duāku‡ *vp.* to discomfit, defeat completely
ana mar'ūti laqû‡ *vp.* to adopt
ana masikti† *adv.* blasphemously, disgracefully
ana mēt *adv.* per cent
ana minâtīšu* *adv.* comparatively, relatively
ana mišlāni parāsu‡ *vp.* to halve
ana mitḫār *adv.* equally, by the same amount, one-to-one
ana nēša *adv.* hither
ana pāni *adv.* forwards
ana pāni alāku‡ *vp.* go ahead, advance, proceed, progress
ana qanni *adv.* out, outdoors, outward[s]
ana qāti mallû‡ *vp.* to hand over
ana qinniš *adv.* aback, backward[s]
ana qinniš alāku‡ *vp.* to be in vain, fail, regress, retrogress
ana qinniš saḫāru‡ *vp.* to retrograde, turn back
ana qinniš saḫḫuru‡ *vp.* to reverse
ana rabā šamši *adv.* to the sunset, to west, westward[s]
ana rēmi šakānu‡ *vp.* to make find mercy
ana rēšūti alāku‡ *vp.* to become a slave; (Š) to enslave
ana sadīr aḫāiš *adv.* in chronological order, in sequence
ana simini *adv.* temporarily*
ana ṣirê◊ *adv.* galore, full to the brim, to the limit
ana ṣirê mallû‡ *vp.* to fill to the brim
ana ṣirê malû‡ *vp.* to be fed up, be at the end of the tether; brim, brim over; overflow
ana ṣīt šamši *adv.* eastward[s], to the east
ana ṣuḫīti šakānu‡ *vp.* to be made a laughingstock, object of mockery
ana ṣuḫri turru‡ *vp.* (D) to rejuvenate
ana ša-rēši turru‡ *vp.* to castrate
ana šaparti šakānu *vp.* to mortgage, pledge
ana šapliš *adv.* downwards
ana šiddi X naṭālu† *vp.* to keep an eye on
ana šīmti alāku‡ *vp.* to die a natural death
ana šinīšu *adv.* in two, in half; pair of; of two kinds
ana šubti šēšubu‡ *vp.* to waylay
ana šupāl* *adv.* downwards
ana tarṣi◊ *prp.* over against, towards; during
ana ūmi *adv.* on schedule, promptly
ana urdānūti kabāsu‡ *vp.* to enslave
ana zaqīpē šēlû* *vp.* to impale
ana zaqīpi šakānu *vp.* to impale; to hang
ana ziqīpi zaqqupu* *vp.* to impale
ana X kullu‡ *vp.* to consider, regard as
ana X mašālu‡ *vp.* to take after
ana/ina pūḫi našû‡ *v.* to borrow, take as a loan
anāḫu  *v.* a/a to be weary, be tired, be exhausted, tire, run down; to labor, toil, overwork, take trouble, weary; to sigh, whine; to become dilapidated
anāḫu*  *v.* a/a (Št) to endure, last, outlast, take (time), hold [out], to take pains, makean effort
anāḫu  *v.* a/a (Š) to exhaust, wear down, exert, tire s.o., frustrate, make work hard, overwork
anāku  *pron.* I, ego*
anāqutu  *nf.* she-camel
anāšu  *v.* i/i to be weak, dilapidated; (D) to weaken, deaden, impair
anāšu+ *v.* i/i (D) to enfeeble
andaḫšu  *n.* [1] small onion, crocus(?)
anduḫallutu  *nf.* (a type of lizard)
andurāru*  *n.* debt remission
anēnu *pron.* we
angāšu  *n.* plum
angāšu+ *n.* pear
angubbû* *n.* (a constellation; a class of priests)
anḫu *adj.* exhausted, weary, run-down, haggard, jaded, fatigued
anḫullīmu *n.* (a medicinal plant)
anḫullu* *n.* storm, hurricane, tornado
anḫurašru  *n.* (a climbing plant)

anḫūtu *nf.* exhaustion, fatigue, weariness; dilapidation
ānīḫu* *adj.* tiring, weary
anīna *int.* hear me!
ankūnu *n.* (a metal object)
annāka *adv.* here, hereabouts
annēša *adv.* hither
anni* *int.* ay[e], yea
annīu *pron.* this
annīumma *pron.* same
annu *n.* consent, assent, approval; yes, sanction*
annu⁺ *int.* ay[e]
annu kēnu *np.* positive answer, affirmative
annuku *n.* lead, tin
annūrig *adv.* at present, at the moment, just, (just) now, presently, this instant
annūti ... annūti *pron.* some ... others
annu B* *n.* crime, punishment
anpatu* *n.* (a bird)
anpatu⁺ *n.* heron, egret
anqullu *n.* glow, fire
anqullu* *n.* feverish heat, fiery glow
anṣabtu *nf.* earring
anšiš *adv.* weakly*
anšu *adj.* weak, feeble, fragile
anšu⁺ *adj.* fretful
anšūtu *nf.* weakness, fragility
antu *nf.* maid, slave-girl, female servant, wench
anuntu* *nf.* battle
anūt akāli *nf. cp.* cutlery*
anūt bēti *nf. cp.* domestic fittings, domestic accoutrements, household utensils
anūt erê *nf. cp.* bronzes
anūt ēṣi *nf. cp.* woodwork
anūt ḫūli *nf. cp.* luggage*
anūt kabbê* *nf. cp.* haberdashery, notions, sewing materials
anūt kamādi* *nf. cp.* knitwear
anūt tāḫāzi* *nf. cp.* armament, munitions
anūtu *nf.* utensils, tools, implements, wares; goods, possessions, property
anzaḫḫu *n.* frit
anzanunzû* *n.* subterranean waters, abyss; water-table
anzillu* *n.* abomination, taboo
anzû *n.* lion-eagle, thunderbird
apāl bēt ili *n. cp.* service
apālu *v.* [a/u] to answer, reply, respond, retort; to echo, react; (Gtn) to echo, respond; (D) to pay; (Š) to answer
apālu B *v.* to provide (food), supply, cater, serve, attend to, minister to, administer, do for
apāniš* *adv.* through the window
aparakku *n.* [1] (a headdress)
apāru* *v.* [i/i] to cover; (D) to put on; (N) to be crowned
apiltu* *nf.* heiress
apiš* *adv.* like a marsh
āpītu *nf.* female baker
āpiu *n.* [2] baker
apkallatu* *nf.* wise woman
apkallu *n.* sage, savant
aplu *n.* heir
apparrītu* *nf.* tufted hair, strand of hair
apparrû* *adj.* dishevelled, shaggy
appāru *n.* marsh, marshy meadow, swamp
appāt ubānāt šēpi* *nf. cp. pl.* tips of the toes, tiptoes
appāti *n. pl.* reins
appi arê* *n. cp.* aquiline nose
appi tulê* *n. cp.* nipple
appi ušāri* *n. cp.* glans
appu *n.* nose, beak; tip; top, apex, acme, peak
appu labānu* *vp.* adore, worship, bow down to, beg humbly, exhibit humility
apputtu† *int.* please
aprušu *n.* siderites
apsammikku* *n.* trapezoid
apsasītu* *nf.* sphinx
apsû *n.* abyss, subterranean waters
apšānu* *n.* yoke
apšinnu* *n.* furrow
apšitû* *n.* ratio
aptu *n.* [3] window, opening; balcony; niche, pigeon-hole
apu *n.* hole, opening
apû* *v.* to be visible, be manifest; to shine forth, appear, stand out, turn up; (Š) to proclaim; to make visible, make manifest, visualize, to elicit*
apû a.* *adj.* apparent, visible, noticeable, overt, manifest, palpable, plain
apu B* *n.* reed, giant reed, reed thicket, canebrake
aq-qāt† *prp.* more than, over
aqqābu *n.* [2] hind part(?)
aqû* *v.* [i/i] to wait; (D) to await, heed
araḫḫu* *n.* (a song)
araḫsamnu *n.* Marchesvan, November
arāḫu* *v.* [a/a] to be urgent; to hurry, hasten, scud; (D) to accelerate, precipitate, quicken, speed, speed up
arāk ikki◊ *n. cp.* forbearance, patience

arāku *v.* $^{i/i}$ to be long; (D) to make long, lengthen, prolong, protract; to continue doing; (Š) to extend, lengthen, prolong
arāku+ *v.* $^{i/i}$ (D) to dwell upon; (Š) to draw out
arallû* *n.* underworld
arammu* *n.* (siege) ramp, causeway
arāmu *v.* $^{i/i}$ to envelop, cover, blindfold
arāniš* *adv.* like an eagle
arānu* *nf.* coffin, sarcophagus
arāpu *v.* $^{u/u}$ to be cloudy, overcast
ararrūtu* *nf.* work of a miller
arāru* *v.* $^{a/u}$ to curse
arāru B* *v.* $^{u/u}$ to tremble, shake, panic; to convulse
arāšu *v.* $^{a/u}$ to cultivate; (Š) to put under cultivation
arattû* *adj.* excellent
arbâ *num.* forty
Arbail *n.* Arbela, Erbil
Arbāiu *adj., n.* Arab, Arabian
arbēšerīu* *num.* fourteenth
arbīšu *adv.* four times
arbittu *nf.* four, tetrad, quartet
Arbītu *nf.* Arabic; Arabian woman
arbīu* *num.* fortieth
arbūtu* *nf.* rout, flight
ardatu* *nf.* young woman, maiden, virgin
ardu◊ *n.* servant, slave
ardūtu◊ *nf.* servitude, vassalage
argamannu *n.* purple, flaming red, crimson
argamannu+ *n.* hyacinthine, purple garment
argannu *n.* (a conifer)
arḫiš *adv.* quickly, swiftly, hurriedly, shortly
arḫiš arḫiš *adv.* very quickly, very soon
arḫiš šaṭāru *vp.* to jot down*
arḫišam* *adv.* monthly
arḫu* *nf.* cow
arḫussu◊ *adv.* each month
aribiš* *adv.* like locusts
āribu* *n.* [1] raven, crow; rook, jackdaw
āridu* *adj.* downhill, sloping
ariktu* *nf.* long design
āriru *n.* miller
āriru B* *n.* blazing
ārišūtu *nf.* cultivation
arītu *nf.* (round) shield
arītu B *nf.* pregnant woman
arkāniš* *adv.* afterwards
arkānu* *adv.* afterwards
arkatu* *nf.* background, circumstances; rear part
arki* *prp.* after, behind
arkiš* *adv.* later (on), afterwards, backward[s], behind
arkītu◊ *nf.* later time, future
arku *adj.* long; tall; lengthy
arkû* *adj.* second, junior; later
arku+ *adj.* prolonged, slow, wide
armaḫḫu* *n.* thick woods(?)
Armāiu *adj., n.* Aramean
armanniš* *adv.* like an armannu-pomegranate
armannu *n.* mountain apple, pomegranate
Armītu *nf.* Aramaic; Aramean woman
armu *n.* buck
arnabānu* *adj.* harelip
arnu *n.* sin, guilt
arnu* *n.* crime, punishment, penalty
arnubu *n.* hare, rabbit
arrābātu *nf.* female dormouse
arrābû *n.* dormouse
arraku* *adj.* very long, tall
arratu* *nf.* curse, malediction, swearword*
arsallu *n.* [1] (an iron implement)
arsānu *n.* barley groats
arsu *n.* [1] barley groats
arsuppu* *n.* carp
aršu* *adj.* grubby, smudged, soiled, sordid, stained, unclean, untidy
aršūtu* *nf.* impurity
arû *n.* [3] millstone, grindstone; (hand) mill
āru *n.* [3] frond, branch
âru* *v.* $^{a/i}$ to go, march; (D) to instruct; to control, govern
arû F* *v.* $^{u/u}$ to lop, prune, sever
Arubu *n.* Arabia; Arab(s)
Arumu *n.* Aram; Aramean(s)
aruppu* *n.* armpit
arūru* *n.* outlet of a canal
arūrūtu *nf.* wailing, lamentation
aruštu* *nf.* dirtiness, pollution
aruštu B* *nf.* famine, hunger
arutḫē *n.pl.* tongs
arûtu *nf.* conception*

arû B v.$^{i/i}$ to be pregnant, conceive

arû C* v.$^{u/u}$ to bring, take to; (Gtn) to guide, educate; to administer, steer, to develop*, nurture*

arû D* n. eagle

arû E* n. multiplication (table), mathematics*, result, product; factor, multiplier

arzallu n. (a plant or stone)

asakkiš* adv. like taboo

asakku n.^{1} epidemics; taboo; (a disease-causing demon)

asallu n.^{3} (a cooking vessel of metal)

asāmu* v.$^{a/i}$ to fit, befit, suit, be proper; (D) to fit, adorn

asarru n.^{1} diagram

asḫar* n. black kohl

asīdu* n. heel

asītu† nf. tower

askuppu* n. stone slab

askupputu nf. threshold, door-sill

asliš* adv. like fat sheep

aslu* n. fat sheep

aslu B* nf. (great) cubit

asmarû* n.$^{1/2}$ spear, lance, javelin

asmāti* n. pl. (a type of horse trappings?)

asmiš* adv. suitably

asmu* adj. fit for, fitting, suitable, proper, applicable, apposite, suited; seasonable

aspu* n. sling

asqūdu n. hamster

assammu* n.^{1} pitcher, jug

assāru* n. charioteer

assinnu n. she-man, effeminate man, man-woman, pansy, transvestite

asu n. myrtle

asû n.^{2} physician, doctor

asû+ n.^{2} healer, leech

asû ša ēnāte+ np. oculist

asumit qabūri n. cp. gravestone*, tombstone*

asumittu n.^{3} inscribed slab, stele, memorial, monument

asuppu◊ n.^{3} shack, shed

asurrakku* n. subterranean waters; culvert

asurrû* n. foundation structure, damp course of a wall, latrine, toilet

asûtu nf. medicine, medical skill

asûtu+ nf. healing art, medical science

asu B n.^{3} bear

aṣābu◊ v.$^{a/i}$ to add, increase

aṣābu v.$^{a/i}$ (D) to add to, multiply

aṣappu coll. pack-animal

āṣītu nf. exit, export*

āṣītu* nf. projection, protrusion

āṣiu adj. departing, outgoing, outward bound, prominent; outcoming, resulting, consequent, apparent*, salient*

aṣūdu n.^{3} kneading bowl, fruit bowl; fruit offering

aṣūdu+ n.^{3} kneading-trough, dough, lump of dough

ašāgu n. acacia, camel thorn, thistle, thorn bush

ašamšāniš* adv. like a dust storm

ašamšūtu nf. dust storm

ašannu◊ n.^{2} (an emblem)

ašar* subj. where

ašar šēpu parsat* phr. privacy, seclusion, isolation

ašarēdu n. leader, champion*

ašarēdu a. adj. foremost, best, first-class, pre-eminent, ranking

ašarēdūtu nf. leadership, first rank, pre-eminence

ašarissu* nf. crack troops, shock troops

ašāru v.$^{a/u}$ to check, review; to take care of, provide with; to superintend

ašāru B v.$^{i/i}$ to be right; to prosper; to go directly

ašāru C* v. to be humble, pious

ašāšu* v.$^{u/u}$ to be desperate, be stressed, be worried, worry; (D) to distress, disturb, grieve, stress, worry, torment; to maltreat, mistreat

ašāti* nf. pl. reins

ašāṭu* v. to be stiff, be obdurate

ašbu* adj. inhabited

ašgugu* n. battle, fray, fight

ašḫulu n.^{1} (a box made of metal, wood or reed)

āšib gimri* adj. cp. ubiquitous, omnipresent

āšibu n.^{4} inhabitant, inmate, occupant, resident, tenant

āšipu n. exorcist, magician, conjurer

āšipūtu nf. exorcism, magic

aširtu nf. review, inspection, census

āširtu nf. providence

ašišû* adj. miserable, wretched

ašītu◊ nf. tower

aškāpu n.^{2} leather-worker, shoemaker

aškāpu+ n.^{2} cobbler, shoemaker

aškikītu ṣalintu* np. f. blackbird

aškiqû n. arsenic(?)

aškuttu* *nf.* wedge, bar
ašlāku *n.* bleacher (of garments), washerman, launderer
ašlu
n. $^{1/2}$ tow, string, rope; tow rope; measuring rope (60 metres)
ašlukkatu* *nf.* storeroom; lobby, hallway
ašnan A* *n.* fossiliferous limestone
ašnan B* *n.* grain, cereal(s)
ašpû *n.* ^{1} jasper, pale-blue chalcedony
ašqulālu* *n.* water lily(?); lasso(?)
ašrāti* *nf. pl.* (pl.) holy places, divine abodes
ašrāti še'û* *vp.* to strive constantly for, to be assiduous toward
ašriš* *adv.* humbly
ašru* *n.* ^{3} place, site, locality, location
ašru a. *adj.* controlled, checked, reviewed
ašru B* *adj.* humble, pious
ašša◊ *subj.* as soon as
aššat ili* *n. cp.* (a priestess, liter. god's wife)
aššatu* *nf.* wife
aššu* *subj., prp.* because, inasmuch as; so that; because of, concerning, regarding, as to
Aššūrāiu *adj., n.* Assyrian
Aššūrītu *nf.* Assyrian (language, woman)
Aššūru* *n.* Assyrian(s)
aššut◊ *prp.* concerning
aššutu† *nf.* wife
aššūtu◊
nf. marriage, matrimony
aštammu* *n.* hostel, brothel
aštapīru* *n.* ^{1} dependent, client
aštillu* *n.* (part of a chariot?)
ašṭu* *adj.* hard, adamant, harsh, rigorous, stern, stiff; bullheaded, headstrong, obdurate, obstinate, refractory, pertinacious*, problematic*
ašṭūtu* *nf.* obduracy; stiffness, rigor
ašû* *adj.* distinguished, noble
ašû *v.* (Š) to confuse, throw into confusion
ašūḫu *n.* pine
ašuštu* *nf.* dejection, depression, distress, grief, worry, stress
atâ *q., int.* why?
atā'išu* *n.* (a medicinal plant)
atāku* *v.* (D) to bend, twist
atalluku* *n.* perambulation
atānu *nf.* mare; she-ass, donkey-mare
atappiš* *adv.* like a canal
atappu *n., nf.* (small) canal, ditch
atappu+ *n., nf.* (small) stream, creek
atartu* *nf.* excess
atbāru *n.* basalt
atḫê* *n. pl.* brotherhood
atḫusu *n.* carrying stick
atkuppu *n.* reed worker
atkuppūtu* *nf.* basketry
atmāṣu* *adj.* stubborn
atmû* *n.* utterance, speech
atmunu *n.* ^{1}, *nf.* cella, sanctum
atra ḫasīsi* *adj. cp.* exceedingly wise, genial, genius, ingenuous
atta *pron. m.* you, thou, ye
attalû *n.* eclipse
atti *pron. f.* you (f.)
attû* *prp.* own, belonging to
attunu *pron. pl.* you (pl.), ye
atû *n.* gateguard, doorman
atūgallu *n.* chief doorkeeper
atūnu *n.* kiln, oven
atūnu+ *n.* furnace
atû B* *v.* $^{u/u}$ to find, discover, locate; (D) to select, choose; (Št) to meet; to be in opposition
aza'illu† *n.* ^{3} sack
azannu *n.* ^{3} quiver
azarru *n.* lynx
azāzu* *v.* $^{a/a}$ to buzz
azugallatu *nf.* chief woman physician
azupirānu* *n.* saffron
ba'ālu *v.* $^{i/i}$ to be bright, be dominant, be exceptionally big
ba'āru *v.* $^{a/a}$ to catch, hunt
ba'āšu◊ *v.* $^{i/i}$ to be bad, become worse; (D) make bad, worsen
bāb bēt tinūri *n. cp.* bakery
bāb bitqi◊ *n. cp.* sluice gate
bāb ēkalli *n. cp.* gate of the palace
bāb kamî* *n. cp.* outer gate
bāb pūti *n. cp.* front door*
bāb sekri+ *n. cp.* floodgate
bāb tinūri *n. cp.* bakery, oven door
bāb zīqi* *n. cp.* ventilation hole, air vent
bābānû* *adj.* outer
babbanītu◊ *nf.* beauty, belle
babbanû◊ *adj.* good, excellent, wonderful, beautiful
Bābilāiu *adj., n.* citizen of Babylon, Babylonian
Bābili *n.* Babylon
bābti muškēnūti* *nf. cp.* slum
bābtu *nf.* neighbourhood, city quarter, district*

bābu n.[2], nf. gate, doorway
bābu* n.[2], nf. item
bābu† n.[2], nf. supply
badāqu v.[a/u] to repair
baddudu v. to squander, waste, dissipate
bādisu n.[2] (a profession)
badqu n. repair work
bādu n. evening
baḫāru* v. evaporate*, vaporize*, to steam, fume; (D) evaporate*, vaporize*, to boil, heat, to keep boiling
baḫru n. sea salt
baḫru* n. boiling hot, piping hot, steaming hot, red-hot
baḫrû n.[1] coral(?)
baḫrūssu* adv. while hot
baḫrūtu* nf. boiling state, boiling point
baiādu n. nocturnal ceremony, vigil
baiāšu* adj. ashamed*, decent, respectable; bashful, modest, coy, shy
bā'ilu* adj. prevailing, prevalent
bā'ilūtu* nf. prevalence
bā'ir nūni n. cp. fisherman
bā'iru n. fisherman
bā'irūtu nf. fishing
ba''ītu* nf. sought one, desire
bakāru v. to sprinkle(?)
bākītu nf. wailing woman
bakkânu* nf. crybaby
bakkiu n. mourner, weeper
bakru* n. foal
bakû v.[i/i] to weep, cry, bewail; to complain, protest; (Gtn) to complain in tears, blubber, holler, wail
balālu v.[a/u] to mix, blend, mingle, alloy, temper; to mix up, confuse; to concoct; (N) to intermingle
balāmu* v.[i/i] to gag
balāmu+ v.[i/i] to muzzle, check
balāṣu* v.[i/i] to stare (with wide-open eyes), glower; (D) to fix eyes in a stare
balāt prp. apart from, without
balāṭu v.[a/a] to live, survive, subsist; to recover, recuperate, perk up, freshen, quicken; (D) to keep alive; to enliven, revive, refresh, invigorate, pep up, regenerate, resuscitate, heal
balāṭu n. n. life, lifetime; recovery, resurgence
balballû* n. (mng. unkn.)
bāliṭu* adj. convalescent
ballu adj. mixed, confused; promiscuous
ballukku n. (an aromatic plant)
ballukku+ n. oleander(?)
ballulu adj. halfbreed*, mongrel*
ballussu nf. medley, mixture
balluṭu adj. revived
balṣu adj. starey, staring
baltānû* adj. good-looking
baltu nf. thorn bush
bāltu* nf. pride, shame
balṭītu nf. woodworm, wood fretter, termite
balṭītu+ nf. boring-worm, caries
balṭu adj. alive, living; lively, vivid, vigorous, surviving, intact; fresh, raw, uncooked
balṭūssu* adv. alive
balṭūtu nf. being alive; liveliness, vigour, vividness, vivacity; lifetime
balu* prp. without
balû* v.[i/i] to be extinguished, come to an end, go out, peter out, burst
balû v.[i/i] (D) to blow out, extinguish, terminate, put out, quell, quench, stanch, turn off
bâlu* v.[a/a] to beseech
balû+ v.[i/i] to molder, wear out, waste away
bamāti* n. pl. open country, plain
bandillu n.[1] belly, tummy
bandû* n. quotient
bandudû n. pail
banītu* nf. beautiful girl, belle, beauty
bāniu adj. constructive
bāniu+ adj. creative
bannāiu+ adj. constructive
bāntiš* adv. like a mother
bāntu* nf. mother
bāntu B* nf. ribcage, chest, thorax
banû v.[i/i] to build, create, generate
bānû* n. creator, begetter; builder, originator*
banû a.* adj. good, beautiful
banūtu* nf. handsomeness, beauty
banû B* v.[i/i] to be good, beautiful
baqālu* v. to malt, sprout
baqāmu v.[a/u] to pluck
baqāru v.[a/u] to claim, allege, contest, dispute
bāqilu* n. maltster, coster[monger], greengrocer
baqqālu+ n. greengrocer
baqqālūtu+ nf. grocery
baqqu* n. fly, gnat, mosquito
barāḫu* v. to beam, shine, radiate; (D) to irradiate*
barakku* n. corridor, outbuilding
barāmu v.[i/i] to seal
barāmu B* v. to be variegated, multico-

lored, speckled; (D) to color, paint in several colors; to weave colored cloth

bārānû* *adj., n.* rebel, rebellious

barāqu* *v.* $^{i/i}$ to flash, shine; (Š) to strike by lightning

barārītu *nf.* evening watch, dusk, twilight

barārīu *adj.* dusky

barāru *n.* to be dim, be dusky, be obscure; to grow dim, grow dimmer; to glimmer, wink; (D) to dim, obscure

barāru n. *n.* dimness, obscurity, unsteadiness

barāṣu* *v.* $^{u/u}$ to light up, shine, glare

barāṣu+ *v.* $^{u/u}$ (D) to make lucid, make luminous

barbarānu *adj.* wolfish, wolf-like

barbartu* *nf.* she-wolf

barburu *n.* wolf

barḫu *adj.* shining, radiant, shiny, glistening*, glossy*, translucent*, transparent*

barīlāti* *n.pl.* sagapenum, sage

barīlu *n.* sagapenum, sage

bariu *adj.* hungry, famished

bāriu *n.* haruspex, diviner

barmāti *n. pl.* speckled, multicolored wool

barmu* *adj.* multicolored, motley, mottled, pied, speckled, variegated

barraqtu* *nf.* emerald, smaragd

barraqtu+ *nf.* emerald

barrāqu *n.* maltster(?)

barru* *adj.* dim, blurry, filmy, obscure, opaque

barrumu *adj.* multicolored, colorful

barruntu *nf.* colored wool

barruqu *adj.* red-haired, redhead

bārtu *nf.* rebellion, insurrection, revolt

barû *v.* $^{i/i}$ to be hungry, starve, famish; (Š) to make hungry

bâru* *v.* $^{a/a}$ to revolt

bārûtu *nf.* extispicy, divination

barû B* *v.* $^{i/i}$ to study, examine, check through, collate, scrutinize; to revise, to analyze*, research*; (Gt) to look at thoroughly; (Gtn) to look at repeatedly, admire, marvel, wonder; (Š) to show, exhibit, reveal

barû B *v.* $^{i/i}$ (D) to announce, apprise, reveal, divulge, give out, promulgate, to blazon*

bâru B* *v.* $^{u/u}$ to be firm, durable

barû C* *v.* $^{i/i}$ (Št) to continue, go on, persevere, stay permanently

bāsi *adv.* in order to, so (that); duly, in due course, soon

basû* *n.* cube root, square root

baṣāru *v.* $^{a/u}$ to cut, pick, harvest (grapes); (D) to tear apart

baṣāru+ *v.* $^{a/u}$ to bate, debase, detract from, devalue, take away

bāṣiš* *adv.* like sand

baṣru+ *adj.* petty

bāṣu* *n.* sand

bašālu *v.* $^{a/a}$ to cook, boil, scald, stew, simmer; to ripen; to refine; (Š) to cook, let boil, let simmer, stew; to fire, melt; to solder

bašālu+ *v.* $^{a/a}$ to seethe

bašāmu* *v.* $^{i/i}$ to fashion, lay out, create

bašāmu B* *n.* sackcloth

bašāmu C* *v.* $^{a/u}$ to carry away, kidnap

bašā'u *v.* to despise

bašā'u+ *n.* disdain, scorn

bašiu *adj.* available, existent, existing

bašlu *adj.* cooked, boiled, refined, ripe, mature

bašlu+ *adj.* mellow

bašmu *n.* viper, adder; dragon; Hydra

bašmu+ *n.* asp

bašû *v.* $^{i/i}$ to exist; (Š) to give birth, create, produce; to make happen; (N) to come into being, become, materialize, come about, originate; to happen, take place

bâšu *v.* $^{a/a}$ to be ashamed, be abashed, be bashful, come to shame; (D) to put to shame, dishonor, disgrace, embarrass, abash

bâšu+ *v.* $^{a/a}$ (D) to disappoint

batāqu *v.* $^{a/u}$ to cut, cut off, amputate; to cut out, lop, prune; to cut up, hew; to parcel out, partition; to divert; to accuse, to dismember*

batāqu† *v.* $^{a/u}$ to go beyond the price, reduce price, cheapen

batiqtu *adj.* information, detail, denunciation; rumour(?)

bātiqu *n.* [4] informer, denouncer

batqu *n.* breach, deficit, shortage, damage

batqu a. *adj.* cut, missing, unavailable

batqu a.† *adj.* expensive, in short supply, low; cheap

batqu kaṣāru *vp.* to repair

batqu ṣabātu *vp.* to repair, restore

batqu tadānu *vp.* to supply the deficit

battatāia *adv.* one by one, one after another

battibatti *prp.* around, about

battu *nf.* side, party*
battu ana batti *adv.* edgeways, edgewise
batūlāiu+ *adj.* maidenly
batūlu *n.* [1] young man, adolescent, youngster, youth
batūlūtu *nf.* virginity*
batūlūtu+ *nf.* celibacy
batūssu *nf.* girl, virgin
baṭāl kakkē* *n. cp.* armistice, truce
baṭālu *v.* $^{i/i}$ to cease, stop, pack in, pack up, shut down
baṭālu⋆ *v.* $^{i/i}$ (Š) to interrupt, discontinue
baṭālu+ *v.* $^{i/i}$ to die out
baṭālu n.+ *v.* $^{i/i}$ abatement, annulment, overriding
baṭiltu⋆ *nf.* interruption
baṭlu *n.* strike, interruption, cessation, walkout, intermission*, interval*
baṭlu a. *adj.* interrupted, ceased
baṭṭālu+ *n.* loafer
baṭṭilu* *n.* striker
ba''û *v.* to look for, enquire for, search, rummage, forage; to seek, seek out; to try, attempt; to demand, claim, call to account
bâ'u⋆ *v.* $^{a/a}$ to pass over, pass by, walk along; to sweep across; (Š) to inundate
bâ'u *v.* $^{a/a}$ (Š) to move alongside
ba''û+ *v.* to solicit
ba'ulāti⋆ *n. pl.* subjects, people, population; troops, crews
bazāḫu† *v.* $^{a/u}$ badger, entail, extort, press strongly, pressgang, put pressure on
Bāzu *n.* Arabian Desert
bazūšānu *n.* (mng. unkn.)
be'āšu *v.* $^{i/i}$ to be bad, smell bad, smell rank, stink
be'āšu+ *v.* $^{i/i}$ to be evil, displease, seem evil; (Š) to do evil, harm, hurt, make seem evil
be'ēšu◊ *v.* $^{i/i}$ to be bad, smell bad, stink, reek
Bēl *n.* Jupiter
bēl abiti *n. cp.* adversary
bēl adê *n. cp.* confederate, guardian of a treaty
bēl āli *n. cp.* city lord
bēl ālūtu *n. cp.* city-lordship
bēl amati◊ *n. cp.* adversary
bēl arīti *n. cp.* shield-owner
bēl arni⋆ *n. cp.* sinner, wrongdoer, culprit
bēl batqi *n. cp.* repairer, restorer
bēl bēti *n. cp.* master of the house, househusband, host
bēl birki⋆ *n. cp.* runner, constable
bēl dabābi *n. cp.* adversary, legal opponent, enemy
bēl dāmē *n. cp.* mortal enemy, archenemy; avenger
bēl de'iqti *n. cp.* friend, favorite
bēl dēni *n. cp.* adversary in court, prosecutor
bēl dulli *n. cp.* work master
bēl eleppi *n. cp.* boat-owner, ship-owner
bēl emūqi⋆ *n. cp.* strong man, athlete
bēl eqli *n. cp.* landed, landowner
bēl eqli* *n. cp.* leaseholder
bēl gimilli⋆ *n. cp.* one who owes somebody a favor
bēl ḫabulli *n. cp.* creditor
bēl ḫarimti *n. cp.* pander*, pimp*
bēl ḫarrāni *n. cp.* caravan entrepreneur, travel companion
bēl ḫiṭṭi *n. cp.* evil-doer, criminal
bēl ilki *n. cp.* labor-duty superior
bēl iškāri *n. cp.* holder of state property
bēl kusāpi *n. cp.* guest
bēl lemutti⋆ *n. cp.* wrongdoer, enemy
bēl lišāni *n. cp.* one who speaks the language; languaged
bēl maḫāri *n. cp.* recipient
bēl maṣṣarti *n. cp.* office holder
bēl mugirri *n. cp.* chariot owner
bēl mūtāti *n. cp.* mortal enemy
bēl nakāri *n. cp.* enemy
bēl niqê *n. cp.* sacrificer
bēl palluḫi *n. cp.* worshipper(?), penitent(?)
bēl parṣi *n. cp.* officiant
bēl pīḫati◊ *n. cp.* governor
bēl piqitti *n. cp.* official
bēl piqittūtu *n. cp.* office
bēl pirri *n. cp.* (cavalry) unit commander
bēl qarīti *n. cp.* organizer of banquet
bēl qātāti *n. cp.* guarantor
bēl salāmi◊ *n. cp.* ally
bēl sīḫi *n. cp.* insurgent
bēl simmilti *n. cp.* staircase owner
bēl ṣāssi *n. cp.* (legal) opponent, litigant
bēl šumi+ *n. cp.* namesake
bēl šumi damqi *n. cp.* reputable*
bēl tadāni *n. cp.* vendor
bēl tādirti *n. cp.* mourner
bēl taḫūmi *n. cp.* neighbour

bēl ṭābti *n. cp.* friend, patron
bēl ṭābtūtu *nf. cp.* friendship, patronage
bēl ṭēmi *n. cp.* reporter, information officer
bēl umāši *n. cp.* athlete
bēl zakār šumi* *n. cp.* aforementioned person
bēl zarrūti◊ *n. cp.* (an office)
bēl zitti *n. cp.* co-owner, shareholder, sharer, partner
bēlānu *adj.* lordlike, lordly
bēlat bēti *n. cp.* lady of the house, housewife, hostess
bēltānu *adj.* ladylike, ladyly
bēltu *nf.* lady, mistress, dame, madam
bēlu *n.* lord; owner, proprietor, possessor; master, employer; sir, sire
bêlu* *v.* $^{i/i}$ to rule, be victorious
bēlūtu *nf.* lordship; ownership, control, domination, sway; mastery; ascendancy, dominion, empire
bennu *n.* epilepsy
bēr kaqqiri *n. cp.* league
berāti* *n. pl.* swamp waters, lagoons
bēru *n.* double hour, hour
Bērû *n.* Beirut
bêru* *v.* $^{i/i}$ to put aside
berūtu* *nf.* hunger, starvation
bērūtu* *nf.* foundation pit; mound
bēru B *adj.* chosen, elite
bēru B+ *adj.* adept
be'šu *adj.* stinking, stale, rank
bêšu* *v.* $^{i/i}$ to go away; to withdraw; to fork, part, branch
bēt *conj.* where, whereto; when; what
bēt ...ni *phr.* whereabouts
bēt abi *n. cp.* father's house, paternal house; dynasty; patrimony
bēt abulli *n. cp.* gatehouse
bēt abūsāti *n. cp.* magazine
bēt aḫi *n. cp.* arm-piece(?)
bēt akkulli *n. cp.* tool shed
bēt āli *n. cp.* city house, city hall, town hall
bēt āpie *n. cp.* bakery
bēt appāti* *n. cp.* portico
bēt ararri* *n. cp.* mill
bēt āriri* *n. cp.* mill
bēt asalli *n. cp.* kettle room
bēt asê+ *n. cp.* clinic
bēt bēli *n. cp.* government
bēt būṣinni *n. cp.* lamp
bēt dēni *n. cp.* tribunal
bēt dūri *n. cp.* fortified place, fortification, fortress
bēt ekiri *n. cp.* (a building)
bēt eleppi* *n. cp.* ship's cabin
bēt erši *n. cp.* bedroom
bēt esēri* *n. cp.* cage
bēt ēṣi *n. cp.* wood store
bēt gabê* *n. cp.* pharmacy
bēt gallābi *n. cp.* barbershop, hairdresser's [salon]
bēt ginê *n. cp.* room for regular offerings
bēt giṣṣiti *n. cp.* firewood container
bēt Gula *n. cp.* temple of Gula, hospital
bēt ḫabūbāti* *n. cp.* beehive
bēt ḫašīmi *n. cp.* granary
bēt ḫidāti* *n. cp.* house of celebrations
bēt ḫillāni *n. cp.* portico, stoa
Bēt Humrî *n. cp.* Israel
bēt ḫurši *n. cp.* storehouse, pantry, canteen*
bēt ḫuruppi *n. cp.* kitchen cabinet, sideboard
bēt ilāni *n. cp.* house of god(s), temple
bēt ili *n. cp.* house of god, temple
bēt isāti *n. cp.* women's quarters, harem
bēt kalbi+ *n. cp.* doghouse
bēt kanīki *n. cp.* sealed house
bēt kaqqidi *n. cp.* moneybox(?)
bēt karāni *n. cp.* wine cellar
bēt kāri *n. cp.* trading post; custom-house, customs
bēt karmi *n. cp.* grain store, granary
bēt kāsāti *n. cp.* container for cups, cupboard
bēt kīli* *n. cp.* prison, dungeon, gaol
bēt kūdini *n. cp.* mule stable
bēt kutalli *n. cp.* Rear Palace
bēt kuzippi *n. cp.* container for cloaks, closet, wardrobe
bēt limmi† *n. cp.* office of the eponym official
bēt maḫītāti *n. cp.* whip container
bēt maiāli *n. cp.* bedroom
bēt maqarti *n. cp.* icebox*
bēt mardēti *n. cp.* road station, post-stage, roadside inn
bēt maṣṣarti *n. cp.* garrison
bēt māšarti *n. cp.* review palace, armory,

arsenal
bēt maškenē+ *n. cp.* camping ground
bēt mê  *n. cp.* water tank, reservoir
bēt mēsiri* *n. cp.* penitentiary
bēt milki* *n. cp.* conference room
bēt musâti* *n. cp.* lavatory, convenience, rest room, toilet, water closet
bēt mussa''īti *n. cp.* pleasure-house, pavilion
bēt mutirrēti* *n. cp.* portico, porch
bēt nappāḫi* *n. cp.* smithy
bēt naptini *n. cp.* dining room
bēt napṭarti *n. cp.* barracks
bēt napṭiri* *n. cp.* lodgings, guesthouse
bēt natḫi* *n. cp.* (a chapel)
bēt niṣirti* *n. cp.* treasure house
bēt nuḫatimmi  *n. cp.* kitchen
bēt nūni+ *n. cp.* aquarium
bēt nūri* *n. cp.* lantern
bēt pagri† *n. cp.* morgue, mortuary
bēt paṭīrāti *n. cp.* room for portable altars
bēt puḫri* *n. cp.* assembly hall, venue
bēt pūli  *n. cp.* limestone store
bēt pūṣāie *n. cp.* laundry
bēt pūti *n. cp.* front room*
bēt qabūri+ *n. cp.* burial ground
bēt qassi  *n. cp.* bow-case
bēt qāti *n. cp.* storehouse, closet, vestry
bēt quppi *n. cp.* bursary*
bēt qurši *n. cp.* bridal chamber
bēt ramāki  *n. cp.* bathroom
bēt rēdûti *n. cp.* Succession Palace; house of government
bēt rē'ê *n. cp.* shepherd's hut
bēt rēšāti *n. cp.* room for first fruits
bēt rēši 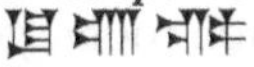 *n. cp.* (a garment or kind of cloth)
bēt rinki *n. cp.* ablution ritual
bēt rugbi *n. cp.* upper storey
bēt sābê* *n. cp.* pub, tavern
bēt salā' mê* *n. cp.* (a purification ritual)
bēt siḫri *n. cp.* turning point*
bēt ṣabti *n. cp.* prison
bēt ṣibitti *n. cp.* prison
bēt ṣīri* *n. cp.* embassy
bēt ša-kubšēšu *n. cp.* millinery*
bēt šammāni+ *n. cp.* drugstore
bēt šammi *n. cp.* fodder store
bēt šamni 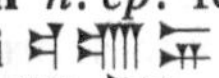 *n. cp.* oil container
bēt šarri 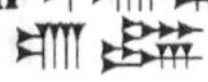 *n. cp.* royal residence, royal tomb
bēt šikāri *n. cp.* tavern, pub
bēt šumēli *n. cp.* Left House/Palace
bēt talpitti *n. cp.* barn(?)
bēt tankāri *n. cp.* bank*
bēt tārīti *n. cp.* nursery*, nursing home*
bēt tilli *n. cp.* house of equipment, supply room, arsenal
bēt ṭābiḫi *n. cp.* slaughterhouse*
bēt ṭābti *n. cp.* salt mine
bēt ṭuppāti *n. cp.* archive, registry, scriptorium
bēt ṭuppi *n. cp.* school
bēt ubri *n. cp.* inn, hostel, hotel, lodging inn
bēt umāmi *n. cp.* stable
bēt unqi  *n. cp.* sealed storeroom
bēt urḫi *n. cp.* road house
bēt ūri 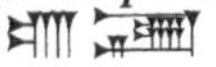 *n. cp.* roof pavilion, gazebo
bēt ušābi* *n. cp.* living space
bēt utnannāti† *n. cp.* carriage shed, cart shed, coach house
bēt zibāni  *n. cp.* housing for scales
bēt zibli *n. cp.* dung house
bētāiūtu+ *nf.* familiarity
bētāniāti *nf. pl.* inner parts, internal organs, intestines
bētānīu *adj.* inner, inmost; internal, domestic
bētānu  *adv., n.* interior, inside, indoors; domestic quarters, women's area
bētu  *n.2/3, nf.* house, home, room, building, edifice; household, domain, premises; temple, bureau*, office*
bētu+ *n.2/3, nf.* family, mansion, nation, race
bētu dannu  *np.* hall, main building
bētu elīu *np.* upper storey, second floor
bētu šaniu *np.* outhouse, annex
bētu šaplīu *np.* bottom floor, first floor, ground floor
bētūtu *nf.* economy*
biādu  *v.* to spend the night, pass the night, stay overnight, remain all night, stay, tarry
biādu*  *v.* (Š) to leave overnight, simmer overnight
biādu  *v.* (D) to put s.o. up for night, lodge, accommodate, billet
biālu  *v.* to rule, control, hold sway over, dominate, prevail
biāru  *v.* to examine, check, test; to choose, elect, select, cull, pick out, opt [for]

bibâni *n. pl.* plumbing, pipes
bibbu 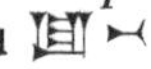 *n.* planet
bibil libbi* *n. cp.* wish, desire; caprice, emotion, fancy, impulse, passion, vagary, whim
bibil libbi rašû* *vp.* to covet
bibil libbi B* *n. cp.* favorite
bibil pāni* *n. cp.* reconciliation
biblu  *n.* [2] hemerology
biblu B* *n.* flood; (pl.) produce
biblu C◊ *n.* favorite
bību  *n.* [1/2] drainage pipe,waste pipe, pipe, gutter, duct, sewer
bidurḫu◊  *n.* bdellium
bikītu  *nf.* weeping, wailing, crying, sobbing, blubbering
bilat maltakti* *n. cp.* assayed talent
billu  *n.* alloy; (blended) beer, (diluted) ale
billu*  *n.* complexity
billutu 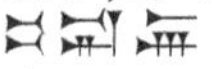 *nf.* (blended) beer, (diluted) ale
billutu*  *nf.* mixture, admixture
billu B *n.* (a plant)
biltu  *nf.* load, burden; talent; tax, tribute, rent; yield
binītu* *nf.* form, structure
bintu  *nf.* daughter
bīnu  *n.* tamarisk
binût nūni* *nf. cp.* fish egges, roe
binût tânti* *nf. cp.* marine creature, sea animal, seafood
binûtu 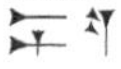 *nf.* form, shape; creation, creature
bir kabti◊  *n. cp.* nobleman(?)
birbirru  *n.* sheen, sparkle, flash; radiance
birdu* *n.* pockmark
birḫu  *n.* (mng. unkn.)
biri-* *prp.* among, between, amidst
birimtu  *nf.* seal impression
birīt* *prp.* between, through, in the midst of
birītu* *nf.* fetter
birītu B* *nf.* distance; interspace, interval, space between; partition, dividing baulk; alley
birku* *n.* knee, lap; loin
birmu  *n.* multicolored textile
birmu*  *n.* painting, fresco
birnu  *n.* (mng. unkn.)
birqu  *n.* lightning, thunderbolt
birru *n.* lattice, trellis, grid, mesh, net
birṣu* *n.* glow, luminous phenomenon, sheen
biršu *n.* cotton wool, wool felt, (pressed) felt
birti  *prp.* between, among, in the midst of, through
birti ēnē maddudu‡ *vp.* to make clear, impress upon, inculcate
birti X birti Y ḫakāmu‡ *vp.* to distinguish, differentiate between
birti X parāsu‡ *vp.* to arbitrate between, interpose, mediate
bīrtu  *nf.* fort, fortress, castle, bastion, military base
bīrtu+ *nf.* court
bīrtūtu* *nf.* fortification
bīru  *n.* extispicy, divination, examination*, analysis*, autopsy*, scrutiny*
bīru B* *n.* baulk, ridge
bīru C* *n.* bull calf, bullock
bis  *adv.,conj.* soon(?); so that(?)
biṣṣūr atāni  *n. cp.* donkey's cunt; cowrie, clam, mussel
biṣṣūru*  *n.* vulva, vagina, cunt, female genitals
bišīt milki* *n. cp.* intuition
bišīt uzni* *n. cp.* intelligence, wisdom
bišītu* *nf.* property, assets; being, existence
biškānu  *n.* cocoon
bišru 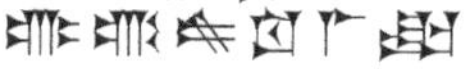 *n.* (a kind of leek)
bīštu* *nf.* obscenity, slander, abuse
bīšu◊ *n.* bad, malicious, infamous, disgraceful, dishonorable, scandalous, notorious
bīšu+ *adj.* bad, evil, deplorable, malignant, sinister, unfortunate, unlucky
bīšu B* *n.* property, belongings
bīt siggi◊ *n. cp.* detention room, jail
bitiqtu 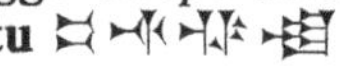 *nf.* deficit, detriment, loss
bitqē batāqu‡ *vp.* to make accusations
bitqu  *n.* accusation, allegation, charge; (a tax)
bitqu†  *n.* loss
bitqu+ *n.* chink, crack, cranny
bitqu B◊ *n.* cutting, opening, sluice; channel
bitrû* *adj.* outstanding, superb, magnificent, enormous
bitrumu* *adj.* multicolored
bu'āru* *n.* health, happiness, prosperity
buāru† *v.* [a/u] (D) to affirm, fortify, prove
bubāti◊ *nf. pl.* starvation
bubbulu *n.* flood, spate

bubû  *n.* (part of a kiln)
bubu'tu* *nf.* boil, pustule
bubūtu  *nf.* hunger, starvation, famine; sustenance
bubūtu B* *nf.* axle
budê  *n.* (a fruit confection or sweet sauce)
būdu◊ *nf.* shoulder
budurḫu  *n.* bdellium
bugurru  *n.* (a cut of meat)
buḫlalû* *n.* (an Elamite class of priests)
buḫra* *adv.* cooked
buḫru* *n.* fume*, steam*, vapor*
bukānu* *n.* pestle
bukāšu* *n.* duke
bukinnu  *n.* [1] trough, water vessel
bukru* *n.* [1] (first-born) son
bukurtu* *nf.* daughter
bulê  *n.* dry wood, firewood
būltu◊ *nf.* embarrassment, shame; modesty; dignity
bulṭu *n.* [1/2] remedy, cure, therapy; medical recipe, medical literature
bulṭu libbi *n. cp.* delight
būlu  *n.* cattle, livestock
būn abni *n. cp.* (a precious object)
bunbullu  *n.* cone(?)
bunnannê* *n. pl.* (facial) features, outer appearance, likeness, figure
bunnu  *n.* [1] countenance, features, outward appearance; face
būnu  *n.* [1] countenance, features, looks, appearance, semblance, complexion; aspect, temperament; face; race
būnu B◊ *n.* goodness
buppāniš* *adv.* face down, head first, headlong
buqāqu* *n.* gnat, mosquito
buqlu  *n.* malt
buqurrû◊ *n.* [2] legal claim
burallu  *n.* beryl
burāšu 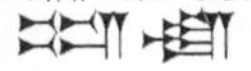 *n.* cade, (prickly) juniper, prickly cedar
burbāni *n. pl.* (mng. unkn.)
burbillutu  *nf.* (an insect)
burbu'tu* *nf.* bubble
burdišaḫḫi *n.* caterpillar
burgû* *n.* (a kind of offering)
burku 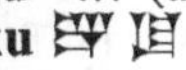 *n.* [1] knee, lap; loin
burmāmu* *n.* porcupine
burmu* *n.* color(ed part)
bursaggû* *n.* (a kind of offering)
būrtu  *nf.* well, cistern
būrtu B  *nf.* heifer calf
burṭiš *n.* yak
būru  *n.* [2] well, cistern
burum ēni* *n. cp.* iris
burummu*  *n.* celestial firmament
būru B  *n.* young calf, veal
burzibandû*  *n.* (a small container)
burzigallu* *n.* (a large bowl)
bussurtu*  *nf.* good news
buṣaṣê* *n. pl.* trifles
būṣinnu *n.* mullein, verbascum; wick, candlewick; lamp
būṣinnu+ *n.* light
būṣu  *n.* byssus, fine linen, mussel silk, sea silk
būṣu B* *n.* hyena
bu'šānu* *n.* diphtheria
bušlu* *n.* smelting, melting
buššu a.* *adj.* shamed, ashamed
būštu* *nf.* dignity, modesty, decency, sense of shame, shame; abashment, embarrassment, scruple
būštu+ *nf.* degradation, disappointment, embarrassment
bu'šu* *n.* reek, stench, stink
bušû*  *n.* [1] property, goods, belongings
būšu* *n.* [1] goods, property
butiqtu  *nf.* water conduit(?)
butuqtu*  *nf.* water channel
buṭnānu *n.* pistachio-like (garden herb)
buṭnu *n.* terebinth, pistachio (nut)
buṭnu+ *n.* pistachio nut; (pl.) terebinth-berries
buṭuttu *nf.* terebinth, pistachio
būzu  *n.* [3] glass vessel
da'āmu*  *v.* [i/i] to be dark; (D) to darken
da'āni *adv.* by force, forcibly
da'āni erābu‡ *vp.* to intrude
da'ānu  *v.* [i/i] to be strong, hard, difficult, severe, tough; (D) to strengthen, intensify; to harden, reinforce, enforce, to force*
da'ānu n. *n.* compulsion
da'āpu  *v.* [i/i] to push, shove, jab, knock, knock down; (D) to press
dabābti šapti *n. cp.* lip service
dabābtu  *nf.* talk, chatter
dabābu  *v.* [u/u] to talk, speak; to plot; to contest, litigate, dispute, argue, plead; to negotiate, discuss; to confess, speak out;

(Gtn) to blabber, chatter, talk idly, quibble; (Š) to persuade, convince, make compliant; to exhort, urge; to abet, agitate, incite, instigate, foment; to provoke

dabābu issi‡ *vp.* to connive with, conspire

dabābu n. *n.* litigation, process; talk, rumour; argumentation, argument; speech, discourse, discussion; wording, text

dabāqu+ *v.* $^{u/u}$ to adhere to, cohere, cling, get along, stick to, to cleave, adhere, keep close to; (D) to glue, join together, splice

dabbābītu+ *nf.* midge

dabbu ša namli+ *n.* antbear

dabdû* *n.* defeat

dābib ṣalipti* *n. cp.* teller of lies

dābib šāri *n. cp.* windbag*

dābibānu *n.* ^{4} plotter

dābibtu* *nf.* gossip, gossipy (woman), telltale

dābibu* *n.* ^{4} speaker, teller

dābiqānu+ *adj.* tenacious

dābiqu+ *adj.* sticky, viscous

dabūbu* *n.* conversation, dialog[ue]

dadāni* *n. pl.* neck muscles

daddammu *n.* mule

daddaru* *n.* (an ill-smelling, thorny plant, centaury(?)), centary(?), thistle

dadmē* *n. pl.* habitable world

dadmī* *n. pl.* habitations, inhabited regions

dādu* *n.* pet*, poppet*, love, lust

dagālu *v.* $^{a/u}$ to see, look, look at, scan, spy; to aim, behold, consider, gaze, regard, to fantasize*, foresee*; (Š) to make look, show, to visualize*; (N) to be looked upon as, pass for; to belong to, be subject to

dagālu* *v.* $^{a/u}$ to envisage, imagine

dāgil iṣṣūri *n. cp.* augur

dāgil nāri *n. cp.* river watcher

dāgil pāni *n. cp.* vassal; obedient

dāgil rūqi* *adj. cp.* far-sighted

dāgilu *n.* observer, watcher, spy, spectator*, viewer*; onlooker*, bystander*

daḫru* *adj.* angry, furious

daḫû *v.* $^{a/u}$ to push, exclude, rebuff, refuse

daḫû+ *v.* $^{a/u}$ to cast down, cast out, drive away, expel, impel, reject, repel, thrust, thrust out

daiāltu *nf.* (synodic) revolution, circuit, rotation

daiāltu* *nf.* excursion, hunting expedition, hunting foray

daiālu *n.* ^{1} scout, spy; courier; constable

daiānānu *adj.* judge-like

daiānu *n.* ^{1} judge

daiānūtu* *nf.* judgeship, judicature, judiciary

daiaštu* *nf.* threshing sledge

dā'ikānu◊ *n.* ^{1} killer, murderer, assassin

dā'iku* *n.* killer, murderer, assassin, murderous

dā'inūtu* *nf.* judgeship

dā'iqu* *n.* siege wall

dakāku* *v.* $^{u/u}$ to gambol, romp

dakāšu* *v.* $^{a/u}$ to pierce, stab, thrust; to accentuate, emphasize

dakāšu+ *v.* $^{a/u}$ to pierce through, transfix

dākiu *adj.* summoner, mobilizer

dakkannu* *n.* doorway

dakšu* *adj.* pierced; accentuated, emphasized

dakû *v.* $^{i/i}$ to call up, summon, mobilize, levy; to stir up, incite, excite; to unleash; to raise, rouse, arouse, awaken, wake up; to remove, censure, to evoke*

dakû◊ *v.* $^{i/i}$ (D) to incite, instigate, stimulate

dakûtu *nf.* levy, muster, calling up

dalāḫu *v.* $^{a/u}$ to stir, stir up, roil, muddle, blur, ruffle; to agitate, disturb, perturb, trouble, vex, embarrass, pester; to perplex, bewilder, confuse, confound, bewilder, baffle; to upset, disorganize; to fuss, do hastily; (D) to do s.th. hastily, hasten

dalāḫu+ *v.* $^{a/u}$ to annoy, bestir, discomfit, disquiet, harry, unnerve

dalāḫu epāšu *vp.* to make too quickly, do hastily, bungle

dalālu *v.* $^{a/u}$ to praise, recite benedictions

dalālu B* *v.* to be small, be stunted, be wretched; (D) to oppress

dalāpu *v.* $^{i/i}$ to be sleepless, stay awake, stay up, sit up; to linger on; (D) to keep awake, disturb, harass, vex; (Š) to harass

dalāpu ina muḫḫi *vp.* to fuss over

dalāqu◊ *v.* $^{i/i}$ to burn

dalbānu* *n.* corridor, alley, passageway

dalḫu *adj.* mixed up, turbid; perplexed, confused, baffled; disturbed, disquieted, troubled, agitated, desperate; distracted; disorderly

dalḫu+ *adj.* annoyed, blurred, fouled, ruffled, tempest-tossed, unsettled, wrought up

daliḫtu* *nf.* confusion, mess; distress, disturbance
dāliḫu* *adj.* noxious*, puzzling*, tantalizing*, worrying*, disturbing, perplexing
dāliḫu⁺ *adj.* annoying
dalīlu *n.* ^{1} praise, doxology, thank(s)
dāliu *n.* ^{4} water drawer
dallāqu⁺ *n.* glow-worm
dallu a.* *adj.* small, stunted, wretched, abject
dalpu *adj.* sleepless, restless, bleary-eyed, weary-eyed; watchful; vexed, harassed
dalû *v.* $^{u/u}$ to draw water, hoist
dālu *n.* $^{1/2}$ bucket
dām erēni *n. cp.* cedar balsam
damāmu* *v.* $^{u/u}$ to wail, moan, bemoan; to creak, rustle; to coo
dāmānāiu⁺ *adj.* bloody
damāqu *v.* $^{i/i}$ to be good, beautiful, fine, skilled, fortunate; (D) to do (something) well, improve, refine, embellish, beautify, make pleasant, to approve*, qualify*
damāqu ana *vp.* to be qualified for, be suitable for
dammû *v.* to make weep, draw tears
dammuqu *adj.* excellent, refined, dapper*
dammuqu epāšu *vp.* to do well, do a good job
damqāti saḫāru* *vp.* to do good deeds
damqiš† *adv.* kindly, benevolently; well, luckily, fortunately
damqu *adj.* good, nice, fine; beautiful, fair, handsome, pretty, shapely, bonny, comely, cute; chic, elegant; fortunate, happy, lucky; well-off, well-to-do; noble, aristocratic; benevolent, kind, genteel, benign; qualified, able-bodied
da'mu* *adj.* dark
damû◊ *v.* $^{u/u}$ to jerk, convulse
dāmu *n.* ^{1} blood
da'mutu *nf.* pigment
danāniš* *adv.* by force, by might
danānu* *v.* $^{i/i}$ to be strong, hard, difficult; (D) to strengthen, fortify, intensify
danānu n.* *n.* power, strength, severity
dandannu* *adj.* strongest, all-powerful
dandannūtu* *nf.* all-powerfulness
dannat miḫṣi *nf. cp.* brunt*
dannatānu *n.* powerful (person), big shot
dannatti *adv.* by force, by might, forcibly
danninu *n.* solid ground
dannu *adj., n.* strong, powerful, potent; big, gross; hard, tough, rough, rugged; harsh, severe, austere, strict, serious; forcible, compulsive, stringent, imperative; vehement, violent, intense
dannutu *nf.* stronghold; hardship, difficulty, predicament; intensity, severity; valid document, title deed
dannūtu* *nf.* strength, power; stronghold, power base
dannutu amāru‡ *vp.* to experience hardship, rough it
dannu B *n.* ^{2} barrel
da'nu *adj.* strong; big; hard, difficult, unlikely, improbable; dangerous, rough, tough, rugged
dapānu* *n. a/u* to roll along, butt
dapānu⁺ *n. a/u* (D) to wrench
dapāru* *v.* $^{i/i}$ to frequent, swarm, teem; (D) to go away, stay clear (of)
dāpinu* *adj.* belligerent, heroic, martial, militant, warlike, overpowering
dāpi'u *n.* (a bowl or goblet)
dapniš* *adv.* aggressively
dapnu* *adj.* aggressive
dappastu *nf.* bedcover, blanket; (pl.) bedclothes, bedding
dappu* *n.* $^{1/2}$ crossbeam; board, plate, panel
dappu⁺ *n.* $^{1/2}$ page, leaf, plank
daprānu *n.* (Syrian) juniper
daqāqu◊ *v.* to be small, thin, minute; (D) to crush minutely
daqāqu⁺ *v.* to beat, bray, maul, pound
daqqiqu* *adj.* insubstantial, very tiny
daqqiqu⁺ *adj.* itsy-bitsy, itty-bitty
daqqu* *adj.* minute, tiny, little
daraggu* *n.* way, path, track
darāku† *v.* to pack
darāku⁺ arrive at, tread; (D) to thrash, thresh
darāru *v.* $^{a/u}$ to intercalate
darāsu *v.* $^{i/i}$ to tread, tread harshly, trample down; to expound, debate; (D) to thresh
dārat aḫāiš *adv.* in succession, successively
dargu* *n.* stair
dargu⁺ *n.* class, degree, grade, rank, rating
dargu ana dargi* *adv.* gradually
darīku *n.* (a container)
dāriš* *adv.* forever
dārišam* *adv.* forever
dariu *n.* ^{3} regular sheep offering

dārīu *adj.* everlasting, eternal, immortal*
darru*  *n.* bearded man
darsu *adj.* deposed
darsu^{+} *adj.* trodden, trite, trivial, worn
darû  *adj., n.* to be eternal, endure, last for ever
dāru *n.* era, eternity
dāru^{+} *n.* age, century, time
dārūtu *nf.* eternal life, immortality
darû B  *v.* $^{i/i}$ to intercalate
dassu  *nf.* door; plate, page
dāṣtu*  *nf.* violence
dâṣu* *v.* $^{a/a}$ to treat unjustly, with disrespect; to dupe, cheat, falsify, to force, compel
dašāpu* *v.* to be sweet; (D) sweeten
dašnu* *adj.* mighty(?)
dašpu* *adj.* sweet
daššu *n.* ^{2}, *nf.* (a small metal implement)
dāt *prp.* after
da'ummatu*  *nf.* dark ness
debqu^{+} *n.* glue, solder
de'iqtu 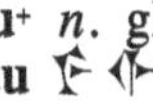 *nf.* goodness, good deed, good word, courtesy, kindness
dēktu  *nf.* defeat, massacre, fighting
dēnāiu^{+} *adj.* judicial
dēnānu *adj.* judgmental, judgment-like
dēnu  *n.* ^{2} judgement, verdict, sentence, conviction; lawsuit, trial, case, proceedings
dēnu a.$^{+}$ *adj.* doomed
dēnu garû *vp.* to litigate, start a process
dēnu ša muāti *np.* death sentence*
dēnūtu^{+} *nf.* prosecution
dēpu* *n.* warp
dešû* *adj.* to sprout; (Dt) to abound, flourish
diānu  *v.* to pass judgement, judge
diāšu* *v.* to trample upon, tread down; to thresh; to destroy; (D) to trample
diāti* *n.pl.* (pl.) tears
dibbē *n.pl.* words, argument
dibbē lā dibbē *np.* gibberish
dibbē lā šalmūti *np.* false allegations, bullshit
dibbē lammadūti *np.* password, watchword
dibbē ša šāri *np.* twaddle, drivel
dibiru* *n.* trouble, calamity, catastrophe*, plague*, pestilence*, (a calamity)
didabû 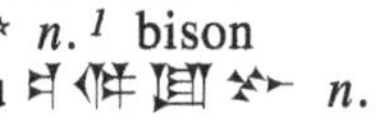 *n.* ^{1} novice
didānu* *n.* ^{1} bison
didibbu 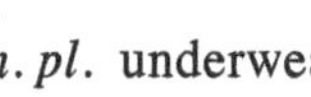 *n.* water-clock, clepsydra
dīdû† *n.pl.* underwear
digilu  *n.* ^{1} gem, precious stone inlay
Diglat *n.* Tigris
diglu  *n.* vision; sight; view, prospect*, scene*
diḫḫu *n.* ^{1} cyst
diḫipu  *n.* (a wooden object)
dikšu* *n.* ^{1} accent, emphasis, point, protuberance*, bulge, swelling; diaphragm; piercing pain
dīku  *n.* arousing, awakening; summoning, mobilization, incitement*, stimulus*
dikûtu *nf.* levy, muster, calling up
dilḫu* *n.* trouble, vexation, confusion, disturbed state, disruption
diliḫtu* *nf.* distraction*, disturbance
diliptu 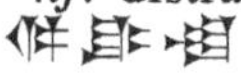 *nf.* sleeplessness, restlessness, unrest
dilpu *n.* ^{1} effort
dilûtu* *nf.* drawing of water, bucket irrigation; water drawing device, shaduf
Dimašqa *n.* Damascus
dimmatu* *nf.* moaning, wailing, lamentation
dimmu* *n.* moaning
dinānu  *n.* substitute
dintu  *nf.* tear
dintu B* *nf.* tower; pile, pyramid
dīnu* *n.* ^{2} legal provision, statute, law
dipāru 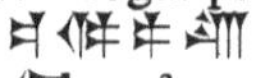 *n.* ^{3} torch, lantern
diqāru  *n.* ^{3} cooking pot
diqqu* *adj.* small, meagre
diqugallu*  *n.* supreme judge
diri  *adj., n.* intercalary
dirratu* *nf.* lash (of whip)
diru'u  *n.* (a kind of bread)
dišānu *n.* (an official)
dišarru* *n.* oats
dišpu  *n.* honey, syrup
dīšu* *n.* grass; spring
dīšu^{+} *n.* lawn
di'u* *n.* throne-platform
dī'u  *n.* malaria
duāku  *n.* to kill, murder, assassinate, do away with, do in; to defeat; to try to kill, fight
duālu  *v.* to run about, move about, patrol; to loiter; to serve
duālu^{+} *v.* to waddle
duālu n.$^{+}$ *v.* service, attendance
duāru† *v.* to surround, enfold
dubāqu *n.* bird-lime
dubāqu^{+} *n.* adhesion [to], glue
dubdubbu *n.* (a musical instrument)

dubqu⁺ *n.* adherence [to]
dūdu *n.*^{1} (a round-bottomed cooking pot)
duḫšiu *n.*^{1} tanned leather; quartz, rock-crystal
dulbānu *n.* passageway, corridor
dulbu* *n.* plane tree
dulīqāti *n. pl.* groats
dulli bēti *n. cp.* housework*
dulli qabāri *n. cp.* funeral service*
dullu *n.*$^{2/3}$ work, task; ritual, treatment
dullu* *n.*$^{2/3}$ misery
dullu epāšu‡ *vp.* to work
dullu issāḫaiš epāšu *vp.* collaborate, co[-]operate
dullu utru *np.* overwork*
dulluḫiš* *adv.* in confusion; hurriedly
dullulu a.* *adj.* oppressed, wronged
duluḫḫû* *n.* trouble; confusion, disorder; turbidity; perplexity
duluḫtu◊ *nf.* concern, flurry, hurry
dumāmu* *n.* tiger
dumāqu *n.* jewellery
dumuqqû* *n.* sign of gratitude
dunānu *n.*^{3} (a type of chariot)
dunnamû* *n.* feeble-minded person, simpleton
dunni qaqqari* *n. cp.* bedrock, solid ground
dunnu* *n.* strength, power; hardness; ground
dunnu† *n.* fortified farm(stead), fort, fortress
dunnuniš* *adv.* solidly, firmly
dunnunu* *adj.* firm, solid; highly respected
dunqu *n.* beauty, good luck, fortune, prosperity; niceness, nicety
duppussû* *n.* younger brother
duprānu *n.* (Syrian) juniper
duprānu* *n.* juniper, Juniperus drupacea
duqdu *n.* almond (tree)
duqdu⁺ *n.* truncheon
dūr abni* *n. cp.* stone wall
dūr šinni* *n. cp.* gums
durāru *n.* amnesty, debt remission, freedom
durāru šakānu‡ *vp.* to liberate, manumit, set free; to emancipate*, enfranchise*
durā'u *n.* arm, foreleg
durgu* *n.*^{1} innermost, central part, core, nucleus
dūru *n.*^{2} city wall, bulwark, rampart, fence*
dūru⁺ *n.*^{2} gum
duruššu* *n.* base, foundation
dūru B *n.* continuity, duration
duššû* *adj.* abundant, copious
duššupu* *adj.* sweet, sweetheart*
dūtu* *nf.* nook, secret place
du'u* *n.* podium*, stage*, throne-platform, platform
e'ālu *v.*$^{i/i}$ to hang, hang up
ebābu *v.*$^{i/i}$ to be pure, shining, clean; (D) to clean, keep clean
ebāru *v.*$^{i/i}$ to cross, cross over, get across; (Š) to bring across, take across, make go across
ebāru ina birti *vp.* to intervene*
ebbītu *nf.* thick (loaf)
ebbu *adj.* shining, polished, clean, pure, shiny
ebbūb ḫašî* *n. cp.* windpipe
ebbūbu *n.* flute, pipe
ebēḫu* *v.*$^{i/i}$ to gird, belt up
Eber nāri *n. cp.* Across-the-River, Transpotamia
eberti tānti* *adv.* overseas
ebertu *nf.* fired brick, tile
ebertu šaḫittu *np.* glazed tile*
ebertu B *nf.* pace, step; step (of a staircase)
ebertu C* *nf.* the other bank
ebēru B* *v.*$^{a/u}$ to paint (the face)
ebēṭu* *v.*$^{i/i}$ to swell up; (D) make swollen, plump up
ebēṭu⁺ *v.*$^{i/i}$ to grow thick
ebḫu *n.* belt
ebiānu⁺ *n.* blister, bunion, callus, tumour
ebīḫu* *n.* belt, girdle
ebirna *int.* (mng. unkn.)
ebissu *nf.* bundle
eblu *n.*^{1} rope, thong, string
ebru* *n.*^{1} comrade, friend, fellow merchant, partner
ebru a.* *adj.* painted, made-up
ebrūtu* *nf.* friendship, partnership; alliance, confederation
ebrūtu⁺ *nf.* fellowship
ebṭu* *adj.* swollen
ebṭu⁺ *adj.* dense, thickly grown, fleshy, thickset
ebû *v.* to be thick, be tumid, be tumescent
ebû⁺ *v.*$^{i/i}$ to swell, thicken, harden

ebû a. *adj.* thick, swollen, turgid, turbid, tumid; fleshy, portly, stocky

ebû a.+ *adj.* dense, gross, swollen, thick

ebû n.+ *n.* bulging, swelling, thickness

ebūru  *n.* harvest, crop; harvest time; summer, summer-time

edādu *v.* $^{u/u}$ to be pointed

edālu  *v.* $^{i/i}$ to bar, close, lock; to shut off; (N) to shut o.s. up

edamukku* *n.* amniotic fluid, amniotic sac

ēdānītu *nf.* single door

ēdānīu  *adj., n.* single, singular; lone (horse)

edānu  *n.* term, deadline

ēdānu-* *adv.* alone

eddettu *nf.* boxthorn

eddu *adj.* pointed

edēḫu* *v.* to be covered with patches

edēpu* *v.* $^{i/i}$ to blow down, blow away

edēqu* *v.* $^{i/i}$ to dress, don, clothe; (N) to get dressed

edēru* *v.* $^{i/i}$ to embrace, meet; (N) to embrace one another (in affection), hug

edēšu* *v.* $^{i/i}$ to be new; (D) to renew, renovate, restore, re-establish, repair, reform

ēdissu *nf.* door, door leave

ēdissu+ *nf.* (pl.) door with two leaves, double doors

ēdiš*  *adj.* alone

ēdiššī-*  *adj.* alone

edlu *adj.* locked, shut

edû  *adj.* renowned, well-known, notable, famous, famed, illustrious, acknowledged, celebrated, distinguished, noteworthy, remarkable

ēdu  *adj.* one, single, only, unique, exclusive*

ēdumānu  *adj.* single, solo, unaccompanied, lonely, solitary

ēdumānūtu *nf.* solitude*

edûtu* *nf.* celebrity*, publicity*, knowledge

edû B* *n.* tidal wave, flood, spate, high water, tide

egalkura◊  *n.* (a ritual)

egalturrû* *nf.* little palace

egertu *nf.* letter, document

egertu+ *nf.* epistle

egēru* *v.* $^{i/i}$ (Gt) to be perverse, be twisted, be cross; (D) to twist, pervert; (N) to hobble; (Ntn) to falter, stumble, stammer, stutter

egītu  *nf.* carelessness, negligence, omission

egru *adj.* transverse, crossed; crooked, perverted, perverse, twisted, tortuous

egû  *v.* $^{i/i}$ to be lazy, disregard, neglect

egû a. *adj.* lazy, negligent, slothful, slug, sluggard

egûtu *nf.* negligence, indolence, laziness, sloth

e'iltu* *nf.* bond, obligation; debt, liability

ēkâ◊ *q.* where?

ekāku  *v.* $^{i/i}$ to itch; (D) to scratch

ēkal māšarti *n. cp.* review palace, arsenal

ēkallu *n.* ^{3} palace; the state

ēkallu* *n.* ^{3} ark

ēkallu+ *n.* ^{3} church, temple, nave

ēkamma◊  *q.* where?

ēkānu◊ *q.* where?

ekdu* *adj.* fierce, ferocious, savage, wild

ekeltu* 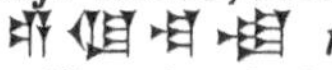 *nf.* darkness

ekēlu* *v.* $^{i/i}$ to be dark; (D) to darken

ekēmu*  *v.* $^{i/i}$ to take away, deprive, wrench out; to absorb

ēkīam* *q.* where?, whither?

ekkēmu* *n.* robber, thief

ekketu* *nf.* itching, scabies

ekkimu* *adj.* rapacious, thieving

ekletu*  *nf.* darkness

eklu* *adj.* dark, sombre

ekmu* *adj.* taken away, stolen

ekṣiš* *adv.* insolently

ekû*  *adj., n.* impoverished; bereaved, orphaned, orphan

ēkurru *n.* ^{3} temple

ekūtu*  *nf.* impoverishment; orphan girl

ela*  *adv., prp.* apart from, besides; in the absence of, except (for)

elāḫu† *v.* $^{i/i}$ (D) to adorn, deck

elallu  *n.* dolomite, calcite

elālu  *v.* $^{i/i}$ to be pure; (D) to purify

elammakku* *n.* (a tree, precious wood, almug)

Elamtu *n.* Elam

elān* *adv., prp.* above, upstream, upwards

elāniš* *adv.* above, upwards

elānu◊ *adv., prp.* above, over; upwards, upstream, uphill, upstairs

elapûa *n.* duckweed, algae, seaweed; moss

elat* *adv., prp.* in addition to, beyond, apart from; additionally

elât šamê*  *n. cp.* zenith

elēlu*  *n.* cheerful song, joyous song, jubilation

elēnīu*  *adj.* upper; upper-

most, topmost
elep nēberi* *n. cp.* ferry boat
elep qarābi *n. cp.* warship*
eleppu *n.* ^{2}, *nf.* boat, ship, galley, ark
elēpu* *v.* $^{i/i}$ (Gt) grow together, be interlocked; (Št) grow densely, interlock, intertwine, tangle
elēṣ libbi* *n. cp.* joy
elēṣu* *v.* $^{i/i}$ to rejoice
eli* *prp.* over, upon, more than, on account of, on behalf of
eli minâtīšu* *adv.* abnormally, beyond measure, exceptionally
eliāti* *nf. pl.* (pl.) upper lands, upper world; upland, highland, tableland
eliš *adv.* above, upwards, uphill; over
eliš† *adv.* even more
elīta dabābu* *vp.* speak up
elītu *nf.* upper garment, (fringed) shawl; upper part, heading*
elītu* *nf.* prefix
elītu+ *nf.* attic
elīu *adj., n.* upper, superior; paramount, topmost, uppermost
ēliu *n.* ascender, climber*
ellāmū-* *prp.* before, in front of
ellatu* *nf.* band, group, host; family group, clan; army, (enemy) troops
elliš* *adv.* purely, clearly
ellu *adj.* pure, holy
ellūtu* *nf.* purity, holiness
ellūtu B* *nf.* (a tree)
ellu B* *n.* sesame oil
elmessu *nf.* darnel(?)
elmessu† *nf.* chickling vetch
elmēšu *n.* amber; electrum
elmēšu+ *n.* diamond
elṣiš* *adv.* gaily, joyfully
elṣu* *adj.* blissful, gay, happy, jolly, jovial, joyful, merry
elû *v.* $^{i/i}$ to go up, ascend, climb
elû* *v.* $^{i/i}$ (Št) dedicate o.s. to*, be raised high
elû *v.* $^{i/i}$ (D) to raise, lift; to deduct; to remove, put away, set aside, tuck away; (Š) to raise, bring up, move up; to boost, uplift; to promote, dedicate, devote, donate, offer, escalate*
elû a.* *adj.* upper; high, tall, exalted
elû n. *n.* ascent, climb, rise, rising
Elūlu *n.* (month) Elul, September
ēma* *conj.* wherever
emādu *v.* $^{i/i}$ to lean on; to lean against, recline; to join; to collide, bump into, run into, land, dock; to impose; (D) to impose, press, put on; (N) to combine, join up, get together, meet up, meet with; to converge
emādu n. *n.* landing*
emāmu *v.* $^{i/i}$ to be hot, hot up; (D) to heat up
emātu *nf.* (part of intestines?)
emēṣu* *v.* to be sour
emēṣu+ *v.* to turn sour, turn acid; (D) to ferment, leaven
emēṣu n.+ *n.* fermentation
emētu* *nf.* mother-in-law
emmu† *adj.* hot
emmu+ *adj.* stuffy
emṣānūtu+ *nf.* acidity
emšu* *n.* lower body, abdomen
emu *n.* father-in-law, son-in-law
emû* *v.* $^{i/i}$ to become, change shape, turn into; (Š) to transform, change into
emû qišubbiš‡ *vp.* to turn into uncultivated land
emūq ramāni* *n. cp.* own strength, resources
emūqatti† *adv.* by force, violently
emūqu *n.* ^{1} strength, force; power, value; (pl.) armed forces, troops, legion(s), army
emūtu* *nf.* wedding
enāqu *v.* $^{i/i}$ to suck; (Š) to suckle, breastfeed, nurse, wet-nurse
enāqu n. *n.* suction
ēnē nappulu* *vp.* to tear out eyes
ēnē šakānu‡ *vp.* to pay attention to
ēnē tarruṣu‡ *vp.* to expect, long for
ēnē X dagālu‡ *vp.* to look for s.o.'s favor, curry favor with
enēbu* *v.* bloom*, blossom*, flourish*, to fruit; (D) to fruit; (Dt) to pick fruit; to bear fruit
enēnu* *v.* $^{i/i}$ to punish
engisû* *n.* (a stone)
enguratti *adv.* (mng. unkn.)
ēniqu* *n.* ^{4} sucker, suckling, unweaned child
enīta* *adv.* conversely, vice versa
enītu* *nf.* changed order
enna◊ *adv.* now
ennānāti† *nf. pl.* (pl.) clemency, dispensation, favor, indulgence
ennettu* *nf.* (divine) punishment
ennu† *n.* favor, mercy
enqu* *adj.* wise, skilled, crafty, sagacious
enṣu *adj.* sour
enṣu+ *adj.* acid
enṣu n. *n.* sour bread

enşu n.⁺ *n.* leaven, leavened bread
enšu* *adj.* weak, feeble
enšūtu* *nf.* weakness; dilapidation
ēntu*  *nf.* priestess
enû*  *v.* $^{i/i}$ to alter, change; (Št) to exchange, to alternate*; (N) to be altered, revoked
ēnu  *nf.* eye; eyesight; eye-stone; spring, well
ēnu našû* *vp.* to covet, greed, lust for
enūma* *conj.* when
Enūma Anu Illil* *phr.* (astrological omen series)
enūru*  *n.* (an incantation formula)
ēnūtu* *nf.* lordship
ēnu B* *n.* high priest
enzu  *n.* ^{3} goat
epāqu† *v.* $^{i/i}$ encircle, encompass, grow round; (D) to pack
epāšu  *v.* $^{a/u}$ to do, act, make, commit, effect; to perform, carry out; to prepare, draw up, accomplish, work out; to build, manufacture, fabricate, undertake; to treat
epāšu*  *v.* $^{a/u}$ (Gtn) to perpetrate; (Š) to have built, have made; to assign work; to employ
epāšu  *v.* $^{a/u}$ (D) to do, do up, process; to practice, exercise; operate, treat; to enact, personate, impersonate; (N) to happen
epāšu n. *n.* making, working, doing, acting; manufacture, preparation
eper šaššāri* *n. cp.* sawdust
epinnu  *nf.* plough
ēpissu *nf.* she who acts
ēpiš dulli 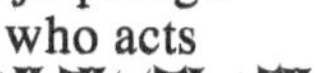 *n. cp.* worker, laborer, workman
ēpiš gabbu *n. cp.* all-around*, all-round*
ēpiš namūti† *n. cp.* flirt, flirtatious; jester, joker, jokester, prankster
ēpiš šēni* *n. cp.* shoemaker
ēpiš tāḫāzi* *n. cp.* fighter
ēpišānu  *n.* ^{4} instigator, perpetrator
ēpišānūtu◊ *nf.* agency
epištu* 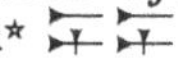 *nf.* ritual
ēpišu *n.* ^{4} maker, manufacturer, author; actor, achiever, doer
ēpišu a. *adj.* active, effectual, efficient, industrious, studious
ēpišūtu *nf.* industriousness*, efficiency*
epqēnu* *n.* dandruff, flake, scale
epqu* *n.* psoriasis
epriš* *adv.* with earth
epru  *n.* dust, earth, soil, ore
epru*  *n.* volume
epšetu *nf.* act, action, activity; achievement, accomplishment, deed; operation, enterprise; workmanship; handiwork, work, construction; manufacture, product; fabrication, machination
epšu *adj.* made, built, worked, prepared, well constructed, made-up, manifactured, produced
epû◊ *v.* $^{i/i}$ to bake
eqbu  *n.* heel
eqbu⁺ *n.* footprint
eqīdu  *n.* ^{1} cheese
eqlu  *n.* ^{3} field, land, estate, area, territory
eqlu⁺ *n.* ^{3} column (of a book)
eqû  *v.* $^{i/i}$ to anoint, smear, daub; (Gt) to paint o.s.*, make up*
ēqu  *n.* (a cultic object, sacred tree(?))
ēqūtu 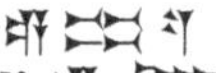 *nf.* (an offering)
erāb āli  *n. cp.* entrance into city, triumph
erāb bēti* *n. cp.* homecoming
erābu  *v.* $^{a/u}$ to enter, accede, go into, visit; to penetrate, move in, intrude; to set (sun); (Š) to introduce, bring in, send in; (vent.) to come in
erābu ina muḫḫi‡ *vp.* to participate in
erābu n. *n.* advent, arrival, coming; entrance, entry; admittance, admission; setting (of sun)
erāqu *v.* $^{i/i}$ to be green, be pale, be yellow; (D) to turn pale
erāšu *v.* $^{i/i}$ to request, desire, wish for, ask for, call for, require, demand, to necessitate*
erbettu*  *nf.* (group of) four, tetrad
erbi *num.* four
erbīšu  *adv.* four times
erbiu  *n.* grasshopper, locust
erēb šamši*  *n. cp.* sunset, west
erēḫu* *v.* $^{i/i}$ to act aggressively, be insolent, be provocative; to attack, rush against
erēnu  *n.* cedar
ereqqu* *n.* ^{1}, *nf.* wagon, cart; Ursa Major, the Plough, truck*
erēru* *v.* to be parched, dry; (D) to parch
erḫu* *adj.* aggressive, provocative; boldfaced, cheeky, impudent, insolent, outrageous, impertinent*, pert*, saucy*, rude*
erḫūtu* *nf.* aggressiveness
ērib bēt ili  *n. cp.* temple enterer, clergyman
ērib bēti  *n. cp.* clergyman,

cleric; clergy

ērib ēkalli *n. cp.* palace enterer, courtier

erib garābi *n. cp.* leprosy(-covered) locust

eribiš* *adv.* like locusts

ēribtu *nf.* enterer, incomer; immigrant (group)

ēribu  *n.*[4] enterer, incomer; next, following, upcoming; coming month, next month

erijāti* *n. pl.* cold wind

erimmatu* *nf.* (egg-shaped) bead, necklace

erinnu* *n.* neck-stock, halter

erintu *nf.* necklace; cover, covering, envelope

erišti libbi* *nf. cp.* qualms, nausea

erištu*  *nf.* request, demand, need, requisition*

ērišu* *n.* bridegroom

erītu* 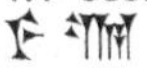 *nf.* pregnant woman

ermiānu* *n.* (Anu's) canopy; sky, heaven

ermu* *n.* baldachin, canopy

erpetu*  *nf.* cloud

erpu *adj.* clouded, cloudy

erpu* *adj.* overcast

erqu *adj.* green, pale, pallid, yellow, yellowish, sallow

errē *n.*[1], *nf.* intestines, bowels, entrails

errēšu◊  *n.*[1] tenant farmer

errēšūtu* *nf.* cultivation (contract)

erretu* *nf.* curse

erretu B* *nf.* weir, barrage; pigsty

erru* *adj.* moldy, musty, stale

errutu† *nf.* dam of reeds, weir, barrage

erṣutu*  *nf.* ground, earth, soil, land; netherworld

eršaḫungû  *n.* penitential psalm

eršemmû *n.* psalm

eršu  *nf.* bed, litter, bier; tray; cradle, crib, manger

eršu a. *adj.* desired, requested; mandatory, necessary, requisite

eršu B* *adj.* wise

e'ru  *n.* magic wand

erû  *n.* copper

ēru* *adj.* awake

êru  *v.* i/i to be awake, conscious; (D) to waken

ērūtu* *nf.* wakefulness, consciousness

erû B† *v.* i/i to be naked, be empty-handed; (D) to empty, strip, strip bare, denude*

esāku 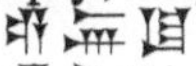 *v.* i/i (mng. uncert.)

esāpu 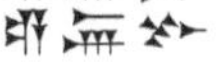 *v.* i/i to gather together, put together, collect up, to compile*

esāpu*  *v.* i/i (D) to scoop up

esāpu  *v.* i/i (Š) to scrape up; (N) to be decanted

esāru 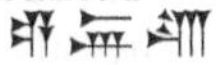 *v.* i/i to besiege, blockade, shut in, shut off, seclude, confine, enclose, include, frame

esāru*  *v.* i/i (Dt) to be shut in

esāru  *v.* i/i (N) to shut o.s. in

esāru+ *v.* i/i to captivate

esēqu* *v.* i/i to incise, engrave, carve, chisel; to depict

esīgu* *n.* ebb, low water; ebb-tide, reflux

esiḫtu  *nf.* assignment, task, duty; allocation

esirtu *nf.* concubine

esittu* *nf.* pestle

eṣ qāti *n. cp.* handcuffs

eṣādu  *v.* i/i to reap, harvest, mow down

eṣādu n. *n.* harvest

eṣānu  *v.* i/i to smell, scent; to sniff at, snuff at, snuff, snuffle; to pry

eṣāpu  *v.* i/i to double, redouble, multiply; to drape, flex, plait

eṣāpu tadānu *vp.* to pay double

eṣāru  *v.* i/i to draw, design, depict, portray

eṣāru+ *v.* i/i to characterize, delineate, describe, envisage, figure, form, imagine, paint, represent, typify

ēṣe *adv.* a bit*, a little*, somewhat*

eṣennû* *n.* tube, spout

eṣenṣēr eleppi* *n. cp.* keel, keel plank

eṣenṣēru  *n.* backbone, spine, spinal column, vertebral column

eṣentu *nf.* bone; foot; skeleton

eṣidītu◊  *nf.* (travel) provisions, victuals

ēṣidu  *n.*[1] harvester

ēṣiru* *n.*[4] designer*, draftsman*, draughtsman*, drawer*, (stone) carver

ēṣiš† *adv.* soon, shortly

eṣpu* *adj.* double; twined

eṣru *adj.* drawn, figured*, graphic*

eṣṣu'u  *nf.* gecko

ēṣu  *n.*[1] tree, wood, lumber

ēṣu dariu* *np.* hardwood

eṣurtu* *nf.* drawing, plan, design

ēṣu B *adj.* few, little; scarce, sparse, scant, meagre; shallow; insufficient

ešāšu *v.* i/i to be new; (D) to renew, renovate

ešer  *num.* ten

ešertu  *num., nf.* ten, decad, platoon*

ešēru* *v.* $^{i/i}$ to be right, straight, fair; to go straight, directly; to prosper, thrive; (Š) to straighten, set straight, set right, rectify, unbend; to throw up, purge; to sweep; (Št) to set aright; to guide to the right path, rule justly; to set in order, normalize
eširtu* *nf.* sanctuary
ešītu* *nf.* confusion, perplexity, political disorders
ešmarû* *n.* (a silver alloy)
ešqu* *adj.* solid, massive, strong
ešrā *num.* twenty
ešrāia *adv.* ten (times) each, tenfold
ešrāti *adv.* one-tenth; tithes
ešrīšu *adv.* ten times
ešrīu* *num.* twentieth
ešru† *num.* tenth
ešrû* *n., num.* tenth; one tenth
ešrūtu *nf.* tenth part, tithe
eššebu *n.* owl
eššēšu *n.* ^{2} (a festival)
eššiš* *adv.* anew, afresh
eššiš epēšu* *vp.* to reconstruct
eššiš šakānu* *vp.* reestablish
eššu *adj.* new, modern*
eššūtu* *nf.* novelty, newness
ešû* *adj.* to be confused, be turbid, confuse, perplex; (N) to become confused
ešû a.* *adj.* confused
etāku *v.* to be alert, be wary, be watchful; (D) to alert, alarm; to attend, guard
etallūtu* *nf.* sovereignty, domination, dominion
etāqu *v.* $^{i/i}$ to go past, pass over, pass by; to advance, go ahead, proceed, move on, parade; (Š) to bring over; to convey, pass on, forward; to carry out; to transfer, channel; to avert, ward off, bypass, skip; (Štn) to ignore continually
etāqu alāku *vp.* to go straightaway, move on
etāqu ina muḫḫi‡ *vp.* oblige s.o.
etellu* *n.* king, monarch, lord, champion, sovereign
etellutu* *nf.* lady, princess
etinnu *n.* $^{2/3}$ master builder
ētiqu *adj.* passing, transient*, transitory*
ētiqu* *n.* ^{4} passer[-]by
etku *adj.* alert, cautious, wary
ettūtu* *nf.* spider
eṭāru *v.* $^{i/i}$ to save, spare, take away, to preserve*
eṭāru B *v.* $^{i/i}$ to pay; (D) to pay in full, pay off (a debt), settle up
eṭemmu *n.* ^{1} spirit of the dead, ghost, spectre, spook
ēṭiru *n.* saviour
eṭlu *adj., n.* ^{4} young man, manly man
eṭlūtu* *nf.* call-up age*, manhood, manliness
eṭrāti* *nf. pl.* savings
eṭû* *v.* $^{i/i}$ to be dark
eṭû a.* *adj.* dark, shadowy
eṭûtu* *nf.* darkness
ezābu† *v.* $^{i/i}$ to leave, leave behind, abandon, disregard; to divorce; to spare, save, wink at*; (Gt) break up*, get divorced*, split up*
ezābu *v.* $^{i/i}$ (Š) to escape, get off, be left over, survive; to rescue, save, to
ezābu+ *v.* $^{i/i}$ (Š) to deliver, preserve, ransom, redeem, salvage
ezāḫu *v.* $^{i/i}$ to gird
ezbu* *adj.* abandoned, derelict, divorced
ezēzu* *v.* $^{i/i}$ to be angry, furious
ezib* *prp.* except
ezibtu* *nf.* exception
ezû* *v.* to be fast, be hasty, hurry
ezziš* *adv.* angrily, furiously
ezzu* *adj.* angry, fierce, furious, choleric
gabābu *v.* $^{a/u}$ (D) broil, grill, fry, singe
gabadibbu* *n.* parapet
gabaraḫḫu* *n.* rebellion
gabāru+ *v.* to enforce, use force
gabāṣu* *n.* contraction (of eye)
gabbē- *n.* every one [of]
gabbu *adj., pron.* all; whole, entire; every one [of]
gabbubu *v.* broil, grill, fry, frizzle, sizzle
gabbubu a. *adj.* broiled, grilled, fried
gabdi *adj.* beside, next to, adjoining to
gabnu◊ *n., adj.* hunchback, humpback; hunchbacked, humpbacked, gibbous
gabrû *n.* reply, response, answer; copy
gab'u *n.* lair, pit
gabû *n.* alum
gabūdu *n.* (a kind of food)
gadālu+ *v.* to twist, plait, interweave, twine, circle in the air, gyrate, soar
gadāmu† *v.* $^{i/i}$ to cut off
gadāmu+ *v.* $^{i/i}$ to cut down, hew down, mow
gaddāiu *n.* (a profession)
gadiu *n.* (male) kid
gadu* *prp.* with
gagû◊ *n.* cloister, nunnery

gāgu *n.* [1] necklace
galādu *n. u/u* to fear, be afraid
galādu* *v.* u/u (Š) to frighten, terrify, scare off
galādu *v.* u/u (D) to frighten, scare, intimidate, deter; to terrify, terrorize
galālu *v.* a/a to roll
galālu+ *v.* a/a to reel, trundle
galālu B◊ *n.* gravel, pebble
galītu *nf.* deportation; deportees, settlers
gallu+ *n.* [4] emigrant
gallābtu *nf.* female barber
gallābu *n.* barber, hairdresser
gallābūtu *nf.* shaving, haircut
gallatu* *nf.* rolling
gallû *n.* [1] demon, devil
gallubu *v.* to shave, shear, clip
gallulu *v.* to blind
gallulu a. *adj.* blind, boss-eyed, squint-eyed
galtiš* *adv.* awfully, fearfully, terribly
galtu* *adj.* awful, fearful, fearsome, scaring, terrible, terrifying
galû *v.* i/i to go into exile, emigrate, migrate; (Š) to carry away, deport, exile, lead into exile; to displace, dislocate
galû+ *v.* i/i to emigrate
galûtu+ *nf.* captivity, emigration, exodus, migration
gamādu+ *v.* to haggle, mangle, press heavily
gamalnemru+ *n.* camelopard, giraffe
gamālu *v.* i/i to spare, do a favor
gamartu* *nf.* totality; termination; preterite
gamāru *v.* a/u to finish, complete, use up; to annihilate, exterminate, liquidate, destroy, do away with, do for
gamāru* *v.* a/u (N) to end, be used up, wear off
gamāru *v.* a/u (D) to complete, do completely, finish doing s.th.; (Dtt) to end, be finished, run down
gamāru+ *v.* a/u (D) to carry out
gamāzu+ *v.* to crinkle
gamēsu *n.* crystal
gāmilu* *adj.* merciful, gracious, cordial, hearty
gamirtu *nf.* entirety
gamīru◊ *adj.* effective, strong
gāmiru* *adj.* effective, dynamic; annihilating, finishing
gamīrūtu* *nf.* complete dominion
gāmirūtu* *nf.* efficacy, dynamism
gamlu *n.* [3] hooked or curved staff, crook, crank; scimitar, sabre
gammaltu *nf.* she-camel
gammalu *n.* [1] camel
gammalu+ *n.* [1] dromedary
gammīdu *n.* [3] (a kind of garment)
gammīdutu *nf.* (a kind of cloth)
gammilu* *adj.* friendly, forgiving, obliging, sympathetic
gammīzu+ *adj.* crinkly, dingy, grubby, squalid
gammurti libbi *n. cp.* loyalty, solidarity
gammurtu *nf.* totality
gammuru a. *adj.* accomplished
gammuru tadānu *vp.* to pay completely
gammuzu *v.* to press hard(?)
gamru *adj.* finished, done with; final, ready, perfect; complete, total; exhaustive, through; bygone, past, elapsed
gana* *int.* come on!
ganāḫu* *v.* i/i to cough
ganāṣu* *v.* to lift (nose, lip); (Dt) to wrinkle, sneer
gangannu* *n., nf.* pot stand
ganṣir* *n.* underworld
ganūnu* *n.* treasury
gapāru* *v.* to be superior; (Dt) to contend
gapāšu *v.* u/u to be huge, mighty; to rise up, swell; (D) to enlarge
gapnu *n.* bush, shrub, tree
gapnu+ *n.* vine
gapru* *adj.* superior
gapšu *adj.* huge, numerous, mighty, imposing
garābu *v.* to be leprous
garābu* *n.* mange, scab, scabies, scurvy
garādu* *v.* to be mangy, bald
garādu+ *v.* to abrade, erase, rasp, scrape, scrape off, lay bare
garāmu* *v.* i/i to follow a course
garānu* *v.* a/u to store, pile up; (D) to heap up, stack up, pile on
garāru *v.* u/u to become scared, wince; (Š) to frighten, scare, unnerve; (Ntn) to tremble all over
garāṣu* *v.* to scurf
garāšu *v.* a/u to trim, carve
garbānu *n.* leper
gardu* *adj.* mangy
Gargamis *n.* Carchemish
gargīru *n.* rocket
gargīru+ *n.* horseradish
garīdu* *n.* beaver

garinnu *nf.* mother
garīṣtu *nf.* loaf
garīṣtu+ *nf.* cake
garmartu *nf.* (a festival)
garruṣu *adj.* scurfy
garû* *v.* $^{i/i}$ to turn hostile, begin hostilities, challenge, start fight, make war
gārû* *n.* ^{1} adversary, foe, opponent; polemic
gaṣāṣu *v.* $^{u/u}$ to grind, grate, gnash (teeth); to be anguished, suffer
gaṣāṣu B* *v.* $^{i/i}$ to be cruel
gaṣṣānu *adj.* calcareous
gaṣṣiṣu *n.* ^{1} hater, foe
gaṣṣu *adj.* gypsum, lime
gaṣṣu+ *n.* lime, mortar, plaster
gaṣṣutu *nf.* firewood
gaṣṣūtu* *nf.* atrocity, cruelty
gaṣṣu B* *n.* abominable, atrocious, brutal, cruel, hideous, horrid
gašāru* *v.* $^{i/i}$ (Dt) to strike with great force; to bully; to cascade
gašīrūtu* *nf.* furniture
gašīšiš* *adv.* on stakes
gašīšu *n.* stake
gašru *adj.* strong, powerful, robust
gašru+ *adj.* ravenous
gašû* *v.* to belch, burp
gašūru *n.* log, timber, roof-beam, rafter
gattu *n.* form, stature
gazālu *v.* to steal, carry off
gazālu+ *v.* to rob, plunder
gazāru *v.* to cut
gazāru+ *v.* to circumcise
gazāzu *v.* $^{a/u}$ to shear, bob
gazzizu *n.* shearer
gennû* *n.* mountain
gentu *nf.* (mng. unkn.)
gerdu *n.* plucked wool
gerginakku* *n.* library
gergiššu* *n.* strawberry
gerru* *n.* ^{1,2,nf} campaign; road, way, path
gerrû *n.* utterance, formula; reputation, mood
gerseqû* *n.* courtier, eunuch
gêšu* *v.* to turn over, gash, grub up
gibillu??◊ *n.* chips for kindling
gīdānu *n.* outside
giddagiddû* *n.* twitching, twitch, jerk, spasm
gidgiddānu *adj.* spasmatic, spasmodic, twitchy
gidiltu+ *nf.* bight
gidimmu *n.* ^{3} ladle, water scoop
gidlu *n.* braid, plait, twining
gīdu *n.* ^{1} sinew, tendon, gristle, nerve
gigallu* *adj.* wise
gigallūtu* *adj.* wisdom
gigunû* *n.* ^{1} raised temple
gildu *n.* (ox) hide, skin
gildu+ *n.* hide, fur
gilittu* *nf.* fright
gilittu rašû* *vp.* to take fright, be frightened
gillatu* *nf.* crime, sin, sacrilege, misdeed, misdemeanour
gillu* *n.* wave
gillu+ *n.* billow
giltu *nf.* (mng. unkn.)
gimillu* *n.* kindness, compassion, mercy, favor; revenge, vengeance
gimillu turru* *vp.* to return a favor, avenge, requite
gimirtu *nf.* totality, entirety; all, whole, wholly
gimlu *n.* compassion, sympathy, requital; revenge, vengeance
gimru *n.* ^{1} total, totality, all, altogether
gimru† *n.* ^{1} cost, expense
ginâ* *adv.* constantly, usually
gingīru *n.* rocket salad, roquette
ginisû *n.* ^{1} (a leather object)
ginnu* *n.* hallmark
ginû *n.* ^{1} ordinary, regular offering; contribution
gipāru* *n.* pasture, meadow
gipāru B* *n.* residence (of high priestess)
gipiš libbi* *n. cp.* pride
gipiš ummāni* *n. cp.* massed body of troops, massed might
gipšu* *n.* mass, expanse, might, swelling, congestion
gipšūtu* *nf.* bulk, numerousness, multitude
girginakku* *n.* library
girgiššu* *n.* strawberry tree
girim-ḫilibê *n. cp.* (a semi-precious stone)
girīṣu* *n.* cherry(?)
girmadû* *n.* launching roller
girrānu* *n.* wailing, lamentation
girru* *n.* fire
giršānu *n.* (a large variety of leek)
girtablilû* *n.* scorpion-man

girūtu *nf.* hostility
gisallāti* *nf. pl.* (pl.) eaves, ledges
gisgallu* *n.* station, position
giskimmu* *n.* omen, portent
giṣṣu *n.* thorn
gišallu* *n.* oar
gišallû* *n.* (part of roof, perhaps eaves)
gišburru *n.* (a cultic object, tree of absolution)
gišgallu* *n.* seat, pedestal, throne-base, column-base
gišginû* *n.* (a heavy stick, perhaps clamp)
gišgirru *n.* ^{1} spill
gišḫummu* *n.* bench
gišḫurru* *n.* magic circle; plan, design, model, archetype
gišimmaru *n.* date palm
gišimmaru* *n.* palm tree
gišmaḫḫu* *n.* ^{1} beam, column, tree-trunk
gišnugallu *n.* alabaster
gišparru* *n.* trap, snare
gišru *n.* bridge
giššu *n.* hip, hipbone, flank, haunch
gišṭû* *n.* writing board
gišūtu* *nf.* eructation, belch
gitmāliš* *adv.* perfectly
gitmālu* *adj.* perfect, ideal
gitmālūtu* *nf.* perfection
giṭṭu◊ *n.* $^{2/3}$ oblong tablet, document
giṭṭu+ *n.* $^{2/3}$ (parchment) document, will
gizilû *n.* torch of reed, brand
gizzu *n.* ^{2} shearing
gizzutu *nf.* yield of wool, clippings
gubāru◊ *n.* neck, nape of the neck; mane, bun
gubāru B◊ *n.* (a gold ornament)
gubbu *n.* ^{2} cistern, well, pit
gubbuḫu* *adj.* bald
gubbutu+ *nf.* cavern, den, hole, pit
gubību *n.* ^{3} roasted barley
Gubla *n.* Byblos
gubru* *n.* ^{1} shepherd's hut
gudūdu◊ *n.* ^{2} patrol
gugallu *n.* canal inspector
gugamlu *n.* paddock(?)
guggalīpu *n.* hump, hunch
guggupinnu *n.* pectoral(?)
guḫaṣṣu *n.* ^{3} wire cable
guḫḫu* *n.* cough
guḫlu *n.* antimony (paste), kohl
gukkallu *n.* fat-tailed sheep
Gula* *n.* Aquarius
gulbūtu *nf.* (a cereal)
gulēnu *n.* ^{1} tunic
gulgullāiu+ *adj.* cranial
gulgullu *n.* ^{1}, *nf.* skull
gulībtu* *nf.* clipping
gullultu* *nf.* misdeed, crime, sin, sacrilege
gullutu *nf.* column-base
gumakilu *n.* (mng. unkn.)
gumāru *n.* [live] coal, ember
gumāru+ *n.* red-hot stone, carbuncle
gummāḫu* *n.* ^{1} choice bull
gummurtu* *nf.* totality
gum'u *n.* (an ornament)
gungulīpu* *n.* ^{1} camel's hump
gunnu* *n.* ^{1} elite, elite troops, main force
gupnu *n.* ^{1} tree, tree-trunk
gupnu+ *n.* ^{1} bryony, (wild) vine
gupšu* *n.* surge, swell, mass
guqqanû* *n.* (a monthly offering)
gurnu* *adj.* average quality
gurpissu *n.* ^{1} helmet; hauberk
gurrudu* *adj.* manged, bald, balding, baldish, mangy
gurruṣu◊ *adj.* leprous(?)
gurṣiptu *nf.* butterfly
gurunniš* *adv.* into a heap
gurunnu* *n.* ^{3} heap, pile
gusīgu *n.* (a piece of jewellery)
guššuru* *adj.* strong(er), (more) powerful
guzallu* *n.* ruffian, scoundrel
guzalû* *n.* (an official, liter. chair-bearer, throne-bearer)
guzguzu◊ *n.* (a garment)
ḫabābu* *v.* $^{u/u}$ to buzz, croon, hum, gurgle, mumble, murmur, mutter, purl, purr, slur
ḫabalkinnu* *n.* (a metal or alloy used for weapons)
ḫabālu *v.* $^{a/u}$ to borrow, be indebted, owe; (D stat.) to be in debt; (D) to lend
ḫabālu n.* *n.* injustice, oppression, violence, wrong, wrongdoing, exploitation*
ḫabālu B *v.* $^{i/i}$ to oppress, wrong; to defraud, take advantage, embezzle, exploit; to deprive, bereave
ḫabālu B* *v.* $^{i/i}$ (D) to damage
ḫabālu B+ *v.* (D) to deform, disconcert
ḫabaraḫḫu *n.* (a wooden box or case)
ḫabāru *v.* $^{u/u}$ to be noisy, babble,

blab, clatter, gab

Habaṣirānu* *n.* Centaurus

ḫabaṣiru* *n.* rat

ḫabāṣu*  *v.* $^{u/u}$ to be exuberant, be luxuriant

ḫabāšu *v.* $^{a/u}$ to break, chop

ḫabātu *v.* $^{a/u}$ to plunder, rob, maraud, pirate, prey

ḫabbābitu+ *nf.* thrush

ḫabbālu+ *adj.* abusive

ḫabbaqūku *n.* (a garden herb)

ḫabbāt tānti* *n. cp.* buccaneer, pirate

ḫabbātu 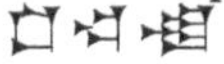 *n.* [1] robber, bandit, pirate

ḫabbilu* *n.* evildoer, wrongdoer, oppressor, hoodlom*, gangster*

ḫabbiru *n.* [4] babbler*, prattler*

ḫabbulu *adj.* indebted, debtor

ḫabburu  *adj.* corpulent, dense, gross, bulky, solid

ḫabbūru *n.* shoot, stalk, sprout, scion

ḫabību* *n.* happy hubbub

ḫābilu* *adj., n.* [4] oppressive; oppressor

ḫābilu B* *n.* [4] trapper

ḫābiru *n.* [4] husband, lover

ḫābītu *nf.* woman drawing water

ḫābiu  *n.* water drawer

ḫabnutu *nf.* (a container)

ḫabru* *adj.* clamorous, busy, noisy, tumultuous

ḫabrû *n.* (a kind of food)

ḫabṣu* *adj.* abundant, luxuriant, plentiful; bounteous, fertile

ḫabṣu+ *adj.* crowded, overcrowded, mushed (together)

ḫabšu *adj.* shattered

ḫabû *v.* $^{u/u}$ to draw water; to deplete

ḫabû* *v.* $^{u/u}$ (Dt) to exhaust o.s.

ḫābû* *n.* (a storage jar)

ḫabūbītu* *nf.* bee, buzzer

ḫabullu  *n.* [1] debt

ḫabūnu  *n.* bosom, tuck

ḫabû B  *n.* cushion(?)

ḫadādu  *v.* $^{a/u}$ to rustle, swish

ḫadaššû* *n.* bridegroom

ḫaddânūtu* *nf.* glee, jealousy

ḫadi *conj.* either

ḫadi ... ḫadi *conj.* either ... or

ḫādi-ūa* *n. cp.* sadist

ḫādiānu  *n.* [4] ill-wisher, gloater; jealous, envious person

ḫadīš* *adv.* gaily, gladly, happily, joyfully, with pleasure; advisedly, voluntarily, willingly

ḫadiu *adj.* happy, joyful, glad, merry, carefree, jocund; voluntary, willing

ḫadû *v.* $^{u/u}$ to be happy, be glad, be merry; to rejoice, gloat over; to be willing, will, wish; to like

ḫadûtu *nf.* joy, happiness, gladness, rejoicing; voluntariness

ḫaḫḫu *n.* peach; plum

ḫaḫḫūru* *n.* raven

ḫaḫḫu B* *n.* mucus, phlegm, slime, snot

ḫaḫû* *v.* $^{u/u}$ to spew, spit out, vomit

ḫaḫû B* *n.* slag, clinker

ḫaiāltu  *nf.* woman in labor

ḫaiattu*  *n.* panic, terror

ḫaiāṭu* *n.* spy, surveyor, inspector, watchman

ḫā'iru*  *n.* husband, lover, suitor

ḫā'irūtu* *nf.* marital status

ḫā'iṭānu* *n.* [4] weigher

ḫā'iṭu* *n.* watchman, night-watchman, vigilante

ḫakāmu *v.* $^{i/i}$ to understand, comprehend, perceive, distinguish (between), to imply*; (Š) to explain, make clear, clarify, put across; to instruct, inform, let know, brief; (N) to be distinct, become clear

ḫakāmu+ *v.* $^{i/i}$ to discern

ḫakāmu birti‡ *vp.* to distinguish

ḫakê* *adv.* crooked, askew(?)

ḫakimtu* *nf.* connotation, implication, notion, perception, realization

ḫākimu *adj.* comprehending, understanding

ḫākimu+ *adj.* canny

ḫakmu *adj.* clear, distinct, intelligible, understandable, implied*

ḫalābu  *v.* $^{i/i}$ to milk

ḫalālu  *v.* $^{a/u}$ to slink, skulk, sneak, creep, crawl, creep in, infiltrate, permeate

ḫalālu B *v.* $^{u/u}$ to sound, wheeze, whine, whistle, pipe; to clink, jingle, chime, ring; (D) to make sound

ḫalāpu*  *v.* $^{u/u}$ to cover, clothe, clothe with, wrap up, envelope; (Gt) to cover each other, be enveloped, be tangled

ḫalāpu  *v.* $^{u/u}$ (N) to cover o.s.

ḫalāpu B* 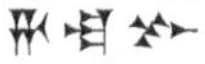 *v.* $^{u/u}$ to slip in, slip through

ḫalāpu C *v.* $^{i/i}$ to milk

ḫalāpu D+ *v.* to exchange, substitute

ḫalāqu *v.* $^{i/i}$ to disappear, run away, slip away, get away, abscond, escape, flee, slip out, make off; to be lost, perish; (Gtn) to dodge; (D) to lose, mislay; to destroy, ravage,

dispose of; (Š) to make disappear, help escape
ḫalāṣu *v.* $^{a/u}$ to comb out, filter, strain, distill
ḫalāšu* *v.* $^{a/u}$ to scrape off, grub up
ḫalbu* *n.* forest
ḫalgatû* *n.* barbarian, rabble
ḫalḫallatu* *nf.* tambourine
ḫalīdu *n.* cavity, burrow(?)
ḫālilānu* *adj.* sneaky
ḫālilu* *n.* (a kind of canal or ditch)
ḫalīlu* *n.* tone
ḫalip qissi* *adj. cp.* wooded
ḫāliptu *nf.* (an object, mng. unkn.)
ḫālipu* *n.* ^{4} milker
ḫaliqti šīri *n. cp.* loss of weight
ḫaliqtu *nf.* loss
ḫāliqu* *adj.* elusive, evasive, fleeting
Hallaba *n.* Aleppo
ḫallālāniš* *adv.* stealthily, furtively
ḫallālatti *adv.* like a centipede
ḫallam *adj. or n.* (a qualification of meat)
ḫallāni *n. pl.* hind legs
ḫalli-arkāti *adj. cp.* longlegged
ḫallimu◊ *n.* ^{2} raft
ḫallu *n.* crotch, upper thigh
ḫallu patû* *vp.* to open thighs, sit astride, ride
ḫallulâ *n.* centipede
ḫalluptu *nf.* armor, armory, harness
ḫallupu *adj.* covered, protected, armorclad
ḫallūru* *n.* chick-pea, peas
ḫalpu a.+ *adj.* fickle
ḫalputu *nf.* successor
ḫalpūtu† *nf.* condemnation, indictment
ḫalqu *n.* fugitive, refugee, runaway, slacker
ḫalqu a. *adj.* fled, lost
ḫalṣu *adj.* filtered, strained, limpid; combed
ḫaltappānu *n.* (a plant)
ḫaltappû* *n.* (a stone)
ḫalû* *v.* to be bright, shine; (Gt) to shine brightly; (Š) to make bright, brighten
ḫālu *n.* vinegar
ḫaluppu *n.* oak
ḫalzu *n.* district, county
ḫalzu* *n.* ^{2} fort, fortification
ḫamadīru* *adj.* parched, shrivelled, withered
ḫamāmu* *v.* $^{a/u}$ to gather, collect, concentrate, to compile*
Hamānu *n.* Amanus
ḫamartu *nf.* (mng. unkn.)
ḫamāṣu◊ *v.* $^{a/u}$ to take off, strip by force, rob; (Š) despoil, rape
ḫamāšu* *v.* to be fifth, be five times as great; (D) to quintuple
ḫamāti* *n. pl.* help, rescue; assistance, aid; auxiliary force
ḫamāṭu* *v.* $^{a/u}$ to glow, burn, flame, be inflamed, flare up; (D) to burn up, make glow; (Š) to set aglow; to work up
ḫamāṭu B* *v.* $^{u/u}$ to hasten, be quick, hurry; (D) to hurry up, quicken; (Š) to do quickly
ḫambaṣūṣu* *n.* (a garden herb)
ḫamiš šeš *num. phr.* several
hami&&er[et]* *num.* fifteen
ḫamiššerīu* *num.* fifteenth
ḫammar ṭīṭi *n. cp.* (a fig-like tree)
ḫammā'u* *n.* ^{1} usurper, pretender
ḫammu◊ *n.* ^{3} family head
ḫammurtu *nf.* (a kind of beer)
ḫammūtu *nf.* nuptial chamber
ḫamru *n.* sacred precinct
ḫamṣu* *adj.* bald
ḫamû* *v.* $^{i/i}$ to immobilize, stun
ḫāmu *n.* litter, rubbish, chaff
ḫamussu *nf.* one fifth; (a tax)
ḫamussu† *nf.* week
ḫamuttu* *nf.* haste, speed, celerity, swiftness
ḫamû B◊ *v.* $^{u/u}$ to rejoice
ḫanābu *v.* $^{u/u}$ to be luxuriant, flourish, thrive
ḫanānu* *v.* $^{u/u}$ to flow
ḫanāpu* *v.* $^{i/i}$ to flatter, fawn
ḫanāqu *v.* $^{a/u}$ to strangle, press, throttle, suffocate, choke, stifle
ḫanāṣu* *v.* $^{i/i}$ to raise the lip, bare the teeth, grimace; (D) to contort; to grimace, scowl
ḫanāšu *v.* $^{i/i}$ to submit o.s.; (D) to subjugate, subdue, subject
ḫanāṭu+ *v.* to embalm, stuff
ḫandūru* *n.* projection
ḫanduttu* *nf.* clitoris
ḫangarānu *adj.* dagger-like
ḫangaru *n.* dagger
ḫāniqu *n.* ^{1} strangler; choking, stifling, suffocating
ḫannāka *adv.* here
ḫannēša *adv.* hither
ḫannīu *pron.* this
ḫanṣāti* *n. pl.* hips

ḫanša  *num.* fifty
ḫanšāiu* *num.* fiftieth
ḫanšat tuāmē⁺ *nf. cp.* quints, quintuplets
ḫanšīšu  *adv.* five times, fivefold
ḫanšu *num.* fifth
ḫanšūtu* *nf.* dependence, submissiveness, subordination
ḫanšu B *adj.* submissive, subordinate, dependent
ḫanṭiš* *adv.* quickly, offhand
ḫanṭu *adj.* hot, fervent; flaming, inflamed
ḫanṭūssu* *adv.* hastily, at once
ḫanṭu B* *adj.* quick, swift, sudden, hasty; immediate, instantaneous, offhand; preterite
ḫanû* *v.* $^{i/i}$ to browbeat
ḫanzizītu  *nf.* horsefly
ḫapāpu◊ *v.* to wash, clean
ḫapāpu⁺ *v.* to freshen up, soap
ḫapāru* *v.* $^{i/i}$ to dig (up)
ḫapiu *adj.* asunder, broken, fragmentary, fragmented
ḫappu  *n.* rogue, villain, rascal, scamp, scoundrel
ḫappūtu* *nf.* villainy
ḫapû  *v.* $^{i/i}$ to break, crush; to crack, shatter, fracture, shiver; to ruin, destroy; to divide, halve; (N) to be broken, break down, crash
ḫâpu* *v.* $^{a/i}$ to cleanse, purify
ḫapûtu *nf.* destruction
ḫarābu* *v.* $^{i/i}$ to be deserted, lie waste; (Š) to lay waste, ravage, waste, render desolate
ḫarādu  *v.* $^{i/i}$ to be awake, be on guard; to wake, watch, attend; (D) to waken, place on guard, warn, alert, caution, prompt; (N) to be attentive, vigilant, watch out
ḫarāku◊ *v.* to post (troops)
ḫarammāma 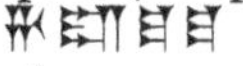 *adv.* later; thereupon, subsequently
ḫarāmu* *v.* $^{i/i}$ to isolate, keep apart
ḫarāmu† *v.* $^{i/i}$ (D) to envelop, put in envelope
ḫarāmu⁺ *v.* $^{i/i}$ to be forbidden, banned; (Š) to excommunicate, ban
ḫarāpu 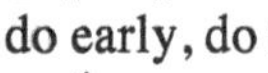 *v.* $^{u/u}$ to be early, be first; to do early, do first, anticipate, forestall, to be eager*
ḫarāpu alāku *vp.* to go first, go earlier
ḫarāru* *v.* $^{a/u}$ to dig, hollow out, root about
ḫarāsu* *v.* to itch, scratch
ḫarāsu n.* *n.* itch, scabies
ḫarāṣu 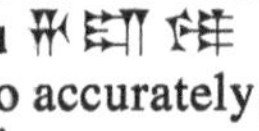 *v.* $^{a/u}$ to clear up, find out; to do accurately; to dig, delve into; to cut into, incise, groove, notch; to subtract
ḫarāṣu†  *v.* $^{a/u}$ (Št) to deduct, deduce, infer, ponder
ḫarāṣu šapāru *vp.* to send a detailed report
ḫarāšu* *v.* to bind (on); (D) to bring together, collect; to plant (trees)
ḫarāšu B* *v.* $^{i/i}$ to be in labor, be in confinement [of women in labor]; (D) to give birth, deliver
ḫarāšu C* *v.* to be silent
ḫarāšu C⁺ *v.* to be dumb, be mute, be tongue-tied; (D) to silence, make dumb
ḫarāṭu *v.* $^{i/i}$ to mince, strip off, pick clean
ḫarbakannu  *n.* bay(?), warhorse
ḫarbāti *nf. pl.* ruins
ḫarbatu*  *nf.* wasteland, ruins
ḫarbiš* *adv.* like a wasteland; into ruins
ḫarbu  *n.* [1] subsoil-plough
ḫarbubu  *n.* (mng. obscure)
ḫarbūtu *nf.* untilled land, depopulation*
ḫarbūtu⁺ *nf.* bollocks, bunk[um], havoc
ḫardu *adj.* vigilant, waking, wakeful, watchful; diligent, attentive, careful, solicitous; conscientious, meticulous, punctilious, scrupulous;
ḫarduttu *nf.* attention, watch; vigilance, wakefulness, diligence
ḫargullu* *n.* lock, locking ring; muzzle
ḫargullu nadû‡ *vp.* to put on a lock
ḫarḫarru  *n.* [1] chain
ḫarḫaru* *n.* villain, rogue, scoundrel, rascal
ḫarintu *nf.* prostitute, whore, slut, hooker, hussy, streetwalker
ḫāripānu  *n.* early riser, early bird
ḫarīpu⁺ *adj.* acute, agile, eager, keen, quick-witted, sharp
ḫarīru  *n.* [3] (a kind of garment or textile)
ḫariṣtu  *nf.* detailed report
ḫarištu* *nf.* woman in confinement
ḫariu  *n.* [3] vat, basin
ḫarmāku  *n.* (a devotee of I&tar)
ḫarmu*  *n.* consort, husband, lover
ḫarmu†  *adj.* covered, enveloped, certified
ḫarmu⁺ *adj.* banned, forbidden, illicit, prohibited, untouchable
ḫarmūtu *nf.* prostitution(?)
ḫarpē *n. pl.* early summer
ḫarpiš* *adv.* early
ḫarpu *adj.* early, premature*

ḫarpūtu *nf.* early moment
ḫarrānu *n., nf.* road, way, path, course; journey, trip; trade route, business venture, caravan; campaign, expedition
ḫarrānu išartu* *np.* beeline
ḫarrānu šutēšuru‡ *vp.* to proceed, set course, take the direct road
ḫarrā'u* *n.*[4] miner
ḫarriru *n.* vole, mole*
ḫarru *n.*[3] canal, moat
ḫarru a. *adj.* dug up, hollow
ḫarrupu šapāru *vp.* to send earlier, send first
ḫarrušu⋆ *adj.* bound, tongue-tied, dumb
ḫarrūšu+ *adj.* hoarse
ḫarṣiš* *adv.* exactly, precisely
ḫarṣu *adj., adv.* specific, precise, exact, accurate
ḫarṣūtu* *nf.* accuracy
ḫaršu *n.* (a culinary dish)
ḫaršūtu+ *nf.* dumbness, deafness
ḫaršu B+ *adj.* dumb, deaf; deaf-mute
ḫarṭibu *n.*[1] (Egyptian) dream interpreter, magician
ḫarû *v.*[i/i] to dig, excavate
ḫarû n. *n.* mining*
ḫarūbu *n.*[1] carob (tree)
ḫarūbu+ *n.* locust tree, (carob) husk, (carob) pod
ḫarūrānu *adj.* holey, pored, porous, pore-skinned
ḫarurtu *nf.* throat
ḫarūru⋆ *n.* hole (in grindstone)
ḫarūru+ *n.* hole, perforation, pore
ḫarušḫu *n.* (an animal)
ḫasāpu *v.*[i/i] to pluck out, tear away; to remove
ḫasāru⋆ *v.*[i/i] to blunt, chip off, trim, flake away, flake off
ḫasās ṭābti⋆ *n. cp.* gratitude
ḫasāsiš lā naṭû⋆ *adj. cp.* inconceivable, imponderable, unthinkable
ḫasāsu *v.*[a/u] to be conscious; to think of, be mindful of, remember, recall (to mind), recollect, come to; to note, conceive
ḫasāsu⋆ *v.*[a/u] to understand
ḫasāsu *v.*[a/u] (Gtn) to think constantly, long for; (Š) to remind, adduce; to commemorate
ḫasāsu* *v.*[a/u] (Š) to memorize
ḫasā'u *v.*[i/i] to mistreat, misuse, harass, molest, assault
ḫasḫaltu⋆ *nf.* leaf, foliage; green leaves
ḫāsis ṭābti⋆ *adj. cp.* grateful
ḫasīsu *n.* ear; intelligence, wisdom, understanding, comprehension; consciousness
ḫāsisu *adj.* conscious, cognizant, thoughtful; intelligent, clever, wise
ḫasru⋆ *adj.* blunt
ḫassē⋆ *n. pl.* salad
ḫassu *adj.* clever, smart, intelligent, quick-witted; wise, sapient
ḫassu+ *adj.* conscious of, cognizant, privy to, sympathetic
ḫassūtu⋆ *nf.* wisdom, perspicacity
ḫāsu *n.* lettuce
ḫaṣābu◊ *v.*[a/u] to cut, break off
ḫaṣānu *v.*[i/i] to shelter, protect, defend, stand up for, patronize; to take care of, cherish, nurse; to embrage, hug, welcome
ḫaṣāṣu *v.*[a/u] to cut, cut down, break; to build a reed hut
ḫaṣbattiš⋆ *adv.* like a pot
ḫaṣbattu⋆ *nf.* potsherd
ḫaṣbu *n.*[1] clay pot, pot, crock, sherd; pottery, crockery, terracotta
ḫaṣbu+ *n.*[1] (clay) vessel (with two handles), (large) wine-jar
ḫaṣṣinnu *n.*[1/3] axe
ḫašaddu *n.* betrothal, marriage festival
ḫašādu *n.* to propose to*, propose marriage*, court*, woo*
ḫašaḫtu† *nf.* need, requirement
ḫašaḫtu+ *nf.* use, utility, necessity; (pl.) amenities, facilities, necessaries, needs
ḫašāḫu⋆ *v.*[a/u] to desire, need, require, appreciate
ḫašālu *v.*[a/u] to bruise, crush, shatter; (Š) to make crush
ḫašānu *n.* thyme
ḫašdānu *adj.* marriageable
ḫašḫaltu *nf.* foliage, green leaves
ḫašḫu⋆ *n.* need
ḫašḫu a.⋆ *adj.* needy; needed, required, necessary
ḫašḫūr api *n. cp.* marsh apple
ḫašikku⋆ *adj.* deaf-mute
ḫašīmu *n.* granary
ḫašlāti *n. pl.* groats
ḫašmānu *adj., n.* light blue, greenish blue
ḫašû *n.* lungs
ḫašurru⋆ *n.* (a kind of cypress)
ḫašû B *n.* thyme
ḫâšu B⋆ *v.*[a/a] to be anxious; to ail; (D) to worry
ḫatamlu *n.* (a type of flour)
ḫatannu *n.*[3] brother-in-law;

son-in-law, bridegroom
ḫatānu* *v.* $^{i/i}$ to protect, shelter
ḫatāpu *v.* $^{i/i}$ to slaughter; (D) to make a slaughter-offering
ḫataššu◊ *n.* (a profession)
ḫatnūtu+ *nf.* espousals, nuptials, marriage ceremony, wedding ceremony
ḫattu* *nf.* panic, terror
ḫaṭāmu *v.* $^{i/i}$ to block, muzzle, stop up, shut, close, muffle
ḫaṭāṭu *v.* $^{a/u}$ to excavate, dig out
ḫaṭāṭu+ *v.* $^{a/u}$ to delineate, dig
ḫaṭāṭu B* *v.* $^{a/u}$ to ferment
ḫāṭiu *adj.* faulty, sinful, sinner
ḫāṭiu* *adj.* erring, fallible, liable to err
ḫaṭṭā'u* *n.* delinquent, sinner
ḫaṭṭi balāṭi *n. cp.* (a herb, staff of life)
ḫaṭṭu *nf.* sceptre
ḫaṭû *v.* $^{i/i}$ to err, go astray, blunder; to act amiss, do wrong, harm; to sin, offend, transgress, violate, trespass, to miscalculate*
ḫaṭû◊ *v.* $^{i/i}$ (D) to damage, destroy, spoil
ḫaṭû* *v.* $^{i/i}$ to fail, miss, omit, miss out, neglect; (D) to render culpable
ḫâṭu* *v.* $^{a/i}$ to search, explore, investigate, examine, scrutinize; to watch over, supervise
ḫaṭû a.* *adj.* faulty, erroneous, misguided, amiss; sinful
ḫa'ūtu *nf.* cushion, pillow
ḫazannu *n.* [3] superintendent, inspector
ḫazannūtu *nf.* office of superintendent
ḫazû* *v.* to fizz, hiss; to be husky
ḫazû a.* *adj.* husky, inarticulate
Hazzat *n.* Gaza
ḫegallu* *n.* prosperity
ḫerṭu+ *n.* gash, groove, scratch
ḫesû* *v.* $^{i/i}$ to break up, hack
ḫi'ālu◊ *n.* [2] army
ḫiālu *v.* to be in labor, be in pain, labor; to wriggle, writhe, squirm
ḫiāqu *v.* to mix, blend, mingle; to dilute, temper
ḫiāru *v.* to choose, select, seek out, pick out; to inspect, scrutinize
ḫiāru+ *v.* to peek, peep
ḫiāšu* *v.* to hurry, hasten, rush
ḫiāṭu *v.* to weigh
ḫiāṭu* *v.* to watch over,supervise, control; to survey, scan, spy, pry; to explore, examine, analyze, assess, investigate; to trace, retrace
ḫiāṭu *v.* (D) to seek out, search out
ḫibiltu *nf.* debt
ḫibiltu* *nf.* wrong, wrong-doing, crime; damage, loss, bereavement
ḫibiltu *nf.* (pl.) arrears, damages
ḫibištu* *nf.* cuttings, shavings
ḫibṣu *n.* blister, bump
ḫibšu *n.* recess, niche
ḫiburnu *n.* [1] (a large container for beer or barley)
ḫidâtānu *n.* [4] joy-maker, merrymaker
ḫidâti *nf. pl.* joy, jubilation, rejoicing
ḫiddu *n.* bead, ornament(?)
ḫidûtu *nf.* joy
ḫidûtu* *nf.* joy, rejoicing, merriment, mirth
Hilakku *n.* Cilicia
ḫilbānāiu+ *adj.* lactic, milky
ḫilēpu* *n.* willow
ḫili ṣarbiti *n. cp.* resin of poplar
ḫilimmu *n.* (a locust)
ḫillu *n.* cover, wrapping; haze
ḫillutu *nf.* creeping, slinking
ḫilpu *n.* milk
ḫilpu B+ *n.* relay
ḫīltu† *nf.* secretion, exudation
ḫīlu *n.* resin
ḫīlu B* *n. pl.* labor pain
ḫimātu *nf.* butter, ghee
ḫimiṭ libbi* *n. cp.* (excessive) ardor, fervor, vehemence
ḫimiṭ ṣēti* *n. cp.* heat stroke, sunstroke, sunburn
ḫimmatu* *nf.* sweepings, refuse, rubbish; collection, compilation, hoard
ḫimṭēti* *nf. pl.* heartburn
ḫimṭu* *n.* fever, heat
ḫinḫinu *n.* (a cereal preparation made with oil, hummus?)
ḫiniqtu* *nf.* constriction, stranguary; (urine) retention
ḫinnu* *n.* ship's cabin
ḫinqu* *n.* narrows, stricture, strangulation, suffocation
ḫinsāti *n. pl.* spoils, wrongful possessions
ḫinṣu *n.* fat, fatty tissue
ḫintu *nf.* leather bag, handbag, purse
ḫinziribu *adj.* b lue-green, bluish green
ḫīp libbi *n. cp.* anxiety, panic
ḫīp šaddî *n. cp.* mountain-quarried, genuine
ḫipītu* *nf.* break, breaking
ḫippu *n.* break
ḫīpu *n.* hewing off; break, breakdown, fracture

ḫīqu *adj.*, *n.* mixed, diluted, mild*, temperate*
ḫirdu *n.* precaution
ḫirgalû *n.* (a kind of flour)
ḫiriṣ gallê lemni* *np.* devil itself
ḫirīṣu *n.*[2] moat, trench, channel, groove*, notch*
ḫirītu *nf.* canal
ḫirṣu *n.* cut, slice, sliver; piece, portion; track, rut
ḫīrtu *nf.* wife, spouse
ḫirūtu* *nf.* digging work, excavation
ḫisiāti *nf. pl.* flogging, harassment
ḫisiʾtu *nf.* maltreatment, mistreatment
ḫissat libbi* *n. cp.* understanding, intuition, insight, idea, imagination, fantasy
ḫissat X ḫasāsu‡ *vp.* to be mindful of, think of
ḫissutu *nf.* reminder, memorandum, notice, notification; note, reference; memory, recollection, reflection, remembrance, reminiscence, souvenir
ḫiṣbu* *n.* yield, abundance
ḫiṣibtu* *nf.* chip, fragment
ḫiṣnu* *n.* protection, defence
ḫiṣṣu* *n.* rubble, gravel, grit
ḫišaḫtu+ *nf.* use, utility, necessity, need
ḫišiḫtu* *nf.* desire, need; requisite, requirement; necessaries, necessities, materials needed, raw material(s); material, ingredient, constituent
ḫiššamû* *adj.* thoroughbred, superb, fine
ḫitmutiš* *adv.* very quickly, speedily
ḫitmuṭu* *adj.* inflamed
ḫitpu *n.*[2] (a type of sacrifice)
ḫitrubu* *adj.* very desolate
ḫittu* *nf.* architrave, lintel
ḫittu+ *nf.* plank (resting on pillars), plank bridge
ḫittu B* *n.* enigma, problem, riddle
ḫiṭītu* *nf.* crime, guilt, sin, vice, flaw; errance, erratum, lapse, shortcoming, slip-up
ḫiṭṭu *n.*[2/3] error, failing; fault, shortcoming; crime, sin, misdemeanor; misconduct, malpractice; blame; defect, harm; punishment, penalty, deformity
ḫiṭṭu dannu *np.* felony
ḫiṭṭu emādu *vp.* to condemn, convict, incriminate, punish
ḫiṭṭu ḫaṭû *vp.* to make a mistake, commit an error, err; to commit a crime, commit an offence, sin against
ḫiṭṭu ša muāti *np.* deadly crime, mortal sin
ḫubbu* *n.* buzz, hum
ḫubburu *adj.* noisy
ḫubburu* *adj.* (D) to make solid, thick
ḫubtu *n.*[2] booty, loot; captives, prisoners of war, abduction*
ḫubtu ḫabātu *vp.* to plunder, sack, despoil
ḫubūru* *n.* clamour, din, noise, hubbub, hullabaloo; bustle, ado, commotion, riot, rumpus, uproar, tumult
ḫūd libbi *n. cp.* joy of heart, contentment; free will, spontaneity
ḫūd pāni* *n. cp.* mirth
ḫuddudu* *adj.* deeply cut, deep
ḫudû *n.* joy, happiness, gladness, rejoicing
ḫūdu *n.* joy
ḫuḫāriš* *adv.* as with a bird-snare
ḫuḫāru *n., nf.* bird-snare, trap
ḫuḫḫurāti *n. pl.* (a dye or kind of wool)
ḫuḫḫuru *n.* (a kind of bread)
ḫūl šarri *n. cp.* royal road, highway
ḫulālu *n.* onyx, striped agate, chalcedony
ḫulamēšu *n.* chameleon
ḫūlāpu+ *n.* alteration
ḫuliam* *n.* helmet
ḫullānu *n.* cloak, wrap, hood
ḫulmiṭṭu* *n.* (a lizard)
ḫultuppu* *n.* (a demon)
ḫulû *n.* shrew
ḫūlu *n.*[2] road, way; trip, tour, voyage
ḫūlu ana šēpi šakānu‡ *vp.* to prepare for journey or career, smooth the path
ḫūlu karmu* *np.* cul-de-sac, dead end
ḫūlu lābiu* *np.* roundabout route, roundabout way
ḫūlu nakkuru‡ *vp.* (D) to change course, deviate, turn aside from normal route
ḫuluḫḫu *n.* (light-colored) frit, slag
ḫuluppāqu *n.* (a small brazier of clay or metal)
ḫulūtu *nf.* female shrew
ḫulūṭu *n.* dumpling(?)
ḫumbābarītu *nf.* Humbaba-figurine(?)
ḫumbābītu *nf.* gecko
ḫumbiṣutu *nf.* yeast bread
ḫummuru◊ *adj.* shrunken, shrivelled; lame, crippled, cripple
ḫummuṭu◊ *adj.* quick
ḫummuṭu B* *adj.* very hot, scorching
ḫunduraiu *n.* carpet

weaver(?)
ḫunnunu◊ *v.(?)* (mng. uncert.)
ḫunṭu *n.* fever, inflammation
ḫunṭu ša ēnāti *np.* eye infection
ḫunṭu ša errē* *np.* enteritis
ḫunṭu ša eṣmāti* *np.* rheumatic fever, rheumatism
ḫunṭu ša ḫašê* *np.* pleurisy
ḫunṭu ša uzni* *np.* ear infection
ḫunzû* *adj.* lame, limp
ḫuppu *n.* hamper, crate; socket
ḫuppudu* *adj.* blind, dazzle
ḫuppu B *n.* hole
ḫuppu C *n.* wickerworker
ḫupšiš* *adv.* like a plebeian
ḫupšu* *n.* common people, mob; rank and file
ḫuptu *nf.* hole, hollow
ḫūptu◊ *nf.* purity(?)
ḫupû* *n.*[1] fragment, flake; (a cloud formation)
ḫūpu *n.* fear
ḫūpu B* *n.* (wheel) rim, tyre; ring
ḫūqu *n.*[1] crossbar, rung; landing stage(?)
ḫūqu B* *n.* death rattle
ḫurādu *n.*[3] military assignment
ḫurāptu *nf.* female spring lamb
ḫurāpu *n.* spring lamb
ḫurāṣānu* *n., adj.* (a bird, perhaps goldfinch)
ḫurāṣānu† *n., adj.* gold-like, goldy
ḫurāṣu *n.* gold
ḫurāṣu uḫḫuzu *vp.* gold plated
ḫurbabillu *n.* hedgehog
ḫurbāšu* *n.* frost, hoarfrost, rime; (cold) tremors, ague; awe, dread, horror, terror
ḫurbu *n.* desert(ed place), wasteland
ḫurdatu* *nf.* cunt, pussy, vulva
ḫurdu *n.* posthumous son
ḫurḫummatu* *nf.* foam, scum, sud
ḫurībtu* *nf.* desert
ḫurnu *n.*[1] (mng. unkn.)
ḫurri pê* *n. cp.* mouth cavity
ḫurru *n.*[3] hole, burrow; cave, cavern, mine, grotto; cavity, slot; gorge, ravine
ḫurru+ *n.*[3] hole, aperture
ḫurrutu *nf.* hole
ḫursān *n.* ordeal
ḫuršāniš* *adv.* like a mountain
ḫuršānu* *n.*[1] mountain
ḫuršu† *n.*[1] cookery, larder, pantry
ḫurtu *nf.* (mng. unkn.)
ḫuruppu* *n.*[3] (metal) dish
ḫūrutu *nf.* madder
ḫusāru† *n.* (a precious stone)
ḫusû *n.* (a kind of owl)
ḫuṣābu *n.*[1] chip, splinter, stick, piece; twig, branch
ḫuṣannu* *n.*[1] belt
ḫuṣṣutu *nf.* reed hut
ḫušaḫḫu *n.* famine, need
ḫušê *n. pl.* (metal) scraps, fragments
ḫušê parzilli* *n. cp.* scrap iron
ḫuššû* *adj.* red
ḫutennu* *n.* javelin, missile
ḫutnû* *n.* (a wooden part of a chariot)
ḫutû *n.* platform(?)
ḫutugu *n.* (an implement)
ḫuṭārtu* *nf.* rod, sceptre
ḫuṭāru *n.* staff, stave, rod, sceptre
ḫuṭṭimmu* *n.* snout, muzzle
ḫuzālu *n.* young gazelle
ḫuzālu+ *n.* gazelle
ḫuzīqutu *nf.* (a kind of textile or garment)
ḫuzīrānu* *adj.* piggy
ḫuzīrtu *nf.* sow, female pig
ḫuzīrtu+ *nf.* mumps; (pl.) sores, swellings, scrofula
ḫuzīru *n.* pig, swine
ḫuzīru+ *n.* hog, boar
ḫuzīrūtu+ *nf.* piggishness, swinishness
ḫuzūnu *n.*[3] (a piece of clothing)
ḫuzzû* *v.* to limp, hobble
ḫuzzumu◊ *adj.* stupid
iābilu *n.*[1] ram
Iadnāna *n.* Cyprus
iaḫilu *n.*[1] (a garment)
iaḫudû* *adj.* simple, daft
Iamnāiu* *adj., n.* Ionian, Greek
iamnuqu *n.* (a garment)
iāmuttu *pron.* each, everybody, every one [of], apiece*
iannusu *n.* sledge, sled, sleigh*
ia'nu◊ *part.* is not
ianūqu *n.* (a meat, milk chicken(?))
ianūqu+ *n.* suckling
Iappû *n.* Yafo, Jaffa
iarḫu *n.* pond, pool, puddle
iarītu *nf.* (a garment)
iāši *pron.* me
iāti* *pron.* me
Iaūdāiu *adj., n.* Jewish, Jew
Iaūdītu* *nf.* Jewess

Ia'ūdu* *n.* Judah
Iauna *adv.* Ionia, Greece
Iaunāiu *n.* Greek, Ionian
ibāru* *n.* scar
ibašši *v.* there is; absolutely, actually, in fact, indeed, fairly*, practically*, preferably*, rather*, reasonably*, tolerably*, virtually*
ibbû  *n.* wrath
ibissu  *nf.* bundle
ibratu* *nf.* bay, niche, recess
ibrēti* *n.pl.* radius and ulna
ibsû* *n.* square root
idatūtu◊  *nf.* (mng. uncert.)
iddāt *prp.* after
iddāt aḫāiš *adv.* in succession, one after the other
iddāti *adv.* afterwards, thereafter, then; accordingly, consequently, subsequently, thence
idē patû‡ *vp.* to get ready for battle
idirtu  *nf.* sorrow, trouble, dismay
idrānu* *n.* potash, salt
idru* *n.* saltpetre
idu*  *n.*$^{1/3}$ arm; side; strength
idû◊  *v.* (Št) familiarize o.s., familiarize
idû*  *v.* to know; (D) to announce; to recognize, identify, mark; (Š) to acknowledge, announce, assert, confess, inform, make known, proclaim, profess, state, to publicize*
idu naparkû‡ *vp.* to leave someone's side, to desert someone
igāru  *n.*^{3} wall
igiarû* *n.* calculation, mathematical problem
igibû* *n.* reciprocal of reciprocal
igiltu *nf.* darkness
igirû* *n.* heron, stork
igisû  *n.*^{1} present, contribution
igitennu* *n.* fraction, quotient
igizaggû 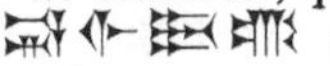 *n.* (a semi-precious stone)
igrē *n.pl.* salary, wage(s)
igrē+ *n.pl.* fee
igû* *n.* reciprocal
igulû* *n.* fine ointment, perfumed oil
iḫzēti* *n.pl.* decorative inlay, mountings
iḫzu* *n.*^{1} learning, erudition, education, study; instruction, teaching, precept(s); coating, setting, mount
ijû  *poss.pron.* mine
ikīsu  *n.* brother-in-law, husband of wife's sister
ikiš* *adv.* like a ditch
ikkanû *poss.pron.* your, yours
ikkār ēkalli *n.cp.* palace farmer
ikkāru  *n.*^{3} farmer, peasant
ikkāru+ *n.*^{3} ploughman, husbandman
ikkārūtu* *nf.* farming; cultivation
ikkārūtu+ *nf.* agriculture, rusticity
ikkibu  *n.*^{1} taboo, abomination; privilege
ikkibu*  *n.*^{1} forbidden
ikku  *n.* temper, mood
ikkû 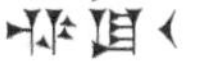 *poss. pron.* yours, your, thine, thy
ikku+ *n.* gusto, palate
ikku karû* *vp.* (D) to irritate, peeve
ikku karû‡ *vp.* to be irritable, be impatient, be anxious
ikku kaṣāru‡ *vp.* to bear a grudge, resent
ikku kullu‡ *vp.* to bear a grudge, mope, sulk
ikku urruku‡ *vp.* to be patient, be forbearing
iklu* *n.* victim
ikribu  *n.*^{1} blessing; prayer, dedication
ikû  *n.* acre; Pegasus
iku  *n.* dyke, ditch
ikūku* *n.* rancid oil
il āli  *n.cp.* city god
ilāni *n.pl.* gods, God
ilāni ētapšū‡ *vp.* accidentally, by chance
ilānû* *adj.* favored by god, lucky
ilā'u *n.* god
ilittu  *nf.* birth; offspring, scion; born (in); brat, brood; descent, nativity, stock
ilkakāti *nf. pl.* contributions (of food), dues, payments
ilku  *n.*^{2} state service, duty, due
illidiš *adv.* the day after tomorrow
Illil *n.* Enlil; god of gods, highest god, supreme god
illilūtu 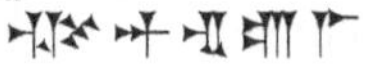 *nf.* Enlilship, divine supremacy
illu* *n.* playmate, comrade, partner
illūr pāni* *n.cp.* rouge
illūrānu *adj.* pinkish, pinky
illūri  *int.* hurrah!
illūriš* *adv.* pinkily, pinkly
illurtu* *nf.* manacle
illūru* *n.* pink, pink carnation, clove pink
ilṣu *n.* joy
iltānu*  *n.* north wind, north, northwest
iltēniš* *adv.* together
iltēnšu* *adv.* once, one time; firstly
iltēt* *num.* one

iltu *nf.* goddess
iltu B *nf.* chaff, husk
i'lu *n.* band (for head or feet)
ilu *n.* [2] god
ilu mušallimu* *np.* tutelary god
ilu rabiu *np.* great god
ilumma *int.* by God!
il'ūtu *nf.* (a vegetable)
ilūtu *nf.* divinity, godhead
im-magāni *adv.* gratuitously, gratis, in vain
im-magāni+ *adv.* freely, without expense
im-matāḫi *adv.* at sunrise
imāru *n.* donkey, jackass; homer, hectare
imat mūti* *n. cp.* deadly poison
imbāriš* *adv.* like a fog
imbāru *n.* fog, mist
imbû* *n.* loss, deficit
imḫullu* *n.* storm, hurricane
imittānu* *adj.* right-handed
imittu *nf.* right side, right hand; south; shoulder
immanakku *n.* sandstone, tin ore
immatēma *adv.* whenever, any time, ever
immati *q.* when?
immatimēni *adv.* any time, ever
immatimēni lā *adv.* never
immer šaddi *n. cp.* mountain sheep, wild sheep
immerānu *adj.* sheepish
immertu* *nf.* ewe; sheep
immeru *n.* [1], *nf.* sheep, wether; mutton
immeru gabbubu *np.* kebab
immu◊ *n.* tablet, record
immu B* *n.* day, daytime
imnu *n.* right side
imratu* *nf.* look, gaze, glance
imsuḫḫu* *n.* whirlwind, cyclone, tornado
imšu* *n.* abdomen
imtu *nf.* poison, venom
in nūni◊ *n. cp.* pearl
ina *prp.* in; by means of, with; into, to; from; during
ina aḫītēšu *adv.* secretly, in secrecy
ina appāt ubānāti* *adv.* on tiptoe
ina appāt ubānāti alāku* *vp.* to tiptoe
ina barāri† *adv.* at dusk
ina bēt kīli šapāru‡ *vp.* to send up
ina bētāni *adv.* indoors
ina birīt *adv.* intermittently, occasionally, sometimes, sporadically
ina birti šakānu *vp.* to interpose
ina danāni* *adv.* by force, by might, forcibly
ina danniti‡ *adv.* by the heavy (weight) standard, by the large (measure)
ina dāt *prp.* after
ina ebertān tānti* *adv.* overseas
ina gammurti libbi *adv.* loyally, wholeheartedly
ina gum libbi‡ *adv.* heartily, wholeheartedly
ina ḫadûti *adv.* at pleasure, gratuitously, voluntarily, willingly
ina ḫidâti‡ *adv.* joyfully
ina ḫūd libbi‡ *adv.* deliberately, intentionally, purposely, spontenously
ina ḫūli‡ *adv.* abroad
ina idi alāku‡ *vp.* to accompany, protect
ina idi uzuzzu‡ *vp.* to assist, stand at someone's side
ina irti *prp.* against, toward(s)
ina irti X alāku‡ *vp.* to come upon, meet, run into
ina irti X maqātu‡ *vp.* to bump into
ina issēt šēpi uzuzzu‡ *phr.* to be handicapped
ina išāti šarāpu‡ *vp.* to destroy by fire
ina kaspi *adv.* for money, moneywise
ina kētti *adv.* honestly, sincerely, truly, truthfully
ina kibri *adv.* ashore
ina kūm *prp.* instead of, in lieu of
ina kūmi *prp.* instead
ina kussê ušābu‡ *vp.* to accede to the throne
ina kutalli *adv.* behind, in the back, in the rear, abaft; instead
ina lā minātīšu* *adv.* incalculably, unpredictably, unforeseenly, unexpectedly
ina lā mūdānūti‡ *adv.* inadvertently, inexpertly, unawares, unwittingly
ina lā simānīšu* *adv.* unseasonably, prematurely, untimely
ina lā simini *adv.* prematurely
ina lā ūmi *adv.* precociously
ina libbi *prp.* in, among; with; within
ina maḫar* *prp.* before
ina maḫirti *adv.* previously(?)
ina marušti* *adv.* reluctantly
ina mar'ūti nasāḫu‡ *vp.* disinherit
ina māt nakiri‡ *adv.* abroad
ina matēma *adv.* whenever, anytime, ever, always
ina matimēni *adv.* ever

ina memmēnī-‡ *prp.* at s.o.'s own expense
ina mēreštī‡ *adv.* deliberately
ina mišil ḫūlī‡ *adv.* halfway, midway
ina mūdānūtī‡ *adv.* consciously, willingly
ina muḫḫi *prp.* on, upon, on top of; against, contra, versus; onto, to; about, concerning, regarding, with regard to, as to; apropos [of]; owing to
ina muḫḫi aḫāiš *adv.* all together
ina muḫḫi ašli *adv.* at once, directly, immediately, offhand, outright, straightaway
ina muḫḫi maqātu‡ *vp.* to run into
ina muḫḫi pê‡ *prp.* at the command of
ina muḫḫi X saḫāru‡ *vp.* to turn against
ina mūši mašil* *adv.* at midnight
ina nakiri‡ *adv.* abroad
ina nēbarti tānti* *adv.* overseas
ina pān *prp.* before, in the presence of
ina pānāt *prp.* before, in the presence of
ina pāni dagālu‡ *vp.* to await, expect, look for, look forward to
ina pānīti *adv.* formerly, before; beforehand
ina pēthalli *adv.* on horseback, astride
ina pī ḫūli† *adv.* (to be) in the way, in s.o.'s way
ina pirṣātī‡ *adv.* deceitfully
ina pitti *prp., adv.* according to; accordingly
ina pūḫi *adv.* in exchange, instead, on loan
ina pūḫi tadānu‡ *vp.* to loan
ina puḫur* *prp.* among
ina pūt *prp.* contrary to, opposite; according to
ina pūt aḫāiš* *adv.* face to face
ina pūti *adv.* accordingly
ina qanni *adv.* outdoors, outside
ina qāt *prp.* at the disposal of; through, care of
ina qāti *adv.* manually
ina qāti ba"û‡ *vp.* to hold responsible for, call to account
ina qāti kullu‡ *vp.* to maintain
ina qāti manû‡ *vp.* to deliver to, hand over
ina qereb* *prp.* inside, in, within, among, amid, in the midst of
ina qīti* *adv.* at the end; eventually, finally, ultimately
ina rēši *adv.* at the beginning, ahead of
ina ṣerreti kullu‡ *vp.* to tether
ina ṣilli *adv.* under the aegis of; in shadow
ina šalši ūmi *adv.* the day before yesterday
ina šapliš *adv.* downstairs
ina šapti šakānu‡ *vp.* to put on one's lips, utter
ina šēpi *adv.* afoot, on foot
ina šēṭūti* *adv.* carelessly, inadvertently, negligently
ina šiāri *adv.* tomorrow
ina šīmti* *adv.* inevitably, naturally, necessarily, of course
ina šulmi alik* *phr.* bye [bye], goodbye, farewell
ina tarṣi *prp.* at the time of, in the reign of; during, towards
ina timāli *adv.* yesterday
ina tukulti‡ *prp.* with the support of
ina ṭēbūti ša *prp.* by grace of
ina ṭūbi‡ *adv.* accurately
ina ūmīšu‡ *adv.* at that time, then
ina X elû‡ *vp.* to forfeit, run out
inanna* 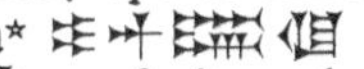 *adv.* now
inbu  *n.* fruit; embryo, flower*
inbu bēl arḫi *n. cp.* (royal) calendar, hemerology
indu *n.* obligation to work, imposition
ingallu 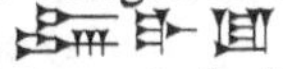 *n.*[1/3] sickle
ingirāšu* *n.* (a fruit tree)
ingu 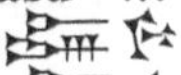 *n.* (an object)
inḫu  *n.*[1] sigh, whine
iniānu◊  *n.* (a copper object)
inimmû* *n.* word
innamāri  *adv.* at daybreak, in the morning
innidi *prp.* beside, near, close to
inninnu 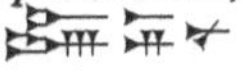 *n.* (a cereal, perhaps a type of barley)
innirti *prp.* against, towards
innû 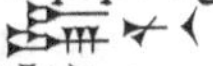 *poss. pron.* ours
inu* 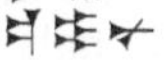 *n.* (a stringed instrument)
īnu* *n.* lore, job, craft
inum* *conj.* when
inūma* 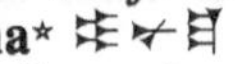 *conj., prp.* then, when
inūmīšu* *adv.* at that time, in those days, then
inūšu* *adv.* at that time, then
inzurātu  *nf.* scarlet
ipinnutu  *nf.* (a wooden object)
ippiru*  *n.* confusion, struggle
ipqu* *n.* embrace
ipqu⁺ *n.* hug
ipšu* *n.* action, deed
ipu* *n.* membrane; afterbirth, placenta; blinkers
iqabbûniššu *vp.* so-called, titled
iqnû  *adj., n.* sky-blue, azure; lapis

lazuli
iqqur īpuš *n.* (hemerological omen series)
irat šēpi* *n. cp.* instep
irbu *n.* income, revenue[s]
irgilu *n.* (a locust)
irginu *n.*[1] (a breed or color of horse, mauve(?))
irīšu* *n.* smell, scent, fragrance, odour
irnittu* *nf.* triumph, victory
irṣiṣu *n.*[1] (a precious item)
irti barāri *adv.* at dusk
irtu *nf.* breast, chest, thorax
irtu nē'u‡ *vp.* to turn the breast, withdraw, flee; (D) to repel
irtu ša qāti* *np.* back of the hand
irṭu *n.* (mng. unkn.)
isāti *nf. pl.* (pl.) womankind
isḫappu* *n.* crook, rogue, villain
isḫu◊ *n.* allocation
isḫunnu *n.* bunch of grapes
isḫunnutu *nf.* bunch of grapes
isḫu B* *n.* string
isḫu C* *n.* arm; fin, flipper; wing
isikku* *n.* (potter's) clay
isiltu* *nf.* swelling, inflation; constipation, constriction
isinnu *n.*[3] festival, festivity
isinnu epāšu‡ *vp.* to hold a festival
isītu *nf.* tower, turret; pile, pyramid
ispillurtu *nf.* cross, crossroads; intersection, junction
isqu *n.*[3] share, lot; prebend
isru* *n.* (a part of the exta)
issēn *num.* one; unique; first
issēn ... issēn *num. phr.* one ... the other
issēn ana šinīšu *adv.* in two, in half
issēniš *adv.* also, in addition; likewise, as well; at the same time, simultaneously
issēnīu *adj.* single, individual
issēnšerīu* *num.* eleventh
issēnūti ... issēnūti *num. phr.* some ... others
issēššerīu *num.* eleventh
issēt *num. f.* one
issi *prp.* with
issi aḫāiš *adv.* together
issi aḫāiš sammuḫu *vp.* to intermingle
issi aḫi‡ *nf. cp.* sister-in-law
issi ēkalli *nf. cp.* queen
issi libbi dabābu‡ *vp.* to be concerned about, think about, ponder, worry
issi nišē māti manû‡ *vp.* to naturalize
issi qanni *prp.* instead
issi X dalāpu‡ *vp.* to be occupied with, stay awake with
issi X šakānu‡ *vp.* side with
issi X udû‡ *vp.* to conspire with
issi X uzuzzu‡ *vp.* to stand by, assist, help
issu *prp.* from
issû* *n.* clay pit
issu bēt *subj.* since, ever since; from where
issu ḫaramme *adv.* recently, of late, lately
issu kutalli maḫāṣu‡ *vp.* to stab in the back
issu libbi *prp.* from
issu māka issu māka‡ *adv.* from various directions, crisscross
issu mār *subj.* since
issu maṣi *subj.* since, inasmuch as; if indeed
issu maṣin *subj.* as though, as if; if indeed, really
issu muḫḫi *prp.* concerning
issu pān *prp.* because of, owing to; from (the presence of)
issu pān X ḫalāqu‡ *vp.* to shirk
issu pî *prp.* by order of
issu pī ḫūli paṭṭuru† *vp.* to clear from the way
issu pūte *adv.* especially, expressly
issu rēši *adv.* from the beginning, initially, originally
issu šapal *prp.* from under
issu šiddi arki‡ *adv.* in detail
issurri *adv.* perhaps, perchance, maybe; possibly, probably, presumably; surely, certainly, doubtless; assuming that, supposing
issūtu *nf.* wifehood, womanhood; marital status
issu B *nf.* woman, wife
isu* *n.* cheekbone, jaw
iṣṣu nāš šīpāti* *np.* silk tree
iṣṣūr ḫurri *n. cp.* partridge
iṣṣūr ṣēri* *n. cp.* wildfowl
iṣṣūr šāri* *n. cp.* vane, weathercock
iṣṣūr tānti* *n. cp.* seabird
iṣṣūriš* *adv.* like a bird
iṣṣūrtu *nf.* female bird
iṣṣūru *nf.* bird, poultry*
iṣṣūru rabiu *n. cp.* duck, goose
išānû* *adj.* possessive
išariš* *adv.* straight, correctly, fairly, duly, normally, easily

išartu◊ *nf.* justice
išaru* *adj.* straight, direct; correct, normal; just, righteous; straightforward, upright
išarûtu* *nf.* righteousness
išât api* *nf. cp.* wildfire
išât ṣimirti+ *nf. cp.* inflammatory fever
išâtiš* *adv.* on fire, ablaze
išâtu *nf.* fire; lightning; bonfire, (bon)fire beacon, pyre
išâtu karâru‡ *vp.* to kindle fire
išâtu šaḫuzu‡ *vp.* to set on fire, set fire to
išâtu ummudu‡ *vp.* to set afire
išdâiu+ *adj.* fundamental
išdi bukâni *n. cp.* (an insect)
išdi tânti* *n. cp.* seabed
išdiḫu *n.* lucre, prosperity
išdu *n.*^{3} foundation; base, bottom, stump, root; stance, basis
išḫu *n.* (a cloth or leather item)
išḫu† *n.* allocation
išḫu B *n.* (a precious stone)
išid eleppi* *n. cp.* bilge, hull of a ship
išid šamê* *n. cp.* horizon
išippu* *n.* purification priest, exorcist
išippûtu* *nf.* (position of a purification priest)
išittu* *nf.* treasure
iškâru *n.*^{3} quota, impost, allotment; series; curriculum, syllabus; (institutional) field
iškâru+ *n.*^{3} field of labor, farm
išku *nf.* testicle
iškûrtu* *nf.* candle
iškuru *n.* wax
išpattalu† *n.* overnight accommodation
išpikku *n.*^{1} storage bin, silo; bucket
išpu *n.*^{1} (a container)
išputu *nf.* quiver
išqillatu* *nf.* shell, pebble
išqippu *n.* (a worm)
išqûqu *n.* (a fine quality of flour, white flour)
iššakku* *n.* vice-regent, vicar, representative
iššakkûtu* *nf.* vice-regency
iššanû *poss. pron.* theirs, their
iššaššûmi *adv.* the day before yesterday
iššiari *adv.* tomorrow
iššû *poss. pron.* his
ištâru* *n.*$^{1/2/3}$ goddess
ištêniš* *adv.* entirely, together
ištênûtu* *nf.* unit
ištîššu* *adv.* once
ištu* *conj., prp.* from, since, after, as soon as

ištuḫḫu* *n.* whip
išû* *v.* to have, possess
itannu* *n.* mesh, interstice
itât* *prp.* around
itâti* *n. pl.* surroundings, environs
itbârtu* *nf.* club, consortium
itbâru† *n.* friend, colleague; shareholder
itbârûtu† *nf.* business partnership, partnership*
itê* *prp.* alongside, adjacent to, next to
itguru* *adj.* entangled, intertwined; complex, complicated, tricky; crooked
itgurûtu* *nf.* complication, entanglement*
itḫiṣu *n.* (a type of field)
itḫurânûtu* *nf.* posthumous fame
itḫuru *n.*^{3} emblem, token
itḫusu* *n.* sobbing
itḫuzu* *adj.* interconnected, well versed
itmû* *v.* to nod the head
itpâlu* *adj.* responsive
itpêšu* *adj.* expert, competent
itqânu* *adj.* fleecy
itqu *n.* fleece, lock of hair, wad, tuft of wool, fuzz*
itqurtu ša abâri* *np.* eye salve, collyrium
itqûru *n.*^{3} spoon, dipper, bowl, pan*
ittêltu◊ *adv.* once; first
itti* *prp.* with
ittimâli *adv.* yesterday
ittimma◊ *adv.* in addition
ittu *nf.* mark, sign, signal, omen, portent, augury, prognostic, token, manifestation*, trait*; gesture*
ittu* *nf.* marker, road marker, signpost; feature, characteristic, peculiarity; analogy; password
ittû* *n.* pitch, tar
ittu tadânu *vp.* to beckon, signal, motion
ittussu *nf.* grain sack(?)
ittû B* *n.* funnel, seed-funnel
itu◊ *prp.* beside, near
itû* *n.*$^{1/3}$ border, boundary
Itu'âiu *adj., n.* Itu'ean; (light) archer, auxiliary archer
itûtu* *nf.* discovery, finding; selection
Itu'u *n.* Itu'ean(s); (light) archer, auxiliary archer
itû B* *n.* neighbor
iṭṭû *n.* crude bitumen, pitch
izbânu* *adj.* monstrous
izbu *n.* anomaly, malformation, malformed birth, monster, oddity*
izimtu* *nf.* desire, wish; object, objective
izirû *n.* arm, upper arm

izru* *n.* curse
izzirtu  *nf.* curse, damn*, swear-word*
kabābu* *n.* 1/3 (heavy) shield
kabābu B◊ *v.* a/u to burn
kabādu *v.* i/i to be important, respected; (D) to honor
kabādu+ *v.* i/i (D) to chafe
kabakku  *n.* (a type of land)
kabālu* *v.* a/u to be crippled; be paralysed; to hobble, limp; (D) to constrict, disable, immobilize, paralyse
kabāru  *v.* i/i to be thick, be fat, thicken (itr.); (D) to fatten, thicken (tr.)
kabāsu  *v.* a/u to tread upon, step, trample; to tread down, put down, quell, repress, suppress, subdue, curb; to domesticate; to forgive, remit, stamp out
kabāsu*  *v.* a/u (D) to extinguish, pardon; (Š) to subjugate, have trampled
kabāsu+ *v.* a/u to break in, keep under, press hard upon, subjugate, tame; to filch, pilfer
kabattu  *nf.* liver; mind, mood, humor, temper, spirits; innards
kabātu*  *v.* i/i to be weighty, be important, be respected; to outweigh, preponderate; (D) to honor
kabbīru+ *adj.* considerable
kabbû *v.* (D) to sew, stitch; to mend, patch
kabbudu *adj.* honored
kabbulu 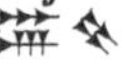 *adj., n.* lame, cripple(d), disabled, invalid, limping
kabbulūtu* *nf.* disability
kabburu *adj.* fattened; fat, fatty, plump, obese, portly, pudgy
kabbusītu  *nf.* outline, relief(?)
kabdu *adj.* heavy; important, honored
kabdūtu* *nf.* gravity, heaviness, prestige, solemnity
kabittu*  *nf.* main part, bulk
kablu  *n.* 3 leg (of a piece of furniture)
kabnu* *n.* casing, tyre(?)
kabra irti* *adj. cp.* burly, stalwart, stocky, sturdy
kabru  *adj.* thick, fat; chubby; corpulent, gross, ponderous, stout
kabrūtu* *nf.* fatness, obesity, thickness
kabsu  *n.* 1 young sheep, young ram
kabsu a. *adj.* broken up, domesticated
kabsu a.+ *adj.* broken in, downtrodden, pent-up, subdued, tamed
kabsutu  *nf.* young ewe
kabsūtu* *nf.* repression
kabsūtu+ *nf.* bondage, subjection; self-control
kabtu* 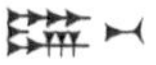 *adj.* heavy, weighty; important, salient, prestigious; dignified, honored, honorable, respectable, venerable; grave, momentous, serious, solemn
kabtu n.* *n.* 4 dignitary
kabû◊ *n.* 1 excrement, dung
kabūt alpi *nf. cp.* cow-dung
kabūt sissê *nf. cp.* horse-dung
kabūtu  *nf.* dung
kadammu  *n.* 3 storeroom
kadāru  *v.* i/i to mark off, delimit
kadāru B *v.* i/i to toil
kadāru B+ *v.* i/i to become weak, become sickly, be wearied; (D) to enfeeble
kadāru C* *v.* i/i to be wild, arrogant, insubordinate; (Š) to make fierce, incite
kaddāru+ *adj.* meddlesome, obtrusive
kadibbidû* 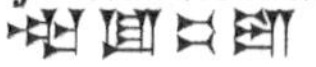 *n.* aphasia, oral paralysis
kadru* *adj.* wild, goring, aggressive
kādu◊  *n.* fort
kaiamānlu  *adj., adv.* constant, permanent; everyday, regular, routine; customary, usual, habitual; familiar, homely; veritable, natural*
Kaiamānu *n.* Saturn
kaiamānu  *adv.* constantly, regularly; usually, mostly; always
kaiamānūtu* *nf.* habit, routine
kaiāna* *adv.* constantly, regularly
kaiānu*  *adj.* constant
kak dāmi  *n. cp.* bloodstained weapon
kakkab Marduk*  *n. cp.* star of Marduk (Mercury)
kakkabānu  *n.* 3 (gray) partridge; starry
kakkabtu  *nf.* star-shaped object, rosette, asterisk*
kakkišu  *n.* 3 weasel, polecat
kakku  *n.* weapon, warfare
kakkû* *n.* lentil
kakku sakku  *n.* (an esoteric compendium)
kakkubu  *n.* star; constellation; celestial body, orb
kakkubu rabiu *np.* big star, falling star, shooting star, meteor, meteorite
kakkubu ṣalmu* *n.* black star (Saturn)
kakkul zibli* *n. cp.* dustbin, rubbish bin,

trash can, waste bin

kakkullânu *adj.* basket-like, basket-bodied

kakkullânu+ *adj.* dappled, speckled, spotted

kakkullu *n.* ^{1} scuttle, fruit-basket, waste-basket

kakkultu *nf.* eye-ball

kakkultu+ *nf.* pill, spot

kakkussu *n.* ^{2} (an ornament)

kakugallu* *n.* ^{1} exorcist, magician

kakugallûtu* *nf.* magic, exorcism

kal muššuli* *np.* perfect likeness

kal ûmi *n. cp.* daytime

kalab mê* *n. cp.* otter

kalab urṣi* *n. cp.* badger

kalakku *n.* ^{1} kelek, raft

kalakku B* *n.* mortar

kalakku C◊ *n.* ^{3} underground store, grain silo, basement, cellar

kalâma* *pron.* all, all kinds of; whole, entire; everything; in every respect, everywhere

kalamâḫu *n.* chief chanter, chief lamentation priest

kalappu *n.* ^{3} axe, pick axe

kalâṣu* *v.* $^{i/i}$ to contract o.s., shrink, pucker [up]

kalbâniš* *adv.* like a dog, doggedly

kalbânu* *n.* (a siege engine)

kalbânu B* *adj.* canine

kalbatânu* *adj.* bitchy

kalbatu* *nf.* bitch, female dog

kalbu *n.* ^{2} dog, hound

Kalbu* *n.* (constellation) Hercules

kalbûtu+ *nf.* hydrophobia

Kalḫu *n.* Calah

kališ* *adv.* completely

kalîš* *adv.* overall, totally, throughout, wholly

kalîtu *nf.* kidney

kâliu* *n.* (a bird, perhaps crane)

kalkaltu* *nf.* lever, sweep

kallabûnu *n.* migratory locust

kallamâri *adv.* early morning, dawn; tomorrow morning

kallâp šipirti *n. cp.* dispatch rider

kallâpu *n.* $^{2/3}$ (armored) horseman, knight, outrider

kallat Šama&* *nf. cp.* dragonfly

kalli kaqqidi* *n. cp.* cranium

kalliu *n.* mule express, post service; post-stage; post-rider, postman, courier

kallu *n.* $^{1/3}$ bowl, dish, urn; shell

kallulu *v.* (D) to veil; to crown

kallulu+ *v.* (D) to adorn with garlands, crown as bride, unite in marriage

kallumu* *v.* (Š) to reveal, disclose

kallumu *v.* (D) to show, display, exhibit; to demonstrate, declare, divulge, expose, reveal, make apparent, set forth; to indicate, betoken, point out, assign; to teach

kallutu *nf.* bride, daughter-in-law

kallûtu *nf.* status of a daughter-in-law/bride

kalmutu *nf.* parasite, louse, vermin, bug; insect(s)

kalu* *adj., pron.* all, whole, every

kalû *v.* $^{a/a}$ to hold back, hold up, keep back, detain, retain; to stop, stunt; to withhold, refuse, deny, ban, forbid, hinder, prevent, prohibit, restrain; to imprison, shut up; (Gtn) to delay; (Š) to reserve; (N) to cease, stop; to remain, stay

kal'u* *adj.* stuck

kalû+ *v.* $^{a/a}$ to intercept

kalûmiš* *adv.* like lambs

kalûmu◊ *n.* ^{1} lamb

kalûtu *nf.* lamentation texts

kalû B *n.* ^{1} chanter, lamentation priest; (pl.) choir

kalzu *n.* ^{2} community, contingent

kamâdu◊ *v.* $^{a/u}$ to knit

kamâdu+ *v.* to fade

kamâmu* *v.* $^{a/u}$ to nod the head, bob

kamantu *nf.* (a plant)

kamânu *nf.* (a sweetened cake), wafer*

kamâru *v.* $^{i/i}$ to heap, pile up, accumulate

kamâru* *v.* $^{i/i}$ to add up, sum up, total (up), tot (up); (Gt) to be heaped up, accumulated; to add up to

kamâru *v.* $^{i/i}$ (D) to heap up, pile up, amass, mass, clump

kamâru šakânu‡ *vp.* to defeat

kamâru B* *n.* defeat

kamâsu *v.* $^{i/i}$ to gather, assemble; (D) to sit, live, stay, be resident

kamâsu B* *v.* $^{i/i}$ (Š) to have kneel down, make submit

kamâṣu *v.* $^{i/i}$ to crouch, kneel, squat, cower

kamâtiš* *adj.* to outside

kameššeru* *n.* pear (tree)
kamēšu *n.* (a kind of food)
kāmidu *n.* knitter, carpet-knitter
kamīš* *adv.* like a captive, in fetters
kamīš šūšubu‡ *vp.* to make live in bondage
kamītu* *nf.* outside; (pl.) environs
kammu* *n.*^{3} (esoteric) composition, text
kammutu *nf.* shield-boss
kammu B* *n.*^{2} mildew
kamru* *adj.* piled up
kamû* *v.*$^{i/i}$ to vanquish, bind
kamunû *n.* mo[u]ld (fungus)
kamūnu *n.* cumin
kamūssu* *adv.* in fetters
kamūšu* *n.* blight
kamûtu* *nf* *b* bondage
kamû B* *adj.* outer
kanakku* *n.* (mng. uncert.)
kanaktu *nf.* frankincense(?)
kanāku *v.*$^{a/u}$ to seal
kanānu* *v.*$^{a/u}$ to twist, coil, wrap up, roll up; to tuck up, cuddle up, curl up, snuggle
kanānu† *v.*$^{a/u}$ (Štn) to bed down, bow down, kowtow
kanāšu* *v.*$^{u/u}$ to bend, bend down, bow down, give in, ply, submit to; (D) to subject, subjugate, make bow; (Š) to subjugate, make submit, bear down, force into submission
kanāšu n. *n.* obeisance
kanāšunu *obl. pron.* you
kandalānu *adj.* kettle-stand-like
kandalu* *n.* kettle-stand
kandirši *n.*^{2} (a garment or item of attire)
kandu *n.* pitcher
kanīku *nf.* sealed document
kankannu *n.*^{1} pot stand
kanku *adj.* sealed, opaque, closed off*, hidden*
kannāšu+ *n.* scavenger
kannu *n.*^{1} pot stand
kannû† *v.* (D) to accommodate, put up
kannû *v.* (D) to make up, spruce up, dress up, smarten, prepare (for burial)
kannu+ *n.* support, base, candlestick
kannû a. *adj.* honored, cared for, cherished, smart, dapper*, neat*
kannušu *v.* to gather, collect
kannušu+ *v.* to aggregate, assemble, bring together, compile, convoke, epitomize
kannu B *n.* sprig, shoot
kannu B+ *n.* stalk, stem
kanšiš* *adv.* submissively
kanšu* *adj.* submissive, docile, yielding, pliable
Kanūnu *n.* (month) Kanun, December
kanūnu *n.* brazier, fireplace, hearth
kanzabu* *n.* clapper
kāp tānti* *n. cp.* reef
kapādu *v.*$^{u/u}$ to plan, project, scheme ?kapa:pu to bend, curve, bow; to subdue, surround, to attempt*
kapālu* *v.*$^{i/i}$ to roll up, wind up; (Gt) to intertwine
kaparru* *n.* shepherd boy
kapāru *v.*$^{a/u}$ to wipe, wipe clean, cleanse, burnish, polish, purify, scour; to smear, coat with
kapāṣu* *v.*$^{i/i}$ to be curled, be bent, bend back, crumple; (D) to bend, distort
kapāṣu+ *v.*$^{i/i}$ to constrict, contract, flinch, put shortly, recapitulate, restrain; (Gt) to stagnate
kapātu◊ *v.*$^{i/i}$ to extend
kapātu* *v.*$^{i/i}$ to accrue(?); (D) to collect, roll into ball, form ball; to form a pellet, pill
kapātu+ *v.*$^{i/i}$ to accede, ball, form into a pod; (D) to thicken, form into a knot
kapdu◊ *adv.* at once, fast
kapdu a.* *adj.* planned, projected
kāpidu* *n.*^{4} planner
kāpilu *n.* (a leather object)
kāpir diqāri *n. cp.* pot caulker, dishwasher(?)
kappaltu* *nf.* groin
kappi ēni* *n. cp.* eyelid, eyelash
kappu *n.*$^{1/2}$ drinking bowl
kappu ṣapāpu‡ *vp.* to teach to fly
kappupu *adj.* bent, hunched, stooped
kappu B* *n.*$^{1/2}$ wing, plumage; feather, quill; arm
kappu C* *adj.* convex, curved
kapru *n.*$^{2/3}$ village, hamlet
kapṣu* *adj.* bent up, bent, crumpled, distorted
kapṣu+ *adj.* abbreviated, brief, concise, curt, self-contained, terse
kapšarru *n.* engraver
kapšarrūtu* *nf.* carving, sculpting
Kaptara* *n.* Crete
kaptukku *n.* two-seah jar
kāpu *n.*^{2} embankment, cliff,

rock

kāpu* *n.*^{2} crag, precipice, steep rock

kaqqad Pazūzi *n. cp.* Pazuzu head (amulet)

kaqqad šiltāḫi† *n. cp.* arrowhead

kaqqad ubāni *n. cp.* fingertip

kaqqadānu *adv.* bigheaded; headlong

kaqqar bāṣi* *n. cp.* sand desert, sands

kaqqar giṣṣi* *n. cp.* moorland

kaqqudu *n.*^{3} head; beginning; capital, principal; personage

kaqqudu nakāsu *vp.* behead, decapitate

kaqquru *n.* earth, ground, soil, underground; plot of land, land; location, territory, terrain, region; surface, area; room, space, tract

karābu *v.*$^{a/u}$ to bless, adore, invoke, to congratulate*, thank*

karābu n. *n.* benediction, blessing

karāku *v.*$^{i/i}$ to gather; to wrap, twine; to fold, roll up; to do jointly; (N) to be assembled

karāku+ *v.*$^{i/i}$ to fold up, roll round, roll together, shroud, swathe, wrap; (N) to go around with

karāku epāšu *vp.* to perform s.th. jointly

karallu* *n.* goad

karāmu *v.*$^{i/i}$ to hinder, restrain, delay; to grasp, seize, to clutch*

karāmu B *v.* to stock up, store; to heap, pile up

karān ḫāli *n. cp.* vinegar

karān lā'i *n. cp.* (a kind of wine)

karān šēlibi* *n. cp.* fox-wine

karān šēlibi+ *n. cp.* bittersweet, nightshade, horse nettle

karānu *n.* wine; grapes

karānu ḫabburu *np.* full-bodied wine

karapḫu *n.*^{1} fallow

karāru *v.*$^{a/u}$ to lay, place, put down, set, set up; to locate, situate; to throw, cast, launch; to dispose, discard, throw up; (stat.) to be located, be situated

karāsu *v.* to be cold, cool

karāṣu *v.*$^{i/i}$ to pinch off, break off

karāṣu+ *v.*$^{i/i}$ to nip

karaš alpi+ *n. cp.* tripe

karašû* *n.* annihilation, catastrophe, disaster, calamity, concentration camp*

karāšu B* *n.* camp

karātu *v.*$^{i/i}$ to slice, break off, cut off, to whittle*

karballutu *nf.* crest, helmet crest

karballutu+ *nf.* bird's crest, cock's comb, tuft

kāribu *n.* blesser, pilgrim, thankful*

kāriṣu* *n.*^{4} miser, niggard, penny-pincher, skinflint

karkadinnu *n.*$^{1/3}$ confectioner

karkadinnutu *nf.* female confectioner

karkartu *nf.* (a condiment)

karku *adj.* amassed, gathered

karmiš* *adv.* to ruins

karmu *n.*^{2} heap, pile of grain, granary

karmu* *n.*^{2} (ruin) heap

karmūtu* *nf.* ruin

karpāniš* *adv.* like a pot

karpassu* *n.* cotton(?)

karpatiš* *adv.* like a pot

karputu *nf.* (clay) vessel, pot, earthenware

karrāṭu+ *n.* carving knife

karru* *n.* knob, pommel

karrû* *adj.* short

karrû+ *v.* (D) to deplore

karru B* *n.* mourning garment

karsu *adj.* cool

karṣē akālu‡ *vp.* to backbite, blaspheme, calumniate, cavil, defame, denigrate, denounce, inveigh against, libel, nag, nibble, slander

karṣu *n.* morsel; (pl.) slander, calumny

karšāiu+ *adj.* abdominal

karšānu *adj.* big-bellied, paunchy

karšānu+ *adj.* voracious

karšu *n.*^{1} stomach; mind; interior

karšu+ *n.*^{1} abdomen, belly, cavity, paunch, womb

karšu B *n.* leek

kartappu◊ *n.*^{1} groom

karû *v.*$^{u/u}$ to be short, draw in

karû† *v.*$^{u/u}$ (D) to amortize, make a payment on

karû *v.*$^{u/u}$ (D) to shorten, abbreviate, abridge

kāru *n.*^{2} quay, quay-bank, landing-place; pier, jetty, wharf; port, harbor, haven; trading station, trade colony, colony

kâru* *v.* to be benumbed, dazed, fall into stupor, become unconscious; (D) deaden, dope

karû ikki *n. cp.* bad mood, moping, sulking, impatience

karû B *n.*^{2} grain-heap; grain-store, pile of barley

karû C* *n.* yardarm, mast(?)

karzillu* *n.* lancet, scalpel

kasāmu† *v.*$^{a/u}$ to chop up, chip, mince

kasânītu *nf.* (beet-like) carnelian

kasap kīsi* *n. cp.* small money, change

kasāpu *v.*$^{a/u}$ to break off, chip, chop off

kasāru *v.*$^{i/i}$ to block, stanch, clog, jam; to pave

kasāsu *v.*$^{a/u}$ to chew, gnaw; to encroach on

kasāsu+ *v.*$^{a/u}$ to munch, to blame, chide, rebuke

kasilaqqu◊ *n.* treasure, sealed tablet(?)

kāsip libbi* *adj. cp.* harrowing, heart-breaking

kasītu* *nf.* (magical) constraint

kasītu B* *nf.* (a stone)

kasītu B+ *nf.* coral

kasiu *n.* common beet

kaskāsu *n.* breastbone

kaspānāiu+ *adj.* financial

kaspu *n.*^{1} money, cash

kaspu* *n.*^{1} silver

kaspu tadānu‡ *vp.* to pay down

kassupu *adj.* chopped

kasû *n.* to bind

kāsu *n., nf.* goblet, cup

kasû+ *v.*$^{i/i}$ to enfold

kāsu+ *n.*^{3} beaker, chalice, drinking-vessel

kasūsu *n.* falcon, hawk

kasūtu *nf.* hop(s); dodder

kasû B* *v.*$^{i/i}$ cuscuta

kaṣābu* *v.*$^{a/u}$ to reduce, pare off(?)

kaṣāpu *v.*$^{i/i}$ to reckon, calculate, estimate, evaluate, to assume*, presume*, suppose*, surmise*; (D) to make plans, speculate, think

kaṣāru *v.*$^{a/u}$ to tie, knot; to organize, construct, compose, form; to put together, collect; to concentrate; to prepare; to re-establish, rehabilitate

kaṣāru+ *v.*$^{a/u}$ to complicate, full

kaṣāru n.+ *n.* coercion

kaṣāṣu* *v.*$^{a/u}$ to cut short, trim, clip, snip

kaṣâtu* *nf.* morning

kāṣir ikki* *adj. cp.* resentful

kāṣir nērti* *adj. cp.* murderous

kāṣir qarābi* *n. cp.* warmonger

kāṣiru *n.* tailor, edifying*

kaṣriš* *adv.* briefly

kaṣru *adj.* tied, knotted, well-packed; organized, well-organized; grouped, clustered; concentrated, compact, concise; firmly joined, solid

kaṣru† *adj.* well-packed

kaṣṣāru† *n.* packer, packing-supervisor

kaṣṣû† *v.* to tilt

kaṣṣuru+ *adj.* obsessed

kaṣṣurūtu+ *nf.* obsession

kaṣû* *adj.* to be cool, cold, chilly; (D) to cool, chill

kaṣû a.* *adj.* chilly, cool, cold

kāša *obl.pron.m* you

kašādu *v.*$^{a/u}$ to reach, arrive at; to catch, catch up, catch up with, come by, outstrip; to achieve, get, get at, obtain, attain; to conquer, occupy, take possession of; to vanquish, defeat, win, overcome; (D) to chase away, dispel; to chase, pursue

kašāpu* *v.*$^{i/i}$ to bewitch, enchant, lay under spell

kašāru *v.*$^{i/i}$ to accomplish, achieve, succeed, be successful

kašāru+ *v.*$^{i/i}$ to do with success, be fortunate, prosper

kašāru B* *v.*$^{i/i}$ to repair, restore, compensate

kašāšu* *v.*$^{a/u}$ to assume control of, expropriate

kašāṭu* *v.*$^{i/i}$ to cut down, cut off, chop down

kašdu *adj.* achieved, conquered

kāši *obl.pron.f* you (f.)

kāšidu *adj.* conquering, victorious

kāšidu* *adj., n.*^{4} conqueror, victor, winner

kāšipu* *adj.* charming, enchanting, fascinating

kāširu+ *adj.* advantageous, assiduous, dexterous, diligent, energetic, excellent

kaškaššu* *adj.* overpowering, almighty

kašmaḫḫu* *n.* first class beer

kašpu* *adj.* bewitched, charmed

kašru *adj.* successful

kaššadūtu *nf.* (a device for weighing)

kaššāptu *nf.* sorceress, witch, hag

kaššāpu *n.* sorcerer, witch

kaššu* *adj.* massive, strong

kāšunu *obl. pron.* you (pl.)

kašurrû* *n.* basalt (from Gasur)

kašūšu* *n.* overpowering (weapon)

kataduqqû* *n.* utterance

katāmu  *v.* $^{a/u}$ to cover, cover up, tuck up, conceal, hide; to occult, stain, eclipse; to overwhelm

katāmu*  *v.* $^{a/u}$ (Š) to cover, overwhelm

katāmu  *v.* $^{a/u}$ (D) to cover, cover up, shroud, veil, mask, hush up, connive at

katarru  *n.* lichen

katāru  *v.* $^{i/i}$ to help, aid; get as help, recruit as ally

katāru+ *v.* $^{i/i}$ to abide, await, bide, delay, outstay, stay on, tarry, wait for

katāru B *v.* $^{i/i}$ to wait, hesitate

katātu* *v.* to quiver, ripple, vibrate

katimtu* *nf.* secret

kātiru* *adj.* cooperative, helpful

katmu* *adj.* covered up, concealed, hidden, masked, mysterious*, surreptitious*, ulterior*

katrû*  *n.* gift, present, bribe

katû* *adj.* destitute, poor

kātu  *nf.* (a cereal)

kazābu* *v.* to be charming, be attractive; to tell stories, entertain; (D) to charm, fascinate; to allure, lure, attract, entice; to fawn, cajole, flatter, wheedle; to seduce, vamp

kazāru *v.* $^{i/i}$ to coiffure, curl, dress (hair)

kazbatu* *nf.* allure, attraction

kazbu* *adj.* entertaining; alluring, attractive, charming; inviting, tempting

kazbūtu* *nf.* entertainment, funny stories, lies

kazru *n., adj.* (a devotee of I&tar, coiffured man)

kazrutu *nf.* (a devotee of I&tar, coiffured woman)

kēn* *int.* yes

kēnāti  *n. pl.* righteousness, loyalty, truthfulness, virtues*

kēniš  *adv.* justly, truly, duly, positively

kēniš+ *adv.* fairly

kēnu  *adj., n.* true, authentic, real, actual, factual; truthful, reliable, honest; faithful, loyal; right, righteous, just, virtuous, proper; rightful, legitimate

kēnūtu  *nf.* authenticity, veracity; truthfulness, reliability, honesty, sincerity; faithfulness, fidelity, loyalty; righteousness; legitimacy

kēnūtu+ *nf.* equity, fairness

keppû* *n.* skipping rope; rhombus

kepû* 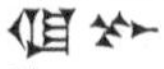 *v.* to bend (back); to blunt, dull

kepû+ *v.* to roost

kepû a.* *adj.* blunt

kerṣappu* *n.* footstool, socle, pedestal

kēru* *adj.* benumbed, dazed, numb, torpid

kēšu* *adj.* awkward, clumsy

kēttu *nf., adv.* truth, candour, fact, reality; truly, really, actually, in fact, indeed; nevertheless, nonetheless

kēttumma *adv.* verily

kî  *conj., prp.* as, like; if, whether

kî aḫāiš *adv.* together

kî annie *adv.* thus

kî annimma *adv.* in the same way, in like manner, likewise, similarly

kî bādi *adv.* in the evening, at night

kî da'āni *adv.* by force, forcibly, violently

kî dannati* *adv.* harshly, roughly

kî lā *prp.* contrary to, against

kî lā libbi *prp.* agaist the will

kî libbī- *adv.* ad-lib, at one's pleasure, arbitrarily

kī maṣi *q.* how much?, how many?

kī maṣi aḫḫūr *q.* how long still?

kī maṣīma *subj.* as if

kī maṣin *subj.* since; as though, as if

kī pî issēn‡ *adv.* unanimously

kî raminī- *adv.* arbitrarily

kî ṣūḫi* *adv.* for fun

kî ša *subj.* (just) as

kī ša kāiamānu‡ *adv.* as usual

kī X dagālu‡ *vp.* to take for

kiādu *v.* (mng. unkn.)

kīam*  *adv.* thus

kibarru* *n.* boat of inflated skins(?)

kibbāni *n. pl.* harrow(s)

kibir ēni* *n. cp.* rim of eye

kibir nāri *n. cp.* river bank

kibirru* *n.* taper, fire-brand

kibrāt erbetti*  *n. pl.* the four quarters, whole world

kibrāti*  *n. pl.* regions, horizons; the world

kibri tānti* *n. cp.* sea-shore, lake-shore

kibrītu* *nf.* sulphur

kibrītu+ *nf.* brimstone

kibru  *n.* ^{3} shore, bank; beach, coast, seashore

kibsu  *n.* $^{1/3}$ track, vestige, trail, path

kibsu+ *n.* $^{1/3}$ footprint

kibsu radû‡ *vp.* to trace, track down

kibšu* *n.* dandruff, mildew, mold

kibtu  *nf.* wheat

kīdānu* *adv.* outside

kīdānû◊ *adj.* outer, external

kidinnu  *n.* divine protection;

protégé

kidinnû◊  *n.* protégé

kidinnūtu *nf.* privileged status

kīdītu* *nf.* exterior, outer part

kīdu* *n.*[1] countryside

kīdû* *adj.* exterior, external

kidudê* *n. pl.* ceremony, rite

kigallu  *n.* pedestal, socle; underworld

kiḫullû*  *n.* mourning-place

kīkî* *q.* how?

kikiṭṭû* *n.* ritual procedure

kikkisu  *n.* reed hut; reed fence, wall

kīku *n.* (mng. unkn.)

kilallān* *pron.* both

kilallē *pron.* both

kilattān* *pron. f.* both

kilīl lumāše+ *n. cp.* sphere, zodiac, Zodiacal circle

kilīliš* *adv.* like a wreath, mural crown; as with a garland

kilīlu *n.* crown, mural crown

kilīlu+ *n.* garland, wreath, chaplet; circle; rim

kilītu* *nf.* restraint

kilītu+ *nf.* attitude

killu  *n.* scream, cry for help, cry of distress; clamour, noise, uproar; cry, wail(ing), lamentation

kilṣu* *n.* contraction, shriveling, shrinkage

kīlu* *n.* break, pause, standstill, stop, interval; cadence; finale

kīma *conj., prp.* when, after, if; like, as

kīma◊ *q.* how much?

kīma atartimma* *adv.* besides, in addition, extra

kimaḫḫu *n.* tomb, mausoleum, sepulchre

kimarru* *n.* infantry

kimru  *n.*[2] (a kind of sheep offering)

kimtu  *nf.* kin, family

kīmu* *prp.* instead

kināltu *nf.* congregation, committee*

kināltu+ *nf.* choir, congress, covey, gentry

kinattu *n.* colleague, employee, fellow-craftsman, fellow worker, relative

kindabassu  *n.* shawl, scarf, tablecloth

kinnāru* *n.* zither

kinṣu  *n.* lower leg, calf of the leg, shin, shank, tibia

kinšu* *n.* curve*, downhill, incline, slope

kinūtu* *nf.* nickname

kipdu* *n.* plan

kiplu  *n.* twine, braid; mole

kippat erbetti *nf. cp.* four quarters (of the earth)

kippu  *n.* snare, noose, loop, trap

kipputu  *nf.* circle, disc; hoop, loop; circumference, perimeter

kipṣu* *n.* constriction, contraction

kipṣu+ *n.* constipation

kīpu *n.*[2] rock, stone

kiqillānu *adj.* dumpy

kiqillutu  *nf.* dung heap, dunghill, refuse dump

kiqillutu+ *nf.* dust-heap

kirbīnu *n.* (a garment)

kiri tilliti *n.* vineyard

kiribtu *nf.* blessing

kiriktu* *nf.* collection, accumulation

kirimāḫu* *n.* arboretum, park

kirimmu* *n.* bosom; shawl

kirinnu* *n.* lump, potter's clay

kirissu* *n.* hairpin, hairslide; pin, clasp

kirītu *nf.* garden

kiriu 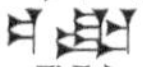 *n.*[3] orchard, garden

kirku  *n.*[1] scroll, roll

kirku+ *n.*[1] armlet

kirnāiu *n.* (a garment)

kirru  *n.*[1/2] storage jar, pithos

kirrutu  *nf.* (a meal)

kirru B* *n.* collarbone, clavicle

kirṣu  *n.* crumb, clot, bit*, jot*

kīrtu* *nf.* daze, coma(?)

kīru *nf.* oven, kiln

kīs libbi  *n. cp.* colic

kisallu *n.*[3] courtyard, patio*

kisalluḫḫatu* *nf.* female courtyard sweeper

kisalluḫḫu* *n.* courtyard sweeper

kisalmāḫu *n.* main courtyard

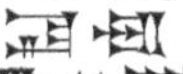

kisibarru 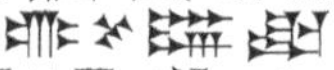 *n.* coriander

kisirtu  *nf.* paving (block), facing

kisittu* *nf.* stem, trunk; stump; line, lineage; descent, ancestry, parentage; origin, pedigree

kiskilāti *n. pl.* clappers

Kislīmu *n.* (month) Kislev, December

kismu* *n.* cutting, weeding

kispu 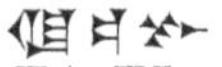 *n.*[1] funerary offering

kissu  *n.* (mng. uncl.)

kissutu  *nf.* fodder

kissutu+ *nf.* forage, hay, provender

kisû* *n.* supporting wall; footing, plinth

kīsu *nf.* money bag, purse
kisukku *n.*[1] grate, grating
kisurru* *n.*[1] territory, border
kiṣallu *nf.* ankle bone, astragal
kiṣiptu *nf.* calculation, computation, appraisal*, assessment*, assumption*, estimation*, evaluation*
kiṣir ammiti *n. cp.* elbow
kiṣir šaddê *n. cp.* bedrock
kiṣir šarri *n. cp.* royal corps, standing army
kiṣirtu *nf.* case, envelope, packing*
kiṣru *n.*[2] group; (military) unit, troop; company, cohort; army corps, corps; joint, knot, node; structure; concentration, link*, section*
kiṣṣu* *n.*[1] cella, chapel, shrine
kišād tānti* *n. cp.* lakeside, seaside
kišādu *n.*[3] neck; neck-stone, amulet, cylinder seal; bank, shore, talisman*
kišdu *n.* attainment, acquisition
kišinnu *n.* bitter vetch
kišittu* *nf.* conquest, walkover; booty, spoil
kiškanû *n.* lime(?), lime-tree
kiškattû* *n.* craftsman, forge
kišpē *n. pl.* sorcery, witchcraft
kišpu* *n.* enchantment
kišru *n.* success
kiššāti* *nf. pl.* expropriation
kiššatu* *nf.* world, universe; totality; full flood
kiššūtu *nf.* hegemony, might, (world) power
kišubbāniš* *adv.* into a waste
kišubbiš* *adv.* into a waste
kišubbû* *n.*[1] fallow field, uncultivated land
kitkittû *n.*[1/3] military craftsman, paramilitary troops
kitmuru* *adj.* heaped up
kitrānūtu* *nf.* alliance(?)
kitru *n.* help, aid; ally; auxiliary troops, auxiliaries; cooperation
kitturru *n.*[3] bench, stool
kitturru B *n.* large frog, toad
kitû *n.* flax, linen; linen garment
kitullu* *n.* (a troop formation?)
kiūru* *n.*[1] cauldron, basin
kizirtu *nf.* emblem, symbol; lock of hair, curl, ringlet, tress; coiffure, hairdo
kizû* *n.* groom, personal attendant
kizzu *n.* (male) goat, buck
kuānu *v.* to be firm, be solid, be loyal, be true, be steady, be stable; (D) to affirm, assure, certify, verify; to confirm, corroborate, prove; to consolidate, stabilize, secure; to attest, testify, vouch; to justify; to set up, establish, institute, found, to convict*, normalize*, ratify*; (Dtt) to be tried, establish o.s.
kuāṣu *v.* to flay
kuāšu *v.* to be late, dawdle, tarry; (D) to be delayed; to tarry
kubādu *n.* honors, veneration
kubru *n.* thickness, diameter
kubšānu* *n.* hoopoe*, (a crested bird)
kubšānu+ *n.* fig-pecker, lark
kubšu *n.* cap, hat, headgear, mitre; (pl.) millinery
kubtu *n.* block, lump; weight, gravity, heaviness; importance
kūbu* *n.* foetus, still-born child, premature baby
kubukku* *nf.* strength, power
kudāru *n.* boundary mark[er]
kudimmu *n.* cardamom; cress
kūdunu *n.*[1] mule, pony*
kūdunu ša kallie *np.* post-horse
kudurrānu *n.* bounder
kudurru *n.*[2] boundary stone, boundary mark[er]
kudurru B* *n.* carrying basket, builder's hod; forced labor
kuḫlu+ *n.* eyeliner
kukittu* *nf.* (mng. uncert.)
kukku *n.* (a cake)
kukkupu *n.* (a small container for libations)
kukkušu* *n.* (a cheap type of flour)
kulbābiš* *adv.* like ants
kulbābu *n.*[1] ant
kulīlītu* *nf.* dragonfly
kulīltu *nf.* fish-woman; dragonfly, mermaid*
kulīlu *n.*[1] fish-man, merman; mayfly
kulīlu* *n.*[1] dragonfly
kullatu* *nf., pron.* totality, all
kullu *v.* to deal with*; (D) to hold, take for; to keep, hold on, keep up, hold to, keep to, retain; to have, wear; to handle, steer, wield; to hang on, keep on; to linger, stay, live in; (Dtt) to be taken for, hold good, hold up, remain valid

kullu ša rēši* *np.* upkeep
kullultu* *nf.* coronation; crenellation(?)
kullumūtu* *nf.* exhibition, display(?)
kullutu *nf.* totality, everything
kullu B *n.*[2] nut, kernel, nutmeat
kulmašītu *nf.* (a hierodule)
kultāru* *n.*[1/3] tent
kulūlu *n.* battlement, crenellation, cornice; crown, mural crown
kuluppu *n.* (an insect)
kulu'u *n.* (an emasculated devotee), choir boy*
kūm *prp.* lest
kūm X apālu‡ *vp.* to represent
kumāru *n.* shoulder
kummu* *n.* cella, cell, inner room, cabinet, compartment
kumû* *n.* pelican
kūmu *adv., conj* instead (of), in lieu of
kūn libbi* *n. cp.* foresight, forethought, prudence
kūn qāti* *n. cp.* procedure
kunāšu
nf. emmer
kundirašši *n.*[2] (a garment or item of attire)
kuninnu *n.* trough
kuniphu *n.*[1] (an alliaceous plant)
kunnu *adj.* confirmed, firm, solid, steadfast, stable; fixed, settled, established, tenable; certified, proved, assured, certain, sure; justified,
kunnû* *v.* (D) to treat kindly, treat with care, cherish, care for
kunnupu* *v.* (D) to take under one's wing, protect
kunnūtu◊ *nf.* care, cherishing; favorite, fosterling
kunnūtu* *nf.* certainty, certitude, sureness
kunšu* *n.* braid, ball (of wool)
kūnu* *n.* firmness, stability
kunuk kišādi* *n. cp.* cervical vertebra
kunukku *n.*[1] seal; gem; vertebra
kunzu* *n.*[1] leather bag
kupartu◊ *nf.* purification
kupatinnu* *n.*[1] globule, pellet, pill, pastille
kupātu *nf.* bird fodder
kupīru *n.* bitumen
kupītu *nf.* (a bird)
kuppu* *n.*[2] cistern, water-source
kuppû *n.* reed, reed-bed, reed thicket, rushes
kuppupu* *adj.* (very) bent, bowed, hunched, stooped
kupputu* *adj.* conglomerated
kuppû B* *n.* eel
kupû *n.* snow, snowfall; ice
kuraggu *n.* rice
kurbān eqli *n. cp.* (a medicinal plant)
kurbānu *n.*[1] clod, lump, clump
kurdinnu *n.* (an aromatic plant)
kurdiššu *n.* pile (of straw)
kurgarrû *n.* corybant, gallus
kurgarrutu *nf.* female corybant
kurḫu *n.* workshop, shop*
kurḫu+ *n.* cabin, cottage, hovel, hut, shanty, shed
kuribtu *nf.* (a kind of field)
kurību *n.*[1] cherub
kurillu* *n.* shock, sheaf, stook, haystack, hayrick, rick, stack
kurinnu *n.* (a neck ornament)
kurissu *nf.* leek
kurītu* *nf.* shin, shin[bone], tibia
kuriu *adj.* brief, curt, short
kurkānû *n.* turmeric(?)
kurkizānu *n.* piglet, young pig
kurkû *n.* crane
kurkurru *n.*[1] (a metal container)
kurru *n.* tanner's paste
kurru B* *n.* cor, kor (c. 8 bushels)
kurru C* *n.* flexure of the groin, fold of the groin
kursinnu *n.*[3] ankle, knuckle; fetlock
kursissu* *n.* (a rodent)
kursiu *n.* leather strap(?)
kurṣipti eqli* *n. cp.* nettle
kurû* *adj.* dwarf, midget, pigmy, pygmy, stumpy
kūru *nf.* kiln, furnace, crucible, refining-pot
kurullu* *n.* funeral pile, pyre
kurummutu *nf.* barley ration; food offering
kurunnu* *n.* date beer or wine, nectar*
kuruppu *n.*[1] basket, hamper
kurussu *n.* strap
kurûtu* *nf.* brevity, shortness

kūrūtu+ *nf.* sultriness
kūru B* *n.* daze, depression, stupor, torpor
Kūsāiu *adj., n.* Cushite, Ethiopian
kusāpu *n.*[1] bread
kusarikku*  *n.*[1] bull-man
kusīpu* *n.*[3] flat, thin bread, pita
kusītu  *nf.* robe, toga
kuspē *n. pl.* husks, bran, residue (of sesame)
kussimtu  *nf.* scale, plate
kussiu  *nf.* throne, chair, seat; sedan chair
kūsu *n.* (a topographical feature)
kusup dišpi *n. cp.* wax
kusup libbi  *n. cp.* broken heart, bleeding heart*
kuṣṣu  *adj., n.* cold, coldness, cold temperature, cold weather, winter; ague, chill, shivering
kuṣurtu* *nf.* necklace clasp
kušīru *n.* success, profit, benefit, good fortune*
kušīru+ *n.* advantage, activity, assiduity, diligence, prosperity
kušru *n.* (a plant)
kuššû* *v.* to expand
kušû* *n.* crocodile(?)
kutāḫu *n.*[1/3] lance
kutallānu† *adj.* backward
kutallu 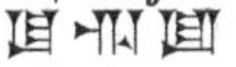 *n.* back, rear; reserves
Kutê *n.* Cutha
kutlu† *n.*[3] rail, fence
kutmu* *n.* cover, covering, mask
kuttimmu  *n.* goldsmith
kuttumu* *adj.* covered; inaccessible
kūtu *nf.* (a vessel for wine, beer and oil, flagon)
kutummu*  *n.* mat; cover; veil; scabbard, sheath
kuzallu† *n.* (eleventh month)
kuzbānu* *adj.* alluring, graceful, sensual, erotic, sexy
kuzbānû* *adj.* attractive
kuzbu 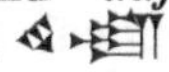 *n.* charm, charisma, grace; allure, attractiveness, attraction, (sex) appeal; sexual potency, sex, sexuality
kuzippu  *n.*[1] garment, cloth, suit (of clothes), costume
kuzubtu† *nf.* flattery, seduction, temptation*
kuzzubu* *adj.* (highly) attractive, very charming, luscious, ravishing, winning
la *prp.* from
lā *part.* no, not, nor; shan't, won't; un-, (...) qabu^ to deny, forbid
lā+ *part.* nay
lā ... lā *part.* neither ... nor
lā ... šina *phr.* aren't
lā ... šunu *phr.* aren't
lā a'āri* *adj.* inaccessible
lā ādiru* *adj.* fearless, intrepid; impudent, disrespectful
lā akālu *n.* fasting
lā akī *prp.* unlike
lā ālidu* *adj.* barren, sterile
lā ālidūtu* *nf.* barrenness, sterility
lā āliku *adj.* immobile, motionless
lā amēlu *n.* inhuman, no gentleman
lā amru *adj.* not seen, unforeseen, unnoticed, unseen, unseemly
lā āniḫu* *adj.* indefatigable, strenuous, unflagging
lā apru* *adj.* bareheaded
lā balṭu* *adj.* inamimate, lifeless
lā bašiu* *adj.* nonexistent
lā bašlu *adj.* crude, immature, unrefined, unripe
lā būštu* *n.* indecency, infamy, impudence
lā dāgilu *adj.* blind
lā dāgilūtu* *nf.* blindness
lā damāqu* *v.*[i/i] to disqualify
lā damqu *adj.* bad, ugly, unfortunate, unpropitious, unqualified
lā elê* *np.* unsurmountable
lā ēpišu *adj.* ineffectual, inefficient, inert; do-nothing
lā ēpišūtu* *nf.* inefficiency
lā erpu* *adj.* cloudless
lā eršu *adj.* needless, uncalled-for, unnecessary
lā etāqi* *vp.* impassable
lā gāmilu* *adj.* grim, remorseless, ruthless, implacable
lā gamru *adj.* incomplete, unfinished
lā gitmālu* *adj.* imperfect
lā ḫādiu* *adj.* involuntary
lā ḫakāmu* *v.*[i/i] to misunderstand, misapprehend, misinterpret
lā ḫakmu *adj.* inarticulate, unclear, unintelligible
lā ḫanšu *adj.* insubordinate, unbending, unsubmissive, unyielding, independent*
lā ḫanšūtu* *nf.* independence, insubordination
lā ḫarṣu* *adj.* inaccurate, inarticulate, inexact
lā ḫasās amāti* *n. cp.* forgetfulness, amnesia

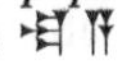

lā ḫasās ṭābti⋆ *n. cp.* ingratitude
lā ḫāsis ṭābti⋆ *adj. cp.* ungrateful
lā ḫāsisu⋆ *adj.* forgetful, heedless, oblivious, thoughtless
lā ḫāsisu* *adj.* unconscious
lā ḫassu⋆ *adj.* unwise, witless, fool
lā ḫāṭiu* *adj.* unerring
lā īdû⋆ *adj.* unknown
lā kabsu* *adj.* unbroken, untamed, wild
lā kaiamānīu* *adj.* extraordinary, inconstant, irregular, uncommon, unnatural
lā kaiamānūtu* *nf.* irregularity
lā kallulu* *adj.* barefaced, unveiled
lā kapdu* *adj.* desultory
lā kāribu* *adj.* thankless
lā kāṣir ikki⋆ *adj. cp.* forbearing
lā kašru* *adj.* unsuccessful
lā kēnu *adj.* false, disloyal, illegitimate, incorrect, insincere, irreal*
lā kettu *n.* untruth
lā kettu dabābu *vp.* to misinform, deceive
lā kunnu* *adj.* unestablished, unjustified
lā kušīri⋆ *np.* profitless, disadvantageous
lā kušīri+ *np.* ineffectual, of no use, unprofitable, useless
lā lamdu⋆ *adj.* inexperienced, innocent
lā lammudu⋆ *adj.* uninitiated, untrained, untried
lā lē'û⋆ *adj.* incompetent, inefficient, inept, hopeless, powerless, unskilled
lā lē'ûtu⋆ *nf.* inability, incompetence
lā magāru *v.* u/u to be disobedient, be uncompromising, gainsay; (N) to be contrary, disagree, dissent, differ; to refuse
lā magāru n. *n.* disagreement*, refusal*
lā māgiru⋆ *adj.* discordant, dissident; disobedient, unobliging; uncooperative, irreconcilable; loath, unwilling
lā magru *adj.* disobliging, unfriendly
lā maḫār⋆ *np.* irresistible, unopposable
lā māḫir šulmāni* *adj. cp.* incorruptible
lā mamman⋆ *pron.* nobody
lā mammāna⋆ *pron.* nobody, no one
lā manê⋆ *np.* countless, numberless
lā māqitu* *adj.* infallible
lā marṣu* *adj.* painless
lā memmēni *pron.* nothing at all, nothing whatever
lā mīnānu *adj.* unspecified, vague
lā mīnu⋆ *adj.* countless, numberless, uncountable, innumerable, untold
lā mitgurtu⋆ *nf.* discord, disobedience, dissension
lā mitguru* *adj.* incompatible, incongruous, irreconcilable
lā mitḫāru⋆ *adj.* disproportionate, diverse, unequal
lā mitḫārūtu* *nf.* disproportion, inequality
lā mitḫuru *adj.* illogical, incoherent, inconsistent
lā mitluku⋆ *adj.* inconsiderate, ill-adviced
lā mūdânūtu *nf.* ignorance
lā mūdû⋆ *adj.* unaware, ignorant
lā mūdû abiti *adj. cp.* ignorant, ignoramus
lā muktappu* *adj.* inflexible
lā mupparkû⋆ *adj.* incessant, never ceasing, unceasing, unfailing
lā mūqā- *np.* cannot, can't
lā mušlu *adj.* unlike
lā mušpēlu *adj.* irreversible, unchangeable
lā muštālu* *adj.* imprudent
lā muštannû* *adj.* invariable
lā muttalliku* *adj.* immovable
lā nakkuru* *adj.* unchanged
lā naparkû⋆ *adj.* ceaseless, incessant
lā nāriṭu* *adj.* unflinching, unshakable
lā naṣru* *adj.* unattended, unguarded
lā nāš kakki* *adj. cp.* unarmed
lā nāši pūtuḫi* *adj. cp.* irresponsible
lā nāṭilu⋆ *adj.* blind
lā naṭû⋆ *adj.* impossible, unsuitable, inadequate
lā nībi *adj.* countless, innumerable, numberless, untold
lā pādû⋆ *adj.* cold-blooded, heartless, inclement, inexorable, grim, remorseless, unrelenting
lā pāliḫu *adj.* disrespectful, fearless, intrepid, irreverent
la pān◊ *prp.* from
lā pārisu* *adj.* indiscriminate
lā parsu* *adj.* bland, indefinite, vague
lā pašāḫi⋆ *np.* incurable
lā patītu  *adj.* virginal
lā paṭāri *np.* incurable
lā pitqudu* *adj.* indiscreet
lā qā'ipu* *adj.* doubtful, sceptical
lā qariu* *adj.* unbidden
lā qatru *adj.* smokeless
lā qēpu *adj.* doubtful, dubious, suspicious, incredulous; incredible, unbelievable
lā qiāpu *n.* disbelieve, doubt, question, suspect
lā qīptu* *nf.* disbelief, doubt, suspicion, misgiving
lā qītu* *n.* infinity
lā qurbu *adj.* absent, unavailable; absen-

tee; irrelevant, unconcerned
lā qurbūtu* *nf.* absence
lā radiu+ *adj.* impolite, misguided, undisciplined, badly brought-up
lā rā'imu *adj.* unloving
lā raksu *adj.* unattached, uncommitted
lā rāš tašīmti* *adj. cp.* half-wit, imbecile
lā rāš ṭēmi* *adj. cp.* unreasonable
lā rāš ṭēmi u milki* *adj. cp.* irrational
lā riddu* *n.* improper conduct
lā sakru* *adj.* unlocked
lā salmu *adj.* unfriendly
lā sapqu* *adj.* inadequate, insufficient
lā simāti* *adj.* inapt, objectionable, undue, unfit
lā simāti-* *np.* unduly
lā simtu* *n.* indignity
lā simunu *n.* wrong moment
lā ṣaḫātu* *n.* apathy, listlessness
lā ṣāḫitu* *adj.* apathetic, listless
lā ṣaḫtu *adj.* undesirable, unwanted
lā ṣālilu* *adj.* restless, sleepless, uneasy
lā šādidu* *adj.* intolerant
lā šaḫsasūtu *nf.* oversight
lā šakru* *adj.* sober
lā šalāmu* *n.* incorrect behavior, unseemly behavior
lā šalmu *adj.* insincere; precarious, unsafe, unfounded, unwarranted; unhealthy, unsound
lā šalṭu* *adj.* unauthorized
lā šāmiu* *adj.* deaf, disobedient
lā šamû *v.* $^{i/i}$ to disobey
lā šanān* *np.* incomparable, insuperable, matchless, peerless, unrivalled, unmatched
lā šāniu+ *adj.* unvaried
lā šaṣbutu* *adj.* unequipped, unprepared
lā šēmû* *adj.* deaf
lā šēzubi* *np.* inescapable
lā šitqulu* *adj.* imbalanced, unbalanced
lā šitqulu+ *adj.* lop-sided
lā tadānu* *n.* non-payment
lā taiār* *np.* relentlessly, without respite
lā takālu* *n.* distrust, mistrust
lā taklu* *adj.* distrustful, fishy, shady, shifty, suspect, unreliable
lā taqnu* *adj.* insecure, questionable
lā tarṣu *adj.* inconvenient, incorrect
lā tēbû* *adj.* incurable
lā ṭābtānu *n.* malefactor
lā ṭābtu *nf.* disfavor
lā ṭābu *adj.* displeasing, inauspicious, insipid, tasteless, uncomfortable, unkind, useless
lā ṭēmānu *adj.* mad, senseless, unreasonable
lā ṭūb libbi *n. cp.* unhappiness, malaise
lā ṭūb libbi* *n. cp.* dissatisfaction
lā ṭūb šīri *n. cp.* infirmity, bad health, unhealthiness
lā unnubu* *adj.* fruitless
lā utar† *int.* no further, that's enough!, no exaggeration
lā zēzu *adj.* undivided
lā ziqnānu* *adj.* beardless
la'āšu* *v.* to dirty, defile
la'ātu* *v.* $^{u/u}$ to absorb, gobble, gulp, swallow (up)
la'ātu+ *v.* $^{u/u}$ to glut
la'āzu+ *v.* to lisp, chant
labābu* *v.* $^{a/u}$ to rage; (N) to become furious
labāku *v.* $^{i/i}$ to be soft, supple; (D) to soften up, moisten, soak, to extenuate*, lubricate*, mollify*
labān appi* *n. cp.* humble prayer, humility, adoration, devotion, prostration, worship
labānu *v.* $^{i/i}$ to mold bricks
labānu B* *v.* $^{i/i}$ to stroke (nose), exhibit humility
labār ūmē *n. cp.* long duration; longevity; distant future
labāriš* *adv.* to old age
labāriš alāku‡ *vp.* to become old, dilapidated
labāriš ūmē‡ *adv.* in days to come, with the passage of time
labāru* *v.* $^{i/i}$ to be old; (D) to make long-lasting; (Š) to prolong
labāšu *v.* $^{i/i}$ to dress
labāšu* *v.* $^{i/i}$ (Gt) to clothe o.s.; (Š) to cover, overlay, bedeck
labāšu *v.* $^{i/i}$ (N) to put on, get dressed, clothe o.s.
labbānu *adj.* lionly, lion-like
labbatu* *nf.* lioness
labbiš* *adv.* like a lion
labbu* *n.* [1] lion
labbunu *n.* [3] (a stand or pedestal)
lābinu *n.* brick maker
labīru *adj.* old, ancient, antique, dated; long-standing, traditional; original, obsolete*, second-hand*
labīru n. *n.* olden times, past
labīrūtu *nf.* old age
labīrūtu alāku‡ *vp.* to grow old, to become dilapidated
labītu *nf.* circuit; circulation,

circumambulation, encircling
labītu labû *vp.* to make the round, circumambulate
lābiu *adj.* encircling, surrounding, circular, roundabout
labku *adj.* moist, supple, soft, tender
Labnāna *n.* Lebanon
labšu* *adj.* clad, clothed, worn
labšu+ *adj.* armed, mailclad, endued
lab'u† *n.* lion
labû  *v.* $^{i/i}$ to go around, get around, go round, circumambulate, circle; to besiege, circumvent, encircle, fence in, surround, wrap up; to turn round, veer, to fence*, hedge*; (Š) to surround, put around, carry around, to circulate*
labû+ *v.* $^{i/i}$ to accompany, convoy, go with
labû a. *adj.* besieged
labussu *nf.* clothing, attire, garment, dress, outfit
lādiru* *adj.* fearless
lādunu* *n.* rockrose, ladanum, labdanum, rose water
lagāru* *n.* (a priest)
laḫannu  *n.* [1] bottle
laḫāšu  *v.* to whisper, murmur, to intimate*
laḫāšu+ *v.* to connive with, insinuate, murmur, speak low, sing softly
laḫātu+ *v.* to pant
laḫḫennu *n.* (temple) steward, caterer
laḫḫennutu *nf.* female caterer, stewardess
laḫīmu* *adj.* hairy
laḫmu* *adj.* hairy
laḫru*  *nf.* ewe
laḫšu* *n.* gum(s)
lā'i gabbi* *adj. cp.* omnipotent
lā'i mê* *adj. cp.* able to swim
lā'i tānti* *adj. cp.* seaworthy
lā'iu *adj.* adroit, competent, meritorious, skilled
lakû  *n.* baby, infant, newborn
lakūtu  *nf.* childhood
lakûtu *nf.* infancy*
lalânu* *adj.* luxuriant, lusty, flourishing, florid
lalgar* *n.* cosmic subterranean water, abyss
laliu  *n.* kid, young goat
lallarītu* *nf.* wailing woman
lallāru* *n.* white honey
lallû  *v.* (D) to give pleasure, fondle
lallû B+ *v.* (Dt) to act foolishly, be a fool, be infatuated, turn stupid, make a fool

lalû  *n.* luxury, luxuriance, exuberance; pleasure, delight; vigour, vitality, prime of life, charisma*
lalû šebû‡ *vp.* to be satisfied
lām* *adv., prp.* before
lamādu  *v.* $^{a/a}$ to apprehend, find out, learn, fathom
lamādu†  *v.* $^{a/a}$ to know, know (sexually); (Gtn) to study, familiarize o.s., take cognizance of
lamādu  *v.* $^{a/a}$ (D) to instruct, teach, explain, make clear, clarify; (Š) to inform, brief
lamaḫuššû  *n.* (a robe)
lamāmu* *v.* $^{a/u}$ to chew, munch; (D) to masticate
lamānu  *v.* $^{i/i}$ to be bad, evil, malignant, unsatisfactory, unfavorable; (D) to make bad, to make unfavorable; to deteriorate, impair, worsen
lamassu  *nf.* angel, protective spirit, tutelary deity
lamdu* *adj.* conversant, erudite, experienced, initiated, learned
lammu *n.* almond tree
lammudu *adj.* broken in, initiated, instructed, taught
lammunu *adj.* very bad, crummy, ill-fated, miserable, pathetic*, piteous*, pitiful*
lamniš† *adv.* badly, poorly*, unfortunately*, unhappily*
lamnu *adj.* bad, evil, malignant, unfortunate, untoward, inauspicious, worst*
lamutānu◊  *n.* attendant, temple servant
lamuttu *nf.* evil, misfortune, wickedness
lānu  *n.* body, figure, outward form, stature; height, size, profile*
lapānu*  *v.* $^{i/i}$ to be poor; (D) to impoverish
lapāpu+ *v.* (D) to compile
lapat armanni  *n.* pomegranate-like turnip
lapātu  *v.* $^{a/u}$ to touch, strike, affect, afflict, infect, to influence*
lapātu*  *v.* $^{a/u}$ (D) to play (a stringed instrument); (Š) to ruin, destroy, defeat, defile, desecrate
lāpitu* *adj.* touching, affecting
laplaptu  *nf.* parching thirst
lapnu  *adj., n.* poor
laptu  *adj.* turnip
laptu B *n.* touched, affected, injured; unlucky, ominous
laputtû◊  *n.* lieutenant;

mayor

laqānu *v.* (mng. unkn.)

laqātu *v.* [u/u] gather, gather up, glean; pick, pick up, collect; subdue

laqātu+ *v.* [u/u] to embroider, peck, pick

laqlaqqu* *n.* stork

laqqātu* *n.* [4] collector*, gatherer

laqqātu+ *n.* [4] embroiderer

laqtu+ *n.* bait

laqû *v.* [i/i] to take; to buy, acquire, purchase; to adopt (child), to shop*

laqû† *v.* [i/i] to receive

lardu  *n.* nard, alkali, soap

larû *v.* to branch (out)*, ramify*

larû n. *n.* branch, twig, bough*

lasāmu *v.* [u/u] to run, race, gallop; to serve

lāsimu *n.* runner, sprinter

lasmu *adj.* cursory, fast, fleet, hurried, rapid, speedy, swift, rash*

lassumu *adj.* speedy, nimble

laššu
part. there is not, is void, is missing, ain't, aren't, isn't

laššu a. *adj.* invalid, idle, null and void

laššu lā *part.* absolutely not, certainly not, really not

laššūtu *nf.* lack of things

lâšu B* *v.* to lick

latāku *v.* [a/u] to check, test, try out, to probe*, try on*

latāku* *v.* [a/u] (Gtn) to experiment

latku *adj.* checked, tested, proven*

lattu *n.* [1] creel (for fish)

laṭiru* *n.* chickling vetch, grass pea

lâṭu* *v.* [u/u] to confine, keep in check, curb, control; to encircle, enclose, to prohibit*

la'û *n.* to be able

lā'u *adj.* (a qualification of wine)

lazānu *v.* [i/i] to banter, deride, flout, gibe, jeer (at), make fun of, mock, ridicule, slander

lazāzu *v.* [a/a] to continue, go on, go ahead, carry on; to endure, persist, perpetuate, persevere, hold [out]

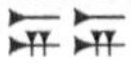

lazāzu+ *v.* [a/a] to be boring, importune, tease

lāzinu* *adj.* impish, mischievous, sarcastic

lazziš* *adv.* persistently

lazzu *adj.* continual, chronic, enduring, perpetual, persistent, drab*, dreary*, humdrum*, monotonous*

lazzu+ *adj.* boring, grievous, importunate, injurious, tiresome

lazzūtu* *nf.* perseverance, persistence

lazzuzu* *adj.* tedious

lazzuzu+ *adj.* bore, importunate person

lebû* *v.* [u/u] to bellow, bleat, hiss, howl, hum, squeal; to whine, groan, cry out

leḫēmu◊  *v.* [i/i] to eat, taste

leḫmu  *n.* food, victuals

lē'i ini* *adj. cp.* expert, specialist, alert

lē'îš* *adv.* ably, competently, mightily

lemniš* *adv.* badly

lēpu 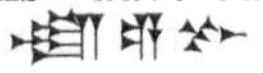 *n.* generation; descendant

lēqu◊ *n.* steering paddle

lēqu+ *n.* paddle, scull

lēru 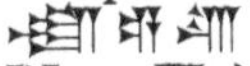 *n.* (a gold paste)

lēšu 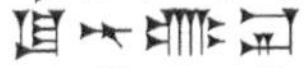 *n.* dough

letû* *v.* [i/i] to split; (D) to shatter, crush

lētu *nf.* cheek; side

lētu nadû‡ *vp.* to drop one's cheek, to pay attention, give one's attention to; to be careless

lē'u  *n.* [2] writing board; sheet, plaque of metal

lē'û* *adj.* able, capable, competent

lē'u ḫurāṣi *np.* gold plate

lē'u siparri *np.* copperplate

lē'u ša balāṭi *np.* book of life

lē'ûtu* *nf.* ability, capability, competence, expertise, skill, proficiency, talent; might, power

liāku* *v.* to lick (up)

liāmu *v.* to taste

liāru* *n.* white cedar

libānu *n.* [1] neck

libbānāiu+ *adj.* cordial, hearty

libbānu* *adv.* inside; inner, inmost (part), essence*

libbāt X malû‡ *vp.* to get angry with s.o., get mad at s.o.

libbāti *n. pl.* anger, wrath, indignation

libbi abiti *n. cp.* bottom line

libbi āli *n. cp.* inner city, downtown

libbi gišimmari*  *n. cp.* date palm branch

libbi māti *n. cp.* inland

Libbi-āli *n.* Inner City, Assur

libbu  *n.* heart; courage, morale, spirit; mood, mind; wish, choice, preference; inside, interior; essence, substance; content

libbu†  *n.* thought

libbû◊ *adv., prp.* like, exactly as, instead of, according to

libbu balāṭu‡ *vp.* to become happy, be delighted

libbu balluṭu‡ *vp.* to cheer up, delight

libbu gammuru‡ *vp.* to give one's heart

entirely, be loyal
libbu lummunu‡ *vp.* to displease
libbu marāṣu‡ *vp.* to be concerned, sorry
libbu marṣu‡ *adj. cp.* sad, sorry
libbu nammuru‡ *vp.* to make carefree, cheerful, merry
libbu nasāḫu‡ *vp.* to discourage, dishearten
libbu nuḫḫu‡ *vp.* to comfort, condole, console
libbu pašāru‡ *vp.* to relax, be(come) friendly with
libbu pašru‡ *adj. cp.* warmhearted
libbu patû‡ *vp.* to give satisfaction, unburden o.s.
libbu rabbu‡ *adj. cp.* softhearted, tenderhearted
libbu rapšu‡ *adj. cp.* broadminded, liberal, magnanimous
libbu rašû‡ *vp.* to buck up, muster courage
libbu ṣabātu‡ *vp.* to take hold of o.s., pull o.s. together, control o.s., keep calm
libbu šakānu‡ *vp.* to encourage, hearten
libbu šapālu‡ *vp.* to be depressed, be discouraged, be down, feel blue, feel down
libbu šappulu‡ *vp.* to depress, discourage, sadden
libbu ṭubbu‡ *vp.* to please, satisfy, content, gratify
libbu urruku‡ *vp.* to have patience
libbuḫu *n.* bladder
libbu B *n.* heart-shaped cake
libbu B+ *n.* patty
libīt ēkalli *nf. cp.* royal entourage, courtiers
libīt šarri *nf. cp.* royal entourage
libittu *nf.* brick, brickwork
libītu *nf.* entourage, surroundings
libītu† *nf.* packaging, wrapping
libītu+ *nf.* accompaniment, attendance, escort, company, companionship
li'bu* *n.* burning fever, inflammation
lidānu *n.* 1 young (of animals), duckling
līdiš *adv.* the day after tomorrow
līdu *n.* 2 child, litter
liginnu *nf.* one-column tablet, school exercise tablet, homework, lesson
lignu *n.* (a wooden container?)
liḫšu *n.* whisper
likalka *int.* go!
līlāti* *n.pl.* evening

lilissu *n.* 2/3 kettledrum
lilītu* *nf.* Lilith
lillatu* *nf.* foolish woman
lillidu *n.* offspring
lillu* *n.* fool, moron, idiot, boob, booby, dunce, dumbbell, dummy
lillu+ *n.* fool; brutish, dull, fatuous, foolish, senseless, stupid
lillūtu* *nf.* foolishness, foolery, idiocy, stupidity
lillūtu+ *nf.* folly, nonsense
lilû* *n.* (a demon)
līm šanāti *n. cp.* millennium, thousand years
limītu* *nf.* perimeter, environment, surroundings, vicinity; enclosure, enceinte, fencing, hedge
līmīu* *num.* thousandth
limmu *n.* 2 eponym year, eponymate
līmu *num.* thousand
līp līpi *n.* descendant
lipiššāti* *nf. pl.* labia
lipit qāti* *n. cp.* handicraft, handiwork
lipittu *nf.* craft, work, collision*
lipit Erra* *n. cp.* plague
lippu *n.* 1 tampon, wad
lipšutu *nf.* scrotum(?)
liptu *n.* 3 affliction, touch
līpu *n.* marrow, pith; fat, grease, tallow
līq pî* *n. cp.* palate
liqtu *n.* 1 assortment, collection, gleaning
lisnu *n.* footrace, race; running, gallop
lišān girri* *n. cp.* tongue of flame
lišān kalbati+ *n. cp.* cockle, darnel, lolium
lišān kalbi* *n. cp.* hound's-tongue, cynoglossum
lišān kalbi+ *n. cp.* hounds-tongue
lišān nišē* *n. cp.* slang
lišān ummâni* *n. cp.* jargon
lišānu *nf.* tongue, language, dialect; information, (oral) tidings; rumour, gossip, hearsay; informant, informer; nationality; blade; ingot
lišānu+ *nf.* people, nation, pronunciation, speech, spit (of land), isthmus
lišānu šakānu* *vp.* to establish communication, converse, negotiate
lišdu* *n.* cream
lištāḫu† *n.* arrow
li'šu *n.* desecration
litiktu* *nf.* test, probe

litku  *n.* experiment, test, trial; sample(?)
litmudu* *adj.* learned
littu  *nf.* cow
littūtu  *nf.* extreme old age
lītu*  *nf.* victory, triumph, power
lītu šakānu‡ *vp.* to establish victory
liṭṭu *n.* [1] draft, sketch; chart, map, plan
līṭu* *adj., n.* [1] confined; hostage
līṭu† *adj., n.* [1] prisoner of war
līṭūtu* *nf.* condition of being a hostage
liznu* *n.* derision, jeering, mocking, mockery, ridicule, sarcasm
lū  *part.* be it, let, may; hope that; ought, shall, should, would; even if, even though, although, notwithstanding
lû *n.* bull
Lû* *n.* Taurus
lū ... lū *conj.* either ... or; both ... and
lū lā *part.* may not, must not, shouldn't
lū maḫrāka* *int.* welcome!
luādu  *v.* to bend down, come to shame
luāšu* *v.* to knead
luʼāti* *nf. pl.* uncleanliness, impurity
lubāru* *n.* [1] clothing, garment; piece of cloth, rag
lubku* *n.* lubricant, salve
lubšu* *n.* clothing, garment
lubussu  *nf.* clothing, attire, garment, dress, outfit
lubūšē šaḫāṭu‡ *vp.* to denude, undress
lubūšu *n.* [1] clothing, attire
lukannu  *n.* [1] (a container of leather)
lulimitu *nf.* (a siege-instrument?)
lulīmu  *n.* red deer, stag
lūlītu◊ *nf.* arrowhead
luliu  *n.* slag(?)
lullû* *v.* to provide with charm, pleasure
lullû a.* *adj.* charming, graceful
lullû B* *n.* primal man, primitive man
lulû* *n.* splendour, charm, glamour, abundance
luludānitu  *nf.* (a multicolored stone)
lumaḫḫu* *n.* (a priest)
lumāšu  *n.* [1] constellation, sign of the zodiac, zodiacal sign
lummu  *n.* (a small dish for mutton)
lumnānû* *adj.* ill-fated, unfortunate, unlucky
lumnu  *n.* [2] bad luck, ill fate, mischance; ill turn, disservice
lumun libbi  *n. cp.* annoyance, displeasure, grief, unhappiness
luppu 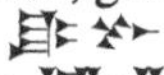 *n.* (leather) bag
lurintu  *nf.* pomegranate
lurmu  *n.* ostrich
luʼtu* *nf.* debility, feebleness, inertia, lack of strength, lassitude, powerlessness
luṭṭu* *n.* [1] (soup) plate, mug*
luʼʼû* *adj.* to defile, pollute, oil
luʼu* *n.* gullet, oesophagus, throat
luʼʼû a.* *adj.* defiled, polluted, soiled, dirty, sullied
mā  *adv., part.* thus, as follows, meaning, quote
maʼad *adv.* frequently, often; much, too much; enough
maʼādu  *v.* [i/i] to be much, become many, increase, grow in number, multiply; (Š) to make numerous, increase; to give more, make more, make much of
maʼassu  *nf.* corral, stud
maʼʼatta *vp.* who are you (sg.)?
maʼʼattunu *vp.* who are you (pl.)?
maʼda *adv.* much
madādu  *v.* [a/u] to measure, survey
Mādāia *n.* Media, Medes
madāktu  *nf.* military camp
madālu 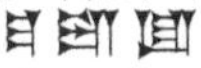 *v.* [i/i] to pickle, preserve in salt, put in salt
madbarāiu+ *adj., n.* hermit, solitary
madburu *n.* desert, plateau, steppe
madburu+ *n.* wilderness
maddattu  *nf.* taxation, tax, tribute
madgaltu  *nf.* watchtower
madgulu* *n.* observation, observation tower, border post, viewpoint*, perspective*
mādidu  *n.* [2] measurer
maʼdiš* *adv.* much, greatly, vastly
madlu *adj.* picked, salted, salty
madlû 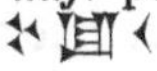 *n.* bucket, pail
maʼdu *adj., adv.* much, many, numerous, significant; many-sided, multi-, multiple, plenty of, plural, versatile
mādû* 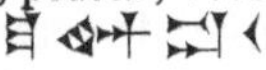 *n.* large quantity, multitude
maʼdūtu* *nf.* numerousness; plural, plurality
magādu  *v.* [a/u] to pick fruit; to pick quarrel, pick on, nag at
magāgu  *v.* [a/u] to become rigid, become stiff, have an erection; to cramp; to stick out, jut [out], protrude

magāgu* *v.* $^{a/u}$ (Gtn) to have cramps, spasms

magāgu *v.* $^{a/u}$ (D) to stiffen, pull taut; to project

magal* *adv.* much

magallatu◊ *nf.* parchment

magallatu* *nf.* parchment scroll

Magan* *n.* Makran, Oman

magānu *n.* gift

magarru *n.* wheel, chariot

magāru *v.* $^{u/u}$ to accept, be in agreement, obey

magāru* *v.* $^{u/u}$ to deign, endorse, sanction; (Gt) to come to terms, make up with, to adapt o.s.*, adjust o.s.*, be compatible*; (D) to make obey, conciliate, reconcile; (N) to compromise*

magāru *v.* $^{u/u}$ (N) to agree, comply, consent, concur, fall in with, go along with, oblige, settle for

magazzutu *nf.* clippers, shears

maggu *adj.* rigid, stiff, taut, tight, tense

magguru *v.* to tear down

magguru+ *v.* to destroy, knock out, overwhelm

magillu* *n.* barge

māgiru *adj.* obedient, compliant, obliging, submissive, yielding

magrītu* *nf.* spite(ful act), insult, malice, abuse

magru *adj.* agreeable, favorable, welcome; obedient, in agreement

magrû* *adj.* insulting

magulû* *n.* (a big raft)

maḫāḫu *v.* $^{a/u}$ to decompose, dissolve

maḫāru *v.* $^{a/u}$ to accept, receive, welcome; to appeal to, apply to, approach, turn to; to face, confront; to defy, resist, withstand; to counterbalance

maḫāru* *v.* $^{a/u}$ (Gt) to be consistent*, cohere*, conform*, to face one another; be proportional, be harmonious

maḫāru *v.* $^{a/u}$ (D) to be adverse; to present, offer, to make face*, orientate*; (Š) to compare; to make like, do likewise

maḫāru n. *n.* acceptance, reception, receipt

maḫāru ša eleppi* *v.* to row, propel a boat

maḫāṣu *v.* $^{a/a}$ to beat, flick, hit, knock, pounce, punch, slap, strike, whack; to bang, clap, clash, rap, slam, sound; to slay, smite, defeat; to bruise, injure, wound; to let blood, whack;

maḫāṣu* *v.* $^{a/a}$ (Gt) to fight; (D) to hurt, stab

maḫāṣu *v.* $^{a/a}$ (N) to fight; to collide

maḫāṣu B *v.* $^{i/i}$ to weave

māḫāzu *n.* $^{1/2}$ cult center, city

maḫḫû *n.* ecstatic, prophet , ascetic*

maḫḫû* *n.* crazy, delirious, insane, lunatic, mad, madman, nuts, possessed

maḫḫuriš* *adv.* as an offering

maḫḫuru *adj.* averse, adverse, conflicting, contrary

maḫḫûtiš alāku* *vp.* to go mad, become crazed

maḫḫûtiš alāku‡ *vp.* to become frenzied, ecstatic

maḫḫūtu *nf.* prophetess

maḫḫûtu* *nf.* craze, craziness, madness

māḫir igrē* *n. cp.* wage earner

māḫir šulmānāti* *n. cp.* corruptible

māḫirānu† *n.* recipient, buyer, purchaser, addressee*, consignee*, receiver*

māḫirānu+ *adj.* hospitable

maḫīriš* *adv.* cheaply

maḫirtu *adv., nf.* past; upstream direction

māḫirtu *nf.* (boat) moving upstream

maḫīru *n.* exchange rate, exchange, market price, turnover; market place, market; business, commerce, trade

māḫiru *n.* ^{1} stockade

māḫiru a. *adj.* corresponding; facing; opposing, withstanding

māḫiru B* *n.* opponent, antagonist, adversary; resister, resistant

māḫiṣāti* *n. pl.* (a wooden calculator, perhaps abacus)

māḫiṣu *n.* ^{2} archer; beater, striker, fighter*

maḫītu *nf.* whip

maḫru *n., prp.* front

maḫrû *adj., num.* previous, earlier, first

maḫru a. *adj.* acceptable, likeable, pleasing, preferable, welcome

maḫruṣu *n.* ^{1} cutting(?) table, rack(?)

maḫṣu *adj.* smitten, wounded

maḫû* *v.* $^{i/i}$ to rave; (N) to become frenzied

maḫû* *v.* $^{i/i}$ (D) to craze, madden

maiāltu* *nf.* bed

maiālu *n.* bed, resting place, stretcher*

maitānu* *adj.* moribund
makaḫalūtu *nf.* kohl pen, eyeliner
makāku◊ *v.* $^{a/u}$ to stretch out
makallû* *n.* mooring place, anchorage, berth
mākālu *n.* food, dish, meal
makāru* *v.* $^{i/i}$ to water, irrigate; (Š) to provide irrigation
makāru B† *v.* to do business, retail*, shop*
mākassu *nf.* wooden dish, saucer
makāsu *v.* $^{i/i}$ to collect taxes
makāṣu* *n.* slaughter-bench
mākisu *n.* [2] toll collector, tax collector
makiu *adj.* destitute, helpless, needful, powerless, wanting, weak
mākiu *n.* idler, loafer, sluggard
makiu+ *adj.* poor, meek, paltry
makiu B *adj.* indolent, lazy, negligent, sloppy, slothful
makkāsu* *n.* cutting tool
makkūru *n.* property, means
makkūtu* *n.* cargo ship, freighter
makkūtu+ *n.* barge, float, raft
makkūtu B◊ *nf.* tile(?)
makkūtu B+ *nf.* stone cover, stone lid
maklulu *n.* headscarf(?)
maklūtu* *nf.* anchorage, berth
maknaktu† *nf.* (sealed) envelope
maknuku† *n.* sealed container, sealed room
makru+ *n.* cinnabar, ochre, red pigment, vermilion
maksūtu *nf.* incense stand
makṣaru* *n.* factor, common factor; bridle-bit, snaffle; bundle, bale
makû *v.* to be weak
makūtu *nf.* winch, windlass, (shaduf) pole
makūtu* *nf.* shaduf
makûtu *nf.* weakness, destitution
makûtu+ *nf.* humility, meekness
makûtu B *nf.* absence, indolence, laziness, negligence, sloth
makû B *v.* $^{i/i}$ to be lazy, be negligent, loaf, neglect
mala* *pron., prp.* as much/many as; everything that
māla *adv.* once
māla šinīšu *np.* more than once
malāḫu *v.* $^{a/u}$ to tear out(?); (D) to flicker(?)
malāku *v.* $^{i/i}$ to advise, counsel, propose, suggest
malāku* *v.* $^{i/i}$ (Gt) to confer, deliberate
malāku *v.* $^{i/i}$ (N) to take counsel, confer, deliberate, discuss
malālu* *v.* $^{a/u}$ to eat clean, eat one's fill, gluttonize
maldu* *n.* edge(?), side(?)
maldudu *n.* curtain(?)
malduru *n.* permanence
malʾētu† *nf.* contingency, possibility
malgūtu *nf.* (mng. unkn.)
māliku *n.* [1/2] adviser, councillor, counsellor
malīlu *n.* flute
malkatu* *nf.* queen
malku* *n.* [1] king, sovereign
malkūtu* *nf.* kingship
mallāḫu *n.* boatman, sailor, skipper, seaman; boatwright, shipwright
mallāḫu+ *n.* mariner, pilot
mallāḫūtu* *nf.* navigation, sailor's trade, seamanship
mallatu* *nf.* bowl, dish
maltaktu* *nf.* test, check
malṭuru *n.* text, prescription, inscription
malʾu *adj.* filled, full; fed up, stuffed
malû *v.* $^{a/a}$ to be full, fill up, be fulfilled
malû* *v.* $^{a/a}$ (Š) to fill; (Št) to cover with
malû *v.* $^{a/a}$ (D) to fill, fill out, fulfil, refill, replenish, stuff; to load (the bow)
malʾu+ *adj.* fraught with
malû+ *v.* $^{a/a}$ to replenish; (Š) to accomplish, do thoroughly, finish, perfect; (Št) to be initiated, be perfected
māluku *n.* journey, course, march, travel, walk; procession; access road, walkway; river-bed, promenade*, walking distance*
malûtu+ *nf.* abundance, adequacy, fullness
malūṭu* *n.* ring, clasp; bridle; stocks, pillory
malû B* *n.* filth
māmītu *nf.* oath
māmītu* *nf.* oath, wow; curse
māmītu+ *nf.* adjuration
mamlu* *adj.* heroic, noble
mamma* *pron.* anyone
mamman* *pron.* somebody, anybody
mammāna* *pron.* somebody, anyone
mammannu* *n.* relative
māmū* *n.pl.* water
manāḫtu *nf.* resting place, resort*

mānaḫtu  *nf.* toil, exertion, toiling; tool; fatigue, weariness, elbow grease*, drudgery*; (pl.) proceeds, earnings
mānaḫu* *n.* labor
manāma* *pron.* somebody
mandītu◊ *nf.* information
mandītu B◊ *nf.* surprise (attack); attachment, mounting, cap
mangu  *n.* paralysis
mangu B* *n.* (a type of bean?)
mangu B+ *n.* Indian pea
manītu  *nf.* amount
mānitu* *n., nf.* wind, breeze
mannu  *pron. q.* who?
mannu aḫḫūr *q.* who else?
mannu ša *pron. subj.* anyone who, whoever
manû  *v.*[u/u] mina; kilogram
mânu◊ *v.*[u/u] to provide
manû a. *adj.* counted, numbered
manû ana‡ *vp.* to assign to, count as, turn into
manû ina libbi‡ *vp.* to reckon in
manû ina muḫḫi‡ *vp.* to charge against
manû ina qāti‡ *vp.* to hand over
manû issi‡ *vp.* to consider, count as, count among, reckon among, reckon as;
manû B  *v.*[u/u] to count, calculate, reckon; to enumerate, number, recount, recite; to deliver to, hand over; to assign to
manû B†  *v.*[u/u] to charge (an account), debit, take account of
manzāt* 
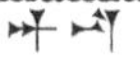 *n.* rainbow
manziaše* *n.* (a metal container or weapon)
manzû  *n.* copper drum
mappūḫītu+ *nf.* volcano
maqaltānu  *n.* (a priest)
maqalūtu *nf.* burnt-offering, combustion, conflagration
maqarrutu  *nf.* bale
maqartu  *nf.* cooling
maqātu  *v.*[u/u] to fall; to fall off, desert; to come off, fall out, happen, occur; to attack, invade, plunge, pounce upon, swoop; to fall down, collapse, succumb, tumble (down), to fall through*, plump down*; (Š) to make fall, overthrow, defeat; (vent.) to strike
maqātu ana‡ *vp.* to fall for, fall to, fancy
maqātu ina muḫḫi‡ *vp.* to assail, attack, befall, fall upon, surprise
maqāṭu *n.*[1/3] gown
maqāṭutu *nf.* gown
maqittu* *nf.* dilapidation, disrepair

maqlû  *n.* burning, combustion
maqqabu* *n.* hammer
maqqītu  *nf.* libation
maqqû  *n.* libation
maqtu  *n.*[4] deserter, defector
maqtu a. *adj.* fallen; ruined, decadent*, prostrate*
mār *pron., prp.* as much/many as, all that
mār abi 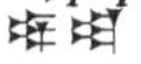 *n. cp.* half-brother(?)
mār aḫ-abi *n. cp.* cousin
mār aḫāti  *n. cp.* nephew, sister's son
mār aḫi  *n. cp.* nephew, brother's son
mār ālānūtu* *nf. cp.* citizenship
mār āli  *n. cp.* city dweller, townsman, townie, citizen
mār atāni* *n. cp.* donkey foal
mār banî◊ 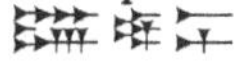 *n. cp.* nobleman; nobility
mār damqi  *n. cp.* aristocrat, nobleman; chariot fighter, chariot-knight
mār damqūtu  *n. cp.* chariot-knighthood; aristocracy
mār ēkalli *n. cp.* courtier, palace official
mār emi* *n. cp.* brother-in-law
mār ḫabbāti* *n. cp.* robber, plunderer, bandit
mār karšāni *n. cp.* (an occupation)
mār mār aḫ-abi* *n. cp.* second cousin
mār mar'i  *n. cp.* grandson, grandchild
mār masenni  *n. cp.* fellow treasurer
mār māt nakiri* *n. cp.* foreigner
mār māti  *n. cp.* citizen, native, compatriot, countryman
mār mātūtu* *nf. cp.* citizenship
mār muškēnūtu *n. cp.* the poor, proletariat
mār nagie  *n. cp.* local (inhabitant)
mār qāti  *n. cp.* adjutant
mār rēdûti* *n. cp.* successor, heir
mār simini+ *n. cp.* contemporary
mār šarri  *n. cp.* crown prince
mār šarri*  *n. cp.* prince
mār šarrūtu *n. cp.* princeship
mār šatti  *n. cp.* one year old
mār šīmi  *n. cp.* bought slave
mār šipri  *n. cp.* messenger
mār zēri* *n. cp.* field laborer
marādu 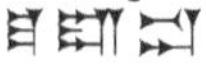 *v.* (N) to suffer damage

māraku* *n.* length, extent
marāqu 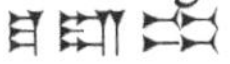 *v.* $^{a/u}$ to crush, grind
marāqu+ *v.* $^{a/u}$ to cleanse, disinfect, enamel, polish, rub off rust, scour
marāru  *v.* $^{i/i}$ to be bitter
marāru◊  *v.* $^{i/i}$ (D) to make bitter, embitter
marāru*  *v.* $^{i/i}$ (Š) to make bitter, rankle
marāru  *v.* $^{i/i}$ (D) to scrutinize
marāru+ *v.* $^{i/i}$ to be sour, acid; (Š) to sour, exacerbate
marāsu  *v.* $^{a/u}$ to mash, squash
marāsu+ *v.* $^{a/u}$ to bruise, crush, saturate, steep
marāṣu  *v.* $^{a/a}$ to be ill, be sick, sicken; be painful, be arduous, be troublesome, be displeasing, be sad
marāṣu*  *v.* $^{a/a}$ (Št) to concern o.s., take trouble
marāṣu  *v.* $^{a/a}$ (Gtn) to be sickly; (Š) to trouble, make suffer, hurt, give a hard time, pester
marāṣu+ *v.* $^{a/a}$ to fall ill
mar'at aḫāti *nf. cp.* niece
mar'at aḫi *nf. cp.* niece
mar'at damqi* *nf. cp.* noblewoman
mar'at emi* *nf. cp.* sister-in-law
mar'at mar'iti  *nf. cp.* granddaughter
mar'at šarri *nf. cp.* king's daughter, princess
mar'at šatti  *nf. cp.* yearling, one-year-old (ewe)
mar'atūtu *nf.* daughtership
marāṭu *v.* $^{a/u}$ to rub, scratch, scrape off, abrade; to wear out, to rub away*, scrub*; (N) to suffer damage, be damaged
marāṭu+ *v.* $^{a/u}$ to pluck, pull out, tear off
mardītu  *nf.* stage, stretch, distance; journey, march
mardû  *n.* successor
mardutu  *nf.* rug, tapestry; (pl.) drapes*
mardûtu+ *nf.* culture, education, discipline, instruction
marḫītu* *nf.* wife
marḫuṣu  *n.* [1] lotion, rinse
markastu* *nf.* compress
markāsu  *n.* bond; moorings; closure
marmēna  *n.* (a milk product?)
marqītu* *nf.* asylum, refuge, recourse
marqītu aḫāzu* *vp.* to take refuge, go into hiding, hide

marrāṣu* *adj.* sickly
Marratu* *nf.* Persian Gulf
marratu* *nf.* salt water, sea-water, ocean
marru  *n.* shovel, spade
marrutu  *nf.* (a wild bird)
marru B *adj.* bitter; acrid, brackish; acrimonious, bitter-tempered, embittered; bilious, rancorous, snappish*
marru B+ *adj.* acid, cruel, embittered, harsh, morose, peevish, sad, sour
marṣa'u* *n.* awl
marṣiš *adv.* bitterly, painfully, sadly; laboriously; poorly, sorely
marṣu  *n.* [4] sick person, patient
marṣu a. *adj.* diseased, sick, ill, unwell, indisposed, morbid; agonizing, grievous, bitter; hurtful, troublesome; difficult, arduous, exhausting, gruel[l]ing; laborious, painstaking
marṣu a.+ *adj.* ailing
marṣu ša tānti* *adj.* seasick
maršītu *nf.* property, possessions, livestock
maršu 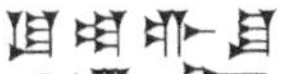 *n.* [2] leather strap
martakal  *n.* (a medicinal plant)
martu  *nf.* gall (bladder), bile; ill temper, malice, peevishness, rancour, spite*
martû* *n.* rig
martu+ *nf.* bitterness
marturrû* *n.* small vehicle
marṭu *adj.* rubbed, worn-out
mar'u  *n.* [1] son, boy
marû*  *adj.* to be fat, fatten, do slowly, be slow; (Š) to fatten, provide with fodder
mâru◊ *v.* $^{i/i}$ to buy
marû a.* *adj.* fat, fattened; obese, phlegmatic, ponderous; slow
marû n.* *n.* present (tense)
marurtu+ *nf.* chicory
maruštu*  *nf.* trouble, hardship; inconvenience, misadventure, misfortune; menstrual period
mar'utu 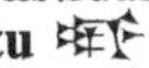 *nf.* daughter
mar'ūtu  *nf.* sonhood, sonship; adoption; boyhood, membership*
mārûtu* *nf.* fattening (technique)
masāku*  *v.* (D) to make bad, spoil; to disgrace, revile; (Š) to give a bad name, consider as bad
masāku†  *v.* to be bad, be ugly, be rotten, rot
masappu  *n.* basket
masennu  *n.* treasurer
masennutu 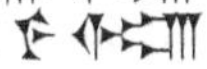 *nf.* female treasurer

masiktu† *nf.* bad feelings, bad reputation, disgrace, ugliness
masiu *adj.* washed, cleaned
masku† *adj.* bad, despicable, disgraceful, ugly, rotten
maslaḫ ušāri* *n. cp.* semen duct
masla'tu* *nf.* disease, infection
masnaqtu* *nf.* control, checking, inspection
masrāḫu *n.* (a vessel for wine)
massāru* *n.* saw
massāru+ *n.* porpoise
massītu *nf.* drink, beverage; drinking-pot, drinking-vessel of ten seahs
massû◊ *n.* leader
massuḫu† *adj.* to treat badly, treat with contempt, insult
massuḫu a.† *adj.* spoiled, bad, of bad quality
massuku *n.*^{1} chamber; (a textile)
masû *v.*$^{i/i}$ to wash
māsunu *n.* (a bowl or jug)
maṣallu *n.*^{3} resting place, shelter
maṣallutu *nf.* rest room, rest-house
maṣarru *n.* (a wooden object)
maṣāru◊ *v.*$^{a/u}$ to circle, enclose; (D) to limit, demarcate
maṣātānu *n.* influential person, big fish
maṣḫutu *n.*^{3} (a kind of scented flour)
maṣi *adv.* already; enough, suffiently; well enough, full well
māṣiru *adj.* enclosing, delimiting
maṣraḫu* *n.* cystic duct
maṣṣar bābi *n. cp.* gate guard, janitor
maṣṣar ēni *n. cp.* well guard
maṣṣar qabli *n. cp.* forester, ranger
maṣṣar šulmi u balāṭi *n. cp.* guardian angel
maṣṣar ṭiṭṭi *n. cp.* earthworm
maṣṣartu *nf.* watch, guard, vigilance
maṣṣarūtu◊ *nf.* guard duty
maṣṣuru *n.* guard, sentry, warder
maṣû *v.*$^{i/i}$ to match; to be enough, be sufficient, suffice; to be up to, come up to, cope with; to prevail over, surmount
maṣû* *v.*$^{i/i}$ (D) to make reach; (Št) to try hard, make an effort, get as far as
maṣû *v.*$^{i/i}$ (Š) to be able; to make overcome
mâṣu* *v.*$^{i/i}$ to be too little, insufficient
maṣû+ *v.*$^{i/i}$ (D) to enable
mašaddu *n.*^{3} (yoke) pole
mašādu* *v.*$^{i/i}$ to strike with palsy; (N) to be stricken
mašādu B* *v.*$^{i/i}$ to brush*, to comb, comb out, card; (D) to massage, rub
mašāḫu *v.*$^{a/u}$ to measure, compute
mašāḫu+ *v.*$^{a/u}$ (D) to moderate, proportion
mašāḫu B* *v.*$^{a/u}$ to flare up, shine brightly
mašak arabê *n. cp.* (bag of) dormouse skin
mašak pēri *n. cp.* elephant skin
maš'altu* *nf.* inquest*, question; questioning, interrogation; examination, exam
mašālu *v.*$^{u/u}$ to be alike, resemble; to be equal, be identical, match; to be even, be smooth
mašālu* *v.*$^{u/u}$ (D) to copy, make similar, imitate; equalize, make equal, equate, try to equal; match, reflect; replicate, reproduce
mašālu *v.*$^{u/u}$ (Š) to do likewise, do similarly; to emulate, imitate, mime, mimic, simulate; to make equal
mašālu+ *v.*$^{u/u}$ to exemplify, speak in parables; (D) to compare; (Š) to use a simile, utter parables
māšartu *nf.* review, inspection
mašāru *v.*$^{a/u}$ to drag, trail
mašāru* *v.*$^{a/u}$ to drive around
mašāru *v.*$^{a/u}$ (Gtn) to drag around
maša'u *v.*$^{a/u}$ to plunder, rob; to abduct, kidnap, to ransack*
mašdaḫu* *n.* procession (street), parade
mašennu *n.* shoe, sandal; sole
mašḫaṭu* *n.* stairs, ladder
mašḫultuppû* *n.* scapegoat, kid as expiatory sacrifice
mašḫulu *n.*^{3} sieve
māšiḫ eqli* *n. cp.* land-surveyor
māšiḫu* *n.* geometrician*, measurer, surveyor
mašīru* *n.* (a kind of chariot)
mašītu *nf.* (a votaress of Adad)
mašiu *adj.* forgotten
maškadu* *n.* arthritis, joint disease
maškakāti* *nf. pl.* harrow(s)
maškānu *n.* hostage; deposit, guarantee, pledge

maškānu⁺ *n.* pawn

maškānūtu *nf.* pledge, detention

maškānūtu⁺ *nf.* pawning, condition of a hostage

maškattu◊ *nf.* depot; ingredients, materials

maškittu *nf.* offering table

mašku *n.* ^{1} skin, hide, pelt; leather, parchment

maškunu *n.* tent; place, location, settlement, site

maškunu⁺ *n.* habitation, tabernacle

maškuru *n.* ^{1} wineskin raft; water-skin, pontoon

mašlû* *n.* leather bucket; wrapper

mašqalālu* *n.* suspense

mašqaltu† *nf.* weight, pendant

mašqālu⁺ *n.* criterion

mašqītu *nf.* potion, drink; watering place

mašqû *n.* drinking place, drinking utensil

mašru *adj.* gnarly, roughened

mašrû *n.* opulence, riches, wealth

mašrutu *nf.* (a wooden object)

maššânu *n.* ^{1} tongs

maššartu* *nf.* foodstuffs set aside; deduction, withdrawal

maššītu* *nf.* tampon

maššī'u* *adj.* rapacious, predatory; robber

maššiu *n.* (a leather bag for carrying)

maššû* *adj.* twin

maššuḫu⁺ *adj.* average, modest, moderate, temperate

maššuḫūtu⁺ *nf.* economy, frugality, moderation

maššu'u *v.* to rub, massage

maštaku* *n.* living quarters, chamber, cell

maštilû* *n.* (a magical text)

maštītu* *nf.* flagon; drink

maštu* *nf.* bump

mašṭāru⁺ *n.* archives

mašṭû* *n.* drying place

mašû *v.* $^{i/i}$ to forget; (D) to make forget; (N) to fall into oblivion, become forgotten

māšu* *n.* twin; Gemini

mašû B *n.* (a votary of Adad)

māt nakiri *nf. cp.* enemy land

māt nukurti *nf. cp.* enemy country

māt tānti *nf. cp.* Sealand

matāḫu *v.* $^{a/u}$ to lift, fetch, pick up, raise; (N) to be lifted, elevated, rise, rise higher

matāqu *v.* $^{i/i}$ to be sweet; (D) to sweeten

matāru* *v.* to be speckled(?)

matgiqu* *n.* (part of a gate)

mātitān* *adv., n.pl* all countries; in every country

matnu *n.* ^{3} bowstring, string, cord, tendon; penis

matnutu⁺ *nf.* lumbago

matqu *adj.* sweet

mattuqu *adj.* candied, sweetened

mātu *nf.* land, country, native land; nation, state, territory

māt Akkadî *nf.* Babylonia

māt Aššūr *nf.* Assyria

maṭi *part.* less, minus

maṭiu *adj.* deficient, defective, incomplete, insufficient, lacking; of lower rank

maṭiu† *adj.* low-value, of inferior quality; humble

maṭṭaltu* *nf.* mirror image, reflection; counterpart

maṭû *v.* to lessen, diminish, decrease; to lack, be defective, be in want, be missing, be lacking, be wanting, to fail*; (D) to inflict loss; to decrease, lessen; to cut down, curtail, reduce, retrench

maṭû* *v.* (Š) to understate, underestimate, undervalue

mâ'u* *v.* $^{a/a}$ to vomit

ma''unu *v.* nourish, support (with food)

ma''uttu *nf.* alimony, nourishment, subsistence, sustenance

mazāqu *v.* $^{a/u}$ to suck; (D) to suck out; (Dtt) to dry

mazā'u *v.* $^{i/i}$ to squeeze, press; to compress, press out, wring; (D) to rape

maziu *n.* $^{1/2}$ (a dish for serving soup, tureen)

mazluqu† *n.* fork, trident

mazrūtu *nf.* cultivation

mazūru* *n.* fuller's stick, wringer

mazūru⁺ *n.* fuller's mallet, mallet

mazzassu *nf.* podium, stand, position; post

mazzassu⁺ *nf.* station

mazzā'u *n.* ^{1} squeezer, water-skin

mazzāz ēkalli *n. cp.* courtier, palace personnel

mazzāz ēkurri *n. cp.* temple personnel

mazzāz pāni *n. cp.* courtier, entourage

mazzāz pānūtu *n. cp.* courtier status, court position, courtier training

mazzāzu *n.* $^{1/2}$ station; stand,

post; personnel, staff
mê *n. pl.* water, juice, sap, fluid, bodily fluids
mê bībi* *n. cp.* effluent, sewage
mê ēni *n. cp.* spring water
mê ḫâli *n. cp.* water of delivery
mê kibrīti+ *n. cp.* sulphuric acid
mê la'û‡ *vp.* to swim
mê nūni* *n. cp.* fish brine
mê sasqî* *n. cp.* semolina broth
mê šīri *n. cp.* meat stock, bouillon
mê tānti* *n. cp.* sea water
mēat *num.* hundred
mēdelu* *n.* bar, bolt, hasp, latch
medû◊ *adj.* known
me'elu *n.* phylactery, poultice
meḫānu* *adj.* stormy, tempestuous, turbulent
meḫret* *prp.* in front of, facing, opposite; in the likeness of
meḫretu* *nf.* opposite side; front, facade
meḫru *n.* [1] fir
meḫû *n.* storm, tempest
meḫû ša kuppi* *np.* snowstorm
mekku *n.* (raw) glass
mekkû* *n.* driving stick
mēkūtu◊ *nf.* lack
melammu* *n.* [1] nimbus, splendour, radiance
mēlê *n. pl.* stairs
mēleṣu* *n.* joy
mēlītu* *nf.* step (of a staircase), staircase, stairway
mēliu *n.* [2] height, altitude; ascent; hill, hillock; stair, staircase, stairway; (pl.) ladders
Meluḫḫa* *n.* Ethiopia, Nubia
Meluḫḫāiu* *adj., n.* Ethiopian, Nubian; negro
Meluḫḫītu* *nf.* negress
mēlulāiu* *adj.* playful
mēlultu* *nf.* game
mēlulu *n.* play
mēlulû* *n.* actor, player
mēlulu issi‡ *vp.* to trifle with
memmēni *pron.* anybody, anyone, anything; someone, something; any kind of, some kind of, some or other
mēnēšu *n.* weariness
mēqītu* *nf.* eye paint
mēqû* *n.* cosmetics
mērânû* *adj.* naked, nude
mērānūtu* *nf.* nakedness
mēreḫtu* *nf.* insolence, insult, outrage, presumption, provocation
mērešīu *adj.* naked, needy
mēreštu* *nf.* request, wish, need; necessaries, needs, requisites
mēreštu B* *nf.* planting, cultivation
mērešu* *n.* need, wish
mērēšu *n.* [1] cultivated land, cultivation, plantation; crop year
merḫu* *n.* sty, trachoma
mer'ītu* *nf.* pasture
mērû* *n.* pregnancy
meserru* *n.* band, belt, girdle
mēsēru* *n.* confinement, detainment, imprisonment, hemming in; isolation
messūtu* *nf.* identification
mēsu* *n.* cosmic tree
mêsu* *v.* to destroy, crush
mēsu+ *n.* scarlet oak
mesukku *n.* [1] falcon
mēṣēru *n.* drawing, outline
mēṣu *n.* (a stone)
mēšāru *n.* justice, righteousness
mēšertu* *nf.* abundance(?)
mešrēti* *n. pl.* limbs, organs
mêšu* *v.* to despise, scorn, spurn, disregard, neglect; to fail, miss; to forgive; (D) to treat with contempt
mētāia* *adv.* hundredfold, a hundred times
mētāiu* *num.* hundreth
mētellūtu* *nf.* rulership, excellence
mēteqtu* *nf.* march-past, parade
mētequ* *n.* course, passage, road
mētu *adj.* dead
mētuqu *n.* course, passage, road
mētūtu *nf.* death
mētūtu+ *nf.* deadness, mortality [rate]
meṭēnu* *n.* mill
meṭlūtu* *nf.* manhood, prowess, excellence
mēzīu* *adj.* juicy, succulent
mēzu *n.* (a kind of wine), cider*, cyder*, extract*, juice*
miāru *v.* to buy, deal in, to shop*
miāru+ *v.* to import, supply, transport
middat balāṭi* *nf. cp.* lifespan
middutu *nf.* measure, dimension, quantity*, rate*
midlu *n.* salted meat
midru *n.* (a kind of bread)
migirtu* *nf.* challenge, insult
miglu *n.* scroll
migru* *n.* consent, approval, acceptance, acquiescence, endorsement, sanction

migru B* *n.* favorite
miḫḫu  *n.* (a type of beer)
miḫir šumi* *n. cp.* synonym
miḫirtu  *nf.* counterpart, copy
miḫirtu*  *nf.* complaint against, opposition, resistance
miḫirtu B* *nf.* income, produce, production
miḫiṣtu  *nf.* cuneiform sign
miḫret* *prp.* opposite
miḫru  *n.*[1] copy, counterpart, duplicate, equivalent; response, antiphon; equal, compeer, peer; mishap, misfortune, adversity, accident, setback; weir, barrage
miḫrūtu* *nf.* parity, equality
miḫsu *n.* (mng. unkn.)
miḫṣu  *n.*[1] blow, flick, knock, punch, slap, strike, wallop, whack; percussion, rap; concussion, impact, shock, thrust; prick, sting, stroke; bruise, injury, contusion, wound
miḫṣu* *n.*[1] shock
mikru* *n.* irrigation
miksi kāri nēberi *n. cp./pl.* quay and ferry dues
miksu  *n.*[1] tax, toll, fee, customs, customs duty, duty, tariff
milḫu  *n.* extraction, tearing out
milītu* *nf.* corpulence
milku  *n.*[2] advice, counsel, deliberation, proposal, proposition, suggestion
milu  *n.*[1/2] flood
mimma*  *pron.* anything
mimmû  *n.* possessions; anything, everything, every kind of
mīnānu* *n.* numeral
mināti* *n. pl.* (pl.) normal size, time; measure, dimension; limbs, proportions
mindēma* *adv.* maybe
mindīnu* *n.* cheetah, gepard
minimmēni  *pron.* whatever
minītu  *nf.* reckoning, computation; observed part
mīnu  *pron., q.* what?, what for?, why?
mīnu aḫḫūr *q.* what else?
mīnu ša *pron. subj.* that which, anything which, whatever
minūtu  *nf.* amount, number
mīnu B* *n.* number, amount
miqit pāni◊ *n. cp.* attitude, disposition
miqit pê* *n. cp.* impudence, effrontery, blasphemy
miqit ṭēmi* *n. cp.* despair, desperation; loss of reason, insanity
miqitti išāti *nf. cp.* stroke of lightning, thunderbolt
miqittu  *nf.* collapse, crash, fall, downfall, tumble; collapsed part
miqittu rašû‡ *vp.* to become dilapidated, fall into ruin
miqtu  *n.*[2] occasional need, incident, occurrence; incidence; epilepsy, accident*, chance*, coincidence*, fluke*
mirsu  *n.* (a confection made of dates, oil, butter, etc., baklava)
mirṭu *n.* abrasion, scratching, friction*
mīru◊ 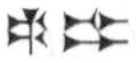 *n.* young bull
mīs pērti* *n. cp.* hairwash
mīs pî* 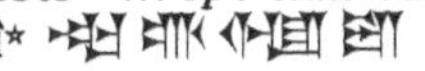 *n. cp.* mouthwashing (ritual)
mīsu*  *n.* wash, washing, washing-up
miṣirānu *adj.* (a qualification of horses)
miṣru* 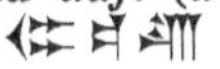 *n.*[1] boundary, border, frontier; territory
miṣru B  *n.* (decorative) band
mīšariš* *adv.* justly, in justice
mīšartu◊ *nf.* justice
mišḫu* *n.* flare, flare-up, flash, train of a meteor
mišiḫtu* *nf.* measurement, size, length, dimension; measured area
mišil *n.* demi-, hemi-
mišil mūši* *n. cp.* midnight
miširtu* *nf.* produce
mišitti libbi* *nf. cp.* heart failure
mišittu* *nf.* (apoplectic) stroke, apoplexy, coronary, palsy, paralysis
miši'tu* *nf. cp.* plundering, pillage
mišītu* *nf.* oblivion
mišlāti ša ebūri* *np. pl.* midsummer
mišlu  *n.*[3] half
mišlūtu *nf.* (a wooden container?)
mitgāru* *adj.* favorable, propitious
mitgurtu  *nf.* acceptance, agreement, concord, benignity, concession*, compromise*
mitguru* *adj.* adaptable*, adjustable*, compatible*, congenial*, harmonious, accordant, concordant, congruous, congruent
mitḫāriš*  *adv.* equally, proportionally, alike, similarly; uniformly, unanimously, with one accord, collectively, respectively*
mitḫartu* *nf.* harmony, correspondence; quadrangle, quadrilateral, square
mitḫāru* *adj.* equal, equivocal, identical;

uniform, even, homogeneous, harmonious, proportional, proportionate, symmetric(al); unanimous, relative*

mitḫurtu* *nf.* contrast, opposition; convergence, coincidence; harmony, unanimity

mitḫuru* *adj.* coherent, consistent

mitḫuṣ kakkē* *n. cp.* clash of weapons, combat

mitḫuṣu* *n.* fight, combat, clash

mitḫuṣūtu* *nf.* fighting

mitluktu* *nf.* advice, deliberation

mitluku* *adj.* considerate, prudent

mitru* *adj.* strong, powerful

miṭirtu* *nf.* irrigation canal, (watered) orchard

miṭītu *nf.* demerit

miṭītu◊ *nf.* decrease, deficit, loss, reduction, shortfall

miṭru* *n.*[3] irrigation ditch

miṭṭu *n.*[1] mace, (divine) weapon

Mūab *n.* Moab

muāqu *v.* to miss(?)

muāqu+ *v.* to boo

mu'āru* *n.* man, hero

muāṣu* *v.* to churn

muāšu+ *v.* to feel, grope [about]

muātu *v.* to die; (Š) to cause the death of s.o., execute, put to death, kill, slay

mubabbilu* *n.*[4] weight-lifter, weight-carrier

mubaddidu* *adj.* wasteful, prodigal

muballiṭānu† *n.* maintainer

muballiṭu *n.*[4] healer

mubarrimu *n.*[4] polych rome dyer

mubarriu* *n.*[4] announcer, proclaimer

mubbirtu◊ *nf.* (female) accuser

mūbû *n.* thickness

mudabbirānu+ *n.* hermit

mudāburu *n.* desert, steppe

mudakkītu* *nf.* impetus, incentive, motive

mudakkiu *n.* (part of an ornament)

mudammiqtu *nf.* (palm branch) fan

mudammiqu *adj.* profitable, remunerative, rewarding

mūdānû◊ *n.*[1] connoisseur, expert

mūdânūtu *nf.* awareness, consciousness, knowledge

mudarriktu *nf.* (a cultic ceremony)

mudasû* *n.* list of names, register

muddišu* *n.*[4] renewer, renovator, innovator, restorer, reformer

muddû◊ *v.* to notify(?)

mudduru* *adj.(?)* (mng. uncert.)

mūdê abiti *adj. cp.* well-informed

mu'dû *n.* multitude

mūdû *adj.* acquainted with, aware of; conversant with, knowing, knowledgeable, versed in; erudite, well-versed, wise; initiate; learned (man), savant

mūdû īni* *n. cp.* expert

mūdû kalāma* *adj. cp.* omniscient

mūdû pirišti* *adj. cp.* possessor of secret knowledge, initiated, mystic*

mūdût šipri *nf.* know-how*

mūdûtu* *nf.* knowledge, wisdom, gnosis

mugallitu* *n.*[4] intimidator, terrorist, troublemaker

muggu *n.* paralysis, cramp, stiffening, convulsion

mugirru *n.* chariot, two-wheeled vehicle; wheel

mūgu *n.* contingent, squadron, brigade*

muḫḫalṣû* *adj.* sliding, slippery

muḫḫu *n.* top, upper part, surface; crown of the head; head, skull, cranium; brain

muḫḫurtu* *nf.* facing, opposite direction

mu'irru* *n.* commander

muk *adv., part* thus

mukabbītu* *nf.* seamstress

mukabbû *n.* clothes mender, seamster, stitcher, dressmaker

mukallimtu *nf.* commentary

mukallimu* *adj.* explicit, expressive

mukannišu+ *adj.* sweeping

mukappirānītu+ *nf.* swab

mukarrisu *n.*[1] (a copper dish for oil)

mukaṣṣītu *nf.* cooler

mukazzibu* *adj.* flattering

mukīl appāti *n. cp.* chariot driver

mukīl ašāti* *n. cp.* chariot driver

mukīl dassi* *n. cp.* door holder, door hasp, doorstop; hinge

mukīl nūri* *n. cp.* lamppost

mukīl rēš lemutti* *n. cp.* (an evil demon)

mukīl sissê *n. cp.* horse keeper

mukillu *n.* holder, keeper, user; support

mukinnu  *n.*[1] witness; establisher, founder
mukinnūtu◊ *nf.* testimony, evidence, proof
mukīntu  *nf.* proof, evidence
muklulu *n.*[1] headscarf(?)
mūku *part.* thus (I/we)
mulammidu* *n.* instructor, teacher
mulappitu  *n.*[1] spatula
mullilu 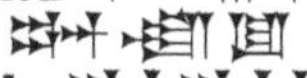 *n.* purifier
mulmullu  *n.*[1] arrow
multablakkitu◊ *adj.* rebellious
multaḫṭu* *n.*[1] survivor, escapee
multāmu 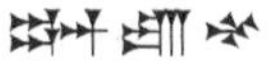 *n.* (mng. uncert.)
multarḫu* *adj.* arrogant, haughty, vainglorious; conceited, presumptuous, presuming, pretentious, pompous*
multarḫūtu* *nf.* arrogance, vainglory; conceit, ostentation, presumptuousness, pomposity*
multa''ūtu* *nf.* leisure, pleasure
multēpišu* *n.* wizard, sorcerer
multēširu* *adj.* orderly
mūlû  *n.*[1] height, hill, high ground; ascent, climb
muma''iru*  *n.*[4] command er, ruler
mumalliānu+ *n.* fulfiller, supplier
mumaššilu* *adj.* reflecting, reflective
mummillu* *n.* actor
mummiltu* *nf.* actress, dancing-girl
mummilu* *adj.* stirring, exciting; whirling; obscuring(?)
mummirtu† *nf.* matchmaker, procuress
mummu  *n.* temple workshop
mummu*  *n.* creator
muna''išu* *n.* horse-doctor, veterinarian, veterinary surgeon
munammiru* *n., adj.* illustrative*, brightener
munammû*  *n.* loveliness
munappiḫu* *n.* lighter; stirrer, inciter, rumor-monger
munaqqītu  *nf.* libation bowl
munattu* *nf.* morning slumber, doze, nap
mundagru* *adj.* compliant, obedient
mune''û◊ *n.* (bridle) bit(?)
muniḫḫu* *n.* vanquisher, subduer
munnabbitu◊  *nf.* fugiti ve
munnabtu* *n.*[1] fugitive, refugee
munnagru  *n.*[4] hir eling, migrant worker
munnagrūti* *n. pl.* migrant labor
munnaḫzu* *n.* flaring-up
munnapḫu* *adj.* inflammable
munnarbu* *adj., n.*[1] runaway, fugitive; runner, racer
munqu◊ *n.* (mng. unkn.)
muntaḫṣu* *n.*[1/4] fighter, combatant, warrior
muntaḫṣūtu* *nf.* soldiering
muntalku* *adj., n.*[1] circumspect, cautious; counsellor
mūnu  *n.* caterpillar, larva
munūtu* *nf.* counting, accounting; quota, dividend
mupaggiānu+ *n.* entertainer, imitator, mimic
muparrisu+ *n.* magistrate
muparrisūtu+ *nf.* criticism
mupassiru  *n.* bringer of news, harbinger
mupazziru* *n.* smuggler, bootlegger
mupeggû* *n.* imitator, mimic
muppalsu* *n.* observer
mupparkû* *adj.* ceasing
mupparšu* *adj.* winged, flying, volatile
muppišu  *n.* dealer, practitioner, agent
muqallilu* *adj.* defamatory, degrading, derogatory, disparaging
muqappil zê* *n. cp.* dung beetle, dorbeetle
muqarribu* *n.* presenter
mūqaru* *n.* soft mass
mūqaru+ *n.* brain matter, yolk (of an egg)
muqattirtu  *nf.* censer, thurible
muqāṭutu *nf.* gown
muqqelpû* *adj.* drifting, gliding, random*
muqqu* *v.* to be weary, be slow, be sluggish, to delay
muqqu a.* *adj.* weary, tired, sluggish, restive, languid, feeble
muqtablu*  *n.*[1] fighter, warrior
murabbânu *n.* tutor, trainer
mūraddu* *n.* descent, way down
murakkibānu+ *n.* composer
mūrānu  *n.*[1] young dog, puppy, pup, whelp; cub, kitten*
muraqqītu  *nf.* female perfume maker
muraqqiu  *n.* perfume maker
murāru* *n., nf.* endive, chicory
murasû *n.* wildcat
murdû* *n.* filigree, grating
murdu+ *n.* hemlock
mūrnisqu* *n.* select young animal; war

horse, stallion
murqu* *n.* intellect, reason
murrânu *n.* ash (tree)
murrânu+ *n.* beech
murriḫu* *adj.* urgent
murru *n.* myrrh; bitterness
murrû◊ *v.* to interrupt
murruqu◊ *adj.* clear, intelligible
murruru◊ *v.* to check, examine
murrutu◊ *nf.* (an edible plant)
murṣânu+ *n.* ailment, ill health, pallor, sickness
murṣânûtu+ *nf.* pallor, paleness
murṣu *n.* disease, illness, sickness; ailment, ache, (continuous) pain
murṣu šatti *n. cp.* seasonal disease, flu*, influenza*
murtâmu* *n.*[1] lover, lovebird
murtaṣnu* *adj.* roaring
mûrtu† *nf.* filly
mûru *n.*[1] calf, foal
mûruku* *n.* length
muruṣ êni* *n. cp.* eye disease
muruṣ eṣenti* *n. cp.* rheumatism
muruṣ ḫašê* *n. cp.* pneumonia
muruṣ kalbi* *n. cp.* distemper
muruṣ kutalli* *n. cp.* backache
muruṣ libbi *n. cp.* heartache, heart disease; compunction, remorse; preoccupation, concern, worry
muruṣ niâki* *n. cp.* venereal disease
muruṣ qabli* *n. cp.* ischias
muruṣ qaqqadi* *n. cp.* headache, head disease
muruṣ râmi* *n. cp.* lovesickness
muruṣ šinni* *n. cp.* dental infection, toothache
muruṣ šuburri* *n. cp.* anal disease
muruṣ tânti* *n. cp.* seasickness
muruṣ uzni* *n. cp.* earache
musaḫḫiru◊ *n.* buyer, buying agent
musakkiltu *nf.* (mng. unkn.)
musalliḫtu *nf.* sprinkler
musallimu* *adj.* peacemaker*, conciliable, conciliatory, placable
musappiḫu* *n.*[4] wastrel, spendrift
musarû* *n.* inscription
musâru *n.* belt, girdle
musarû B* *n.* garden bed, flower-bed, vegetable-bed, seedbed*
musâti* *nf. pl.* washing water; toilet, lavatory
musku *n.*[1] (a tree)

mussa"îtu *nf.* leisure, relaxation; amusement, pleasure, leisure time*, spare time*
mussipu* *n.* scoop
mussû◊ *v.* to distinguish, find out, identify, specify, tell apart
mussû* *v.* to identify, locate; to distinguish, discriminate
mussuku* *adj.* ugly-looking, ugly
musukkannu *n.*[1] (Indian) rosewood
musukkatu* *nf.* unclean woman
musukku* *n.* ritually unclean, impure person
muṣa"irânu *n.* frog
muṣallu *n.* (mng. uncert.)
muṣallutu *nf.* sleeping place, shelter
muṣappîtu *nf.* female dyer
muṣappiu *n.* dyer
muṣarrirtu *nf.* libation vessel
muṣiḫḫu* *n.* clown, jester
muṣiḫḫu a.* *adj.* amusing, comical, droll, funny
muṣiptu◊ *nf.* piece of cloth
muṣlâlu *n.* midday, noon, noontime; afternoon, siesta
Muṣrâiu *adj., n.* Egyptian
muṣṣâlu* *adj.* quarrelsome, hostile, pugnacious
mûṣu *n.* (a stone)
mûṣû *n.* exit, way out, departure
Muṣur *n.* Egypt
mušabbiu* *adj.* satisfactory
mušadbibu *n.* agitator (of conspiracy), incendiary, instigator, conspirator, demagogue*
mušadbibu a.* *adj.* cogent, convincing, persuasive
mušadbibûtu *nf.* agitation, abetment
mušâdu* *n.* combings
mušaḫḫinu *n.* stove
mušaḫkimu* *adj.* instructive, suggestive
mušaḫribu* *adj.* ruinous
mušaḫsisu* *adj.* reminiscent
mušâkil alpi *n. cp.* ox fattener
mušâkil iṣṣûri *n. cp.* fowl fattener
mušâkilu *n.* (a stone implement, feeder)
mušâkilu B* *n.*[1] supplier of food, purveyor
mušâlittu* *nf.* midwife
mušallimânu *n.* healer
mušallimu *n.* saving, salutary, wholesome

mušamḫiṣu *n.*[1/4] instigator of rebellion
mušamḫiṣūtu *nf.* instigation to rebellion
mušamšû* *adj.* wandering by night, wakeful
mušāniḫu* *adj.* exhausting, painstaking, tiresome, tiring
mušanmirtu *nf.* candelabrum, chandelier, lamp
mušanniānu+ *n.* narrator
mušanniktu *nf.* (a tool)
mušanniu* *n.* narrator
mušannû◊ *n.* (mng. unkn.)
mušanziru* *adj.* invidious
mušappilu* *adj.* degrading, discreditable
mušapšiqu* *adj.* aggravating
mušarkisu  *n.*[2] recruitm ent officer, horse collector
mušarkisūtu  *nf.* of fice of horse collector
mušaršidu* *n.* founder
mušaṣbiru* *adj.* giddying
mušašnītu  *nf.* (temporary) dam for diverting watercourse, coffer-dam
mušatbiu* *adj.* exciting
mušēbirtu *nf.* ferry
mušēdû* *n.* confessor
mušēltu *nf.* whet-stone
mušēniqtu  *nf.* wet nurse, milch camel
mušēpišu* *n.*[4] organizer
mušērittu* *nf.* oesophagus, gullet
mušērtu *nf.* (mng. unkn.)
mušēṣītu* *nf.* drainage channel
mušēṣiu *adj., n.*[2] outlet pipe, outlet canal
mušētiq sāri* *n. cp.* sweeper
mušēzibtu  *nf.* protective shield, siege-shield
mušēzibu *n.* rescuer, savior
mušḫalṣītu* *nf.* slippery ground
mušḫalṣû* *adj.* slippery
mušḫuššu*  *n.* dragon
mūšiš* *adv.* at night
mūšīta* *adv.* at night
mūšītiš* *adv.* at night
mūšītu* *nf.* night
muškēnu 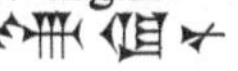 *n.*[4] poor man, beggar, mendicant, pauper, wretch; destitute, miserable, needy
muškēnu+ *n.*[4] poor, meagre; poverty-stricken, wretched
muškēnūtu *nf.* beggary, penury, poorness, poverty, want
muškēnūtu+ *nf.* poorness, meagreness
mušlaḫḫu* *n.* snake charmer
mušlallilu* *n.* reptile
mušlālu *n.* (a gate or gatehouse)
mušlānūtu* *nf.* resemblance, similarity
mušlu *adj.* similar, akin, alike, like, equal, identical*
mušpalu* *n.*[1] depression, lowland, dale, valley, low-lying place, depth
mušpēlu* *adj.* changeable, capricious, fickle
muššarû *n.*[2] inscription
muššāru  *n.* serpentine
muššipu* *n.* exorcist
muššultu* *nf.* reflection, imitation, replica
muššulu* *n.* likeness, replica; mirror
muššu'tu* *nf.* ointment, cream, paste
muštābilu* *adj.* contemplative, meditative, musing, pensive
muštabrītu* *nf.* seaworthy ship
muštaddinu* *adj.* communicative
muštaḫalqu◊ *n.*[4] deserter
muštaḫḫizu* *adj.* infectious, contagious
muštaḫmiṭu* *adj.* blazing, glowing, everignited
muštālu* *adj., n.* judicious, thoughtful, circumspect, prudent, deliberate; adviser, councillor
muštālūtu* *nf.* consideration, deliberation; conference, council
muštamḫiru* *adj.* comparative
muštaprišu* *adj.* flying, winged
muštapṣu* *n.*[4] wrestler
muštapšiqtu† *nf.* woman in labor, travailing woman
muštarriḫu* *adj.* arrogant, overweening, self-important, conceited, proud
mušta''û* *adj.* idle, at leisure
muštēmiqu* *adj.* devout, suppliant, supplicating
muštēnû* *adj.* changing, variable, adolescent, growing towards maturity
muštēpišu* *adj., n.* crafty; sorcerer, bewitcher
muštinnu* *n.* urethra
mušṭu* *n.* brush*, comb, card[ing device]
mūšu  *n.* night
mūšu annīu *np.* tonight
mūšubu *n.*[1] apartment, domicile, dwelling; dwelling house; accommodation, housing, lodging
mušuttu *nf.* dream ritual
mūtānu  *n.*[1] pestilence, plague, epidemic
mūtānu+ *n.*[1] mortality, slaughter
mūterrišu* *adj.* demanding, requester
mutḫummu* *n.* fruit, fruit tree

mutinnu* *n.* choice wine
mutīr gimilli* *n. cp.* avenger
mutīr ṭēmi *n. cp.* information officer
mutirru 
 *n.*[1] fire rake, poker
mutīrtu* *nf.* double door
mutlellû* *adj.* exalted
mutnāru  *n.* (a wooden object)
mutnennû* *adj.* pious
mutqītu  *nf.* candy, sweet cake, delicacy, tidbit
mutqû* *n.* sweet bread
muttabbiltu* *nf.* furnishings, furniture; female servant
muttabbilu*  *n.* servant, domestic, waiter*
muttaddinu* *n.* salesman, seller
muttaggišu* *adj.* restless
muttalliktu* *nf.* pavement, processional way, avenue
muttalliku  *adj.* mobile, movable, portable, ambulatory
muttallu* *adj.* noble, princely
muttanbiṭu* *adj.* bright, shining
muttaprašš̌idu* *adj.* fugitive, homeless
muttaprišu* 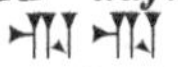 *adj.* flying, winged
muttāqu *n.* confectionery
muttarrittu* *nf.* perpendicular (line)
muttutu* *nf.* half
mutu  *n.* husband, man
mūtu  *n.*[2] death
muṭê *n. pl.* deficit, shortfall; missing (sum); deficiency, shortage, lack
muʼuntu◊ *nf.* field of sustenance
muʼʼuru*  *v.* to send, guide; to command
muzakkû* *n.* cleaner
muzzīqu* *n.* raisin
naʼādu*  *v.* $^{a/a}$ to praise, extol; (Gt) to pay attention, observe, revere
naʼādu  *v.* $^{a/a}$ (D) to praise, commend, laud, to acclaim*, applaud*
naʼālu* *v.* $^{i/i}$ to moisten
naʼāpu* *v.* $^{u/u}$ to be dry, wither
naʼāru* *v.* to roar, snarl
naʼāru+ *v.* to growl, bray, creak
naʼāšu* *v.* $^{i/i}$ to have difficulty breathing, pant, wheeze, sneeze(?)
nabābu* *v.* $^{u/u}$ to pipe, play the flute
nabāḫu◊ *v.* $^{u/u}$ to bark, yelp
nābališ turru‡ *vp.* to turn into dry land
nabalkattānu*  *n.* rebellious, rebel, revolutionary, mutineer
nabalkattu*  *nf.* revolt, revolution, uprising, insurrection, mutiny, coup; desertion; reversal, retreat; scaling, climbing over; ladder, ramp, inversion*, overthrow*, burglary
nabalkutu  *v.* to rebel, revolt, defect, transgress; to turn over, be inverted; to spring back; to surmount, topple over, cross over, traverse, transcend
nabalkutu*  *v.* to do a somersault, toss about, be capricous; (Gtn) to do somersaults
nabalkutu  *v.* (Š) to excite to rebellion, revolutionize; to displace, invert, turn over, capsize, tip over; to overturn, turn upside down; to overthrow, upset, reverse; to push over, bring over, take across
nabalkutu a. *adj.* inverted, awry; inverse, reverse; rebellious
nabalkutu n.* *n.* somersault
nābalu* *n.* dry land, mainland, terra firma, continent
nābartu* *nf.* trap, cage
nabāsiš* *adv.* like red wool
nabāsu* *n.* red(-dyed) wool
nabāṭu* *v.* $^{u/u}$ to shine; (Š) to make shine; (Ntn) to gain radiance
nabāʼu* *v.* $^{u/u}$ to gush*, gush out*, jet*, spout*, spurt*, squirt*, stem from*, to rise, swell up; (Š) to cast(?), to jet*
nabāʼu+ *v.* $^{u/u}$ to spring up, flow; to shoot up; to burst forth; (Š) to pour forth, bring forth, eject, overflow
nābiʼu* *n.* plunderer
nablāṭu* *n.* healing, cure
nablu  *n.* flame, flash
nabnītu*  *nf.* creation; creature(s); nature; stature, figure, physique
nabrarû* *n.* open field, plain
nabraštu+ *nf.* chandelier, candlestick, pendant lamp
nabšaltu+ *nf.* cuisine
nabṭû* *n.* horizon
nabû*  *v.* $^{i/i}$ to call; to name, nominate, dub; (D) to lament, wail, moan
nābu* *n.* insect egg, nit
nābu+ *n.* louse's egg
naburriš* *adv.* like battlements
naburru* *n.* battlement
nadādu† *v.* $^{i/i}$ (D) to curry, comb
nadādu B* *v.* $^{i/i}$ to budge*, move*, to cede, give way(?)
nadānu*  *v.* $^{i/i}$ to give; (Št) to intermingle, confer, converse, ponder
nadāqu* *v.* to tickle(?)
nadāru* *v.* to roar, growl, be wild, be furious, rage; (N) to become enraged, go on a

rampage

nadbâk dîši* *n. cp.* turf

nadbâk mê* *n. cp.* cataract, waterfall

nadbâktu *nf.* ravine, gully, waterfall

nadbâku *n.* $^{1/2}$ expenditure; brick course, layer, stratum; ravine, gully, waterfall

naddinu* *adj.* permissive

nâdinu* *n.* giver, donor

na'diš* *adv.* attentively, reverently, piously

nadîtu* *nf.* nun

nâdîtu* *nf.* miscarrying woman

nadru* *adj.* raging, furious, wild, aggressive

na'du* *adj.* attentive, considerate, heedful, given up to; reverent, respectful, pious; observant, solicitous

nadû* *v.* to throw, cast, toss, lay down, put; to pitch; to inflict, impose; to abandon, renounce, drop, abort; (Š) to depopulate; (stat.) to lie, be situated

nâdu *nf.* waterskin

nadunnû *n.* marriage gift, dowry

na'du B* *adj.* praised, praiseworthy

nagâgu* *v.* $^{u/u}$ to guffaw*, to bray, neigh, whinny; to bellow, bawl

nagalmušu *adj.* (specification of a chariot)

nagaltû* *v.* to awake, wake up

nagâlu* *v.* to glisten, glow

nagarruru *v.* to grovel, roll, roll about, wallow; (Š) to roll out, allow to wallow

nagâšu* *v.* $^{u/u}$ to go; (Gtn) to wander about, travel about, ramble, straggle

nagbu* *n.* ^{1} spring, well, fountain, source, underground water

nagbu B* *n.* totality, all, entirety

naggâr magarri *n. cp.* cartwright, wheel-maker

naggâr mugirri *n. cp.* cartwright

naggâr pâši *n. cp.* axe maker

naggâru *n.* ^{2} carpenter, joiner

naggâru+ *n.* ^{2} sawyer

naggulu* *adj.* glowing, phosphorescent

nagiânu* *adj.* insular

nâgir êkalli *n. cp.* palace herald

nâgiru *n.* ^{4} herald

nagîtu* *nf.* district

nagiu *n.* $^{1/2}$ district, region

naglubu *n.* shoulder blade; shaving blade, razor

nagmuru *adj.* final, ultimate

nagû* *v.* $^{u/u}$ to rejoice, be hilarious, exult; to sing joyfully, carol

nâgurtu *nf.* hire(?)

nagû B* *n.* island, isle

nagû B+ *n.* (pl.) archipelago

naḫalṣû *v.* to slip, slide, stumble; to err, make an error, trip up

naḫâlu* *v.* $^{a/u}$ to sieve, sift

naḫanṣû *n.* (a type of wine)

naḫarmumu* *v.* to collapse, break down

naḫarmuṭu* *v.* to dissolve, melt, melt away, thaw, crumble; (Š) to disintegrate, liquidate, liquefy, melt

naḫarmuṭu a.* *adj.* liquid, molten, runny

naḫarmuṭu n.* *n.* dissolution

naḫâru* *v.* $^{u/u}$ to hoot, snore, snort, snorting, toot, wheezing

naḫâru+ *v.* $^{u/u}$ to bray, creak, growl, honk, roar

naḫâru B* *v.* to be shrivelled, withered; (D) to invalidate

naḫâsu◊ *v.* $^{i/i}$ to cede, recede, return; to withdraw, yield, shrink from; to abate, subside

naḫâsu B* *v.* to snivel, sniffle, sob

naḫâšu* *v.* $^{i/i}$ to prosper, thrive; to be fertile, be lusty; (D) to grant prosperity

naḫâtu *v.* to be small, diminished; (D) to clip

naḫbû *n.* ^{1} bucket, bailer

naḫbuṣu *n.* oil flask, ointment vase

naḫbutu *n.* robbery

nâḫirânu* *n., adj.* puffer, snorter

naḫîru *n.* ^{1} nostril

nâḫiru* *n.* dolphin, siren, whale

naḫîru+ *n.* ^{1} nose, nostril(s), nozzle, flange (of folding-doors)

naḫlaptu *nf.* coat, (felt) armor, mail-shirt

naḫlu *n.* ^{3} brook, gorge, rivulet, stream, wadi

naḫlu+ *n.* ^{3} torrent, dry bed of torrent, valley

naḫlu B† *adj.* sieved, strained

naḫnâḫutu *nf.* cartilage

naḫru† *adj.* invalid, not binding

naḫsu* *adj.* (very) thin, narrow; delicate, fine

naḫšâti* *n. pl.* haemorrhage

naḫšu* *adj.* prosperous, thriving, healthy,

lusty
naḫtu *n.* (an intestine; a garment)
naḫtu+ *n.* (long) outer garment
nāḫu *n.* pig fat, lard
naiabtu* *nf.* cartilage, floating rib
naiāktu* *nf.* adulteress
naiāku* *n.* adulterer, fornicator, womanizer, hustler, stud
naiākūtu* *nf.* promiscuity
naiālu *n.* parasite, lazybones
nā'ikānu† *n.* rapist
nā'iku *adj.* promiscuous
na'īlu* *n.* ^{3} flooded valley
nā'imu* *adj.* adventurous*, bold
nā'iru* *n.* ^{1} rager, roarer; predatory bird, eagle
naiulu* *adj.* bedridden
naiumu+ *adj.* drowsy
nakādu *v.* $^{u/u}$ to beat, throb, palpitate; to worry
nakālu *v.* $^{i/i}$ to be artful, be dexterous, be skilful; to act cleverly, contrive, feign, invent, pretend, trick
nakālu* *v.* $^{i/i}$ (D) to make skilfully, execute artistically, to make artificially*; (Š) to execute skilfully
nakālu+ *v.* $^{i/i}$ to act deceitfully, beguile, betray, defraud, to betray, gull
nakāmu* *v.* $^{a/u}$ to stock, heap up, pile up, store, amass
nakāpu* *v.* $^{i/i}$ to push, thrust; to butt, gore, mutilate, stub; (Gt) to butt each other, lock up horns; (Gtn) to abut; (D) to knock down
nakāru *v.* $^{i/i}$ to be hostile, strange, different; to rebel, revolt; to refuse; (D) to change; to remove, depose, to do exceptionally*; (Š) to make inimical, cause enmity, alienate, estrange
nakāru+ *v.* $^{i/i}$ to disclaim
nakāsu *v.* $^{i/i}$ to cut, cut down, fell, cleave; to cut off, clip, sever, mutilate, maim; (D) to chop, hack to pieces
nakātu+ *v.* to nettle
nakbāsu *n.* floor, step (of a staircase)
nakbusu *n.* carpet, mat
nakdu* *adj.* critical, earnest, serious
nakīru *n.* ^{1} enemy
nākisu *n.* ^{4} butcher, lumberjack*
nakkamtu *nf.* treasure; treasury, storehouse, store, stock; resources
nakkaptu* *nf.* temple
nakkāpu* *n.* promontory, protuberance
nakkulu+ *adj.* crafty, wily
nakkuru *adj.* changed, different, odd, weird
nakliš* *adv.* artistically, skilfully
naklu *adj.* artful, artistic; intricate, sophisticated; clever, dexterous, ingenious, skilful, slick, sly; astute, crafty, cunning, shrewd, wily; artificial, factitious
naklu+ *adj.* crooked, deceitful, faithless, perfidious
nakmu* *adj.* heaped (up), amassed
nakmû* *n.* branding, branding-iron
nakmuru *n.* reed basket, pannier
nakriš* *adv.* inimically, like an enemy; strangely
nakru *adj.* strange, different; foreign, alien; barbarous, unintelligible, unknown; hostile
nakru n. *n.* ^{4} enemy
nakrumu† *n.* storage
nakrūtu* *nf.* hostility
naksu *adj.* cut (off), felled
naktumu *n.* cover, lid
nâku* *v.* to browse on(?)
nakuppu *n.* circumference
nakuttu *nf.* fear, distress
nalbân* *adv.* all around, completely
nalbâna† *adv.* all around
nalbantu* *nf.* brick mold, frame, framework, matrix, square(-form), trapezoid
nalbanu* *n.* brick mold
nalbaš ṣēni* *n. cp.* fleece
nalbaš šamê* *n. cp.* clouds
nalbašu* *n.* attire, cloak, costume, outfit
nalbētu† *nf.* overlay, wrapper, wrapping
nalbubu* *adj.* raging, ferocious
nalšu *n.* dew
nālu *n.* roe deer
namaddu *n.* ^{3} measurement, dimension
namaddu B* *n.* beloved one, darling, favorite
namārītu *nf.* daybreak, twilight, morning watch
namarkû *v.* to be late, delayed, lag [behind]; to fall behind; to tarry; (Š) to delay, retard
namarkû a. *adj.* overdue, retarded, tardy
namāru *v.* $^{i/i}$ to be bright, be brilliant, shine, burn brightly, radiate, beam; to clear up
namāru* *v.* $^{i/i}$ (D) to brighten, illuminate, lighten; to make happy, make radiant
namāru *v.* $^{i/i}$ (Š) to let shine, make brilliant, brighten, light up, lighten, illuminate; to

cheer up; to kindle, to illustrate*
namāṣu* *n.* churn
namāšu† *v.* $^{u/u}$ to be agile, move, move on
namāšu *v.* $^{u/u}$ (D) to depart, get about, set forth, set off, set out, start out; to set in motion
namba'u* *n.* seep, water hole, source, spring
namba'u+ *n.* fount, fountain
nambūbtu *nf.* wasp
namburbû  *n.* apotropaic ritual
namēlulu *v.* to play
namḫartu* *nf.* receipt
namḫaru* *n.* mooring pole
namḫāru† *n.* vat, receptacle
namḫaštu* *nf.* oar
namirtu* *nf.* brightness, light, illumination
nâmiru  *n.* ^{2} watchtower
namkūru* *n.* ^{1} possession(s), property, capital
namlaktu* *nf.* realm
nammaššû*  *n.* *pl.* wildlife, wild animals
nammaštu*  *nf.* wild animal
nammuru+ *adj.* enlightened
nammušīšu* *adj.* mobile, agile
nammušīšu alāku‡ *pl.* to pass away, die
namrāṣiš* *adv.* with difficulty
namrāṣu* *n.* difficulty
namrirru* *n.* (pl.) brilliance, luminosity
namriš* *adv.* brilliantly, brightly, radiantly, splendidly
namru  *adj.* bright, brilliant; clear, lucid; luminous, shiny, shining, sunny; beaming, radiant; blithe, cheerful, merry, obvious*, unmistakable*
namrūtu* *nf.* mother-of-pearl
namsētu* *nf.* wash-basin
namsû* *n.* washbowl, washing place, washing tank
namṣāru* *n.* ^{1} sword
namtāru* *n.* fate
namû* *n.* ^{1} pasture, pasturage, desert, steppe
nam'udu  *n.* majority, plenty; luxury
namullu  *n.* (plank) bed
namurratu*  *nf.* terrifying splendour, brilliance
namurru* *adj.* awe-inspiringly radiant, brilliant, resplendent
nāmurtu *nf.* audience gift
nāmuru *n.* ^{1} tower, watchtower, lookout
nāmuru B  *n.* mirror
namūtu† *nf.* flirt, jest, mischief, prank
namûtu* *nf.* desolation, wasteland
namūtu epāšu† *vp.* to flirt, jest, dally, trifle
namû B*  *v.* to be abandoned, lie in ruins; (D) to lay waste, turn into ruins
namzāqu* *n.* ^{1} key
nanduqu* *adj.* clad, clothed
nanduru* *adj.* raging, furious, wild; fearsome, inhospitable
nanḫaṣtu  *nf.* target*
nanḫuṣu *n.* rod, driving stick
naniḫu  *n.* mint, spearmint*
nanmurtu* *nf.* heliacal rising
nannabu*  *n.* progeny
nannaru*  *n.* luminary, light
nanzāzu* *n.* position, station
napādiš* *adv.* treacherously(?)
napāḫ šamši *n. cp.* sunrise, east
napāḫu *v.* $^{a/u}$ to blow, hiss, puff; to ignite, kindle, light, light up; to rise (heliacally)
napāḫu* *v.* $^{a/u}$ (D) to light, ignite
napāḫu *v.* $^{a/u}$ (N) to become inflated, become swollen
napāḫu+ *v.* $^{a/u}$ to blow out, breathe into, erupt, exhale, inspire, fan, puff up, swell
napalkû* *v.* to be wide
napalsuḫu* *v.* to throw o.s. down, prostrate o.s.; to squat, grovel, cringe; (Š) to make squat
nāpaltu† *nf.* answer, reaction, reflex
napālu* *v.* $^{a/u}$ to raze, demolish, pull down; (D) to gouge out eyes, blind; to turn up (soil)
nāpalû* *n.* interpreter, translator
napāqu* *v.* to clog up, be blocked, be constipated
napardû* *v.* to shine, to be radiant, bright, pleased, cheerful; (Š) to brighten, lighten, illuminate; to cheer up
naparkû* *v.* to cease, stop, end, fail; (Š) to stop
naparqudu* *v.* to lie flat, lie on back, lie supine
naparqudu a.* *adj.* supine, face up
naparrurtu* *nf.* divergence, dispersal
naparšudu* *v.* to escape
napāru+ *v.* to moult
nāpassu *nf.* answer, reply, reaction
napāṣu *v.* $^{a/u}$ to push away, push down; to beat up, bruise, maul; to bang, kick, slam, strike down, dash; (D) to smash, crush, shatter; to smite, slay

napāṣu+ *v.* $^{a/u}$ to shake off, throw down; (D) to break to pieces, dash to pieces, shake off
napāšu *v.* $^{u/u}$ to breathe, draw breath, ease off, ease up, inhale, puff; to snort; to distend, expand; (D) to set at ease; to air, ventilate
napāšu+ *v.* $^{u/u}$ (D) to enliven
napāšu B *v.* $^{a/u}$ to comb, card, pluck (wool)
napḫar murṣi*  *n. cp.* (a medical compendium, all diseases)
napḫaru*  *n.* totality, sum, all, whole, entirety
napḫu *adj.* blown-up, inflated, swollen; enkindled
napḫu* *adj.* ablaze, alight, blown on, bright, kindled, shining
napḫu+ *adj.* puffed-up, elated, inspired; puffy, out of breath
nāpilu* *n.* battering ram
napīšu* *n.* breath; breeze; breathing, panting, respiration; scent, smell, aroma
nāpi'u* *n.* plunderer
nappāḫ erê  *n. cp.* coppersmith
nappāḫ parzilli  *n. cp.* blacksmith
nappāḫ siparri  *n. cp.* bronzesmith
nappāḫtu  *nf.* female smith
nappāḫu 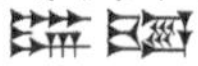 *n.* ^{2} smith
nappaltu* *nf.* rubble, debris
nappaltu B* *nf.* difference
nappāšu* *n.* air vent, vent
nappilu  *n.* caterpillar
nappītu  *nf.* sieve
nappu+ *n.* rhubarb
nappû??◊ *n.* sieve
nappuḫu*  *n.* inspired*
napraku* *n.* bolt, (cross)bar, hasp; barrier, obstacle
napšaltu *nf.* ointment, salve
napšāru* *n.* uvula
napšu *adj.* plentiful, ample, abundant, bounteous; spry, brisk
napšurtu* *nf.* dissolution, release
napšuru *n.* forgiveness
napšutu  *nf.* life; throat; soul; person, individual, psyche*
napšutu qatû‡ *vp.* to perish, lose one's life
naptāḫu+ *n.* clue
naptan līlāti* *n. cp.* dinner
naptan muṣulāli* *n. cp.* lunch, luncheon
naptan šēri* *n. cp.* breakfast
naptaqu* *n.* (metal) mold
naptû* *n.* key, opening device, opener
naptunu  *n.* ^{1} meal, dinner, repast
napṭartu* *nf.* key
napṭaru* *n.* guest-friend, acquaintance
napṭu *n.* naphtha, mineral oil*
napû◊ *v.* $^{i/i}$ to sift, sieve
napūḫu *n.* bellows
naqābu* *v.* $^{a/u}$ to penetrate sexually
naqābu+ *v.* $^{a/u}$ to perforate, pierce, puncture
naqādu* *v.* to be in danger(ous condition), be critical, cause concern
naqāḫu+ *v.* to caw, croak, peck, crack
naqallulu  *v.* to glow, shine
naqāpu+ *v.* to cleave, haunt, stick to
naqāqu+ *v.* to croak
naqāru  *v.* $^{a/u}$ to demolish, dismantle, pull down, raze, tear down; to carve, cut (stone), hew, scratch, scrape out, to engrave*
naqāru*  *v.* $^{a/u}$ (Š) to wreck
naqāru+ *v.* $^{a/u}$ to hew out, hollow out, incise
naqāšu+ *v.* to click
naqbītu 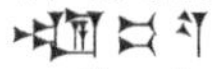 *nf.* litany, recitation, diction*, wording*
naqburu  *n.* burial place, grave, sepulchre, tomb
naqdu* *adj.* critical(ly ill); solicitous
nāqidu 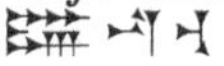 *n.* herdsman, stockbreeder
nāqidu+ *n.* custodian, sheepmaster
nāqiru* *n.* ^{1} wrecker; (wall) hook
nāqiru+ *n.* ^{1} woodpecker
naqmūtu* *nf.* conflagration, burning
naqqār arê *n. cp.* millstone cutter
naqquru+ *adj.* pitted
naqrabu*  *n.* battleground
naqû  *v.* $^{i/i}$ to shed, pour, libate; to sacrifice
naqû*  *v.* $^{i/i}$ (D) to offer
naqû+ *v.* $^{i/i}$ (D) to devote o.s. to
naquttu◊ *nf.* crisis, critical situation
narāmtu*  *nf.* beloved, darling
narāmu*  *n.* beloved, darling
nar'antu  *nf.* mace, club, cudgel
nārārūtu* *nf.* help, aid
narāṭu *v.* $^{u/u}$ to quake, shake, tremble, quaver, quiver; to stagger, totter; to hesitate, vacillate, waver; (D) to shake, wiggle, jolt; to make tremble, perturb, bother
narbāṣu* *n.* lair
narbû*  *adj.* greatness; great

achievements, great deeds, feats
narbû a.* *adj.* increasable, expandable
narbûtu* *nf.* greatness
nargallu  *n.* (senior) singer, musician
nargallutu  *nf.* female singer
nargu+ *n.* axe
nāriš* *adv.* like a river
nāriṭu *adj.* hesitant, shaky, scrupulous*
nāriṭu* *n.* marsh, swamp, mire
narkabtu 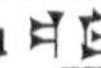 *nf.* chariot
narmaktu 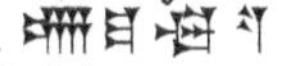 *nf.* washbasin, washbowl, sink*
narmuku† *n.* washbowl, bathtub, sink*
narqītu* *nf.* remoteness, place of refuge
nārtu *nf.* canal
narṭubu *n.* beer wort
narû  *n.* stele; annals; autobiography, chronicle, legend, memorial, biography*, history*, memoirs*
nāru *n.* river, stream, current
naruqqu  *nf.* leather bag, sack; investment capital, investment*
nârūtu* *nf.* musicianship, music, musical arts
nasāḫu  *v.* $^{a/u}$ to tear out, tear away; to eradicate, pull off, pull out, root out, uproot, weed; to displace, dispose of, banish, expel; to exact, remove, withdraw; to extract, copy, quote, cite; to subtract
nasāḫu paqādu‡ *p* *t* to relegate
nasāku  *v.* $^{u/u}$ to throw down, toss; to eject, shoot; to reject, throw out; to overrule, refute, void; to belch forth
nasāku* 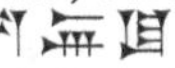 *v.* $^{u/u}$ (Š) to shrug off, remove, eliminate, abolish, repeal
nasāku+ *v.* $^{u/u}$ to pump
nasāqu  *v.* $^{i/i}$ to choose, select, elect, single out
nasāru* *v.* $^{u/u(?)}$ to saw
nasāsu* *v.* $^{u/u}$ to moan, wail
nasḫuru  *n.* benevolence, attention, penitence*, repentance*
nasīḫu* *n.* displaced person, laborer; deportee
nasīku  *n.* $^{2/3}$ sheikh
nasku *adj.* thrown down; horizontal, level
naspantu* 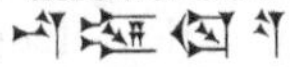 *nf.* devastation
naspuḫtu* *nf.* dissipation, disintegration
nasqu *adj.* selected, choice, elect, precious
nasramû  *n.* (a cult object)
nassiqu* *adj.* choosy, fastidious
nassu* *adj.* groaning, wretched, anguished
naṣābu* *v.* $^{a/u}$ to suck, lick
naṣālu* *v.* $^{i/i}$ to go away, leave(?)
naṣāru  *v.* $^{a/u}$ to guard, defend, protect, safeguard; to watch, beware of; to cherish, preserve, prize, treasure
naṣāru*  *v.* $^{a/u}$ (Š) to guard, appoint a guard over
naṣāru+ *v.* $^{a/u}$ to conserve
naṣāru n.+ *n.* conservation
naṣbutu  *n.* ^{3} sash holder; grip, handle
Naṣībina *n.* Nisibis
naṣību+ *adj.* congenital, implanted, ingrafted, innate
nāṣiru  *adj.*, *n.* protective, watch-; guardian, protector, preserver
naṣmadu* *n.* ^{1} team
naṣraptu  *nf.* crucible; dyeing vat
naṣru  *adj.* rack, hook, peg
naṣṣubu  *n.* drain pipe; (a cucurbitaceous plant)
naṣû *v.* $^{i/i}$ to strive(?)
nāṣu* *n.* plumage, feathers
naṣû+ *v.* to contend
nāš ēni* *adj. cp.* avaricious, avid, greedy
nāš kakki* *adj. cp.* armed
nāš qašti* *n. cp.* archer
našābu* *v.* $^{u/u}$ blow away, clear off, scatter, winnow
našāku *v.* $^{a/u}$ to bite; (D) to bite up, crunch
našāqu  *v.* $^{i/i}$ to kiss
našarbuṭu* *v.* to flit; to chase around
našāru *v.* $^{a/u}$ to take away, remove, withdraw, deduct; (N) to be taken away, fall off; to improve
našāšu B* *v.* $^{i/i}$ to sniff
našbaṭu◊ *n.* trimmed palm-frond
nāši pūtuḫi* *adj. cp.* liable, responsible
nāšiu *n.* ^{2} carrier, porter; laden with
našmaṭu* *n.* pulled-out (part)
našmû* *n.* hearing, sense of hearing
našmû+ *n.* obedience
našpantu *nf.* devastation
našpartu *nf.* letter, message
našpāru◊ *n.* envoy, messenger
našpirtu† *nf.* message
našpu  *n.* (a type of thin beer)
naštuq* *n.* (leather) bag, purse
našû  *v.* $^{i/i}$ to lift; to carry, bear, tote; to get, receive; to remove, take; to prop [up], support, uphold; to stand, sustain, tolerate; (vent.) to bring, fetch
nâšu* *v.* $^{u/a}$ to quake, shake; to lurch, tot-

ter; to budge, shift, dislodge, give way; to be weakened, become shaky; (D) to jolt

našû ana‡ *vp.* to multiply

našû rammû *vp.* to drop dead, cease doing, abandon

našû rēši *n. cp.* summoning, summons

natāku *v.* u/u to drip, drop, ooze, trickle; to leak; (D) to (let) drip

natāru* *v.* (Š) cut through, split, cleave, demolish

nātiku *adj.* runny

naṭālu* *v.* a/u to look, see, gaze; (N) to appear, be visible

nāṭilu* *adj.* seeing

naṭpu* *adj.* (mng. unkn.)

naṭû *v.* u/u to beat, slash, whip, scourge, spank

nāṭu *n.* 2 (a ritual)

naṭû a.* *adj.* possible, potential, feasible, practicable; fitting, appropriate, adequate

naṭû B* *v.* i/i to be possible, be feasible, be proper

nazālu◊ *v.* a/u to pour out, drain

nazāmu *v.* u/u to creak, grouch, grouse, groan, moan, to patter*; (Dtt) to grumble, growl, murmur, complain

nazāqu* *v.* i/i to worry, despair; to bawl, howl, squeak, squeal, whine, yowl; (D) to grieve; (Š) to exasperate, irk, vex, annoy

nazāru *v.* i/i to curse, cuss, damn; to accurse, condemn; (Š) to make hateful, make detested

nazāzu* *v.* u/u to moan, grunt, rustle, snort, splutter; (D) to hush(?)

nazīru+ *n.* 4 ascetic, celibate, hermit

nazmatu* *nf.* wish, desire

nazru *adj.* accursed, damned, detestable

nazziqu* *adj.* plaintive, querulous, fretful*, irritable*, grumpy*, peevish*, pettish*, petulant*, squeaking

nazzītu *nf.* brewing vat, mash tub

nazzītu+ *nf.* cask

nēbartu* *nf.* crossing (place), ford; other side, transition*

nēbartu+ *nf.* pass

nēberānu+ *n.* isthmus

nēbettu *nf.* girdle, sash

nebrītu* *nf.* hunger, famine

nebû* *v.* to gleam, shine, sparkle

nebû a.* *adj.* shining, bright

nēbuḫu *n.* 1 band, belt, sash; frieze

nēburu *n.* 3 crossing, ford, transit

nēburu+ *n.* 3 duct, canal; passage, strait; vestibule; ferry, ferryboat

nēḫiš* *adv.* calmly, quietly, leisurely*

nēḫtu* *nf.* peace, quiet; security, composure, tranquility; equanimity, peace of mind, sobriety, condolence*, comfort*, consolation*, solace*

nēḫu *adj.* peaceful, calm, quiet, tranquil, unmoved; composed, contented, dispassionate, placid, self-possessed, sober; imperturbable

nēḫu+ *adj.* tranquil, gentle, meek, at rest

nekelmû* *v.* to frown, glare, look angrily

nēkemtu* *nf.* removal, plundering; atrophied part

nēku *adj.* raped, ravished, violated

nēmattu *nf.* couch, sofa, back(rest); crutch, support, armchair*

nēmel *subj.* because

nēmēqu *n.* wisdom

nemru *n.* 2 panther

nemru+ *n.* 2 leopard

nemrutu+ *nf.* leopardess, she-leopard

nēmudu *n.* 1 couch

nēmulu *n.* profit, gain, benefit

nentû* *v.* to follow closely

nēpeštu* *nf.* ritual; workmanship

nēpešu* *n.* 1 tool, gadget, implement, machine, (siege) engine, construction

nēpēšu *n.* 1 ritual; procedure, mode of performance

neplu+ *n.* clover

neqelpû* *v.* to drift, glide, float, to cruise*, to dizzy, giddy

nērab tānti* *n. cp.* bay, gulf

nerāku *n.* (mng. uncert.)

nērāru* *n.* aid, help, helper; auxiliary troops, ally

nērārūtu* *nf.* help, aid

nērtu* *nf.* murder, assassination, homicide, manslaughter

nerṭû* *n.* sin, misdemeanour

nêru* *v.* to kill, slay, strike, conquer

nērubu *n.* 2 entrance, pass; deep valley, defile, gorge; ingress, way in

nērubu+ *n.* 2 abrupt valley, deep pool, precipice

nesû* *adj.* to go far, be distant; to withdraw; to shun, shy at, shy from, shy away (from); (D) to remove, deport

nesû a.* *adj.* far-away, distant, remote, exotic, from afar

nēsupu *n.* 1 shovel

nēšakku* *n.* [1] (a priest)
nēštu* *nf.* lioness
nēšu *n.* lion
nê'u* *v.* to turn back, turn away, deflect; to stanch; (D) to stave off
niāku *v.* to rape, ravish; to have sexual intercourse, copulate, fornicate, fuck, bonk, diddle
niāku† *v.* (Gtn) to sleep around*
niāku *v.* (Gtn) to have illicit sex repeatedly, be promiscuous
niāku n. *n.* copulation, sexual intercourse, fornication
niālu *v.* to lie down, sleep; (D) to lay flat; (Š) to make sleep
niāru *n.* [1] papyrus, paper*
niāši* *pron.* us
niāwu+ *v.* to mew
nībit šumi* *n. cp.* giving of name, name-giving
nībītu* *nf.* name, call, vocation; nomenclature; called, chosen one
nibṣu* *n.* young bird, fledgling
nib'u* *n.* flux, swelling up
nību* *n.* [2] amount, number, name; utterance, declaration
nibzu *n.* [2] (clay) tablet, document
nibzu+ *n.* [2] receipt
nīd aḫi* *n. cp.* negligence, laxity
nīd kussî* *n. cp.* base of the throne
nīd libbi* *n. cp.* abortion, premature birth
nidbû *n.* (food) offering
nidin pê* *n. cp.* promise
nidintu◊ *nf.* present, gift
nidnakku† *n.* censer
nidnu* *n.* gift, payment, reward
nīdu* *n.* (cumulus) cloud(?)
nidūtu* *nf.* uncultivated land, untilled land, uninhabited land, wasteland
nigdimdimmû* *n.* form, shape
nigiṣṣu* *n.* crack, crevice
nigūtu* *nf.* merry-making, (joyful) music
nigūtu epēšu‡ *vp.* to make music
nigūtu šakānu‡ *vp.* to make merry, hold a festival
niḫru+ *n.* honk
niḫsu *n.* inlay
nikil libbi* *n. cp.* ingenuity
nikiltu *nf.* ingenuity, cleverness, dexterity, subtlety; art, skill; affectation, cunning, deception, trick; (pl.) arts, ingenious ideas
nikimtu† *nf.* heaping up, accumulation
nikiptu *nf.* spurge
nikittu *nf.* anxiety, preoccupation, fear, worry
nikkassu *n.* [1] account, accounting; assets, estate, property, funds
niklāti nukkulu‡ *vp.* to make artistically
niklu *n.* cunning, trick; bluff, gimmick, hoax, intrigue, knack, stunt
niklu+ *n.* guile, deceit, dissimulation, feigning, perfidy, plot
niklu nakālu *vp.* to play a trick, bluff, deceive, hoax, invent a ruse
niksu *n.* [2] breach, cut, cutting, incision; (a garment)
nīku *n.* adultery, coition, coitus, sexual intercourse, fucking; rape
nīlu *n.* semen, sperm, fluid
nimgallu* *n.* (a siege engine, liter. big fly)
nimrā'u *n.* (a garment)
nindabû* *n.* [1] (food) offering
nindānu* *n.* measuring rod (c. 6 m)
nindānu B* *n.* knowledge
niniu *n.* ammi
Nīnuwa *n.* Nineveh
nipḫu *n.* sun disk, disk, boss, protuberance; (heliacal) rising, blazing, blaze, eruption*, outbreak*, inspiration*
nipiḫ šamši* *n. cp.* sunrise, east
nipṣu* *n.* smashing, shattering
nipšu *n.* tuft of wool, fluff, wisp
nipšu B *n.* breathing, snort; smell, odour
nīpu *n.* [2] amount, number
niqiu *n.* [1/3] offering, sacrifice, victim*
niqru* *n.* wreck, wreckage
nirit *subj.* because; towards
nirriṭu *n.* trembling, tremor; doubt, hesitation
nīru *n.* yoke
nīru+ *n.* bondage, service, servitude, weft
Nisannu *n.* (month) Nisan, April
nisḫāni *n. pl.* cold cuts
nisḫu *n.* [1/2] portion, cut; extract, citation, quotation; payment; tariff
nisḫu* *n.* [1/2] velocity
nisḫutu† *nf.* subtraction; import tax
nisiqti abnē* *nf. cp.* choicest gems
nisiqtu* *nf.* choice, selection
nisiu *n.* (a profession)
nisku* *n.* shot
nisqu* *n.* choice, choicest, selection
nissābu* *n.* corn, grain
nissatu* *nf.* worry

nişirtu*  *nf.* secret, treasure
nīš* *prp.* by
nīš ēni* *n. cp.* look, glance; chosen one, favorite
nīš libbi* *n. cp.* desire, libido, lust, passion, potency, sexual desire, sexual drive, excitement
nīš libbi rašû* *vp.* to be excited, get potency
nīš qāti* *n. cp.* lifting of the hands, prayer
nīš rēši*  *n. cp.* honor; head-lift (part of the exta); uplift
nišē *n. pl.* people, population
nišē+ *n. pl.* folks
nišē bēti *n. cp. pl.* domestic servants
nišē ēkalli *n. cp. pl.* palace people, courtiers
nišē māti *n. cp. pl.* inhabitants of the country, citizenry
nišḫu* *n.* diarrh[o]ea
niširtu* *nf.* deduction, removal, withdrawal
nišīt ēni* *adj., n.cp* glance (of favor); choice, favorite
nišītu* *nf.* lifting, raising, elevation; chosen one, favorite
nišku* *n.* bite
nišru  *n.* deduction, removal; slab(?)
ni'šu* *n.* sneeze, wheezing
nīšu *n.* lifting, raising
nišūtu* *nf.* relatives
nīšu B* *n.* oath
nitiru 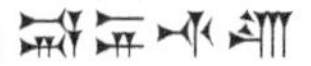 *n.* nitre, soda ash, washing soda
nitku 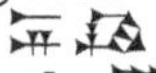 *n.* drop, dripping(s)
nittamēlu  *n.* burglar
nītu 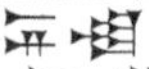 *n.* (a precious item)
nītu* 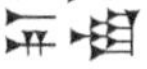 *n.* siege, encirclement
niṭil ēnē *n. cp.* eyesight
niṭlu* *n.* sight, look, view, glance, gaze
nīṭu* *n.* bloody excrement
niṭūtu* *nf.* beating, thrashing
niziqtu*  *nf.* grief, sorrow, worry, worries
nizirtu  *nf.* curse, malediction
nizmatu* *nf.* desire, objective
nuāḫu *v.* to be calm, be quiet, rest; to retire, relax, unbend; to relent, subside, blow over; (D) to allay, appease, calm, placate, soothe, sedate
nuāḫu+ *v.* to be at rest, be assuaged, stay quiet, cease; (D) to assuage, relieve, give rest
nuāmu+ *v.* to doss, doze, doze off, drowse, nap, nod off, slumber, snooze
nuāqu* *v.* cry, groan, wail, whimper
nuārtu 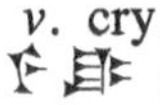 *nf.* female singer, female musician
nuāru  *n.* singer, musician
nuā'u† *adj.* barbarian, brute, brutish, rude, uneducated
nuballu* *n.* wing; vanguard, eagle-bearer*, trap
nubattu  *nf.* evening
nūbtu* *nf.* honey-bee
nūbu+ *n.* tarragon
nuggatu* *nf.* anger, wrath
nuguššû* *n.* bustle, fuss
nuḫatim bēt ili  *n. cp.* temple cook
nuḫatim bēti  *n. cp.* temple cook
nuḫatimmu *n.* cook
nuḫatimmu+ *n.* baker
nuḫatimmūtu* *nf.* culinary art, cook's prebend
nuḫḫuru* *adj.* emaciated, skinny(?)
nuḫḫuṭu* *v.* (D) to hiccup, sob
nuḫšu *n.* abundance, affluence, prosperity; fertility
nūḫtu* *nf.* calm, peace, tranquility
nuḫurtu *nf.* asafoetida
nuk 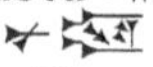 *part.* thus (I, we)
nukarib urqi 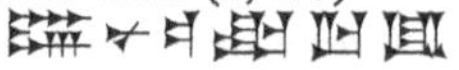 *n. cp.* vegetable gardener
nukaribbu  *n.* gardener
nukaribbūtu* *nf.* gardening; date cultivation
nukkulu* *adj.* artful, artistic, elaborate, sophisticated
nukkusu* *adj.* torn, cut in pieces
nukru* *n.* curiosity, curio
nūku *part.* thus (I, we)
nukurrû† *n.* denial
nukurtu  *nf.* enmity, feud, hostility; act of aggression
nukuššû *n.* hinge, pivot
nullāti*  *n. pl.* improprieties, maliciousness; foolish talk, foolishness, bluster
numāti* *n. pl* movables
nummur kabatti* *n. cp.* happy mood
nummur libbi* *n. cp.* cheerful mood, gaiety, hilarity
nummur pāni* *n. cp.* radiant face, joy
numru* *n.* brightness
numūru  *n.* [1] torch, light
nūn apsê* *n. cp.* freshwater fish
Nūnē* *n.* Pisces
nūnu *n.* [3] fish

nūpāḫu+ *n.* blister
nupāru* *n.* heart, mood
nupḫu+ *n.* bulge
nūptu◊ *nf.* gift, payment
nupūšu† *n.* airing
nūr iškūrti* *n. cp.* candlelight
nūr sīn *n. cp.* moonlight
nūr šamši *n. cp.* sunlight
nurbu* *n.* moist spot; soft place, tender part, juicy part
nurmû  *n.* pomegranate
nurrubu* *adj.* very soft; yielding
nurruṭu* *adj.* quivering
nūrtānu *adj.* Ninurta-like, godlike
nūru  *n.* light, lamp; shine, gleam
nusāḫu  *n.*^{1} (pl.) grain tax
nusāḫu B *n.*^{3} torn-out (piece)
nussuqu* *adj.* select, well-chosen, splendid
nussusu* *v.* to shake, wave
nušurrû* 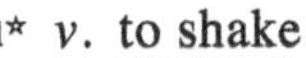 *n.* decrease, reduction
pâ ēda šuškunu‡ *vp.* to unify, unite
pâ ištēn šuškunu‡ *vp.* to make unanimous, unify, integrate
pâ itti X šakānu‡ *vp.* to conspire with
pa'āṣu  *v.*$^{a/u}$ to withdraw; (D) to remove, abduct, make disappear, steal(?)
Pabilsag* *n.* Sagittarius
padakku 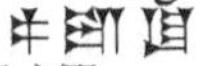 *n.*^{3} corn-bin, silo
padānu  *nf.* path
padattu* *nf.* form, frame
paddi'u* *n.* redeemer
padû  *v.*$^{i/i}$ to absolve, forgive, pardon, spare; (D) to ransom, redeem
pādû* *adj.* forgiving
pâdu*  *v.*$^{i/i}$ to shut in, confine, imprison, put in fetters, take captive
paggû* *v.* (D) to ape, imitate, mimic
pagguru+ *adj.* embodied, incarnate
pagrānu+ *adj.* bodily, carnal, fleshly
pagrānūtu+ *nf.* bodily nature, incarnation
pagru  *n.*^{1} body; corpse, cadaver, carrion, carcass; flesh; trunk
pagû* 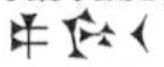 *n.*^{1} monkey, ape
pagulu 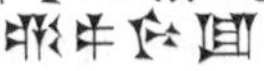 *n.*^{1} libation bowl
pagūtu* *nf.* (female) monkey
paḫāḫu *v.* to abate, be weakened
paḫāḫu+ *v.* to be dried up, be porous, be shattered
paḫāru  *v.*$^{u/u}$ to gather, assemble, congregate, rally, get together; (D) to bring together, assemble, collect, congregate, round up; (Dtt) to band together
pāḫatūtu  *nf.* governorship
paḫāzu  *v.*$^{i/i}$ to be insolent, be loose, be reckless, run wild; to boast, brag, swagger; (Š) to leave loose
paḫāzu+ *v.*$^{i/i}$ (D) to act lewdly; (Dt) to be voluptuous, be licentious; (Š) to cause to wanton, make impudent
paḫḫāru  *n.* potter
paḫḫārūtu+ *nf.* ceramics
paḫḫizu  *n.*^{2} boaster, braggart; grotesque performer
paḫḫu+ *adj.* brittle, crisp, futile, hollow, porous, untrustworthy
paḫḫurtu  *nf.* collection, assemblage
paḫḫuzû◊  *n.* boisterous, boastful, caddish, insolent; cad
paḫiu *adj.* blockheaded, stupid
pāḫizu  *n.* comic actor, comedian, buffoon
paḫû  *v.*$^{i/i}$ to block, close, confine, lock up; to store away
pāḫutu  *n., nf.* province; governor, satrap
paḫûtu* *nf.* dumbness, stupidity
paḫzānūtu+ *nf.* impetuosity, rashness
paḫzu *adj.* boastful, boisterous; immoderate, inordinate, uninhibited, unchecked, vulgar*
paḫzu+ *adj.* lascivious, lewd, licentious, loose, obscene, unrestrained, voluptuous, wanton
paḫzūtu+ *nf.* debauchery, intemperance, lasciviousness, wantonness
pakku  *n.*^{1} (a metal object)
pakku B* *n.* reason, sense, wits
palāḫ ili *n. cp.* piety, religiosity, religiousness; religion, worship
palāḫu  *v.*$^{a/a}$ to fear, be afraid, be frightened, dread; to respect, revere, serve, venerate, worship; to shy at, to suspect*
palāḫu* 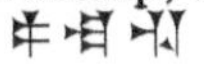 *v.*$^{a/a}$ (Š) to make reverent, inspire awe, to endanger*, hazard*, imperil*, jeopardize*
palāḫu  *v.*$^{a/a}$ (D) to frighten, frighten off, scare, stampede; to shock, terrify, horrify, deter
palāḫu+ *v.*$^{a/a}$ to serve God
palāḫu n. *n.* reverence, adoration, veneration
palāku* *v.*$^{a/u}$ to divide off, demarcate, delineate
palāqu* *v.*$^{i/i}$ to slaughter, smite, strike down
palāsu*  *v.*$^{a/u}$ (N) to look at, gaze at, glance at, glimpse; (Ntn) to examine, look

over, stare

palāšu *v.* $^{a/u}$ to pierce, perforate, puncture; to bore, drill, drill through; to make breach, break into, penetrate; to break through, tunnel

palāšu+ *v.* $^{a/u}$ to dig through, undermine

palgiš* *adv.* like a ditch

palgu *n.* ditch

palḫiš* *adv.* fearfully, timidly, reverently, repectfully

palḫu *adj.* afraid, frightened, timid; fearful, reverent; feared, fearsome, respected

pāliḫ ili *n. cp.* pious, religious

pāliḫ šarri *adj. cp.* lawabiding

pāliḫu *adj.* worshipper; reverent, respectful

palka uzni* *adj. cp.* intelligent, broad-minded, enlightened

palkû* *adj.* wide, broad; comprehensive, extensive, vast; wise, accomplished, enlightened

pallāḫu* *n.* coward, craven, timid person

pallāḫūtu* *nf.* cowardice

pallissu *nf.* female stoneborer

pallišu *n.* driller, stoneborer; plumber, tunneller; burglar, housebreaker

palšu *adj.* pierced, breached

palšu+ *adj.* broken into, nicked

palû *n.* reign, dynasty, period, epoch

pān *prp.* before

pān muṣlāli *n. cp.* forenoon

pān mūši* *n. cp.* nightfall

pān šāri* *n. cp.* windward

pān šatti *n. cp.* spring, springtime

pān X amāru‡ *vp.* to visit

pān X dagālu‡ *vp.* to obey, to look forward to, expect, wait for

pān X šudgulu‡ *vp.* to hand over, entrust to, subject to

pāna* *adv.* before

panāgu *v.* $^{i/i}$ to cap, wrap; (D) to complete(?)

panantu *nf.* fender

pānāt *prp.* in front of, in the presence of; before, prior to, previous to

pānāti *n. pl.* vanguard, front part; presence, reception

pandugānu *n.* (a festival or ceremony)

pānē ana X šakānu‡ *vp.* to aim at, bend one's mind towards, incline towards, take aim, make for, orientate o.s., turn towards

pānē guddudu‡ *vp.* to be downcast; to slouch

pānē ḫardūti‡ *n. cp. pl.* poker face

pānē našû‡ *vp.* to long for

pāniš* *adv.* in front

pāniš u arkiš* *adv.* to-and-fro

pānītu *nf.* past time[s], past

pānīu *adj., num.* previous, earlier, first, former, senior; anterior, ex[-], preceding, preliminary

panû *v.* $^{i/i}$ to go in front, go ahead, move ahead of; to be ahead, anticipate, precede, to outdistance*

pānu *n.* $^{1/3}$ front, fore; presence; (pl.) appearance, face; aspect

pānu+ *n.* $^{1/3}$ face, aspect

pānu B* *n.* bushel; (an area measure)

papāḫu *n.* ^{3} cella, holy of holies

papallu* *n.* shoot, sprout, offspring

pappardaliu *n.* agate with one white band

papparmīnu *n.* agate with two white bands

pappāsu *n.* porridge, pudding, gruel, pap*

pappāt ēni* *nf. cp. pl.* eyelashes

pappīru* *n.* beer bread

pappūtu *nf.* (mng. unkn.)

paqādu *v.* $^{i/i}$ to appoint; to allocate, delegate, consign, assign, confide, entrust, vest in; to review, check

paqādu+ *v.* $^{i/i}$ to constitute

paqāru *v.* $^{i/i}$ to claim, lay claim to, arrogate; to challenge, contest, dispute

paqdu *adj.* appointed, entrusted

pāqirānu◊ *n.* claimant

pāqu *adj.* narrow, tight

pār nūbti* *n. cp.* honey, beeswax

parādu* *v.* $^{i/i}$ to be scared, be disturbed, be terrified, be afraid; (Gtn) to be nervous, be diffident; (D) to appall, frighten, dismay, shock, startle, terrify, upset; (Dt) to become confused

parādu+ *v.* $^{i/i}$ to be scared away, flee away; (D) to scare away, drive away

parāḫu *v.* to flee; (D) to squander

parāḫu+ *v.* to fly, float, pervade, spread; (D) to dissipate, waste

parakku *n.* ^{1} dais, shrine, altar

parakku+ *n.* ^{1} (small) temple, shrine

parāku *v.* $^{i/i}$ to lay across, draw across; to bar, block, obstruct, refuse access, thwart; to object, oppose; to contravene; (D) to debar, impede, inhibit, hinder, prevent, prohibit, preclude, obstruct

paramaḫu *n.* high temple

parāmu *v.* to hack, rend, shred, splinter

parāqu* *v.* to divide off, isolate, segregate, separate

parāqu+ *v.* to dislocate, dissociate, separate from, break loose, break off

parāru *v.*[u/u] to be powerless; (D) to disperse, scatter, shatter, break up, rupture; (N) to be crushed

paras *n.* fraction, part

paras+ *n.* half-mina

parās birti* *n. cp.* mediation

parās šēpi *n. cp.* exclusion*

parasrab *n.* five sixths

parāsu *v.*[a/u] to separate; to decide, define, determine, interpret; to differentiate, discriminate, distinguish; to isolate, shut off, separate from, set apart from, alienate from, wean; to divide, split up, divert; to cut off, sever, stop

parāṣu *v.*[a/u] to break, transgress; to break into, break through; to proceed

parāṣu* *v.*[a/u] to breach, break law, trespass: to deceive, lie, tell lies; (Š) to deceive

parāšu* *v.* to fly; (Š) to let fly; (N) to fly, flee; (Ntn) to fly about, hover about, soar

parāṭu *v.*[a/u] to tear; to flicker

parāṭu+ *v.*[a/u] to rend, tear away, drop off

parā'u *v.*[u/u] to spring up, bud, burst out, sprout

parā'u B* *v.*[a/u] to cut off, sever, slit, slice

parāzu *v.* to winnow(?)

pardiš* *adv.* fearsomely, horribly

pardu* *adj.* afraid, dismayed, disturbed, frightened, scared, terrified; fearful, frightful, upset; bloodcurdling, frightening, shocking, terrifying; horrible, ghastly, grisly, gruesome

pardu+ *adj.* sleepless

pargāniš* *adv.* undisturbed

pargāniš rabāṣu‡ *vp.* to live in peace

pariangu* *n.* harpoon

pariktu *nf.* injustice; curtain, drapes; crossbar, strut

pāriku* *adj.* preventive

pāris birti* *n. cp.* arbiter, go-between, intermediary, mediator

parīsatti+ *adv.* chiefly, particularly

parīsu* *n.*[1/3] punting pole

pārisu *adj.* crucial, decisive, determinative

pārisu n. *n.* decider, decision-maker

parititu *nf.* (a garment)

parkiš* *adv.* crosswise, athwart

parku *adj.* reluctant, cross, cranky; crosswise, transverse; awkward; misfit

parkullu *n.* stonecutter, stonemason, sculptor

parparḫû† *n.* purslane

parrāiu+ *n.* furrier

parrāṣu* *n.* liar

parratu* *nf.* she-duckling

parriku* *n.* autocrat(?)

parrisu* *n.*[2] boatman

parriṣu *n.*[4] bandit, criminal, crook, outlaw, traitor

parritu *n.* ripper(?)

parrû† *v.* to contaminate, abuse, blaspheme

parruḫu+ *adj.* spendtrift, dissolute

parsīgu* *n.* headband

parsu *adj.* separate, private, secluded, sequestered; weaned; decided, definite; definitive, conclusive, determinate, discrete, distinct, particular, special; divided, schismatic

parsu+ *adj.* differentiated, distinctive, insular

parsuāiu *n.* Persian (sheep), blackhead Persian

Parsumaš *n.* Persia, Fars, Persis

parsutu *nf.* (a bowl)

parsūtu+ *nf.* discrimination, disparity

parṣu *n.*[1] function, office; cult, rite, ritual, ceremony; custom, practice, manner, usage*

paršamūtu *nf.* old age, senility*; senate*

paršu+ *n.* cobblestone, flagstone, slate

paršum āli *n. cp.* city elder

paršumāti *nf. cp.* grayness, gray hairs

paršumu *v.* (D) to grow old, age; to live longer than, outlive; (Dtt) to reach a great age

paršumu a. *adj.* aged, senile

paršumu n. *n.*[4] old man, senior, elder; witness

paršuntu *nf.* old woman

paršu'u* *n.* flea

parû *n.*[1] onager, mule

pāru* *n.* skin, hide

pâru* *v.*[a/a] to seek, look for

paruššu* *n.* goad, sharp stick

paruššu+ *n.* barb

parūtu* *nf.* marble

pāru B* *n.* product

pāru C† *n.* hymn

parzillu *n.* iron

parzillu sakru *np.* wrought iron, steel
pasâku *v.* (D) to clear away, clear out, empty out, evacuate, remove, rid
pasâlu* *v.* $^{i/i}$ to turn back, turn around, twist
pasâlu† *v.* $^{i/i}$ to distort
pasâsu *v.* $^{a/u}$ to annihilate, annul, blot out, cancel, delete, invalidate, nullify, obliterate, strike out; to smash
paslu* *adj.* crooked, twisted
paspasu* *n.* duck, goose
pasqu* *n.* ^{1} ledge, cornice
pasru *n.* (a kind of bread)
passu* *n.* doll, puppet, toy; pawn, game-piece, piece, token;
passu+ *n.* ballot, lot
passuku n.* *n.* removal
passulu* *adj.* bandy-legged, bowlegged
passurtu *nf.* news, good news, tidings
passuru *v.* to announce, relate, bring tidings, bring good news
paṣâdu *v.* $^{i/i}$ to cut into; (Dtt) to crack
paṣânu† *v.* $^{i/i}$ (D) to disguise, veil
paṣâṣu *v.* to withdraw
paṣîtu *nf.* white cow
paṣiu *adj.* white, pale; bleached
paṣiu† *adj.* cleared (plot of land)
paṣiu+ *adj.* blameless
paṣiu ṣalmu *adj. phr.* piebald, pied
paṣṣû *v.* to break up, crush
paṣṣuntu *nf.* veil
paṣṣunu† *adj.* veiled
paṣû *v.* $^{i/i}$ to be white, whiten (itr.), be white-hot; to turn pale; (D) to bleach, whiten, whitewash; to sinter
pašâḫu *v.* $^{a/a}$ to be tranquil, rest, relax; to calm down, cool down, ease off; to abate, subside; (Š) to calm, sedate, soothe; to allay, alleviate, ease, relieve
pašâku+ *v.* to doubt, suspect; (D) to make to doubt, puzzle
pašâlatti* *adv.* crawling
pašallu* *n.* (a kind of) gold
pašâlu* *v.* $^{i/i}$ to creep, crawl, cringe
pašânu* *v.* $^{i/i}$ to yank, pull violently
pašâqu *v.* (D) to explain
pašâqu+ *v.* to ease off, ease up, make easy, make plain
pašâqu B* *v.* $^{u/u}$ to be narrow, difficult; (Š) to aggravate, complicate, straiten; (Št) to have a hard time, labor, travail
pašâru *v.* $^{a/u}$ to solve, explain, interpret; to dissolve, loose, loosen, undo, release, absolve; to relax, appease; to convert, to digest*
pašâru† *v.* $^{a/u}$ to break a promise
pašâru *v.* $^{a/u}$ (N) to relent
pašâru+ *v.* $^{a/u}$ to digest, liquefy, mature, ruminate
pašâru n. *n.* current value
pašâru n.+ *n.* fusion
pašâšu *v.* $^{a/u}$ to smear, anoint, oil, grease; (N) to anoint o.s.
pašâšu n. *n.* anointing, unction
pašâṭu *v.* $^{i/i}$ to abrade, delete, efface, erase, expunge, obliterate, rub out; to exstirpate
pašḫu *adj.* placid, relaxed, restful, resting, sedate
pašîqatti+ *adv.* easily, readily, plainly, distinctly
pašîqu+ *adj.* cushy, easy
pašîqûtu+ *nf.* ease, easiness, facility
pašîratti◊ *adv.* secretly
pâširtu *nf.* (a container for grain and fruit, dispenser)
pašîru* *n.* secrecy
pâširu *n.* interpreter, expositor; releaser, absolver, explanatory*
pâširu† *n.* retail merchant
pašîšu* *n.* (a priest, liter. anointed one)
pašqiš* *adv.* barely, hardly, with difficulty
pašqu* *adj.* narrow; arduous, cumbersome, difficult, gruel[l]ing, precipitious, steep
pašqu+ *adj.* concise, succinct
pašru* *adj.* appeased; gracious, kind, gentle; liquid
paššûr gerri* *n. cp.* picnic table
paššûru *n.* ^{1}, *nf.* table, desk; mess
paššûru karâru *vp.* set the table
paššûru rakâsu‡ *vp.* to set the table
pašû* *v.* $^{u/u}$ to exhale
pâšu* *n.* axe, adze
pašultu* *nf.* (a kind of knife)
pašurtu* *nf.* sale, selling
pašûtu *nf.* expectoration(?)
patâḫu *v.* $^{a/u}$ to pierce, puncture, bore through; to broach, stab
patâlu* *v.* $^{i/i}$ to twine, twist, wind
patâlu+ *v.* $^{i/i}$ to twist awry, pervert
patânu◊ *v.* $^{i/i}$ to be strong; (D) to strengthen
patâqu* *v.* $^{i/i}$ to fashion, form, cast; to create, devise, fabricate, forge
pati *adv.* away, off
pâti êni *n. cp.* eye-opener
patinnu◊ *n.* headband, sash
patiu *adj.* open, patent; distant, far, far-away, far-off, remote

patlu* *adj.* entwined, twisted

patlu+ *adj.* crooked, distorted, perverse, pervert

patlūtu+ *nf.* kink

patnu* *adj.* tough, hardy, resistant

patqu* *adj.* formed

patru *n.* 1 sword; knife

pattiš* *adv.* like a canal

pattu *nf.* canal; edge, border, border-line, border area

pattû *adj.* opened, opened-up, open; bare, naked

pattūtu *nf.* open chariot

patû *v.* i/i to open; to bare, detect, disclose, expose, reveal, uncover, unmask, unseal, unveil, unfold, unfurl, unravel, unwind, unwrap; to distance o.s., move farther, part from; (D) to dismiss, discharge, fire, lay off, remove from office, sack

pātu *n.* canal

patû+ *v.* i/i to open up, unbutton

pāṭ gimri* *n. cp.* full extent, entirety

paṭāru *v.* a/u to loosen, undo, unfasten, unlock, untie; to free, liberate, ransom, redeem, release; to demobilize, dismiss; to clear away, dismantle, unbuckle, unhitch; to unload, unpack; (D) to clear away, demolish; (N) to be loosened, be ungirt, come off; to disappear, fade out, vanish

paṭīru *n.* 3 reed altar

paṭru *adj.* liberated, loosed, released, unhitched

pāṭu* *n.* border, limit, area

pa'û* *n.* peacock(?)

pa'û+ *v.* to baa, bleat

pazāzu+ *v.* to frisk, leap, wince

pazīzu+ *adj.* agile, nimble, skittish

pazriš* *adv.* in secret

pazru* *adj.* concealed, covert, surreptitious, ulterior

pazû *v.* (mng. unkn.)

pazzurtu *nf.* secret mission, contraband*, smuggling*

pazzuru *v.* to conceal, hide; to bootleg, smuggle

pe'ettu *nf.* coal, charcoal

pēgu *adj.* taken away

peḫû* *v.* i/i to close, block, obstruct; to shut up, bar; to caulk, fuse, lute, seal (an opening), insulate; to confine, enclose

peḫû a.* *adj.* closed off; blockheaded, stupid, dumb; deaf-mute, stone-deaf; watertight

pelludû* *n.* cult(ic rites)

pelû◊ *n.* egg

pelû a.* *adj.* red-hued, reddish

pelû B◊ *v.* i/i to be red

pēmu *n.* (upper) thigh

pe'mu+ *n.* carbon, coal

pennigu *n.* pastry, honey cake

pēntu *nf.* charcoal, coal(s)

peqqû* *n.* colocynth

per'ānu+ *adj.* fruitful

perdu+ *n.* fright, sleeplessness

pērtu *nf.* hair

pērurūtu *nf.* (house) mouse

per'ūtu+ *nf.* cornucopia

pesēnu◊ *v.* i/i to veil; to hide, cover up, conceal, keep secret, hush up

pesnu◊ *adj.* concealed, secret, clandestine, surreptitious

pessû* *adj.* lame, crippled, halt, limping; deformed, gnarled

pētān birki* *n. cp.* swift runner

pētḫallu *n. cp.* riding horse; cavalry

pētu *n.* opening, aperture

petû a.* *adj.* open, cloudless

pī aḫāmiš* *n. cp.* dialogue

pī karši* *n. cp.* epigastrium

pī mappūḫiti+ *n. cp.* crater

pī māti* *n. cp.* public opinion

pī nāri *n. cp.* mouth of the river, delta, estuary

piālu *v.* to rule, hold sway over

piāqu *v.* to be narrow, slight

pi'āru *n.* blotch, spot, freckle*

piāti *n. pl.* confluence

piāzu* *n.* mouse

pidānu* *n.* assay

pīdu *n.* redemption, pardon, indulgence

pīgu* *n.* lying, deception(?)

pīḫatu* *nf.* province

piḫiu *n.* beer jug

pilaggu *n.* harp

pīlāniš* *adv.* like limestone

pilaqqu *n.* spindle, distaff

Pilistu *n.* Philistea, Palestine

pilku *n.* 2 work assignment; zone, sector; section, faction*, sect*

pillû* *n.* mandrake

pilšu *n.* breach; borehole, perforation, tunnel; breakthrough, penetration

pilšu ša ušāri* *np.* urethra

pindû
n. (a mottled type of limestone)

pindû*
n. blemish, red mole

pingu *n.* 1 knob, cap, finial

pīnu *n.* (an ornamental button or

knob)

piqatti *adv.* perhaps(?)

piqittu *nf.* allocation; charge, ward; appointment, investiture, nomination, office; check-up, confirmation, control, verification; stocktaking

piqittūtu *nf.* mandate, office, position of authority

piqtatti *adv.* perhaps; surely, undoubtedly

pīqu* *adj.* narrow, tight

piriggallû* *n.* big lion

piriktu* *nf.* opposition, hindrance*, impediment*, handicap*, prevention*

piriṣtu* *nf.* deceit

pirištu* *nf.* secret (lore), mystery

pirittu* *nf.* fright

pirʾtu *nf.* shoot, sapling

pirku *n.* injustice, obstruction(?)

pirku* *n.* chord, radius

pirru *n.* $^{2/3}$ tax collection; cavalry unit, squad

pirsu *n.* weaned child; division, section, chapter, part, separation*

pirṣāti* *nf. pl.* deceit

pirʾu *n.* bud, scion, shoot

pirʾû* *n.* pharaoh

pīru *n.* elephant

pisannu *n.* ^{3} gutter, drain pipe, water trough

pisnuqiš* *adv.* wretchedly, miserably

pisnuqu* *adj.* rickety*, feeble, helpless, powerless, wretched

pispisu *n.* bug

pissatu* *nf.* cancellation, erasure

pisurru* *n.* gizzard

pisurru+ *n.* crop (of a bird), stomach (of a ruminant)

pišannu◊ *n.* box, chest

pišāti uppušu‡ *vp.* treat abusively, scandalize

piširtu *nf.* solvent, solution

pišru *n.* ^{3} interpretation, meaning, sense, significance, signification

piššatu* *nf.* unguent, ointment

piššatu B* *nf.* cancellation

pištu* *nf.* abuse, calumny, insult, invective; scandal

pīt bābi◊ *n. cp.* (a ceremony, opening of the gate)

pīt ḫasīsi* *n. cp.* intelligence, wit

pīt pāni* *n. cp.* clear solution, resolution

pīt pî* *n. cp.* opening of the mouth

pīt purīdi* *n. cp.* stride

pīt upnē* *n. cp.* prayer

pīt uzni* *n. cp.* insight, intelligence

pitennu *n.* food, meal

pitḫu *n.* wound

pitiltu *nf.* cord, lace, rope, string

pitiltu+ *nf.* strand, wick

pitiqtu* *nf.* mud wall, mud masonry

pitluḫu* *adj.* terrifying

pitnu* *n.* safebox, casket, strong-box, lock-box

pitnu B* *n.* string (of a musical instrument), chord, mode, tuning

pitqu *n.* fold, sheepfold, pen

pitqu* *n.* casting; mud wall

pitqudu* *adj.* cautious, prudent, circumspect, discreet, wary

pitqu B+ *n.* card

pitru* *n.* open area, clearance, clearing

pitrustu* *nf.* disengagement

pitrusu* *adj.* ambiguous, contradictory, inconsistent

pitruštu* *nf.* ambiguous omen, ambiguity

pitti *adv., prp.* according to; accordingly; in consideration of, considering that

pittu *nf.* ambit, sphere of responsibility

pitūtu *nf.* diadem, (royal) headband

piṭru *n.* shank

piṭru+ *n.* shank-band

piṭru B* *n.* fissure, split

piṭru C* *n.* liberation, release

pizallūru *n.* gecko

pû *n.* ^{3} mouth; utterance, declaration, statement, wording, command; oral tradition; opening, aperture, inlet, orifice; jaws, beak

pû ēdu* *np.* unison, unity

pû ištēn‡ *np.* unanimity

pû patû‡ *vp.* to protest, speak out

pû ṣabātu‡ *vp.* to deal with

pû tadānu‡ *vp.* to assure, commit o.s., promise

puāgu *v.* to deprive, grab, snatch, take away, take by force, wrest; to abduct, bereave, hijack, usurp

puāqu+ *v.* to gape, yawn

puašḫu* *n.* ^{3} (a javelin)

pudri sūqi *n. cp.* (a pigeon, street dung)

pudru *n.* (animal) droppings, dung, dung

cake, muck

pu'ē  *n.pl.* hay; chaff, husk

puggulu* *adj.* robust, strong, massive

puglu  *n.* radish

pūgu* *n.* net

puḫādu  *n.*[2] (male) lamb

puḫālu  *n.*[2] ram, (breeding) bull, stud, drake

puḫattu 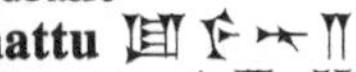 *nf.* (female) lamb

puḫḫu  *v.* to change, exchange, substitute; to modify, to barter*

puḫpuḫḫu* *n.* squabble, brawl

puḫru 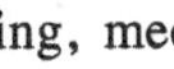 *n.* assembly, council; assizes; gathering, meeting, reunion; congress, convention, congregation

puḫru*  *n.* totality, all

puḫru+ *n.* mess, company

puḫru ša āli* *np.* city council, town council

puḫru ša māti *np.* national assembly

puḫru ša nišē *np.* public assembly, mass meeting

pūḫtu  *nf.* item of exchange, substitute

pūḫu  *n.* exchange, loan; makeshift, stand-in, substitute

pukku* *n.* ball

pulḫu  *n.*[1] fearsomeness; fear, respect

pūlu  *n.*[2] limestone, foundation stone, cornerstone

puluggu* *n.*[1] boundary, territory

puluḫtu  *nf.* fear, respect, danger*, hazard*, peril*, risk*, suspicion*

pulukkiš* *adv.* like a mountain peak

pulukku* *n.* needle, stake; (mountain) peak, pinnacle; boundary (stake), border

pulukku+ *n.* bodkin

pūlu B* *n.* bean, broad bean

pungulu* *adj.* robust, strong, massive

puqdutu  *nf.* thorn plant, brier; spike

puqqu  *v.* to pay attention to, observe; to yearn, crave (for), long (for), look forward to, hope*

puqqu n.* *v.* craving, expectation, yearning

pūqu+ *n.* gaping, yawning

pūrāḫu+ *n.* extravagance

Purattu *n.* Euphrates

purīdu  *n.*[1] leg

purīṭu *n.* (mng. unkn.)

purpuḫinnu  *n.* purslane

purqidam* *adv.* on(to) the back, supine

purruku* *adj.* transverse

pursānu+ *n.* detachment, differentiation, distinction, franchise, prerogative

pursāsu* *n.* wig

pursītu  *nf.* (offering) bowl

purṣīnu *n.* pomegranate seed

purṣīnu+ *n.* grape-stone, raisin

purṭû *n.* (a metal object)

pur'u *adj.* sprouted

pūru  *n.*[2] cube, dice; lot, lottery; plot of land; term of office

pūru karāru‡ *vp.* to draw lots for, raffle [off]

purussu* *n.* bung, plug, stopper

purussû  *n.* decision

pūru B *n.* stone bowl, jar (for ointment)

pussumu* *adj.* veiled

pussunu◊ *adj.* covered up, veiled

pusummu* *n.* veil

pūṣ ēni* *n.cp.* white of the eyes

pūṣāiu  *n.* launderer, bleacher

pūṣammūtu* *nf.* laundry work

pūṣānu  *n.* paleface

puṣû 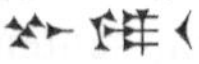 *n.* white color, whiteness; blank space; bare, undeveloped plot of land

pūṣu  *adj.* white glow, white spot; paleness, pallor

puṣuddu* *n.* mongoose(?)

puṣūnu† *n.* disguise, veil

pušḫu *n.*[3] shrew

pušku *n.*[1] hand's breadth, palm

pušqu* *n.* distress, strait, travail, vicissitude(s); narrow pass, gorge, defile

pušurtu+ *nf.* digestion

pūt *prp.* opposite, toward(s), in front of

pūt alpi* *n.cp.* trapezoid

pūt šiddi* *adv.* lengthwise

pūt upni 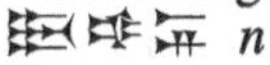 *n.cp.* prayer bowl

pūtu  *adv,nf,prp* forehead, brow; front (side), foreground

pūtuḫu 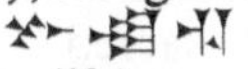 *n.* responsibility

pūtuḫu našû‡ *vp.* to bail, ensure, guarantee, bear the responsibility

puṭrānu *adj.* fungous, fungy, spongy

puṭuru *n.* champignon, fungus, mushroom, truffle

puzru  *n.*[3] refuge, shelter

qabāru  *v.*[i/i] to bury

qabassīu  *adj.* middle, central

qabassu  *nf.* middle, center

qabbiru* *n.*[4] gravedigger, undertaker

qabḫu 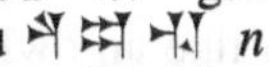 *n.* (a container)

qābiānu  *n.* speaker

qābiu* *adj.* commanding

qablē rakāsu‡ *vp.* to brace o.s. [up], compose o.s., get ready, perk [up], prepare o.s. [for war]

qabli tânti *b. cp.* open sea

qablītu *nf.* middle watch

qablītu B *nf.* (a container for money)

qablīu* *adj.* central; intermediate; median; infixed

qablu *n.* [1] middle; (pl.) middle parts, hips, loins, waist

qablu ša madbāri* *np.* oasis

qablu B *n., nf.* grove (of trees); coppice, copse, plantation

qablu C* *n.* [3] battle, warfare

qabsi *prp.* in the middle of, inside

qabsi āli *n. cp.* city center; citadel

qabsīu *adj.* middle, central

qabsu *nf.* middle, center

qabû *v.* [i/i] to say, speak; to communicate, inform, tell; to comment, note, observe, remark, state; to declare, to promise; to command, order, enjoin, bid, prescribe; to decree, designate, dictate, ordain, sentence; to mean, indicate, imply

qabû ana *vp.* to bode, connote, indicate, mean, signify, refer to

qabû ina libbi *vp.* to think

qabūru *n.* [2] grave, cemetery

qabuttu *nf.* stall, mews

qabūtu *nf.* cup

qadādu *v.* [a/u] to cut off

qadādu+ *v.* [a/u] to cut away, rend off, tear away

qadādu B* *v.* [u/u] to bow, bend down, stoop; to humble o.s.

qadāpu* *v.* to row(?)

qadaruttu *nf.* (mng. unkn.)

qadāšu* *v.* to be sacred, pure; (D) to sanctify, purify

qadissu *nf.* sacred woman, sacred prostitute

qadīšu *n.* holy person, sacred man

qadīšu+ *n.* saint

qadû *n.* owl

qâdu* *v.* [u/u] to ignite, kindle, burn

qadurtu *nf.* (mng. unkn.)

qadurtu+ *nf.* small pot, vase

qadūtu *nf.* wheat bread

qadūtu* *nf.* mud, sediment; dregs; pus, matter

qadû B* *v.* [i/i] to screech like an owl

qaiālu* *adj.* attentive; reticent, taciturn

qaiāpu* *adj.* inclining, liable to collapse, prone, sagging, tottering

qaiāšu* *adj.* generous, liberal

qā'ipānu† *n.* creditor, lender

qā'iu* *adj.* queasy

qalālu *v.* [i/i] to be small, be light, be slight, be insignificant; (D) to belittle, discredit, slight, vilify; to admonish, castigate, scold, rebuke, reprimand, reproach

qalāpu *v.* [a/u] to peel, peel off, pare, scale off, shell, skim, skin

qalāpu* *v.* [a/u] to hatch, come forth (from an egg)

qalāpu+ *v.* [a/u] to hull, pare

qalâti *n. pl.* roasted barley

qālīš* *adv.* silently

qallassu *nf.* young girl, girl, lass

qallīlu *adj.* unimportant; harmless, inessential, immaterial, trifling, wee

qallīlu+ *adj.* little, small; light, slight; brief, fleeting, rapid, swift; a little, a few

qalliš* *adv.* easily, frivolously, lightly, slightly

qallu *n.* boy, lad; slave

qallû* *n.* genitals, vulva

qallu a. *adj.* little, small, tiny; light, slight

qallu dannu‡ *np.* everyone, everybody, (liter. weak and strong)

qallulu *adj.* despicable, frivolous, light-minded, petty, trivial, vile

qallupu *adj.* peeled

qallutu *nf.* (slave) girl

qalpē+ *n. pl.* peelings

qalpu *adj.* peeled, scaled, shelled; worn, shabby, napless, threadbare

qalû *v.* [u/u] to burn, roast, sear; to refine

qālu *adj.* noiseless, quiet, quiescent, silent, tacit

qalû+ *v.* [u/u] to fry, parch

qamāru *v.* [a/u] to strap(?)

qamû *v.* [u/u] to burn, cauterize, destroy by burning, sear, scorch

qamû* *v.* [u/u] (Š) to let burn

qan ṭuppi* *n. cp.* reed pen, stylus

qanānu *v.* [u/u] to nest, make a nest, nestle

qanītu *nf.* (an object)

qāni'u* *adj.* jealous, envious, zealous

qanni *prp., conj.* at, by, next to; together with; out of, outside; as soon as, once

qanni aḫāiš *adv.* close together

qanni āli *n. cp.* suburb

qannu *n.* fringe, border, verge; environs, outskirts; outside

qannu ṣabātu‡ *vp.* to grasp the hem, sub-

mit, declare allegience
qannunu* *adj.* curly, rolled up
qanû *n.* $^{1/3}$ reed, cane; rod, measuring rod, shaft; pipe
qanû+ *n.* $^{1/3}$ haulm, reed pen, stalk, straw, stylus
qanû ṭābu *np.* sweet reed
qanû ṭābu+ *np.* aromatic cane, sweet calamus
qanūnu *n.* measuring rod(?)
qanû B *v.* $^{u/u}$ to acquire, buy, gain
qanû B+ *v.* $^{u/u}$ to earn
qapālu* *v.* $^{i/i}$ roll up, wind up; (Gt) intertwine
qapālu+ *v.* $^{i/i}$ to draw back, roll aside, roll away
qapāpu+ *v.* to brood, incubate, keep quiet, sit (on eggs)
qapīru *n.* ^{2} (a container or measure for fish and dates)
qaplu+ *adj.* wrinkled
qâpu* *v.* $^{u/u}$ to incline, slant, sag, buckle; to cave in, fall down, collapse
qāqullu* *n.* cardamom
qarābtānu+ *adj.* warlike, belligerent
qarābu *v.* $^{i/i}$ to approach, arrive, come by, show up; to be close, be imminent, be present; (D) to present, offer, hold out; to bring, forward, produce, procure; to introduce
qarābu+ *v.* $^{i/i}$ to come near, draw nigh, touch (a woman); to approximate; (D) to apply, carry near, lay near, sacrifice
qarābu ina libbi *vp.* to be implicated, be involved in s.th.
qarābu ina muḫḫi *vp.* to apply to, be relevant, concern, pertain to
qarābu n. *n.* battle, fight
qarābu n.+ *n.* war
qarādu *v.* to be warlike, be courageous; (D) to encourage, urge, strengthen
qarāḫu *v.* $^{u/u}$ to be frozen, freeze, freeze up, ice up; (D) to freeze, to ice*
qarāmu *v.* to cover, overlay with
qarāmu+ *v.* to cover with skin, encrust, overlay, overspread, plate
qaran aiāli* *n. cp.* antler
qarānu* *v.* $^{a/u}$ to stack up, pile on
qarāqu+ *v.* to chuckle, clack
qarāru* *v.* $^{u/u}$ to undulate, be wavy; (D) meander
qarāšu *v.* $^{a/u}$ carve, trim
qarāšu B* *v.* $^{?/u}$ to copulate
qarbāti- *adv.* personally(?)
qarbatu* *nf.* field, pasture land
qardammu* *n.* enemy, adversary
qardu *adj.* heroic, warlike; audacious, bold, brave, courageous, daring, dauntless, gallant, stout, undaunted, valiant
qardūtu* *nf.* audacity, bravery, fortitude, gallantry, valiantness, valour
qarētu *nf.* banquet, party
qarētu+ *nf.* invitation
qarḫu *n.* ^{3} ice, frost
qāribu *n.* ^{1} raven, crow; rook, jackdaw
qarīḫu+ *adj.* bald
qarittu *nf.* heroine
qarnānu* *adj.* horned, sprouted
qarnīu *adj.* horny
qarnu *nf.* horn; germ, sprout; fringe
qarrādu *adj., n.* hero, warrior, champion
qarrādūtu* *nf.* heroism
qarrāru *n.* ^{3} bedcover, bedspread, counterpane
qarrātu *nf.* (a festival)
qarruḫu* *adj.* frozen, ice-cold
qarrurtu *nf.* (an internal organ)
qarruru *v.* to spray, sprinkle
qarṭuppu *n.* ^{3}, *n.cp* stylus, writing reed, reed pen, pen
qarû *v.* $^{i/i}$ to invite, call
qāru *n.* ^{3} table top
qarūḫu *adj., n.* bald, old animal
qarūḫu+ *adj.* hornless
qarūmu+ *n.* covering, crust layer, membrane, skin
qarūru* *n.* receding (water)
qaspu *n.* (an iron implement)
qassu *nf.* bow; Bow-star, Canis major
qassu+ *nf.* arch; semicircle
qasūru+ *n.* pumice [stone]
qašāpu+ *v.* to discolor
qašdu* *adj.* holy, sacred, saintly, sanctimonious, untouchable
qašdu n.* *n.* holy man, saint
qašdūtu* *nf.* sanctity
qāt ṣibitti *adv., n.* red-handed; stolen property
qātā- *adv.* personally, in person
qatānu* *v.* $^{i/i}$ to be thin, be fine, be narrow; (D) to attenuate, narrow, thin (out)
qatānu+ *v.* $^{i/i}$ to be narrowed, grow thin, grow frail
qatāpu *v.* $^{a/u}$ to crop, pick off, pluck, pull off
qatāru *v.* $^{u/u}$ to smoke, reek; (D)

to fumigate

qatattu *nf.* thin fabric, fine garment

qatā'u* *v.* to titter

qatinnu *n.* tiller, serf, peasant

qatinnūtu *nf.* serfdom, peasantry

qatnu *adj.* thin, slender; slim, fine, delicate; junior, weak, puny; shallow, tenuous, frail*, fragile*

qatnu+ *adj.* lean, meagre; strait, narrow; sharp; high, shrill; acute, keen, subtle

qatnūtu+ *nf.* mildness, precision

qatrānu* *n.* cedar resin, tar

qatru *adj.* smoky

qattanu* *adj.* thin, fine

qatturu *adj.* smoked, smoky, foggy*, misty*

qatû* *adj.* to end, finish; (D) to bring to an end, destroy

qātu *nf., n.* 1 hand; paw; handwriting; part; custody, charge, possession; list

qātu+ *nf., n.* 1 broomstick, handle

qatû a.* *adj.* finished, completed

qātu napāṣu‡ *vp.* to thrust away the hand, refuse to obey, reject alliance

qātu šakānu‡ *vp.* to lay hands on, confiscate

qātu ubālu‡ *vp.* to interfere

qātu ummudu‡ *vp.* to lay hands on

qa''û *v.* to wait on; to await, wait for

qê ettūti* *n. cp.* spider-web, cobweb

qēmu *n.* flour, powder

qenû* *v.* to burn with zeal*, to be jealous, envy

qēptu *nf.* belief; credit, credence, trust; merchandise

qēpu *n.* 2 royal trustee, confidant[e], legate, delegate

qēpu a. *adj.* believable, credible, plausible; trusted, entrusted, confidential

qēpūtu *nf.* legateship; credibility, legation*

qerbēnu* *adv., prp.* inside

qerbiš* *adv.* immediately, promptly

qerbītu* *nf.* interior, center

qerbu* *adv., prp.* inside; close, near

qereb mūšīti* *n. cp.* midnight

qēssu *nf.* gift, present; bequest

qiālu† *v.* to fall; (D) to fell

qiāpu *v.* to believe, trust; to devolve, entrust; to give credence, give credit; to confide, lend, vest in

qiāšu *v.* to grant, bestow, present; (D) to give out, distribute gifts

qiā'u *v.* to throw up, vomit

qibīt pî* *nf. cp.* promise

qibītu* *nf.* command, order; pronouncement, sentence, statement

qību *n.* 2 command, commandment, statement; diagnosis, forecast, prediction, prognosis, comment*, observation*, remark*

qību šakānu *vp.* to forecast, make a statement, make a prediction, make a prognosis, predict, prognosticate

qiddat ūmi* *nf. cp.* (late) afternoon

qīltu *nf.* lye

qīlu *n.* burning, burn-mark

qimmatu* *nf.* hair, mane, topknot; crown, top; tuft, plume

qimmu *n.* top, crown

qinītu *nf.* purchase, acquisition, property

qinnāzu *n.* whip

qinnāzu+ *n.* scourge

qinniš *adv.* backward[s]

qinnītu *nf.* (a type of offering)

qinnu *nf.* nest, family

qinnu+ *nf.* ant's nest, anthill, beehive, brood, rookery

qinnutu *nf.* anus, ass, asshole; buttocks

qiplu* *n.* fold, ply

qīptu* *nf.* office, position of trust; belief, credence

qīqu+ *n.* jay

qirmu *n.* 1 overcoat, wrap

qirsu *n.* 1 cart

qirsu B *n.* arbor, pergola

qiršu *n.* (pl.) trimmings

qīru *n.* 3 pitch, tar

qissu
nf. wood, forest

qiššāti bašlāti *n. cp. pl.* ripe melon

qiššāti marrāti *n. cp. pl.* green melon

qiššû *n.* 3 melon, gourd, cucumber

qīšu* *adj.* granted, given

qitpu† *n.* gathering, plucking

qīttu* *nf.* lighting, kindling

qītu *n.* destination, goal

qītu* *n.* end, termination, expiration

qi''u *n.* envy

qû *n.* litre

quālu *v.* to be silent, passive, inactive, stay quiet; to heed; to shut up

quaqua *n.* caw-caw

qūbāti *n. pl.* ague(?)
qubbû* *n.*[1] lamentation
qubūru *n.* grave
qudāsu *n.*[1/3] earring, nose-ring
quddušu* *adj.* holy, sacred, consecrated, sanctified
qudīni lā *adv.* not yet
qudmu* *n.* front; primeval time
qū'iš* *adv.* like threads
qulālē šakānu‡ *vp.* to affront, disparage, bring dishonor on, discredit
qulālu *n.* belittlement, discredit, disparagement*, fault-finding*, insult*, scolding*
qulālu+ *n.* belittling, contempt, ignominy, reproach, slighting
qulāptu† *nf.* bark, cortex, husk, peel, rind, scale, shell, skin of scales
qulāptu+ *nf.* parchment
qulāpu+ *n.* card
quliptu* *nf.* scale, scaly skin, upper eyelid
qulkullānu *n.* cassia
qullītu *nf.* roasted grain
qulliu *n.*[3] bowl, pitcher
qullu *n.*[1] clasp, collar, buckle, fastening
qulmû* *n.*[1] axe
qulpu *n.* rind, bark
qulpu+ *n.* husk, peel, shells; scales (of fish), flakes
qūltu* *nf.* silence, dead of night
qūlu *n.* quietness, quietude, silence
qumāšu* *n.*[3] capital (of a column)
qumbutu *nf.* (a building)
qumbutu+ *nf.* pavilion, tabernacle; arch, dome, vault
qummû* *adj.* sunburnt
qundu *n.* (an object made of copper)
qunnabtu *nf.* hemp flower
qunnubu *n.* cannabis, hemp, hashish*
quppu *n.*[3] box, basket; money-box; cage, bird-cage; guffa
quppû* *n.*[1] sharp knife, scalpel, stiletto
quppu+ *n.* cash-box, till, coop
quppu B* *adj.* inclined, sagging, propense; buckled, collapsed
qūptu* *nf.* inclination, propensity
quqqubānu* *n.* stomach (of a pig)
quqqubānu+ *n.* crop (of a bird), gullet
qurādu *n.*[1] warrior, hero
qurbu *adj.* close, close to, near; present, at hand, available, handy; imminent, impending; intimate, nearest; neighbouring, next-door, kindred
qurbu+ *adj.* forthcoming; nigh, nearly
qurbu ana *adj. phr.* akin, cognate, related to
qurbu ina libbi *adj. phr.* implicated, involved
qurbu ina muḫḫi *adj. phr.* applicable, pertinent, relevant to, related to
qurbu n. *n.* neighbour, follower
qurbūtu *nf.* closeness, nearness, proximity; imminence; intimacy; affinity, relationship, connection*, involvement*
qurdu *n.*[1] heroism; bravery, feat(s), great deed(s), valor
qurnû* *n.* (a herb, perhaps marjoram)
qurpissu *n.*[1] armor, hauberk
qurqurru* *n.* metal-worker, coppersmith
Qurrāiu *adj., n.* Gurrean; (light) spearman, auxiliary spearman
Qurru *n.* Gurrean(s); (light) spearman, auxiliary spearman
quršu *n.* wedding, wedding night, wedding banquet; sexual union
qurubtu *nf.* king's stand-by
qutānu *n.*[3] strip (of field)
qutāru *n.*[1] fumigant
qutnu *n.* thinness, thin part
qutratu *nf.* (a plant)
qutrinnu *n.* incense offering
qutru *n.* smoke, fog
qutturu* *adj.* smoked, smoky
Qutû* *adj., n.* Gutian; barbarian
qû B* *n.* thread, string; web; filament, capillary; (measuring) line
ra'ābu *v.*[u/u] to be angry, rage; to reprimand, reproach, blame
ra'āmu *v.*[a/a] to be fond of, love, fall in love with, fancy, take a fancy to; (D) to make love, fondle
ra'āmu+ *v.*[a/a] (D) to to endear
ra'āmu n. *n.* love; adherence, fondness
ra'āzu* *v.* to inlay
rab abullāti *n. cp.* commander of city gates
rab ālāni *n. cp.* village manager
rab āli *n. cp.* town manager, city manager
rab āpie *n. cp.* chief baker
rab asê *n. cp.* chief physician, chief doctor
rab aṣappi *n. cp.* commander of pack-animals

rab āšipi *n. cp.* chief exorcist
rab aškāpi  *n. cp.* chief leatherworker
rab ašlāki  *n. cp.* chief fuller
rab atê  *n. cp.* head porter
rab bānî  *n. cp.* master builder
rab bārê  *n. cp.* chief haruspex
rab bārūti *n. cp.* office of chief haruspex
rab batqi 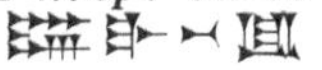 *n. cp.* official in charge of levy
rab bēt šarrāni *n. cp.* overseer of the royal tombs
rab bēti  *n. cp.* major-domo
rab bētūti *n. cp.* office of major-domo
rab birti  *n. cp.* fort commander
rab daiāli  *n. cp.* chief scout
rab danibāti 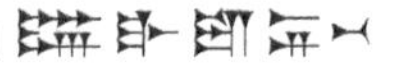 *n. cp.* chief victualler
rab darî◊ *n. cp.* manager of the regular sheep offerings
rab dēnāni  *n. cp.* president of the court of justice
rab ēkal mašarti *n. cp.* manager of Review Palace
rab ēkalli *n. cp.* palace manager
rab ēkurrāti *n. cp.* chief of the temples
rab ešerti  *n. cp.* commander-of-ten, decurion, corporal*, platoon commander*
rab etinnāti  *n. cp.* head of master builders
rab ḫalzi  *n. cp.* fort commander
rab ḫanšê  *n. cp.* commander-of-fifty, lieutenant*
rab ḫarbi  *n. cp.* chief of untilled land
rab ḫi'āli◊ *n. cp.* army commander
rab ḫunduräie  *n. cp.* chief hundurean
rab ikkāri  *n. cp.* head farmer
rab isāti  *n. cp.* master of (harem) women
rab Itu'āiē *n. cp.* commander of Itu'eans
rab kalê  *n. cp.* chief chanter
rab kallāpi  *n. cp.* commander of outriders(?)
rab kallî  *n. cp.* mule express commander, postmaster
rab kaqqulti *n. cp.* basket(?) master
rab karāni  *n. cp.* wine master
rab kāri  *n. cp.* chief of trade
rab karkadinni  *n. cp.* chief confectioner
rab karmāni  *n. cp.* chief of granaries
rab karmi *n. cp.* granary master
rab kāsāti  *n. cp.* cup master
rab kāṣiri  *n. cp.* chief tailor
rab kibsi  *n. cp.* track master
rab kirie  *n. cp.* garden manager
rab kissiti  *n. cp.* fodder master
rab kiṣri  *n. cp.* cohort commander, captain*
rab kiṣrūti *n. cp.* rank of cohort commander
rab kitê  *n. cp.* linen master
rab kurgarrê  *n. cp.* chief gallus
rab kūtāti  *n. cp.* wine-can master
rab līmi  *n. cp.* commander-of-thousand, chiliarch
rab mallāḫē+ *n. cp.* boatswain
rab mallāḫi  *n. cp.* chief boatman, chief of the sailors, boatswain
rab maṣṣiri 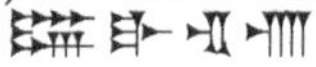 *n. cp.* commander of guards
rab mašiāti  *n. cp.* master of votaresses
rab maški  *n. cp.* leather master
rab ma'utti [illegible] *n. cp.* manager of sustenance field(s)
rab midli *n. cp.* salt-meat master
rab mūgi [illegible] *n. cp.* general (of cavalry or chariotry), brigadier*
rab naggāri [illegible] *n. cp.* chief carpenter
rab nappāḫi [illegible] *n. cp.* master of smiths
rab nikkassi [illegible] *n. cp.* chief of accounts
rab nuāri [illegible] *n. cp.* chief singer
rab nuḫatimmi [illegible] *n. cp.* chief cook
rab nukaribbi [illegible] *n. cp.* chief gardener
rab paḫḫāri [illegible] *n. cp.* master of potters
rab pētḫalli [illegible] *n. cp.* cavalry

commander
rab pilkâni *n. cp.* chief of public works
rab pilki *n. cp.* chief of public works
rab piqitti *n. cp.* office holder
rab pirrâni *n. cp.* commander of cavalry units
rab puḫri* *n. cp.* chairman, chairperson, head of assembly
rab qaqqulâti *n. cp.* (an official in charge of food)
rab qatinnê *n. cp.* serf master
rab râdi kibsi *n. cp.* chief tracker
rab râ'î *n. cp.* chief shepherd
rab raksi *n. cp.* commander of recruits
rab râqûti *n. cp.* chief oilpresser
rab sagullâti *n. cp.* overseer of the herds
rab sasinni *n. cp.* chief bowmaker
rab sêpî *n. cp.* chief felt worker
rab sikkâti *n. cp.* peg master
rab sikkûri *n. cp.* lock master
rab sirâšê *n. cp.* chief brewer
rab sukkalli *n. cp.* chief vizier
rab sûti *n. cp.* seah master, controller (of grain deliveries)
rab ṣâbi *n. cp.* troop commander
rab ṣâḫiti *n. cp.* chief oilpresser
rab ṣarrâpi *n. cp.* chief goldsmith
rab ša-muttâqi *n. cp.* chief cake-baker
rab ša-rêši *n. cp.* chief eunuch
rab ša-rêšûtu *n. cp.* office of chief eunuch
rab šaddâni *n. cp.* coffer master
rab šaglûti *n. cp.* master of deportees
rab šamni *n. cp.* oil master
rab šâqê *n. cp.* chief cupbearer
rab šelappâie *n. cp.* chief architect
rab šibirti *n. cp.* message master
rab šiknâni *n. cp.* chief planner, designer(?)
rab šîmâni *n. cp.* purveyor
rab širâšê *n. cp.* chief brewer
rab širki◊ *n. cp.* master of temple oblates
rab tallakti *n. cp.* wagon master
rab tankâri *n. cp.* chief merchant
rab tilli *n. cp.* chief of equipment, quartermaster*
rab ṭâbiḫi *n. cp.* chief butcher
rab ṭupšarri *n. cp.* chief scribe
rab ummânâti *n. cp.* commander of troops
rab ummânâti rapšâti *n. cp.* supreme commander
rab ummâni *n. cp.* army commander
rab urâsi *n. cp.* chief mason
rab urâti *n. cp.* team commander
rab urdâni *n. cp.* slave master
rab ušpâri *n. cp.* chief weaver
rab zammâri *n. cp.* chief singer
rabâ šamši *n. cp.* sunset, occident, West
rabâbu *v.* $^{u/u}$ to be soft, be feeble, be weak, be languid, languish, relax; (Š) to soften, let languish, let relax, weaken, to extenuate*, mitigate*, mollify*
rabâku† *v.* $^{a/u}$ to decoct, boil away, consume, waste
rabannu* *n.* ^{1} magnate
rabâsu *v.* $^{a/u}$ to beat
rabâṣu *v.* $^{i/i}$ to be recumbent, lie down, rest, repose; to loll, recline; to lie in wait, lurk
rabbiš* *adv.* gently, softly, tenderly
rabbu *adj.* fourth
rabbû* *adj.* great, magnificent, large
rabbu B *num.* soft, gentle, tender, cuddly*, lenient*, mild*, suave*
râbiṣu *n.* lurker (demon), bailiff*
râbiṣu† *n.* advocate, attorney, solicitor
rabîš* *adv.* greatly, magnificently, abundantly; solemnly
rabiu *adj.* big, great, large, major; grown-up, adult, old
rabiu n. *n.* ^{4} chief, magnate, warden*
rabrabâni *n. pl.* high-ranking officers, grandees, ministers*
ra'bu *adj.* angry, miffed, upbraiding

rabû  *v.* $^{i/i}$ to be great; to grow, grow up, outgrow; to accrue, build up, increase; to bear interest

rabû*  *v.* $^{i/i}$ (Š) to extol, exalt, magnify; to enlarge, aggrandize, to maximize*

rabû  *v.* $^{i/i}$ (D) to bring up, develop, foster, nurture; to raise, rear, train; to promote

rabû+ *v.* $^{i/i}$ (D) to to foster

rabušeni *adv.* three years ago

rabuttu  *nf.* one fourth, quarter

rabûtu *nf.* grandeur, greatness, magnificence, majesty; magnanimity, generosity; magnitude, size

rabû B  *v.* $^{i/i}$ to set

radādu  *v.* $^{a/u}$ to chase, drive away; to pursue, persecute

radāpu  *v.* $^{i/i}$ to pursue, persecute; to drive on, urge on; to hasten, hurry, rush on; to insist

radāpu+ *v.* $^{i/i}$ to dragoon

raddādu* *n.* persecutor

raddīdu *n.* (a textile or garment)

raddīdu+ *n.* bridal veil

rādi gammali  *n. cp.* camel driver

rādi imāri  *n. cp.* donkey driver

rādi kibsi  *n. cp.* tracker

rādi litti* *n. cp.* cow driver

rādi masenni  *n. cp.* attendant of the treasurer

rādi qāti 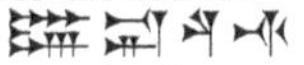 *n. cp.* adjutant

rādipu* *adj.* insistent

rādiu  *n.* ^{2} driver; leader, guide; infantryman, soldier, private

radiu+ *adj.* cultivated, civilized, disciplined, educated, well-bred

radpi◊ *adv.* quickly, suddenly

radû  *v.* $^{i/i}$ to drive, guide, lead; to accompany, convey, go along with, escort, see off; to follow, march, proceed, pursue; to administer, manage, govern, rule

radû*  *v.* $^{i/i}$ (Š) to advance, proceed; to make flow, tap

radû  *v.* $^{i/i}$ (D) to add to, attach, append; to do in addition, do more

rādu*  *n.* cloudburst

râdu* *v. u:* to quake, shake, tremble

radû+ *v.* $^{i/i}$ to continue, derive, emanate, flow, follow after, issue, go forward, journey, move along, travel; (Š) to discharge, let flow

ragāgu* *v.* $^{i/i}$ to be mischievous, wicked, bad

ragāmu  *v.* $^{u/u}$ to call, call out, cry out, exclaim, shout, yell; to roar, sound, peal; to raise claim, sue, prosecute; to declaim, preach, prophesy, remonstrate; (vent.) to address, call for

ragāšu* *v.* $^{i/i}$ (N) be excited

ragāšu+ *v.* $^{i/i}$ to be aware, be in commotion, feel, perceive, sense

raggimu  *n.* ^{2} prophet, preacher

raggintu  *nf.* prophetess

raggu*  *adj.* evil, malicious, mean, naughty, spiteful, vicious, wicked

raggūštānu+ *adj.* impressionable, sensitive, sentimental

raggūšu+ *adj.* sensible, susceptible

ragšu* *adj.* excitable, touchy

raḫāṣu  *v.* $^{i/i}$ to be confident, trust; (Š) to encourage, make confident

raḫāṣu B  *v.* $^{i/i}$ to rinse, wash out; to flood, inundate; to devastate, sweep away, swill, wipe out; to spatter, splash, splatter

raḫāšu* *v.* $^{a/a}$ to move

rāḫiṣu* *adj.* destructive, devastating, ruinous

raḫṣu* *adj.* flooded, submerged

ra'i* *adv.* definitely, without question

rā'i alpi  *n. cp.* ox herder

rā'i enzi *n. cp.* goat herder

rā'i gammali  *n. cp.* camel herder

rā'i immeri  *n. cp.* shepherd

rā'i iṣṣūri  *n. cp.* fowl herd

rā'i sagulli *n. cp.* herder, drover

rā'i ṣēni* *n. cp.* sheep and goat herder

rā'imānu  *n.* ^{1} lover, well-wisher; in favor of, pro-; adherent, supporter

rā'imānû◊ *adj.* affectionate, amorous

ra'imtu+ *nf.* girl friend

ra'īmu *adj.* loved, beloved, loved one

rā'imu *n.* ^{4} loving, in love, fond; amorous, enamoured; lover, well-wisher, hearty*

rā'imu ša nišē *np.* lover of people, philanthropist

rā'imūtu* *nf.* affection, friendship

rā'imūtu+ *nf.* civility

ra'intu *nf.* beloved, loved one

rā'iu  *n.* ^{1} shepherd, herdsman

rā'iūtu  *nf.* shepherdship, leadership

rā'iūtu+ *nf.* pastoral care, shepherding, tending

rakāb sissê* *n. cp.* riding, horseback riding

rakābu  *v.* $^{a/a}$ to ride, mount, surmount; to board, sail

rakābu* *v.* $^{a/a}$ (Gt) to copulate, have sexual intercourse; (D) to pollinate

rakābu *v.* $^{a/a}$ (Š) to make ride; to breed, mate, have served; to load, embark

rakābu+ *v.* $^{a/a}$ to embark, get on; (D) to put together, rig up, make up, compose, compound, write (songs)

rakāsu *v.* $^{a/u}$ to attach, tie; to tie up, moor; to bandage, bind, bind up; to tie together, pack up; to tie on, gird; to harness, hitch up; to assemble, fit together, join, link; to summarize, sum up; to bind legally, regulate; (Š) to equip, have hitched up, have constructed; to enlist, recruit; (N) to be tied; to commit o.s.

rakbu* *n.* ^{4} rider

rakbû* *n.* mounted messenger, rider

rakkābu* *n.* crew

rakkābūtu* *nf.* sailing

rakkubu+ *adj.* compound, composite

raksu *n.* ^{4} recruit, mercenary(?)

raksu a. *adj.* bound, tied, scheduled; attached, committed, contracted, harnessed, packaged, plaited, spellbound

raksūtu* *nf.* attachment, commitment

ramāku *v.* $^{u/u}$ to wash o.s., bathe o.s.; to dilute, soak; (D) to bathe

ramāmu* *v.* $^{u/u}$ to roar, rumble, thunder; to bellow, groan, growl, rattle

ramanka *pron.* yourself

ramankunu *pron.* yourselves

ramanšu da'āpu‡ *vp.* to become retrograde, tumble down

ramanšu dakû* *vp.* bestir o.s.

ramanšu kallumu *vp.* present o.s., reveal o.s.

ramanšu naṣāru *vp.* fend for o.s., take care of o.s.

ramanšu paṭāru* *vp.* resign

ramanšu šannû *vp.* disguise o.s.

ramanšunu *pron.* themselves

ramini *pron.* myself

ramku* *n.* ^{4} bathed, holy man

rammāku+ *n.* ostler, stableman

rammû *v.* (D) to leave, reject, discard, disregard, dump, drop, quit, throw away, forsake, release, disband; to abandon, repudiate, divorce; to abnegate, cast off, dispose of, give over, give up, lay off, pack in, renounce, skip (out)

rammûti *n. pl.* released troops

ramninni* *pron.* ourselves

ramû *v.* $^{u/u}$ to be loose, be limp, slacken, slack off; to ease off, give way, indulge

ra'mu+ *n.* chum, crony

ra'mu a. *adj.* loved, beloved, popular

ramû a. *adj.* slack, flabby, flaccid, lax, limp

ramunu *pron.* self

ramû B* *v.* $^{i/i}$ to settle down, take up residence, dwell, be seated; (Š) to install in a place of residence, settle

ranānu+ *v.* to clang

rapādu *v.* $^{u/u}$ to run away, run off, stampede; to hike, ramble, roam, rove, trek, wander

rapāqu *v.* $^{i/i}$ to fix, nail, rivet, secure; (D) to fasten

rapassu *nf.* pelvis; rump, haunch; chine

rapāsu *v.* $^{i/i}$ to beat together, clap; to beat, flog; to thresh; to scuffle, thrash, tussle

rapāsu+ *v.* $^{i/i}$ to beat the ground, dance, kick, paw, prance

rapāš libbi* *n. cp.* magnanimity

rapāšu *v.* $^{i/i}$ to be broad, be wide, be extensive; (D) to amplify, extend, expand, enlarge, widen, dilate, escalate*, propagate*; (Š) to make wide

rappu* *n.* ^{2} bridle, grip, clamp

rapšiš* *adv.* largely*, expansively, extensively, widely

rapšu *adj.* ample, large-scale, large, broad, roomy, spacious, extensive, wide, widespread, vast

rapšūtu* *nf.* vastness

rapšu B* *n.* shovel for winnowing

rapšu B+ *n.* winnowing-fan, shoulder-blade

rāpu+ *n.* bevy, shelf

raqādu *v.* $^{u/u}$ to dance, skip, to hop*, frisk*; (Š) to toss

rāqānūtu+ *nf.* bankruptcy, frivolity

raqāpu+ *v.* to floor, lay a floor

raqāqu *v.* $^{i/i}$ to be thin, fine; to be sparse; (D) to hammer thin, roll out thin, to rarefy*, tone down*

raqāqu+ *v.* $^{i/i}$ (D) to make thin, draw fine; (Š) to attenuate, beat thin

raqpu+ *n.* booth, planking

raqqatu* *nf.* swamp, marsh, river-flats

raqqidu* *n.* dancer

raqqiu *n.* malingerer, hider

raqqu* *n.* tortoise, turtle

raqqû *v.* to make perfume

raqqu a. *adj.* thin, fine, slim

raqqu a.* *adj.* thin, fine, slim
raqqû a. *adj.* perfumed*, spiced*, spicy*, tasty*
raqqu a.+ *adj.* shallow, subtle, thin-drawn
raqqûtu *nf.* perfume, spice
raqrāqu+ *n.* shoal, shallow
rāqtu* *nf.* space, vacuum, void
raqû 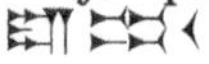 *v.* $^{i/i}$ to hide, give refuge to
rāqu *adj.* empty, vacant, void; available, free, unoccupied; at leisure, idle, unemployed; futile, meaningless, vapid, valueless, worthless
rāqu+ *n.* cuckoo
rāqūtē- *adv.* empty-handed
rāqūtu *nf.* emptiness; availability, vacancy; free time; idleness, unemployment; vacation, leave; futility, vanity
rasābu* *v.* $^{i/i}$ to smite, strike down; to cut down, fell, thrash
rasānu *v.* $^{i/i}$ to soak, steep; to brew
rasmu *adj.* unpredictable, quick-tempered, impetuous, fiery, sultry, rash; hothead
ra'su  *n.* ^{2} chieftain
raṣānu* *v.* $^{u/u}$ to make a loud noise, resound, blare; (Dt) to rumble, roar, thunder
raṣāpu *v.* $^{i/i}$ to brick up, build, construct, wall up
raṣāpu+ *v.* $^{i/i}$ to make solid, ram in, pave
raṣāpu gamāru *vp.* to build completely
raṣāpu šaklulu* *vp.* to build completely
raṣīnu+ *n.* bayou, brooklet, rill
raṣmu*  *adj.* loud-voiced, sonorous
raṣpu *adj.* built
raṣpu+ *adj.* paved, solid
raṣṣīṣu* *n.* chicken
rāš ili* *adj. cp.* fortunate, lucky, blessed
rāš libbi* *adj. cp.* courageous, gutsy, spirited
rāš tašīmti* *adj. cp.* discerning
rāš ṭēmi u milki* *adj. cp.* rational
rāš uzni* *adj. cp.* intelligent, intuitive
rašābu* *v.* to be terrifying
rašādu* *v.* (Š) to found, lay foundations of
rašbu* *adj.* awesome, fearsome, frightening, imposing, terrifying
rašdu* *adj.* firmly founded, well-founded
rāšilūtu* *nf. cp.* fortune, luck, blessedness
rašû*  *v.* $^{i/i}$ to get, obtain, acquire, come to have, incur; to experience, be affected by; (Š) to let acquire, cause to suffer
rāšû◊ *n.* ^{4} creditor
rašubbatu* *nf.* terrifying appearance, chilling fear
rašubbu* *adj.* awesome, awe-inspiring, terrific, terrifying
rašûtānu◊ *n.* creditor
rašûtu◊ *nf.* credit
rašû B* *v.* $^{i/i}$ to itch
ratānu◊ *v.* to whisper
ratātu* *v.* $^{u/u}$ to shiver, tremble, vibrate
ratātu+ *v.* $^{u/u}$ quake, shake, shudder
ratītu* *n.* shivering, trembling, vibration
rattitu* *adj.* shivery, tremulous
raṭābu *v.* to be moist, damp; (D) to soak
raṭābu+ *v.* to be wet; (D) to moisten, wet, water
raṭbu *adj.* damp, dewy, humid, moist; watery, wet; fresh
raṭībūtu+ *nf.* humidity, moisture, wetness
raṭṭubu *adj.* soaking [wet], wetted through
rāṭu *n.* $^{2/3}$ drainpipe, pipe, drain, chute, gutter; water-channel, channel, trough, tube
ra'û  *v.* $^{i/i}$ to shepherd, pasture, tend; to graze
ra'ūmtānu+ *adj.* humane
rebītu* *nf.* square, plaza; main street, thoroughfare, forum*
rēdût māti* *nf. cp.* public administration, government
rēdûtu *nf.* succession; government, regimen
rēdûtu* *nf.* administration, regime
rēḫāti *nf.pl.* (pl.) leftovers, remains, relics
rēḫtu  *nf.* remainder, rest, remnant, leftover
reḫû* *v.* $^{i/i}$ to pour in, ejaculate, impregnate, imbue, fertilize, beget; (Dt) to get pregnant
rēmānu *adj.* merciful, clement; benignant, charitable, compassionate, gracious, pitiful, tenderhearted
rēmānû◊ *adj.* merciful
rēmēnānû* *adj.* compassionate
re'mu◊ *n.* friend
rēmu *n.* compassion, grace, clemency, mercy, pity
rēmu ina muḫḫi/ana X šakānu‡ *vp.* to have mercy upon, have compassion on, have mercy, have pity, feel pity for, pity, show mercy, sympathize
rēmu rašû‡ *vp.* to have mercy, have pity, forgive, pardon
rēmuttu  *nf.* grant, donation, reward*
rēmūtu* *nf.* mercy, pardon
rēmu B* *n.* womb

rēntu *nf.* beloved(?)
reqdu+ *n.* pantomimic dancing, revelling
rēqu* *adj.* distant, far, remote
rēssu◊ *adv.* earlier
rēṣu* *n.* [1] helper, supporter, ally
rēṣūtu* *nf.* help, aid
rēš dabābi* *n. cp.* foreword
rēš gišri+ *n. cp.* bridgehead
rēš namkūri* *n. cp.* liquid capital, available funds
rēš šarrūti* *n. cp.* accession year
rēš šatti *n. cp.* new year, New Year's Day
rēš tānti* *n. cp.* cape, headland, peninsula
rēšāti *n. pl.* choicest things, first fruits; summits, peaks
rēšēti* *nf. pl.* basics, essentials, fundamentals
rēštu* *nf.* first quality, first-class; summit, peak
rēštû* *adj.* eldest, first; first-ranking, foremost; first-rate, prime, primary; primeval, primitive
rešû* *adj.* reckless, inconsiderate
rēšu *n.* head; top; beginning; prow
rēšu+ *n.* nob
rēšu kullu‡ *vp.* to take care of, look after, care for, wait for; to provide, make available, make ready; to be available, be ready, serve
rēšu našû‡ *v.* to summon; to honor; to check; to begin with; to prepare, to pick out, uplift; employ; get ready with; to inspect, check on
rēšūtu* *nf.* slavery, servitude
retû* *v.* [i/i] to rig, to drive in, set in place, install, fix, erect, pitch
reṭbu+ *n.* moisture, verdure, wet ground
rezpu+ *n.* poppy
riābu *v.* to compensate, make up for, recompense, remunerate, repay, replace, requite, to reward*
riāḫu *v.* to remain, be left over; (Š) to leave behind
riāmu *v.* to remit, excuse, pardon, exonerate, exculpate; to grant, bestow, donate, give away
riāqu *v.* to be empty; to be free, be available; to be idle, lack work, be unemployed, be unoccupied; to be meaningless, be in vain; (Š) to empty, empty out; to vacate, void, unload; to release, lay off, free of work, set free; to make available; to cast (metal)
riāqu+ *v.* to potter [about]
riāšu *v.* to rejoice, exult
ribku* *n.* decoction, concoction, infusion
rību *n.* [2] earthquake
rību riābu‡ *vp.* to pay compensation
rību B* *n.* setting (of planet)
rību C* *n.* replacement, recompensation, requital
riddu *n.* conduct, behavior, education; ideal behavior, mores, demeanor*, paragon*
riddu* *n.* ideal, model, paragon, example
riddu kēnu* *np.* proper behavior
riddu šakānu‡ *vp.* to educate
ridpu *n.* pursuit, chase, persecution*
rīdu* *n.* driving, droving, drive; succession; pursuit, persecution
rigāmu *n.* bunch(?)
rigbu* *n.* storey*, superstructure; upper level, top level, top part; upper storey
riggatu *nf.* injustice, villainy
riggu+ *n.* instant, moment, while
rigim Adad *n. cp.* thunder
rigmu *n.* voice, sound; pronunciation; call, exclamation, shout, shriek; bark; roar, rumbling; clangor; clamour, tumult, uproar; crying, screaming; complaint, lament, chink*, clink*, twang*
rigšu+ *n.* sense, feeling, perception
riḫiṣtu* *nf.* destruction, devastation, flooding
riḫṣu *n.* blizzard, downpour, violent rain; flooding, devastation; splash, splashing
rihu:t Šulpaea* *nf. cp.* epilepsy, epileptic
riḫūtu *nf.* sperm, spawn, ejaculation*
rikalla *n.* netherworld, hell*
rikbu* *n.* crew
rikibtu* *nf.* mounting; coitus, copulation, sexual intercourse, sexual union; pollination
rikis gerri* *n. cp.* directory, itinerary, overview
rikis qabli◊ *n. cp.* loin-girding, equipping, equipment; readiness, preparedness
rikistu* *nf.* decree, contract, agreement; (pl.) regulations
riksu *n.* band; binding, tie, link; bundle, package; bond, agreement, obligation; set-up, arrangement; schedule; regulation, rule, ordinance; gist, summary, synthesis, substance
riksu dannunu‡ *vp.* to reinforce the construction
rīmāniš* *adv.* like a wild bull
rimītu* *nf.* dwelling, residence

rimmatu* *nf.* rumble, humming
rîmtu* *nf.* wild cow
rimṭu *n.* venereal disease
rîmu *n.*[2] wild bull, aurochs
rimûtu* *nf.* numbness, paralysis
rimûtu rašû* *vp.* to suffer paralysis
rinku *n.*[2] bath, ablution
ripittu* *nf.* straying, trek
ripîtu *nf.* (a kind of bread)
ripsu *n.* haze, mist
riqdu *n.* dance, dancing
riqiu *n.*[1] aromatic, perfume, spice, seasoning*
riqû* *n.* (mng. uncert.)
rîqu* *adj.* empty; unemployed, unoccupied
rîqûtu* *nf.* emptiness; empty-handed
risittu◊ *nf.* tanning, tanned leather
risittu* *nf.* soaking, soaked malt
riṣiptu* *nf.* revetment, masonry, construction*
riṣiptu+ *nf.* (tesselated) pavement, mosaic
riṣpu* *n.* edifice, building
riṣpu+ *n.* floor, pavement
riṣpûtu+ *nf.* paving
rîṣu* *n.* assistance
rîšâti *n. pl.* joy
rîštu◊ *nf.* celebration, exultation, jubilation, merrymaking, rejoicing
rišûtu* *nf.* itch, scurf
ritkubu* *n.* copulating, mating
ritpâšu* *adj.* extensive, vast, expansive*
rittu *nf.* hand, wrist; paw; handle
rîtu* *nf.* herbage, pasturage
ruâbu *v.* to quake, tremble; (D) to shake, dislodge
ru'âmu* *n.* love, affection, lovemaking, love affair
ruâqu *v.* to be distant; be profound; to distance o.s., withdraw, make off, elude, evade, avoid, shirk, shun, shy from
rubâia *pron.* four each
rubâtu* *nf.* queen, empress
rubâ'u† *n.* king
rubbu* *n.* billows, waves
rubbu'u* *adj.* fourfold, quadruple
rubê *n.* interest; increase
rubṣu* *n.* litter, bedding; dung
rubû* *n.* ruler, prince, nobleman
rûbu *n.* growth, maturity, adulthood, development*
rubû'â◊ *pron.* four each
rubûtu* *nf.* queen, princess
rubûtu B* *nf.* kingship, rulership, rule
rûbu B *n.* setting (of planet)
rûbu B* *n.* anger, turmoil
ruggubu* *v.* to furnish with a deck, roof
ruggubu a.* *adj.* roofed
rugubu *n.* loft, room on roof, upper room
rugummû* *n.* claim
rukûbu* *n.*[1] vehicle, carriage; boat
ruppušu* *n.* expansion
rupšu *n.* width
rupuštu* *nf.* froth, foam
rûqiš* *adv.* far, afar
ruqpu *adj. or n.* (a qualification of silver)
ruqqi uzni* *n. cp.* cavity of the ear, auditory meatus
ruqqu *n.* kettle, caldron, cauldron
ruqqu B* *n.* cavity
rûqu* *adj.* distant, remote, far-away; deep, profound, unfathomable, inscrutable
rûqu+ *adj.* far-away, farthest
rûqu n.* *n.* long distance, far-away place
ruṣṣunu* *adj.* loud-voiced, resonant, vociferous
ruššû* *adj.* red, reddish, auburn*
rûštu* *nf.* fine oil, virgin oil
rušundu* *nf.* swamp, marsh; mud, sludge
ru'tîtu* *nf.* sulphur
ruttu* *nf.* girl friend
ru'tu* *nf.* spittle, saliva; sap
ruṭbu* *n.* dampness, moisture
ruṭibtu *nf.* irrigated field
ruṭibtu* *nf.* wet ground; dampness, moistness
rûṭu *n.* span, half-cubit
ru'u* *n.* friend, comrade
ru'ubtu◊ *nf.* anger, outrage, rage, tantrum
ru'ûmtu* *nf.* darling
ru'ûtu* *nf.* friendship
sabâku *v.* [i/i] to assail
sabâku* *v.* [i/i] to interweave
sabâku *v.* [i/i] (D) to seize, catch in
sabâku+ *v.* [i/i] to attack, cling [to], fasten on, set on; (D) to cling [to], lay hold [of]
sabâ'u *v.* [u/u] to billow, fluctuate, rock, roil, roll; to move back and forth, pulsate, oscillate; to wag one's tail
sabirru *n.*[1] ring, bracelet, anklet, torc
sâbîtu* *nf.* barmaid
sabiu *num.* seventh
sâbiu *n.* inn-keeper, barman
sabsûtu *nf.* midwife
sâbu* *n.* (a red stone)
sabubânu

 *n.* black cumin
sabubu *n.* (a gold object)
sadāru 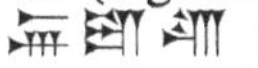 *v.* $^{i/i}$ to do regularly, do usually; to put in order, set in order, arrange, array, line up, draw up; to maneuver; to exercise, drill; (D) to do in an orderly manner, do systematically, do methodically, to normalize*, regulate*; (Š) to accustom*, habituate*, inure*; (stat.) to occur regularly
sadāru+ *v.* $^{i/i}$ to lay in order, set in array, marshall; to follow in order, happen successively
sadāru n. *n.* maneuver, manoeuvre
sadduru *adj.* orderly, proper
sadēia* *n.* rhinoceros
sadirtu  *nf.* line of battle, battle array, battalion, phalanx, commonplace*, manoeuvre*
sadīru *n.* order
sadīru* *n.* section
sâdiu  *n.* [2] slinger
sadru  *adj.* normal, regular, ordinary, average, common, standard, usual; regularly occurring, continual, continuous, sequential, mediocre*, mean*
sa'du  *n.* meadow, pasture
sādu 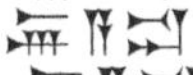 *n.* (an alloy of gold)
sādu◊  *n.* meadow
sâdu*   *v.* $^{a/a}$ to slay
sagalmušu  *n.* (a plant)
sagbû* *n.* vanguard
sagdilû* *adj., n.* single, bachelor
saggilatu* *nf.* sedge tuber
saggilmut *n.* azure, azurite
sagû *n.* to flinch, swerve
sāgu  *n.* [3] (short) tunic, kilt
sagû+ *v.* to err, stray, swerve, wander; (Š) to delude, lead astray, mislead, seduce
sagû a.+ *adj.* absent-minded
sagullu  *n.* [3] herd, flock, drove
sagullu+ *n.* [3] bunch, cluster
sagûtu+ *nf.* aberration, deviation
sāgu B* *n.* [1] shrine, holy room
saḫāl šīri* *n. cp.* annoyance, nuisance
saḫālu  *v.* $^{a/u}$ to pierce, prick
saḫaptu* *nf.* devastation
saḫāpu  *v.* $^{a/u}$ to cover, overwhelm, overthrow, defeat; to lay flat, flatten
saḫāpu+ *v.* $^{a/u}$ to cast down, demolish, dethrone, overturn, pull down, throw down, thrust, to confute, desolate, subvert, undermine
saḫār ūme *n. cp.* turn of the day, late afternoon, early evening
saḫargû *n.* dust-guard, mud-guard, footboard (of a chariot)
saḫaru *n.* tower(?)
saḫāru  *v.* $^{u/u}$ to turn, turn about; to do again, redo s.th.; to turn back, return; to retreat, retrograde, revolve; to turn to; to go round, gad about, peddle
saḫāru*  *v.* $^{u/u}$ (Š) to put around, surround; (Št) to encircle
saḫāru†  *v.* $^{u/u}$ to delay, tarry, linger, loiter
saḫāru  *v.* $^{u/u}$ (D) to bring back, get back, regain, restore, retrieve; to do again, repeat; (N) to relent, regret, repent; (stat.) to be round, lie round
saḫāru+ *v.* $^{u/u}$ to go round begging
saḫāru alāku *vp.* to go again, go back, come back
saḫāru erābu *vp.* to re-enter, come back again
saḫāru n. *n.* turn, return
saḫḫāpu+ *adj.* subversive
saḫḫirtu  *nf.* vagabond, pedlar woman
saḫḫiru  *n.* vagabond, hawker, pedlar, peddler, retailer, tramp, vagrant
saḫḫu* *n.* meadow, waterlogged land
saḫḫuru mallû* *vp.* to refill
saḫḫuru manû* *vp.* to re-count
saḫḫuru tadānu‡ *vp.* to give back, pay back, restore
sāḫilu* *adj.* poignant
saḫimtu* *nf.* yeast
saḫimtu B* *nf.* valley(?)
sāḫipu* *adj.* daunting, overwhelming, swooping
sāḫirtu*  *nf.* free-roaming cow, heifer
sāḫiru  *n.* (part of a bed)
sāḫiru B *n.* [4] peddler, salesman, vendor
saḫlû  *n.* cress
saḫmaštu*  *nf.* anarchy
saḫru *adj.* round
saḫunu  *n.* (a spice or vegetable)
sa'ītu *nf.* revetment, battlement, parapet
sāiu  *adj.* knotted(?)
sakāk uzni* *n. cp.* ear blockage
sakāku  *v.* $^{a/a}$ to block; to be blocked, clogged, impenetrable
sakālu* *v.* $^{i/i}$ to acquire, hoard; to appropriate, annex; (D) to scrape up, scratch up, scratch together
sakālu B* *v.* $^{i/i}$ to balk, be shy
sakannu  *n.* [1] band(?)
sakāpu* *v.* $^{i/i}$ to overturn, overthrow; to beat off, fend off, drive back, push back,

repel, repulse; (D) to reject

sakâpu B* *v.* $^{u/u}$ to lie down, rest

sakâru *v.* $^{i/i}$ to refine (metals), gild

sakâru n.+ *n.* shutdown

sakâru B *v.* $^{i/i}$ to dam, block, close, clog, stew

sakâru B+ *v.* $^{i/i}$ to barricade, close, confine, curb, hinder, hold in, keep from, occlude, restrain, sequester, shut

sakâtu◊ *v.* $^{u/u}$ to be silent; (D) to silence

sakâtu+ *v.* $^{u/u}$ to perch, rest, settle dowb, stay quiet, cease from war; (D) to tranquillize, give rest

sakikkû *n.*[1] symptom; diagnostics; pulse

sakîku* *n.*[1] silt, sediment

sâkilu* *adj.* acquisitive

sâkipu* *n.* resting

sakkâpu* *n.* pusher

sakku* *adj.* obtuse, obscure, impenetrable

sakkû* *n.*[1] ritual regulation

sakkuku *adj., n.* deaf, hard of hearing; obtuse, limited; ignoramus; mentally handicapped, dumb

sakkukûtu *nf.* deafness; idiocy, dumbness, stupidity

sakku B* *n.*[1] (an ornament on doors and columns)

sakliš* *adv.* simply

saklu *adj.* simple; simple-minded, silly, foolish; illiterate, incompetent; barbarous, ninny*, credulous*, gullible*

saklu+ *adj.* foolish, stupid; fool

saklu n. *n.* simpleton; common man, upstart

saklûtu* *nf.* simplicity, laity

saklûtu+ *nf.* folly, senselessness

sakru *adj.* refined; gilded, gilt, gold plated

salâḫu* *v.* $^{a/u}$ to sprinkle, spatter, rain down; (stat.) to be damp

salâmu *v.* $^{i/i}$ to make peace, to capitulate*; (D) to appease, reconcile, conciliate

salâmu+ *v.* $^{i/i}$ to assent, give in, surrender, yield

salâqu *v.* $^{a/u}$ to boil

salâtu *v.* $^{a/u}$ to split, cut up

salâtu* *v.* $^{a/u}$ (D) to cut through, split

salâtu B* *nf.* kin by marriage, family, clan

salâ'u *v.* $^{a/u}$ to sprinkle

salḫu† *adj.* damp, clammy*

salîm kiššati* *n. cp.* universal peace

salîmu* *n.* peace, reconciliation, amity

salîtu *nf.* net

saliu+ *adj.* abominable, castaway

sallu *n.*[1] basket

sallu+ *n.*[1] basket

salmu *adj., n.*[1] acquiescent, friendly, peaceful, peaceable; ally

salmu+ *adj., n.*[1] compliant

salmûtu+ *nf.* compliance

salqu *adj., n.*[2] boiled (meat)

sâlti ana libbi X alâku‡ *vp.* to go to fight against

salṭu *n.*[2] quiver, bow-and-arrow case

salû *v.* $^{i/i}$ to lie, cheat, deceive; (Gtn) to lie

saluppu *n.* date

samâdiru *n.* flower

samâdiru+ *n.* blossom of the vine, tendril, wine-bud

samâḫu *v.* $^{a/u}$ to merge, mingle; to cohere, be unified; (D) to unite, mix, integrate with; (Dtt) to be united, mixed; to mingle with, collaborate with, to join in*

samâku *v.* $^{a/u}$ to be bad; (D) to make bad, treat harshly, damage, worsen

samânâ* *num.* eighty

samâne* *num.* eight

samânšerîu* *num.* eighteenth

samânu *n.* (a noxious insect)

samânu B* *n.* chicken pox, smallpox

samâru* *n.* bracelet

samîdu *n.* (a spice)

samîdu B* *n.* fine flour

samîdu B+ *n.* finest wheaten flour

samiktu *nf.* misdeed, enormity*

Sâmirîna *n.* Samaria

Sâmirînâiu *adj., n.* Samarian, Samaritan

samîtu* *nf.* battlemented parapet; wall-plinth, revetment

samku *adj.* bad, malodorous, evil

sammânu+ *adj.* toxic

sammû *n.*[1] lyre

sammuḫu *adj.* assorted, mixed, miscellaneous

sammumu+ *v.* (D) to poison

sammûru+ *n.* sable

sammûtu* *nf.* fragrance

samnu* *n.* oath, eighth

samû *v.* $^{u/u}$ to hesitate, vacillate; to be inept, to be drift*; (Gtn) to deviate, stray; (D) to cause to stray, lose direction, distract

sāmu *adj.* red; brown; ruddy, blond*
samû a. *adj.* inept
samullu◊ *n.* (a tree)
samuntu *nf.* one eighth
sanāqu*  *v.* $^{i/i}$ to approach, come close; to check, examine
sanāqu  *v.* $^{i/i}$ (D) to question, interrogate, cross-examine
sanāqu+ *v.* $^{i/i}$ (D) to abuse, inflict severe pain, punish, torture
sanbuku  *n.* cluster, bunch
sandāniš* *adv.* like a fowler, like a bird-catcher
sandû  *n.* fowler
sangilû* *n.* difference, discrepancy
sangu* *n.* ^{2} mountain path(?)
sangû 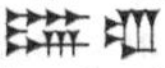 *n.* ^{2} priest
sangû karkadinnu  *n. cp.* priest-confectioner
sangûtu *nf.* priesthood
sanḫu *adj.* assorted
sanku *adj.* obnoxious*
sanqu* *adj.* disciplined, prudent, obedient
sanqūtu* *nf.* discipline, prudence, obedience
santak*  *adv.* constantly
santakku* *n.* wedge, cuneiform wedge; triangle, right triangle
sāntu  *nf.* carnelian
sāntu B  *nf.* redness, red light, dawn
sanû  *v.* $^{i/i}$ to be angry(?)
sapādu* *v.* $^{i/i}$ to mourn
sapāḫu *v.* $^{a/u}$ to scatter, spill, disperse
sapāḫu* *v.* $^{a/u}$ to squander, waste; (N) evaporate
sapāḫu *v.* $^{a/u}$ (D) to squander; to splash
sapalgīnu* *n.* elecampane
sapan tānti* *n. cp.* coastal plain
sapannu* *n.* ^{1} flatland, expanse, depression
sapānu  *v.* $^{a/u}$ to level, deface, flatten, lay flat, smooth [away, out, down], wipe out
sapānu+ *v.* $^{a/u}$ to make even
sapāqu  *v.* $^{i/i}$ to suffice, be enough, be sufficient
saparru 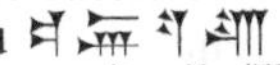 *n.* ^{3} cart, car
saparru B*  *n.* ^{1} net
sapḫu* *adj.* scattered
sapīqu+ *adj.* adequate, competent, eligible, fit, sufficient
saplišḫu *n.* (a meat preparation)
saplu  *n.* ^{1} bowl, basin, dish
sapnu* *adj.* even, flat, smooth
sapnu issi‡ *adj. phr.* level with
sappāru  *n.* mountain ram
sappiḫu* *adj., n.* wasteful, prodigal, spendthrift
sapqūtu+ *nf.* adequacy, benignancy, contentment, fitness, qualification, sufficiency
sapsupu *n.* moustache
sapsupu† *n.* fringe
sapulḫu *n.* ^{1} (a culinary dish)
sapūnu+ *n.* badger, rock badger
saqāru  *v.* $^{a/u}$ to mention, utter, invoke
saqqu† *n.* sack, sackcloth
saqqu+ bag, haircloth
sāqu *adj.* narrow, straitened, tight
sarābu *n.* drought
sarādu† *v.* $^{i/i}$ to pack, tie up; packing
sarāḫu+ *v.* to range, rove; (Š) to captivate, enrapture, fascinate, ravish
sarame *n.* (part or decoration of a door)
sarāpu* *v.* to sup
sarāpu+ *v.* to sip
sarāqu 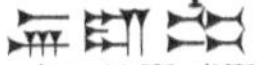 *v.* $^{a/u}$ to strew, scatter
sarāru†  *v.* to be a criminal; to lie, be fraudulent; to cheat, dupe, fool, hoodwink, swindle
sarbu  *n.* ^{3} slush, mash, mush, squash
sārē šētuqu‡ *vp.* to sweep the floor, sweep up
sarḫu *adj.* ecstatic, rapturous, delirious*, rapt*
sarḫu+ *adj.* enraptured, fanatical, immoderate, unrestrained
sarḫu B *adj.* (a qualification of wine)
sariānu  *n.* armor, scale armor, coat of mail
sarnu+ *n.* axis, hub
sarrāti* *n. pl.* lies, falseness, fraud
sarrīqu  *adj.* empty, vainglorious
sarru*  *adj.* mock, false, dishonest, deceptive, foxy, fraudulent, misleading
sarru n.* *n.* liar; con man, swindler, impostor
sarruru  *v.* to pray, implore
sarrūtu* *nf.* cheating, dishonesty, swindle
sarsarru *n.* ^{2} gangster, archi-traitor
sartatti◊ *adv.* deceptively, fraudulently
sartennu*  *n.* chief judge

sartu  *nf.* crime, fraud, theft; falsehood, dishonesty; fine, penalty

sāru  *n.* $^{2/4}$ thief, burglar, housebreaker

sâru* *v.* $^{u/u}$ to whirl, circle, dance, dance (in a circle), rotate, twirl, whirl; (D) set up in a circle

sāru B  *n.* $^{1/2}$ palm frond, broom

sasin qašāti  *n.* *cp.* bow-maker

sasin šiltāḫi *n. cp.* arrow-maker

sasin uṣṣi  *n.* *cp.* arrow-maker

sasinnu  *n.* bow-maker, arrow-maker

sasiu  *adj., n.* ^{4} invited (guest)

sāsiu* *n.* ^{4} reader

sasqû* *n.* semolina

sassaptu* *nf.* eyelash

sassu  *n.* base-board (of a chariot), driving-platform

sassutu 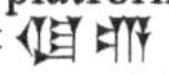 *nf.* grass, turf, underbrush*, undergrowth*

sasû  *v.* $^{i/i}$ to read (out), shout, call (out)

sāsu  *n.* moth

sāsu+ *n.* decay, maggot, mite, worm

sasuppu  *n.* ^{3} napkin, towel, sheet, apron*, bib*

sasuppu+ *n.* ^{3} covering, handkerchief, veil

sasûtu *nf.* reading

satālu* *v.* $^{i/i}$ to plant

sataru* *n.* (a herb, perhaps thyme or savory)

sattukku*  *n.* ^{1} regular offering

sa'uru  *n.* ^{3} bracelet

sebâ* *num.* seventy

sebāiu* *num.* seventieth

sebe*  *num.* seven

sebe:&er[et]* *num.* seventeen

sebēšerīu* *num.* seventeenth

sebettu*  *num.* seven, heptad

sebīrūtu+ *nf.* imagination, illusion, pretence

sebīšu*  *adv.* seven times

sebru+ *n.* conjecture, supposition

sêdu* *v.* to help, aid, support

sēgallu  *nf.* queen, queen-consort, wife of the king

segû◊ *v.* $^{i/i}$ to go about, go along, move about, wander; (Š) to let go

seḫû* *v.* $^{i/i}$ to rise up, rebel, revolt; (D) to disarrange, disturb, mess up

sēḫû◊  *n.* contestant

sekrutu *nf.* concubine, mistress, harem woman

selû◊ *v.* $^{i/i}$ to despise, reject

selû+ *v.* $^{i/i}$ to cast away, detest, disapprove, throw away, turn down

semēru* *n.* ^{1} manacle

senkurru *n.* cheetah

sepēru◊  *v.* $^{i/i}$ to write in Aramaic script

sepīru* *n.* scribe (of Aramaic)

sēpiu  *n.* felt-worker

sēpu  *n.* pollen(?)

sēpu B *n.* (a cereal)

sēru *adj.* plastered, slipped with clay

se'û◊ *v.* $^{i/i}$ to oppress

siāmu  *v.* to be red; (D) to redden

siāqu  *v.* to be tight, be narrow; be hard-pressed; (D) to constrict, make narrow, restrict, straiten, tighten, give a hard time

siāru  *v.* to plaster, smear, rub down

sibbirru  *n.* (a spice)

sibibiānu† *n.* black cummin

sibkarû *n.* (a piece of temple furniture)

sibrītu  *nf.* (a garment)

siddētu *nf.* (mng. unkn.)

siddu  *n.* (a metal object)

sidirtu* *nf.* line of battle, battle array, battalion, phalanx

sidru  *n.* line; row, register; order, sequence

sidru*  *n.* line of battle

sidru+ *n.* array, rank, series, succession

sigāru  *n.* ^{3} neck-stock

siggu  *n.* tuft of wool

siḫḫāru  *n.* ^{3} shallow bowl, platter, plate

siḫḫu  *n.* (mng. uncert.)

siḫiltu* *nf.* pain, sting

siḫirti X‡ *np.* all kinds of X

siḫirtu*  *nf.* circumference, perimeter, surroundings, environment, periphery; entirety, totality, sum total

siḫlānu* *adj.* prickly

siḫlu  *n.* thorn; piercing pain, pain, pang

siḫpu  *n.* surface, cover, covering, overlay; bark, bast; overwhelming attack

siḫpu B* *n.* strech, extent

siḫru  *n.* turn, turning; setting, surroundings, region; entirety; contact

sīḫu  *n.* wormwood

sīḫu B*  *n.* rebellion, revolt, conspiracy, sedition

sikiltu* *nf.* hoard, accumulated property, hoarding*
sikiptu* *nf.* rejection; defeat, overthrow
sikkannu* *n.* rudder, paddle, steering paddle
sikkat mê* *nf. cp.* plug
sikkat ṣeli *n. cp.* rib
sikkatānu* *adj.* conic[al]
sikkatu *nf.* yeast, leaven
sikkû *n.* mongoose
sikkūru *n.* lock, bolt
sikkutu *nf.* peg, nail, cone, stake, wall cone; pyramid; ploughshare
sikkutu* *nf.* drumstick, stick
sikkutu+ *nf.* pin, splinter, wedge
sikrānu+ *adj.* jagged, jaggy
sikru *n.* abscess, boil, scab
sikru* *n.* barrage, blockage; dam, barrier, hurdle; cloistering, seclusion
sikru+ *n.* drawback
siliāti *n. pl.* lies, rubbish, baloney
silittu* *nf.* splitting off, forking off
sili'tu* *nf.* illness, disease
silītu* *nf.* afterbirth
sillurmû* *n.* night/day blindness
silqu *n.* boiled meat
silqu B* *n.* mangel-wurzel
silqu B+ *n.* beet, beetroot, chard
siltu *nf.* (a kind of groats)
sīlu *n.* (a precious stone)
siluḫ *n.*[3] (rdg. obscure, a textile)
simanīu* *adj.* provisional, temporal, temporary
Simannu *n.* (month) Sivan, June
Simānu* *n.* (month) Sivan, June
simānu* *n.* time
simat pāni* *n. cp.* complexion
simāt šarrūti* *nf. cp. pl.* royal insignia, regalia
simin naptini *n. cp.* mealtime
simin ṣalāli *n. cp.* bedtime
simmagir* *n.* (a Babylonian minister)
simmānû* *n.* food ration, material, equipment
simmatānu *adj.* brand marked(?)
simmiltu *nf.* ladder, staircase
simmu *n.*[1] sore, wound, lesion, contusion, trauma; carbuncle, scab, swelling
simru *n.* fennel
simtu *n.* (person or thing) fit for, befitting, worthy of, worth, appropriate; adornment, ornament, decoration; badge, insignia, ensign, medal; propriety, characteristic, symbol
simunu *n.* time, time for, moment, season, occasion
simurru* *n.* (a whirling wind)
sinbu* *n.* menstrual bandage
Sindāiu* *adj., n.* Indian
sindu *n.* groats
Sindu* *n.* India
sindû* *adj.* Indian wood
sinniš* *adj.* female, feminine
sinnišāniš* *adv.* like a woman, womanly
sinnišānu* *adj.* effeminate
sinnu* *n.* withdrawal(?)
sinnutu *nf.* brand mark
sinpu *n.* (an object)
sinqu *n.* agony, anguish, crisis, distress, plight
sīnu *n.* moon
sinūntu *nf.* swallow
siparrānu *adj.* bronzen, bronzy, bronze-colored
siparrē šakānu‡ *vp.* to cuff
siparru *n.* bronze; shackles
sipḫu◊ *n.* (mng. uncl.)
sipiḫ libbi◊ *n. cp.* consternation(?)
sipittu* *nf.* lamentation, mourning
sippu *n.*[1/2] doorjamb, doorframe, doorpost, jamb, rim; entrance (to a city)
sippu+ *n.*[1/2] porch, sill, threshold; approach (to city)
sipru◊ *n.* letter-scroll, document
sīpu* *n.* prayer
siqqurrutu *nf.* ziggurat, temple tower, spire
siqqurrutu B *nf.* ziggurat-shaped cake, (tiered) cake, wedding cake
siqru *n.* word, command; expression, phrase, utterance
sīqu *n.*[2] thigh; (pl.) lap
sīqu a.◊ *adj.* narrow, tight
sirāšû *n.* brewer
sirdu *n.*[1] olive
sirdû* *n.* shaft (of a sedan chair)
sirḫu* *n.* earthen wall(?), debris
siriam* *n.* armor, coat of mail
siriam+ *n.* armature, armor plate, breastplate, corselet, cuirass
sirīšu* *n.* beer
sirpu* *n.* brown horse, roan
sirqu *n.* offering (of aromatics or flour)
sirrimtu* *nf.* female onager

sirrimu  *n.* wild ass, onager
sīru *n.* (wall-)plaster
sisalḫu 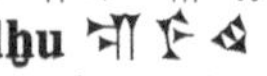 *n.* (a qualification of sheep and oxen)
sisītu *nf.* shank, leg
sissiktu*  *nf.* hem
sissinnu* *n.* spadix
sissû  *n.*[1] horse
sissû ša tânti* *np.* whale
sīsu *n.*[1] teat(?)
Sīsû* *n.* Cassiopeia
sittu*  *nf.* rest, remainder
sittūtu* *nf.* rest, remainder
si'ūtu* *nf.* pressure(?)
sû *n.* red sandstone
suādu *n.* sedge(-tuber), cyperus, incense
suāku *v.* to pulverize, crush, pound
suālu *n.* phlegm; cough with phlegm; bronchitis
Subarû◊ *adj., n.* Subarean
subbusu◊ *adj.* gathered together
sudduru *adj.* orderly, neat
suḫār šēpi* *n. cp.* ball of the foot
suḫātu *nf.* armpit
suḫḫurtu* *nf.* retreat (of army), withdrawal
suḫīru* *n.* young (of animals), foal
suḫsi Issār *n. cp.* (a plant, bed of Ištar)
suḫsilu  *n.* (a locust, god's bed)
suḫurmāšu *n.* goat-fish; Capricorn
Suḫurmāšu* *n.* Capricorn
suḫurrû* *n.* reversal
sukanninu  *n.* turtledove
sukkalmaḫḫu* *n.* chief minister
sukku  *n.*[1] chapel
sukkuku◊ *adj.* deaf
sukru+ *n.* bolt, bar, latch
sukurtu† *nf.* embargo, suspension, closure*, seclusion*, occlusion*, stoppage*
sullû* *v.* to appeal, pray to
sullû B* *n.* disloyal speech, impudence, deception
sulû* *n.* street, track, lane
sūlû+ *n.* disapproval, rejection, refusal
sulummû*  *n.* peace, nonaggression*
sumaktar◊  *adj.* fatherless
sumāmītu *nf.* poisonous matter
sumkinnu* *n.* rot, decayed matter
summatu* *nf.* dove, pigeon
su'mu  *n.* redness
sūmu *n.* redness, red spot, carbuncle
sūmu B* *n.* indecision
sunābu *n.* (a bandage or loincloth)
sungirtu◊  *nf.* (a meadow plant)
sunnāka *adv.* from here
sunqu*  *n.* want, famine
sūntu *nf.* violet wool
sūnu *n.* lap, thigh
sūnu B  *n.* loincloth
supālu* *n.* (a kind of) cypress
supāqu *n.* (a garment)
supīrtu *nf.* clipping(?)
suppinnu* *n.* toggle
suppû* *v.* to pray; prayer
supuḫru  *n.* cedar resin
supuqtu 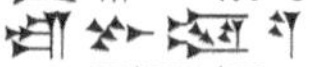 *nf.* (an object)
supurgillu  *n.* quince
supūru* *n.* sheepfold; halo
sūq erbetti* *n. cp.* intersection
sūqāiu+ *n.* huckster
suqāqu *n.*[3] alley, by-street, lane, narrow street, side street, street
suqāqu+ *n.*[3] narrow passage
sūqinnu† *n.* lane, narrow path
sūqu *n.*[2/3] street
sūqu+ *n.*[2/3] bazaar, market, open space, square
surāru *n.*[1] prayer
surdû* *n.* falcon, hawk
surḫu* *n.* rapture
surqinnu*  *n.*[1] offering
surqu* *n.* strewn offering(?)
surrāti* *n.pl.* lies, treason
surriš* *adv.* in a moment, for a moment, quickly, soon
surru* *n.* fallacy
sūrtu* *nf.* twirl
sūsabinnu* *n.* paranymph, groomsman, best man
sūsabinnūtu* *nf.* role of best man
sūsān nakkanti *n. cp.* trainer of reserve horses
sūsān ša-pattūti *n. cp.* horse trainer of open chariot
sūsān ša-šēpi *n. cp.* horse trainer of the royal guard
sūsānu *n.*[1] horse trainer, chariot-man, groom
sūsānu+ *n.*[1] ostler
sussullu  *n.* box, chest
sūsu *n.* liquorice, liquorice tree
sūsu B* *n.* (bubalis) antelope

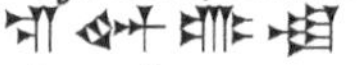

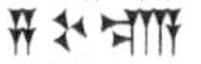

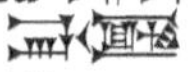

suttinnu*  *n.* bat

sūtu  *nf.* seah, peck; decare

su''u  *n.* [1] dove, pigeon; carrier pigeon

ṣāb ēkalli *n. cp.* palace personnel

ṣāb eleppi* *n. cp.* seaman, marine; ship's crew

ṣāb ḫupši* *n. cp.* common man, commoner, plebeian; common soldiers, common people

ṣāb kakki* *n. cp.* warrior(s), troops

ṣāb qassi  *n. cp.* archer(s), archery unit, archery

ṣāb ṣēri* *n. cp.* nomad(s)

ṣāb šarri  *n. cp.* draftee; king's men

ṣāb šarrūtu  *n. cp.* military service, conscription

ṣāb tāḫāzi* *n. cp.* combat troops

ṣabāru  *v.* $^{u/u}$ to twinkle, blink, wink; to chirp, chirrup, peep, prattle, twitter, warble; tochat, chatter, mutter; to flit

ṣabāru+ *v.* $^{u/u}$ to talk foolishly, brawl, gossip, prate, twaddle, babble

ṣabāru B *v.* $^{a/u}$ to spin; (Š) to make spin, swirl

ṣabātu  *v.* $^{a/a}$ to seize, grasp, grip; to apprehend, arrest, capture; to take hold of, confiscate, grab, take over; to take on, take up, undertake; to conceive; to adopt

ṣabātu*  *v.* $^{a/a}$ (Gt) to wrestle

ṣabātu  *v.* $^{a/a}$ (D) to fasten, fix in place, affix; (Š) to install, put in place, set up, settle; to prepare, make ready; to equip, furnish, provide with, supply with

ṣabbutānu *adj., n.* disabled, incapacitated, lame

ṣabbutu *adj.* fastened, fixed, installed; arrested, captured; connected

ṣabbutu* *adj.* consecutive; successive; lame

ṣābirtu* *nf.* spinster

ṣābiru* *adj.* chatterbox, telltale, talebearer, tattletale, tattler

ṣābit abbūti *n. cp.* intercessor, mediator

ṣabītu  *nf.* gazelle

ṣābitu  *nf.* keeper, depositary

ṣabītu+ *nf* doe, roe [deer]

ṣābitu a. *adj.* arresting, catchy, magnetic

ṣābitūtu* *nf.* magnetism

ṣabtu  *n.* prisoner, convict, inmate; captured, possessed, taken, stuck

ṣabû◊  *v.* $^{i/i}$ to wish, desire; to need

ṣābu  *n.* [2] [able-bodied] man, soldier; men, troops

ṣabû+ *v.* $^{i/i}$ to be willing, prefer, seek to, will, wish

ṣābu pānīu *np.* veteran, vet

ṣadānu*  *n.* (a tree or bush)

ṣādānu  *n.* vertigo

ṣadāru* *v.* squint, twitch, blink

ṣaddu*  *n.* sign, signal

ṣadīdu  *n.* antimony

ṣâdu *n.* *a/u* to prowl, spin, whirl, swirl, twiddle

ṣâdu◊ *v.* $^{a/u}$ to whirl; to prowl, roam about; to turn about

ṣâdu* *v.* $^{a/u}$ (D) to make dizzy

ṣâdu *v.* $^{a/u}$ (Gtn) to spin round and round, whirl, to become dizzy*, faint*

ṣaḫāru  *v.* $^{i/i}$ to be small, be young, be minor; to shrink; (D) to deduct, diminish, lessen, reduce; (N) to shrink

ṣaḫāru+ *v.* $^{i/i}$ to dwindle

ṣaḫātu  *v.* to want; to be greedy for, covet, desire, hanker for, lust for

ṣaḫātu B*  *v.* $^{a/u}$ to press (out), squeeze

ṣaḫittu  *nf.* wish, desire; luxury item, article of value

ṣaḫittu kašādu‡ *vp.* to attain goal

ṣāḫitu 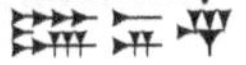 *n.* oilpresser, desirous*, covetous*, lascivious*

ṣaḫtu *adj.* desired, wanted

ṣaḫūrānīu* *adj.* boyish, juvenile, youthful

ṣaḫūrānūtu  *nf.* puberty, teens, youth

ṣaḫurtu 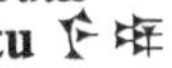 *nf.* adolescent, juvenile; youth, teenager

ṣaiādu* *n.* vagrant; hunter

ṣaiāḫu* *adj.* desirable*, elegant*, delicious, delightful, dainty, enjoyable, fancy, lovely

ṣaiāḫû* *adj.* coquette, coquettish, flirtatious

ṣā'idu* *adj.* roaming about, restless

ṣalālu* 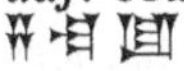 *v.* $^{a/a}$ to be at rest, kip [down], lie down, lie still, sleep, sleep in; (Š) to let sleep, put to rest

ṣalam ili *n. cp.* image of god

ṣalam šarri  *n. cp.* image of king, royal statue

ṣalāmu  *v.* $^{i/i}$ to be black; (D) to blacken

ṣalāpu* *v.* $^{i/i}$ to cut (at an angle), dissect; to distort

ṣalāpu+ *v.* $^{i/i}$ to bruise, cut, wound; (D) to open a little, set ajar

ṣalā'u† *v.* $^{i/i}$ to cast, throw, cast off, throw off; to put, put down, lay (down), set up; to miscarry, abort; (Š) to make abort; (stat.) to be situated

ṣalilu* *adj.* sleeping, sleepy, sleepy-head

ṣalintu *nf.* black woman

ṣaliptu* *nf.* lying, dishonesty, treachery

ṣalīpu+ *adj.* wounded; divided, dissentient

ṣalittu  *nf.* indigo-blue, blue-black wool

ṣallamtu* *nf.* black stone, basalt(?)

ṣallu 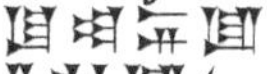 *n.* [1] tanned hide

ṣallû  *v.* to beg, entreat, pray, supplicate

ṣallu a.* *adj.* sleeping, sleepy, asleep

ṣallulu  *v.* to cover, roof

ṣallulu+ *v.* to shade, overshadow, ceil, lay rafters or planks

ṣallulu a. *adj.* covered, shaded, obscure, mystic[al]*

ṣallummû*  *n.* comet

ṣallumu  *n.* [2] (an amulet of wood)

ṣallumu a. *adj.* swarthy

ṣallupu* *adj.* ajar

ṣallūtu* *nf.* sleep

ṣalmāt kaqqidi* *n. cp.* human being

ṣalmu *adj.* effigy, figure, icon, image, likeness, statue

ṣalmu+ *n.* [2] idol, picture

ṣalmu B  *adj.* dark, black

ṣalpiš* *adv.* askance*, askew*

ṣalpu* *adj.* sliced; crooked, wicked, oblique*, skew*

ṣâltu* *nf.* fight

ṣâltu epēšu* *vp.* to fight a battle, engage in a fight

ṣâlu† *v.* to fight, contradict, object, quarrel, argue, bicker, contend, contest, wrangle, hassle, be contrary*, fall out*, jangle*

ṣalūlu *n.* shelter, protection

ṣâlūtu† *nf.* argument, debate, dispute

ṣamadāni* *n. pl.* teams

ṣamādu *v.* $^{i/i}$ to harness, hitch, yoke; to couple, join, link together; to combine, compound, connect; to attach; to bandage

ṣamādu*  *v.* $^{i/i}$ (N) to be harnessed, be conjoined

ṣamādu+ *v.* $^{i/i}$ to bind, bind up, bind together, buckle (on/up), fasten, fasten together, tie

ṣamāru* 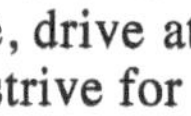 *v.* to strive for, aim for, aim, aspire, drive at, intend, wish; (Gt) to be intent on, strive for doggedly

ṣamdu+ *adj.* affiliated, bound, closely joined

ṣāmiru* *adj.* intent

ṣammuru* *n.* aim, intention, wish, goal

ṣamru* *adj.* intentional, premeditated

ṣamû◊ *adj.* to be thirsty, thirst; (D) to make thirsty

ṣanāḫu* *v.* $^{a/u}$ to excrete, have diarrhoea

ṣandu *adj.* coupled, joined

ṣandu* *adj.* bound up, harnessed, hitched up

ṣapāpu*  *v.* $^{u/u}$ to spread wings; to flap, flutter; (D) to keep aloft; (Š) to teach to fly

ṣapāru*  *v.* $^{i/i}$ to press down, inlay, inset; to wink; to strand, dress (hair), trim away

ṣāpītu* *nf.* tower

ṣāpiu  *n.* dyer

ṣappuḫu* *v.* to scatter, spill, run out (of s.th.)

ṣapû *v.* $^{u/u}$ to soak, drench, color, tinge

ṣapūnu◊ *n.* north

ṣarāḫu  *v.* $^{a/u}$ to be hot, be feverish, be warm; (D) to keep warm, warm up, to heat; (N) to become angry, hot, enraged

ṣarāḫu B* *v.* $^{a/u}$ to cry out, utter a cry; to sing a lamentation, lament, to yowl; (Š) to utter cries of mourning

ṣarāḫu B+ *v.* $^{a/u}$ to cry aloud, groan, screech, scream, squall

ṣarāḫu C* *v.* $^{u/u}$ to flare up, flash, scud

ṣarāḫu C+ *v.* $^{u/u}$ to catch fire, take fire, coruscate, crackle, crash

ṣarāku* *v.* to gut, disembowel

ṣarāmu  *v.* $^{i/i}$ to endeavour, make an effort, strive, try to

ṣarāmu+ *v.* $^{i/i}$ to be determined, dare, venture

ṣarāpu  *v.* $^{a/u}$ to dye (red); to burn, bake; to smelt, refine; (D) to give burning pain, torture

ṣarāpu+ *v.* $^{a/u}$ to clear, purge, refine; (D) to afflict, clarify, chastise, punish

ṣarāru  *v.* $^{u/u}$ to drip, ooze, trickle; (D) to libate, let drop

ṣarāru B* *v.* $^{u/u}$ to flare up, flash, twinkle

ṣarātu *v.* $^{i/i}$ to fart

ṣarbutu  *nf.* Euphrates poplar; poplar wood

ṣarḫiš* *adv.* ardently, warmly

ṣarḫu *adj.* hot, warm; muggy, sultry, sweltering; inflamed;ardent, hot-tempered

ṣarḫu lā ṣarḫu* *adj. phr.* lukewarm, tepid

ṣarḫūtu  *nf.* heat

ṣarip duḫšî *n. cp.* tanner of colored leather

ṣaripu *n.* tanner

ṣâripu+ *adj.* pungent

ṣâriru*  *n.* fine gold

ṣarmu+ *adj.* daring, determined, intrepid, plucky

ṣarmūtu+ *nf.* determination, hardihood

ṣarpiš* *adv.* loud and bitterly

ṣarpu  *n.* silver

ṣarpu a. *adj.* fired, baked; refined

ṣarramu* *adj.* very keen, eager

ṣarrāp kaspi  *n.* *cp.* refiner of silver, silversmith

ṣarrāpu 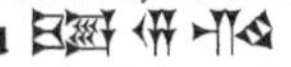 *n.*[2] goldsmith

ṣarrāpu+ *n.*[2] metal-worker, refiner of silver

ṣarrat šamê  *n.* *cp.* (lead rope of heaven, an astrological work)

ṣarritu  *n.* farter

ṣarru 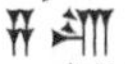 *n.*[1] sheaf

ṣarṣāru  *n.* cooler

ṣarṣāru B* *n.* cricket

ṣarṣūru+ *n.* canker-worm, grub, locust

ṣâssu *nf.* argument, dispute, fight, quarrel, run-in; conflict, strife, controversy, confrontation; polemics, contradiction*

ṣâssu garû *vp.* to have a quarrel, have a dispute; to quarrel, argue, wrangle, fight, litigate, fall out; to initiate proceedings, start a lawsuit, sue

ṣaṣumtu*  *nf.* (a medicinal plant, perhaps manna)

ṣâti *n. pl.* distant time, far-off days; antiquities, archaisms; scholastic explanations, scholia

ṣâtiš* *adv.* for ever, for the future

ṣēdu *adj.* melted, molten, smelted

ṣeḫer iṣṣūrē *n. cp.* fowlherdboy

ṣeḫer u rabi‡ *np.* everyone, everybody, (liter. small and great)

ṣeḫertu *nf.* young girl

ṣeḫēru n.* *n.* boyhood, infancy, youth

ṣeḫḫeru  *adj.* very small, tiny, diminutive; young

ṣeḫrānu* *adj.* childish

ṣeḫru  *adj.,n.2,4* small, minor, lesser; juvenile, underage; child, apprentice, manservant

ṣeḫru◊  *adj.,n.2,4* (pl.) rank and file

ṣēlāniš* *adv.* sideways

ṣelpu+ *n.* chink, cranny, rift

ṣelû◊ *v.*[i/i] to fight, object

ṣēlu  *nf.* rib

ṣēlūtu* *nf.* quarrel, dispute, enmity, contest, conflict

ṣemēru* *v.* to swell up, be swollen, bloated

ṣennītu* *nf.* (a skin disease)

ṣennītu+ *nf.* gout

ṣennu* *adj.* wicked

ṣēnu* 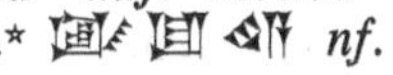 *nf.* flock of sheep and goats

ṣēnu B* *adj.* laden [with]

ṣēnu B+ *n.* dependant, freight, load

ṣepru+ *n.* small bird, finch, sparrow

ṣēr* *adv., prp.* over, upon; above, on top of, in addition to; towards, against

ṣēriš* *prp.* towards, against; above, over

ṣerrānu *adj.* snake-like, snakish, snaky

ṣerret šamê *nf. cp.* Galaxy; Milky Way

ṣerretu*  *nf.* lead, lead rope, leash

ṣerretu šakānu‡ *vp.* to tether

ṣerretu B* *nf.* breast, tit, udder

ṣerru  *n.* snake, serpent

ṣēru*  *n.* open country, plain, steppe, wilderness; back, upper side; battlefield

ṣeṣru+ *n.* cockroach

ṣēt sīn* *n. cp.* moonlight

ṣēt šamši  *n. cp.* sunlight

ṣētu  *nf.* heat, light, drought

ṣê'u  *v.* to throw, hurl, repulse(?)

ṣiāḫu* *v.* to laugh, smile; to cry; (Gtn) to laugh a lot, behave coquettishly, giggle, snigger; (D) to make laugh, amuse

ṣiānu  *v.* to heap, load, pile, stow

ṣibāru*  *n.* excrescence

ṣibāru B* *n.* sparrow

ṣibit appi* *n. cp.* instant, moment

ṣibit libbi *n. cp.* presence of mind, self-control

ṣibit ṭēmi* *n. cp.* action, decisive action, decision

ṣibittu*  *nf.* imprisonment, captivity; work procedures, training(?)

ṣibtu  *n.*[3] grip; seizure, fit; hold, capacity

ṣibtu B†  *nf.* interest (on money etc.)

ṣiburu *n.* aloe

ṣibūtu* *nf.* wish, desire; need; objective, intention, plan; enterprise

ṣidītu*  *nf.* viaticum, travel provisions

ṣidru+ *n.* mania, headache, dizziness

Ṣīdūnu Sidon

ṣiḫittu  *nf.* desire, wish

ṣīḫtu  *nf.* coquetry*, amorous dalliance*, flirtation*, love play*

ṣīḫtu*  *nf.* laughter

ṣilbānu 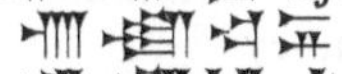 *n.* (a poultice)

ṣiliptu* 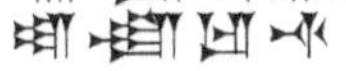 *nf.* (diagonal) dissection; diagonal, hypotenuse

ṣillānu* *adj.* shade-loving, shady, shadowy, dusky, sombre
ṣillānu+ *adj.* seeming, apparent
ṣillu *n.* shadow, shade; protection, shelter; auspices, aegis
ṣimirtu* *nf.* bloatedness, distension
ṣimirtu+ *nf.* gallstone, kidney stone, strangury
ṣimittu* *nf.* (yoked) team; pair, couple
ṣimmittu *nf.* (an architectural feature)
ṣimtu *nf.* (a type of beer)
ṣindāti* *nf. pl.* connections
ṣindatu* *nf.* regulation, ordinance, edict
ṣindu *n.* bandage; team; coupling, fastening
ṣindu u birtu* *np.* mob, rifraff, proletariat, common people
ṣinḫu* *n.* excretion
ṣinnutu *nf.* double-pipe, oboe
ṣipirtu *nf.* (woven) girdle, sash, waist-belt, cummerbund
ṣippatu* *nf.* orchard
ṣippirrāti *nf. pl.* early morning
ṣippu *n.* (mng. uncert.)
ṣippu† *n.* (seventh month)
ṣipputu *nf.* cover
ṣippūtu *nf.* (a tree)
ṣiprāti+ *nf. pl.* daybreak, dawn
ṣipru* *n.*[3] crest, coma (of a comet); spike, beak, point
ṣīpu *n.* dyeing; submersion, soaking, drenching, hue*
ṣīr āli* *n. cp.* city emissary
ṣirḫu* *n.* flare, flash
ṣiriḫ libbi* *n. cp.* inflammation
ṣiriḫtu* *nf.* moan, groan, wail
ṣiriptu* *nf.* reddening, discoloration
ṣirpu *n.*[2] red dyed wool
ṣirru* *n.* door-pivot, socket for doorpost
ṣirru+ *n.* (upper or lower) door socket, lower stone (of door)
ṣirû◊ *n.* brim
ṣīru *n.*[2] ambassador, envoy, (foreign) chieftain, noble, diplomat*
ṣīru+ *n.*[2] emissary, delegate
ṣīru a.* *adj.* elevated, exalted, lofty, sublime; august, eminent, noble, outstanding
ṣīrūtu* *nf.* eminence, exaltedness, highness, loftiness, supremacy
ṣiṣītu* *nf.* heddle
ṣiṣṣu* *n.* bar, manacles(?)

ṣīt libbi* *n. cp.* offspring, child
ṣīt pî* *n. cp.* command, utterance
ṣīt šamši* *n. cp.* sunrise, east
ṣītān* *adv.* in the east
ṣītu* *nf.* exit; issue; outcome; loss, consequence*, effect*, aftermath*, repercussion*, upshot*
ṣuādu *v.* to melt (down), fuse, become molten, smelt; (D) to melt, refine, smelt
ṣubāt balti* *nf. cp.* festive garment
ṣubāt ēni* *nf. cp.* blinder(?)
ṣubāt qabli* *nf. cp.* loincloth
ṣubātu *nf.* cloth, textile; garment, dress
ṣubbû* *v.* to observe, inspect, look at; (Š) to plan
ṣūd pāni* *n. cp.* dizziness, giddiness, vertigo
ṣūdāru+ *n.* drowsiness, heaviness, headache
ṣuddê* *n. pl.* (travel) provisions
ṣudduru* *adj.* squinting, cross-eyed
ṣūdu *n.*[3] molten metal, fusion*
ṣūdu B* *adj.* whirling
ṣuḫāru* *n.* employee
ṣuḫḫu* *adj.* amused*, laughing, smiling; laughable, ridiculous, trivial
ṣuḫḫuru* *adj.* very small
ṣuḫītu◊ *nf.* laughingstock, mockery
ṣuḫrītu* *nf.* youth
ṣuḫru* *n.* youth
ṣūḫu* *n.*[3] humor*, laugh, laughter, fun, amusement, frolic, mirth; love play
ṣuḫurtu *nf.* youth, adolescence
ṣūlāti* *n. pl.* fighting, battle
ṣullû* *n.*[1] prayer, observance
ṣullulu* *adj.* obscure, dark
ṣulmu* *n.* blackness; black spot, blackhead; black wood, ebony
ṣulūl ēni+ *n. cp.* eye shadow
ṣulultu* *nf.* roofing, covering; diaphragm
ṣulūlu *n.* roofing; shade, shadow; shelter, protection, coverage*, lee*
ṣulūlu+ *n.* defence
ṣumāmītu *nf.* thirst
ṣumbu* *n.*[2/3] wagon
ṣumlaliu *n.* (a spice plant)
ṣummû* *n.* thirst, need, want
ṣummurtu* *nf. pl.* (pl.) wish, objective, goal, endeavour
ṣummuru* *n.* desire, wish, purpose

ṣumrāt libbi* *nf. cp. pl.* aim, ambition, aspiration, intention
ṣumru* *n.* intent*, desire, purpose
ṣūmu *n.* thirst
ṣūmu+ *n.* fasting
ṣuppān* *n.* half-rope (60 cubits = 30 metres)
ṣuppu† *v.* to rub down
ṣuppu a. *adj.* polished
ṣupru *n.* [1] nail, fingernail; claw, talon; hoof; nailmark
ṣupur ubān šēpi* *n. cp.* toenail
ṣupur ubāni* *n. cp.* fingernail
ṣūrāmu+ *n.* determination, resolution, spunk
ṣurārītu* *nf.* lizard
ṣurārītu+ *nf.* eft, (yellow) lizard, newt, salamander
ṣurāru *n.* [1] libation
ṣūrat ṣilli+ *nf. cp.* silhouette
ṣurḫu *n.* heat; warmth; temperature
ṣurīrītu *nf.* lizard
ṣurīrû *n.* lizard
ṣurru *n.* obsidian, flint
Ṣurru Tyre
ṣurrušu* *v.* to sprout, branch (out)
ṣurru B* *n.* heart, mind
ṣurtu* *nf.* flint blade, obsidian
ṣūṣû* *n.* reed thicket
ṣūṣunu *n.* (a fruit tree, possibly walnut or mulberry)
ṣu'ubtu *nf.* (a designation of sheep)
ša *pron.* that; what; of; per; (he) who; although, though
ša adanni* *adj. cp.* periodical
ša aḫāiš *adj., adv.* mutual(ly)
ša akāli *adj. cp.* eatable, edible
ša amāri* *adj. cp.* appreciable
ša ana epāši lā illakūni‡ *adj. phr.* impracticable
ša ana epāši ṭābūni *adj. phr.* practicable, viable
ša bādi *adv.* in the evening
ša bētāni *adj. cp.* inner
ša birti *adj. cp.* intermediary, intermediate
ša da'āni *adv.* by force, forcibly
ša ēnšu namratūni‡ *adj. phr.* sharp-sighted
ša ḫalāqi* *adj. cp.* perishable
ša ḫapê *adj. cp.* breakable, destructible
ša ḫasāsi* *adj. cp.* memorable
ša iḫakkimūni* *adj. phr.* comprehensible, conceivable, perceptible
ša kil *adv.* by express
ša kušīri* *adj. cp.* profitable, serviceable, useful
ša lā *prp.* without; -less; without permission; against the will, contra; regardless of
ša lā balāṭi *adj. cp.* incurable
ša lā bēli *adj. cp.* ownerless, without an owner
ša lā bēti *adj. cp.* homeless
ša lā dulli *adj. cp.* without work, easily, effortlessly
ša lā ḫiṭṭi+ *adj. cp.* seamless
ša lā iggammaru* *adj. phr.* inexhaustible
ša lā iḫakkimūni *adj. phr.* incomprehensible, unintelligible, ununderstandable
ša lā ilāni* *adv.* godless(ly)
ša lā immaḫḫaru* *adj. phr.* irresistible
ša lā innennû* *adj. phr.* inalterable
ša lā iššabbû* *adj. phr.* insatiable
ša lā iššannanu* *adj. phr.* unrivalled
ša lā mašê *adj. cp.* unforgettable
ša lā memmēni *adv.* without any trouble
ša lā naparšudi* *adj. cp.* from which there in no escape
ša lā nībi* *adj. cp.* countless
ša lā paqāri *adj. cp.* infallible, incontestable, indisputable, peremptory, undeniable, unobjectionable, unquestionable
ša lā pašāri *adj. cp.* indissoluble, inexplicable, insoluble
ša lā paṭāri *adj. cp.* incurable
ša lā pî *adv.* without permission, unauthorized
ša lā šunnê *adj. cp.* immutable, inalterable, unchangeable, unalterable
ša madādi* *adj. cp.* measurable
ša maḫāṣi* *adj. cp.* vulnerable
ša mūši *adv.* in the night, during the night, at night, by night
ša pān *adj. cp.* pre-
ša pān abūbi* *adj. phr.* antediluvian, prehistoric
ša pašāri* *adj. cp.* digestible, explicable, soluble
ša pî *adj., np.* oral, (oral) tradition, lore
ša pî nišē *adj. cp.* colloquial, vernacular; popular
ša pitti *adj. cp.* consistent with, subject to
ša pūti *adj. cp.* opposite
ša qāt *adj. cp.* under the command of
ša raddê *np.* addendum
ša ramini- *adj. cp.* own
ša simini* *adj. cp.* temporary
ša šatti *adj. cp.* yearly
ša šatti ša šatti *adv.* every year
ša šiāri nubatti *adv.* morning and evening

ša šiddi tānti* *adj. cp.* coastal, seaside
ša šunāia guggalīpi-* *adj. phr.* two-humped
ša šunāia karrūni *adj. phr.* two-humped
ša šunāia ṣēri-* *adj. phr.* two-humped

ša tabrâti* *adj. cp.* amazing, astonishing, admirable, marvellous, wonderful, wondrous
ša tadāni* *adj. cp.* payable, saleable
ša ūmi *adv.* by day, at daytime
ša ūmi ana ūmi *adv.* as of now, at present
ša ūmi ša ūmi *adv.* every day
ša urḫi *adv.* monthly
ša urki *adj. cp.* post-
ša ušābi* *adj. cp.* habitable
ša- *part.* to cause to, compel, force to, make to
ša-abāri* *n. cp.* wrestler
ša-akussēšu *n. cp.* soup vendor
ša-ālāni *n. cp.* administrator of towns
ša-arīti *n. cp.* shield-man, (regular) spear-man
ša-bābi  *n. cp.* janitor
ša-bēt-kīli* *n. cp.* jailer, prison official
ša-bēt-kiṣri *n. cp.* (linen) attendant
ša-bēt-kūdini 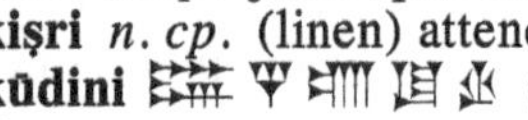 *n. cp.* mule-stable man
ša-bēt-qiqî  *n. cp.* (a domestic)
ša-bēt-šaknūti *n. cp.* (employee) of the house of the prefects
ša-bēt-šumēli *n. cp.* (employee) of the Left House
ša-bēti-šanie *n. cp.* lackey, valet
ša-billēšu *n. cp.* ale-monger
ša-birme *n. cp.* garment with multicolored trim
ša-bīrti  *n. cp.* garrison troops
ša-būri *n. cp.* well administrator
ša-dabābi *n. cp.* (a court official)
ša-dannēšu *n. cp.* cooper*
ša-dēnāni *n. cp.* lawman
ša-dūdēšu *n. cp.* kettler
ša-ebissēšu *n. cp.* bundle carrier(?)
ša-ēkallāti *n. cp.* (a palatial profession)
ša-ēkurri *n. cp.* clergyman, temple warden
ša-endēšu *n. cp.* incense dealer
ša-epinni  *n. cp.* ploughman

This space intentionally left blank.

ša-eqli *n. cp.* peasant(?)
ša-erêšu  *n. cp.* copper peddler
ša-gabêšu *n. cp.* alum maker, druggist*, pharmacist*
ša-gaṣṣātēšu *n. cp.* firewood peddler
ša-ginêšu *n. cp.* official in charge of the regular offering
ša-gišalli* *n. cp.* oarsman
ša-ḫalluptēšu *n. cp.* harness-maker, armor-maker, armorer
ša-ḫallupti  *n. cp.* harness-suit
ša-ḫassupi *n. cp.* tweezers
ša-ḫimātī† *n. cp.* butter trader, ghee trader
ša-ḫuppānēšu *n. cp.* basket-seller
ša-ḫurdati *n. cp.* petticoat, sanitary towel
ša-ḫusinnēšu *n. cp.* (a peddler)
ša-ḫuṭārēšu *n. cp.* staff maker
ša-ḫuṭāri *n. cp.* staff-bearer, officer
ša-imitti *n. cp.* right-sider (he who sits at the right side), second-in-esteem
ša-irti  *n. cp.* infant at the breast, nurseling
ša-irti B *n. cp.* pectoral, breastplate, chest-plate
ša-issi *n. cp.* accomplice, collaborator
ša-kalbāni *n. cp.* keeper of (hunting) dogs
ša-kaqqidi  *n. cp.* head covering, head-scarf
ša-kāribi  *n. cp.* votive offering
ša-karri *n. cp.* (mng. uncert.)
ša-kīma† *n. cp.* representative
ša-kitturrēšu *n. cp.* stool-bearer
ša-kubšēšu *n. cp.* cap-maker, fez-maker, hatter, milliner*
ša-kūdini *n. cp.* mule man
ša-kurrēšu *n. cp.* seller of tanning fluid
ša-kuzippēšu* *n. cp.* dressmaker
ša-libbi  *n. cp.* foetus, embryo
ša-lišāni  *n. cp.* informer, orator*
ša-manê *n. cp.* abacus
ša-maṣṣarti  *n. cp.* guard, sentry, sentinel
ša-mê-qāti  *n. cp.* ewer
ša-mēlê *n. cp.* hill guard
ša-midlēšu *n. cp.* salt-meat trader
ša-muḫḫi-āli  *n. cp.* mayor
ša-muḫḫi-ālūtu *nf. cp.* office of the mayor
ša-muḫḫi-bābi  *n. cp.* overseer of the gate
ša-muḫḫi-bēt-Aššūr *n. cp.* overseer of the temple of A&&ur
ša-muḫḫi-bēt-ilāni *n. cp.* overseer of the temple
ša-muḫḫi-bēt-ili *n. cp.* temple overseer
ša-muḫḫi-bēt-rēdûti *n. cp.* overseer of the Succession Palace
ša-muḫḫi-bēt-šarrāni *n. cp.* overseer of the royal tombs
ša-muḫḫi-bēt-šarri *n. cp.* overseer of the royal residence
ša-muḫḫi-bētāni  *n. cp.* chamberlain
ša-muḫḫi-bēti  *n. cp.* overseer of the household
ša-muḫḫi-ēkalli *n. cp.* overseer to the palace
ša-muḫḫi-kanni *n. cp.* keeper of the wine cellar
ša-muḫḫi-kezrēti *n. cp.* overseer of the coiffured women
ša-muḫḫi-mê *n. cp.* water administrator
ša-muḫḫi-Nīnua *n. cp.* overseer of the city of Nineveh
ša-muḫḫi-nīri  *n. cp.* yoke finial
ša-muḫḫi-qanāti  *n . cp.* overseer of reeds
ša-muḫḫi-qāti *n. cp.* overseer of the storehouse(?)
ša-muḫḫi-quppi *n. cp.* cashier
ša-muḫḫi-šaḫūri *n. cp.* overseer of the šahūru building
ša-muḫḫi-x *n. cp.* overseer of [...]
ša-mušēzibti *n. cp.* protective shield carrier
ša-mutqītēšu *n. cp.* candy peddler
ša-muttāqi *n. cp.* cake man
ša-naḫbêšu◊ *n. cp.* drinks vendor
ša-naptini *n. cp.* dinner-attendant, waiter
ša-narkabti *n. cp.* charioteer
ša-nukuššēšu *n. cp.* hinge maker
ša-pān-bābi 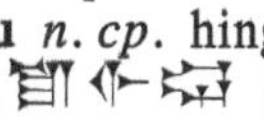 *n. cp.* gate supervisor
ša-pān-bēt-qāti  *n. cp.* supervisor of the storehouse
ša-pān-bēt-ṭuppāti* *n. cp.* archivist
ša-pān-bēti *n. cp.* supervisor of the house
ša-pān-daiāni *n. cp.* president of tribunal
ša-pān-dēnānī 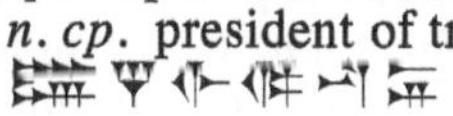 *n. cp.* president of the court
ša-pān-ēkalli *n. cp.* palace supervisor
ša-pān-ēkurri *n. cp.* supervisor of the temple
ša-pān-girginakki* *n. cp.* librarian
ša-pān-manê *n. cp.* accountant
ša-pān-mugirri *n. cp.* chariot supervisor

ša-pān-nērebi *n. cp.* concierge
ša-pān-nuḫatimmi *n. cp.* supervisor of cooks
ša-pān-sūqi *n. cp.* supervisor of the streets, street inspector
ša-pān-ša-šadādi *n. cp.* rickshaw supervisor
ša-pānīti *n. cp.* (a bodyguard)
ša-paqādi* *n. cp.* candidate
ša-parzillēšu *n. cp.* iron peddler
ša-patrēšu* *n. cp.* cutler
ša-patri *n. cp.* (a topographical term)
ša-pattūti *n. cp.* open chariot
ša-pê *n. cp.* information; (a garment)
ša-pētḫal qurubte *n. cp.* cavalry(man) of the royal guard
ša-pētḫalli *n. cp.* cavalryman, equestrian, horseman, rider
ša-pētḫallūtu* *nf. cp.* horsemanship
ša-pūlēšu *n. cp.* limestone peddler
ša-qabli *n. cp.* loincloth(?)
ša-qassi *n. cp.* bowman
ša-qašti* *n. cp.* bowman
ša-qātāti *n. cp.* guarantor
ša-qāti *n. cp.* bowl for washing hands; hand towel
ša-qurbūti *n. cp.* bodyguard
ša-qurubti *n. cp.* stand-by cavalryman, buddy*
ša-rēš šarri *n. cp.* royal eunuch
ša-rēši *n. cp.* eunuch, castrate
ša-rēšūtu *n. cp.* eunuchship, castration, emasculation
ša-sāgātēšu *n. cp.* tunic peddler
ša-salā'i *n. cp.* sprinkling can, sprinkler
ša-sikkāti *n. cp.* (a high military official)
ša-siqqurrātēšu *n. cp.* baker of seven-tiered cakes
ša-suādēšu *n. cp.* perfume peddler
ša-ṣallēšu *n. cp.* dealer in leather hides
ša-ṣilli *n. cp.* sunshade, parasol, umbrella
ša-ṣubātēšu* *n. cp.* mercer
ša-ṣūdi *n. cp.* melting pot
ša-ṣupri *n. cp.* nail-cutter
ša-šadādi *n. cp.* rickshaw
ša-šamni† *n. cp.* oil trader
ša-šāpti† *n. cp.* wool trader
ša-šarri *n. cp.* man of the king
ša-šēḫi *n. cp.* ecstatic, maniac, madman
ša-šēpi *n. cp.* (personal) guard, bodyguard
ša-šērāti *n. cp.* morning
ša-šēzubi† *n. cp.* rescuer, savior
ša-šīmi *n. cp.* bought slave
ša-šipri† *n. cp.* worker
ša-šipti *n. cp.* exorcist
ša-šumēli *n. cp.* left-sider (he who sits at the left side), first-in-esteem
ša-taḫlīpi *n. cp.* groom of armored chariot
ša-tāluk-ṣirri *n. cp.* (a garment, moving like a snake)
ša-tāmarti *n. cp.* looking glass, lens(?)
ša-tēlissi *n. cp.* purification device
ša-ṭābti† *n. cp.* salt trader
ša-umāši *n. cp.* athlete, combatant, wrestler
ša-urâni *n. cp.* attendant of teams(?)
ša-uzni *n. cp.* ear-man
ša-ziqni *n. cp.* bearded courtier
ša-zizibēšu *n. cp.* milk trader, milk seller, milkman, milk-dealer, milk-vendor
ša-zizibi *n. cp.* suckling, sucker
ša-zumbē *n. cp.* fly whisk
ša-zuqiti *n. cp.* (a cultic object)
ša'altu⁺ *nf.* petition, request, requisite
ša'ālu *v.* $^{a/a}$ to ask, consult, interrogate, question; to ask about, enquire, inquire; to ask for
ša'ālu⁺ *v.* $^{a/a}$ to beg, borrow, question, entreat, interrogate
ša'ālu uṣṣuṣu *vp.* to investigate thoroughly
ša'āru *v.* to be dirty
ša'āru* *v.* (Š) to make dirty
ša'āru *v.* (D) to make dirty, soil
ša'āru⁺ *v.* to be black, sooty; (D) to blacken, foul, char, make sooty
šabābu* *v.* $^{u/u}$ to glow, burn
šabābu⁺ *v.* $^{u/u}$ to break out, burn up, smolder, take fire slowly
šabāḫu◊ *v.* $^{a/u}$ to sprinkle; (D) to disperse(?)
šabalkutu *n.* upheaval
šabalkutu a. *adj.* helter-skelter, topsy-turvy, upside down
šabāru *v.* $^{i/i}$ to break, break up
šabāru⁺ *v.* $^{i/i}$ to refract

šabāsu* *v.* $^{u/u}$ to be angry
šabāšu *v.* $^{a/u}$ to collect, gather, gather together; to scoop up, to round up*
Šaba:#u *n.* (month) Shebat, February
šabāṭu B* *v.* $^{i/i}$ to blow, blast, hit, sweep
šabbaliltu* *nf.* fenugreek
šabbāsu* *adj.* angry, irascible
šabbiṭu* *n.* staff, sceptre
šabbiṭu+ *n.* truncheon
šabbu *adj.* contented, sated, satisfied
šabburtu* *nf.* tilled land
šābišu *n.* collector of straw tax
šabru *adj.* broken
šabrû* *n.* seer, dreamer; visionary, clairvoyant
šabsu◊ *adj.* angry, indignant
šabû *v.* $^{i/i}$ to get sated, be full, enjoy; to be satified; (D) to sate, fill with, satisfy
šâbu* *v.* $^{u/u}$ to sway, shake down, swing, waver to and fro; (stat.) to be flattened
šaburru* *n.* anus; bottom, deck
šad erēni* *n. cp.* cedar mountain
šadādu *v.* $^{a/u}$ to drag, haul, tow, tug, pull; to extend, stretch
šadādu* *v.* $^{a/u}$ to bear, endure, tolerate
šadādu *v.* $^{a/u}$ (Gtn) to endure
šadāḫu* *v.* $^{i/i}$ to march; to walk, stride, move forward, proceed, parade
šadālu* *v.* $^{i/i}$ to be broad; (D) to widen, broaden, enlarge, increase
šadattūnu *n.* (mng. uncert.)
šaddāiu* *n.* highlander, mountain-dweller, mountaineer
šaddānu *n.* haematite
šaddānu ṣābitu *n. cp.* magnetite, lodestone
šaddaqad◊ *adv.* last year
šaddaqdiš *adv.* last year
šaddidu* *n.* hauler, tower; draught(-animal)
šaddīnu *n.* [1] satin, silk
šaddīnu+ *n.* [1] sheet, wrapper
šaddu◊ *n.* [2] chest, trunk
šaddû *n.* [1/2] mountain; east wind, east, northeast
šaddu a.◊ *adj.* tense
šaddû'a* *n.* mountain-dweller
šadê◊ *n.* (a plant?)
šādid ašli *n. cp.* surveyor
šādidat ašli *n. cp.* female surveyor

šādidu* *adj.* patient, tolerant
šadlu* *adj.* broad, roomy, spacious, sumptuous
šadussu *nf.* one sixth
šagāgu* *v.* to stiffen, harden
šagammāḫu* *n.* exorcist
šagammu* *n.* door pivot
šagāmu *v.* $^{u/u}$ to roar, thunder; to resound, buzz; to chime, peal, ring
šagapīru* *adj.* mighty, majestic
šagāšu *v.* $^{i/i}$ to strike down, slay, annihilate; to slaughter, kill, murder, massacre
šagāšu+ *v.* $^{i/i}$ to be boisterous, rough up, rage, ruffle
šagbānu* *n.* chicken pox, smallpox
šaggaštu* *nf.* slaughter, massacre, murder, carnage; bout (of illness)
šaggāšu* *n.* robber, murderer, thug
šaggāšû* *adj.* murderous
šaggāšu+ *n.* partisan, ruffian
šaggīšu+ *adj.* disorderly, dangerous, unsettled
šagigurû* *n.* free-will offering
šāgimu* *adj.* roaring, thundering
šaglû *n.* [4] deportee
šaglūtu *nf.* deportation, exile
šaḫāḫu *v.* $^{u/u}$ to disintegrate, erode, flake off, waste away, to degenerate*
šaḫāḫu† *v.* $^{u/u}$ (D) to corrode, waste
šaḫālu◊ *v.* $^{a/u}$ to sift, sieve, filter
šaḫālu+ *v.* $^{a/u}$ to distill, drip, exude, strain, pour off, trickle
šaḫānu◊ *v.* $^{u/u}$ to be warm
šaḫāpu *n.* marsh boar, wild boar
šaḫarrāti *nf. pl.* (pl.) leggings
šaḫarru* *adj.* porous(?)
šaḫaršuppû *n.* leprosy
šaḫāru *v.* $^{a/u}$ to marry(?)
šaḫātu* *nf.* side, inside corner, hiding place
šaḫātu† *nf.* assistance, support
šaḫātu+ *nf.* armhole, armpit
šaḫātu emādu‡ *vp.* to seek refuge, to go into hiding
šaḫātu B* *v.* $^{u/u}$ to fear, be afraid; (D) to scare, intimidate
šaḫātu C+ *v.* to grow dull, rust; (Š) to befoul, cover with rust, sully, tarnish
šaḫāṭu *v.* $^{a/u}$ to strip, tear off, take off; to pull, pull off, detach, cast off
šaḫāṭu B *v.* $^{a/u}$ to rinse, swill, wash (away); to enamel, glaze

šaḫāṭu C* *v.* i/i to leap, jump, spring; to dart, bolt, scamper, scud, scurry, sprint; to assail, attack, come suddenly upon, fly at, plunge; to become angry; (Gtn) to leap up and down, bounce, caper, frisk, gambol
šaḫḫītu* *nf.* sailboat, sailing boat
šaḫḫu◊ *n.* canvas, cloth
šaḫḫû* *n.* canvas, sail
šaḫīlu *n.* (a garment)
šāḫilu◊ *n.* filter
šaḫīmu+ *adj.* greasy, swarthy
šaḫīnu+ *adj.* snug, warm
šaḫītu* *nf.* sow, female pig
šaḫītu B+ *nf.* condiment, sauce
šaḫluqtu* *nf.* annihilation, destruction, disaster, perdition
šaḫrartu* *nf.* deathly silence
šaḫruru *v.* to devastate, lay waste, make desolate
šaḫsasūtu *nf.* reminder, recollection
šaḫšaḫḫu* *n.* slanderer, scandalmonger
šaḫšūru *n.* apple (tree)
šaḫtu* *adj.* reverent, humble
šaḫû *n.* pig, boar
šāḫu *n.* can
šaḫurratu* *nf.* awesome silence, stillness
šaḫūru *n.* (a sanctuary)
šaiāṭu+ *n., adj.* despiser, scorner; contemptuous, disdainful, scornful
šā'iltu* *nf.* female dream interpreter, pythia
šā'ilu *n.* dream interpreter, interrogative*
šā'ilu B *n.* mantis, praying mantis
šā'imānu* *n.* buyer, purchaser
šakāku* *v.* a/u to harrow
šakāku† *v.* a/u to thread, string, string together
šakālu *v.* a/u (mng. unkn.)
šakānu *v.* a/u to place, set, set up, set down, put; to install, arrange, establish; to conclude; (Š) to provide with, institute; to settle; (N) to take place, ensue, result
šakartu *nf.* drunkenness
šakāru *v.* i/i to be drunk, be inebriated; (D) to make drunk, inebriate
šakāru+ *v.* i/i to be dull, be dizzy; (D) to intoxicate
šakātu *v.* (Š) to dispatch
šakin māti* *n. cp.* governor
šakintu *nf.* female administrator, manageress, directress
šakirūtu *nf.* henbane
šakkanakku* *n.* 1 governor, viceroy, representative
šakkiru *n.* 4 drunkard
šakku *n.* 1 (a wooden object)
šakkullu *n.* willow(?)
šakkulu *v.* to wipe, mop
šaklulu* *v.* to perfect, complete, restore; to carry to term, finish doing
šaklulu+ *v.* to finish, rebuild
šaklulu a. *adj.* immaculate, perfect, unblemished; uncastrated
šaklulu a.+ *adj.* finished, complete; adult, full-grown
šaklulu n. *n.* 4 perfect bull, ungelded bull
šaknu *n.* 4 (acting) governor; prefect; administrator; representative
šaknūtu *nf.* governorship, prefectship
šakrānu *n.* 4 drunkard, alcoholic*
šakrānūtu* *nf.* drunkenness, alcoholism
šakru *adj., n.* 4 drunk, tipsy
šakru+ *adj., n.* 4 intoxicated
šakrūnu+ *n.* henbane, soporific
šakṣu* *adj.* wild, wicked, scowling(?)
šākussu *nf.* feeding
šakuttu *nf.* jewellery, decoration, ornament
šalāgu* *v.* a/a to snow
šalāḫu *v.* a/u to pull out, take out, retrieve, tear off; to jerk, tug, twitch, yank
šalāḫu+ *v.* a/u to lay aside, put off, shed, slough [off], strip off, take off
šalāḫu B† *v.* a/u to dispatch, send off
šalāḫu B+ *v.* a/u (D) to expedite
šalāliš* *adv.* surreptitiously
šalālu* *v.* a/u to loot, plunder, take into captivity, prey
šalālu+ *v.* a/u to exploit
šalālu B* *v.* to creep, slither
šalām šamši* *n. cp.* sunset, west
šalamtu* *nf.* corpse, body, carcass
šalāmu *v.* i/i to be sound, whole, safe, be finished, be successful, to succeed, to manage to*; (D) to complete, restore; to look after, keep well; to defray, indemnify, make up for, replenish; to do completely, finish doing, to atone for*
šalāmu+ *v.* i/i to be complete, be concluded, be fulfilled, come to an end, end up, expire; (D) to break up with, conclude, deliver up, fulfil, hand over, make restitution, recompense
šalāmu n. *n.* health, well-being, welfare, survival
šalānu◊ *prp.* without

šalāpu *v.* a/u to pull out, tear out, extract, draw, unsheathe
šalāqu *v.* a/u to cut, slit open; to lacerate
šalāšā* *num.* thirty
šalāšāiu* *num.* thirtieth
šalāšīšu *adv.* three times, thrice
šalāšīšu arbīšu *adv.* repeatedly, several times
šalāšer(et)* *num.* thirteen
šalāššerīu* *num.* thirteenth
šalāšu *num.* three
šalāšu B* *v.* a/u (D) to do for a third time; to multiply by three, triple, treble
šalāṭu *v.* i/i to have authority over, dispose of (property); to control, dominate, rule; to claim authority
šalāṭu* *v.* i/i (Gt) to prevail, predominate
šalāṭu *v.* i/i (Š) to authorize, give authority over, entitle to do s.th.
šalāṭu⁺ *v.* i/i to be in charge, hold rule, hold sway, have power, have the mastery, prevail; (Š) to give permission, give power, vest in
šalā'u *v. a.u, u/u* to fling, hurl, shoot
šalbābu* *adj.* furious, raging; wise
šalgu* *n.* snow, sleet, slush
šalḫiu *n.* outer wall, rampart
šālilu* *n.* plunderer, looter
šalintu *nf.* safety, peace
šālipu *n.* (a profession)
šallāmu *n.* complement, resupply
šallāqītu⁺ *nf.* variola
šallaru* *n.* mortar, plaster
šallašatti◊ *adv.* the year before last
šallu* *adj.* snatched away, deported, plundered
šallumu⁺ *adj.* accomplished, finished, integral, perfected, whole
šallumu epāšu *vp.* to perform completely
šallumu tadānu *vp.* to pay in full, pay completely
šalluntu *nf.* completion, compensation; (complete) repayment, restitution, final accounting
šallūru *n.* cherry plum, prune, apricot
šallussu *nf.* one third
šallušu *adj.* treble, trebled, triple, threefold
šallutu *nf.* booty, plunder, loot, prey, spoil; prisoner of war, captive
šallūtu* *nf.* captivity
šalmiš *adv.* safely
šalmu *adj.* complete, whole, intact; undamaged, unhurt; innocuous, safe; healthy, sane, sober, sound; propitious, successful; honest, sincere, reliable; solvent
šalmūtu* *nf.* good condition, health, well-being
šalmūtu⁺ *nf.* approval, familiarity, integrity
šalputtu *nf.* ruin, ruination
šalšāiu* *adj.* third (in age)
šalši ūmi *adv., n.* day before yesterday
šalšiš* *adv.* thirdly
šalšu *num.* third
šalšūtīšu *adv.* for the third time
šalṭāniš* *adv.* haughtily, imperially, imperiously, victoriously
šalṭānu* *adj.* haughty, imperial, imperious
šalṭiš* *adv.* imperially
šalṭu *adj.* bow-case
šalṭu⁺ *adj.* lawful, permitted
šalṭūtu⁺ *nf.* predominance
šalṭu B *n.* authoritative, having authority
šalû* *v.* i/i to dive, plunge under water, submerge; to immerse o.s., wade
šalultu* *nf.* third (extispicy)
šalummatu* *nf.* luminous splendour
šalušševi *adv., n.* the year before last, two years ago
šalû B* *v.* u/u to spit, fling, kick up
šamādu *v.* i/i to apply
šamāḫu* *v.* u/u to grow abundantly, flourish, thrive; to be profuse, grow thickly; (D) to make flourish
šamallû *n.* apprentice, journeyman
šamallûtu *nf.* apprenticeship
šamāmī* *n.pl.* heaven(s)
šamāmiš* *adv.* like heaven
šamāmu* *v.* a/u to lame, paralyse, numb
šaman pūri* *n. cp.* oil from bowl
šaman rūšti* *n. cp.* first class oil
šaman samādiri *n. cp.* oil of blossom
šaman sirdi *n. cp.* olive oil
šamānāiu *num.* eightieth
šamāni *num.* eight
šamāru* *v.* u/u to be wild, be fierce, be spirited
šamāru B* *v.* (Gt) to extol, praise
šamaškillu *n.* onion, shallot
šamaššammē *n.pl.* sesame
šamātu◊ *v.* i/i to mark, brand
šamāṭu *v.* a/u to pluck out, brush off, wipe away, tear off, strip off, rip off, snatch
šamāṭu⁺ *v.* a/u to draw, draw out, pull off, pull out, tear out, unsheathe
šamê *n.pl.* heaven, sky
šamḫatu* *adj., nf.* harlot, prostitute
šamḫiš* *adv.* proudly

šamḫu* *adj.* luxuriant, lush, plush; gaudy, showy, tawdry; prosperous; bushy, profuse, thickset
šāmiānu* *n.* hearsay witness
šāmiu* *n., adj.* hearer, listener, obedient
šammāḫu* *n.* large intestine; paunch
šammi nipši  *n. cp.* lupin
šammi pašāri *n. cp.* medicine, drug
šammu  *n.* ^{2} plant, herb, drug
šammu+ *n.* ^{2} medicine, remedy, poison, pigment
šammu arku *n. cp.* (a climbing plant, long plant)
šammu balāṭi *n. cp.* medicine of life
šammu ša muāti *np.* fatal drug, poison
šammu ša muāti šaqû‡ *vp.* to poison
šammunu *v.* to anoint; (Dtt) to be anointed
šammušu+ *v.* (D) to bask
šammu B* *n.* emery
šamnu  *n.* oil; fat; cream
šamnu ṭābu *n. cp.* sweet oil, perfume*
šamriš* *adv.* impetuously, fiercely, furiously
šamru *adj.* fierce, furious, grim; impetuous, passionate, spirited; savage, wild, violent
šamšiš* *adv.* like the sun
šamšu  *n.* sun
šamṭu+ *adj.* bare, unshod, barefoot
šamû  *n.* to hear; to hark, heed, listen to, obey; (Gtn) to listen; (Š) to inform, notify, impart
šâmu* *v.* $^{a/a}$ to buy, purchase
šamû n. *n.* obedience
šamû ša Ani* *np.* seventh heaven
šamuttu† *nf.* beet
šamūtu* *nf.* rain
šanānu  *v.* $^{a/u}$ to rival, equal, vie
šanānu*  *v.* $^{a/u}$ (Gt) to compete, contend, contest
šanāṣu* *v.* $^{i/i}$ to sneer, scorn, scoff at, taunt
šanā'u* *v.* $^{a/u}$ to stifle, block
šandabakku*  *n.* chief accountant, governor of Nippur
šanduppu 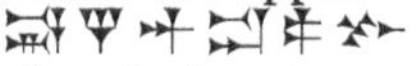 *n.* bead(?)
šanētu *nf.* female deputy
šaniānu* *adv.* secondly, for the second time
šāninu  *n.* competitor, contender, rival
šāniṣu* *adj.* sarcastic
šanīš  *adv.* differently, alternatively; ditto
šanītu *nf.* another thing, secondly
šanītu alāku* *vp.* to change course

šaniu  *num.* second, secondary*
šaniu a. *adj.* other, different
šaniu n. *n.* ^{4} deputy, assistant, adjunct
šannu'u *adj.* double(d)
šanšāntu *nf.* sun disk
šanšānu *nf.* sunlike, sunny
šanšu *n.* sun
šanû *v.* $^{i/i}$ to be different, to change
šanû* *v.* $^{i/i}$ to do again, do for a second time; (Gt) to be changeable, be conflicting, be contradictory, diverge from; (Gtn) to alternate, keep changing, vary, fluctuate; (Št) to duplicate, double, do again
šanû *v.* $^{i/i}$ (D) to do again, repeat; to relate, to narrate*, recount*, rehearse*, reiterate*; (Š) to change, alter, to alter*
šānû* *n.* runner, trotter
šanukkatu* *nf.* princess
šanuttēšu *adv.* once more, once again
šanu''udu* *adj.* illustrious, praised
šapāku*  *v.* $^{a/u}$ to pile, heap up; to pour, cast; to invest
šapāku†  *v.* $^{a/u}$ to invest
šapāku+ *v.* $^{a/u}$ to pour out, empty out, slop
šapal  *adv., prp.* under, below
šapal qāti *adv.* secretly, in secret, clandestinely, discreetly, underhand
šapālu *v.* $^{i/i}$ to be low, be humble; to go deep, go down, reach the lowest point; to be depressed
šapālu* *v.* $^{i/i}$ (Š) to abase
šapālu *v.* $^{i/i}$ (D) to lower; to degrade, demote, humiliate, mortify; to bend down, incline; (Dtt) to move downstream
šapālu+ *v.* $^{i/i}$ (D) to abase, bring low, cast down, lay low; (Š) to bring low, overpower
šapāpu* *v.* to move along, drift, glide
šapāpu+ *v.* to move softly, crawl, sneak
šapartu  *nf.* pledge, gage
šapāru  *v.* $^{a/u}$ to send; to send word, write to; to direct, enjoin, order, rule
šapāru*  *v.* $^{a/u}$ to govern, administer
šaparziqqu* *n.* (a wind)
šapassu *nf.* sealing
šapāṣu* *v.* $^{i/i}$ to clasp, grip, to enfold; (Gt) to wrestle, grapple, grapple with; (D) to keep enfolded
šapattu* *nf.* fifteenth day, fortnight
šapāṭu* *v.* to issue strict orders, threaten
šapêlu *v.* to barter, exchange, trade, trade in; to transfer; to answer (by), counter
šapiltu* *nf.* anvil, anvil-stone; lower part
šapīnutu *nf.* boat
šapīnutu+ *nf.* ship

šāpiru *n.* [1] administrator; sender
šāpirūtu* *nf.* sovereignty
šapku* *adj.* cast; dense
šapla *prp.* below, under
šapla qāti‡ *adv.* discreetly, secretly
šaplān šēpi* *n. cp.* sole of the foot
šaplāniš* *adv.* underneath, below
šaplānu- *prp., adv.* below, under; inwardly
šaplāti* *n. pl.* lower parts, netherworld
šapliš *adv.* below, down; downward[s], downhill, downstream
šaplītu* *nf.* bottom part; suffix
šaplīu *adj.* lower, nether
šaplu *n.* underside, bottom
šaplu a. *adj.* low, lowly, humble, mean; lower, nether, inferior
šaplu a.+ *adj.* base, wretched, cowardly
šappu *n.* [1] bowl
šappulu *adj.* abased, abject, degraded, downcast, humiliated
šapputu *nf.* (a large wine jar, jug)
šapru *n.* [3/4] envoy, messenger, errand boy*
šaprutu *nf.* (a kind of real estate)
šaprūtu *nf.* delegation, embassy
šapru B *n.* [3/4] pledge
šapru C* *n.* thigh
šapṣu* *adj.* defiant, obstinate, recalcitrant, wayward
šapšāqu* *n.* constraint, hardship
šapšuqu *adj.* recondite
šaptu *nf.* lip; rim, brim, edge
šāptu *n. pl.* wool
šaptu+ *nf.* brink
šapû* *v.* u/u to be dense, intense, keen, loud; to surge, swell up und down; (D) to intensify, to condense*, emphasize*, highlight*
šāpû *adj.* manifest, illustrious, shining, splendid, apparent, obvious*, evident*
šapû a.* *v.* u/u dense, loud, thick, concrete, material, sonorous, substantial, tangible
šapūlu *n.* inner thigh, groin
šapūssu *nf.* exchange
šapû B* *v.* i/i to wrap, lace
šaqālu* *v.* a/u to weigh, pay; to balance, suspend; (Gt) to be in balance, equilibrium
šaqāru* *v.* i/i to pierce
šaqiš* *adv.* high up; highly, loudly, aloud
šāqītu *nf.* female cupbearer
šaqiu *adj.* high, lofty, elevated; prominent, sublime
šāqiu *n.* cupbearer, butler
šaqlu* *adj.* weighed out
šaqû *v.* i/i to give to drink, serve drinks; to irrigate, water
šaqummatu* *nf.* silence, gloom
šaqummiš* *adv.* silently
šaqû B *v.* u/u to be high, elevated; to climb
šaqû B* *v.* u/u (D) to exalt, make high, raise up; (Š) to elevate, heighten, make higher
šār* *adj., num.* saros (3600); countless, myriad
šār ilāni *n. cp.* spirit of God
šar pūḫi *n. cp.* substitute king, regent
šarābu+ *v.* to deny, negate
šarāḫu* *v.* u/u to be glorious, splendid, proud; (D) to make proud, splendid; to glorify; (Dt) to act arrogantly, be haughty, boast, bluster, brag, glory in, pride o.s., show off, vaunt
šarāku *v.* a/u to present, endow
šarāku B* *v.* i/i to fester, suppurate, discharge pus
šarāmu *v.* a/u to cut, cut to size, trim
šarāmu† *v.* a/u to break open
šarāmu+ *v.* a/u to cut off (tip of nose)
šārānu *n.* empty talker, flatulent*, wind-bag*
šarāpu *v.* a/u to burn, burn down
šarāqu *v.* i/i to steal
šarāru* *v.* u/u to bend
šarāṣu *v.* a/? to clutch, claw onto
šārat lēti* *nf. cp.* whiskers
šārāti *n. pl.* (pl.) twaddle, drivel
šarāṭu* *v.* a/u to tear; (D) to tear into strips, shred
šarbābu* *n.* impotence
šarbillu* *n.* breeze
šarbu *n.* rainy weather, cold
šarbubu *adj.* languid, languishing; devoted to, obedient, impotent*
šarḫu* *adj.* proud; glorious, splendid, resplendent; fantastic, magnificent, superb
šāriku* *n.* donor
šarissu *nf.* crack troops
šarku *n.* pus, suppuration
šarku a.* *adj.* festering, purulent
šarmu *adj.* sharply incised, clear-cut
šarmu+ *adj.* flat-nosed, lop-nose, snubnose
šarnuppu◊ *n.* (an Elamite class of persons receiving rations)
šarqiš* *adv.* stealthily, secretly
šarqu* *adj.* stolen
šarqūtu *nf.* larceny, theft
šarrāiu+ *n.* amateur, beginner, freshman,

novice, postulant, tyro
šarrâiu a.+ *adj.* elementary, incipient, initial
šarrâku◊ *n.*^{3} donor(?)
šarrâqiš* *adv.* like a thief, furtively, in stealth, in secret
šarrâqu* *n.* thief
šarrat bêti *nf. cp.* lady of the house, housewife, landlady, matron
šarriqu* *adj.* furtive, stealthy, thievish
šarru *n.*^{2} king, monarch
šarrû *v.* to begin, commence, start, start out, start up; to kindle; to inaugurate
šarrû+ *v.* to fall to
šarrû n. *n.* beginning, inauguration, outset
šarru rabiu *np.* great king, emperor
šarrušu+ *adj.* deep-rooted, inveterate
šarrutu *nf.* queen, lady
šarrûtu *nf.* kingship, kingdom, royalty, monarchy, principality
šarrûtu epâšu‡ *vp.* to exercise kingship, rule
šaršarrânu◊ *n.* rebel, gangster
šaršarru *n.* would-be king(?)
šaršarruttu *nf.* would-be kingship(?)
šaršudu* *v.* to build firmly, establish; to ground
šaršudu a. *adj.* firmly fixed
šartennu *n.* chief judge, minister of justice
šârtu *nf.* hair, pelt, plumage
šârtu+ *nf.* fuzz
šarṭu *adj.* ragged, rent, tattered
šarû *v.*$^{i/i, u/u}$ to be rich, wealthy
šâru *n.*$^{1/2/3}$ wind, blast; air; gas, flatus; breath, spirit; vanity, vain (words); cardinal point, direction
šarû a. *adj.* affluent, opulent, rich, wealthy, well-off; rich man, tycoon
šarûr šanši *n. cp.* sunbeam, sunshine
šarûriš* *adv.* like sunlight
šarûru *n.* brilliance, lustre, radiance; ray
šassukku* *n.*^{1} bookkeeper
šassûru* *nf.* womb, uterus
šasû* *v.*$^{i/i}$ to shout, call; to read (out); to invoke, appeal to; to summon; to caw; (Gtn) to read, peruse
šaṣbutu *n.* provisioning, supplies, preparations
šaṣbutu a. *adj.* equipped, prepared
šâša *pron.* her
šašallu *n.* hoof tendon, Achilles tendon
šâši *pron.* her
šâšina* *pron.* them
šâšîtu* *nf.* lantern
šašluṭu *adj.* authorized, entitled
šaššûgu *n.*^{1} (a tree)
šaššûmi *adv.* the day before yesterday
šâšu *pron.* him
šâšunu *pron.* them
šât mûši *n. cp.* night-time
šât mûši* *n. cp.* nighttime
šât urri* *n. cp.* morning watch
šatâḫu◊ *v.*$^{a/u}$ to be tall, elongated; (D) to make grow long
šatam ekurrâti* *n. cp.* chief temple administrator
šatammu* *n.* prelate, 'bishop'; administrator, government auditor
šatammûtu* *nf.* prelacy
šatânu* *v.*$^{i/i}$ to urinate
šatâqu* *v.*$^{a/u}$ to cut, split; (D) to fissure, split in many places
šatâqu+ *v.*$^{a/u}$ to tear asunder, divide, lacerate, rend, rive, separate, cause a schism
šâtina* *pron.* them
šâtiu *n.*^{4} drinker, heavy drinker
šattišam* *adv.* year by year; yearly
šattu *nf.* year
šattu ana šatti *adv.* year after year
šattu diri‡ *np.* leap year
šattu eššutu‡ *np.* new year
šatû *v.*$^{i/i}$ to drink, imbibe, gulp down, toss off
šâtunu* *pron.* those
šatûtu† *nf.* weaving
šatû B* *v.*$^{u/u}$ to weave, spin; to entangle, entwine, interlace, knot together
šaṭâpu* *v.*$^{a/u}$ to preserve life, save
šaṭâru *v.*$^{a/u}$ to write, write down, inscribe; to register; to scribble, spell
šaṭâru* *v.*$^{a/u}$ (D) to have written; (Š) to have written
šaṭâru+ *v.*$^{a/u}$ (Š) to ascribe, lay on
šaṭâru gammuru *np.* to finish writing up
šâṭir šumi* *n. cp.* undersigned
šâṭiru *n.*^{4} author, writer
šaṭru *adj.* written, inscribed, recorded, written down, documentary
šaṭṭâru *n.*^{2} copy, document, exemplar, text, writing, writ
šaṭṭiru* *adj.* eager to write
šâṭu* *v.*$^{a/u}$ to draw, pull, toil
šâṭu B* *v.*$^{a/u}$ to ignore, despise, be negligent
ša'ûdu *v.* (Š) to acquaint with, communi-

cate, inform, indicate, make known, point out; (Štn) to spread tales, spread a rumour, gossip(?)
ša''uru *adj.* dirty, filthy, smutty, soiled
ša''uru+ *adj.* sooty
šazamû *n.*[3] wine flask
šazbussu *nf.* shipmen t, delivery, consignment, carriage, batch, conveyance
šawaššammē+ *n. pl.* grains of sesame, sesame seed(s)
šebītu *nf.* small harp
šebû* *adj.* satisfied, sated
šēbulti kaspi* *nf. cp.* remittance
šēbultu* *nf.* despatch, shipment, consignment
šeburtu *nf.* (a color or quality of wool)
šēdānu+ *n.* little devil, gnome, imp
šedišširīu* *num.* sixteenth
šedû *n.* (a tree)
šēdu *n.* genie
šēdu+ *n.* demon, devil
šegû* *adj.* to be wild, rave, rage; (N) to become wild, furious
šegû a.* *adj.* frantic, furious, howling, infuriated, mad, rabid
šegunû* *n.* grain crop
šegûtu* *nf.* rabies
šēḫānu *n.* ecstatic, madman, lunatic
šeḫenītu* *nf.* (part of a citadel wall?)
šēḫtu *nf.* censer
šēḫu *n.* frenzy, lunacy, madness
šēḫu B* *adj.* tall, high, stately, eminent
šē'i bābi *n. cp.* neighbor
še'ītu† *nf.* mattress, bolster, stuffing*
šēlabiš* *adv.* like a fox
šēlabtu *nf.* vixen
šelappāiu *n.* architect(?), constructor(?), engineer(?)
šelappû *n.* turtle
šelluru *n.* mortar, plaster, cement, concrete
šelû◊ *v.* [i/i] to be negligent, careless, inattentive, neglectful
šēlu* *adj.* sharp, astringent, piquant, trenchant
šêlu* *v.* to sharpen, whet
šēlubu *n.* fox
šēlūtu *nf.* votive gift; votary, votaress, devotee
šēlûtu *nf.* dedication, devotion, promotion
šēmu* *adj.* predestined, predetermined, resolute
šemuru *nf.* bracelet; ankle-chain, anklet, bangle
šēnu *nf.* shoe, sandal
šênu* *v.* to put on shoes
šēpē pašāru‡ *vp.* to move off
šēpītu *nf.* foot, foot end, lover end; piedmont
šēpu *nf., n.*[1] foot
šēpu ana šēpi‡ *adv.* unanimously
šēpu parāsu‡ *vp.* to exclude, isolate, keep from, keep out, seclude
šer'ān izirê* *n. cp.* biceps
šer'ānīu* *adj.* muscular, wiry
šer'ānu *n.*[1] muscle, sinew, tendon, ligament; nerve; vein, artery
šer'ānu+ *n.*[1] joint, membrane, pulse
šer'ānu ša dāmi+ *np.* blood vessel
šer'ītu *nf.* (a divine garment)
šernu *n.* axle, axis
šerru* *n.*[1] (young) child, infant, baby, newborn
šeršerru* *n.* link
šeršerrutu *nf.* chain, string of beads, necklace(?)
šērtu *nf.* tomorrow; morning
šērtu B* *nf.* sin, guilt, offence; vice, crime, misdeed; punishment
Šer'u* *n.* Virgo
šerû* *v.* [i/i] to thrive(?), lay down(?)
šēru* *n.* morning, morning star; dawn, aurora
šērubtu* *nf.* introduction
šēru B* *adj.* terrible, devastating, fierce
šēssu *nf.* blade
šēssu* *nf.* cutting edge
šeššā *num.* sixty
šeššīšu *adv.* six times, sixfold
šeššu *n., num.* sixth; one sixth
šētiš* *adv.* like a net
šētu* *nf.* web, net
šêtu* *v.* to be spared, left over; to remain, escape
šeṭû* *v.* [i/i] to spread, lay out
šēṭu *n.* idler, do-nothing, sluggard; careless, indifferent, neglectful, negligent, perfunctory, remiss, indolent, slipshod, slothful
šêṭu* *v.* to miss; to neglect, disdain, disregard
šēṭu+ *adj.* despicable, despised, contemptible, worthless
šeṭūtu *nf.* contempt, disdain, scorn; neglect, negligence; idleness, indifference, sloth

šeṭūtu+ *nf.* contempt, scorn; contemptibility, desecration
še'u *n.* grain, kernel, corn
še'û* *v.* i/i to seek, search, strive for; (Gtn) to frequent, haunt
šê'u† *v.* to pad, upholster; (stat.) to be stuffed with
šēzubtu* *nf.* relief, holiday
šî *pron.* she, it
ši' ši' *int.* hush-hush
šiāḫu *n.* earnest talk(?)
šiāḫu B* *v.* to be tall, grow, grow tall, spring up
šiāḫu B+ *v.* to flourish, spring from, sprout, thrive
šiālu *v.* to coat, cover
šiāmu *v.* to decree, destine, determine, define, enact, ordain, specify; to foreordain, bequeath; to constitute, establish as
šiāmu+ *v.* to affirm, declare, postulate, presume
šiāmu B *v.* to sell; to buy
šiānu *v.* to piss, urinate
šiāru *n.* (the) morrow, tomorrow
šiāru nubattu *np., adv.* morning and evening
šiāṣu *v.* to become insufficient, decline, diminish, wane
šiāti* *pron.f.* her; that
šiāṭu *v.* to be negligent
šiāṭu+ *v.* to neglect, treat with contempt
šibbu* *n.* belt, girdle
šibḫu* *n.* deposit, layer
šibiḫ mūti* *n. cp.* pall of death
šibirru* *n.* shepherd's staff; staff, sceptre, crook
šibirtu *nf.* block, piece, lump, fragment
šibistu* *nf.* anger, wrath
šibittu* *nf.* dill
šibqu* *n.* plan, stratagem, plot, trick
šibru* *n.* broken piece
šibšu *n.* [1] straw tax
šibšutu *nf.* door-beam, frame
šibṭu *n.* plague, epidemic
šību *n.* [4] witness; elder
šibūbu* *n.* spark, scintillation
šībūti u ṣeḫrūti‡ *np.* high and low
šībūtu *nf.* old age; the elderly
šiddi *prp.* along, alongside
šiddi arki‡ *adv.* extensively, in detail
šiddi nāri *n. cp.* riverside
šiddu *adv., n.* long side; furlong, stadium; deferment, respite
šidlu+ *n.* queue
šigāru* *n.* bolt, lock
šigūšu *n.* late barley
šiḫḫutu *nf.* decay, disintegration, erosion, flaking off, rot, degeneration*
šiḫiltu+ *nf.* distillation, liquefaction
šiḫītu+ *nf.* swimming
šiḫlu *n.* [1] replacement, runner-up*
šiḫlu a. *adj.* second-best, second-rate
šiḫṭu *n.* assault, attack, foray, incursion, inroad, raid, razzia, sudden onslaught, surprise (attack); scurry
šiḫṭu B *n.* rinse, rinsing
šīḫu* *n., adj.* full-scale, full-grown, giant
šikāru *n.* (strong) beer, ale
šikin adanni* *n. cp.* time frame
šikin napišti* *n. cp.* animate, living being
šikin pāni* *n. cp.* orientation
šikin pî* *n. cp.* speech
šikin qāti* *n. cp.* appointee
šikin ṭēmi *n. cp.* commandant; command
šikin ṭēmūtu *n. cp.* commandership
šikinnu◊ *n.* (mng. unkn.)
šikintu *nf.* allocation
šikittu* *nf.* appearance, construction, form, layout, shape, stature, structure
šikkatu* *nf.* flask (of perfume)
šikkatu B* *nf.* tassel, trimmings
šikkatu C* *nf.* alum
šikkidirru* *n.* marten
šikku *n.* (a piece of jewellery?)
šikkû* *n.* mongoose
šiknat napišti* *n. cp.* living being
šiknu *n.* [2] setting, layout, arrangement; appearance, character, nature; kind, type; definition, description; imposition; position, posture; situation
šikru* *n.* alcoholic drink, (strong) beer
šikru B* *n.* haft, hilt
šiliḫtu◊ *nf.* (part of a canal)
šilītu* *nf.* sharpness(?)
šillān* *adv.* in the west
šillatu* *nf.* blasphemy, impudence, shamelessness; iniquity, sacrilege
šilpu* *n.* plundering
šiltāḫiš* *adv.* like an arrow
šiltāḫu *n.* [1] arrow
šilû *n.* (a bird)
šīlu* *n.* hole, depression
šilūtu† *nf.* shot
šimētān* *n.* evening
šimit uzni* *n. cp.* ear-mark; birthmark
šimmatu *nf.* paralysis
šimšālu *n.* box-tree

šimšālu+ *n.* juniper

šimtu* *nf.* mark, token; color, paint

šīmtu *nf.* fate, destiny; will, testament, disposition, nature of things*, necessity*, resolution*

šīmtu šiāmu *vp.* to decree fate; to make a will

šimṭu+ *n.* breakage

šīmu *n.* price, cost; purchase; merchandise, value*

šīmūtu◊ *nf.* purchasing venture

šina *pron.* they (f.)

šina šalāš *np.* a few

šināšina *obl.pron.f* them

šināti* *pron.f.* those, the aforementioned

šīnāti *n.pl.* urine, piss

šina B *num.* two

šindu◊ *nf.* brand mark

šinešertu+ *nf.* dozen

šingutu *nf.* (mng. unkn.)

šinintu* *nf.* equality(?)

šinip *n.* two thirds

šinīšu *adv.* twice

šinīšu šalāšīšu *adv.* often, several times

šinītu* *nf.* metamorphosis*, transformation*, alteration, change

šinītu+ *nf.* frenzy, trance

šinnānu+ *n.* cog

šinnatu* *nf.* rival; equal

šinni pīri *n. cp.* ivory, elephant's tusk

šinni ṣabīti* *n. cp.* (a stone)

šinnu *n.* tooth, tine, fang

šinnu rabītu* *np.* canine tooth

šinnu ša ḫilbi+ *np.* deciduous tooth

šinṣu* *n.* irony*, sarcasm*, sneer, scoff, taunt, gibe

šinšerû* *num.* twelfth

šinūntu* *nf.* swallow

šipāru* *n.* regulations, instructions; assembly

šipik bāṣi* *n. cp.* sand-dune, dune

šipik šaddê* *n. cp.* bedrock, rock bottom

šipir nikilti* *n. cp.* skilful technique; work of art, artefact, artifice; contrivance; craftiness deceit, trickery, masterpiece*, technique*

šipir qāti *n. cp.* activity, handiwork

šipirtu *nf.* message, dispatch

šipītu* *nf.* suture, seam

šipku *n.* casting, pouring; forming, formation; mass, bulk, solidity

šipru *n.* message, mission; work, task; art, artefact, manufacture; skill, craft; ruse

šipṣu* *n.* obstinacy, obduracy; defiance, noncompliance

šiptu *nf.* incantation, spell

šipṭu *n.* penalty, punishment; threat, menace*

šipṭu* *n.* judg[e]ment, verdict, strict orders

šipṭu emādu *vp.* to inflict punishment, penalize, punish

šipṭu šakānu‡ *vp.* to give strict orders

šīpu* *n.* gray hair; mold, decay

šīpu B* *n.* yellow paste

šīpu B+ *n.* salve, eye-salve

šiqlu *n.* shekel

šīqu *n.*[3] irrigation

šīqu B* *n.* eczema

šīr alpi *n. cp.* beef

šīr šaḫî* *n. cp.* pork

šīr šumê *n. cp.* roasted meat; scent, whiff

širiat *adj.* meaty(?)

širiktu *nf.* present, grant

širku *n.*[1] oblate

širpu *n.* combustible, fuel

širqu *n.* flour offering

širṭānu+ *adj.* striped

širṭu *n.* lint, bandage, gauze, shred, strip, tatter

šir'u* *nf.* furrow

šīru *n.*[2] flesh, meat; physical condition

šīru saḫālu‡ *vp.* to annoy

šisīt nāgiri* *n. cp.* call of herald; proclamation, announcement

šisītu* *nf.* call, cry, shout, summons; clamour, noise

šišanibu *n.* (a garden vegetable)

šišītu* *nf.* membrane, film; hymen; skin; layer

šīšnu* *n.* (a rush)

šīšnu+ *n.* butomus, flowering rush

šit'āru* *adj.* iridescent

šitassû* *n.* reading

šiti *pron.* she, it

šitimgallu* *n.* master builder, chief builder

šitluṭiš* *adv.* imperially, triumphantly, unopposed

šitluṭu* *adj.* autocratic, dominant, imperial, triumphant

šitmāru* *adj.* strong-willed, impetuous

šitmuriš* *adv.* impetuously, vehemently

šitmuru* *adj.* raging, impetuous, high-mettled

šitnû* *adj.* conflicting, different, unlike, at variance

šitnuntu* *nf.* rivalry, competition, contention, match*
šitnunu* *adj.* combative, vying
šitpuru* *v.* to outfit, attire oo.s.
šitpuṣu* *adj.* wrestling
šitqu* *n.* cleft, crack, crevasse, crevice, gap, rift, split, tear
šitqu+ *n.* chasm, schism
šitqultu* *nf.* conjunction, opposition; equinox
šitqulu* *adj.* balanced
šitrāḫu* *adj.* magnificent, splendid, superb, swanky
šitru* *n.* orchestra, choir
šitruḫu* *adj.* proud, splendid
šitta  *num.* two
šittālu* *adj.* consulting
šittān* *n.* two thirds
šittu* *nf.* sleep, dream
šittu B◊ *nf.* rest, remainder
šītu *nf.* (a textile)
šitūltu* *nf.* consultation, discussion; deliberation, interview*
šiṭir arāni* *n. cp.* epitaph, funerary inscription
šiṭir šumi* *n. cp.* inscription
šiṭirtu* *nf.* essay*, text, writing
šiṭru* *n.* writing, inscription
šizû* *n.* one third cubit
šû *pron.* he; this, that; it (is)
šuāšu* *pron.* him; that
šuāti* *pron.* that, said
šuātina*  *pron.* those
šuātu*  *pron.* that, aforementioned
šuātunu* *pron.* those
šuā'u *v.* to buoy, float, swim, soar(?)
šubabītu  *nf.* (an insect)
šubarrû* *n.* freedom, amnesty; released, exempted person
šubat nēḫti šūšubu‡ *vp.* to let dwell in security
šubê  *n. pl.* roast meat, cooked meat, steak
šubiltu  *nf.* ear (of barley)
Šubiltu+ *nf.* Virgo, Spica
šubtu  *nf.* seat, abode, dwelling, residence, settlement; ambush
šubû  *n.* (a semi-precious stone)
šūbu* *n.* (a kind of sheep)
šubû+ *n.* agate
šūbulti inbi* *adj.* junior, young
šūbultu*  *nf.* present, gift, shipment
šuburru  *n.* rectum, anus
šubû B*  *n.* battering ram

šudlupu* *adj.* sleepless, exhausted
šūdûtu* *nf.* confession*, profession*, thanksgiving*, announcement, edict
šūdûtu+ *nf.* assurance, commitment, declaration, warrant
šugarruru† *v.* to roll, seal (with a cylinder seal)
šugludu* *adj.* terrifying, awe-inspiring
šugummû *n.* buzzing; chime, peal
šugurru *n.* [1] (a reed mat?)
šugurrû* *n.* basket for dates
šuḫ  *prp.* concerning, as to, apropos [of]
šūḫānu+ *n.* ulcer
šuḫarruru* *v.* to become dazed, become dumb, become petrified; to abate, subside, to die down*
šuḫarruru a.* *adj.* awestruck, dazed, silent, still, dumb, numb with fear, petrified, stupefied*, thunderstruck*
šuḫattu  *nf.* cloth, rag (for wiping), tissue
šuḫdû◊ *adj.* amused, arbitrary, high-handed
šuḫḫu* *adj.* very long
šuḫḫu† *n.* buttock
šuḫḫû* *adj.* destroyed(?), ruined(?)
šuḫru* *n.* eyebrow
šuḫrubu* *v.* desolate, uncultivated, waste
šuḫruru* *v.* to lay waste
šuḫtānu+ *adj.* grimy, rusty, foul
šuḫtu *n.* patina, rust, verdigris, mo[u]ld, tarnish
šuḫtu+ *n.* squalor, tartar (on the teeth)
šūḫu  *n.* [2] (a small melon or cucumber)
šuḫuppu* *n.* rim, tyre
šuḫupputu† *nf.* boot
šuḫuṭ libbi* *n. cp.* anger
šuillakku  *n.* [2] hand-lifting prayer
šu'ītu* *nf.* lord
šukānu*  *n.* ornament, jewellery
šukênu *v.* to prostrate o.s.
šukkallu 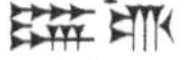 *n.* vizier
šukkallu rabiu *np.* grand vizier
šuklultu* *nf.* perfection, completion, completeness
šuklulūtu *nf.* perfection
šuknušu* *adj.* obedient
šukû* *n.* door pole
šukuddu* *n.* arrow; Sirius
šukūniš* *adv.* humbly
šukunnû◊ *n.* blasphemy, false accusation
šukurru* *n.* [1] spear

šullāmu *n.* complement
šullāmu+ *n.* completion, consummation, end, epilogue, expiration
šullu* *n.* (big) wart, pockmark(?)
šulluṭu* *adj.* masterful, triumphant
šulmānati tadānu‡ *vp.* to bribe
šulmānu  *n.* [3] present; bribe, inducement
šulmu  *n.* health, well-being, welfare, hail; state of health; greeting, salutation; salvation
šulmu qabû *vp.* to salute
šulpu  *n.* stalk, straw; drinking tube; stubble, stem
šulputu* *adj.* defeated
šulšaia 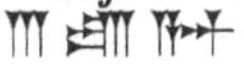 *pron.* three each
šulšu◊ *n.* one third
šūlû* *n.* garrison troops
šuluḫḫu*  *n.* purification (ritual)
šūluku* *adj.* fit, suitable
šūlulu* *v.* to rejoice, make jubilant
šulum šamši* *n. cp.* sunset, west
šulum ṭēmi* *n. cp.* sanity
šulūšâ◊ *num.* three each
šulušīu *adj.* three-year-old
šūlūtu* *nf.* garrison
šumāku+ *n.* patronage, prop
šumēlānu* *adj.* left-handed
šumēlu  *n.* left, north
Šume:ru *n.* Sumerian
šumḫu* *n.* abundance, luxuriance; decoration, adornment
šumku†  *n. pl.* onion
šumlû+ *n.* fulfilment
šumma  *conj.* if; whether; (in oath) not
šumma ... šumma *conj.* either ... or; whether ... or
šummannu* *n.* rope, halter, tether
šummu *conj.* if; whether
šummu* *n.* conditional clause, relative clause; (pl.) terms
šumšû* *v.* to stay overnight, spend the night
šumu  *n.* [2/3] name, proper name; reputation, repute, fame; line, sentence, noun*
šūmu 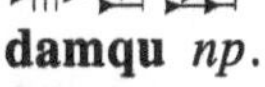 *n.* garlic
šumu damqu *np.* good name, good reputation, renown
šumu lā damqu *np.* bad name, bad reputation, infamy, notoriety
šumu nabû‡ *vp.* to call by name, give a name, nominate
šumu šaṭru* *np.* written name, inscription, autograph*, signature*
šumu zakru‡ *np.* sworn name
šumūdu◊ *n.* increase
šumuttu* *n.* beet, beetroot
šunāgu *n.* (a commodity)
šunāia *num.* two each
šunannu  *n.* [1/3] (a kind of tray)
šūnāqu+ *n.* torment, torture
šunāšunu *pron.* them
šunātunu* *pron.* those
šundulu* *adj.* wide, extensive, of great expanse; abundant
šungallu  *n.* [1] dragon
šunkē *n. pl.* onions
šunnû* *adj.* double(d)
šunnūtu* *nf.* alteration, change
šunquttu* *nf.* adjustment, deduction
šunu  *pron. m.* they (m.)
šunû*  *n.* chaste tree
šunû+ *n.* tree of chastity
šūnuḫiš* *adv.* laboriously, wearily, miserably
šūnuḫu* *adj.* miserable, much troubled, weary, worn-out, frustrated*
šunu'lu *adj.* two-year-old
šunūši◊ *pron. m.* them
šunūti*  *pron. m.* them, those
šupāl* *prp.* beneath, under, below
šupālītu  *nf.* lower garment, shirt, underwear
šupālītu ḫalluptu  *nf. cp.* mail shirt
šupālu*  *adv., prp.* depression, lowland; underside; subordination
šupālû◊ *adj.* lower
šuparruru* *adj.* to spread out, broaden, extend
šuparzuḫu* *v.* to make abundant
šupêlu* *v.* to change, exchange, switch
šūpîš* *adv.* openly, overtly, plainly, publicly
šupku* *n.* base, firmament
šuplu *n.* depression, depth
šuplu libbi *n. cp.* melancholy, downheartedness, dejection, depression, low spirits, sadness
šuppulu* *adj.* very deep, profound
šupšuqiš* *adv.* with difficulty, very laboriously
šupšuqu* *adj.* narrow, strait, difficult, laborious
šupšutu 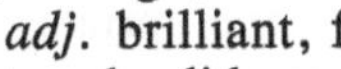 *nf.* doorpost(?), pailing*, railing*, stockade*
šūpû* *adj.* brilliant, famous, manifest, resplendent, splendid; considerable, conspicuous, evident, flagrant

šupuk šamê* *n. cp.* horizon
šuqallulu* *v.* to hang (down), dangle, hover
šuqallulu a.* *adj.* hanging, pendent
šuqammumu* *v.* to be silent; to amaze, silence
šuqammumu a.* *adj.* amazed, silent, speechless, still
šuqdu *n.* almond
šuqdu+ *n.* tonsil
šuqlu† *nf.* bulk, load, packet
šūqu* *n.* height, ascension
šuqullālu* *n.* pendant
šuqultu *nf.* weight
šūquru* *adj.* most precious, invaluable
šūr īni* *n. cp.* eyebrow
šurānu* *n.* cat
šūrānu *n.* cat
šuratḫu* *n.* (a tree)
šurbû* *adj.* exalted, supreme
šurdu *n.*[1] shaft, arrow-shaft
šurdû* *adj.* leaking, overflowing
šurdunû *n.* (a plant, possibly rocket)
šurdūtu◊ *nf.* inundation
šuribtu* *nf.* terror, awe(?)
šurinnu *n.* standard, banner*
šurīpiš* *adv.* like ice
šurīpu* *n.* ice, frost
šur'ītu *nf.* (a kind of wool)
šurmēnu *n.* cypress
šurpu* *n.* (a ritual, burning)
šurrâti* *nf. pl.* beginning
šurru* *v.* to bend forwards; to peer in at
šurruḫu* *adj.* dashing, gorgeous, splendid; gaudy, showy, lavish; arrogant, haughty
šurruḫu B* *v.* to drool, dribble
šurrû B* *v.* (Dt) to abstain*, do without*, to fast, stop eating
šuršē+ *n. pl.* (pl.) rudiments
šuršiš* *adv.* by the roots; radically
šuršu* *n.* root, base, foundation
šuršummu* *n.* sediment, dregs
šūru *n.*[2] reed marsh
šu'ru+ *n.* blackness, lampback, soot
šuruppû* *n.* frost
šuruptu *nf.* burning, combustion; fuel; burnt-offering, funeral burning, cremation, pyre*
šūru B* *n.*[1] bull
šūsumu* *adj.* fitting, appropriate
šūṣūtu* *nf.* lease
Šūšan *n.* Sidon
šūšan unqi+ *n. cp.* lily of the valley
šūšanu+ *n.* lily, lotus
šūši *num.* sixty
šūšīu* *num.* sixtieth
šuškallu* *n., nf.* net
šušlušu* *adj.* trebled, triple
šušrāti *n. pl.* (a type of leek)
šūšu* *n.* liquorice
šūšuru* *adj.* straight
šūt* *pron.* of; (he) who
šūt-abnī* *n. cp. pl.* stone amulets
šūt-rēši* *n. cp.* eunuch
šutābulu* *v.* to argue
šutaddunu* *v.* to exchange advice, deliberate
šutāḫû* *adj.* matched, teamed; identical, matching
šutaktutu* *v.* to descend
šutāpu* *n.* associate, partner
šutāpu+ *n.* chum
šutāpūtu* *nf.* joint venture, partnership
šutāpūtu+ *nf.* collaboration
šutarruḫūtu* *nf.* magnificence
šutātû* *adj.* facing each other, opposite
šutēlupu* *v.* to flourish; to intertwine, entangle, enmesh
šutēmudu* *adj.* consecutive, superimposed
šutēmuqu* *n.* to pray devoutly, entreat; intense prayer
šutērsû* *v.* to make ready, prepare
šuteṣlup* *adv.* criss-cross
šuteṣlupu* *adj.* criss-crossed
šutlumu* *v.* to bestow, grant, present
šuttatu* *nf.* pit, pitfall, trap
šuttu *nf.* dream
šuttu amāru *vp.* to dream
šuttu parittu* *np.* nightmare
šutû† *n.* woven material, warp
šūtu *pron.* he
šutukku *n.* reed hut, bundle
šutummu* *n.* storehouse, silo; treasury
šūtuqtu* *nf.* averting
šūtuqu* *adj.* surpassing, outstanding
šūturu* *adj.* enormous, gigantic, tremendous; excellent, superior, supreme; extreme, utmost, uttermost
šūtu B *nf.* south wind, south, southeast
šūt B* *prp.* because of, concerning
šu'u *n.*[1] chick-pea, pea
šu''uru* *v.* to be hairy
šu''uru a.* *adj.* hairy, unshorn, unshaven
šu'u B* *n.*[1] sheep

ta'ādu+ *v.* to be astonished, stupefied; (Š) to astonish, astound, fascinate, surprise
tabāku *v.*$^{a/u}$ to pour, shed, infuse; to pour out; to store, pile up, to slop*, spill*
tabāku* *v.*$^{a/u}$ (D) to excrete; (Š) to make pour out
tabāku *v.*$^{a/u}$ (N) to flow, pile o.s. up
tabāku+ *v.*$^{a/u}$ to slop
tabālu *v.*$^{a/a}$ to carry away; to disappear
tabarru* *n.* red wool
tabbilu* *n.*^{1} (a bronze object)
tabbītu* *nf.* moaning
tābīlu† *n.* powder
tabiu *adj.* loose
tābiu *adj.* rampant
tabku *adj., n.*^{2} stored grain; poured out, spilt, stored, stratified*
tablittu* *nf.* recreation*, regeneration*, resuscitation*, revival*, refreshment, victual, nourishment
tablu *n.* theft
tablu tabālu *vp.* to commit a theft
tablu tabbulu *vp.* to commit thefts
tabnīt tānti* *nf. cp.* sea monster
tabnītu* *nf.* creation
tabrâti* *nf. pl.* miracle*, prodigy*; (pl.) astonished gaze, astonishment, admiration, amazement, wonderment; wonder, marvel
tabrību *n.* red wool
tabrīmu *n.* multicolored, polychrome wool
tabrītu* *nf.* appearance, apparition, vision
tabriu *n.*^{3} hay field, forage
tabšūtu* *nf.* creation
tabû *v.*$^{i/i}$ to rise, arise, get up, stand up; to assault, attack; to be excited, get an erection
tabû* *v.*$^{i/i}$ (Gtn) pulsate, pulse, throb
tabû *v.*$^{i/i}$ (Š) to raise, erect; to remove, dethrone; to excite, turn on; (stat.) to be loose
tabūtu *nf.* procession
tadānu *v.*$^{a/i}$ to give, deliver, hand over, provide; to give away, give over, sell; to cede; to let, allow, permit; (Š) to collect, make to pay
tādinu *n.* giver, seller
tādirtu *nf.* mourning, eclipse
tadmiqtu† *nf.* profit-making, amelioration*, improvement*, refinement*
tadnintu* *nf.* reinforcement, strengthening
tagmirtu* *nf.* completion
taḫāḫu* *v.* to pour (over)(?); (D) to drench
taḫapšu *n.* (woven) felt, rug, saddlecloth; saddle
tāḫāzu* *n.*^{3} battle, combat, skirmish
taḫbātu* *nf.* (a wrapping); casing
taḫḫūtu* *nf.* support, procuration
taḫlīpu *n.* (defensive) covering, armoring; armored chariot; covering-board, cover-plate, screen
taḫluptu* *nf.* covering
taḫsistu* *nf.* reminder, memorial, recommendation
taḫsītu* *nf.* ambush, assault
taḫṣību* *n.* rupture
taḫtānu *prp.* under, beneath
taḫtû* *n.* defeat
taḫūmu *n.*$^{2/3}$ border, boundary, frontier, front line, limit; confines, territory, domain
taiārtu* *nf.* compassion, forgiveness; return; repetition
taiāru *n.* return, revenue
taiāru* *n.* mercy
taiāru a.* *adj.* relenting, returning, merciful, recurrent*
ta'īdu+ *adj.* delightful, miraculous
takāku* *v.* to injure
takāku+ *v.* to harm, oppress
takāltu* *nf.* pouch, bag, pocket; case, sheath
tākaltu* *nf.* stomach, stomach-ache
takālu *v.*$^{i/i}$ to trust in, rely on, hope in; (D stat.) to depend on; (D) to give confidence, give faith, assure; (N) to put one's trust in
takālu+ *v.*$^{i/i}$ to depend, place confidence in, put trust in, count on, reckon on
takālu ana‡ *vp.* to rely on
takālu ina muḫḫi‡ *vp.* to rely on
takāpu *v.*$^{i/i}$ to prick, puncture, cup; to impress, imprint; to stitch, sew
takbāru *n.* fattened sheep
takbittu* *nf.* honor, honorific ceremony
takiltu* *nf.* (blue) purple (wool)
takiltu+ *nf.* dark blue, violet, purple; (pl.) purple robes
takiltu B* *nf.* reliability, trustfulness, trustworthiness
takittu* *nf.* confirmation
takkapu* *n.* hole
takkassu *n.*^{1} piece

takkīru* *n.* diversion (canal)
takkulu *adj.* reliant, trustful, trusting
takkussu *n.*^{3} tube, pipe, pipette
taklimtu *nf.* (funerary) display; exhibition, presentation, spectacle, (cultic) drama; disclosure, revelation; exhibit
taklīmu* *n.* demonstration
taklu *adj.* reliable, staunch, trustworthy, trusty, foolproof*, infallible*
taklu+ *adj.* faithful, trustful
takmīsu *n.*^{2} (a sheep offering); offering table
taknītu* *nf.* loving care, make-up*
taknû* *n.* loving care, tenderness; comfort, hospitality
takpirtu *nf.* purification
takpu *n.*^{1} (a basket)
takrimāti *nf. pl.* autumn(?)
takrītu* *nf.* abbreviation, abridgement, shortening
takṣiāti *n. pl.* cold weather, winter
takšīru* *n.* repair, restoration
taktīmu *n.* cover, covering
tākultu *nf.* feeding ritual
talālu* *v.*$^{a/u}$ to stretch out; to stick out
talammu* *n.* rump
talbītu* *nf.* circumference
talbuštu* *nf.* clothing, costume
talīmāni* *n. pl.* both hands
talīmu *n.* brother, equal brother, twin brother
talittu *nf.* birth, childbirth, natality
tal'ītu *nf.* (absorptive) dressing
tallakku *n.* (a cult object)
tallaktu *nf.* carriage, cart, wagon, convention*
tallaktu B* *nf.* walkway, way; gait
tallaktu B† *nf.* (pl.) procedures
tallu *n.* crossbar
talluku* *n.* course, gait, progression, advance
tallultu *nf.* trappings
tallulu *adj.* equipped, fitted out
talmīdu *n.*^{2} disciple, pupil, student; apprentice; schoolboy, schoolchild
talmīdu+ *n.*^{2} disciple, follower
talmīdūtu+ *nf.* teaching, education; discipleship, pupillage, novitiate
talmittu† *nf.* girl student, female student, studentess, female apprentice
taltallu *n.*^{1} stamen (of date palm)
tamāḫu* *v.*$^{a/u}$ to grasp, hold fast
tāmartu *nf.* observation, viewing; visibility; appearance, apparition; audience gift
tamāru *v.*$^{i/i}$ to bury
tamarzu *n.* (mng. unkn.)
tamgirtu† *nf.* hush-money, reconciliation payment, gratuity*, recompense*
tamgītu* *nf.* rejoicing, frolic, gaiety
tamgussu *n.* small kettle
tamḫāru* *n.* battle
tamḫīru† *n.* presentation, offering; (a month)
tamḫīṣu* *n.* overlay, veneer(?)
tamirtu* *nf.* meadow
tamīt šapti tamû‡ *vp.* perjure o.s., commit perjury
tamītu *nf.* oath; oracle query
tamītu ša dabābti šapti *np.* perjury
tamlītu *nf.* inlay, filling, lining, padding, stuffing
tamlīu *n.* terrace
tamriqāti *n. pl.* (a cultic act or ritual)
tamšāru *n.* strap, whip-lash, whipcord
tamšīl* *n.* equalling, corresponding to, quasi*
tamšiltu* *nf.* mold, matrix, template, equation*, parable*, simile*
tamšīlu *n.* wild pigeon, wood-pigeon
tamšīlu B* *n.*^{3} likeness, equivalent, peer; replica, reproduction
tamṭīt pî* *nf. cp.* humiliation
tamṭītu* *nf.* diminution, privation
tamû *v.*$^{a/a}$ to swear, vow; (D) to adjure
tamû B* *v.*$^{u/u}$ to be amazed
tanattu* *nf.* praise, compliment, oration
tanēḫtu† *nf.* mollification, pacification
tanīḫtu* *nf.* pacification, mollification
tānīḫu* *n.* sighing, weariness, exhaustion
tānīštu† *nf.* impairment, weakness
tanittu* *nf.* praise, eulogy, panegyric
tankār sissê *n. cp.* horse trader
tankārānu* *adj.* businesslike*
tankārānû* *adj.* like a merchant, mercantile
tankāru *n.* merchant, trader, businessman; investor, banker, money-lender
tankāruttu† *nf.* merchanthood; business, commerce, trade
tāntu *nf.* sea, ocean, lake
tāntu elītu* *np.* Mediterranean Sea

tāntu rabītu* *np.* ocean
tāntu rabītu ša Amurri* *np.* Mediterranean Sea
tāntu ša Kaldi* *np.* Persian Gulf
tāntu ša Nairi* *np.* Lake Urmia
tāntu ša šalām šanši* *np.* Mediterranean Sea
tāntu šaplītu* *np.* Persian Gulf
tanūku  *n.* (a container)
tapḫīru† *n.* collection, roundup*
tapḫu *n.* $^{1/2}$ (a large kettle, cauldron)
tappinnu  *n.* coarse flour
tappû  *n.* ^{1} comrade, companion, chap, fellow, fellow traveller; partner, mate; schoolfellow, schoolmate
tappû† *n.* ^{1} trading partner, business associate
tappūti alāku‡ *vp.* to come to assistance, to help, to aid
tappūtu* *nf.* comradeship, companionship, partnership; solidarity, assistance
tapqirtu*  *nf.* dispute
tapšīḫu* *n.* alleviation
tapšû  *n.* ^{1} cover, covering, quilt
tapšuḫtu* *nf.* rest, relief
taptiu  *n.* (land newly brought into cultivation, clearing)
tapṭirtu* *nf.* release
tapṭīru* *n.* castration
tâpu* *v.* $^{u/u}$ to devote o.s.
tapzirtu* *nf.* concealment, cover-up
taqānu  *v.* $^{u/u}$ to be secure, be in order; (D) to make secure, put in order, set in order
taqānu+ *v.* $^{u/u}$ to be in good order, be stable; (D) to amend, set right
taqdīšu† *n.* consecration, purification
taqnu *adj.* in order, secure, safe
taqnu+ *adj.* established, stable, staunch, trusty
taqnūtu+ *nf.* rectitude, stability
taqribtu* *nf.* offering; lamentation, dirge
taqribtu epāšu‡ *vp.* to perform a lamentation
taqribtu šakānu‡ *vp.* to set up a lament
taqrintu*  *nf.* accumulation, collection
taqrubtu* *nf.* battle, combat
taqtītu* *nf.* termination
taraḫḫu* *n.* slope
tarāḫu† *v.* $^{a/u}$ to delve, dig up, grub, grub up
tarāku  *v.* $^{a/u}$ to beat, throb, pound, thump, palpitate; to bang, pat, tap; (Š) to shake, agitate; to wield
tarāku B* *v.* to be dark
tarāmu *n.* grain heap, shock
tarāmu+ *n.* layer of straw (under or over a stack of corn), thatch
tarāmu B† *n.* darling
tarānu* *n.* roof, shelter
tarāpu* *v.* to be covered with color, be painted; (D) to paint, tinge
tarāru* *v.* $^{u/u}$ to shake, shiver, thrill, tremble
tarāṣu *v.* $^{a/u}$ to stretch out, spread out, reach out, extend, diffuse
tarāṣu*  *v.* $^{a/u}$ (Š) to stretch over
tarāṣu B *v.* $^{u/u}$ to be proper, be feasible, be in order, be all right
tarāṣu B*  *v.* $^{u/u}$ (Gt) to be mutually satisfactory
tarāṣu B  *v.* $^{u/u}$ (D) to adjust, edit, revise, set straight; to direct; (stat.) to be correct
tarāṣu B+ *v.* $^{u/u}$ (D) to do rightly, set right, direct; to set upright; to amend, reform; to emend, correct
tarbāṣu  *n.* ^{3} courtyard, yard; stall, pen, cow-house, cow-shed; halo
tarbāṣu+ *n.* ^{3} forecourt, entry
tarbītu  *nf.* aggrandizement, enlargement; stem(?); foster child, fosterling; product
tarbītu*  *nf.* (pl.) promotion
tarbītu+ *nf.* growth, increase; education, upbringing
tarbiu  *n.* ^{2} trainee, apprentice, alumnus, pupil; foster son
tarbu'tu* *nf.* (cloud of) dust
tarbûtu *nf.* upbringing, rearing; education, schooling, training
tardennu* *adj., n.* younger; second, secondary, subsidiary, minor
tardītu  *nf.* addendum, addition, adjunct, attachment, augment, supplement
targīgu* *n.* evildoer
targumānu 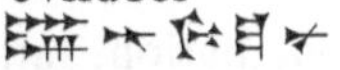 *n.* interpreter, translator, dragoman
targumu+ *v.* to interpret, translate
tarīntu* *nf.* gift, award
tariṣ 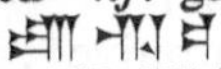 *adv., int.* in order, okay
tārītu *nf.* nurse, nursemaid, nanny
tariu† *adj.* half-grown, adolescent, teenage(d)
tāriu† *n.* (child) minder
tarkibtu* *nf.* fertilization, breeding

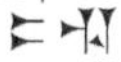

tarkistu* *nf.* guarantor's liability
tarkubtu* *nf.* riding
tarmazillu *n.* [1] (an edible bird)
tarmītu* *nf.* relaxation; release, renunciation, repudiation
tarmuš* *n.* lupin
tarnugallu *n.* cock
tarnugallutu+ *nf.* hen
tarpašu* *n.* otter
tarpašû* *n.* open space, space
tarṣiātu* *nf.* pleasure, enjoyment
tarṣu *adj.* straight, direct, correct, honest; trim, orderly, shipshape; proper, feasible, convenient
tarṣu+ *adj.* upright, straightforward, right
tarṣu B *n.* reach, extent, range, scope; time, reign; direction
taršītu* *nf.* harassment
Tarzi *n.* Tarsus
taskarinnu *n.* boxwood
taslītu* *nf.* prayer, petition
tasniqtu* *nf.* cross-examination*, test
taspītu* *nf.* prayer
tasrirru* *n.* deceitful omen
taṣlītu* *nf.* prayer, petition, plea
taṣpuptu* *nf.* flap, fluttering
taṣriḫtu* *nf.* heating
tašbītu† *nf.* satisfaction, payoff
tašḫītu* *nf.* pregnancy
tašīltu* *nf.* glory, splendour, magnificence; celebration, feast
tašīmtu* *nf.* judgement, discernment, good sense, prudence, sagacity
taškâti *n.pl.* triplets
taškû *n.* triplet; three-legged stool; tripod
tašlimtu *nf.* reimbursement, remuneration, recompensation
tašlīšu *n.* [2] third man, protector (on chariot)
tašlīšūtu *nf.* office of third man (in a chariot team)
tašmû* *n.* reconciliation, attention, concord
tašnintu* *nf.* battle, combat
tašnīqu* *n.* (internal disease)
tašnītu* *nf.* anecdote*, narrative*, tale*, repetition
tašnû* *n.* repetition
tašnuntu* *nf.* rivalry, strife
tašpiltu* *nf.* abasement*, abjection*, degradation*, demotion*, humiliation*, lowering, difference
tašqirtu* *nf.* defamation, deception
tašriḫtu* *nf.* splendour
tašrīḫu* *n.* glorification
tašrītu *nf.* (month) Tishri, October
tašrītu B* *nf.* beginning, commencement, starting point; inauguration feast
tatīdu* *n.* (a tree)
tatidūtu *nf.* francolin
tattiktu* *nf.* dripping, leakage
taturrû* *n.* (a bronze object)
ta''umāti+ *nf. pl.* (pl.) two-valved, double doors
ta''umu *v.* (D) to double, twin
ta''umu a. *adj.* double, twin, dual
ta''umu a.+ *adj.* twofold, paired, fitted to each other
Ta'ūzu *n.* (month) Tammuz, July
tazbiltu* *nf.* delay, retardation
tazkītu *nf.* purification, clearance
tazkītu* *nf.* justification*, acquittal, settlement, manumission; clarification
tazkītu+ *nf.* cleansing, expiation
tazzimtu *nf.* lamentation
tebīru *n.* iron-worker
teb'ītu* *nf.* investigation, quest, rummage, search
tēbû* *n.* [1] insurgent, rebel, aggressor*, assailant*
tēbû a.* *adj.* lively, active, pulsing; lustful; ready; rising; aggressive, offensive
tēdīqu* *n.* apparel, dress, costume
tēdištu* *nf.* renewal, renovation; innovation, reform
tēgimtu* *nf.* anger, rage
tēgirtu *nf.* apology, excuse, fib, pretext(?); bargain(?)
tēgirtu šakānu‡ *vp.* to apologize, bargain, dicker
te'iqtu* *nf.* insult, injury
tēkītu *nf.* shortage, necessity, compulsion
tēkubtu* *nf.* (time) pressure
tēlissu *nf.* purification, cleansing
telītu* *nf.* very competent
tēlītu *nf.* yield
tēltu *nf.* saying, phrase, proverb; pronunciation, enunciation
Tēmâ *n.* Tayma
temennu* *n.* foundation, terrace; foundation document
tēmēqu* *n.* [1] (deep) prayer
tenēšēti* *n.pl.* mankind

tēnintu* *nf.* weeping, lamentation
tēnīqu* *n.* breastfeeding, nursing, suckling
tēnītu* *nf.* changeover*, relief, replacement
tenšû◊ *n.* [1] (a precious metal dress ornament)
tēnû *n.* change (of clothes), spare suit; replacement, successor
tēqītu *nf.* daubing, anointing, ointment
terḫatu*
nf. bridal gift
terinnu* *n.* [3] cone
tērsītu* *nf.* preparation; method; ephemeris
tērtu* *nf.* commission, directive, instruction, commandment, rule; oracle, liver omen, liver; (pl.) ordinances, guidelines*
tērubtu* *nf.* entry
tērubtu† *nf.* bringing in, entrance, entry
tēṣītu* *nf.* rent*, rental*, lease
tēṣītu B* *nf.* debate, dispute; fable, fiction
teṣû* *v.* [i/i] to defecate, shit
tešēšerīu* *num.* nineteenth
tešīu *n., num.* ninth, one ninth
tēšû* *n.* anarchy, confusion, chaos, shambles, turmoil
tiālu *n.* white cedar
tiātu *nf.* asafoetida
tiātu+ *nf.* buttercup
tīb tāḫāzi* *n. cp.* attack, onslaught
tibbuttu *nf.* migratory locust
tibku* *n.* cascade, cataract, waterfall
tibnu *n.* straw
tību *n.* arousal, onset; aggression, assault, attack; twitch, jerk
tibûtu* *nf.* rising, attack, invasion, offensive; swarm(ing); excitement, erection
tidintu *nf.* gift, bounty
tidūku* *n.* combat, fight
tigilû *n.* [3] colocynth
tigû* *n.* bell, cymbal, jingle
tikku* *n.* [3] neck
tiklu+ *n.* confidence
tikpu *n.* [1] brick course, layer
tikpu B *n.* imprint, impression; dot
tīku *n.* raindrop, mist
tillāiu+ *adj.* hilly
tillāti* *nf. pl.* auxiliary troops
tillē *n. pl.* equipment, appendage, attachment, trappings; arms, armament
tillu *n.* [2] hill, knoll, mound, ruin mound, tell
tillutu *nf.* vine, grapevine
Tilmun *n.* Bahrain
tilpānu* *nf.* bow
tilūlītu+ *nf.* knoll
timāli *adv., n.* yesterday
timbuttu* *nf.* drum
timmu *n.* [1] column, pillar
timru *n.* [2] foundation deposit, (apotropaic) figurine
tinūru *n.* oven
tinūru+ *n.* baking pit, furnace
tiqnu* *n.* [1/3] ornament, jewel
tirik libbi *n. cp.* heart-beart, emotion; heart failure, heart-attack
tirik ṣulmi* *n. cp.* black spot
tirimtu *nf.* (a libation vessel)
tiriptu† *nf.* discoloration, coloring*, painting*
tiriṣ qāti *n. cp.* extended hand, prayer; instrument, tool
tirku *n.* throbbing, beating, palpitation; pat, thud, thump, wham
tirku B* *n.* spot, marking
tirṣu
n. duration, extension (of time); time, reign; direction
tīru *n.* [3] coil, spiral; bowel
tīru B* *n.* [1] (eunuch) courtier
tisarru *n.* (a topographical term)
tiṣābu *n.* additional amount, appendix*
tišʾā* *num.* ninety
titābē *n. pl.* beer mash, mash
titipu *n.* (a fruit tree and its fruits)
tittu *nf.* fig
titurru *nf.* bridge, viaduct
tizqāru* *adj.* eminent, exalted, prominent
tuāku+ *v.* (D) to check, coerce, contain, forbid, fence, rail
tuāmē *n. pl.* Gemini
tuʾāmu *n.* twin
tuānu *n.* (a breed of horse)
tuānu B *n.* (a bath)
tuānu B+ *n.* room, chamber; garner, grain bin
tuāru *v.* to return, recur; to turn into, become; to refuse (ordeal); to raise a claim, revoke
tuāru† *v.* to repeat, do again; (D) to repeat, do again
tuāru *v.* (D) to send back, return, restore, recover; to swing; to transform, turn in

tuāru n. *n.* return, recurrence, revocation
tubalû* *n.* belt (for climbing palm trees)
tūbāqu *n.* glue, bird-lime
tubkinnu*  *n.* [3] dung heap
tublu* *n.* foundation trench
tubqu*  *n.* [3] corner
tudittu  *nf.* dress pin, brooch
tūdītu+ *nf.* acknowledg[e]ment
tuganû  *n.* bunch, spray (of fruit)
tuḫallu† *n.* basket
tuḫḫu  *n.* garbage, residue, waste product
tuḫnu  *n.* millet
tu'intu 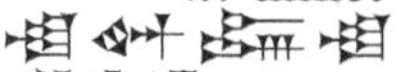 *nf.* double-door
tu'issu 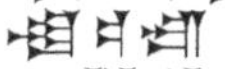 *nf.* maggot, worm
tukkannu  *nf.* leather bag
tukku  *n.* [2/3] oppression, persecution
tukku+ *n.* [2/3] fraud, harm, injury, loss, misery, trick
tukkultu* *nf.* encouragement
tukku B* *n.* alarm, warning, voice (from heaven)
tuklātānu* *adj.* trustworthy
tukpītu  *nf.* kidney-shaped gem
tukšu* *n.* (leather) shield
tuktê* *n. pl.* revenge, reprisal, vengeance
tuktê turru‡ *vp.* to take revenge, to exact vengeance, to retaliate
tūku  *n.* (a merchandise)
tukultu  *nf.* trust, reliance, hope; backing, resource, support
tukultu+ *nf.* confidence
tulīmāni* *n. pl.* both hands
tullal* *n.* (a soapwort)
tullû* *v.* to bedeck, adorn
tulû  *n.* [1/3] breast
tumru* *n.* ash, ashes, cinder
tūmulu  *n.* advantage
tunimmu  *n.* (a kind of leather)
tupninnu  *n.* [3] chest, coffer
tuppisannu* *n.* (a wooden container)
tupru† *n.* juniper
tupšikku *n.* [3] corvée (basket), chores*
tuquntu* *nf.* battle, war
tuqūnu  *n.* good order, security
tūr gimilli* *n. cp.* retribution, revenge
tūra  *adv.* again, once more, a second time; anyway, nevertheless
turāḫu  *n.* mountain goat, ibex
turāḫu+ *n.* chamois
tūrāṣu+ *n.* amendment, correction, emendation, revision
turbu'u* *n.* dust storm
turminabandû  *n.* (a red-black stone, volcanic breccia)
turminû  *n.* breccia
turru tuktê* *np.* revenge, retribution
turrūtu  *nf.* turn(ing), reversion
turtānu  *n.* commander-in-chief, minister of defense
tūrti amati◊ *nf. cp.* answer, reply, response
tūrtu 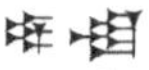 *nf.* backing out, turning; return, reversal, reversion
tūru† *n.* return, retreat
tušaḫruṣu† *n.* deduction, inference, pondering
tušāru* *n.* battlefield
tuššu* *n.* insolence
tuttu◊ *n.* mulberry (tree), sycamore
tūtu+ *n.* mulberry, berry
tutūru *n.* (mng. unkn.)
tū'u* *n.* chamber
tū'u+ *n.* cabin, cell, compartment
ṭabāḫu *v.* [a/u] to slaughter, butcher, cut (up), massacre
ṭābāti *nf. pl.* vinegar
ṭābāti* *nf. pl.* vinegar
ṭābat Amāni *nf. cp.* ammonia
ṭabbāḫāiu+ *adj.* culinary
ṭābiḫu *n.* [2] butcher, slaughterer; executioner, hangman; swordman
ṭābiš* *adv.* well, kindly, graciously, gladly, properly, smoothly
ṭabiu* *adj.* sunken
ṭābtānu *n.* benefactor; bounteous, charitable, generous, liberal, open-handed
ṭābtu *nf.* goodness; favor, charity, goodwill; salt
ṭābtu epāšu‡ *vp.* to do a favor
ṭābtu ḫasāsu‡ *vp.* to feel gratitude
ṭabû *v.* [u/u] to sink, submerge, dip; to drown, be submerged; (D) to sink
ṭābu *adj.* good; good-tasting, palatable, tasty, yummy; pleasant, pleasing, proper, satisfactory; sweet, fresh; aromatic, fragrant; happy, content, satisfied; gentle, friendly, benevolent, gracious, kind, well-meaning; auspicious, favorable, opportune; advantageous, beneficial, helpful, serviceable, useful; comfortable, easy
ṭābūtu* *nf.* alliance, amity, friendship
ṭaḫādu *v.* [u/u] to be abundant, flow over, overflow, run over; (D) to provide abundantly, supply abundantly
ṭaḫdu *adj.* affluent, bountiful, luxuriant,

opulent, overflowing

ṭāḫi *prp.* adjoining

ṭaḫiu* *adj.* contiguous

ṭaḫû *v.* i/i to approach; (D) to bring close; to include

ṭalāmu+ *v.* to cheat, deceive, treat unjustly

ṭalūmu+ *adj.* faithless, ungrateful, unjust

ṭamû* *adj.* to spin, plait

ṭamû a.* *adj.* spun, plaited

ṭamû B* *v.* to totter, go shakily, reel, stagger, toddle, wobble

ṭanāpu◊ *v.* u/u to be dirty, be stained; (D) to befoul, besmirch, foul, soil, taint, smudge, stain, sully, tarnish

ṭanāpu+ *v.* u/u (D) to defile, deflower, pollute, profane

ṭanīpu◊ *n.* rotten dates, spoiled dates

ṭanpu+ *adj.* defiled, filthy, polluted

ṭapālu* *v.* i/i to slander, insult, revile, rail at; (Š) to disseminate slanders

ṭapāšu* *v.* to be plump, chubby, fat

ṭapiltu* *nf.* slander, denigration, invection

ṭapiltu dabābu‡ *vp.* to speak slander, denigrate

ṭaplu* *adj.* slandered

ṭappilu* *adj.* slanderous

ṭappīlu+ *adj.* corrupt, defiled, depraved

ṭappīlūtu+ *nf.* corruption, depravity

ṭappušu* *adj.* plump-bellied, plump-faced

ṭapšu† *adj.* chubby, fat, plump, clownish

ṭapû *v.* i/i to expand, add, apply

ṭarādu* *v.* a/u to drive away, drive off, turn out

ṭarādu+ *v.* a/u to drive out, excommunicate, expel

ṭardu* *adj.* driven off, chased away, outcast

ṭarīdūtu* *nf.* exile

ṭarīdūtu+ *nf.* banishment, expulsion

ṭarkullu* *n.* mooring rope, mooring pole, bollard; pole, mast

ṭarpu'u *n.* [1] tamarisk

ṭarru* *adj., n.* beard

ṭa'tu, ṭātu* *n.* gift, bribe

ṭa'tūtu* *nf.* bribery

ṭa'ūmu+ *n.* snack, meal

ṭeāmu+ *v.* to perceive, taste, try

ṭēbūtu *nf.* kindness, grace

ṭēbūtu+ *nf.* beneficence, goodness, loving-kindness

ṭēḫi *adj.* adjoining, adjacent to

ṭeḫû* *v.* i/i to come near, come close, approach, to accost, approach sexually, have sex with

ṭēḫu *n.* immediate vicinity, proximity

ṭē'inu† *n.* miller

ṭēmānu *adj.* reasonable, rational, wise, sane

ṭēmtu+ *nf.* appreciation, perception, taste, flavor, quality

ṭēmu *n.* reason, opinion, intellect; meaning, mind; order, decree; communication, intelligence, news, report, story, notice; frame of mind, mood, disposition, will, history*; taste*

ṭēmu+ *n.* savor

ṭēmu šakānu‡ *vp.* to give orders

ṭēmu turru‡ *vp.* to report back

ṭerdu* *n.* investigation

ṭerû *v.* i/i to strike, lash

ṭēru* *n.* mud, silt

ṭiābu *v.* to be good, sweet; to be useful

ṭiābu* *v.* (Š) to make good, pleasant, friendly, acceptable

ṭiābu *v.* (D) to make good, make better, improve, ameliorate; to content, satisfy

ṭiābu+ *v.* (D) to render firm, brace, prepare, ready

ṭiānu *v.* to grind, pulverize

ṭibḫu *n.* impression, impress, print

ṭību *n.* yarn, thread, twine

ṭību B* *n.* submersion

ṭikmēnu* *n.* ashes

ṭimītu *nf.* thread, yarn, twine, string

ṭiplu* *n.* slander

ṭīpu* *n.* addition, supplement; application; poultice, wrapping

ṭīru *n.* lash

ṭiṭṭu *n.* clay

ṭīṭu *n.* fig(?)

ṭuānu *n.* (fine) thread, (fine) fabric

ṭūb libbi *n. cp.* peace of mind, gratification, pleasure

ṭūb šīri *n. cp.* (physical) fitness

ṭubbāti* *n. pl.* friendliness, happiness, goodwill, negotiations

ṭubbātiš* *adv.* comfortably

ṭūbtu◊ *nf.* kindness

ṭūbu *n.* goodness, happiness, prosperity, comfort, convenience

ṭūdu *n.* (an ornament)

ṭūdu B* *n.* [1], *nf.* road, path

ṭuḫdu *n.* abundance, affluence, plenty; climax

ṭuḫḫudu* *adj.* very plentiful

ṭulīmu *n.* spleen

ṭullumâ *adj.* treacherous, deceitful

ṭūnāpu+ *n.* outrage, scandal

ṭup šīmāti* *n. cp.* tablet of destinies

ṭuppišu *adv.* punctually, within agreed

time
ṭuppu *n.* $^{2/3}$ tablet, document
ṭupšar āli *n. cp.* city secretary
ṭupšar arê *n. cp.* mathematician
ṭupšar bēt ili *n. cp.* temple scribe
ṭupšar bītūtu◊ *nf. cp.* office of scribe of the house
ṭupšar ēkalli *n. cp.* palace scribe
ṭupšar ēkurri *n. cp.* temple scribe
ṭupšar lē'i *n. cp.* scribe writing on waxed boards
ṭupšar šarri *n. cp.* royal secretary
ṭupšar tibni *n. cp.* accountant of straw
ṭupšar ummāni *n. cp.* military scribe
ṭupšarru *n.* scribe, omen-expert; bookkeeper, clerk, notary, registrar, secretary
ṭupšarrutu *nf.* female scribe
ṭupšarrūtu *nf.* scribal art, scribal practice, tradition; scribal corpus, literature
ṭupšarrūt Enūma Anu Illil* *nf. cp.* astrology
ṭupšarru Enūma Anu Illil *n. cp.* astrologer, astronomer
ṭupšinnu *n.* tablet box
ṭupullû* *n.* slander, suspicion
ṭurru *n.* ^{1} band, string, wire, ribbon*
ṭuṭumēsu *n.* (a kind of grain)
u *conj.* and, however, but; even
ū *adv., conj.* but, however; further, furthermore, also; anyway, anyhow; nonetheless
u kî◊ *subj.* even if, even though
u lū *conj.* even if, even though
ū lū *conj.* or
ūa *int.* woe!
ubālu *v.* $^{a/i}$ to bring, carry, bear, deliver; (Š) to send, deliver, dispatch
ubān* *adv.* by a whisker, all but
ubān ḫašê* *n. cp.* (part of lung, finger of the lungs)
ubān lā* *adv.* nearly
ubān qāti* *n. cp.* finger
ubān šadê* *n. cp.* mountain top, peak, summit
ubān šēpi* *n. cp.* toe
ubānu *nf., n.* ^{1} finger; inch; toe; peak
ubānu qablītu* *np.* middle finger
ubānu rabītu* *np.* thumb
ubānu ṣeḫertu *np.* little finger
ubānu šanītu* *np.* forefinger, index finger
ubāru *n.* stranger, foreign guest, visitor, resident alien, immigrant, metoikos
ubārūtu *nf.* residency
ubārūtu◊ *nf.* immigration
ubburu* *v.* to accuse, denounce
ubbuṭu* *n.* famine
ubbuṭu a.* *adj.* plump, swollen
ubru *n.* ^{1} guest, client
ubrūtu *nf.* clientage, clientele, clientelage
ubsāti *n. pl.* storehouse
ubšukkinakku* *n.* divine assembly hall
uburtu *nf.* female guest, clientess
uddi† *adv.* certainly, probably
udduru *adj.* darkened, disconsolate*, mournful*
udê *n. pl.* utensil, ware[s]; constituents, paraphernalia; tableware
udē- *adj.* alone, on one's own
udēšu *adv.* merely, only, purely, solely
udīna lā *adv.* not yet
udīnu* *n.* (a mountain bird)
udru *n.* $^{1/3}$ (Bactrian) camel
udû *v.* $^{a/i}$ to know, be aware
udû† *v.* $^{a/i}$ (D) to inform, make known, publicize*, spread abroad*
udû+ *v.* $^{a/i}$ to ken
udû a. *adj.* known
Udūmu *n.* Edom
udutilû* *n.* live sheep
ugallu* *n.* ^{1} (a lion-headed demon)
ugāru *n.* ^{1} field
uggatu* *nf.* wrath, rage, fury
uggugu* *adj.* very angry, furious, infuriated, choleric; spitfire
uḫḫu* *n.* phlegm, sputum
uḫḫuru *v.* to be late, tarry; to do later, delay, postpone, put off
uḫḫuru+ *v.* to adjourn
uḫḫuru n.+ *n.* hold-up
uḫḫuzu *adj.* plated with, set in
uḫinnu *n.* dried date
uḫīru* *n.* weed
uḫulgalê* *n.* evil day
uḫūlu* *n.* potash
uḫūlu+ *n.* alkaline plant, salicornia
uḫummiš* *adv.* like a cliff
uḫummu* *n.* cliff
u'iltu *nf.* (horizontal) tablet, report; promissory note; (pl.) liabilities
ukālu *n.* ^{3} morsel; tidbit
ukkubu* *v.* (D) to arrive, draw close
ukkulu* *adj.* pitch dark
ukkušu *v.* to move on, progress
uklu *n.* food, nourishment, victuals
uklu B* *n.* overseer

uklu B+ *n.* caretaker
uklu C* *n.* darkness
ukû* *n.* shuttle
ukullu◊ *n.* food
ukultu* *nf.* devouring
ul* *adv.* not
ulâ *adv., conj.* if not; or, else, otherwise, alternatively; unless
ulādu *v.* $^{a/i}$ to give birth, bear (young); to breed, engender
ulādu* *v.* $^{a/i}$ (Š) to breed
ulāltu *nf.* feeble-minded woman
ulālu *n.* feeble-minded, imbecile; helpless, weak
ulālūtu* *nf.* helplessness
ulamâ *adv.* or else, otherwise
ulāpu *n.* sanitary towel, sanitary napkin, menstrual bandage; rag
uldu *adj.* born, innate*
ulla◊ *n.* antiquity
ullânu* *prp.* before, previous to, prior to; apart from; without, there and then
ullānumma◊ *adv.* suddenly
ullīš* *adv.* later, thereafter
ullu* *n.* negative answer, refusal, denial, negation
ullû* *adj., pron* that; distant, remote, archaic
ulluṣu* *adj.* swollen
ullūtu *nf.* levy
ulmu *n.* $^{1/3}$ axe
ulṣāniš* *adv.* joyfully
ulṣu* *n.* bliss, exultation, felicity, mirth, pleasure, rejoicing
ultu* *prp.* from; since
ultu qereb* *prp.* from
ultu ulla* *adv.* long time ago
ultu ullānumma* *adv.* suddenly
ūlu* *n.* best oil, virgin oil
ūm bubbuli *n. cp.* new moon day
ūm epēš nikkassi *n. cp.* Doomsday
ūmâ *adv.* now
umām ṣēri* *n. cp.* wildlife
umām tānti* *n. cp.* sea animal
umāmu *n.* $^{1/2}$ animal, livestock, beast; (mythological) monster
umandu* *n.* (an intestine)
umāšu* *n.* ^{1} clamp, clamps and chains (of a battering ram)
ūmē ša nanmurti Qašti* *np.* dog days
ūmiš* *adv.* like daylight; like a storm
ūmišam* *adv.* daily
ūmišamma* *adv.* daily
umm-ummi* *nf. cp.* grandma, grandmother, granny
umma◊ *adv.* thus
ummān-manda* *n. cp.* barbarian horde(s)
ummānāti* *n. pl.* troops, hordes
ummânīu+ *adj.* masterly
ummānu* *nf.* army, troop(s); crowd, throng
ummânu *n.* ^{1} expert, specialist; master, scholar, savant; craftsman, artisan, artist, artificer
ummânūtu *nf.* scholarship, learning; artistry, craftsmanship, workmanship
ummânūtu+ *nf.* art, artistry, craft, employment, industry, occupation, profession, trade, vocation
ummânu B+ *n.* bloodletter
ummatu* *nf.* main body, collective mass; nation, people
ummi šarri *n. cp.* queen mother
ummišallu *n.* (a kind of salt)
ummu *nf.* mother; origin, source; original amount; side road
ummu abi◊ *nf. cp.* grandmother
ummu ālittu *n. cp.* natural mother
ummu ša muḫḫi* *np.* phrenitis
ummuliš* *adv.* twinkingly, sparklingly
ummulu* *v.* to scintillate, twinkle
ummulu a.* *adj.* scintillating, sparkling, twinkling
ummuru *adj.* chosen, reliable
ummūtu* *nf.* motherhood
ummu B* *n.* ^{3} heat, fever
umṣatu* *nf.* blackhead*, birthmark, mole
umšu* *n.* ^{1} heat, heatwave
ūmu *n.* $^{1/3}$ day; (pl.) weather
ūmu ana ūmi *adv.* day after day, day to day
ūmu annīu *adv., np.* today
ūmu lā erpu‡ *np.* fair day, day without rain
ūmu mašil† *adv., np.* midday, (at) noon(time)
ūmu rāqu *np.* holiday
ūmu šemû* *np.* auspicious day
ūmu šētuqu* *vp.* to pass time, while away
umunnû* *n.* ^{1} vein
ūmussu◊ *adv.* daily
ūmu B* *n.* lion
undē *n. pl.* rash
unīnu *n.* chest, trunk, case

unīqu 
 *nf.* young she-goat
unīqu lā patītu *np.* virgin goat
unnātu* *nf.* land
unninnu*  *n.*[1] supplication, petition
unnu *n.*[2] (mng. unkn.)
unnubu* *adj.* abloom*, fecund, fertile, fructified, prolific, thriving, very fruitful
unnutu  *v.* (D) to be dim, be faint, be pale
unnutu a. *adj.* faint, pale, vague
unqu  *nf.* signet ring, stamp seal; sealed order; imprint, stamp
unqu B+ *n.* dale, dell, low-lying country, vale, valley
unṣu* *n.* hunger
unūt libbi  *n. cp.* internal organs
unūtu* *nf.* utensils, tools, implements, wares
unzarḫu  *n.*[1] domestic, house-born (slave); native-born, indigenous, autochthonous
upāṭu *n.* nose mucus
upnu  *n.*[1] fist
upnu*  *n.*[1] handful
uppi aḫi* *n. cp.* armpit
uppu  *n.* tube, pipette; socket; key(?)
uppû *adj.* publicized
uppu a.† *adj.* acquired
uppuqu* *adj.* massive, solid
upput eqli  *n. cp.* (a kind of cricket)
uppuṭu* *adj.* blind
uppu B* *n.* drum, fram drum; drumskin
upû* *n.* cloud
upuntu*  *nf.* (a kind of flour)
upurtu* *nf.* headdress, wig
uqāru  *v.*[i/i] to be rare, be expensive, be precious, to do rarely*
uqāru*  *v.*[i/i] (D) to make rare, make scarce, rarefy, use up; (Š) to make rare, make scarce; to value, esteem, respect, honor, to overvalue*
uqāru+ *v.*[i/i] to be costly; (D) to treat with reverence, worship; (Š) to make valuable, value, give honor, appraise
uqniāti* *n.pl.* blue(-green) wool
uqqû* *v.* to incise, inscribe, prescribe
uqququ* *adj.* tongue-tied, dumb
uqru *adj.* rare, scarce, infrequent; expensive, precious, valuable; dear, esteemed, exceptional*
uqru+ *adj.* costly; dear, beloved; honorable, honored
uqru adanniš *adj. phr.* extravagant, invaluable, priceless, ruinous
uqrūtu+ *nf.* dignity, dignified conduct, seriousness, solemnity
ūqu◊ *n.* people, populace
uqūpu  *n.* ape
uqūputu *nf.* female ape
uqur* *adv.* rarely, seldom
uqurtu* *nf.* rarity; (pl.) valuables
urādu  *v.*[a/i] to descend, go down, flow down; to droop; to alight, come down, dismount, get off; (Š) to send down, bring down
uraḫ Ḫiburt *n. cp.* (sixth month)
uraḫ kalmarte† *n. cp.* (ninth month)
uraḫ muḫur ilāni† *n. cp.* (fourth month)
uraḫ qarrāte† *n. cp.* (eighth month)
uraḫ Sînt *n. cp.* (tenth month)
uraḫ ša-kēnāte† *n. cp.* (third month)
uraḫ ša-sarrāte† *n. cp.* (second month)
uraḫ Bēlat ēkalli† *n. cp.* (first month)
urāku◊ 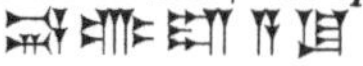 *n.* baton(?), chisel(?)
Urarṭu *n.* Urartu, Armenia
urāsu 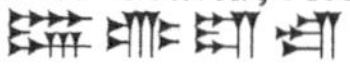 *n.*[1] brick mason, bricklayer, mason
urāsūtu  *nf.* brick masonry
urāšu* *n.* dirty cloth; septic wound, lesion
urballu* *n.* quail
urbānu  *n.* papyrus, paper*
urbānu+ *n.* sedge
urbatu* *nf.* bulrush, rush
urdānīu* *adj.* servile, subservient
urdānūtu  *nf.* servitude
urdānūtu epāšu‡ *vp.* to do obedience
urdimmu*  *n.* (a mythical wild dog)
urdu  *n.*[2] servant; subject, subordinate, underling; follower, retainer; slave
urdu bēti *n. cp.* house slave, servant
urdu ēkalli *n. cp.* palace servant, courtier, civil servant*
urgulû* *n.* hound; Leo
urḫu  *n.*[2] month
urḫu ana urḫi *adv.* month after month
urḫu ūmāti *n. cp.* calendar month, full month
urḫu B*  *n.*[1] road, path
uriānu  *n.* fennel
uridimmu* *n.* wild dog; Lupus
urigallu  *n.* ritual hut; stan-

dard, symbol; banner, pennant, streamer
urimtu◊ *nf.* tablet cover, envelope
urīṣu *n.*[2] male goat, buck
urkat *prp.* after, behind
urkēte *adv.* later, afterwards
urki *prp.* after, behind
urkiš *adv.* in the future
urkītu *nf.* rear, rearguard; later time, future
urkītu* *adv.* lastly
urkīu *n.*[4] surety, guarantee, guarantor, security
urkīu a. *adj.* later, latter; latest, last; hindmost, rearmost; posterior, future; junior
urkutu *nf.* backside; estate, inheritance
urmāḫu* *n.* lion
urmazillu* *n.* stump(?)
urnû *n.* mint(?)
urnutu *nf.* (dressing) gown, frock
urpāniš* *adv.* like a cloud
urpatu* *nf.* cloud
urpu *n., nf.* cloud
urqītu *nf.* greenery, vegetation
urqu *n.*[1] green; vegetable(s)
urqu+ *n.*[1] (pl.) groceries
urra ḫubullu* *n. cp.* (a lexicon or encyclopedia)
urrākūtu* *nf.* sculpture
urru* *n.*[1] day
urruḫiš* *adv.* very quickly, swiftly, very soon, hastily
urruku* *adj.* lengthy, long-drawn-out, prolonged, protracted
urruzu *v.* make dirty, muck up(?)
Ursalimmu *n.* Jerusalem
ursūtu *nf.* magazine, storehouse
uršānatu* *nf.* heroine
uršānu* *n.* hero, warrior
uršānūtu* *nf.* heroism
uršu* *n.* blemish, dark spot, blot, speck, spot, stain, stigma
uršu B* *n.*[1] bedroom
ūrtu* *nf.* order, command, ordinance
urṭû *n.* (a greenish-blue dye; light-blue wool)
urû *nf.* team (of horses)
Ūru *n.* Ur
ūru *n.*[3] roof, ceiling*
urubāti* *n. pl.* wailings
ur'udu* *n.* windpipe
urudû* *n.* copper
urutu* *nf.* observation
ūru B* *n.* sex organ; vagina, womb, vulva
urzinnu *n.* sycamore
usḫu *n.* (a decorative motif)
uskāru *n.* crescent; half-circle, semicircle, arc
usmu* *n.* appropriateness; worthy ornament
ussu* *n.* usage, custom, practice
ussuktu *nf.* assignment, commission
ussuku *v.* (D) to ascribe, assign, attribute, specify
ussu B* *n.* streak, stripe, stroke
usu *n.*[3] swan
usurtu* *nf.* siege
usutu *nf.* assistance, help, aid; means
uṣābu *v.*[a/i] to add, augment, increase
uṣpu *n.* sling, catapult
uṣṣāru◊ *n.* magazine, storehouse
uṣṣu *n.* arrow, arrowhead
uṣṣupu* *adj.* multiple
uṣṣuṣu *v.* (D) to investigate, look into
uṣû *v.*[a/i] to go out, set forth, issue, leave, evade, sally, (Š vent.) to bring out, move out; to redeem, release, set free; (Š) to send out, send away, turn out, banish; to export; to emit; to give out, rent, lease; (vent.) to come out, come forth, emerge, protrude
uṣultu *nf.* dagger, small knife, lancet
uṣurtu *nf.* design, drawing, sketch, plan; layout, scheme, pattern
uṣurtu+ *nf.* form, image, picture
ušābu *v.*[a/i] to sit, dwell, inhabit, live, reside in; to occupy, settle in, sit down; (Š) to settle, install in a place of residence; to colonize, populate, resettle; to enthrone; to install
ušābu n.+ *n.* session
ušallu *n.* meadow, bottom land
ušāmutu *nf.* (an edible bird)
ušandû* *n.* fowler
ušāru *n.* penis
ušburrudû* *n.*[2] anti-witchcraft magic
ušmannu* *nf.* military camp
ušpār birmi *n. cp.* weaver of multicolored trim
ušpār ṣiprāti *n. cp.* sash-weaver
ušpārtu *nf.* female weaver

ušpāru  *n.* weaver
ušpāru*  *n.* ruler's staff, sceptre
uššābu  *n.* lodger, settler, tenant
uššē  *n.pl.* foundation
uššer† *prp.* ignore! except for
uššupu a.* *adj.* spellbound
uššuru  *v.* (D) to abandon, loose; to release, let go, acquit
uššušu *v.* stressed
uššušu a.* *adj.* distressed, stressed, worried
ušû  *n.* diorite; ebony, teak
ušultu* *nf.* vein
ušummu  *n.* mole rat
ušuzzu◊ *v.* $^{a/i}$ to stand
ušuzzu n.◊ *n.* presence
utar* *adv.* excessively; farther, further
utāru  *v.* $^{i/i}$ to be additional; to exceed, surpass, outsize; (D) to augment, increase; to deserve, earn, merit, gain; (Š) to exaggerate, overdo, overstate; to furbish up, poke; to increase, enlarge, to overestimate*, overvalue*
utāru+ *v.* $^{i/i}$ to avail o.s. of, be left over, excel o.s., have over and above, obtain, win; (D) to outbid, to make to abound; (Š) to give over, have enough and to spare
utnannu† *n.* carriage, chaise
utninnu* *n.* supplication
utru *adj.* huge, outsize, superior; additional, excessive, extra, redundant, spare
utru+ *adj.* especial, odd, overmuch, exorbitant, superfluous, surpassing, uneven
utrūtu+ *nf.* majority
uttartu  *nf.* large-wheeled chariot
uttāru  *adj., n.* ^{1} surplus, extra, superfluous; huge, massive, excessive*, exorbitant*, extravagant*
utturu* *adj.* giant*, exaggerated, boastful
utturu† *adj.* expensive
utturu+ *adj.* best, most excellent, virtuous
utukku  *n.* ghost, spirit, spectre, spook
utullu* *n.* ^{3} (chief) shepherd, herdsman
utūlu* *v.* to lie down, sleep
uṭṭuru *adj.* paid off, quit
uṭṭuru issu pān aḫāiš‡ *adj.phr.* quits
uṭṭutu *nf.* grain, barley
ūṭu◊ *n.* span
uznānu *adj.* eared, big-eared, eary
uznē pattû‡ *vp.* to enlighten, inform
uznu  *n.* ^{1}, *nf.* ear, understanding, attention
uznu ana X šakānu‡ *vp.* to give ear, pay attention to, be interested in, see to
uznu bašû‡ *vp.* to be attentive
uzubbatu* *nf.* reprieve
uzubbû* *n.* divorce, separation
uzuntu*  *nf.* earlobe, lobe
uzuntu nītu  *n. cp.* (part of the entrails, lobe of siege)
uzuzzu  *v.* $^{a/i}$ to stand, be present; to become stationary, come to standstill, halt, stop; (Š) to place, set in place, station, set up, erect
uzzatu* *nf.* anger
uzzu* *n.* anger, rage, wrath; fury, fervor, zeal
uzzubu* *adj.* anomalous*, deformed*, degenerate, neglected
uzzu B+ *n.* swan
za'ānu*  *v.* (D) to adorn, decorate, embellish, garnish, redecorate
Zāba elīu *n. cp.* Upper Zab
Zāba šaplīu *n. cp.* Lower Zab
zabābu* *v.* to be in a frenzy, bolt
zabālu  *v.* $^{i/i}$ to carry, haul, transport; to bear, suffer, tolerate; (Š) to ship, convey
zabālu+ *v.* $^{i/i}$ to contribute, put up with, undergo
zabardabbu*  *n.* (a priest)
zabbālu+ *n.* garbage collector
zabbānu+ *n.* customer
zabbu* *adj., n.* ecstatic, frantic, frenzied
zabbu a.* *adj.* fanatic*
zabbūru+ *n.* hornet
zabbūtu* *nf.* fanaticism*, ecstaticism
zābil immeri  *n. cp.* carrier of sheep
zābil kudurri* *n. cp.* basket carrier, corve2e worker
zābilānūtu+ *nf. cp.* endurance, patience, tolerance
zabiltu* *nf.* betrayal
zadimmu* *n.* lapidary, jeweller
zagindurû  *n.* greenish lapis lazuli
zaḫalû* *n.* silver alloy
zā'ir amēlūti* *n. cp.* misanthrophe
zā'irānu*  *n.* ^{1} hater, enemy, foe
zā'iru*  *n.* $^{1/2}$ foe, enemy
zakār šumi*  *n. cp.* invocation, query
zakāru*  *v.* $^{a/u}$ to pronounce, call; to mention, invoke, name; (Š) to adjure

zakīqu *n.* phantom, spirit
zakîš* *adv.* cleanly
zakkāru *n.* ^{1} male
zakkû *n.* $^{1/4}$ exempt; professional (soldier)
zakû *v.* $^{u/u}$ to be pure, clean, free, exempt; (D) to clean, exempt from, free; to ready
zakû+ *v.* $^{u/u}$ to be clear, clear o.s., disown, justify o.s.; (D) to acquit, clear, hold innocent, justify
zakû a. *adj.* clean, candid, chaste, pure; exempt, free; impeccable, spotless, stainless, tidy; faultless, sinless
zakû a.+ *adj.* blameless, clean, free from, guiltless, innocent, sincere
zakūkāiu+ *adj.* glassy, vitreous
zakūkītu* *nf.* glass, glaze
zakūkīu+ *adj.* glass blower, glazier
zakûtu *nf.* exemption, liberty; purity, chastity, cleanliness; candor; cleaned (barley)
zakûtu+ *nf.* holiness, innocence, sincerety
zalāgu+ *v.* to glint, shimmer; (D) to radiate
zalāqu *n.* shiny stone, trinket
zalāqu B+ *v.* to glare, glitter, spangle
zamāmu+ *v.* buzz, tinkle, whir[r]
zāmānu* *n.* enemy
zāmānû* *adj., n.* hostile; enemy
zamar* *adv.* quickly, soon, shortly
zamar ... zamar* *adv.* now ... now
zamār taknê* *n. cp.* hymn of blandishment, song of praise
zamarānu* *adv.* suddenly
zamāru *v.* $^{u/u}$ to sing, chant, intone
zamāru+ *v.* $^{u/u}$ to play (a stringed instrument), sing
zamāru n. *n.* song, poem, epic, ode
zamāru n.+ *n.* music (vocal or stringed)
zambūru* *n.* thyme
zamīmtu+ *nf.* bumblebee
zāmiru+ *n.* nightingale
zamītāiu+ *adj.* angular
zamītānu+ *n.* balcony, bay window, loophole
zamītu* *nf.* corner(?)
zamītu+ *nf* angle, corner
zammāru *n.* singer, minstrel
zammāru+ *n.* flute-player
zammārūtu+ *nf.* music
zammû *v.* to lack, miss; to deprive of
zammukku* *n.* New Year
zamru *n.* fruit
zamru B* *adj.* voiced
zamû* *n.* (outer) corner, corner pillar, angle*
zanānu *v.* $^{i/u}$ to rain
zanānu* *v.* $^{u/u}$ (Š) to bring rain, pour out
zanānu B* *v.* $^{a/u}$ to keep up, pander, procure, provide for
zanānu B+ *v.* $^{a/u}$ to purvey
zāninu* *n.* procurer, provider, provisioner, purveyor, sustainer
zāninūtu* *nf.* sustenance, maintenance
zannu *n.* (a dish made from fermented barley)
zanû *v.* $^{i/i}$ (Š) to cause to be angry, anger, rile
zanzaliqqu *n.* Persian lilac
zanzīru* *n.* starling
zapāru* *v.* $^{a/a}$ to decay, rot, become rotten
zapāru+ *v.* $^{a/a}$ to stink, smell evil, be foul, be rancid
zappu *n.* bristle
zapru+ *adj.* stinking, evil-smelling, foul
zaprūtu+ *nf.* stink, evil smell
zaqānu *v.* to be bearded
zaqāpu *v.* $^{a/u}$ to erect, fix upright, plant; to attack, rise up; to appear in court, lodge a claim, to embed*, fix*, implant*, insert*
zaqāpu* *v.* $^{a/u}$ (D) to impale
zaqāpu+ *v.* $^{a/u}$ to lift up, set up, bristle, hang, crucify
zaqāru *v.* $^{i/i}$ to be high, elevated, culminate; (D) to build high; to boil up
zaqātu* *v.* $^{a/u}$ to sting, goad, prick, prod, spur; to hurt
zaqātu+ *v.* $^{a/u}$ to prod, twinge
zaqiptu* *nf.* vertical
zāqiptu+ *nf.* prong
zaqīpu *n.* $^{1/2}$ stake, picket, pole
zāqipu* *n.* planter
zaqīqiš* *adv.* like a ghost, as nought
zaqnu* *adj.* bearded
zaqpu *adj.* erected, set up; erect, upright, perpendicular, vertical; planted, implanted, ingrafted
zaqpu+ *adj.* erect, poised, hung, crucified
zaqqitu* *n.* mosquito
zaqru* *adj.* high, steep, massive
zaqtu* *adj.* pointed
zār šarri *n. cp.* royal line
zarāpu *v.* $^{i/i}$ to do legally
zarāpu laqû *vp.* to acquire lawfully, ob-

tain legally

zarāpu tadānu *vp.* to sell lawfully

zarāqu *v.* [i/i] to scatter, sprinkle, spray, strew

zarpu laqiu *adj. phr.* lawfully acquired

zarriqu *n.* [1] sprinkler

zar'u *n.* seed; semen; arable field

zarû *v.* [u/u] to sow, seed; to disseminate, distribute, scatter; to winnow

zārû* *n.* [1] father, begetter

zarû n. *n.* sowing, seeding; distributing, scattering; dissemination, distribution

zarūgu† *n.* irrigation hose

zārutu *nf.* tent, canopy, awning

za''û *v.* (mng. unkn.)

za'u* *n.* (aromatic) resin

za''unu* *adj.* adorned, decorated

za'uzzu *n.* distribution

zazabtu *nf.* (a garment or textile)

zazakku* *n.* (a high Babylonian administrative official)

zê *n.* shit, excrement, refuse

zê alpi* *n. cp.* bullshit

zê nissaba *n. cp.* chaff

zê uzni *n. cp.* earwax

zenû* *n. i/i* to be angry, be offended; (D) to make angry, miff, offend

zenû a.* *adj.* angry, irate, miffed, offended

zēqu⁺ *adj.* shrill

zēr ḫalgatî◊ *adj.,n.cp.* barbarian(s)

zēr kitî* *n. cp.* linseed

zēr nērti* *n. cp.* murderer, criminal

zēr šarrūti* *n. cp.* royal line

zērāti* *n. pl.* hateful messages, hostilities, hatred

zērmandu* *n.* vermin

zēru *adj.* hateful, odious, loathful, loathsome, offensive, disagreeable

zēru* *adj.* hated; abhorrent, loathsome, obnoxious, repellent, repugnant, repulsive, disgusting*, nauseating*, revolting*, yucky*

zērūtu* *nf.* antipathy*, aversion*, disgust*, distaste*, repugnance*, hate, hatred, hostility

zēzu *adj.* divided

ziāqu *v.* to blow, waft, drift; to bluster, wail

ziāqu⁺ *v.* to holler, squeal

ziāru *v.* to hate, dislike, detest, loathe; to abhor, resent; to avoid; (N) to be detestable, be disgusting, be repellent, be repulsive, cloy, repel

zibānītu *nf.* scales; Libra

Zibbāti *n. pl.* (pl.) Pisces

zibbitu◊ *nf.* (mng. unkn.)

zibbutu *nf.* tail, tail-end

ziblu *n.* dross, litter, refuse, trash, waste matter, waste

ziblu⁺ *n.* dung, excrement, fertilizer, manure

zibû* *n.* black cumin

zību *n.* vulture; jackal; bird of prey; predator

zību B* *n.* [1] sacrifice

zību B⁺ *n.* [1] immolation

zidubdubbû* *n.* heap of flour

zikārānu* *adj.* mannish

zikāru* *adj., n.* male; man, he-man

zikir šapti* *n. cp.* pronouncement

zikru *n.* name; word, utterance, command, logos

zikru* *n.* male, manly, masculine

zikrūtu* *nf.* manliness, heroism; manhood, masculinity, virility

zikurudû *n.* (throat-cutti ng, a magical rite)

zilītu *n.* (mng. unkn.)

zilliru◊ *n.* (an Elamite official)

zilullû* *n.* vagrant, tramp

zīm pāni* *n. cp.* trophy

zimbānu* *n.* feudal tenure

zimru* *n.* song, melody, tune, intonation*

zīmu *n.* glitter, spendour; (pl.) appearance, countenance, features, lineaments

zinnāti* *nf. pl.* provisioning

zinû *n.* [3] palm-rib, midrib, frond

zīnu *n.* rain, flurry, shower

zinūtu* *nf.* anger

zinzaru'u *n.* ginger (?)

zinzimmu *n.* red onion, shallot

zi'pu* *n.* mold; cast coin

ziqipta* *adv.* vertically

ziqīpu *n.* stake

ziqnānu *n.* bearded man

ziqnu *n.* [1] beard, whisker

ziqpa* *adv.* vertically, upright

ziqpu *n.* [2] sapling, shoot, plant, bush; pole, shaft; blade; peak; culminating constellation, culmination, zenith; perpendicular

ziqqu *n.* [3] wineskin

ziqqu+ *n.* [3] (leathern) bottle
ziqtu *n.* sting, point; sting-mark, pimple
zīqtu *nf.* torch
ziqtu+ *n.* pike
zīqtu+ *nf.* shooting star
zīqu *n.* draught, breeze, flurry, gust
zīqu+ *n.* (violent) rain, cataract
ziqziqqu* *n.* gale, gust, boisterous wind, storm wind
zirqu* *n.* caracal, (desert) lynx
zirqutu *nf.* (female) lynx
zīru *n.* hatred, hate; abhorrence, disgust, loathing, revulsion; resentment, reluctance
zirūtu *nf.* (a body part)
zirzirru* *n.* grasshopper
zittu *nf.* share, portion, division, part; inheritance, heritage, legacy
zittu batāqu‡ *vp.* to divide inheritance, inherit
zizānu *n.* (a locust)
zizibu *n.* milk
zizru *n.* dwarf, minuscule; (a locust)
zīzu *n.* emmer
zīzu B *n.* [1] teat, tit, nipple
zuābu† *v.* to dissolve
zuāmu+ *v.* to hum, hustle, jostle
zuāru† *v.* to twist, turn (round); (D) to turn away, abduct
zuātu+ *v.* to transpire
zuāzu *v.* to divide, share; to allot, impart, portion out; to partake; to give out, pass out, ration out; (D) to distribute
zublānû *n.* wedding gift
zūk šēpi* *n. cp.* heavy infantry
zukiqīpu *n.* scorpion; Scorpio
zukkû◊ *n.* professional troops
zukû* *n.* glass
zūku *n.* infantry
zūku B* *n.* clarity
zumāru *n.* refrain; chorus
zumbi alpi* *n. cp.* gadfly
zumbu *n.* fly
zumru *n.* body
zūmu *n.* colocynth
zunnu *n.* [1] rain, rainfall
zunzuraḫḫu *n.* [1] (a class of soldiers)
zuppu+ *v.* (D) to adulterate, counterfeit, fake, falsify, forge, skew
zupru* *n.* decay, putrefaction, rot
zūpu◊ *n.* hyssop, marjoram
zuqāru *n.* assertion, invocation
zuqqurtu* *nf.* elevation
zuqquru* *adj.* elevated, towering, sky-high
zuqtu *nf.* chin
zuqtu B* *n.* mountain peak, ridge
zūqutu *nf.* (a small metal dish)
zurzu *n.* saddlebag, pack sack
zūtu *nf.* sweat, perspiration
zūtu karāru *vp.* to perspire
zūzu* *n.* half-shekel
zūzu+ *n.* coin